FROMMER'S

COMPREHENSI IDE

NEW ENGLAND
'91

by Tom Brosnahan

PRENTICE
HALL
PRESS

NEW YORK • LONDON • TORONTO • SYDNEY • TOKYO • SINGAPORE

FROMMER BOOKS

Published by Prentice Hall Press
A division of Simon & Schuster Inc.
15 Columbus Circle
New York, NY 10023

Copyright © 1978, 1980, 1982, 1984, 1986, 1988, 1990, 1991 by
Simon & Schuster Inc.

All rights reserved including the right of reproduction in whole or in
part in any form

PRENTICE HALL PRESS and colophons are registered trademarks of
Simon & Schuster Inc.

ISBN 0-13-326786-5
ISSN 1044-2286

Manufactured in the United States of America

CONTENTS

MAPS

For Jane

A Disclaimer

Although every effort was made to ensure the accuracy of the prices and travel information appearing in this book, it should be kept in mind that prices do fluctuate in the course of time, and that information does change under the impact of the varied and volatile factors that affect the travel industry.

Readers should also note that the establishments described under Readers' Selections or Suggestions have not in many cases been inspected by the author, and that the opinions expressed there are those of the individual reader(s) only. They do not in any way represent the opinions of the publisher or author of this guide.

GETTING TO KNOW NEW ENGLAND

1. A SHORT HISTORY

2. PREPARING FOR YOUR TRIP

3. FOR THE FOREIGN VISITOR

4. FROMMER'S DOLLARWISE® TRAVEL CLUB— HOW TO SAVE MONEY ON ALL YOUR TRAVELS

When it comes to American history and culture, New England is where it all began.

Certainly history is not the only thing to attract you to the six states that make up the region: Connecticut, Rhode Island, Massachusetts, Maine, New Hampshire, and Vermont. Each state has natural beauties worth bragging about, like the beaches of Rhode Island, the windswept dunes of Cape Cod, the rugged coasts of Maine, or the Green Mountains of Vermont. And there's the local cuisine, particularly the seafood: lobster, the freshest you can get; clam chowder, easily the best in the world; Vermont cheddar cheese; hotcakes with New Hampshire's maple syrup.

New England is not all cities and civilization, either—despite all the talk about the Eastern megalopolis. The Appalachian Trail has its beginnings here; the sandy shores of Cape Cod are over 100 miles long; Vermont alone has over two dozen challenging ski areas; and if these places are too busy for you, head for the untracked wilderness forests of northern Maine. In fact, it's not really the big cities such as Hartford, Providence, and Boston that set the tone of New England community life, but rather the small New England villages—Litchfield, Conn.; Newfane, Vt.; Kennebunkport, Me.—each with its village green surrounded by the church, school, library, and town hall, each village separated from its neighbor by rolling pastures, lush woodland, and glacial lakes.

Although New England is not just history, one soon discovers that New Englanders love the region because of its history and its traditions. Only here can you see Plymouth Rock, climb Bunker Hill, visit the site of the very first Thanksgiving feast. At Connecticut's Mystic Seaport you can see a New England maritime town of the past, re-created and in full operation; and at Sturbridge Village and Plimoth Plantation the crafts of the colonial period are performed as they were centuries ago.

Even in modern Boston the history of New England is everywhere. From the observatory atop a sleek skyscraper, you can look down upon the charming colonial buildings ranged along gas-lit, cobblestone streets on Beacon Hill. Wander through Faneuil Hall, where American colonists debated the abuses of British rule, then plow through the crowds thronging the renovated Quincy Market, Boston's favorite gathering place. Make an excursion out to the suburban towns of Lexington and Concord, where the first battles of the American Revolution were fought more than two hundred years ago, and you'll cross over Route 128, the nexus of high-technology research and development for the eastern United States.

New England's paradoxical loves of both tradition and innovation have coexisted peacefully from the very beginning, for New England was founded by men and women who escaped the strictures of Reformation Europe to experiment with new religious and societal frameworks. They built a new way of life on this continent, but they included in it the things they loved best about the old countries they had left behind.

---

1. A Short History

To understand New England and its people, you must take at least a quick look at the region's history. To a surprising extent, today's New Englanders think and do as they do because of how their ancestors thought and acted.

THE LAND

The New England landscape, as we see it, is left from the age of the glaciers. But long before the Ice Age, several billion years ago, the earth cooled and shrank, and its crust wrinkled, throwing out towering mountain ranges. The friction and pressure of this "wrinkling" was so intense that sand turned to marble and limestone to gneiss and schist. Molten rock (magma) flowed from the planet's boiling core through faults in the folded crust, but the magma never made it to the surface. Instead it snaked its way into fissures, sometimes reaching a great open "bubble" of air in the crust, filling it. Then the molten rock cooled slowly, insulated beneath the earth's crust, and its liquid minerals slowly took on the crystalline texture we identify as granite.

The results of this geological wonderwork are easily visible throughout New England today, in Vermont's vast quarries of creamy marble, around farmers' fields in the stone fences made of textured gneiss flecked with shiny mica, and in the great domed hills of solid granite (like Mount Monadnock) that were formed deep within the earth.

The lofty mountains formed aeons ago were worn down, subjected to pressure again and again, stretched and mangled, beaten and weathered. Finally they were only a fraction of their former height, yielding today's New England of gentle valleys and easily climbed mountains.

Dinosaurs

Several hundred million years ago, before the mountains were given their final form, New England was in the midst of a tropical climate rich in plant life. The Connecticut River Valley was a paradise for the dinosaurs who thrived here, and who left their footprints—and even their skeletons—in the thick river silt, which later turned to stone. At Dinosaur State Park in Rocky Hill, Conn., you can see these remnants of New England's inhabitants from 200 million years ago.

About eight million years ago, after the passing of the dinosaurs, one final geologic upheaval gave us the mountains we know as the Appalachian range, stretching from Maine to Georgia. New Hampshire's White Mountains, Vermont's Green Mountains, and Massachusetts' Berkshires are part of the range, humble reminders of the ancient Rockies and Alps that once stood here.

The Ice Age

In very recent geological time, about a million years ago, the world's temperature dropped and the polar ice caps thickened. Millions of tons of ice built up on the original ice pack, and the weight of this build-up pushed the edges of the ice pack outward, toward the equator. An enormous blanket of ice slowly moved southward over New England, plowing up the soil, and absorbing dirt and rock into itself by a slow-motion churning. As the climate warmed and the ice retreated, it dumped this debris into long mounds called drumlins, of which Bunker Hill is perhaps the most famous. The ice's bulldozing action also formed thousands of glacial lakes and ponds, including Thoreau's Walden. Across the landscape, huge boulders picked up and carried by the advancing ice were dropped helter-skelter as it retreated. You will come upon these "glacial erratics," as they're called, standing naked in flat fields where they don't seem to belong.

The glaciers came and went, sculpting the terrain of New England at least four times. When they finally retreated, 10,000 to 20,000 years ago, the sea flooded in to cover much of the region. Melting ice added to the oceans' volume, and the weight of the ice had depressed the low terrain beneath the new sea level. But the land rebounded, reaching the level it has today, the oceans retreated, and New England became the New England we know.

THE FIRST NEW ENGLANDERS

In the beginning, there was no one here. Every New Englander, whether of Indian or European stock, is an immigrant.

The western hemisphere was first populated by people of Mongolian stock who came from Asia, perhaps across the Bering Strait, anywhere from 12,000 to 25,000 years ago. They reached New England about 10,000 or 9000 B.C. We know very little about these first inhabitants, not even if they were the ancestors of the Indians who were here when the first European explorers arrived.

New England may be a fount of culture and industry today, but it was not so in ancient times. The greatest advances in ancient American civilization were made by the peoples of the American Southwest, the Valley of Mexico, the Maya lands, and Peru. The great Aztec, Maya, and Inca emperors would no doubt have looked upon the New England peoples of the first thousand years after Christ as the basest barbarians.

When the first European explorers arrived in what would become New England, they found the Algonquian tribes who hunted turkeys, deer, moose, beaver, and smaller animals; angled for fish and collected clams and lobsters; and raised corn and beans, pumpkins, and tobacco. Attuned by tradition to their environment, the Algonquian peoples lived well but simply. They did not always get along with one another, however. Intertribal warfare was common. There was no center of power among the New England tribes as there was in the Iroquois confederacy of New York, which offered a focused and sustained resistance to the encroachments of white settlers. When the Europeans came, they did not need to "divide and conquer" New England's residents, for the indigenous peoples were already divided.

European Explorers

Historians think that the Vikings were the first Europeans to explore North America's shores, but there is evidence, none of it conclusive, that the discoverers may have been Irish, Spanish, or Portuguese. But we know that the Norse came to this area about 1000 B.C., and may have founded settlements in the land they called Vinland. Though the land was fruitful, the settlers found it hard going, mostly because the indigenous peoples fought the settlers ferociously. The great Nordic leaders did not judge the land to be worth the deaths of many of their people, so they withdrew to their more easily ruled settlements in Greenland and Iceland.

By the time the intrepid Columbus set out on his epoch-making voyage 500 hundred years later (1492), Europe had become ready to profit from discoveries of new lands.

Columbus was followed by other explorers, including Giovanni Caboto (known as John Cabot), who sailed under the English flag in 1497 and claimed all of what would become New England for his master, King Henry VII.

It took a century before the English monarch was ready to exploit his claims. During the early 1600s, expeditions were sent out under Sir Humphrey Gilbert,

Bartholomew Gosnold, Martin Pring, and George Weymouth. These brought back useful intelligence on the new land (and Weymouth brought back a Native American named Squanto, who learned English before returning to his homeland), but it was Sir John Smith who studied the land seriously with an eye to colonization, and who gave it the name "New England."

COLONIAL NEW ENGLAND

Before Gilbert, Gosnold, and Smith set out for the New World, several hundred Puritans had already left England for Holland in search of religious freedom. Their stay in Leyden was not a happy one, since they found the morals of the local people to be less than strict; so a number of these Puritan "pilgrims" returned to England and, in late summer of 1620, set sail in the *Mayflower* for the New World. They arrived at what is now Provincetown on the tip of Cape Cod in November, and paused there long enough to draft and sign the Mayflower Compact, which would be their governing law. But Cape Cod's sandy terrain and scrubby vegetation, which delight present-day vacationers, were too poor for the Pilgrims' purposes, and the search for more fertile land finally brought them to Plymouth Rock, south of Massachusetts Bay, in the middle of the frigid month of December 1620.

Half of the Pilgrims died that winter of disease and privation. But luck was with the rest: Squanto, George Weymouth's prisoner, found them and persuaded Massasoit, sachem (chief) of the Wampanoags, to agree to 50 years of peace between his people and the colonists. In 1621 more colonists arrived, and in a few years Plymouth was a sturdy colony. At first land was held and worked in common, but this system was abandoned when it was realized that family plots would be worked more diligently.

Land north and south of Plymouth proved to be more fertile, and soon there were several thriving communities nearby ready to welcome new settlers.

The Founders, as they are called, were followed in 1628 by another group of Pilgrims who established the colony of Massachusetts Bay. By 1637 the colony had several thousand inhabitants, and new towns were being founded up and down the coast, and even inland at Concord, Dedham, and Watertown. The Puritan settlers must have seen a bright future, for in 1636 they set up Harvard College to educate young men for the ministry.

By 1640 there were sturdy communities of settlers in Connecticut and Rhode Island as well as in Massachusetts. By 1680 the indigenous peoples who had lived here before the coming of the settlers were reduced to only a few thousand souls through fierce warfare, European-introduced disease, and alcohol addiction.

Spirit of Independence

The settlers of New England had always governed themselves, though they always paid lip service to the sovereignty of the British crown. They had built their own prosperity despite laws promulgated in London that placed burdens and restraints on their economic activities. Governors sent out by the king were universally disliked, and often forced to return home by the cantankerous colonists.

It was King George III (reigned 1760–1820) who forced the issue, refusing to bear the irritation of the Americans' independent spirit any longer. Taxes were imposed on the colonies, even though the colonists had no elected representatives and no voice in Parliament. Resentment grew as the colonists chafed under the burden of taxation without representation.

The king was determined to force the issue, but it was the colonists who lit the fuse on the powderkeg. In March 1770, a crowd of Bostonians began taunting royal army sentries, and soon the mob got out of hand. Greatly outnumbered, the soldiers fired into the crowd, killing five citizens in what would be known as the Boston Massacre.

Life in Boston was outwardly peaceful for a few years, but king and Parliament were still determined to rule the unruly colonists, and the colonists were determined not to permit interference with their privileges of self-government, now a century and a half old. As a symbol of London's supremacy, a tax was placed on tea shipped to the colonies. Tea was to New England then what coffee is to America today, and the tax was widely reviled, not so much for its economic impact, which was minimal, but because of its symbolic importance: virtually everyone drank tea, and thus everyone was forced to pay the tax. The political temperature rose as American patriots formed secret societies like the Sons of Liberty and the Committees of Correspondence, and worked out plans of resistance to London's control.

In the autumn of 1773, matters came to a head as the patriotic activists insisted that the king's governor order HMS *Dartmouth,* arriving in Boston with a cargo of taxable tea, to go back where it came from. Governor Hutchinson would not give the order, so on the night of December 16, bands of patriots disguised as Indians and blacks emptied the *Dartmouth* and two other ships of their tea cargoes. The tea was dumped into Boston Harbor, and the night's action became known as the Boston Tea Party. When London learned of this rebellious act, laws were passed that were meant to strangle the colonial economy and to teach the nasty colonists a lesson. The political temperature in New England neared the boiling point.

Revolutionary War

Seeing war as inevitable, farmers and tradesmen began to stockpile arms, ammunition, and matériel. Boston and other large towns were under the direct control of sizable royal garrisons, but the countryside and its villages belonged to the revolutionists, so this "arms race" went on uninhibited.

Realizing that the colonists' arms collecting must be stopped, the British ordered an expeditionary force to march secretly to Concord on the night of April 18, 1775, and to make surprise searches of suspected illegal arms caches at dawn.

American spies learned of the plan and set up a system to warn their countrymen. If the redcoats departed Boston along the isthmus that linked it to the mainland, one lantern would be hung in the steeple of Boston's Old North Church. If the troops instead boarded boats to row across the water and march on a different route, two lanterns would be hung. As the British filled the boats, two lanterns appeared in the steeple, easily visible from the far shore where Paul Revere, William Dawes, and Samuel Prescott waited on horseback. These messengers rode into the dark hinterland, sounding the alarm in each village. The American intelligence network was so good that the citizens of Lexington and Concord leapt from their beds long before Major Pitcairn and his royal infantry were anywhere near.

We don't know what went through the minds of the "minutemen," the colonial militia, as they waited in the chilly dawn to hear the crunch of the redcoats' boots in the streets of Lexington and Concord. Whatever their thoughts, they had every right to be frightened, since they, small untrained bands of farmers and tradesmen, were about to face 700 of the world's best professional soldiers. As dawn broke on April 19, 70 Lexington minutemen faced Pitcairn's regiments on Lexington's town green.

The minutemen were ordered by Major Pitcairn to disperse. They stood their ground. Taunts were exchanged. A shot was fired, and that triggered a battle. When the smoke cleared, eight minutemen were dead, and the British troops went on a rampage that was stopped only with difficulty by their commanders, who immediately marched them in the direction of Concord.

Word of the Lexington engagement was rushed to Concord, where the local minutemen retreated across the North Bridge over the Concord River in the face of the powerful British force. The Battle of Concord was fought for command of the bridge. The British forces were unable to take it, which was a victory for the much smaller colonial force. But the redcoats pursued their mission in town, discovering and burning some wooden gun carriages. The smoke rising from the town convinced the minutemen, holding their position at North Bridge, that their homes were in flames, and they fought all the more fiercely.

The "shot heard 'round the world" was fired from a minuteman's musket at Concord North Bridge, where this band of farmers held off professional soldiers. But this first battle of the American revolution was actually won by the colonists as the British retreated. Sniping from behind trees and stone walls along the road back to Boston, minutemen brought the British casualty count up to 200, a grievous and embarrassing loss for the powerful forces of the Crown.

News of the events in Lexington and Concord spread like wildfire through the British colonies in America, forcing every American to choose sides: would one be loyal to the Crown, or committed to the revolutionary cause? There was no middle ground.

On June 17, 1776, full war broke out when the Americans fortified Breed's Hill, next to Bunker's Hill, in Charlestown just across the harbor from Boston. General Gage, the British commander, was forced to attack this threat, but from their entrenched positions the Americans shot more than a thousand of his soldiers. As the battle raged, the Americans' ammunition ran low, and their commander, Col. William Prescott, said to his troops, "Don't fire until you see the whites of their eyes," in order to make every shot count. Their ammunition exhausted, the revolutionary forces abandoned their positions, having won another important victory.

A few weeks later on July 4, in Philadelphia, American leaders signed a Declaration of Independence from Great Britain.

Though many of the most important battles of the Revolutionary War were later to be fought in New York and Pennsylvania, New England prides itself on having been the place where it all began. Patriots' Day (April 19) is a holiday in Massachusetts, and hundreds of citizens and visitors turn out at dawn to witness reenactments of the battles of Lexington and Concord staged by groups in period uniforms.

EARLY AMERICA

By 1781, the Revolutionary War was over and the American colonies were free and independent states. But the forging of a strong and effective central government for the former British territories would not be accomplished until 1789. In the meantime, the removal of British legal restrictions on trade meant that New England merchants were at last free to trade with the world as they liked. New Englanders put to sea in ships built in Maine, Massachusetts, Rhode Island, and Connecticut, and were soon returning with the riches of Europe, Africa, China, and India in trade. Whaling ships out of Salem and New Bedford brought back whale-oil wealth of similar greatness. Though the renewal of war with Great Britain (the War of 1812) disrupted New England's progress for a time, the seas were soon open again.

Industrial Revolution

Across the open sea from England, a young man named Samuel Slater had arrived in 1789. Slater had worked in the new cotton-spinning factories of England. Though it was against British law to "export" knowledge of the machines, which were making Great Britain the world's wealthiest textile producer, Slater slipped out of the country and established a cotton-spinning mill at Pawtucket, Rhode Island, based on his knowledge of English machine design. The mill revolutionized the weaving of textiles in the New World, and set the stage for New England's great weaving industry.

Throughout the 19th century, as New England's clipper ships and whalers swept through the world's oceans, land-bound New Englanders exploited the region's waterpower resources to run their new mills, and industrial towns sprang to life along New England's rivers. The textile factories grew and grew, and some, like the gigantic Amoskeag Mills in Manchester, N.H., had many-windowed facades that marched along the riverbank for more than a quarter mile. Next to the factories were new houses for the armies of workers, many of whom were women. Company stores and company-financed civic buildings filled the streets of the new towns, which were founded on the wealth from weaving.

From some of the factories it was not textiles but machinery, firearms, shoes, watches, and instruments that marched out the doors on their way to the markets of the world. New England inventors and New England engineers gained a reputation for ingenuity that survives today, and samples of "Yankee ingenuity" are still proudly displayed.

New England's commercial success brought New Englanders wealth and so-phistication. Boston, chief city of the region, was proud to call itself the "Athens of America." But times change, and changing times brought changed circumstances to the region in the next century.

THE TWENTIETH CENTURY

After the prosperity of the 1800s, the steamship replaced the New England clipper; natural gas, petroleum, and electricity replaced whale oil lamps; and textile manufacturers moved their operations to southern states where wages were lower. Millions of immigrants who had come from abroad to share in New England's commercial boom were left with minimal skills in a diminishing job market. New England's farms, set on rocky soil in a northern climate, were outproduced and out-sold by the vast farms in other areas of the country.

The stock market crash of 1929 and its aftermath spelled the bitter end of New England's golden age. What had once been America's richest, proudest, and most cultured region was now economically depressed, politically corrupt, and spiritually defeated.

But New England was still beautiful, historic, and proud. In the years after World War II, New Englanders realized that their land had other kinds of wealth. New England's hundreds of colleges and universities were leaders in education. The New England landscape was sprinkled with graceful towns and villages. New Englanders were as ingenious as ever, and the chilly waters of the Atlantic still held a wealth of seafood, so New England survived, and even prospered again.

In recent decades, graduates of New England's universities, no matter where they came from, settled here and founded small companies—Wang Laboratories, Digital Equipment—that became large companies employing tens of thousands. The sturdy old 19th-century textile mills of brick and granite were recycled as com-puter company offices and factories. The name of Route 128, Boston's ring road, became synonymous with the computer industry. New England's picturesque towns and villages found a new vocation as the great old houses were transformed to historic inns, and the more modest houses began to provide bed and breakfast to travelers and vacationers.

Today New England is known for its beautiful landscapes and settlements, its rich history, its technical expertise, its medical research, and, well, its "livability" and charm. More than one New Englander will proudly claim that this is America's first and best, and after your visit here, I think you'll agree.

---

2. Preparing for Your Trip

The smoothest trips are those that are properly prepared in advance. Here's the information you'll need to get ready for your New England sojourn.

INFORMATION

There are both public and private sources of information. Each state has a **tour-ism office,** which issues brochures, maps, lists of festivals and special events, and other useful materials. Municipal governments often have their own tourism offices as well, but the job of providing information in a town or city is done mostly by the local **chamber of commerce** or **convention and visitors' bureau.** I've written the names, addresses, and telephone numbers of these chambers and bureaus in the text of this guide. See also **Travelers Aid** under "Emergencies" in section 4, "For the Foreign Visitor," below.

Anyone passing through New York can benefit from the hundreds of brochures, pamphlets, and maps available at the **New England Vacation Center,** 630 Fifth Ave., Rockefeller Center Concourse Shop No. 2, New York, NY 10111 (tel. 212/307-5780); it's located in Rockefeller Center, between 50th and 51st streets, and Fifth Avenue and Avenue of the Americas.

New England USA, the regional organization promoting tourism, has a toll-free information number: 800/847-4863 (that's 800/VISIT-NE).

Here are the addresses of the state tourism offices:

Connecticut Travel Office, 210 Washington St., Hartford, CT 06106 (tel. 203/566-3385, or toll free 800/243-1685).

Maine Publicity Bureau, Box 2300, 97 Winthrop St., Hallowell, ME 04347 (tel. 207/289-2423).

Massachusetts Division of Tourism, 100 Cambridge St., 13th floor, Boston, MA 02202 (tel. 617/727-3201, or toll free 800/942-6277).

New Hampshire Office of Vacation Travel, 105 Loudon Rd., P.O. Box 856, Concord, NH 03301 (tel. 603/271-2343).

Rhode Island Tourism Division, 7 Jackson Walkway, Providence, RI 02903 (tel. 401/277-2601).

Vermont Travel Division, 134 State St., Montpelier, VT 05602 (tel. 802/828-3236).

WHEN TO GO

Without doubt, the best times to tour New England are summer (June through August) and autumn (September through October), unless you're coming for skiing. You can enjoy a visit here any time of year if you prepare for the weather and are wary of the busy times when hotels, restaurants, and transportation are filled to capacity. Here's a summary of the seasons.

The Four Seasons

Weather in New England is a much-discussed topic, but it is always surrounded by a certain fatalism, not so much because there's a lot of bad weather, but because it's so unpredictable. My rough, personal survey of weather reports has revealed that the weather forecasters are wrong a surprising 60% of the time for Boston! But, after all, Boston does seem to have its own weather: a snowfall may cover all New England, but stop short at Rte. 128, Boston's ring road; or a summer downpour may drench the city while the sun shines everywhere else. However, there are some generalizations that seem to hold true from year to year, and these will affect your plans on when to visit New England.

SPRING   Coming very late and staying very briefly, spring tends to be a disappointment. The week or two of spring days in the normal year are a delight, with cool temperatures in the evening and just the perfect degree of warmth during the day, in bright, clear sun. In the countryside the thaw brings "Mud Time," the period between frost and spring planting. Mud Time is the slowest season for tourist facilities, coming after ski season and before summer warmth and school vacations bring out the city folk. Thus many country inns, resorts, and amusements close for a few weeks in April or thereabouts.

SUMMER   By mid-June, summer is well established and despite the region's northerly and coastal location, it can be pretty hot and sometimes quite humid. When it's 85°F (or even up to 95°F) and humid, as it often is through mid-September, head for the beaches, the islands, mountains, lakes, and riverbanks. Sailing, along the coast or on the rivers, is a choice activity, as is a hike to the top of Mount Washington, or a week at a beach on Narragansett Bay. But a drive through the Berkshires or along the Connecticut coast can also be very satisfying.

AUTUMN   This is undoubtedly New England's glory and its finest season, and if you have a choice of vacation times this is the one to pick. Although you may have to forsake swimming, the famous fall foliage is a worthy substitute; it's at its peak usually in late September and early October, starting in northern Maine, New Hampshire, and Vermont and moving southward as the weeks pass. Days are still warm and very pleasant, nights a bit chilly but not uncomfortably so. City people load their bikes into the car and head for the country, picking up fresh apple cider, pumpkins, and squash from farm stands on the way home. Fresh cranberries are on sale in the markets all autumn, and although the blueberry-picking season is past, many apple orchards open so you can "pick-your-own," and get the freshest fruit possible at a very low price.

People want to get away for the weekend, no matter where they live. Those who don't want to tangle with the traffic on fall weekends can take special bus and rail foliage tours from the major cities. Most tourist resorts and inns stay open through September and often to Columbus Day. Those that stay open all year sometimes close for two weeks or so from mid-October to early December to give the staff a break before the advent of the ski season. By Thanksgiving, everyone's getting in shape for the ski season and shopping for the holidays.

WINTER This season, as they say, depends: in the winter of 1976–77, the region had six inches of snow in November, which is very early; for the first flurries usually come in mid-December, when hopes are high that the accumulation will be sufficient for good skiing during the holiday season. Sometimes snow wishes are too well answered, as in the Great Blizzard of 1978, which piled six feet of snow on Boston, closing the city for a week. Ski reports appear in newspapers and the broadcast media, and the special skiing-condition phone lines go into operation. January through March is cold and snowy, and the skiing may be quite good through April; gray snowy days alternate with brilliant, crisp, sunny days when the air is very cold but the sun's warmth makes it pleasant. Those who aren't skiing take advantage of the cities' cultural season, perhaps escaping to an inn somewhere in the snow-clad mountains for a weekend.

Mount Washington Weather: None of this applies to Mount Washington in New Hampshire, of course. This "highest peak in New England" is said to have the worst weather in all the U.S., and New Englanders delight in exchanging horror stories of the latest report: winds of 150 miles per hour (the record is 211 mph!), temperatures of minus 40° F, wind-chill factors that don't seem earthly. Regional news media often carry the reports even though they don't really affect anyone but the forlorn weather forecasters who have to sit through the storm on the mountaintop.

New England Calendar

Here's what you need to know about New England's year, month by month:

JANUARY New Year's Day (January 1) is a holiday, and transportation services are quite busy on the days immediately preceding and following it. Otherwise, the first two weeks of the month are not a busy time, travel services are unburdened, and prices are lower. The weekend of the third Monday is when **Martin Luther King Day** (January 15) is celebrated. This is the holiday that begins the ski season in earnest. Ski lodges and inns offer money-saving package deals, especially if you stay on weekdays rather than weekends.

FEBRUARY Ski season continues, though many New Englanders fly to the Caribbean or Mexico for a few weeks of warmth and sun. The third Monday is **Presidents' Day,** a holiday honoring the birthdays of Washington (February 22) and Lincoln (February 12). The holiday weekend is particularly busy in ski country.

MARCH Traditional wisdom holds that after St. Patrick's Day (March 17, not a holiday) in the southern New England states (Massachusetts, Connecticut, and Rhode Island), there will be no more big snowstorms—but traditional wisdom is occasionally proved wrong. In any case, ski areas in the northern states (Maine, New Hampshire, Vermont) have plenty of snow until April.

APRIL **Patriots' Day** (April 19) is a holiday in Massachusetts, celebrated on the Monday nearest that date. The day commemorates the first battles of the Revolutionary War, fought in the early hours of April 19 in Lexington and Concord. All state government offices and many local businesses close, though federal government offices and offices of large interstate and international companies remain open. Easter often falls in April, and New England's hundreds of colleges empty out for Easter vacation (or "spring break"). Good Friday, preceding Easter, is not an official holiday though some businesses close and many people travel. Ski season is winding down and spring has not really arrived, so many country inns close for all or part of the month.

MAY Many seasonal services (small museums, campgrounds, flights, etc.) begin operating in May, at least on the weekends. Opening times may be limited, but prices may also be lower. The weekend nearest **Memorial Day** (May 30), signals the official start of the summer tourism season; the holiday is celebrated on the last Monday in the month. Rooms at inns and resort hotels are in great demand on the holiday weekend, and on weekends through Labor Day (the first Monday after the first Sunday in September), but the demand is much lower during the week.

JUNE Early June is not very busy in New England's vacation areas because most children are still in school. But when school ends in mid-June, many families head out for their summer vacations at the beach or in the mountains. Accommodations, campgrounds, and other services are busy by late June.

JULY Early July sees the tourist season in full swing. The **Independence Day** holiday (July 4) is very busy, particularly when it falls on a Friday or a Monday. The six weeks from mid-July through Labor Day are the busiest time of the year. The beach resorts and islands are often filled to capacity.

AUGUST The height of the tourism season continues through August to the Labor Day weekend.

SEPTEMBER The **Labor Day** holiday weekend, the first Monday after the first Sunday, signals the official end of the summer vacation season. The weekend is very busy, but the two weeks following are a good time to travel since children are back in school, few families travel, services are uncrowded, and some price reductions are offered. Foliage season begins in mid-September in the northern states, late September in the southern states.

OCTOBER New England's deservedly famed fall foliage is in full color everywhere in early October. Rooms at country inns are in great demand, especially on weekends. The blazing finale to foliage season is the **Columbus Day** holiday weekend, the second Monday in October. Every room in the countryside is reserved in advance. In Boston, hotels are often filled by conventioneers since October is also a popular month for meetings and conferences. Many inns and seasonal services close for the winter after the Columbus Day weekend, and late October is fairly quiet in the countryside, though busy in the cities.

NOVEMBER This is a slow month for travel. The foliage crowds have departed and the ski crowds have yet to arrive, so many country inns close for part or all of the month. Ski resorts begin to make their own snow if nature has not provided the traditional cover, and some eager skiers take advantage of the **Veterans Day** holiday (November 11, celebrated on the nearest Monday) for a first schuss down the slopes. The big holiday in November is **Thanksgiving,** the fourth Thursday, a holiday when transportation services are strained to the breaking point as *everyone* travels to have

Thanksgiving dinner with relatives. The busiest times are the Wednesday before and the Sunday after Thanksgiving, especially the afternoon and evening. Don't plan to travel at these times if at all possible. If you must travel, expect long delays and inconvenience. Throughout the United States, this is the busiest travel time of the entire year.

DECEMBER The ski resorts are open, and though they may be fairly busy on weekends, innkeepers offer special low prices during the week to lure vacationers. Until the **Christmas** holiday (December 25), this is not a busy month for tourism. Travel is heavy on the day or two preceding Christmas and the day or two following, then there is a lull until New Year's, when travel intensifies again. Between Christmas and New Year's, many New Englanders take short vacations to New York, which is very busy then.

WHAT TO PACK
You won't need any exotic gear for New England. You'll want at least one fairly nice outfit of the dress or jacket-and-tie variety for special evenings in fancy restaurants. Few establishments enforce a strict dress code anymore, but you should be prepared nonetheless. (Newport, R.I., has numerous restaurants requiring jacket-and-tie/dress, and the Ritz-Carlton in Boston also enforces the dress code.)

Rain can come at any time of year. A small umbrella is minimal rain gear in summer; in other seasons a raincoat is necessary as well.

Summer days can get very hot and muggy, so cool cotton clothing is best, but have a sweater or jacket for cool evenings, cruises, and whale-watching expeditions. In spring and autumn moderately warm clothing, including sweater and windbreaker, is essential. In winter, be prepared for freezing weather and snow. Full woolens and foul weather gear are required.

ABOUT THIS GUIDE
This is a complete guidebook, containing everything you'll need to know about New England. I've searched through the cities, towns, and villages looking for the best hotels, the best value-for-money motels, the most charming inns, and also the bed-and-breakfast guesthouses, the small places other guides can't afford to uncover. I've sampled the restaurants that local people enjoy, and I keep track of the chefs and the management. I've described these establishments in enough detail that you'll know what you're getting, and what makes one place different from another. There's plenty of information on how to get from here to there, by every possible means, and I've kept in mind both the traveler with a car and the one without. Every major attraction in New England is thoroughly described in this book, plus many of the charming, lesser-known sights off the beaten path.

If all this sounds sensible and self-evident, think again. These days, some guidebooks are written by committees of editors, others are compiled entirely from data collected on forms sent through the mail, still others charge money (under one scheme or another) for the "privilege" of being included in their pages, or for stickers saying "Featured in Such-and-such Guide," or for signs to hang out front, or for membership in an "association." The only person who pays me anything is you, the reader, by buying this book. I'm working for *you*.

SOME DISCLAIMERS
When I travel around New England looking for the best hotels, bed-and-breakfast guesthouses, country inns, restaurants, and places of amusement, I do my best to keep a secret of what I'm up to, hoping to be treated as any newly arrived customer would be treated, and thus to find out firsthand how an establishment is run. Sometimes it's necessary to confess I'm preparing a guidebook—better that than be mistaken for the Mad Bomber as I peer into kitchens, facilities, and rooms. And so the recommendations found in this book are strictly personal, unaffected by reputations or the blandishments of managers. No establishment in this book has paid to appear in these pages, which means that if I get a lot of complaint letters from

readers (which I read and answer personally), I can remove any establishment without qualm.

But I hasten to add that if you do not find a favorite place of yours listed in these pages, it's because this is not an exhaustive guide, but rather a selection of some of the best, most convenient, unique, quiet, friendly—in short, satisfying—places in New England. They were chosen not according to some inflexible checklist of facilities and luxuries, but with the practical day-to-day needs of discerning travelers in mind.

PRICES AND INFLATION

Remember as you use this book that inflation is a fact of life today, and although I tried to present the most complete, inclusive, and accurate price information of any guidebook, prices may change between the time the book goes to press and when you use it. Check prices when you arrive to avoid confusion.

The prices of rooms, meals, and other expenses given with my recommendations are as accurate as I could make them; if I determined that a price rise was likely between the time of my visit and the time of yours, I figured the rise into the quoted prices. No establishment promised me to keep the prices I quote, and therefore you cannot demand of any establishment that it charge you exactly what is quoted here. When in doubt, a quick telephone call is the best way to determine whether or not prices have changed.

AN INVITATION TO READERS

Like the other books in the Frommer series, *Frommer's New England* hopes to list the establishments that offer the best value-for-money. In achieving this goal, your comments and suggestions can be of tremendous help. Therefore, if you come across a particularly appealing lodging, restaurant, store, even a sightseeing attraction, please don't keep it to yourself. In fact, I encourage you to write to me on any matter dealing with this book. Every now and then a change of management, staff, or ownership will affect the quality of an establishment, and if you find that this is the case with a recommended place, let me know so I can look it over extra carefully for the following edition. And if you found a suggestion of mine particularly good, or found the book helpful in general, I don't mind hearing that either! Finally, you might want to share your extraordinary experiences with other readers: "Go to this museum on weekdays only, it's less crowded and admission is half price."

You have my word that every letter will be read by me personally, and answered as soon as possible in almost every case. Send your notes to Tom Brosnahan, c/o Prentice Hall Travel, 15 Columbus Circle, New York, NY 10023.

NEW ENGLAND ACCOMMODATIONS

In my lodging recommendations, you'll find the full mailing address, with the ZIP code, so that you can write ahead for reservations. Telephone numbers, and a toll-free reservation number if the hotel has one, are included. The hotel or motel room you rent (but not bed-and-breakfast or country-inn rooms) will normally be air-conditioned and will have a private bath and a TV, usually color. The room may have either one or two double beds in it (single beds are rare), and note that prices are for the room, not each bed. To make your life easier, I've figured in the tax as well.

Tips for Families: The most economical way to travel is for several people to stay in the same room, and normally a party of five or even six can use the same room. Here's how it works: Two people are charged the regular room rate, then there is usually a per-person charge for each extra person, but the charge is low. There is also a low cost for rollaway beds. For families there's an extra bonus, because most modern hotels and motels allow children to stay for free with their parents if the parents pay the normal two-person rate and the children use the room's existing beds. So in a room with two double beds, a family of four can stay as cheaply as two. If there are three children and a rollaway bed is necessary, there'll be a small charge ($10 to $20) for it. The age permissible for children under the "family plan" varies.

Weekend Specials: Sometimes there are other special rates, especially at big-city hotels. Many of the more expensive places try to fill rooms on weekends, when business travelers are gone, by offering special mini-vacation rates for two nights (Friday and Saturday), plus some credit toward meals and drinks in the hotel's restaurants and bars. A $180-a-night double might be $125 per night for the two-day period from 5pm Friday to checkout time on Sunday, with perhaps $30 credit toward drinks and dinners, or maybe a free sightseeing tour of the city. These mini-vacation programs and rates vary from year to year and from hotel to hotel, so it's best to call or write ahead for full details.

Some hotels and motels offer a discount to senior citizens who have proper identification, such as a membership card in the American Association of Retired Persons (AARP). Ask about this if you qualify.

Bed-and-Breakfast Guesthouses: The bed-and-breakfast house, long popular in Europe, is sweeping America as travelers discover that they can get charming accommodations at a "B&B." Some houses have a half-dozen rooms, others only one or two; some serve a full, hearty sausage-and-eggs breakfast, others provide home-baked muffins and rolls; some guesthouses provide no breakfast. Rooms can be large or small, with a view or without—in short, nothing is standard. Though I can describe hotel, motel, and inn rooms, which are usually of a certain standard, the only sure way to know what you're getting at a B&B is to look at the room yourself. I've chosen the houses recommended in this guide on grounds of general cleanliness, friendliness, price, location, and charm.

Country Inns: New England is famous for its country inns, delightfully cozy and hospitable or elegant and historic places to stay, often with very fine food. You should realize, however, that country inns are no longer the informal roadside "guesthouses" that they were a generation ago. Rather, they are more like small vacation resorts. Prices tend to be fairly hefty, and requirements for a stay can be complex, very much like those at a resort. For instance, one inn charges $75 for a double room with bath in summer on Monday through Wednesday nights, but $120 for the same room on Thursday through Sunday. To these rates you must add 9.7% room tax, $3 for the maid's tip (required), and $8 if you use the fireplace in the room. All in all, that comes to over $94 for the "$75" Monday-through-Wednesday room, or $144 for the "$120" Thursday-through-Sunday room.

You may have to reserve well ahead for a country-inn room, particularly if you wish to stay during foliage season or when there's some big event nearby. The innkeeper may require a minimum stay of two, three, four, or even more days, with payment in cash (see below).

City hotels offer weekend packages, since the business trade disappears on weekends. But for country inns, weekends are the busy time. What you want to do is plan your city visits for weekends (or at least partly so), and spend Monday through Thursday out in the country.

Pets: By far, pets are not allowed in the majority of hotels, inns, motels, and guesthouses recommended in this book. Although I've done my best to find highway homes for pets, most places just don't allow them. If a hotel or inn does accept pets, I've mentioned this in the text. No mention of pets means that no pets are accepted.

Advance Reservations

At certain times of year, rooms in New England's hotels and inns are in high demand, and you may not be able to get the room you want in the establishment you want unless you reserve it well in advance. The busiest periods are high summer (mid-July through Labor Day), foliage season (mid-September through Columbus Day), Christmas and New Year's Eve, and ski season (late January through March). Low seasons, when business is slack and many inns may be closed, are April, May, and late October through late December.

Know the Rules!

Inn brochures paint rosy pictures of the warm welcome you're bound to receive, and of the friendliness and hospitality of your hosts. But innkeepers are in the lodging business in a sellers' market, and they must make a profit, so they make certain stipulations that you must know about. If you make a reservation and put down a deposit, and the inn or hotel accepts your deposit and confirms your reservation, you have made a legal contract. However, it is usually the inn that spells out the terms of the contract, and this can lead to unpleasant surprises. Though you both want the contract to work out as anticipated, one or the other of you may lose a substantial amount of money if it doesn't, so you must know what to expect.

When making reservations, you can avoid hassles and disappointments by asking some of the following questions. These questions are the distilled wisdom of my experiences with inns, and also that of generations of readers of this guide:

Is smoking allowed in the inn? Are children welcome? What age? What about pets?

Is there a requirement for a minimum stay of two, three, four nights, or even more?

Can you reserve a precise room or sort of room ("with antiques," "in the main inn and not in the annex," "with a canopy bed and full bath," "with a view of the water") or must you take whatever the innkeeper gives you? How many beds does the room have? Real beds or sofa beds? Can you get all this in writing?

Are meals included or required? If breakfast is included, is it store-bought doughnuts and instant coffee, or freshly made French pastries and brewed café au lait? If the inn has no dining room, how close is the nearest restaurant?

Is there a service charge? Is there tax? How much? Are there any other charges, such as for activities or use of a fireplace? They might not tell you if you don't ask.

Are credit cards accepted? Never assume that they are! Many of the most popular inns refuse to accept credit cards, preferring not to pay the 4% to 6% service charge to the credit-card company. They require cash, traveler's checks, or an approved personal check, sometimes for the full amount of your reservation, which might approach $1,000; and sometimes the full amount must be paid upon arrival. Be prepared. (The majority of lodgings listed in this guide do accept credit cards; if it is an inn's policy *not* to accept credit cards, I've noted it in the description.)

How much deposit must you send, and how soon? Under what circumstances can you ask for, and get, a refund of your deposit? What if you are delayed in transit by car problems, a late train or ferry, or weather conditions impossible for flying?

Does the deposit guarantee you a room at the inn absolutely, or does the innkeeper have the option of finding you "equivalent lodgings nearby?"

If your deposit is to be returned, will a "service charge" of 10% to 25% be deducted? What is the deadline for the innkeeper's return of the deposit? Two weeks? Two years?

Camping

See also "Recreational Vehicle Rentals" in chapter II, "Getting There," under "Driving in New England."

New England has many campsites in local, state, and national parks and forests, and on private land. Often there are private campgrounds near popular public ones, just outside the boundaries of a state or national park, for example. Most are open from sometime in May through mid- or late October, though a few private campgrounds stay open all year.

In summer, most campsites fill up quickly on weekends, and they may also be full on weekdays during July and August; this includes even some fairly remote forest campsites. Reservations can be made at some public and virtually all private campsites; usually you must send a deposit to secure the reservation. If you don't (or can't) reserve in advance, plan to arrive early on a weekday to find and hold a spot. For weekends, arrive by midmorning Friday, or, even better, Thursday afternoon. It is usually easy to find a vacant campsite on weekdays in late spring and early autumn, but weekends may be as crowded as summer.

Campsites in public parks and forests are usually simple, consisting of a place to park, flat ground upon which to pitch a tent, a picnic table, and a stone fireplace. Some have facilities for hot showers; most have washbasins with hot and cold water, and flush toilets. Some forest campsites are very basic, with just parking places and tent sites, a drinking water tap, and chemical or composting toilets. Fees for using public campsites range from $5 to $15 per site.

Private campgrounds tend to have less open space, fewer shade trees, more facilities, and higher fees. Some "resort" campgrounds have children's playgrounds, swimming pools, game rooms, cable television and VCR movie rooms, lake swimming and boating facilities, and so on. Virtually all private campgrounds provide hot showers and hook-ups (electrical, sewage, water) for recreational vehicles and trailers (caravans). Fees can range from $15 to $25 or more, depending upon the number of people in your party, and the facilities used.

NEW ENGLAND CUISINE

Seafood is New England's strong suit, of course. Many kinds of fish are taken in New England's waters. In colonial times the codfish was so important to the region's economy that a stuffed codfish had a place of honor in the Massachusetts state house. Filets of choice little codfish are called *scrod*, sautéed in lemon butter or topped with a cheese sauce; it's pretty bland, as is halibut. Bluefish, smoked and served as an appetizer or broiled for a main course, has a fuller flavor. Monkfish sautéed in butter tastes mildly like lobster. Swordfish and fresh tuna steaks are best if grilled over charcoal. Fish chowder, as made in New England, uses bland whitefish, potatoes, corn, and milk.

Shellfish are also important. Everyone knows about Maine lobster, but Massachusetts has a large lobstering fleet as well, and the state supports hatcheries where baby lobsters are raised before being released to sea. Clams are of several varieties. *Soft-shell clams* have shells that chip and crack easily. The clams are usually steamed in the shells, which gave rise to their other name, *steamers*. Hard-shell clams have very hard porcelain-like shells; among the most popular varieties are littlenecks and cherrystones. These can be steamed, baked, or served raw on the half shell with lemon, tomato sauce, or a dab of horseradish. *Quahogs* (pronounced *ko-hogs*) are clams larger than your fist; they're often cut into strips, fried in batter, and served as *fried clams* at roadside or beachfront snack stands, or minced for use in clam chowder. New England clam chowder has clams and potatoes in a base of milk or cream. It's quite different from Manhattan clam chowder, which uses tomato instead of milk. Oysters from Chatham, Wellfleet, and Cotuit on Cape Cod are usually eaten raw on the half shell, or served whole in milk based oyster stew.

Many traditional New England foods are not often served anymore. Boston may be famous for baked beans (navy beans, molasses, salt pork, and onions cooked slowly in a crock), but very few restaurants serve them, and then mostly for sentimental or touristic reasons. New England boiled dinner, a chunk of beef boiled with cabbage, carrots, and potatoes, is also rarely served, and perhaps that's just as well.

Vermont is dairy country, known for cheddar cheese and delicious Ben & Jerry's full-fat ice cream. All of the New England states produce pure maple syrup in the spring. Many inns and some restaurants serve it with breakfast pancakes and waffles.

A Real New England Clambake

Whether on the beach around a driftwood fire, at a backyard cookout, or in a restaurant, chances are you'll encounter the traditional clambake during your stay in New England. The true clambake takes place on the beach, starting with the digging of the clams, but the backyard and restaurant versions are good substitutes provided you observe the rituals properly.

The three essential courses are steamed soft-shell clams, corn on the cob, and lobsters. Here's a recipe: take one very large pot, fill with clean seawater, and place on the fire to boil. Put live lobsters in the bottom, then a layer of seaweed, then ears of corn, more seaweed, and finally a layer of "steamers" (soft-shell clams for steaming). When the clams open, they're ready.

HOW TO EAT STEAMED CLAMS Take a clam, open it completely, and lift out the meat.

The "neck" is black and covered with a wrinkled black membrane. Shuck the membrane off (you pick up the knack for this by about the fifth clam), hold the clam by the neck, and dip it in "clam broth" (seawater that has had clams steamed in it—even in a restaurant you'll be provided with it). The "broth" is strictly for dipping, not for drinking; the dip washes any sand off the clam. Next, dip in the melted butter provided, and then enjoy.

When you've had your fill of clams, it's on to the buttered ears of corn, and finally to the lobsters. Eating a lobster is an art in itself.

HOW TO EAT A LOBSTER   Restaurants will prepare lobsters in any number of elaborate ways, but to a true New Englander there are but two ways to cook a lobster: you boil it or you broil it. To broil, take a live lobster, make a straight cut underneath from head to tail, and place cut-upward under the broiler.

Boiling or steaming is even easier. Put the live lobsters into a pot that has a few inches of boiling seawater in it, cover, bring to a boil again, and let them cook until they turn bright red (10 to 12 minutes, longer for lobsters of several pounds or more). When you take them out, they'll be very hot, and full of hot water, too. Give the lobster a few minutes to cool, and you're ready to begin.

Hold the body in one hand and the tail in the other, and twist the tail off with a side-to-side motion. Holding the tail upside-down, stick a fork (upside-down) between the bottom of the shell and tail meat and pull the whole chunk of tail meat out. The tail is the largest meaty portion of the lobster, but there's lots more.

Each claw should be broken (claw-crackers are always provided) and the meat taken out, even from the joints that connect the claw to the body. This is the most delicious part, a real delicacy. Lobsters molt each year, shedding their hard shells to reveal a new, temporarily soft shell underneath. If you dine on lobster in late July or August, it will have just molted and the soft shell can easily be broken with your fingers. At other times of the year, particularly in May and June, you're certain to need claw-crackers to deal with the year-old, rock-hard shell.

In the larger lobsters (1½ pounds and over), you'll find tender little bites in other places too. Twist the four "flippers" off the end of the tail and chew out the delicate meat inside. Twist off each small leg: in the knuckle next to the body there's a nugget, and you can chew tender meat out of each segment in a leg.

Diehard lobster-lovers (I'm one) go even farther. Take the body apart, and behind where each leg was attached there is a good bit of meat. Of the innards, the gray-colored liver (called "tomalley") is edible—chefs sometimes use it in sauces. If you find a waxy red substance, that's roe (eggs), edible but not choice.

By now you will have discovered that eating lobster is not a refined pastime. The image of the lobster as an item in haute cuisine is justified by its delicious flavor. But simple boiled lobster cannot be improved by even the most creative chef, and eating it should not be an exercise in etiquette. A picnic table, with a newspaper covering to catch the shells, is the perfect setting; a seaside lobster shack is the best location.

---

3. For the Foreign Visitor

Anyone planning a trip to New England must have lots of unanswered questions. Here are the answers to the questions that foreign travelers to New England ask most frequently.

ABBREVIATIONS: In printed text you may see the names of the six New England states abbreviated as Ct. or Conn., Ma. or Mass., Me. (Maine), N.H., R.I., and Vt. In postal addresses the proper abbreviations are CT, MA, ME, NH, RI, and VT. By the way, citizens of Massachusetts in general and Bostonians in particular are famous for abbreviating everything when speaking, especially their state's long Indian name. Massachusetts Avenue becomes "Mass. Ave.," Harvard Business School is

"The 'B' School," Cape Cod is just "the Cape," and Martha's Vineyard is truncated to "the Vineyard." Even Boston's subway, officially the MBTA Rapid Transit System, becomes merely "the T."

BANKS: See "Currency Exchange," "Money and Credit Cards," "Hours."

CONSULATES AND EMBASSIES: Though all embassies are in Washington, D.C., many foreign countries maintain consulates in Boston. If there's no consulate in Boston, your nearest diplomatic representative may be in New York.

Australia
Embassy: 1601 Massachusetts Ave., NW, Washington, DC 20036 (tel. 202/797-3000).
Consulate: International Bldg., 636 Fifth Ave., New York, NY 10111 (tel. 212/245-4000).

Canada
Embassy: 501 Pennsylvania Ave., NW, Washington, DC 20001 (tel. 202/682-1740).
Consulates: 3 Copley Place, Suite 400, Boston, MA 02116 (tel. 617/262-3760); 1251 Ave. of the Americas (Sixth Ave.), New York, NY 10020 (tel. 212/768-2400).

Denmark
Embassy: 3200 Whitehaven St., NW, Washington, DC 20008 (tel. 202/234-4300).
Consulates: Christian G Halby, Honorary Consul, 419 Boylston St., Boston, MA (tel. 617/266-8418); 825 Third Ave., 32nd floor, New York, NY 10022 (tel. 212/223-4545).

France
Embassy: 4101 Reservoir Rd., NW, Washington, DC 20007 (tel. 202/944-6000).
Consulates: 3 Commonwealth Ave., Boston, MA (tel. 617/266-1680); 934 Fifth Ave., New York, NY 10021 (tel. 212/606-3699).

Germany
Embassy: 4645 Reservoir Rd., NW, Washington, DC 20007 (tel. 202/298-4000).
Consulates: 3 Copley Place, Suite 500, Boston, MA 02116 (tel. 617/536-4414); 460 Park Ave., New York, NY 10022 (tel. 212/308-8700).

Ireland
Embassy: 2234 Massachusetts Ave., NW, Washington, DC 20008 (tel. 202/462-3939).
Consulates: Chase Bldg, 535 Boylston St., Boston, MA 02116 (tel. 617/267-9330); 515 Madison Ave., New York, NY 10022 (tel. 212/319-2555).

Italy
Embassy: 1601 Fuller St., NW, Washington, DC 20009 (tel. 202/328-5500).
Consulates: 100 Boylston St., Boston, MA 02116 (tel. 617/542-0483); 690 Park Ave., New York, NY 10021 (tel. 212/737-9100).

New Zealand

Embassy: 37 Observatory Circle, NW, Washington, DC 20008 (tel. 202/328-4800).

Norway

Embassy: 2720 34th St., NW, Washington, DC 20008 (tel. 202/333-6000). **Consulates:** 77 North Washington St., Boston, MA 02114 (tel. 617/523-7078); 825 Third Ave., 17th Floor, New York, NY 10022-7584 (tel. 212/421-7333).

Sweden

Embassy: The Watergate, 600 New Hampshire Ave., NW, Washington, DC 20037 (tel. 202/944-5600). **Consulates:** 6 St. James Ave., Boston, MA 02116 (tel. 617/426-5558); 1 Dag Hammarskjöld Plaza, New York, NY 10017 (tel. 212/751-5900).

United Kingdom

Embassy: 3100 Massachusetts Ave., NW, Washington, DC 20008 (tel. 202/462-1340). **Consulates:** Prudential Tower, Suite 4740, Boston, MA 02199 (tel. 617/437-7160); 845 Third Ave., New York, NY 10022 (tel. 212/752-8400).

CURRENCY EXCHANGE: Only a few banks, mostly in Boston, are prepared to exchange foreign currency. Foreign travelers would be well advised to buy U.S. dollar traveler's checks before leaving home, or upon arrival in the U.S., to solve the problem of exchange.

You can exchange foreign currency at Boston's Logan Airport, at the **Baybanks Foreign Exchange Booths** in Terminals D and E (tel. 617/567-2313); at **Baybank Harvard Trust Co.**, 1414 Massachusetts Ave., Cambridge, MA 02138 (tel. 617/661-3300) in Harvard Square; and at **Deak International Ltd.**, 160 Franklin St., Boston, MA 02110 (tel. 617/426-0016).

CUSTOMS AND IMMIGRATION: Every adult visitor is allowed to bring in, free of duty: 1 liter of wine or hard liquor; 1,000 cigarettes or 100 cigars (but *no* cigars from Cuba) or 3 pounds of smoking tobacco; and up to $400 worth of gifts. If you exceed these amounts, you may have to pay some duty on the excess. In general, Customs officers are very accommodating, even with small excess amounts, if you make a full and complete declaration and don't try to hide something from them.

Do not try to bring in foodstuffs, especially fresh fruit, vegetables, seeds, or other "plant propagative material." If it's important to you to bring in a specific food, or an animal, contact a U.S. consulate and ask how this can be accomplished.

If you are carrying $10,000 or more in currency or negotiable instruments (traveler's checks, bearer bonds, etc.) when you enter or leave the country, you must declare it.

American passport holders complete immigration formalities when the Customs agent examines their luggage; those with other passports must pass through separate immigration and Customs checkpoints, and this can take awhile if several jumbo jets arrive at the same time. It's best to allow at least two or even three hours between the arrival time of your international flight and any onward flight. Coming from Canada, U.S. Customs and immigration formalities are much faster, whether you come by road, rail, or air. Some Canadian, Bermudian, and Caribbean airports have U.S. Customs and immigration officers who clear travelers even before they board their U.S.-bound flights.

DRINKING LAWS: Use of alcohol is governed by federal, state, and local laws. In Maine, New Hampshire, and Vermont, liquor may be bought only in state-operated stores; in Connecticut, Massachusetts, and Rhode Island liquor stores are private.

None of these stores is open on Sunday, though most restaurants and bars with liquor licenses may serve liquor by the drink on Sunday. The minimum age for drinking varies by state, but is usually 18 years.

A restaurant may have a "full liquor license" (for liquor, wine, and beer), a "wine and beer" license, or no license. If a restaurant—typically a small, new bistro —does not have a liquor license of any kind, you may be allowed to "B.Y.O." ("Bring Your Own") or "brown-bag it" (bring your own bottle in a brown paper bag). If allowed, the restaurant will usually provide "set-ups," that is, corkscrews, glasses, ice, ingredients such as soda for cocktails, and so on. But in some restaurants brown-bagging is not allowed, and you'll have to forego alcohol altogether. You are not allowed to drink alcohol, even beer, in most fast-food restaurants—hamburger shops, pizza shops, and the like. It is also against the law to drink any alcoholic beverage in public areas outdoors, such as streets, parks, and beaches. The law is to discourage public drunkenness; if you are discreet, you can usually have wine or beer with your picnic.

A few New England towns (such as Rockport, Mass.) are "dry," that is, it is forbidden for any restaurant or hotel to sell or to serve liquor anywhere in town. In such places you must buy your beverages in another town and serve yourself in restaurants.

ELECTRICITY: Electric current is 110–20 volts, 60-cycle. Appliances built to take 220–40 volt, 50-cycle current (as in Europe) will need a converter (transformer) and a plug adapter with two flat, parallel pins, American-style.

EMERGENCIES: In major cities and many larger towns, dial 911 from any telephone (no coin needed at pay telephones) to contact the local police, fire company, or ambulance. In areas without 911 service, dial "0" (zero, *not* the letter "O") to reach the telephone-company operator, who will direct your call to the proper emergency number. Local numbers for emergency services are also listed on the inside front cover of most telephone directories.

The **Travelers Aid Society,** 711 Atlantic Ave., Boston, MA 02111 (tel. 617/542-7286) is an organization dedicated to helping travelers solve problems large and small. Travelers Aid volunteers at Logan Airport (tel. 617/567-5385 or 569-6284) and South Station (tel. 617/542-9875 or 423-7766) will help you find an address, a hospital, your lost luggage, a way to get money from home, or any other solution to a travel dilemma. For the telephone number of Travelers Aid in another city, look in the local telephone directory under "Travelers Aid."

HEALTH SERVICES: All cities in New England have hospitals; blue signs bearing a white "H" mark the way. Boston is one of the country's most renowned medical centers, with dozens of hospitals and medical facilities treating every known ailment.

To use most of these facilities, however, you will need health insurance, since prices for services are astronomical. A three-day stay in a hospital can cost more than $1,000 just for the room and basic services; medical procedures and doctors' fees might cost several thousand more.

HOLIDAYS: See "New England Calendar," above.

HOURS: Public and private **office hours** are normally 8 or 9am to 5pm, Monday through Friday.

Banks are usually open Monday through Friday from 9am to 3pm, but many banks have extended hours, until 5pm (or even 8 or 9pm on Thursday), and on Saturday from 9am to 2pm or later. No banks are open on Sunday except the currency exchange booths at Boston's Logan Airport. Most banks have automatic teller machines (ATMs) for after-hours transactions.

Post offices are open Monday through Friday from 8am to 5pm; some major post offices in cities stay open until 5:30 or 6pm; the post office at Boston's Logan

Airport stays open until midnight. Weekend hours are normally 8am to noon or 2pm on Saturday, closed Sunday.

Stores open at 9:30 or 10am, and stay open until 5:30 or 6pm Monday through Saturday; many are open from 11am or noon till 5pm Sunday. All cities and many large towns have at least a few **"convenience stores"** for food, beverages, newspapers, and some household items open 24 hours a day; in cities, supermarkets stay open from 8 or 9am to 9 or 10pm, with shorter hours on Sunday, but some are open all the time, closing only from Sunday evening to Monday morning.

Museums normally open at 10am and close at 5pm, Tuesday through Sunday (closed Monday), but you must call and confirm the hours in each case. Many museums and attractions close on Thanksgiving Day (the fourth Thursday in November), Christmas Day, and New Year's Day. If you're in doubt about holiday hours, telephone the museum.

INSURANCE: The United States does not have a national health plan. It is very important for foreign visitors to have health insurance that will cover the very high hospitalization costs in case of sickness, injury, or accident. Even at city, state, and federal government hospitals you will be expected to pay for services if you can afford them.

LAUNDRY: Every city and town has several **Laundromats** where you can wash and dry your own clothes in automatic washing and drying machines at a cost of a few dollars. Some Laundromats have dry-cleaning machines as well. Laundromats are often located in shopping centers. Laundry detergent is usually sold by vending machines in Laundromats, or you can buy some in a nearby supermarket or convenience store.

MAIL: To receive mail at any U.S. post office, have it sent to you **c/o General Delivery,** but be sure to specify the particular post office at which you'd like to pick up your mail. When in doubt, address it to the "main post office." You'll be asked to show such identification as a passport, identity card, or driver's license to get your mail.

An airmail letter between the United States and Europe can take as little as 3 or 4 days to reach its destination, or as many as 10 or 12 days.

MONEY AND CREDIT CARDS: The U.S. dollar is divided into 100 cents. All currency notes (bills) are the same size and color (green). Denominations are $1, $2 (rarely used), $5, $10, $20, $50, and $100; many establishments will balk at accepting a $50 or $100 bill for a small purchase.

Coins are 1¢ ("penny"), 5¢ ("nickel"), 10¢ ("dime"), and 25¢ ("quarter"); the 50¢ ("half-dollar") and $1 coins are collectors' items not often found in circulation. All coins are made of a silvery chromium alloy except the penny, which is of copper.

Foreign visitors to the U.S. can solve currency exchange problems simply by buying U.S. dollar traveler's checks before leaving home. The checks are accepted at face value virtually everywhere—stores, hotels, restaurants, gas stations—with no commission charged upon cashing. You can easily pay for a room, a meal, or a souvenir with a traveler's check, and receive your change in cash; if you just want to exchange a traveler's check for cash, any bank will do so without charge or commission. Having U.S. dollars or dollar-denominated traveler's checks is necessary since currency exchange offices are few, are located only in the largest cities, and often do not offer the best rates of exchange.

Perhaps the easiest and best way to spend money in America is by using a credit card. You get a very good rate of exchange, and you needn't worry about carrying large amounts of cash. All travel agents, airlines, car rental companies, hotels, large stores, most restaurants, and many other establishments accept credit cards, even for purchases as small as $10. Most widely accepted are VISA (BarclayCard in Britain, Chargex in Canada) and MasterCard (EuroCard in Europe, Access in Britain, Diamond in Japan); American Express is sometimes not accepted in smaller, moderately priced restaurants and stores; Diners Club and Carte Blanche are accepted at some establishments.

NEWSPAPERS AND MAGAZINES: Each of the larger cities in New England has its own daily newspaper. The *Boston Globe* and the *Boston Herald* are distributed throughout New England, as is the *New York Times;* the *Washington Post* is also available in most New England cities. Two national newspapers, *USA Today* and the *Christian Science Monitor,* are also on sale. A few newsstands, at Boston's Logan Airport and in the centers of the larger cities, carry the *International Herald-Tribune* and a selection of English, French, Italian, and German newspapers and magazines, usually a day or two after publication.

POST: See "Mail."

RADIO AND TELEVISION: The U.S. has a bewildering variety and diversity of broadcast media, and some of it is available to you through the radio and TV set in your hotel room since even small roadside motels may boast that they provide "color cable TV" in their rooms. All broadcasting is commercial and not government-funded except for the Public Radio and Public Television networks, which get small amounts of government support, but depend mostly upon listeners to send contributions. Many radio and TV stations broadcast 24 hours a day.

"Free TV" includes those television stations that broadcast via the airwaves and that can be received on any TV set with an antenna; Boston has perhaps a dozen of these stations, and other New England cities have their own as well. These stations broadcast a mix of their own local programming and programs from the four large national networks, ABC, NBC, CBS, and PTN.

"Pay TV" includes the several dozen channels available via a cable TV network; many cable stations specialize in a particular type of programming. Subscribers (hotels, motels, and private homes) must pay a monthly fee for cable service, but the service is then provided in your hotel room at no extra charge to you. There are channels broadcasting only sports (ESPN), those with only news (CNN), those covering governmental affairs (C-SPAN), and those that enable viewers to shop at home by buying merchandise displayed on the TV screen. There's a Spanish-language channel (UNO), one that broadcasts nothing but travel information (the Travel Channel), channels with business news, medical news, educational programs, and even a channel that covers only the weather. Several channels show only movies. In the midst of this visual maelstrom are the traditional television networks, ABC, NBC, CBS, and the Public Television Network, or PBS. These broadcast varied programming with news, sports, game shows, "soap operas," and special reports; all except the public have frequent commercials.

Radio broadcasting, both medium wave (AM) and FM, is also commercial and not government-funded, except for the Public Radio stations, which get some government money. You can receive several hundred radio stations in New England. Each station may have a particular "format," or program content, meaning it plays only country music, or jazz, or classical, or rock (or a variation: acid rock, light rock, etc.). There's also "talk radio," stations that encourage listeners to telephone the announcer and give their opinions (on the air) on various topics.

SAFETY: A generation ago, European cities seemed safer than American ones, but now the opposite may be true. With normal traveler's caution, you should have no trouble with crime in New England.

The bigger the city, the more caution you must exercise. Avoid walking or driving through the poorest areas of a city, especially at night; avoid lonely, dark streets and parks. If you must be out on city streets between 10pm and 6am, ask at your hotel about areas to avoid, and whether you should take a taxi rather than walk. Be careful of your wallet or purse in the subway and at open-air festivals and markets, where pickpockets sometimes work the crowds.

TAXES: The U.S. has no national sales tax such as V.A.T. Taxes on hotel rooms, restaurant meals, some transportation services, and on purchases in general are levied by each state and by some cities. Taxes on transportation (bus, rail, and air tickets; gasoline; taxi rides) are included in the prices advertised, and you might not even be aware that you're paying a tax. Taxes on rooms, meals, and other purchases are not included in the price, but are added to your bill. These taxes can add as much as 11% to the cost of a room or a meal, so you must take them into account. In this guidebook I have quoted prices mostly *with the taxes included* so that you can see more accurately what you will have to pay. The exact tax rate for each state and city is given in the text.

TELECOMMUNICATIONS: Telephone, telegraph, and telex services are all operated by private companies, not by the government. With the advent of facsimile (Fax) technology, the telegraph and telex services—and even the mail—are used less these days, and the telephone network is used more.

Telephone service is very good and can be quite inexpensive, but the system is also confusing, even to Americans. There are numerous telephone companies, some for local service, some for long distance, and some companies charge more than others.

Local telephone service is a monopoly granted to one company in each region, in this case New England Telephone. This company carries your call in the local area (say, eastern Massachusetts, or western Massachusetts, or New Hampshire, etc.). From a public coin telephone (call box), all you need do for a local call within a city is insert a coin and press the keys for the local number. If you're calling from a city to a suburb, or from one town to a nearby town, you may have to press "1" first, then the number; then listen as a computer tells you how much money to insert for the call. The initial calling period is three minutes. When it ends, the computerized voice will tell you how much money to insert for an additional three minutes.

For **long distance** (trunk) calls, as when you call from Boston to western Massachusetts, or to another state, your call will be connected automatically via a separate long-distance company such as AT&T, MCI, or US Sprint. Press "1," then the area code, then the number of the person you wish to call. Have ready several dollars in quarters, plus a few nickels and dimes. The cost to call California may not be much more—and may even be less—than the cost to call from Boston to a suburb! You call Canada, Bermuda, the Bahamas, and some Caribbean islands the same way. To make other **international calls** from a coin phone, press "0" (zero), and when the local operator comes on the line, ask for an international operator, who will help you to complete your call.

You can make long-distance and international calls directly from many hotel rooms. Press the number for an outside line (usually marked on the hotel phone; it's often "9"), then "1," area code, and number. For international calls, press the number for an outside line, then "011," country code, city code, and number. Remember that many hotels levy surcharges—perhaps 100%, 200%, or even more —on calls; it's best to ask about these in advance to avoid bill shock.

For a **collect (reverse-charge) or person-to-person call,** dial "0" (zero, *not* the letter "O"), then the area code and the number; an operator will come on the line to help you.

In some airports, railway stations, and large hotels you may find pay phones that accept major credit cards (VISA/BarclayCard, MasterCard/Access/Eurocard, American Express, etc.) or telephone company charge cards (AT&T, MCI, US Sprint, etc.). It is often cheaper and easier to use these phones than to use coin telephones, and you will not need to use an operator for long-distance or international calls. Press "1," the area code, and the number for North American calls. For overseas calls, press "011," then the country code, the city code, and the local number. Here are the most-used country codes:

Australia	61
Austria	43
Belgium	32
Denmark	45
France	33
Germany, E	37
Germany, W	49
Ireland	353
Israel	972
Italy	39
Japan	81
Mexico	52
Netherlands	31
New Zealand	64
Norway	47
Spain	34
Sweden	46
Switzerland	41
U.K.	44

Besides the major telephone companies, which charge low, competitive rates, there are also small companies, which charge much higher rates. For instance, the price for a local intra-city call in Boston is still only 10¢, but some pay phones owned by small companies charge 25¢. For long-distance calls, these small-company phones may use obscure long-distance companies charging two, three, or even ten times the rates of the large, well-known companies. To save money, use only phones that connect your calls via New England Telephone, AT&T, MCI, or US Sprint.

TIME: New England is in the Eastern U.S. time zone, along with New York and Montréal, 5 hours behind Greenwich Mean Time, 6 hours behind Western European time, 15 hours behind Australian time, 17 hours behind New Zealand time.

Auckland	Sydney, Melbourne	Perth	Paris, Rome, Berlin	London	Boston, New York	L.A., San Francisco
5am*	3am*	1am*	6pm	5pm	**noon**	9am

*Next day

TIPPING: Tips are expected in many places, and are often 10% to 20% of the price you are paying. If service has not been particularly good, leave 10% (5% would be an insult); for very good service, leave between 15% and 20%.

Bartenders: 10%–15%.
Bellhops: 50¢–$1 per piece.
Cafeterias, fast-food restaurants: no tip.
Checkrooms: 50¢–$1 per garment.
Cinemas, theaters: no tip.
Doormen (hotel or restaurant): $1 at top hotels for calling a cab, getting your car from the parking lot, or other direct service.
Gas station: no tip.
Hairdressers, barbers: 15%.
Hotel housekeepers: $2–$5 for a stay of several days.
Parking lot: 50¢–$1 if attendant brings your car to you.

Porters ("redcaps" at airports and railroad stations): 50¢ per piece, at least $2–$3 for a lot of baggage.
Restaurants, nightclubs: 15%–20% of the bill.
Sleeping-car attendant: $1–$2 per night to your attendant.
Taxi drivers: 15% of the fare.

TOILETS: Public toilets (known as "rest rooms," "comfort stations," "sanitary facilities," and many other euphemisms) in airports and museums are clean; those in bus stations and railroad stations are perhaps less so, but still usable. Most gas stations have public toilets, but some do not; they vary in tidiness, and some are pretty bad.

Except for these, public toilets are difficult to find. Department stores always have them, usually on an upper floor. Restaurants and bars may post signs reading "Rest rooms for use of our patrons only"; you can ignore the signs, or you can plan to take a break and have some refreshments when you need to use a toilet. Large hotels always have clean toilets, and will not notice your use of them.

---

4. Frommer's Dollarwise® Travel Club—How to Save Money on All Your Travels

In this book we'll be looking at how to get your money's worth in New England, but there is a "device" for saving money and determining value on *all* your trips. It's the popular, international Frommer's Dollarwise Travel Club, now in its 29th successful year of operation. The club was formed at the urging of numerous readers of the $-A-Day and Frommer Guides, who felt that such an organization could provide continuing travel information and a sense of community to value-minded travelers in all parts of the world. And so it does!

In keeping with the budget concept, the annual membership fee is low and is immediately exceeded by the value of your benefits. Upon receipt of $18 (U.S. residents), or $20 U.S. by check drawn on a U.S. bank or via international postal money order in U.S. funds (Canadian, Mexican, and other foreign residents) to cover one year's membership, we will send all new members the following items.

(1) Any *two* of the following books
Please designate in your letter which two you wish to receive:

Frommer $-A-Day© Guides
    Australia on $30 a Day
    Eastern Europe on $25 a Day
    England on $50 a Day
    Europe on $40 a Day
    Greece on $30 a Day
    Hawaii on $60 a Day
    India on $25 a Day
    Ireland on $35 a Day
    Israel on $40 a Day
    Mexico (plus Belize and Guatemala) on $35 a Day
    New York on $60 a Day
    New Zealand on $45 a Day
    Scandinavia on $60 a Day
    Scotland and Wales on $40 a Day
    South America on $35 a Day
    Spain and Morocco (plus the Canary Is.) on $40 a Day
    Turkey on $30 a Day
    Washington, D.C. & Historic Virginia on $40 a Day

($-A-Day Guides document hundreds of budget accommodations and facilities, helping you get the most for your travel dollars.)

Frommer Guides
Alaska
Australia
Austria and Hungary
Belgium, Holland, and Luxembourg
Bermuda and The Bahamas
Brazil
California and Las Vegas
Canada
Caribbean
Egypt
England and Scotland
Florida
France
Germany
Italy
Japan and Hong Kong
Mid-Atlantic States
New England
New York State
Northwest
Portugal, Madeira, and the Azores
Skiing USA—East
Skiing USA—West
South Pacific
Southeast Asia
Southern Atlantic States
Southwest
Switzerland and Liechtenstein
Texas
USA

(Frommer Guides discuss accommodations and facilities in all price ranges, with emphasis on the medium-priced.)

Frommer Touring Guides
Australia
Egypt
Florence
London
Paris
Scotland
Thailand
Venice

(These new, color illustrated guides include walking tours, cultural and historic sites, and other vital travel information.)

Gault Millau
Chicago
France
Hong Kong
Italy
London
Los Angeles
New England
New York

San Francisco
Washington, D.C.
(Irreverent, savvy, and comprehensive, each of these renowned guides candidly reviews over 1,000 restaurants, hotels, shops, nightspots, museums, and sights.)

Serious Shopper's Guides
Italy
London
Los Angeles
Paris
(Practical and comprehensive, each of these handsomely illustrated guides lists hundreds of stores, selling everything from antiques to wine, conveniently organized alphabetically by category.)

A Shopper's Guide to the Caribbean
(Two experienced Caribbean hands guide you through this shopper's paradise, offering witty insights and helpful tips on the wares and emporia of more than 25 islands.)

Beat the High Cost of Travel
(This practical guide details how to save money on absolutely all travel items—accommodations, transportation, dining, sight-seeing, shopping, taxes, and more. Includes special budget information for seniors, students, singles, and families.)

Bed & Breakfast—North America
(This guide contains a directory of over 150 organizations that offer bed-and-breakfast referrals and reservations throughout North America. The scenic attractions, and major schools and universities near the homes of each are also listed.)

California with Kids
(A must for parents traveling in California, providing key information on selecting the best accommodations, restaurants, and sight-seeing attractions for the particular needs of the family, whether the kids are toddlers, school-age, preteens, or teens.)

Caribbean Hideaways
(Well-known travel author Ian Keown describes the most romantic, alluring places to stay in the Caribbean, rating each establishment on romantic ambience, food, sports opportunities, and price.)

Frommer's Belgium
(Arthur Frommer unlocks the treasures of a country overlooked by most travelers to Europe. Discover the medieval charm, modern sophistication, and natural beauty of this quintessentially European country.)

Frommer's Cruises
(This complete guide covers all the basics of cruising—ports of call, costs, fly-cruise package bargains, cabin selection booking, embarkation and debarkation—and describes in detail over 60 or so ships cruising the waters of Alaska, the Caribbean, Mexico, Hawaii, Panama, Canada, and the United States.)

Frommer's Skiing Europe
(Describes top ski resorts in Austria, France, Italy, and Switzerland. Illustrated with maps of each resort area. Includes supplement on Argentinian resorts.)

Guide to Honeymoon Destinations
(A special guide for that most romantic trip of your life, with full details on planning and choosing the destination that will be just right in the U.S. [California, New En-

gland, Hawaii, Florida, New York, South Carolina, etc.], Canada, Mexico, and the Caribbean.)

Marilyn Wood's Wonderful Weekends
(This very selective guide covers the best mini-vacation destinations within a 200-mile radius of New York City. It describes special country inns and other accommodations, restaurants, picnic spots, sights, and activities—all the information needed for a two- or three-day stay.)

Manhattan's Outdoor Sculpture
(A total guide, fully illustrated with black-and-white photos, to more than 300 sculptures and monuments that grace Manhattan's plazas, parks, and other public spaces.)

Motorist's Phrase Book
(A practical phrase book in French, German, and Spanish designed specifically for the English-speaking motorist touring abroad.)

Paris Rendez-Vous
(An amusing and *au courant* guide to the best meeting places in Paris, organized for hour-to-hour use: from power breakfasts and fun brunches, through tea at four or cocktails at five, to romantic dinners and dancing till dawn.)

Swap and Go—Home Exchanging Made Easy
(Two veteran home exchangers explain in detail all the money-saving benefits of a home exchange, and then describe precisely how to do it. Also includes information on home rentals and many tips on low-cost travel.)

The Candy Apple: New York with Kids
(A spirited guide to the wonders of the Big Apple by a savvy New York grandmother with a kid's-eye view to fun. Indispensable for visitors and residents alike.)

The New World of Travel
(From America's #1 travel expert, Arthur Frommer, an annual sourcebook with the hottest news and latest trends that's guaranteed to change the way you travel—and save you hundreds of dollars. Jam-packed with alternative new modes of travel that will lead you to vacations that cater to the mind, the spirit, and a sense of thrift.)

Travel Diary and Record Book
(A 96-page diary for personal travel notes plus a section for such vital data as passport and traveler's check numbers, itinerary, postcard list, special people and places to visit, and a reference section with temperature and conversion charts, and world maps with distance zones.)

Where to Stay USA
(By the Council on International Educational Exchange, this extraordinary guide is the first to list accommodations in all 50 states that cost anywhere from $3 to $30 per night.)

(2) Any *one* of the Frommer City Guides
Amsterdam
Athens
Atlantic City and Cape May
Boston
Cancún, Cozumel, and the Yucatán
Chicago
Dublin and Ireland
Hawaii

Las Vegas
Lisbon, Madrid, and Costa del Sol
London
Los Angeles
Mexico City and Acapulco
Minneapolis and St. Paul
Montréal and Québec City
New Orleans
New York
Orlando, Disney World, and EPCOT
Paris
Philadelphia
Rio
Rome
San Francisco
Santa Fe, Taos, and Albuquerque
Sydney
Washington, D.C.

(Pocket-size guides to hotels, restaurants, nightspots, and sight-seeing attractions covering all price ranges.)

(3) A one-year subscription to *The Dollarwise Traveler*

This quarterly eight-page tabloid newspaper keeps you up to date on fastbreaking developments in low-cost travel in all parts of the world, bringing you the latest money-saving information—the kind of information you'd have to pay $35 a year to obtain elsewhere. This consumer-conscious publication also features columns of special interest to readers: **Hospitality Exchange** (members all over the world who are willing to provide hospitality to other members as they pass through their home cities); **Share-a-Trip** (offers and requests from members for travel companions who can share costs and help avoid the burdensome single supplement); and **Readers Ask . . . Readers Reply** (travel questions from members to which other members reply with authentic firsthand information).

(4) Your personal membership card

Membership entitles you to purchase through the club all Frommer publications for a third to a half off their regular retail prices during the term of your membership.

So why not join this hardy band of international budgeteers and participate in its exchange of travel information and hospitality? Simply send your name and address, together with your annual membership fee of $18 (U.S. residents) or $20 U.S. (Canadian, Mexican, and other foreign residents), by check drawn on a U.S. bank or via international postal money order in U.S. funds to: Frommer's Dollarwise Travel Club, Inc., 15 Columbus Circle, New York, NY 10023. And please remember to specify which *two* of the books in section (1) and which *one* in section (2) you wish to receive in your initial package of members' benefits. Or, if you prefer, use the order form at the end of the book and enclose $18 or $20 in U.S. currency.

Once you are a member, there is no obligation to buy additional books. No books will be mailed to you without your specific order.

GETTING THERE

Three major gateways to New England are New York City, Montréal, and Boston. Most train and bus routes to New England pass through either New York or Montréal, and a large number of transcontinental and transatlantic flights arrive at the airports in these cities. Many travelers choose to fly directly to Boston, of course. All of these routes are covered below, along with information on how to travel around New England by bus, rail, air, and private car.

1. To New England Via New York City

Whether you're coming from London or Los Angeles, Paris or Philadelphia, there's a good chance your trip to New England will take you through New York City. Of cities in this part of the country, New York has by far the most flights arriving at three international airports: Kennedy, LaGuardia, and Newark. From New York, you can continue onward to New England easily by any means.

BY AIR

You can easily catch a connecting flight from New York to Boston if you wish. There are several flights daily from each of the three airports. Airlines flying between New York and Boston include American, Continental, Delta, Northwest, Pan Am, Trans World, and US Air.

If you find no convenient connecting flight, consider taking the airport transfer bus to LaGuardia to catch either the **Pan Am Shuttle** or the **Trump Shuttle**. Trump Shuttle flights depart every hour on the hour, Pan Am Shuttle flights on the half hour, between 6am and 9pm. No advance reservations are needed, and they guarantee that you'll get a seat. The one-way fare is $119 on weekdays, $89 from Saturday morning until 5pm on Sunday.

Flights from New York go daily to these other airports in the region as well: Albany, N.Y.; Bangor, Me.; Bridgeport, Conn.; Burlington, Vt.; Hartford, Conn.; Hyannis, Mass., Lebanon, N.H.; Manchester, N.H.; Martha's Vineyard, Mass.; Nantucket, Mass.; New Haven, Conn.; New London, Conn.; Portland, Me.; Presque Isle, Me.; Providence, R.I.; and Worcester, Mass.

BY RAIL

Amtrak's rail passenger service spans the country from coast to coast. Many, many trains make their way eastward via Chicago, and many of these continue to New York City. From the south, trains speed north along the eastern seaboard, finally entering the Northeast Corridor at Washington, D.C. Any travel agency hooked into the airlines' computerized reservation systems can give you information on Amtrak schedules and fares, and can sell you tickets, since Amtrak's schedules are carried in all the major airline systems.

Here are some facts and figures on getting to New England by train:

First, Amtrak offers the All Aboard America fares, special reduced-rate round-trip excursion fares to various points and seasonal and special reductions. These fares divide the country into three regions: East, from the Atlantic coast to Chicago and New Orleans; West, from the Pacific coast to Wolf Point, Mont., Denver, Albuquerque, and El Paso; and Central, everything in between, including the boundary cities. For only $189 in summer, $179 the rest of the year, you can make a one-way or round-trip journey within any one of these regions, with three stopovers along the way. To tour within two regions costs only $269 in summer, $229 at other times; freedom to plan a three-region, cross-country return trip with three stopovers costs only $309 in summer, $259 at other times.

Another special deal is their $7 Return Fare, especially good for short or medium-length journeys: buy a one-way ticket costing $65 or more (with no change of trains), and the return trip costs only $7.

Only a limited number of tickets are sold at these special fares, so make your reservations as soon as you've decided on your itinerary.

For more information, write to the Amtrak Distribution Center, P.O. Box 7717, Itasca, IL 60143, requesting their free 90-page travel planner entitled "Amtrak's America." For the latest information on ever-changing fares and schedules, call toll free 800/872-7245, which is 800/USA-RAIL.

Sample Rail Fares to Boston (Coach Class)

From:	Full Fare One-way	"$7 Round-trip" Fare	All Aboard America Fare (O/W or R/T)
Atlanta	$200	$207	$189
Chicago	$120	$127	$189
Dallas	$265	$272	$269
New Orleans	$192	$237	$189
New York	$38.50	$45.50	$189
San Francisco	$316	$323	$309
Washington, D.C.	$92	$99	$189

Remember that meals are not included in these coach-class prices; you must pay for meals on the train when you receive them, or carry your own food. If you travel first class in a club or sleeping car, meals are included.

Northeast Corridor Service: Most passengers who come to New England by rail do so along the Northeast Corridor via New York City. Northeast Corridor service includes trains running from Washington, Baltimore, and Philadelphia via New York's Pennsylvania Station ("Penn Station" for short) to New Haven, Hartford, Springfield, Providence, and Boston. Call Amtrak (tel. 212/582-6875 in N.Y.,

617/482-3660 in Boston, or toll free 800/872-7245) to confirm the schedules given below, and to make reservations.

The main line to Boston follows the coast for much of the way, stopping in New Rochelle, Stamford, and Bridgeport before coming to New Haven (Yale University), Old Saybrook (for Old Lyme, Essex, and Ivoryton), New London (U.S. Coast Guard Academy), Mystic (Old Mystic Seaport), Westerly (for Stonington), Kingston (for Narragansett and Port Galilee), and Providence before reaching Boston. Remember, *these schedules will change* (by at least a few minutes, perhaps more) by the time you travel, so call Amtrak for current schedules.

Daily Trains from New York (Penn Station) to Boston

Depart New York	New Haven	Providence	Arrive Boston
8:00am	10:03am	12:08pm	1:17pm
9:17am	11:20am	1:24pm	2:18pm
10:10am	12:09pm	2:09pm	3:01pm
12:10pm	2:17pm	4:18pm	5:09pm
1:59pm	3:53pm	(via Springfield)	8:05pm
4:07pm	6:14pm	8:17pm	9:11pm
4:59pm	6:58pm	(via Springfield)	11:15pm
6:05pm	8:08pm	10:13pm	11:09pm
7:00pm	9:03pm	11:05pm	11:58pm
3:17am*	5:10am	7:39am	8:35am

*The *Night Owl*, having sleeping cars as well as coaches.

Another Amtrak route departs New York's Pennsylvania Station, follows the main line as far as New Haven, then runs up the Connecticut River Valley stopping at the Connecticut cities of Wallingford, Meriden, Berlin (New Britain) and Hartford, then Windsor, Windsor Locks (for Bradley International Airport), and Springfield, Mass. One or two trains daily continue past Springfield to Worcester and Framingham, Mass., then to Boston, but this route takes much longer than the main line via Providence. Again, these times will change (by at least a few minutes, perhaps more) by the time you travel, so call for current schedules.

Daily Trains from New York (Penn Station) to Hartford and Springfield

Depart New York	New Haven	Hartford	Arrive Springfield
8:00am	9:53am	10:45am	11:28am
9:17am	11:10am	12:07pm	12:48pm
12:10pm	2:07pm	2:59pm	3:47pm†
1:59pm	3:53pm	4:48pm	5:35pm*
3:10pm	5:10pm	6:10pm	6:55pm
4:59pm	6:58pm	7:52pm	8:45pm*
7:00pm	8:53pm	9:45pm	10:28pm
9:10pm	11:10pm	12:02am	12:45am

*Continues to Boston (2½ hours).
†Connecting Amtrak bus continues to Northampton, Mass. (4:20pm), Brattleboro (5:10pm), Bellows Falls (5:40pm), White River Junction (6:25pm), Montpelier (7:55pm), Waterbury (for Stowe) (8:15pm), and Essex Junction (for Burlington) (8:45pm) in Vermont.

Besides Amtrak service from Penn Station, there is Metro North train service on the Connecticut Department of Transportation's New Haven Line from New York's Grand Central Terminal to New Haven, Conn., every hour on the hour from 7am until after midnight on weekdays, with extra trains put on during the peak morning and evening hours. Service on Saturday, Sunday, and holidays is almost as frequent, with a train at least every two hours. The trip from Grand Central to New Haven takes 1¾ hours. For exact schedule information, call 212/532-4900 in New York City, or toll free 800/223-6052 in Connecticut.

To Cape Cod: During the peak summer vacation season of July and August (through Labor Day weekend), Amtrak operates special weekend trains from New York City to Hyannis on Cape Cod.

The *Cape Codder* departs New York's Pennsylvania Station on Friday only, at 5:15pm, departs New Haven at 7:07pm, and arrives in Hyannis at 11:38pm. The return trip from Hyannis to New York departs on Sunday at 4:12pm.

The *Clamdigger* departs New York (Penn Station) on Saturday only, at 9:17am, departs New Haven at 11:20am, and arrives in Hyannis at 4:10pm. The return trip from Hyannis to New York departs Saturday only, at 8:05am. If you take the *Clamdigger,* you must change trains in Providence.

BY BUS

New York's main bus station is the **Port Authority Bus Terminal,** Eighth Ave. and 42nd St. (tel. 212/564-8484). From Newark International Airport, shuttle buses go directly to the Port Authority terminal. From LaGuardia Airport or John F. Kennedy International Airport, take a Carey airport bus to Grand Central Terminal, (Park Ave. and 42nd St.) and walk (or take a taxi) five blocks west along 42nd Street to the bus terminal.

From the Port Authority Bus Terminal, various lines run to the different parts of New England:

Bonanza Bus Lines (tel. 212/564-8484, or toll free 800/556-3815): Bonanza's routes go to Albany, N.Y., via the Berkshires (Great Barrington, Stockbridge, Lee, Lenox, and Pittsfield) from New York City; and from New York City to Cape Cod (Falmouth, Woods Hole, and Hyannis) via Providence. During the winter months, service to Falmouth and Woods Hole (for the ferries to Martha's Vineyard and Nantucket) is via connection at Bourne, Massachusetts. Bonanza also operates between New York City and Providence and Newport, R.I., and New Bedford, Mass. Buy your tickets in New York's Port Authority Bus Terminal at the Adirondack Trailways Ticket Plaza.

Greyhound Lines (tel. 212/635-0800): Greyhound operates buses from New York City to Hartford, Springfield, Worcester, New Haven, New London, and Providence. Service to Cape Cod is provided in conjunction with Bonanza. The Boston service has a few buses daily. The direct trip to Boston takes about 4¾ hours. From Boston, connections are made to points in Maine, New Hampshire, and Vermont.

Vermont Transit Lines (tel. 212/594-2000, or toll free 800/451-3292; toll free in Vermont 800/642-3133): Vermont Transit operates in conjunction with Greyhound to serve Vermont's ski and vacation regions as well as Montréal and several points in New Hampshire.

Sample Bus Fares

To reach Boston by bus costs $150 from Chicago, $75 from Washington, D.C., or $40 from New York City if you pay full fare. For long-distance runs like the trip from Chicago or even farther away, discount travel plans often bring the price down substantially. Round-trip fares, by the way, are in some cases only 40% more than one-way fares.

BY CAR

Starting from New York City, choose your route according to your destination: For **northwestern Connecticut, the Massachusetts Berkshires, southern and western Vermont,** follow the Henry Hudson Parkway or I-87 north to the Saw Mill River Parkway, which connects with the Taconic State Parkway north. The

Taconic is a beautiful road, no tolls are collected, and trucks are not allowed, making it the route of choice.

To **southwestern Connecticut, Hartford, central Massachusetts, Boston, eastern Vermont, New Hampshire, and Maine,** take the Henry Hudson Parkway or I-87 north to the Saw Mill River Parkway, and that north to I-684. At the junction with I-84, go east via Danbury and Waterbury to Hartford and beyond.

If you're heading for **points along the Connecticut and Rhode Island coasts** (New Haven, New London, Mystic, Providence, Newport), **Cape Cod and the islands, New Bedford and Plymouth,** follow the Henry Hudson Parkway or I-87 north to I-287. Head east on I-287 to the Hutchinson River Parkway north; after a few miles this road enters Connecticut and becomes the Merritt Parkway. This scenic toll road is not open to trucks, making it even more pleasant. (The alternate route, I-95, has very heavy truck traffic, making it less pleasant for passenger cars.) Beyond Bridgeport, the Merritt Parkway is named the Wilbur Cross Parkway; it continues past New Haven and north to Meriden, where it's best to take I-91 north. To head east along the coast from New Haven you must take I-95, unless you want to slow down and take the older U.S. 1, an interesting route that goes through many coastal towns—and red lights.

---

2. To New England from Chicago and Toronto

Coming from the Midwest, you have the same choices of air, rail, bus, or private car.

BY AIR

Chicago is one of the most important air transportation hubs in the country, and flights take off from the city's four airports—O'Hare International, Midway, Pal-Waukee, and Merrill C. Meigs—daily for New England and nearby destinations, including Albany, N.Y.; Bangor, Me.; Boston, Mass.; Burlington, Vt.; Hartford, Conn.; Manchester, N.H.; New York City; Portland, Me.; Providence, R.I.; and Worcester, Mass. The most active airlines are American, Midway, Northwest, United, and US Air.

BY RAIL

From Chicago: Amtrak's *Lake Shore Limited* travels nightly from Chicago to New England, departing Chicago's Union Station at 6:25pm, making stops at Toledo, Cleveland, Buffalo (5:15am), Rochester, Syracuse, and Albany-Rensselaer (10:40am) before pulling into Springfield, Mass., at 12:55pm the next day. From Springfield, you can continue north by bus, east or south by train.

An Amtrak bus departs Springfield at 3:50pm for Northampton, Mass. (4:20pm); Brattleboro (5:10pm), Bellows Falls (5:40pm), White River Junction (6:25pm), Montpelier (7:55pm), Waterbury (for Stowe, 8:15pm), and Essex Junction (for Burlington, 8:45pm) in Vermont.

Several through cars from the Lake Shore Limited continue to Boston, departing Springfield at 1:25pm, arriving in Boston at 4:15pm.

From Springfield, a train departs at 1:33pm for Windsor Locks (1:53pm), Hartford (2:06pm), and New Haven (2:58pm) before continuing to New York City.

From Toronto: One train daily, the *Maple Leaf,* departs Toronto at 9:35am, departs Buffalo at 1:25pm, and arrives at Albany-Rensselaer at 6:25pm. From Albany, it's a short hop by bus to the Berkshires or southern Vermont. There is only one train a day, the Lake Shore Limited (see above), connecting Albany-Rensselaer with

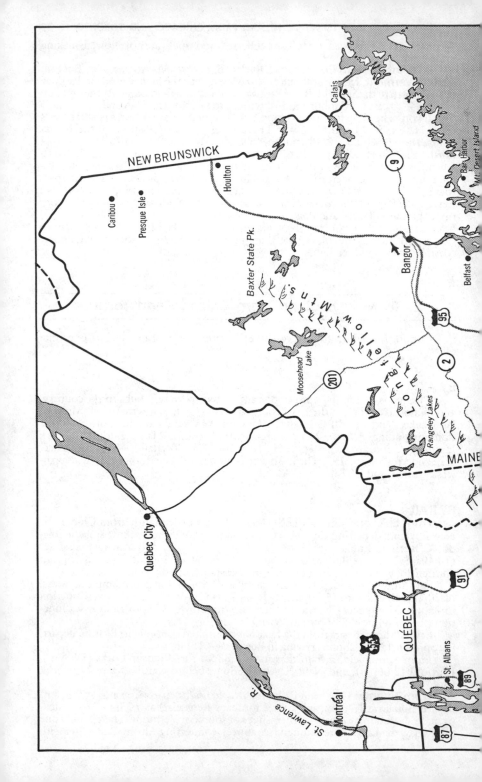

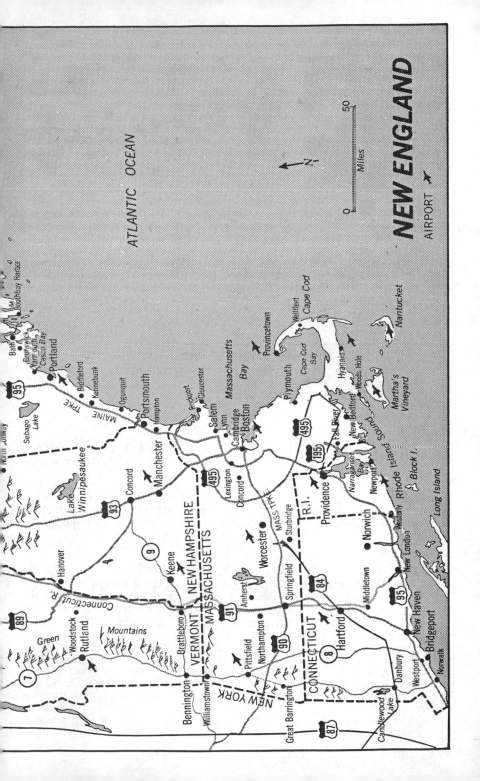

Boston, and this train departs Albany-Rensselaer at 10:40am. If you've come this far on the *Maple Leaf,* you must continue by bus, or stay overnight and catch the *Lake Shore Limited* the next day.

BY BUS

The major bus routes to New England from Chicago and Toronto enter the region at Albany, Montréal, and New York City, and you may find yourself changing buses at one of these points to reach your final destination. The distance by road to Boston from Chicago is almost 1,000 miles (1,500 km), from Toronto 550 miles (860 km).

BY CAR

Interstate 80 between Chicago and Cleveland is very heavily traveled, and not particularly pleasant to drive, but it is the most direct route. For scenery and a more relaxed time, you might consider taking I-94 to Detroit, then crossing the border into Canada to follow Hwy. 401 to Hamilton before heading down via Niagara Falls to Buffalo to pick up I-90, the New York State Thruway, to Albany and Boston. From Toronto, the Hamilton-Niagara-Buffalo-Albany route is the logical choice unless you're headed for northern New England, in which case you might want to drive via Montréal (see below).

---

3. To New England Via Montréal

Though New York City is the most common transit point for New England, Montréal is the northern hub of regional transport.

BY AIR

Delta Airlines operates routes from Montréal's Dorval Airport to Boston and Hartford; Air Canada's commuter line, Air Alliance, flies from Dorval to Boston as well. Either flight takes just over an hour.

If you arrive by air in Montréal and want to continue your trip by road or rail, **Aérocar** airport shuttle buses (tel. 514/397-9999) will take you from Mirabel or Dorval airports to the center of Montréal, stopping at the Queen Elizabeth Hotel (which is right above VIA Rail's Central Station) and the Terminus Voyageur bus station.

BY RAIL

Two **Amtrak** trains run daily from Montréal's Central Station (beneath the Queen Elizabeth Hotel) to New York City, a distance of 450 miles. The schedules given below will almost certainly have changed (perhaps only a few minutes, perhaps more) by the time you're ready to travel, so call Amtrak toll free at 800/872-7245 for current schedules.

The *Adirondack* is a day train (10 hours) departing Montréal currently at 8:40am, traveling down the Hudson River Valley, stopping at Port Kent, N.Y. (ferry to Burlington, Vt.) at 11:53am, and arriving at Albany-Rensselaer, N.Y., at 3:55pm. It continues to New York City, arriving at Grand Central Terminal at 6:43pm. If you get off the train at Albany, you can take a bus to southern Vermont or to the Berkshires.

The *Montrealer* is a night train (12 hours) hauling sleeping cars as well as coaches. It departs Montréal at 5:10pm, stops at Essex Junction, Vt. (for Burlington), at White River Junction, Vt., at 10:40pm, Brattleboro, Vt., at 12:15am, Amherst, Mass., at 1:05am, New Haven at 5:20am, and New York City at 7:35am, before continuing to Philadelphia and Washington.

BY BUS
   Vermont Transit buses depart at least three times daily from Montréal's central bus station, the **Terminus Voyageur,** 505 bd. de Maisonneuve est (tel. 514/842-2281), en route to Boston (nine hours). In the summer months, **Greyhound** operates daily service from Montréal to Burlington, Vt., North Conway, N.H., Old Orchard Beach, Me., and Boston. Other Greyhound buses head due south along Canada 15 and I-87 to New York City, stopping in Albany along the way.
   Sample Bus Fares: From Toronto to Boston costs US$109; from Montréal to Boston, the fare is US$60.

BY CAR
   The most direct route from Montréal to **Vermont, southern New Hampshire, and the southern New England states** is to cross the Pont Victoria and follow Canada 10, the Autoroute des Cantons de l'Est, eastward 22 kms (13 miles) to Canada 35 south; this is all expressway. Beyond Iberville the route is marked as Québec Hwy. 133, and is a fairly fast two-lane highway through flat farming country. At the U.S. border, the road becomes I-89 south, and continues via Burlington and Montpelier to White River Junction, Vt., where it intersects with I-91. Continue on I-89 to Concord and Manchester, N.H., and to Boston; take I-91 south to southern Vermont and New Hampshire, central Massachusetts, and central Connecticut around Hartford.
   For the **western parts of Vermont, Massachusetts, and Connecticut,** take the Pont Victoria or Pont Jacques-Cartier east out of Montréal and follow Canada 15 due south to the U.S. border, where the highway becomes I-87. You can leave this road at Exit 39 north of Plattsburgh, N.Y., to catch a ferry from Gordon Landing over to Grand Isle and thence via U.S. 2 to I-89 and Burlington; or you can take an exit farther south to get to Port Kent and the ferry across Lake Champlain directly to Burlington (for details on this service, see the Burlington section). Near Albany, roads go east to Bennington in southern Vermont, Williamstown, Mass., and the Berkshires; just south of Albany, I-87 intersects with I-90, the Massachusetts Turnpike to Boston. If you're headed farther south, follow I-90 east from I-87 to the Taconic State Parkway, a pleasant, fast road open only to cars, not to trucks.
   From Montréal to **northern New Hampshire and Maine,** take the Pont Victoria, follow Canada 10, the Autoroute des Cantons de l'Est, eastward as far as Magog. Turn south here on Canada 55 to the U.S. border. South of the border the highway is I-93, which leads straight to New Hampshire's White Mountains. To get to Maine, you can take U.S. 2 or U.S. 302 eastward from I-93.
   Another route to Maine, slower and less scenic, with fewer tourist services, is to continue on Canada 10 east from Magog and through Sherbrooke. Beyond Sherbrooke, the road becomes two lane and is numbered Québec 112. Follow 112 to the small town of St-Gérard, then follow Québec 161 through Lac-Mégantic to the U.S. border. In Maine, the road is Maine Hwy. 27, a lonely route through forests and mountains, finally bringing you to Augusta, the state capital.
   By the way, the direct road from **Québec City via Jackman and Skowhegan to Augusta,** Québec Hwys. 171 and 173, and U.S. 201, is also a fairly slow, fairly lonely but scenic road.

---

4. Flying to Boston

   Boston's Logan International Airport is one of America's busiest, receiving flights from throughout the country, the hemisphere, and the world. It's located only three miles from the center of Boston. Nonstop flights connect Boston with these cities:

Albany, NY	Fort Lauderdale, FL	Nashville, TN
Allentown, PA	Fort Myers, FL	Orlando, FL
Amsterdam	Frankfurt	Ottawa, Ontario
Atlanta, GA	Glasgow	Paris
Atlantic City, NJ	Greensboro/Winston-	Philadelphia, PA
Augusta, ME	Salem, NC	Phoenix, AZ
Baltimore, MD	Halifax, Nova Scotia	Pittsburgh, PA
Bangor, ME	Harrisburg, PA	Portland, ME
Barcelona	Hartford, CT	Presque Isle, ME
Bermuda	Houston, TX	Raleigh/Durham, NC
Binghamton, NY	Hyannis, MA	Richmond, VA
Bridgeport, CT	Las Vegas, NV	Rome
Brussels	Lebanon, NH	Saint John, New Brunswick
Buffalo, NY	Lisbon	St. Louis, MO
Burlington, VT	London	Salt Lake City, UT
Cairo	Long Island	San Francisco, CA
Caracas	(MacArthur), NY	Shannon
Charlotte, NC	Los Angeles, CA	San Juan, Puerto Rico
Chicago, IL	Madrid	Syracuse, NY
Cincinnati, OH	Manchester, NH	Tampa/St. Pete, FL
Cleveland, OH	Martha's Vineyard, MA	Toronto, Ontario
Copenhagen	Memphis, TN	Washington, DC
Dallas/Fort Worth, TX	Miami, FL	Westchester City, NY
Dayton, OH	Milwaukee, WI	West Palm Beach, FL
Denver, CO	Minneapolis, MN	Yarmouth, Nova Scotia
Detroit, MI	Montréal, Quebec	Zurich
Dublin	Nantucket, MA	

Besides these nonstop flights, there are hundreds of direct and connecting flights that can get you easily to Boston from anywhere in the world.

OTHER AIRPORTS

Besides Boston's Logan International Airport, several other airports in the region receive national and international flights. These include Albany, N.Y.; Bradley International Airport in Windsor Locks, Conn. (serving Hartford, Conn., and Springfield, Mass.); Bangor, Me.; Burlington, Vt.; Martha's Vineyard, Mass.; Nantucket, Mass.; and Portland, Me.

There are smaller airports receiving regional flights at Augusta, Me.; Presque Isle, Me.; Bridgeport, Conn.; Hyannis, Mass.; Lebanon, N.H.; and Manchester, N.H.

DISCOUNT AIRFARE STRATEGIES

These days, 90% of all air travelers buy tickets at discounted fares. Very few people pay "full fare," which can be surprisingly expensive. At full fare, it can cost as much to make the two-hour flight from Washington, D.C., to Boston, and return, as it does to fly round-trip from Boston to London, Paris, or Rome on an excursion ticket.

The matter of airfares is so complex that only a travel agent with a good knowledge of the airlines' computer reservations systems can get the lowest fare and best flights for you. For a full discussion of how to get the best airfares, how to fly even cheaper using coupons or as an air courier, see my book entitled *Frommer's Beat the High Cost of Travel* (Prentice Hall Press).

Discount Ticket Rules . . .

Discount airfares normally have three constraints attached to them. First, you must make your reservations and purchase your tickets in advance. Usually you must close the deal at least a week before you fly, but some airfares require even more time, perhaps two weeks, or three.

Second, you cannot change your plans without paying some sort of penalty. On the more expensive discount airfares, the penalty for changing your flight dates or for canceling your plans altogether may be 25% of the cost of the ticket; on cheaper fares it may be 50%; and on the very cheapest fares you cannot change your flights or cancel your trip at all without losing the entire amount you've paid.

The third constraint is the number of seats offered at the discount fare. Airlines may offer only a very few seats on each flight at the lowest fare. The reason they are offering the fare is not to fill a lot of seats at that price, but to be able to advertise the low fare in the newspapers! It's a bait-and-switch tactic. You read about an extremely low fare in the newspaper, decide to take a trip, call your travel agent or the airline, discover that all of the seats available at that fare on your chosen flight (perhaps only five or ten seats!) have already been sold, and so you make a reservation at a higher fare.

. . . and How to Change Them

Are there ways around these rules? Yes! Nothing can substitute for good advance planning, so make your plans and talk to your travel agent well in advance of your trip. Find an agent who is willing to "dig" into the plethora of airfares and discover a special fare or a special routing that will save you money. Make your reservations, but don't buy your ticket until you're required to do so. When the time comes to buy your ticket, ask the agent to take another look to see if the situation has changed. The reservations and airfare business is so complex that seats on particular flights may be "reserved" and "released" many times before the plane even leaves the ground, and fares go up and down almost daily.

As for penalties, I have found that airlines rarely levy a penalty if you advance your return date, that is, if you come back to your starting point early. Several times I have bought nonrefundable air tickets at very low fares. The rules said that I could not change my flight plans at all; I must use the flights noted on the ticket, period. But I wanted to come home a day or two early, so I showed up at the airport, non-changeable ticket in hand, and asked if there were seats available on a flight to my destination. There were, and the agent happily changed my ticket and got me a seat on the earlier flight without comment or charge. Note that this strategy works *only if there are seats available* on an earlier flight.

Other Discount Strategies

First of all, avoid holiday "blackout" periods. During these times, when holiday travel is intense, airlines do not allow as many discount fares to be used. Christmas, New Year's, Easter, Memorial Day, Labor Day, and especially Thanksgiving are periods when the discount-fare blackout is in effect.

Another strategy is to fly when airline bookings in general are down: mid-January through March and October through mid-December, except for Thanksgiving. Also, flights on certain days (Tuesday, Wednesday, Thursday, Saturday, Sunday morning) may be cheaper than others, and flights at certain times (10am to 3pm, and after 8pm) may be cheaper as well.

Ask your travel agent if it makes sense to split your trip into segments, or to take an indirect route. The most expensive flights are the most desirable ones: the non-stops. If you are willing to take a direct flight with a stop, or to change planes at a stop, your fare might be lower. In some cases, when there are particularly low promotional fares being offered, it may make sense to buy two tickets, one from your home to an intermediate point and back, another from that intermediate point to your destination and back.

One-way fares tend to be disproportionately expensive, and it is often cheaper to buy a low excursion (round-trip) fare and simply throw away the return portion; or better yet, ask around at the airport and sell the return ticket to someone!

When checking fares, think to ask your travel agent to look into alternate airports. Sometimes fares are cheaper if you avoid the major, most desirable airport and fly to a less-used but still convenient airport instead. The nearest alternatives to Boston, however, would be Worcester, over an hour to the west, or Providence, over an hour to the south.

Special Airfares for Foreign Visitors

Foreign visitors can sometimes take advantage of special air travel passes that offer unlimited flying for a period of time (three weeks, a month, several months, etc.) on a particular airline's routes. Restrictions include provisions that you must buy the pass before you leave home (Europe, Japan, etc.), you cannot fly during holiday blackout periods, you cannot backtrack, and you may have a minimum or maximum number of takeoffs. There is also the constraint of the airlines route system. Does it operate flights to the places you want to visit? But these passes provide indisputable bargains when they are offered.

The United States has nine major airlines (American, Continental, Delta, Eastern, Northwest, Pan Am, TWA, United, and US Air) operating on many national and international routes; a dozen smaller "national" airlines with route systems concentrated in one region, with some national flights; and hundreds of small, local "commuter" airlines which feed passengers to the networks of the larger carriers.

---

5. Getting Around by Bus, Rail, and Air

Good public transportation and a network of Interstate highways make getting around New England very easy. The region is relatively small, and visitors from the wide-open spaces out west may be surprised to find that no two points in New England are more than a comfortable day's drive apart: for example, from New Haven, Conn., to Montpelier, Vt., is a mere 200 miles. A train from New Haven to Boston takes only about three hours.

Details of available public transportation will be given along with lodging, restaurant, and sightseeing recommendations in each chapter, but here are some guidelines:

BY AIR

The large cities (Boston, Providence, Hartford, etc.) all have good air service provided by the larger domestic airlines. Deregulation of the airline industry has brought about the birth of numerous regional "feeder" airlines in New England, and it is now possible to fly between most of the larger cities, even in this small region. There are also many connections by regional carrier to New York City.

Almost all of the small regional airlines operate in conjunction with larger national and international airlines. The regional airlines' flights are included in the flight schedules of the larger airlines, including American, Continental, Delta, Eastern, Pan Am, and US Air. Call these airlines for information on flights, fares, and cities served.

BY RAIL

Amtrak operates trains connecting Boston with Springfield, Mass., Pittsfield, Mass., and Albany, N.Y.; Hartford, New Haven, New London, and Mystic, Conn.; Providence, R.I.; and (via Springfield) Brattleboro, White River Junction, and Montpelier, Vt., and Montréal, Québec. There is no interstate train service northeast of Boston, but there are connecting buses from Boston's South Station to

Portsmouth, N.H., and major cities and towns in eastern Maine. Trains on routes between Boston and points south and west are fast and frequent; but to get to points in Vermont from Boston, connections are not good, and service is infrequent.

BY BUS

Bus service is quite good in New England. Here are some of the major companies, their Boston phone numbers, the terminal from which they operate in Boston, and the areas they serve:

American Eagle (tel. 508/990-0000), Peter Pan Terminal, operates frequent buses daily between Boston and New Bedford.

Bonanza Bus Lines (tel. 617/423-5810), Greyhound Terminal, runs from Boston to Cape Cod (Falmouth and Woods Hole), and Newport and Providence, R.I. Other routes run from Providence to central and western Connecticut and the Berkshires of Massachusetts, and from Providence to Cape Cod.

Cape Cod Bus Lines (tel. 508/775-5524), Hyannis, operates routes serving towns between Hyannis and Provincetown, on Cape Cod.

Concord Trailways (tel. 617/482-6620, or toll free 800/258-3722, 800/852-3317 in New Hampshire). Concord Trailways is the line to take to New Hampshire. Buses start at Logan Airport and the Peter Pan Terminal in Boston, then head north to Concord, Laconia and North Conway, Plymouth, Waterville Valley, and Franconia. Another route goes to Alton and Wolfboro.

Englander Bus Lines (tel. 617/423-5810), Greyhound Terminal, runs its buses from Boston along Mass. 2 all the way to Williamstown, in the northwest corner of the state.

Greyhound (tel. 617/423-5810), with its terminal at 10 St. James Ave. in Boston (any Green Line subway car to Arlington), operates many of the long-distance routes in New England, and connects the region with the rest of the country. Greyhound buses operate from Boston via Hartford and New Haven to New York City; from New York City via New Haven and Hartford to Springfield, Mass., connecting with Vermont Transit buses for points in Vermont, and Montréal, Québec.

Another Greyhound route is from Boston via Portsmouth, N.H., to the Maine coast, stopping at Portland, Freeport, Brunswick, Bath, Wiscasset, Camden, and Bangor (with connecting service to Ellsworth for Bar Harbor); this route connects with Canadian SMT buses headed for New Brunswick and Nova Scotia.

Greyhound also connects New York City via New Haven and New London, Conn., with Providence, R.I., and with connecting service to Hyannis and Provincetown on Cape Cod.

Another route is between Islip, N.Y. (on Long Island), via New Haven and Hartford, Conn., and Boston.

Greyhound also operates buses heading due west from Boston, stopping at Worcester, Springfield, Lee, Lenox, and Pittsfield, Mass., and Albany, N.Y., with connecting service to points west in both the United States and Canada.

Peter Pan Bus Lines (tel. 617/426-7838, or toll free 800/628-8468, 800/332-8995 in Massachusetts), at the Peter Pan (formerly Trailways) Terminal in Dewey Square, opposite Amtrak's South Station, runs between Boston and Albany, Amherst, Bridgeport, Danbury, Hartford, Holyoke, Lee, Middletown, New Britain, New Haven, New York City, Northampton, Norwalk, Pittsfield, Springfield, Sturbridge, Waterbury, and Worcester. Other routes connect Springfield, Mass., with Bradley International Airport and Hartford, Conn. Trailways Bus Lines terminated all of its service in New England in 1987, and Peter Pan Bus Lines took over those routes.

Plymouth & Brockton Street Railway Co. (tel. 508/746-0378, or toll free 800/328-9997 in Massachusetts), Greyhound Terminal, is the one to take from Boston to Plymouth, Sagamore, Barnstable, Hyannis, and Provincetown on Cape Cod. P&B also runs from Hyannis to Chatham on Cape Cod. Many P&B runs start at Logan Airport, then head into Boston for stops at the Greyhound Terminal, the Peter Pan Terminal, and South Station. You can take any P&B bus from Logan Airport, and transfer to another one downtown.

Vermont Transit Lines (tel. 617/423-5810, or 802/864-6811 in Vermont), Greyhound Terminal, in collaboration with Greyhound Lines, operates from New York City via Albany to Bennington, Manchester, East Dorset, Rutland (with connecting service to Killington, Woodstock, and White River Junction), Middlebury, and Burlington. Connecting service from Burlington goes on to Montréal.

Another service is from Boston via Manchester, Concord, Mount Sunapee, and Hanover, N.H., to White River Junction (with connecting service to Woodstock, Killington, and Rutland), then to Barre, Montpelier, Burlington, and Montréal.

Vermont Transit also runs buses between Portland, Me., Burlington, Vt., and Montréal, stopping at North Conway and Bretton Woods, N.H., and St. Johnsbury, White River Junction, and Montpelier, Vt.

Another route takes travelers from New York City or Boston to White River Junction for connections to St. Johnsbury and Newport, Vt., and Sherbrooke and Québec City.

To get to Stowe, Vt., you must first go to Burlington or Newport, Vt.

---

6. Driving in New England

Whether you use your own car or a rental (hired) car, driving is perhaps the best way to see New England. The forested hills, winding river valleys, and historic New England towns and villages are most accessible and best appreciated when seen from a car traveling at moderate speed on secondary roads.

DRIVING DISTANCES

Unlike the western United States and Canada, in New England you will normally drive only an hour or two to your next destination. From Boston, it's only about an hour's drive to Providence, Plymouth, Manchester, or Portsmouth; about two hours to Hartford, Portland, Mystic, or Cape Cod; about three hours to New Haven, the Berkshires, southern Vermont, Boothbay Harbor, or New Hampshire's White Mountains; and only about four hours to New York City or central Vermont. Five hours takes you from Boston to the resort and national park at Bar Harbor, Me., and not much more than six hours' driving deposits you in beautiful Montréal. For more specific mileages, see the mileage chart in this book.

FUEL ECONOMICS

Unleaded regular (89 octane) gasoline costs $1.20 to $1.45 per U.S. gallon in New England; more if you buy it in the very center of Boston, which you need not do. Smaller cars ("subcompact" and "compact" in car-rental terminology) normally have fuel efficiencies of about 30 to 40 miles per gallon, which means that the cost of fuel works out to about 3¢ or 4¢ per mile (that's 2¢ to 3¢ per kilometer). Thus the cost of fuel to drive between Boston and New York City (205 miles) would be $6.15 to $9.90, depending upon the car and your driving habits.

DRIVING LAWS

Highway and street speed limits, licensing of drivers, and all other rules governing automobile use are set by each state's legislature. In general, you must be 18 years old to get a driver's license; maximum speed on most expressways in New England is 55 m.p.h. (89 kmph), though many drivers regularly go 60 m.p.h. (97 kmph) or even 65 m.p.h. (105 kmph). Fines for speeding are $75 to $100 per offense, and after several offenses, your driver's license is revoked for a period of time.

Police use radar to detect speeding drivers, but some drivers use radar detectors to warn them about police speed traps. In Connecticut, it is illegal to mount or to use a radar detector.

Laws requiring use of safety belts are uncommon, but every intelligent driver knows that the chances of surviving an accident and avoiding injury are increased greatly if safety belts are worn. Throughout the United States, infants and small children (under four years of age) are required by law to be placed in child safety seats secured by seatbelts. Child safety seats are available from car rental firms at a small extra charge.

CAR RENTALS

To rent a car in New York or New England you must be 21 years of age, and have a valid driver's license. Though a credit card is not required, it is almost a necessity. Without a credit card you must leave a sizable cash deposit, perhaps $100 per day for the estimated length of the rental, or perhaps a flat $2,000 or more.

Rental rates vary among companies. Most expensive are the well-known international companies with car rental desks right in the major airports; cheapest are small local agencies in major cities. In between are the moderate-sized agencies with airport shuttle buses to take you to their "off-airport" locations.

Cheapest rates are for the smallest cars, rented on "weekends" (Thursday noon through Monday noon), or for an entire week or more with unlimited mileage, and returned to the place of rental, or at least to the city of rental. Always return a rental car to the agency with as much gas in it as when the rental began (usually a full tank). Agencies will charge you if they must refuel the car, and they charge for gas at high rates of $1.50 to $1.75 per gallon.

Car Rental Companies

Rental cars from the national companies may be reserved through any travel agent, or by calling a car rental company directly on its toll-free line. Here are the toll-free numbers of the national companies:

Alamo (tel. 800/327-9633)
American International (tel. 800/527-0202)
Avis (tel. 800/331-1212)
Budget (tel. 800/527-0700)
Dollar (tel. 800/421-6868)
Hertz (tel. 800/654-3131)
National (tel. 800/227-7368)
Rent-A-Wreck (tel. 800/535-1391)
Snappy (tel. 800/669-4800)
Thrifty (tel. 800/367-2277)
USA Rent-A-Car System (tel. 800/872-2277)

Besides the large national companies there are many small, local car rental companies in each New England city. You can find them by looking in the yellow pages telephone directory under "Automobile Renting and Leasing." Many of these small companies specialize in renting cars to local people whose cars have been damaged or stolen, and who are waiting for their insurance companies to process their claims, but they also rent to vacationers and business travelers. Though they do not have the national companies' far-flung systems of agents, these local companies often provide good local service at excellent rates. Most offer free delivery and pickup at the airport or at a hotel, unlimited mileage, and good late-model cars. Since New England is not a large region, you may not be too far from the rental agency if a problem arises.

Below are names and addresses of a few of the larger local car rental agencies in

Boston, picked at random from the hundreds of small companies doing business in the area. I have not sampled the services of any of these, so I cannot endorse any one company. If you have questions about a company's reputation, call Boston's **Better Business Bureau,** 8 Winter St., Boston, MA 02108 (tel. 617/482-9151), which keeps files of complaints on problem companies. If you find that one of these companies gives particularly good service, please write to me and let me know so that I can recommend it to other readers of this guide; and if you get unsatisfactory service, I will remove the offending company from this list.

> **Agency Rent-A-Car,** 214 Lincoln St., Allston, MA 02134 (tel. 617/926-0997).
>
> **Amerex Rent-A-Car,** 36 Bay State Rd., Cambridge, MA 02138 (tel. 617/354-4300, or toll free 800/843-1143).
>
> **Brodie Auto Rentals,** 24 Eliot St. (Harvard Square), Cambridge, MA 02138 (tel. 617/491-7600).
>
> **Excel Car & Van Rental,** 25 River St. (Central Square), Cambridge, MA 02139 (tel. 617/227-7368 or 864-4801).
>
> **Insurance Rentals,** 115 North Beacon St., Watertown, MA 02172 (tel. 617/876-8600 or 232-8877).
>
> **Payless Car Rental,** 220 McClellan Hwy., East Boston, MA 02128 (tel. 617/569-9044).
>
> **Ugly Duckling Rent-A-Car,** 160 Boylston St., Chestnut Hill, MA 02167 (tel. 617/244-3825).

Another source of reasonably priced rentals is local auto dealerships. Several Ford dealerships in the Boston area, including **Jack Madden Ford** (tel. 617/769-4130), **128 Rental** (a division of Tom Ford, tel. 617/245-9560), **Main St. Ford** (tel. 617/899-0300), and **Gibbs Ford** (tel. 617/322-8340 or 233-6850), offer rental cars at competitive rates. Chrysler dealers in the area provide similar service.

ROAD MAPS

New England maps are sold in the region's bookstores and gas stations for $1 or $2. Maps of each state drawn with greater detail are available, usually for free or for less than $1, from official state tourism departments by mail, or from state roadside information centers located on major highways near state borders. For addresses of the state tourism offices, see "Information" in section 3 of chapter I.

BREAKDOWNS

Several interstate highways have Motorist Aid Call Boxes posted at regular intervals along the side of the roadway. State police officers patrol all major highways to assist travelers with car problems. If your car stops and you can't get it going, wait in your car until a patrol stops. The officer can call a repair or tow truck to help you. If you are driving a rental car, remember to call the rental company before authorizing a mechanic to do more than the most minor repairs.

If you are a member of the **American Automobile Association,** 8111 Greenhouse Rd., Falls Church, VA 22047 (tel. 703/222-6000), the AAA will help you to find an authorized mechanic. Authorized AAA mechanics will provide simple towing and breakdown assistance at no charge, although long-distance tows and more expensive repairs are your responsibility. To become a member of the AAA, you join a local AAA-affiliated automobile club near your home, paying that club's normal membership dues; members of some foreign auto clubs that have reciprocal arrangements with the AAA can use AAA services for free. AAA-affiliated clubs issue road maps and guidebooks at no charge to members. The AAA can also provide foreign visitors to the U.S. with "Touring Permits" validating your home driver's license for use in the U.S.

RECREATION VEHICLE RENTALS

Among the most pleasant ways to tour the country is in a rented recreation vehicle ("RV," "motorhome," or "camper"). RVs come in all sizes and shapes, and dozens of models. They usually sleep four to six people comfortably, include a full kitchen with cooking range, refrigerator, and running water, are air-conditioned, and some even come equipped with a shower! Hundreds of campgrounds in New England can provide electrical, water, and sewer hookups for $15 to $20 per night. Some RVs are so self-sufficient that they can operate for several days without hookups. In an RV, you're completely independent, you can save money by cooking your own meals, and you needn't pay for expensive hotel rooms. The advantages to families with young children are obvious. Family travel in a rental RV can be a very cost-effective way to tour New England.

But RVs have disadvantages as well. Rentals are fairly expensive, and you should work out estimated budgets for a trip in an RV versus a trip using a rental car and hotels before making your final decision. When figuring costs, keep in mind that RVs are heavy vehicles, and they use a lot more fuel than do passenger cars. During the busy summer months you may not be able to find the campsite you want in the location you want, since many of New England's choicest campgrounds fill up early in the day. You may have to reserve in advance, which takes some of the fun out of footloose vagabond travel. Finally, New England is a region with many delightful country inns. If you've rented an RV at considerable expense, you may not feel that you can pay to stay in country inns very often.

RV Resources

For more information on RVs you can contact the **Recreation Vehicle Industry Association,** P. O. Box 2999, 1896 Preston White Drive, Reston, VA 22090 (tel. 703/620-6003), and the **Recreation Vehicle Dealers Association,** 3251 Old Lee Hwy., Fairfax, VA 22030 (tel. 703/591-7130). For information on private campgrounds (the ones that most often have hookups for RVs), contact the **National Campground Owners Association,** 804 "D" St., NE, Washington, DC 20002 (tel. 202/543-6260).

Information about campgrounds is available in the *RV Park and Campground Directory* for the Eastern U.S. and Canada, published by Prentice Hall Press. The American Automobile Association gives information on campgrounds in its guide to New England, available to AAA members at no charge.

RV Rental Companies

Companies renting recreational vehicles are listed in yellow pages telephone directories under "Recreational Vehicles—Renting & Leasing," "Motor Homes—Renting & Leasing," and "Trailers—Camping & Travel." (Don't let the word "Trailers" mislead you; this section has lots of listings for RVs, since many businesses rent both trailers and RVs.) Two of the largest national franchisers are **Cruise America** (tel. toll free 800/327-7778, or 617/437-7500 in Boston), and **American Safari National RV Rental System** (tel. toll free 800/327-9668).

Several companies in the Boston area rent RVs. I have not tried any of these, so I can't recommend a particular company. The listing below is for your convenience, since RV rentals should be arranged in advance, and you might otherwise find it impossible to learn who rents RVs in Boston. For information on a company's reputation you can contact Boston's **Better Business Bureau,** 8 Winter St., Boston, MA 02108 (tel. 617/482-9151).

AAT Motor Home Rental & Sales, 1724 Revere Beach Pkwy., Everett, MA 02149 (tel. 387-5560).
Cambridge Rentals, 95 Brighton Ave., Allston, MA 02134 (tel. 787-8225).
U-Haul Center of Medford, 600 Mystic Valley Pkwy., Medford, MA 02155 (tel. 396-9030).

NEW ENGLAND MILEAGE CHART

From \ To	Bar Harbor, ME	Bennington, VT	Boothbay Harbor, ME	Boston, MA	Burlington, VT	Hartford, CT	Hyannis, MA	Laconia, NH	Lenox, MA (Tanglewood)	Litchfield, CT	Montreal, QC	Mystic, CT	New Haven, CT	Newport, RI	New York, NY	Portland, ME	Providence, RI	Provincetown, MA	Toronto, ON	Washington, DC
Bar Harbor, ME		355	125	260	345	355	340	240	375	385	355	350	385	325	460	155	305	375	800	700
Bennington, VT	355		260	130	125	105	250	140	45	90	225	160	130	190	175	200	175	290	420	400
Boothbay Harbor, ME	125	260		165	290	260	245	145	280	275	320	255	300	230	360	60	210	280	700	600
Boston, MA	260	130	165		220	95	80	95	130	125	325	90	135	65	205	105	45	115	550	445
Burlington, VT	345	125	290	220		220	310	140	170	215	100	275	255	285	285	230	235	335	370	510
Hartford, CT	355	105	260	95	220		145	180	70	30	320	55	35	85	105	195	70	185	490	335
Hyannis, MA	340	250	245	80	310	145		175	195	175	390	120	175	75	250	185	75	35	635	480
Laconia, NH	240	140	145	95	140	180	175		185	230	240	205	260	160	295	85	125	210	510	525
Lenox, MA (Tanglewood)	375	45	280	130	170	70	195	185		45	265	125	85	155	140	220	140	255	430	370
Litchfield, CT	385	90	275	125	215	30	175	230	45		310	85	40	115	95	215	100	215	475	325
Montreal, QC	355	225	320	325	100	320	390	240	265	310		375	350	405	355	270	335	440	335	585
Mystic, CT	350	160	255	90	275	55	120	205	125	85	375		55	50	130	195	45	150	545	360
New Haven, CT	385	130	300	135	255	35	175	260	85	40	350	55		105	75	240	35	205	515	305
Newport, RI	325	190	230	65	285	85	75	160	155	115	405	50	105		175	170	35	105	595	405
New York, NY	460	175	360	205	285	105	250	295	140	95	355	130	75	175		300	175	285	455	230
Portland, ME	155	200	60	105	230	195	185	85	220	215	270	195	240	170	300		150	220	640	535
Providence, RI	305	175	210	45	235	70	75	125	140	100	335	45	35	35	175	150		105	555	405
Provincetown, MA	375	290	280	115	335	185	35	210	255	215	440	150	205	105	285	220	105		660	515
Toronto, ON	800	420	700	550	370	490	635	510	430	475	335	545	515	595	455	640	555	660		465
Washington, DC	700	400	600	445	510	335	480	525	370	325	585	360	305	405	230	535	405	515	465	

BOSTON: THE HUB

"**B**oston is the Hub of the Universe," or at least that's what many people remembered Dr. Oliver Wendell Holmes as saying. Actually, his statement about his beloved city was less ambitious: "The Boston State House is the Hub of the Solar System." No matter, because to Bostonians their city is still The Hub, the center of the world. And though outsiders may quibble about its being the Hub of the Universe, they must accept the fact that Boston is and always has been the capital of New England. The Pilgrims settled on the shores of Massachusetts Bay in the 1620s, and the other great cities of the six-state region were offshoots from this early colony: Thomas Hooker, the man who founded Hartford, went there from Cambridge in 1636, and about the same time Roger Williams fled the area to found Providence. The pattern of arriving in Boston and then pushing on into the hills beyond was to be a permanent feature of New England life, and consequently, today the city is a rich mixture of ethnic neighborhoods, almost a little United Nations. Immigrants from all over the world arrived at Boston's docks, and later established communities of their own within the city. From these communities second-generation immigrants would then move out across the state and across the nation.

What gives Bostonians the idea they're special? Well, theirs was the first large town in the region, first in resistance to British measures that brought on the Revolution, and first in science and culture during the 19th and early 20th centuries. And in 1960 their favorite son became president of the United States. Their city is the home of the Celtics, the Bruins, the Red Sox, as well as the Boston Pops and countless other types, famous and infamous.

Although Greater Boston today is home for over half of the 6,000,000 people of Massachusetts, the city of Boston itself is a fairly small area with a population of something over 600,000. But if one adds in the populations of the neighboring cities such as Cambridge, Somerville, Charlestown, Chelsea, Brookline, and so on, the total comes to about 3,000,000. And yet Boston is one of the most "livable" and manageable cities in the world, with the economic and cultural advantages of a great city, but with some of the spirit and ease of a small town. It's a delightful place, and Bostonians know it.

1. Arrival and Orientation

As major American cities go, Boston is eminently approachable. The airport is less than a 15-minute taxi or subway ride from the center of the city. The train station is right downtown, as are the two bus terminals. But once you get here, Boston's famous twisty colonial streets take over, and Boston's notoriously sloppy drivers threaten, so read the sections below carefully.

ARRIVAL BY AIR

Boston's **Logan International Airport** (tel. toll free 800/235-6426) is one of the busiest in the country, but it is well organized, and has the advantage of being very near the center of the city, as airports go. After you get your bags, look for the signs to buses, taxis, and "limo," and after a few steps you'll see the stops.

Downtown by Subway

The **Massport Shuttle Bus** (run by the Massachusetts Port Authority) runs the airport loop, and is free of charge. The bus goes to all the terminals and to the MBTA "Airport" subway stop, where you can take a Blue Line train downtown. The subway into town costs 75¢, and a person in a booth will make change for you except during late-night hours. Trains run every 8 to 12 minutes from 5:30am to 1am; the ride takes only 10 minutes once you board the train. Some of the hotels recommended in this book are within a few blocks of the Government Center stop, but for most places you'll have to change at Government Center from the Blue Line to Green Line trains bound for Boston College, Cleveland Circle, Riverside, or Arborway (all of which pass near the hotels recommended). For Cambridge, take the Green Line to Park Street (only one stop away) and change to the Red Line for Harvard or Alewife. It's a fairly long haul to Cambridge, with these two subway transfers.

Downtown by Water Shuttle

Vehicular traffic through the tunnels connecting the airport to Boston has become very heavy in recent years. One innovative solution to the problem is the **Airport Water Shuttle** (tel. 617/439-3131) service between the airport's own dock and Rowe's Wharf, on Atlantic Avenue in downtown Boston. A one-way ticket for the 10-minute shuttle boat costs $7 for adults, $3 for seniors and children under 12 (infants free). Trips run every 15 minutes between 6am and 8pm on weekdays, every half hour from noon to 8pm on weekends and holidays. From Rowe's Wharf it's only a few blocks to South Station's train, subway, and bus stations.

Downtown by Limo

The **Airways Transportation Company's** minibuses (160 Ipswich St.; tel. 442-2700) will take you from the airport (all terminals) to any downtown hotel for $6.50 per person. The minibuses operate every day from 7am to 7pm running every half hour, 7pm to 10pm running on the hour, and stopping at the "Bus Stop" signs outside each terminal.

Hudson Bus Lines and Hudson Limousine Service (tel. 395-8080) have scheduled service to downtown Boston.

The Westin Hotel in Copley Square has its own limo service. Call 426-8800.

Downtown by Taxi

A taxi from Logan Airport to downtown Boston will cost between $8 and $12 for the ride, plus $1 toll, plus excess baggage charge (if any), plus tip. Figure $10 to $15 altogether.

Beyond Boston

Chances are good that you won't be roaring straight through Boston on your way north, west, or south. But in case you are, you should know about these services: **Share-a-Cab:** In principle it works like this: you call the Massport Dispatcher (tel. toll free 800/235-6426), or simply pick up one of the special Share-a-Cab phones near the baggage-claim areas. You give your name and destination (any suburban community, but not Boston itself) to the dispatcher, and within 15 minutes you're on your way, sharing the expense of the cab with several other passengers going to, or near, the same destination. In practice this excellent idea has been languishing of late due to competition from suburban limo companies. You may or may not find that Share-a-Cab works for you. Best time to try is at rush hour, of course.

Limousines to Eastern Massachusetts: To Lexington, call Hudson Bus Lines or Hudson Limo Service at 395-8080; to Concord, call Townsend Limousine Service at 597-6296; to Plymouth or Hyannis, call the Plymouth & Brockton Street Railway Co. at 773-9400, or South Shore & Cape Cod Airport Limo at 451-1410 or toll free (in Massachusetts only) 800/343-7450.

Buses to Rhode Island: Bonanza Bus Lines (tel. 423-5810) goes from Logan Airport right to Providence, a 1½-hour trip, daily every hour on the half hour between 8:30am and 10:30pm, with a final trip at 11:45pm.

Buses to New Hampshire: Concord Trailways (tel. 482-6620, or toll free 800/258-3722) will take you to Manchester, Concord, Lake Winnipesaukee, North Conway, Jackson, Glen, and Hanover, right from the airport.

Buses to Vermont: Vermont Transit (tel. 423-5810, or toll free 800/451-3292) operates from the airport to New Hampshire, Vermont, and Montréal.

ARRIVAL BY TRAIN

All Amtrak trains operate into and out of Boston's **South Station** (tel. 617/482-3660), the terminus for Boston. If you plan to stay downtown or in Cambridge, go to South Station, the end of the line, and transfer to the Red Line subway inbound, "Alewife." In two stops you'll be at Park Street for downtown hotels, and if you stay on the Red Line you'll get to Harvard Square.

ARRIVAL BY BUS

Boston's masterplan calls for all bus and train terminals soon to be located in a grand South Station Transportation Center, at Amtrak's South Station. Many local, commuter, and regional bus lines already operate from South Station, and **Peter Pan Bus Lines,** 555 Atlantic Ave. (tel. 426-7838), is located in its own terminal in Dewey Square, just across the street from South Station. They offer service to and from Maine, New Hampshire, Connecticut, Rhode Island, and Massachusetts. Want to find your way there from downtown? Look for the towering silver Federal Reserve Bank building, which resembles mightily an enormous truck radiator. Washboard? Cigarette machine? Anyway, it's right in Dewey Square.

Greyhound Lines has its own terminal at 10 St. James Ave. (tel. 423-5810), near Park Square, the theater district, and the Public Garden. Information on service to Portland, Me., can be obtained by dialing 542-3520; to New York City, 542-2380; to Hartford, 542-2991. At the Greyhound Terminal, you're only two blocks from the Arlington (Green Line) subway station.

ARRIVAL BY CAR

The easiest and fastest way to enter Boston by car from the west is via the **Massachusetts Turnpike** ("Mass Pike"), which goes right through the Back Bay to the center of the city; then it connects with the **John F. Fitzgerald ("Southeast") Expressway.** There are exits at Prudential Center and Chinatown (Kneeland Street). The Southeast Expressway (few people call it the Fitzgerald Expressway) is also

Rte. 3 as it comes up from the South Shore (Cape Cod and Plymouth). It's the main commuter route from everywhere south of Boston, and is traveled very heavily; at rush hours there are frequent tie-ups. When it gets right into Boston around Haymarket, the road is sometimes called the "Central Artery." The Central Artery is subject to frequent attacks of arteriosclerosis.

Two divided highways skirt the Charles River toward Cambridge, the faster and busier one being **Storrow Drive** on the southern bank, the more scenic being **Memorial Drive** in Cambridge on the northern bank of the Charles. Take either one to go between Boston and Harvard Square, and go all the way to the Larz Andersen Bridge and Cambridge's John F. Kennedy Street (which used to be named Boylston Street), then turn right (north) for Harvard Square.

Coming from the north, enter Boston on I-93 or U.S. 1 (from I-95), both of which converge on the Mystic River Bridge (also called Tobin Bridge; toll inbound), and at the southern end of the bridge the Central Artery/Southeast Expressway begins. Follow signs on the bridge to get to Storrow Drive for the Back Bay or Harvard Square.

Once downtown, Boston's warren of winding, confusing streets, most of them one way, will try your patience, but once you make your way to a hotel, park the car and try to forget it for the rest of your visit. Driving downtown makes little sense, and driving to Harvard Square even less sense (the parking problem there is worse). Take the car out to go to Lexington, Concord, or the North Shore, but otherwise leave it parked.

ORIENTATION

In its earliest days Boston was called "Trimountain," for the three hills around which the settlement was built. At that time Trimountain was almost an island, connected to the mainland only by the narrow natural causeway called "Boston Neck."

In the 19th century an ambitious development plan resulted in the leveling of two of the hills and the moving of the dirt to fill in around Boston Neck; the marsh and bogs that were filled in to make the Back Bay quarter soon became a prime residential district with a Manhattan-style grid of streets and a wide, shady central boulevard called Commonwealth Avenue.

From the time when Trimountain had only a few winding pathways, the city has grown to be a maze of twisty streets difficult to get through in a car, easy to get lost in on foot. I'll try to make the maze more comprehensible for you by describing the city's more important sections and what you'll find in them when you stroll through.

The North End

Starting at the very northeastern tip of Boston's peninsula, the North End is one of the city's oldest quarters. The graves in **Copp's Hill** burying ground go back to the 1600s, and **Old North Church,** from the tower of which Paul Revere got his famous two-lantern signal, dates back to 1723. Many other sights on the **Freedom Trail** (described below) are here. In successive centuries the North End has been the first landing point for many waves of immigrants, and today the four- and five-story brick buildings packed close around the North End's narrow streets are occupied mainly by Italian families who have made the North End their own. **Salem Street** is the quarter's shopping street, with several Italian groceries featuring all the imported products necessary to the old country's cuisine, as well as a half dozen Italian butcher shops and vegetable stands. The street is always lively, and on Saturday it's closed to traffic so that pedestrians can enjoy the stroll up and down it, perhaps with a stop for a glass of wine and a meal at the small restaurant with a few tables on the sidewalk. **Hanover Street,** one block southeast and parallel to Salem, is the North End's main street, always dotted with groups of men standing on corners and passing the latest news—all in Italian, of course. The best and most authentic espresso and cappuccino in Boston are served in the Italian cafés that line the street, and if you plan to have a cup, stop first at one of the delectable bakeries or pastry shops on the street for a treat to go with it.

Haymarket
Most of the costermongers in Haymarket's Friday and Saturday open-air produce market are oldtimers from the North End, and no wonder—a three-minute walk under the Central Artery via a special passage unites the two areas. The pushcarts and stalls in the market are heirlooms passed down from father to son, or sold at a very high price, because the market is so profitable that a family can live all week from the money made on the two market days.

Faneuil Hall Marketplace
Haymarket's open-air stalls may be packed on Friday and Saturday, but across the street at Faneuil Hall Marketplace shops and vendors are hard put to serve the crowds every day of the week. This phenomenally successful restoration of Boston's historic Quincy Market, North Market, and South Market buildings is not only beautiful and historically important, but also just plain fun. The Marketplace deserves its own restaurant guide for the dozens of places to buy the snacks, lunches, or elegant dinners that are housed here; you can buy sausage, cheese, pastries, Turkish figs, freshly baked French or Italian bread, wine, and on and on for your own picnic as well. Go to buy, or to eat, or just to look.

Waterfront
East of Faneuil Hall Marketplace and south of the North End is Boston's Waterfront, another area in which restoration has brought new life and vitality. The solid old brick and granite buildings, which once served as warehouses for India and China traders, have been modernized and converted to offices, shops, and apartments, and a fine waterfront park brings picnickers, Frisbee-throwers, kids on bikes, and anyone out for a walk. Lewis Wharf, Commercial Wharf, Long Wharf, Rowe's Wharf, and all the rest are well worth a stroll. The New England Aquarium and Marriott Long Wharf hotel are at the southern end of the "new" Waterfront.

Government Center
All of the quarters mentioned above touch on Government Center, a bureaucrats' corral surrounded by striking modern buildings housing city, state, and federal offices and dominated by the **City Hall,** placed in the midst of a brick-paved plaza that covers several acres. The plaza, with its sunken fountain, is a focus of outdoor activities in summer—free concerts, plays, and exhibits. This used to be Scollay Square, the city's tenderloin section, close to the rundown waterfront and peopled by sailors and students out for a good time in the burlesque houses and bars, which were planted thick as mushrooms.
South of Government Center is the city's **financial and commercial heart,** centered on State Street, Milk Street, Devonshire Street, and the surrounding ways.

Beacon Hill
Due west of Government Center is Beacon Hill, last of the three hills of Trimountain and now the very exclusive residential section, with a surprisingly European ambience. The crown of the hill is Bulfinch's great **State House,** topped by its gold dome; the building is the home of the "Great and General Court of Massachusetts Bay" (the state legislature). Be sure to take a walk around Beacon Hill and its famous **Louisburg Square,** where some of the most attractive houses are situated. Today, besides Boston's Old Money, Beacon Hill is home for a good number of students and young professional people.

Boston Common
South of Beacon Hill is Boston Common, the city's "central park," with a Frog Pond—filled with splashing children in summer and skaters in winter—statues and

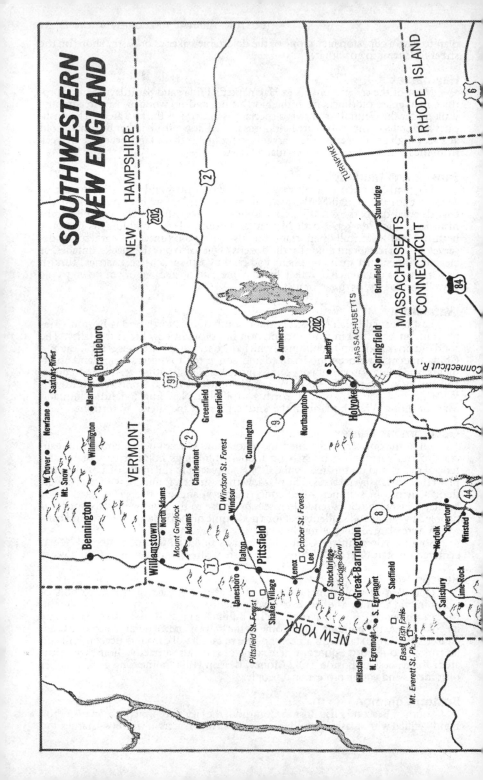

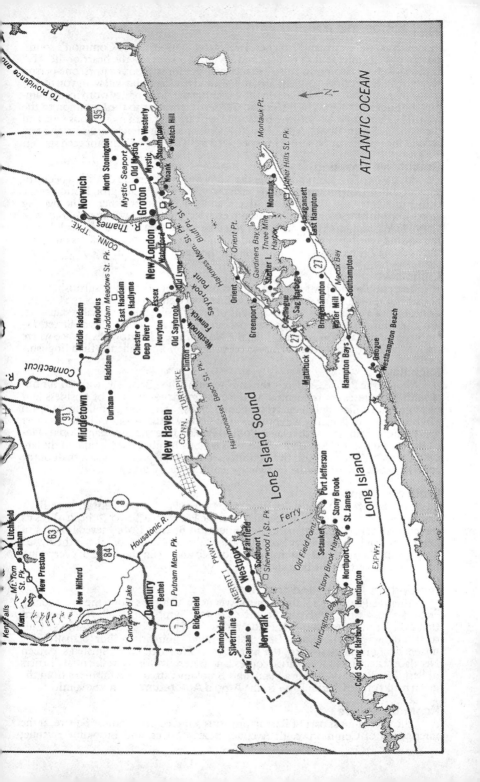

monuments, walkways, and benches. Park Street Station, at the Common's south-eastern corner (intersection of Park and Tremont Streets), is the heart of the "T," Boston's subway system, and also a gathering place for soapbox orators, one-person bands, religious zealots, panhandlers, mimes, and hawkers who will want you to join fringe political groups. The grass on the Common may look pretty worn in late summer, but not so the grass in the **Public Garden,** right next to the Common to the west. The Public Garden's flower beds and lawns are kept with meticulous care, and the famous **Swan Boats** (run by pedal-power), which slowly cruise sightseers around the pond, may be aging, but they get a fresh coat of white paint each spring.

Downtown Crossing

Southeast of the Common is the city's downtown shopping district, a pedestrian zone called Downtown Crossing; take the subway to Washington Station at the corner of Winter and Washington Streets, and you can enter either of the two big stores, **Jordan Marsh** or **Filene's,** without even leaving the subway station. But walk south on Washington Street and soon you'll be in the **Combat Zone,** dead during the day but roaring in the evening and on into the night, its nudie bars and peep shows doing a brisk business most nights of the week.

Chinatown

The jumble and juxtaposition of Boston's neighborhoods is surprising, and perhaps most of all when one discovers Chinatown right on the edge of the Combat Zone, east of Washington Street. Dozens of very presentable Oriental restaurants, groceries, businesses, and churches are packed into the area around Beach Street, Tyler Street, and Harrison Avenue. Like the North End, Chinatown is a place where the language of the old country may greet your ears more frequently than English.

Back Bay

West of the Public Garden is the large section called Back Bay, with **Commonwealth Avenue** as its residential axis, **Boylston Street** its axis of business and pleasure with office buildings, restaurants, clubs, and shops. Walking west on Boylston Street in Back Bay will bring you to **Copley Square,** one of Boston's most genteel areas, bounded by the classic **Boston Public Library,** the elegant **Copley Plaza Hotel,** and Henry Hobson Richardson's famous **Trinity Church,** built in the late 1800s. Modern intruders on this gentility are the striking mirror-glass shaft of the **John Hancock Tower** and the sprawling complex called **Copley Place.**

Prudential Center

Even farther west along Boylston Street is the **Prudential Center,** Back Bay's first large-scale redevelopment scheme, with the Prudential Tower ("the Pru") as its centerpiece, flanked by the mammoth **Sheraton Boston Hotel,** several blocks of luxury flats, and stores such as Lord & Taylor. Also in the Pru complex is the **Hynes Convention Center,** now extensively renovated and again the scene of everything from rock concerts to the boat show.

Huntington Avenue and the Fens

After the Pru Center, Huntington Avenue (which runs along the Pru's southern side) passes the **Christian Science Center, Symphony Hall, Northeastern University,** and the **Museum of Fine Arts** on what might be called Boston's "Cultural Highway." The **Back Bay Fens** sound uninviting, but actually this unappetizing name designates the first links in Frederick Law Olmsted's "Green Necklace," a chain of green parks, copses, and waterways for the residential districts of Back Bay, Roxbury, Jamaica Plain, and Brookline, stretching for miles from the green banks of the Charles River to the **Arnold Arboretum** way to the south.

Kenmore Square

The westernmost part of Boston proper is centered on Kenmore Square, at the intersection of Commonwealth Avenue, Beacon Street, and Brookline Avenue;

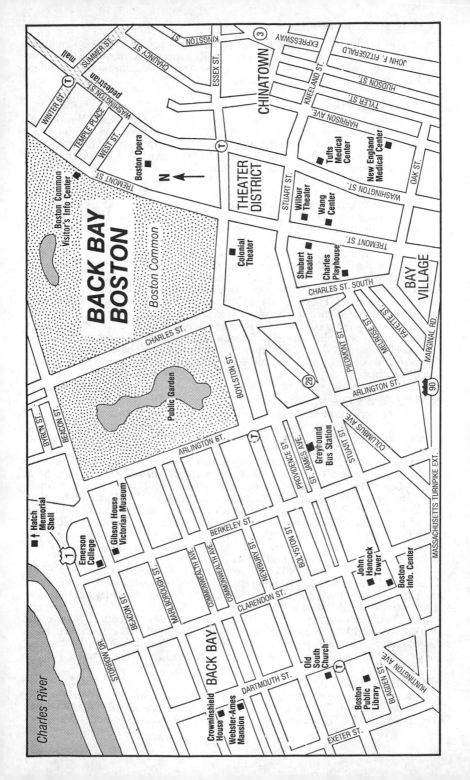

Boston University is just a block or two west from the square, and thus Kenmore's life is dominated by its student denizens, who flock to its cafeterias, book and record stores, movies, and clubs. On the Boston skyline at night, you can always locate Kenmore Square by the huge red Citgo delta.

Outlying Districts

Although the city of Boston is fairly large, it is dwarfed by Greater Boston, officially termed the Metropolitan District, which consists of a dozen other cities as well as some outlying sections of Boston proper. **Charlestown,** north of the tip of Boston peninsula, is dominated by the **Bunker Hill Monument** obelisk; *Old Ironsides* is berthed nearby in the old Boston Navy Yard. **East Boston,** to the northeast, is reached by two tunnels: **Callahan Tunnel** runs north (outbound, no toll), **Sumner Tunnel** runs south (inbound, toll), and the big industry here is Logan International Airport. **South Boston,** southeast of downtown, is separated from the city proper by the Fort Point Channel. "Southie" is the city's Irish bastion, and here St. Patrick's Day is the national holiday. (*Note:* If someone mentions the South End, they're referring to the residential district just south of Back Bay. The South End and South Boston are, confusingly, completely separate places.)

West of Boston is **Brookline,** a large, mostly residential city and the former hometown of the Kennedy family. On the northern banks of the Charles River, **Cambridge** got most of the riverfront land, while **Somerville** had to be content with a mere foothold. The banks of the Charles from the Charles River Dam (topped by the Museum of Science) all the way to Harvard are covered by grass and trees, and in summer the grass is covered with sunbathers, picnickers, readers of paperbacks, and listeners to portable radios. The **Charles River Esplanade** is the river's edge of Beacon Hill, and is perhaps the loveliest part of the Charles's banks, with its marina for small sailboats, the **Hatch Memorial Shell** for summer concerts, a bikepath, and lots of benches.

Several Bird's-Eye Views

The best way to become familiar with Boston's layout is to hover above it in a helicopter. The next best way is to climb to the top of one of the city's tall buildings for the view. Whereas a helicopter ride might be expensive, the skyscraper observatories won't bust your budget.

Take the Green Line (any car you see except "North Station" or "Lechmere") to the Copley Station for the **John Hancock Observatory,** 200 Clarendon St. at Copley Square (tel. 572-6429). The ticket office entrance is on the corner of Trinity Place and St. James Avenue. This, the tallest building in New England, has landmarks picked out for visitors with special telescopelike viewers. Several audiovisual shows outline Boston history and the makeup of the modern cityscape. Hours are Monday through Saturday from 9am to 11pm, year round. On Sunday, summer (May through October) hours are 10am to 11pm; in winter, noon to 11pm. Last tickets are sold at 10:15pm. Adults pay $2.75; seniors, $2; children 5 to 15, $2.

The **Prudential Tower,** 800 Boylston St. (tel. 236-3318), centerpiece of the Prudential Center, has a **Skywalk** on the 50th floor with a full-circle panorama of the city. It's open from 10am to 10pm Monday through Saturday, and noon to 10pm on Sunday. Admission is $2.50 for adults, $1.50 for children (5 to 15) and seniors. Two floors above is the Top of the Hub restaurant and cocktail lounge, and you can see the city for free when you buy a drink or a meal. To get to the Pru, take a Green Line "Arborway" car to Prudential Station, or "Boston College," "Cleveland Circle," or "Riverside" cars to Auditorium Station or Copley Station.

VISITORS' INFORMATION

Before coming to Boston, call 617/536-4100, fax to 617/424-7664, or write the **Greater Boston Convention & Visitors Bureau,** Prudential Plaza, P.O. Box 490, Boston, MA 02199, and they'll send you an information packet.

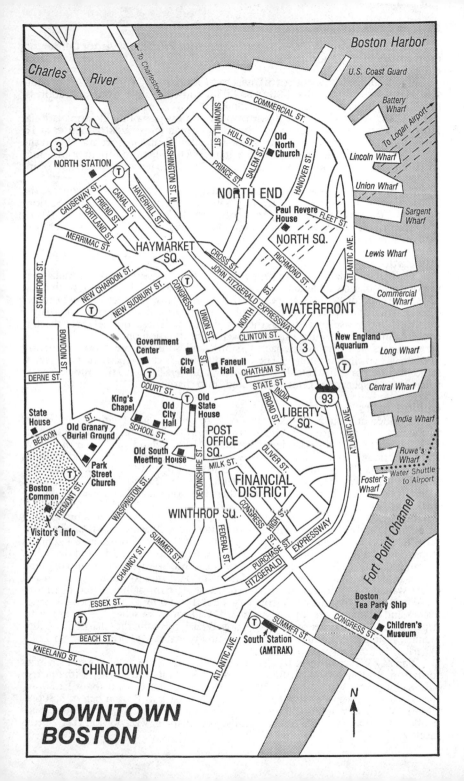

DOWNTOWN BOSTON

The Convention & Visitors Bureau operates the **Prudential Visitor Center,** on the west side of the Prudential Center Plaza (tel. 617/536-4100), open daily from 8:30am to 5pm.

If you call the **Massachusetts Division of Tourism** at 617/727-3201 or (outside Massachusetts) toll free 800/623-8038, and leave your name and address, they'll send you a Massachusetts Vacation Kit.

Much of Boston's historic downtown area is now part of the Boston National Historical Park, and so the National Park Service maintains a **Visitor Center** at 15 State St. (tel. 617/242-5642). Free guided Freedom Trail tours are available in the spring and summer. The Information Center is open daily from 9am to 5pm. You'll see park rangers here and there at historic spots, ready to help with directions or information.

On Boston Common (Green Line or Red Line to Park Street Station), at the intersection of Tremont and Winter Streets just a few steps from Park Street Station, there's the **Boston Common Visitor Information Center** (tel. 617/536-4100), open year round from 9am to 5pm. Come here to get maps and booklets describing the Freedom Trail and other visitor information.

Publications

The best calendar of current happenings for free is *Where* magazine, available at visitors' information desks and in hotel lobbies. It's a complete listing of the best plays, sports events, concerts, special exhibits, and programs. Another way to get current news of current offerings is to buy a copy of one of the city's alternative weekly tabloid newspapers, such as the *Boston Phoenix*. These routinely have theater, concert, cinema, and lecture listings, as well as information on poetry readings and performances at coffeehouses, jam sessions, and some of the most fascinating "Personals" ads in the country. These weekly tabloids can be bought at any newsstand or from street hawkers. If you are near a university, go to the student center where the newspapers are often distributed at no charge.

Guided Tours

A guided bus tour is the easiest way of all to get acquainted with the city and its landmarks, and the price for such an introduction is reasonable. The **Gray Line,** at Park Square (tel. 426-8805), offers 16 tours of New England, one a tour of Boston and Cambridge. Their Tour No. 1 takes three hours, covers 18 miles, and includes many Freedom Trail sights, Beacon Hill, Bunker Hill, and *Old Ironsides.* Harvard and MIT Tours leave every day at various times and cost $15 for people 13 years and older; free if you're 12 or under. Contact them by phone or at the sightseeing desk of one of the larger hotels.

Boat Excursions: A novel way to get acquainted with Boston is by taking a cruise in the harbor and Massachusetts Bay. **Bay State Provincetown Cruises** (tel. 723-7800) operates vessels that tour the waters of Boston. Cruises take 1½ hours (three cruises a day); the price is $5 for adults, half-price for children under 12. A 55-minute cruise of Boston's Inner Harbor is also available with the option of going ashore at the Charlestown Navy Yard. There's also a cruise to Nantasket Beach and whale watches. In addition to these cruises, short trips at lunchtime (12:15 to 12:45pm) are a refreshing break from city life and cost only $1.50 per person. Sandwiches and beverages are for sale on board. Call for exact schedules. These boats depart from the red ticket office at 20 Long Wharf, opposite the Chart House Restaurant, near the Aquarium (Blue Line) subway station. Offices are at 66 Long Wharf.

The M/V *Provincetown II,* also operated by Bay State, journeys to Provincetown from Boston daily in late June, and throughout July and August, with one trip a day sailing from Boston about 9:30am, arriving Provincetown at about 12:30pm, then departing P-town at about 3:30pm to arrive back in Boston before 6:30pm. The M/V *Provincetown* also makes the voyage on weekends in May, early June, September, and October. For more details, see chapter VII, section 11, "Provincetown."

2. Getting Around

THE T

Boston's subway and bus system, one of the oldest in the country, has been revitalized and improved. You'll find the T (short for Massachusetts Bay Transportation Authority, or MBTA) the best way to get around downtown and Back Bay. At this writing, fares are 50¢ on most buses and 75¢ on the subway, but note this: on several lines (most notably the Green Line) the cars surface and serve as trolleys after they leave the central part of the city. When a car emerges, passengers boarding above ground ride for free. If you catch a Green Line trolley inbound, however, you pay the entire fare to your destination (which may cost up to $1.75) when you get on, and then there's nothing to pay later. Children 5 to 11 pay half fare, seniors pay 10¢ for any ride if they have an MBTA identity card. Buses that go to outlying communities (Salem, Marblehead, etc.) charge up to $2.50 one way for the ride. All fares are on an *exact-change* basis: on buses and trolleys you *must* have the exact fare; at subway stations there are change booths open during service hours.

Subway lines are color-coded: the **Red Line** goes from Alewife in Cambridge via Harvard Square through the central station at Park Street and then on to the suburbs of Quincy, Braintree, Dorchester, and Mattapan; the **Green Line** goes from Lechmere Square in East Cambridge through Park Street and downtown and then out to the western suburbs. I'll mention the line—Red, Green, Blue, or Orange—and the appropriate station for most of the sights mentioned in this book, and thus speed your way to your destination.

Special Passes

The MBTA sells a **Tourist Pass** called a "Passport" that allows unlimited travel on the subway and on local buses in Greater Boston. Passes good for three consecutive days cost $8 for adults, $4 for children 5 to 11; seven-day passes are $16 for adults, $4 for children. You can buy your Passport at the "Airport" subway station on the Blue Line, at the Baybanks Foreign Exchange booths in the airport's Terminals C and E, at North Station and South Station subway stops, and at the Boston Common Visitor Information Center. Many hotels also sell the Passports.

Subway Information

The **MBTA Information Booth** is in Park Street Station. For information by telephone, call these numbers: for Lost and Found, 617/722-5000; for route information, 722-3200 or toll free 800/392-6100; for MBTA commuter railroad schedules to places north and west of Boston, 617/227-5070 or toll free 800/392-6099. To points south, 617/482-4400 or toll free 800/882-1220. When in doubt, the central MBTA switchboard number is 617/722-5000.

Hours of Operation

Times on subway and bus lines vary, but you're pretty sure of being able to take the T any day from 5am up to 12:30am (and up to 1am on some lines). After that, be prepared to take a cab, unless you get the final trip time from an officer of the line, and meet the schedule. Hours may vary on Sunday.

Subway Pickpockets

Any big-city transportation system has its pickpockets, and Boston is no exception. The modus operandi is for a group of four or five such types to ride the trains or buses together so the stolen wallet or purse can be passed from one to the other, thus protecting the one who actually lifted it. Watch for people who continually bump people and crowd toward the doors at a stop, and then "decide this must not be the place," and move back in; they'll be carrying coats or raincoats (whatever the weather) to conceal a light-fingered hand and also any prizes they may take. If you see one in action and challenge him or her, the reaction will be aggressive defense—"Who are you calling a pickpocket?"—and then a quick exit.

If you should be so unlucky as to have your pocket or purse picked, call one of the numbers listed in the white pages under "Mass. Bay Transportation Authority, Lost and Found" (the number will depend on the subway line or bus you were on); try a few days later as well, since wallets are often found, minus cash, and turned in.

TAXIS

An ad that runs perpetually in the *Boston Globe*'s "Job Opportunities" classifieds begins, "Sooner or later you'll be a cab driver." There are many long-time professional drivers, of course, but there are also many part-time, out-of-town students, and beginning drivers who may or may not know their way around. There are also those who may know their way around but who will get "lost" because you're paying them by the mile. Such is life in a big city. It could be worse: you could be driving your own car, watching its fenders being bent, battling for parking places. There's no charge for normal luggage, but there is a surcharge for trunks. If you've got a complaint against a driver, get the hackney carriage medallion number, and the driver's name and number (from his permit, posted in the cab), record the date and time of the occurrence, and call the Boston Police Department's Hackney Carriage office at 247-4475. Medallions, or permits to operate cabs, cost in the tens of thousands of dollars, and drivers or companies will do a lot not to lose one.

DRIVING

Boston drivers are famed for being slow of wit and heavy of foot. Traffic control is often minimal, leaving each to fend for her- or himself. It's not so much that Boston drivers are aggressive as that they're thoughtless and inconsiderate. There is a widespread belief that stop signs have no meaning, and that red lights, especially late at night, are mere bagatelles. Although there is a required state vehicle inspection, you may run into five or six cars with inoperative brake lights during even a short drive across town. Horror statistics: A fairly expensive late-model car with full collision insurance can cost its owner over $2,000 a year in insurance premiums alone. One reason is that Boston is the stolen-car capital of the U.S.

Parking is definitely a problem if you want to do it on the cheap. Downtown parking can cost $8 for the first half hour. For the visitor unfamiliar with the city, I'd suggest the large **Boston Common Underground Garage,** entered from Charles Street between the Common and the Public Garden. Here the rates are moderate, and there's a free shuttle bus to take you to nearby points. If you stay for some time in Boston, do not accumulate a backlog of unpaid parking tickets: cars are towed and held hostage until the tickets are paid. By the way, you will see every No Parking zone in the city parked solid almost all the time. It's done, here and in Cambridge, but a few of the scofflaws come back to find their cars towed away or securely locked in place by the big yellow "Denver Boot" (so named after the city that originated its use). The price to get the car back is about $80 plus the cost of overdue tickets.

BIKES

Boston is a good town for bicycling: the hills are gentle, the views are better from a bike, and there are marked bike paths and a new bikeway running from near

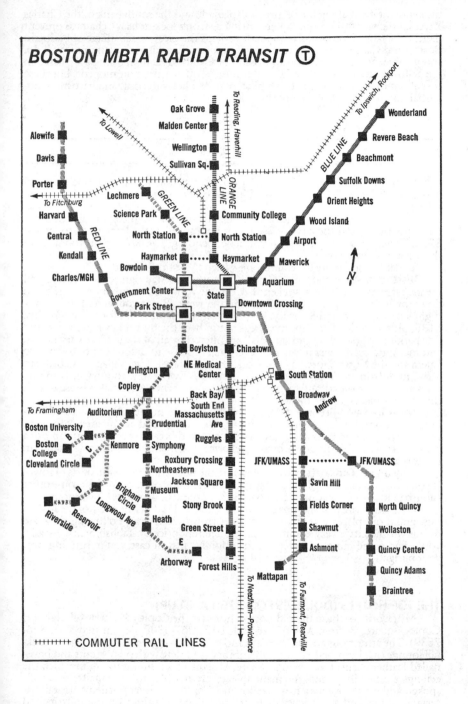

BOSTON MBTA RAPID TRANSIT Ⓣ

the center of town along the beautiful Esplanade and the south bank of the Charles River all the way to Harvard Square. Bring a strong lock or heavy chain to prevent theft, especially if you have a ten-speed. Perhaps the greatest advantage of biking in Boston and Cambridge is the ease and cheapness of parking: any lamppost will do, and it's free. You can rent bikes in Boston or Cambridge. Rental shops are listed in the Yellow Pages under "Bicycles—Renting." You can also rent mopeds, but these cost about three times as much as a bike, require a hefty deposit, and have more potential for problems than a simple bicycle.

---

3. Hotels

Boston has a very fine selection of downtown hotels, and each one seems to have something special to recommend it. The best way to get to know this wonderful city is to stay right downtown, where the action is. This can be expensive, however; a double room in one of Boston's fine hotels often costs nearly $200 or more per night, and the city's 9.7% room tax can hike that lofty price to almost $220. To help you see exactly what you'll be spending, I've *included* the room tax in the prices I quote below.

To get the best value for your money, keep these tips in mind:

Visit on a Weekend: First of all, if you want to stay right downtown, by all means plan your visit for a weekend! A double room at any luxury hotel right in downtown Boston may cost $200 during the week. But if you sign up for a two-night stay on Friday and Saturday, you may get that same room for something like $135, plus a bottle of champagne, breakfast in bed, the morning's newspaper, and free parking. These "weekend specials" are offered by all of the city's luxury hotels, and many are even lower in price. It even makes sense to detour out of town—to Salem and the North Shore, to Cape Cod, or to Old Sturbridge Village—in order to arrive in Boston on Friday afternoon or evening. (By the way, country inns and resorts are most crowded, and highest in price, on weekends; so it makes sense to visit the country places during the week.)

Try a Bed-and-Breakfast: Another way to save money is to try a bed-and-breakfast room. Several agencies will make reservations and arrangements for you, and they're all listed below. By staying in a bed-and-breakfast room, you can pay a half or even a third of the downtown hotel price, and make new Bostonian friends in the bargain.

Stay on the Outskirts: Finally, there are the hostelries on the outskirts of town. If you have a car and are willing to stay in Salem, Lexington, Concord, or some other suburban location, you can save 25% to 50% of the cost of a downtown room.

Here, then, are descriptions of Boston's hotels. I'll describe a few of the luxurious, grand old places you might want to patronize as a treat. Following these are details on the city's very comfortable, moderately priced establishments. Finally, you'll find some hints on lower-priced lodgings, just in case you're running over your budget.

THE TOP HOTELS (DOUBLES FOR $160 AND UP)

My favorite of the grand old Boston hotels is the **Copley Plaza Hotel,** right on Copley Square, Boston, MA 02116 (tel. 617/267-5300, or toll free 800/826-7539). The attractions are the hotel's grand style and original touches: a quiet cocktail lounge that is, in fact, a comfy club library complete with oil portraits and brass-nailed leather chairs; the striking, ornate, elegant Plaza dining room, in which the ceilings are heavily gilded, the mantelpieces are marble, and the maitre d' a soft-spoken and very suave man in a tuxedo; and Copley's, a mirror-laden brass-rail bar serving drinks and sandwiches, with trompe l'oeil paintings on the mirrors and doors. Single rooms are $165 to $215; double or twin rooms run $185 to $240; suites run $300 to $750. Valet parking is $20; nearby parking is $14.

Anyone who's ever come to Boston has considered staying at the **Omni Parker House,** 60 School St. (corner of Tremont), Boston, MA 02108 (tel. 617/227-8600, or toll free 800/843-6664), a traditional beauty that capitalizes on its antiquity, showing off its wood paneling, ornate gilded ceilings, and leather-upholstered furniture. The rooms, although fairly small, are decorated very tastefully with reproductions of antiques. The dining room, Parker's, is a haven of quiet, shining crystal and silver, heavy mirrors, and thick carpets. Lunch here might be $20 to $30, and dinner about $40 to $50 per person. Downstairs from the lobby is The Last Hurrah, an eye-catching collection of Tiffany-style lamps, 1890s bars and booths, brass globe-top lamps, pictures of turn-of-the-century prize fighters, and the like. The Last Hurrah is where many office workers in the nearby government and financial districts come for lunch or after-five cocktails that are served with hot and cold hors d'oeuvres (on the house). The 535 rooms at the Omni Parker House are priced at $145 to $265 single, $160 to $280 double.

"What a perfect place for a hotel!" That's how the **Bostonian Hotel,** Faneuil Hall Marketplace, Boston, MA 02109 (tel. 617/523-3600, or toll free 800/343-0922), introduces itself. It's true: next to Faneuil Hall, Government Center, the weekend open fruit-and-vegetable market, the North End's Italian shops and restaurants, the Bostonian is in the midst of the action. Modern with colonial accents, the hotel boasts tiny balconies overlooking Faneuil Hall on most rooms. It's a small, low-rise (four-floor) luxury hotel with 155 rooms priced at $190 to $240 single, $210 to $260 double. Honeymoon rooms with Jacuzzi tubs and fireplaces cost somewhat more. Kids under 12 stay free.

Four Seasons hotels are noted for their quiet whispering of elegance and status, and the 288-room **Four Seasons Hotel Boston,** 200 Boylston St., Boston, MA 02116 (tel. 617/338-4400, or toll free 800/268-6282), is no exception. This is an impressive addition to Boston's lineup of luxury hotels, and opened in June 1985. Facing the Public Garden, near Back Bay and its chic shopping, a block from the theater district, and a short walk across Boston Common to the central shopping and financial districts, the Four Seasons couldn't have a better location. Facilities are extremely well thought out for guests' comfort, and very plush in an up-to-date style inspired by tradition. Rates are $203 to $357 single, $236 to $390 double, with suites costing up to $1,481 a day. Many rooms, by the way, have views of the Public Garden.

Boston's newest luxury hotel is the **Boston Harbor Hotel,** 70 Rowe's Wharf, Boston, MA 02110 (tel. 617/439-7000, or toll free 800/752-7077), on Atlantic Avenue near the intersection of High Street (from the Central Artery, take the "South Station" exit). Opened in September of 1987, the hotel is part of a landmark redevelopment plan that restored the dramatic old buildings at Rowe's Wharf into a complex that includes the hotel, offices, condominiums, shops, restaurants, a yacht marina, and a ferryboat terminal. You can spot the striking flat-domed main portal easily if you're driving on the Central Artery.

The hotel is wonderfully luxurious, with 230 rooms that are almost junior suites, each with its own sitting area separate from the sleeping area, plus a minibar and remote-control television. There are bathrobes, hair dryers, 24-hour room service, free shoeshine service, fresh flowers, maid service twice daily, windows you can open to let in the sea breezes, and top-class luxury furnishings in classic style. Besides the standard rooms, the hotel has 96 deluxe rooms with harbor or city views, and 28 luxury suites.

The public spaces are classic, conservative, and beautiful, and suggest wealth and richness, from the lavish use of colored marble to the crystal chandeliers, the thick patterned carpets, and the displays of antique maps and charts of Boston and New England. Classical music murmurs in the background, or a piano tinkles in the spacious sea-view lounge. Hotel services include a 60-foot lap pool, a large whirlpool, a sauna, steambaths, massage rooms, exercise equipment, and spa-treatment facilities. There are classes in aerobics and weight-training instruction. The restaurant features New England seafood and other regional American cuisine, and has a sweeping view of Boston harbor.

Single rooms cost $195 to $265, doubles range from $215 to $285, though weekend packages can bring the cost of a room, single or double, down to $175 per night. By the way, the interesting stone pavilion with a copper-clad dome, perched out by the wharf, is the terminus for ferryboats.

A Glance at the Luxury Lineup

The aforementioned are by no means Boston's only luxury hotels, they're just the ones that I think convey a special spirit of the city. In the range of $150 to $250 per night for a double room, you'll also find these excellent places:

The **Hotel Meridien Boston,** 250 Franklin St., Boston, MA 02110 (tel. 617/451-1900, or toll free 800/223-9918) is Air France's elegant hostelry, housed in the handsome former headquarters of the Federal Reserve Bank of Boston, in the heart of the financial district. This stately Renaissance-revival building of granite and limestone has rich, monumental public rooms, but the 326 guest rooms and 22 suites are modern in style and very comfortable in appointments. Julien, the restaurant, is plush, hushed, elegant, satisfying, and expensive; consultant chef Olivier Roellinger presides. The less-formal Café Fleuri has the ambience of a bistro. In the hotel's bar are two patriotic murals by N. C. Wyeth (father of Andrew Wyeth) done in 1923. Rooms cost $225 single, $251 double during the week in summer, but only $173 per room on weekends, tax included.

The **Boston Marriott Hotel Long Wharf,** 296 State St., Boston, MA 02109 (tel. 617/227-0800, or toll free 800/228-9290), is a new luxury hotel with traditional lines, right on the waterfront next to Faneuil Hall Marketplace.

The **Ritz-Carlton Hotel,** 15 Arlington St., Boston, MA 02117 (tel. 617/536-5700, or toll free 800/241-3333; fax 617/536-9340), is Boston's grande dame in the luxury class, with careful service and a prime location right next to the Public Garden.

The modern 500-room **Lafayette Swissôtel,** 1 Avenue de Lafayette, Boston, MA 02111 (tel. 617/451-2600, or toll free 800/992-0124, 800/325-2531 in Massachusetts), one of Boston's newest hotels, is right at Downtown Crossing, in the heart of the shopping district, part of the Lafayette Place complex.

The **Colonnade Hotel,** 120 Huntington Ave., Boston, MA 02116 (tel. 617/424-7000, or toll free 800/962-3030; fax 617/424-1717), concentrates on modern luxuries and European-style personal service in a location near Symphony Hall, Copley Place, the Hynes Convention Center, and the Prudential Center. The 288 rooms in this family-owned hotel have many thoughtful touches, as well as all the luxuries. Rates are $171 to $187 single, $193 to $209 double, tax included. On weekends, rates are $125 to $159, single or double; the higher price includes breakfasts and brunches.

The **Sheraton-Boston Hotel and Towers,** 39 Dalton St., Boston, MA 02199 (tel. 617/236-2000, or toll free 800/325-3535), is New England's largest convention hotel, right in the Prudential Center, with all the facilities imaginable, and 1,250 luxury rooms priced at $180 to $235 single, $202 to $256 double, tax included. The Sheraton Towers, an exclusive 103-room hotel-within-a-hotel, features private registration and a lounge with butler service where you can enjoy free continental breakfast, afternoon tea, and evening hors d'oeuvres. Rooms at the Towers cost $273 to $409 single, $295 to $410 double, tax included.

The **Back Bay Hilton,** 40 Dalton St., Boston, MA 02115 (tel. 617/236-1100), and the **Westin Hotel Copley Place,** 10 Huntington Ave., Boston, MA 02116 (tel. 617/262-9600, or toll free 800/228-3000), are two other additions to the luxury lineup, in an ultramodern complex built right next to traditional Copley Square in the Back Bay.

The **Royal Sonesta Hotel,** 5 Cambridge Parkway, Cambridge, MA 02142 (tel. 617/491-3600), is actually closer to downtown Boston than to Harvard Square. A short trundle from the hotel across the Charles River Dam by the Museum of Science brings you right to Beacon Hill. The Sonesta has 400 modern rooms with views of the river and Boston's skyline. Rooms are priced at $150 to $190 single, $170 to $210 double.

THE UPPER BRACKET (DOUBLES FOR $110 TO $175)

Lower in price than the luxury hotels, these "Upper Bracket" places still offer all the services, such as air conditioning, parking garages, color television, room service, restaurants and bars, and downtown locations. Many also have those marvelous weekend special rates. Be sure to ask about them when you call for information or reservations.

A well-located, upper-range hotel in downtown Boston is the **57 Park Plaza Hotel,** 200 Stuart St., Boston, MA 02116 (tel. 617/482-1800, or toll free 800/468-3557, that's 800/HOTEL-57). The 350-room hotel is only two blocks from Boston Common and the Public Garden, and right near the Greyhound bus terminal, in a multipurpose complex of buildings that includes a parking garage, two cinemas, two lounges, and two restaurants. This is one of the more luxurious establishments in the Howard Johnson chain, with a year-round swimming pool and a sauna. Business meetings provide a big part of its clientele, both because of the facilities and because of its central location. A single person pays $105 to $150; two persons in either one or two double beds pay $115 to $165. Charge for an extra person is $15. Children under 18 can stay for free if their parents pay the standard two-person rate; the hotel gives discounts to AARP senior citizens with ID cards.

Enjoy the pleasures of the Prudential Center and Copley Place by staying at the **Lenox Hotel,** 710 Boylston St., corner of Exeter, Boston, MA 02116 (tel. 617/536-5300, or toll free 800/225-7676 outside Massachusetts). Here you're right in the same block as the Pru, and rooms cost $120 to $180 single, $135 to $210 double; an extra person pays $20, and children under 18 stay free with their parents. An English-style pub is open for lunch, supper, and late-night snacks (till 2am). The Lenox provides its rooms with provincial, oriental, or colonial decor, individually controlled air conditioning, color TV, coffee makers, and soundproofed walls; some rooms have fireplaces. Besides being right in the Prudential Center, the Lenox is right next to the Boston Public Library, and only a block from Copley Square.

The **Holiday Inn at Government Center,** 5 Blossom St., Boston, MA 02114 (tel. 617/742-7630), just off Cambridge Street, between Government Center and the Longfellow Bridge over the Charles River, is a high-rise haven slightly out of the center of things. It's several blocks from Government Center, and then several blocks again from Government Center to the Boston Common. But prices are not too bad in this modern building, and facilities are good: swimming pool (summer months only), free covered parking, and a penthouse restaurant. Rooms cost $125 single, $165 double. Within the same complex as the 300-room hotel are two cinemas, a supermarket, and rows of shops. Children under 18 stay free with their parents.

Boston's famous Statler Hilton is no more, but in its place—actually, in the very same building—you'll find the **Boston Park Plaza Hotel & Towers,** 64 Arlington St. at Park Plaza, Boston, MA 02117 (tel. 617/426-2000, or toll free 800/225-2008; fax 617/426-5545). Most of the 977 rooms have been renovated recently, and all have air conditioning, color TV, and AM-FM radio. The hotel's service includes the Café Rouge restaurant, the Captains piano bar, the lobby lounge, a health club with swimming pool, a cabaret theater featuring "Forbidden Broadway" plays, and 30 of the airline offices in Boston. The location is very central, near the Greyhound bus terminal, and a scant block from Boston Common; the nearest subway station is Arlington. Prices are: $107 to $180 for single rooms, $130 to $202 for double rooms, tax included. Children stay free with their parents.

The **Howard Johnson Hotel Kenmore Square,** at 575 Commonwealth Ave., Boston, MA 02215 (tel. 617/267-3100, or toll free 800/654-2000), is perfectly situated if you're visiting Boston University and well placed for most everything else. A modern 179-room hotel with indoor swimming pool, Profiles Cafe, and Box Seat Lounge, its location allows you to hop right on a Green Line train for the short ride to Park Street Station on Boston Common. Room prices are $112 to $135 single, $128 to $150 double. Kids up to 18 stay free, seniors get discounts, and lots of special money-saving package plans are offered. Call for details.

MODERATELY PRICED HOTELS (DOUBLES FOR $100 TO $125)

Perhaps the best bargain in the area of the Prudential Center, Symphony Hall, and the Christian Science Center is the **Copley Square Hotel,** 47 Huntington Ave. (corner of Exeter), Boston, MA 02116 (tel. 617/536-9000, or toll free 800/225-7062; fax 617/267-3547). Like most of the older hotels in Boston, its rooms have been carefully refurbished and maintained, and are very comfortable, with TV, a coffee maker, and air conditioning. Prices range from $101 to $121 single, $111 to $137 double, $176 for family suites suitable for two, three, or four persons; children under 18 stay free with their parents. This is a full-service hotel with a bar, restaurant, and coffeeshop; $12 overnight parking; limousine service from the airport at $6.50 per person. Be sure to ask about special winter rates and package plans. The hotel is a short block from Copley Square, the Prudential Center, and Boylston Street.

The **Howard Johnson Lodge Fenway,** 1271 Boylston St., Boston, MA 02215 (tel. 617/267-8300, or toll free 800/654-2000), is a 94-room hotel near Fenway Park, home of the Boston Red Sox during baseball season. The Museum of Fine Arts and the Gardner Museum are also close by, and public transportation easily gets you to the city's other sights. Prices are moderate for a city hotel: $100 single, $115 double. As usual at Hojo's, kids under 18 stay for free, senior citizens get discounts, and package plans bring the price down on numerous occasions.

The **TraveLodge Boston** is actually in the neighboring city of Brookline, at 1200 Beacon St., Brookline, MA 02146 (tel. 617/277-1200, or toll free 800/255-3050). The 190 rooms in this residential neighborhood are clean and fairly quiet, with clock-radios and color television sets. Public transportation will take you the several miles into town fairly easily. Single rooms are priced at $88, and doubles at $99.

BUDGET LODGINGS (DOUBLES FOR $45 TO $90)

It's no simple task to find a truly inexpensive, respectable room in Boston, but it can still be done. You'd be well advised to reserve your room in advance, to make sure you can nail down that low price.

A Hotel

The **Chandler Inn,** 20 Chandler St., Boston, MA 02116 (tel. 617/482-3450, or toll free 800/842-3450), at Berkeley Street, only about three blocks from the Greyhound bus terminal, just across the Massachusetts Turnpike from the busy Back Bay commercial district, is a real find. An older hotel, the Chandler has 56 quite small, very simple rooms with renovated bathrooms (including tub and shower), and either a double bed or twin beds. The cost for a room is only $76 single, $87 double, and includes a continental breakfast. Children under 12 can occupy their parents' room for free. Most rooms have only one window and no view, but the corner rooms have two windows and some views; best of all is Room 808, on the top floor (there's an elevator) in the corner. The neighborhood here is undergoing renovation, so ignore its partially rundown appearance.

Bed-and-Breakfast Services

An interesting alternative to commercial lodgings is the bed-and-breakfast room. These are spare rooms or even apartments in private homes, rented to travelers at moderate rates. Bed-and-breakfast services will take your reservation, describe accommodations and prices, and give directions to your lodging. All this is best done in advance, but don't be afraid to call one of the following services if you arrive in town without a reservation.

New England Bed and Breakfast, Inc., 1045 Centre St., Newton Centre, MA 02159 (tel. 617/244-2112), will find you a room in a private home for $45 to $55 single, $60 to $80 double, with a small breakfast included.

A similar service is operated by **Bed and Breakfast Associates Bay Colony, Inc.,** P.O. Box 57166, Babson Park Branch, Boston, MA 02157 (tel. 617/449-5302 from 10am to 12:30pm and 1:30 to 5pm). For $5 they'll send you a 56-page directory describing hundreds of rooms, studios, suites, and apartments located throughout eastern Massachusetts. Prices range from $55 to $85 single, $65 to $125 double, continental breakfast included.

Host Homes of Boston, P.O. Box 117, Waban Branch, Boston, MA 02168 (tel. 617/244-1308), will find you a room in Newton, Brookline, Cambridge, Boston, or another community for about $50 to $85 single, $55 to $100 double, breakfast included. They take credit cards.

Greater Boston Hospitality, P.O. Box 1142, Brookline, MA 02146 (tel. 617/277-5430), makes reservations for private homes, private city clubs, small inns, and condominiums in Boston, Brookline, Cambridge, Needham, Newton, Wellesley, Quincy, Scituate, Gloucester, and Marblehead. You can write, or call 24 hours a day.

Room Rentals

Beacon Guest House, 248 Newbury St., Boston, MA 02116 (tel. 617/262-1771 or 266-7276), will arrange a daily or weekly room rental for you, with private bath and kitchenette with utensils, for $60 per day, $330 per week single; $72 per day, $335 per week double, tax included. All of their rooms are in brownstone apartment buildings located in Back Bay, on Newbury Street near the Prudential Center, the Hynes Convention Center, and public transportation.

Guesthouses

These tend to be plain rather than fancy. Boston's neighbor city of Brookline has several guesthouses, the best being **Anthony's Town House,** 1085 Beacon St., Brookline, MA 02146 (tel. 617/566-3972), a turn-of-the-century brownstone town house with various rooms (private bath or shared bath) for $30 to $55. To get there, take a Green Line subway train ("Cleveland Circle") along Beacon Street from Boston. The street keeps the same name in Brookline. In fact, if you don't keep a sharp eye out, you'll miss the signs announcing that you've entered Brookline. Look for Anthony's on the left-hand side of the street.

Budget Motels on the Outskirts

Although it's preferable to stay downtown and not get snarled in city traffic, you may want to know that Boston has several representatives of the budget-priced **Susse Chalet** motel chain. For reservations, call toll free 800/258-1980 (800/572-1880 in New Hampshire, 800/858-5008 in Canada).

Nearest to the center of Boston are the two motels in Dorchester. Both are on Morrissey Boulevard at Exit 12 (Neponset) or 13 (Freeport St.) off the Southeast Expressway (I-93), five miles south of Boston Common. The 177-room Susse Chalet at 800 Morrissey Blvd., Boston (Neponset), MA 02122 (tel. 617/287-9100), charges $46 to $50 single, $50 to $55 double. Nearby, the 105-room Susse Chalet at 900 Morrissey Blvd., Boston (Neponset), MA 02122 (tel. 617/287-9200), charges $51 to $56 single, $56 to $59 double. The room tax is included in these prices.

There is a similar place in Cambridge. It's the Susse Chalet, 211 Concord Turnpike (Rte. 2 east), Cambridge, MA 02140 (tel. 617/661-7800), west of the Alewife MBTA subway terminus, on the eastbound side of the highway. Rooms here cost $51 to $68 single, $56 to $72 double, tax included. It's about a 15-minute walk to the Alewife station on the MBTA subway's Red Line, which goes directly to Harvard Square in Cambridge and Park Street (for Boston Common) in Boston.

Six miles due west of Boston on Rte. 9 is the neighborhood of Chestnut Hill, and just across the highway from the well-known Chestnut Hill Mall is the Susse Chalet, 160 Boylston St., Newton, MA 02167 (tel. 617/527-9000), with 149 rooms renting for $51 to $54 single, $54 to $58 double, tax included. You can reach this hotel from I-95 (Rte. 128) by taking Exit 20 A (Rte. 9 east); the motel is three miles east of I-95.

The city of Braintree is 11 miles due south of Boston. Take Exit 17 (Union St.) from the Southeast Expressway (I-93 southbound) for the **Susse Chalet, 125 Union Street, Braintree, MA 02184** (tel. 617/848-7890), which charges $46 single, $50 double for a room, and is very near the Braintree MBTA subway station, so you can catch a Red Line train directly into Boston.

Sixteen miles due north of Boston on the way to Cape Ann, New Hampshire, and Maine, there is a **Susse Chalet, 285 Mishawum Rd., Woburn, MA 01801** (tel. 617/938-7575), just west of the intersection of I-95 (Rte. 128) and I-93; take Exit 36 to reach the motel. It's adjacent to the Woburn MBTA commuter rail station. Rates are $51 to $54 single, $56 to $58 double, tax included.

---

4. Restaurants

Dining possibilities in Boston are virtually limitless. The city's array of restaurants includes at least one representative of every notable cuisine in the world, and usually more than one—in the Boston area there are over 150 Chinese restaurants alone. Most of Boston's restaurants take advantage of the fresh seafood that comes to the docks daily, whether the specialty is seafood or not.

For my recommendations, I've tried to help you choose from this bewildering array by sticking to restaurants in Boston proper and excluding the many fine places in the suburbs on the notion that you won't want to fight your way to an unfamiliar town and unfamiliar streets, but would rather spend your time in Boston. Also, I've chosen favorites, places that I've found satisfactory in every way, every time I've been there, and in which I've always felt I've gotten my money's worth. Remember that the many very fine hotel restaurants, lounges, and coffeeshops are covered along with the hotel itself in the preceding section. The good restaurants and coffeehouses in Cambridge are described in the chapter on Cambridge, but it's good to remember that most of them are within walking distance of the Red Line's Harvard subway station, and the trip can be made from central Boston in 10 or 15 minutes. The good restaurant in the Museum of Fine Arts, the best place for lunch if you're seeing the MFA or the Gardner Museum, is described along with the museum itself in the sight-seeing section.

In the more expensive establishments, it's good to call ahead for reservations if they'll take them—many Boston places do not. This is true especially on weekends and holidays, of course. And when you call, ask whether they honor your credit card, and what parking arrangements there are.

Massachusetts has a meal tax of 5.7% added to every meal check over a minimal amount.

THE TOP RESTAURANTS ($50 AND UP)

Any dispute over a city's "best" restaurant is likely to be hot and lengthy, for the simple reason that personal preferences favor certain types of surroundings, service, and cuisine.

Many Bostonians would agree that one of the finest restaurants in town is **L'Espalier,** 30 Gloucester St. (tel. 262-3023), and for the city's ultimate dining experience, it may be equaled but can't be beat. This small, elegant restaurant in an old Back Bay town house serves only dinner, every night except Monday, and you must have reservations, which are sometimes difficult to get. A valet will park your car, and you enter through a vestibule and walk up a flight of stairs to reach the grand high-ceilinged dining room, which is quite nice but not really very "decorated." Waiters in black and white attend to you immediately, and are professional, polished, and friendly in their work. The menu lists the chef's latest creations of French nouvelle cuisine, which, though sometimes exotic, are really inspired and delicious. The wine list is long, good, and fairly pricey. You must be prepared to spend $150 on dinner for two here if you intend not to scrimp, and if you go all out, the tab might come to $200. Whether it does or not, you won't soon forget the meal.

Pride of place on Beacon Hill must go to **Another Season,** 97 Mt. Vernon St., between Charles Street and Louisburg Square (tel. 367-0880). It's small and friendly, with a marvelous feeling of informal elegance; chef Odette Bery puts her personal touch on classic recipes (the menu changes monthly), then makes the rounds of the tables to see how diners have liked them. The wine list is very fine, the cuisine even finer, the service just as good. Get a reservation, then go with about $40 or so to spend for each diner, and you'll find the experience worth far more. Dinner, the only meal, is served Monday through Saturday from 6 to 10pm. Monday through Thursday there are excellent four-course prix fixe menus priced at $15 and $25, plus drinks, tax, and tip.

Among Boston's restaurants of long-standing high quality, few can equal the record of **Maison Robert,** in the old Boston City Hall building at 45 School St., behind King's Chapel (tel. 227-3370). In summer, tables are set outside near the statue of Benjamin Franklin for Ben's Cafe, where you can have a large salad, cold plate, or entree for lunch, and the total bill might be $22 or so. But dinner is the main event here.

Chef Andrée Robert, daughter of the restaurant's founder, creates nouvelle cuisine with American touches. You might start on oysters with raspberry vinegar, or pâté of leeks; go on to lobster with champagne sauce, or sliced breast of duck with apples and blueberries, or perhaps flamed rib of beef for two. Desserts are, of course, sumptuous, from crêpes Suzette through the house gateau (chocolate), to various soufflés. Surroundings are formal and attractive; the service is impeccable. The bill, with wine, tax, and tip, will be in the range of $45 to $60 per person. Hours are 11:30am to 2:30pm and 5:30 to 10pm Monday through Friday, 6 to 10:30pm on Saturday; closed Sunday. Have reservations.

Atop Sheraton World Headquarters at 60 State St., right next to Boston's Old State House, is the **Bay Tower Room** (tel. 723-1666), where every table has a marvelous view of the Custom House Tower, Boston Harbor, Logan Airport, and the hills beyond. A cocktail lounge with a band for dancing (Friday and Saturday) is on the mezzanine level (open 4:30pm to 1am, till 2am on Friday and Saturday, closed Sunday). Dinner is served from 5:30 to 10pm Monday through Thursday, till 11pm on Friday and Saturday (closed Sunday); a jacket is required in the dining room. The menu is long and inclusive, expensive but not outrageous. You can start with lobster ravioli with ginger and basil, or a simple soup. Fish and shellfish, fowl, and grilled meats are all featured; specialties are roast rack of lamb with rosemary, garlic, and cracked pepper in a zinfandel sauce, and a seafood mixed grill of lobster, swordfish, and sea scallops. The bill, per person—tax, tip, and wine included—will be about $55 to $75. It's a good idea to have reservations.

The genteel atmosphere of the **Ritz-Carlton Dining Room** (tel. 536-5700) is a good place for a fine lunch or dinner. From its second-floor location at 15 Arlington St. (corner of Newbury), diners look onto the Public Garden, its trees and flowers, or snow scenes as the case may be. Elegance is all around: gold tracery on the cream-colored ceiling, lofty many-paned windows surrounded by blue-and-white print drapes, crystal chandeliers, and sconces, potted plants, a tinkling piano, and impeccable service. The menu changes daily, but a typical luncheon might offer you roast duckling with cherries, a thin veal cutlet in chive butter, or perhaps a selection from the cold buffet. At dinner, start with lobster bisque with cognac, or Louisiana shrimp, and then go on to a roast leg of spring lamb, or lobster prepared with whisky, or medallions of venison with cranberries and chestnuts. For dessert, have one of the several dessert soufflés, which are first a dream, then ambrosia, then a fond memory. Such a repast will cost $65 to $75 per person, with wine. You can have lunch at the Ritz-Carlton daily from noon to 2:30pm; dinner from 5:30 to 10pm weekdays and Sundays, and to 11pm on Friday and Saturday; Sunday brunch is from 10:45am to 3pm. The dress code is enforced at all times.

Cornucopia, 15 West St. (tel. 338-4600), is in an odd but convenient place:

West Street runs from Tremont Street near the Boston Common Visitor Information Center to Washington Street (Downtown Crossing). Soft muted colors and hanging lamps with diamond-shaped stained-glass shades greet you as you enter; there's an enclosed terrace at the rear, and an attractive upstairs room as well. Original art hangs on the walls, and several black marble café tables with intricate white veining stand waiting near the sidewalk window. The menu is new American, and a meal might begin with chilled duck breast with sun-dried cherry sauce, or veal and walnut terrine with pear, mint, and lime relish, then go on to a main course of grilled scallops, tuna, and shrimp on skewers, or rack of lamb wrapped in pancetta with baked mushroom polenta. The dessert selection changes daily, but is as wonderful as the heartier fare. Lunch should cost $20 to $28 per person; dinner, $30 to $40, tax, tip, and drink included. Hours are Monday through Friday from noon to 2:30pm, and Tuesday through Saturday from 5:30 to 9:30pm. The lighter café menu is available, with drinks, Tuesday through Friday from 2:30 to 10pm, on Saturday from 5:30 to 10pm. Remember the café menu if you need a pick-me-up after shopping or before a night at the opera.

Boston's most famous restaurant is surely the **Hampshire House,** 84 Beacon St. (tel. 227-9605), facing the Public Garden between Arlington Street and Charles Street. While the restaurant is noted for its location in a fine early 20th-century Georgian Revival mansion, its elegant decoration, and its good cuisine, it is far more famous for its Bull & Finch Pub in the basement, which inspired the setting for the television comedy show called **"Cheers."** Every day countless visitors pose by the entrance to have their pictures taken, then descend the stairs to take a look and perhaps to buy a Cheers T-shirt. Let me prepare you for the shock: the pub looks nothing like the set for the show—it is not spacious but rather cozy and crowded, and Sam and Rebecca are not behind the bar. The comfy booths are always crowded with a lively, happy, young, attractive crowd taking in the very English pub atmosphere. The drink to order here is Samuel Adams lager, Boston's own top-quality beer, or Harpoon ale, brewed only a mile or two away on Northern Avenue.

Upstairs is another bar, the Oak Room, as sedate and Beacon Hill–ish as you could imagine. Tall arched windows framed by formal drapes let lots of light into the high-ceilinged room, bringing a glint to the polished glasses and a shine to the grand piano. Dignified gents and ladies, properly dressed, murmur quietly to one another while sipping classic concoctions and munching free hors d'oeuvres. Dinner is served nightly from 5:30 to 10:30pm in the Library and Georgian dining rooms. The menu is interesting without being overly exotic, with some classics such as fettuccine Alfredo, New England clam chowder, and French onion soup gratinée as first courses, then lots of steaks, and also chicken. Expect to pay about $45 to $60 per person for dinner. Lunch, for about $16 or so, can be had Monday through Friday from 11:45am to 2:30pm. Sunday brunch, by the way, is a Hampshire House tradition of many years, served from 10:30am to 2:30pm.

MODERATELY PRICED RESTAURANTS ($35 AND UP)

Because the largest number of recommended restaurants are in the following price brackets, I've divided them up according to location and specialty. Here, then, is the best of the mid- and lower-range dining establishments:

On Beacon Hill

Rebecca's, 21 Charles St. (tel. 742-9747), has lots of strong points. A favorite of the young and beautiful, up-and-coming Beacon Hill set, it is also convenient for visitors to downtown shopping areas and tourist attractions. The food is continental, upbeat, and carefully prepared, interesting without being excessively exotic. Rebecca's serves lunch Monday through Saturday from 11:30am to 4pm, and dinner daily: on Monday from 5 to 10pm, Tuesday through Saturday from 5:30pm to midnight, and on Sunday from 5:30 to 10pm. Lunch costs about $20 per person, and dinner runs about $32 to $45, wine, tax, and tip included. There's paella valenciana, fresh ravioli with spinach and cheese in a cream sauce with shrimp, and roast sea bass with mushrooms cooked with balsamic vinegar, white wine, fresh thyme, bacon, and garlic. You can see the luscious dessert cakes and pastries in the cold cases through the front window as you pass by.

Faneuil Hall Marketplace and the Waterfront

One Boston restaurant which has resisted change is venerable **Durgin-Park Market Dining Room** (tel. 227-2038), 340 Faneuil Hall Marketplace, in the South Market building. Durgin-Park boasts that it was "established before you were born," and adds, somewhat unnecessarily, that "Your grandfather and great-grandfather may have dined with us, too." As you mount the stairs to the dining room, it crosses your mind that you must have taken the wrong stairway and entered some "employees only" door, for there before you is all the dishwashing machinery and hardworking kitchen help, and right next to this, the kitchen itself, with cooks and waitresses scurrying here and there. To left and right are large, plain rooms with steam pipes running about on the ceiling, and several sets of long tables covered with checkered cloths. The menu, plainly printed with notices of daily specials stapled to it, bears pithy reminders and warnings such as "washroom downstairs" and "We are not responsible for any steak ordered well done." The prices have changed since the old days, but the dining room's decor and its food have stayed the same, and portions are big: the prime rib (while it lasts, for this is the specialty) is huge, and costs $16. *Fresh* lobster stew (emphasis theirs) is $12, a roast stuffed duck costs $10, and lowly "frankfort and beans" is $4.50. Clams, oysters, and fish are in the $8 to $14 range. Cocktails are served. Be warned that on weekends for dinner the restaurant is usually very busy, and no reservations are accepted. Perhaps the best time to go is at lunch (11:30am to 2:30pm), referred to as the "dinner bill," when crowds are thinner, portions are more manageable, and prices are lower. By the way, there's an oyster bar in the basement.

Also in Faneuil Hall Marketplace is a good place to dine outdoors, the **Café at Lily's** (tel. 227-3434), in Quincy Market. Actually, there are two Lily's, the Piano Bar at Lily's (a major gathering place for the young and single) and, on the other side of Quincy Market, the Café. In warm weather, tables are set out in the promenades to produce a spacious sidewalk-café atmosphere. Luncheon sandwiches run $5 to $8; a hearty plate of Boston baked beans and knockwurst is in the same range; or an elegant scallop dish named coquilles chablis costs only slightly more. For a very light, diet-conscious lunch, there are salads as well. Lily's is pleasant in summer if it's not too busy (try a late lunch to avoid the jam); in winter the greenhouse—like the main dining area—is under its glass roof.

Seaside Restaurant and Bar, 188 South Market Building (tel. 742-8728), is at the seaside end. Lunch is the time to dine, see, and be seen, although Seaside is busy all day. Elaborate sandwiches, complex salads, omelets, and quiches make up the midday bill of fare, with prices ranging from $5 to $10. Besides the natural-wood tables, Seaside has a bar at which you can sit to have a drink, or a sandwich, or both. At dinnertime, Seaside features steaks, lots of seafood, the chef's daily specialties, and on Tuesday and Thursday a group singing a cappella oldies. Expect to spend about $30 to $45 per person for dinner here. Lunch is served Monday through Saturday from 11:30am to 5pm; dinner is served every night from 5 to 10pm (an hour later on Friday and Saturday). On Sunday there's brunch from 11:30am to 4:30pm.

MONEY-SAVING MEALS ($15 TO $30)

Dining inexpensively does not mean resigning yourself to fast food. This city has hundreds of wonderfully atmospheric and satisfying eating-places charging very little.

The **Commonwealth Brewing Company,** 138 Portland St. (tel. 523-8383), is a working brewery and a restaurant all in one. It's located near North Station and Boston Garden, at the intersection of Portland and Merrimac Streets and Valenti Way. Through the huge windows the antique copper brewing equipment gleams and shines. In the high-ceilinged main dining room are long brass-clad tables and a long stand-up bar running the length of the back wall. There's a spirit of conviviality, inspired by the decor but forcefully encouraged by the Commonwealth's forte:

golden ale, amber ale, bitter, and stout, brewed right here and served live. If you descend to the basement (where there are more tables, and another long bar), you can witness the brewing. The menu is long and satisfying: open-face steak sandwich, shrimp salad, baby back pork ribs, and smoked seafood sampler are a few examples. For a glass of beer and virtually any dish, the bill will be less than $15. Come for lunch, dinner, a late-night snack, or just a glass or two of real beer. Commonwealth is open seven days a week, from 11:30am to midnight Sunday through Thursday, till 1am on Friday and Saturday.

Back Bay: Newbury and Boylston Streets

The two principal shopping and business streets in the Back Bay have a tremendous number of places to nosh, snack, eat, lunch, or dine. Keep this section in mind when you make the rounds of Newbury Street galleries.

Newbury Street's Gallic eatery of long standing (since 1936) is the **Du Barry French Restaurant,** 159 Newbury (tel. 262-2445), between Dartmouth and Exeter Streets (Green Line to Copley). Chef René Rubaud's dinner entrées are classics: filet of sole, daube of beef bourguignon, frogs' legs Provençale, rabbit sautéed in white wine, and beef tongue in a Madeira sauce. Expect to spend $25 to $35 per person at dinner. At lunch, numerous platters are priced below $8. In good weather the outdoor patio and enclosed terrace are the choice places to dine—walk through the restaurant to reach them.

Perhaps the best all-around café on Newbury Street—and certainly the nearest thing to an authentic European café in Boston—is the **Café Florian,** 85 Newbury St. (tel. 247-6600), where you can sit at sidewalk tables or in the air-conditioned rooms down one flight and have a glass of wine or imported beer ($3.50), or a cup of truly excellent Viennese coffee ("Kaffee Wien mit Schlag"); select something from their pastry tray, a sandwich or a bowl of soup, a plate of cheese and bread or an antipasto and cheese plate, or even a full meal. Service is quick and friendly; coffee comes in ten different varieties, priced from $1.25 to $3.50. There are several kinds of tea, and a select wine list. The Florian opens at 8am, and stays open until midnight Sunday through Thursday, till 1:30am Friday and Saturday. There's live music Wednesday through Saturday nights; Sunday brunch is served from 10am, with live jazz at 1pm. On Newbury Street, this is my favorite.

A good place for lunch, dinner, or an evening's sipping and prowling is **Friday's,** 26 Exeter St. at the corner of Newbury (tel. 266-9040), a block from the Boston Public Library, two blocks from Copley Square or the Prudential Center. The space next to the sidewalk has been covered by a greenhouselike shaded glass canopy. The decor is upscale and attractive, and the menu is eclectic: mahimahi fish from Hawaii, or blackened Cajun chicken, or Oriental, Mexican, and American appetizers, or any of a dozen brunch dishes. There are many steaks, sandwiches, and burgers. The drink menu lists every conceivable concoction, plus such pleasant surprises as good champagne at retail-store prices. One might spend $12 to $16 for a light meal, $20 to $28 for a hearty tuck-in. Friday's is open from 11:30am daily; to midnight on weekdays, to 1am on weekends.

The **Harvard Bookstore Café,** 190 Newbury St. (tel. 536-0097), corner of Exeter, has one of the nicest locations in the Back Bay, a shady streetcorner with lots of interesting sidewalk and street activity. If you can grab a sidewalk table, do so; then settle in with coffee and pastry, or order from their menu of fairly substantial luncheon fare. It's sure to satisfy, for the chef here is none other than Moncef Meddeb, formerly of nearby ultra-pricey L'Espalier. With a glass of wine and dessert, a three-course lunch might cost $25 per person, with all that excellent people-watching at no extra charge. The café is open daily from 8am to 11pm (Sunday from noon).

For Seafood

Legal Seafoods (tel. 426-4444) is a Boston institution, a no-nonsense operation that prides itself on freshness and reasonable prices. The restaurant in the Boston Park Plaza Hotel off Park Square (subway to Arlington) is big but nicely arranged in cozy sections, light, and attractive. The menu is encyclopedic, listing close to 100 items, but this is for reference: when fresh stocks run out, that's it for any particular fish. Start with a shrimp cocktail or oysters on the half shell, go on to such choices as scrod, bluefish, mako shark, sea trout. Have a glass or two of wine, and you can expect to pay about $30 for your dinner. Choose carefully and you can spend $22 or so; have lobster, salmon, or scallops, and your bill will be more like $36. Hours are Monday through Thursday from 11am to 10pm, on Friday and Saturday to 11pm, on Sunday from noon to 10pm. Note that there is often a waiting line, especially long on weekends. No reservations accepted.

Jimmy's Harborside (tel. 423-1000), 242 Northern Ave., is at the end of Northern Avenue on Fish Pier, due east of downtown Boston across the Fort Point Channel (Red Line to South Station, then a no. 7 bus, "City Point-South Station"). Jimmy's has a dress code, lots of nautical memorabilia, plush carpets and chairs, and a boat-shaped bar surrounded by little cocktail tables. The lunch special includes chowder or lobster bisque, main course, salad, potato, dessert, and coffee, for about $15; main courses alone cost $6 (for the cheapest sandwich) to about $15. At dinner, have two "chicken" lobsters (the small females, weighing about a pound apiece), with french fries and salad, for $26.75, jumbo shrimp for $16.75, swordfish shish kebab for $13.75, or one of the pasta specialties. The wine list runs to almost 115 items. Jimmy's Harborside, "Home of the Chowder King," is open daily from 11:30am to 9:30pm, Sunday from noon to 8pm.

Chinese Dim Sum

The **Imperial Tea House,** at 70 Beach St. in the heart of Boston's small Chinatown (tel. 426-8439), has been around for a long time, but has only recently been recognized for what it is: the best place in town for dim sum yum chai. The classic meal of Chinese hors d'oeuvres is served every day of the week from 9am to 3pm. The best time to go is between 10 and 11am, or after 1:30pm on weekdays. Other times the crowd is dense. Most of the patrons here are Chinese Bostonians who know a good thing or, rather, things: spareribs, water chestnuts in gelatin, pork dumplings, tofu (soybean cake), green sugarcane leaves stuffed with sweet rice, pork, and quail eggs, even fried duck feet. Sit in the upstairs room for dim sum. The à la carte restaurant downstairs is not as good. The system is this: you pick what you like from the carts, which appear in a steady stream throughout the morning and afternoon. Each plate on the cart has about three portions of the item (so it's good to do dim summing with two friends). When you've had enough, the waiter counts up the plates and gives you the bill, which will be very low (about $10 or $15 per person) considering the amount and quality of the food.

Thai

Bangkok Cuisine, 177a Massachusetts Ave., just down from the corner of Boylston Street, near Prudential Center (tel. 262-5377), is a small, attractive place, always busy serving Thai classics: clear soups made with scallions, shrimp, and hot peppers; savory dishes of duck with pineapple, spices, and Oriental vegetables and mushrooms—once you've tried the food here, you may indeed want to take off for Bangkok. Have soup or an appetizer, a main course based on seafood, pork, beef, or chicken, a dessert, and a bottle of Thai beer, and you'll pay about $20, all in. A warning: Soups are marked "moderately hot," but in my experience they are very spicy-hot (and very good). Bangkok is open for lunch Monday through Saturday 11:30am to 3pm, dinner every day from 5 to 10:30pm.

Mexican

Since **Sol Azteca** (tel. 262-0909) opened, crowds have flocked to its door at 914a Beacon St. in Boston, very near the Brookline town line. The word got around quickly among devotees of Mexican food that the guacamole, enchiladas (rojas, verdes, or Suizas), tacos, and tostadas were authentic, delicious, and moderately priced. Dinner starts with a basket of tortilla chips and a hot sauce dip and perhaps a bottle of Dos Equis or Superior Mexican beer. The combination plates are the best buys, bringing you a little of everything, to the point where you will probably have no capacity left for dessert. Dinner costs $20 to $25 per person, tax, tip, and *cerveza* included. On Friday and Saturday, especially during college term, it's really crowded, and no reservations are accepted. Dinner, the only meal served, is from 6 to 10:30pm (5:30 to 11pm Friday and Saturday, 5 to 10pm Sunday). Get there early. By T, take a "Cleveland Circle" car on the Green Line, and get off at the first stop above ground.

Mexican food on Newbury Street? Yes, at **Acapulco,** 266 Newbury St. (tel. 247-9126), an attractive little restaurant done in brick, butcher block, and Mexican crafts. A typical meal might consist of gazpacho, a tostada, flan for dessert, and a glass of guava juice to drink, all for about $15. Or you could order taquitos, crispy bunuelos for dessert, and drink Dos Equis Mexican beer, and pay somewhat more. Have just a combination plate, very filling, for only $8.50. You can order meatless meals, or dishes put up to take out. Acapulco serves Monday through Saturday from 11:30am to 11pm, on Sunday from 2 to 11pm. In summer, enjoy the outdoor patio tables.

BUDGET RESTAURANTS (MEALS ABOUT $10)

It's not difficult to dine inexpensively in Boston. The variety and cuisine make it possible to eat pleasantly for $10 per day, or less. But the restaurants recommended below are not just for those on a very slim budget. No one wants haute cuisine at every meal—few people's livers can stand it, in any case. For those times when you just want a quick and inexpensive meal, but one that's wholesome and delicious, try one of these places, arranged below according to location:

Along Newbury Street

On fashionable Newbury Street at no. 135 is the **Travis Restaurant** (tel. 267-6388), where a slice of pie à la mode and a cup of coffee, or a hamburger, or perhaps a large salad plate (with tuna, ham, etc.) costs only $4 to $7. The small tables on the sidewalk out front are good for an espresso or capuccino, the interior is the familiar lunch counter and stools (with some tables as well), and it's serve yourself, inside and out. The Travis is open every day from 7am to 4:30pm.

In the North End

Boston's most famous pizza place is **Pizzeria Regina,** 11½ Thatcher St., at the corner of Thatcher and North Margin Streets (tel. 227-0765)—if you have trouble finding it, just ask anyone in the North End. Old dark-wood booths with Formica tables, and a small bar for the solitary lunchers make up the interior. The decor is simple but the pizzas are fancy, for the cooks know the secret of making a good one: the best imported cheese and tomato sauce, and a few dashes of real olive oil. A small, simple ten-inch cheese pizza feeds two moderately hungry people for lunch for as little as $5. You pay somewhat more with mushrooms, anchovies, sausage, or other toppings. The top price is $13, for the elaborate 16-inch Giambotta, which easily feeds a party of three or four. Beer and wine are served.

In Faneuil Hall Marketplace

Good seafood in simple, small surroundings is the formula at **The Salty Dog,** in the basement of Quincy Market (tel. 742-2094; Green or Blue Lines to Government Center). The tiny restaurant is a bit hard to find: facing the front of Quincy Market, with your back to Faneuil Hall, walk to the right of the market facade, and just under the southwest corner of the market is the stairway down to the Salty Dog. It's a seafood bar and grill where you can have fish and chips, clams on the half shell, or any one of several fried or baked fish plates for about $9. Service is hardly elegant, for your food comes in paper containers and you eat with plastic utensils, but the food is very good. The oyster stew seems expensive, but you'll find at least a half dozen whole, succulent oysters in each bowlful. Liquor is served. This tiny place is open from 11:30am to 11pm daily.

Along the Freedom Trail

You're tromping along the Freedom Trail, trying to do it in a few hours, and you just want a quick bite for lunch? Join the be-suited business types grabbing a snack at the **Steaming Kettle,** corner of Cambridge (or Tremont) and Court Streets, very near the Government Center subway station. The huge kettle over the door has been belching steam for years, and inside the waitresses dispense steaming coffee or tea, lemonade or milk, and sandwiches such as hot roast beef, frankfurter and beans, or bologna at prices between $3 and $5 to stand-up customers at the shelflike hardwood counters that line the walls. If it's breakfast or seating you're after, the coffeeshop upstairs is open from 7:30am to 3:30pm.

---

5. Sights

The hundreds of thousands of visitors who come to Boston each year arrive with a purpose. It may be to tour the universities, to attend a meeting or conference, to explore the city's cultural wealth, or to learn about the early history of the United States. Whatever your purpose, you should take your first lesson in Boston history and culture by following the red bricks of the Freedom Trail.

THE FREEDOM TRAIL

The sights of Revolutionary Boston are linked together by the Freedom Trail, an ingenious idea that makes it easy for any visitor to find all the important colonial and revolutionary landmarks. Starting from the Park Street MBTA station on Boston Common, a red line painted on the sidewalk or a double row of bricks laid in the sidewalk leads past the **Massachusetts State House, Park Street Church,** the **Old Granary Burying Ground, King's Chapel,** the **Old State House,** the **Paul Revere House, Old North Church,** and *Old Ironsides* (U.S.S. *Constitution*), as well as other sights. Except for *Old Ironsides,* the trail passes all the important things to see in a mile and a half; *Old Ironsides* is across Boston's Inner Harbor in Charlestown, 2½ miles away, best reached by bus or car.

There is a bus that follows the Freedom Trail: the **Beantown Trolley** (tel. 287-1900). Arrangements for the bus vary with time of year, summer being the time when service is best and most frequent. Fare is $7.50 per adult ($4.50 per child 12 or under) for a day pass entitling you to hop on and off the buses as often as you like; buses run about every 45 minutes from 9am to 5pm. Buy your tickets right near the **Boston Common Visitor Information Center** (tel. 617/267-6446). The Information Center, on Boston Common near the Park Street Station, also hands out maps of the trail and brochures with facts about the sights. Here's a quick rundown so you'll know what there is to see.

Boston Common (1)

This park in the center of Boston was the colonial town's "common pasture land," to which any citizen's cows could be brought. The pasture ordinance is still in effect, so they say, but no one seems to take advantage of it—as if with all the picnickers, sunbathers, soapbox orators, street buskers, and pitch persons there'd be any room left for a cow quietly to graze!

State House and Archives (2)

The Massachusetts State House dominates Beacon Hill and the Boston Common, its gold dome shining and visible for miles. It was designed by Charles Bulfinch, Boston's most famous and best-loved architect, and built at the end of the

1700s. This is where the Massachusetts General Court (legislature) sits today; in its Archives (which you can visit) are curious and famous documents relating to the history of the colony of Massachusetts Bay and the early republic.

While you're up here on **Beacon Hill,** take a detour off the Freedom Trail and explore the back streets of what was once (and in many ways still is) Boston's wealthiest and prettiest residential neighborhood. Wander down the little "mews" (lanes behind the houses) where once the horses and carriages were kept, and don't miss **Louisburg Square,** a tiny private park, which is Beacon Hill's gem. The beautiful old colonial and Federal houses extend to the base of the hill at Charles Street, and down toward the 19th-century developments of Back Bay.

Park Street Church (3)

Right next to Park Street Station is this tall-steepled, graceful church designed by Peter Banner and built in 1809. Take a look inside, so you can compare this early 19th-century church with the earlier churches farther along the Freedom Trail.

Old Granary Burying Ground (4)

Some of the American Revolution's most famous figures, from John Hancock to Crispus Attucks, are buried in this cemetery, which took its name from a nearby granary, now long gone. Take a walk through—you'll constantly be surprised and delighted by the names, dates, and mottoes on the finely carved headstones.

King's Chapel (5)

The building dates from 1754, and in its interesting career changed from being an Episcopal church to a Unitarian meetinghouse. Services are held here, as are lectures and concerts.

Site of the First Public School (6)

Established in 1635, this is where it was.

Statue of Benjamin Franklin (7)

Most people remember the story of Franklin getting off the boat in Philadelphia with very little money and two loaves of bread for sustenance to begin his famous career, but some people forget that he was coming from Boston, his birthplace and childhood home. This statue by Richard Greenough (1856), in front of the city's old headquarters, pays tribute to Boston's famous son.

Old Corner Bookstore (8)

The *Boston Globe* bought and restored this famous house, and it's now a bookstore. The house itself dates from the early 1700s, but its fame began when it became a gathering place for famous American authors in the 19th century. At that time bookstores were also publishers, and Messrs. Ticknor & Fields, who ran the Old Corner Bookstore, published and drank coffee with the outstanding literary men of the age, including Longfellow, Hawthorne, and Whittier.

Old South Meeting House (9)

New England churches frequently call their buildings meetinghouses rather than churches, and it's from this that the Old South Meeting House gets its name, although it was used for town meetings as well. (Old North Church, from which the lanterns hung to signal Paul Revere, is a different building farther along the Freedom Trail.) Built in 1729, the meetinghouse saw its most famous meeting on December 16, 1773, when a group of colonials in Indian dress set out from here to throw the Boston Tea Party. Of the exhibits—old documents, currency, furniture—perhaps the most interesting is a plaster-and-wood scale model of the Town of Boston in 1775, which gives you a very clear idea of the size and layout of the town, and helps your imagination recast the events of the Revolution in their proper setting.

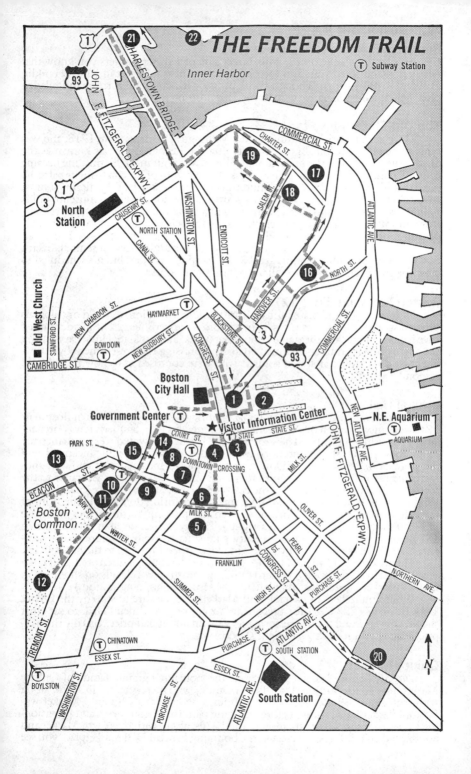

Benjamin Franklin's Birthplace (10)

An obscure plaque on the Milk Street side of a skyscraper lets you know that nearly three hundred years ago there was a house near this spot in which Franklin (1706–1790) was born. Though Franklin made his fame and fortune in Philadelphia, he was a Boston native who learned his printing trade here.

The Old State House (11)

The charming brick building at 206 Washington St. dates from 1713, and was built to house the colonial government; after the Revolution it was known as the State House, and after the present State House was built in 1795, this one became the Old State House. Washington addressed the citizens of Boston from its balcony. Now that it's hemmed in by giant buildings on all sides, much of the dignity it must have held for colonial and revolutionary Americans is lost. Inside, a museum holds military and domestic artifacts, portraits, and a good selection of nautical artifacts, from antique sextants to eight very fine scale models of ships and some dramatic paintings of great ships as well. Historical talks are given on the hour. There's an entry fee to the museum (tel. 720-1713) of $1.25 for adults, 75¢ for senior citizens, 50¢ for children. Summer hours are 9:30am to 5pm every day, but it's scheduled to close for preservation soon, so call to confirm these hours.

Boston Massacre Site (12)

Here, near the Old State House, British soldiers fired into a crowd of colonials protesting what they saw as excesses by the British government. The incident must have happened much as the tragic killings happened at Kent State University during the Vietnam War protests: unarmed civilians expressing their resentment by throwing curses and stones at armed soldiers who were confused as to how they should respond.

Faneuil Hall (13)

Faneuil Hall (pronounced *fan*-yool or *fan*-l) was built by the Town of Boston in 1742 with money given by Peter Faneuil; designed by John Simbert, it was later enlarged by Bulfinch (1805). The ground floor has been devoted to shops since the building was built; the second floor was—and is—used for public meetings; and the third floor houses the headquarters of Boston's most famous chowder-and-marching society, the Ancient and Honorable Artillery Company. Entrance to the second-floor meeting hall is from the east side; National Park Service guides are on hand to tell you all about the building: the huge painting dominating the front of the hall, they will tell you, is of Daniel Webster speaking on the virtues of a close union of states (as opposed to states' rights). The speech was given in Washington in 1830, not in Faneuil Hall, but the painting must have inspired hundreds of less talented, although perhaps equally long-winded, orators. Entrance to the hall is free.

The area around Faneuil Hall has recently been rebuilt and restored, and it is a nice change from the boldly modern buildings nearby. (For details on shopping in Quincy Market, next to Faneuil Hall, see the separate Shopping section.)

While you're here in Faneuil Hall Marketplace, be sure to stop by the **Bostix** kiosk (tel. 617/723-5181 for a recording), right next to Faneuil Hall, to see what shows, concerts, and theater performances are on sale at half price. Usually the half-price seats are for today's (or tonight's) performances.

Quincy Market (14)

Directly behind Faneuil Hall stands the stout grey granite facade of Quincy Market, named for Boston Mayor Josiah Quincy who had it erected in 1826, along with the large Greek Revival market buildings on either side. Quincy Market was Boston's larder for a century before changing patterns of commerce and provisioning led to its decline. Its restoration in the 1970s, along with the North Market and South Market buildings, has created the booming Faneuil Hall Marketplace you see today. (For details on shopping in the Marketplace, see the separate Shopping section, below.)

Paul Revere House (15)

A small clapboard dwelling in Boston's North End, surrounded by crooked cobbled streets, the Paul Revere House, 19 North Square (tel. 523-2338), is the only house left in Boston that was built in the 1600s. Paul Revere moved in about a century after the house was built, and he lived here during the Revolutionary period. The house would be interesting even if the great patriot had never set foot in it, with its quaint weathered exterior, small windows, and wide floorboards. But furnished in colonial style and equipped with an ingenious handrail/barrier, which guides you through the house and gives you information on Revere's life at the same time, the house is worth more than an hour's lecture on Revolutionary history. Admission costs $2 for adults, $1.50 for seniors and students, 50¢ for children 17 and under. No photography is allowed inside the house. Hours are 9:30am to 4:15pm in winter, to 5:15pm in summer. Take a look around North Square, the small cobbled-and-gaslit space near the Revere House, and perhaps rest from your walk on one of its benches. This part of town, the North End, is now very Italian in character—you can hear the local Italian dialect of the mother tongue in the surrounding streets.

Old North Church (16)

You can see by the church's location why it was a good place from which to give a signal. The code, as every schoolchild knows, was "one if by land, two if by sea," and it was two lanterns hung in the tower that started Paul Revere and William Dawes on their fateful night rides to warn the Colonials that British troops were heading out from Boston to search for hidden arms. On April 18, 1975, exactly 200 years from that historic day, President Ford inaugurated the American Revolutionary Bicentennial in Old North Church by lighting a third lantern (hanging at the front of the church). The church is the oldest church building in Boston (1723), and is today officially known as Christ Church, Episcopal. A walk around inside turns up many curiosities that bear on the history of Boston and the United States; memorial plaques to famous men, nameplates on the very high pews. The tall graceful windows of Old North Church are exceptionally fine. After your visit, it's good to drop the requested (not required) donation in the box near the door. Visitors are also welcome for Sunday services at 9:00am, 11am, and 4pm.

Although it's hemmed in by houses and shops on all sides, Old North Church, 193 Salem St. (tel. 617/523-6676), does have a set of tiny terraces and gardens on its north side, open to the public. The small formal garden and the fountain are good to refresh your spirit on a hot day, and the memorial plaques set into the walls are, in some cases, delightful. One reads:

1757–1923
Here on September 13, 1757
"John Childs who had given public notice of his intention to
Fly from the steeple of Dr. Cutler's church, performed it to
The satisfaction of a great number of spectators"
In 1923 the year of the first continuous flight across
The continent this tablet has been placed here by
The Massachusetts Society of the Colonial Dames of America
To commemorate the two events.

The question that comes to mind: would it not have been faster to dispatch John Childs from the steeple to Lexington and Concord by air, rather than Dawes and Revere by land, on that historic night in 1775?

Copps Hill Burying Ground (17)

Walking along Hull Street from Old North Church takes you past 44 Hull, the narrowest house in Boston, to Copps Hill Burying Ground, the second oldest cemetery (1660) in the city. Among the cemetery's permanent inhabitants is fiery Puritan preacher Cotton Mather. Some of the tombstones were marked by stray British musket-balls during the revolution.

Bunker Hill (18)

The 200-foot granite obelisk which towers above Charlestown, north of central Boston, marks the spot where Colonel William Prescott of the Continental army stood with his small force and held off wave after wave of attack by British regulars on June 17, 1775. Their ammunition running low, Colonel Prescott cried to his men, "Don't fire until you see the whites of their eyes" in order to make each shot count. When their ammunition was exhausted the Americans were forced to retreat, but the battle had caused grievous casualties to Boston's British garrison. Most of Charlestown surrounding the hill was burnt by the British during the engagement.

Construction began on the monument in 1828, a half-century after the battle. There's a fine view of Charlestown, the navy yard, and Boston from the top.

U.S.S. *Constitution* (19)

The *Constitution (Old Ironsides)* is still commissioned in the service of the U.S. Navy and could in theory be called to the defense of the country should the need arise. The ship still gets under way once a year, on the Fourth of July, when it's taken a short distance out into the harbor to fire a 21-gun salute. The dock here is right on a former navy base; sailors in 1812 period uniforms will take you through the ship and explain its workings to you free of charge. But the ship is not the only exhibit here: the nearby **Museum** ($2.50 for adults, $1.50 for seniors, $1 for kids 6 to 16; under 6, free) houses many artifacts dealing with the *Constitution*'s history and its 40 battles at sea (all won), besides a "Life at Sea" exhibit, showing what shipboard life was like in 1812. The Boston Navy Yard National Historic Site also offers programs on the yard and the American Revolution every hour in Building No. 5 (between the ship and the museum).

To get to these attractions, and to Bunker Hill with its monument, cross the Mystic River (Tobin) Bridge (toll) or the Charlestown Bridge (free) nearby and follow the signs to the U.S.S. *Constitution*. Bus no. 93 ("Sullivan Square via Bunker Hill") from Haymarket Square will take you fairly close to Bunker Hill and Boston Navy Yard; it runs about every half hour, more frequently during rush hours. You can walk to *Old Ironsides* from Haymarket in about 25 minutes, using the Charlestown Bridge.

Boston Tea Party Ship and Museum (20)

Strictly speaking, this is not on the Freedom Trail, but on a separate excursion called Harborwalk. The events it recalls are very much a part of colonial Boston's struggle for independence. Take the Red Line to South Station, walk north on Atlantic Avenue one block past the Federal Reserve Bank (which looks like a mammoth space-age radiator), turn right onto Congress Street and walk a block to the water, and there's the ship at Congress Street Bridge. A shuttle van operates daily May through October from the rear of the Old State House on the Freedom Trail (corner of Devonshire and State Streets). What you see here is the brig *Beaver II,* a full-size replica of one of the merchant ships emptied by the "Indians" on the night of the tea party raid, and a museum with exhibits outlining the "tea party." At the nearby Tea Party Store you can buy some tea. The ship and museum (tel. 338-1773) are open from 9am to dusk (about 7pm in summer, 5pm in winter) every day except three major holidays, at $5 for adults, $2.75 for children 5 to 14; under-5s are free, and special family rates are available. Complimentary Salada tea is served—iced tea in summer, hot tea in winter.

MUSEUM OF FINE ARTS

The great Greek temple at 465 Huntington Ave. houses one of the world's finest collections of artworks, second in the country only to New York's Metropolitan. Boston's Museum of Fine Arts (tel. 267-9300) is a wonder, a vast collection of beautiful things in a beautiful building. Many pictures you may have admired for years through prints and photos in art books are here: Gilbert Stuart's *Athenaeum Head* portrait of George Washington; Renoir's *Le Bal à Bougival;* Burne-Jones's *The Love Song;* Whistler's *Girl in a White Dress;* works by Van Gogh, Gauguin, Degas, lots of Monets; *Death of Maximilian* by Manet; and works by Japanese, Chinese, European, medieval, Renaissance, and baroque masters are all well represented. A fine collection of Paul Revere silver, several rooms taken from French châteaux, full-size Japanese temples, a 9th-century Spanish chapel, Egyptian mummies, Assyrian seals —the list goes on to the treasures of almost 200 galleries. The way to find what you want is to pick up a floor plan as you enter; you can't possibly see even a fraction of it all, so pick out a few areas or rooms to concentrate on, and enjoy. Before you go, call 267-9377 (or A-N-S-W-E-R-S) for a recording of current special exhibits. If you need the help of a person, call 267-9300, ext. 363.

The entire museum is normally open Tuesday through Sunday from 10am to 5pm (closed Monday), Wednesday evening till 10pm. On Thursday and Friday the main building closes at 5pm but the west wing stays open till 10pm. Admission is $6 for adults, free for those under 16 years, $5 for seniors. If you come on Saturday from 10am till noon, you can get in for free; if you visit when only the new West Wing is open, the fee is $5.

The museum's restaurant is located in the west wing. Lunch is served daily from 11:30am to 2:30pm (except Monday); dinner, on Wednesday, Thursday, and Friday from 5:30 to 8:30pm. Surrounded by glass, the dining room is ultramodern and attractive. The menu is often keyed to special exhibits—Chinese dishes predominated when the impressive Chinese bronzes were on display—and the prices are moderate. You can figure $10 to $12 for lunch, $18 to $22 for dinner. The wine list is short, good, and fairly priced.

For snacks and pick-me-ups, head for the café below the restaurant.

To get to the museum, take a Green Line "E" train ("Arborway" or "Huntington Avenue") and get off at the second stop above ground.

ISABELLA STEWART GARDNER MUSEUM

If you have a full day when you visit the Museum of Fine Arts, plan to spend at least a few hours of it at the Isabella Stewart Gardner Museum nearby (tel. 566-1401), at 280 The Fenway (walk west from the Museum of Fine Arts around its parking lot to the Fenway; turn left and walk two short blocks). "Mrs. Jack" Gardner early developed a love of art, and with her considerable wealth and the services of Bernard Berenson she set about to build an outstanding collection which now includes almost 300 paintings, almost as many pieces of sculpture, close to 500 pieces of furniture, and hundreds of works in textiles, ceramics, and glass. Most of the holdings are from the great periods of European art, but classical and Oriental civilizations are also represented. Not the least of the exhibits is the house itself, which she had built to hold the collection in 1902. "Fenway Court" is not much to look at from the outside, but inside it is Mrs. Gardner's vision of a 15th-century Venetian palace, with many doors, columns, windows, and the like, which were brought from Europe and assembled around an open court topped by a glass canopy. The court is always planted with flowers, in bloom summer and winter, and several fountains bubble merrily at one end. Upstairs in one room is a dramatic portrait of "Mrs. Jack" herself, displayed with various masterpieces above a floor covered in tiles from Henry Mercer's Moravian tile and pottery works in Pennsylvania. Along a corridor nearby, look for mementos of Mrs. Gardner's years, including letters from many of the great and famous of the turn of the century.

In March 1990, this lovely museum suffered a tragedy when art thieves dressed as police officers tricked the guards and made off with 12 masterpieces, including paintings by Degas and Rembrandt and a rare Chinese vase, worth hundreds of millions of dollars. These irreplaceable works will probably end up in a vault somewhere, unavailable to the public, because of some thieves' greed and selfishness.

Admission costs $5 ($2.50 for students and seniors); on Wednesday admission is free. It's open Tuesday from noon to 6:30pm, Wednesday through Sunday from noon to 5pm, closed Monday. Except for July and August, free concerts of chamber music are given on Thursday at 12:15pm, on Sunday at 3pm, and Tuesday evening at 6pm; they're usually very well attended, so go early and claim a seat (for information, call 734-1359). The museum has a nice café serving light meals as well.

OTHER GALLERIES

Perhaps it's the amalgam of college faculty, art-conscious Old Guard families, and artists themselves that makes Boston such a good place to go browsing in galleries. Whatever the cause, Boston is rich in exhibitions of painting, sculpture, and more recent vehicles of artistic expression, such as textiles and welded metal.

Prime among Boston galleries is the **Institute of Contemporary Art,** 955 Boylston St. (tel. 266-5151 for a recording, 266-5152 for a person), across the street from the Prudential Center (Green Line's "Boston College," "Riverside," or "Cleveland Circle" cars to Auditorium Station). The institute is a beautifully modern place inside a historic Richardsonian structure. Shows may be anything from an exhibit of New England photographers' work to works in various media by British artists, or perhaps a show of the outstanding works by modern artists that are in Boston private collections. Special events include video programs, musical concerts, and evening lectures. All exhibitions change about every six to ten weeks. The ICA is open Tuesday through Sunday from 11am to 5pm (and on Thursday and Friday also from 5 to 8pm). Admission is $4 for adults, $1.50 for senior citizens and children under 14, and $2.50 for students. Free admission on Friday evenings. There is never an admission charge for members except for evening events.

The institute never has works for sale. Those interested in browsing and perhaps buying—without any obligation to do so, of course—should pick a day to stroll down **Newbury Street,** where a good many of Boston's better galleries are located. Highlights and dining possibilities for such a stroll are covered in a separate section on "Newbury Street" in this same chapter. Other streets with galleries and antique shops are **Charles Street** at the base of Beacon Hill, and **Boylston Street.**

Boston City Hall, the Boston Public Library in Copley Square, and other public organizations and private corporations sponsor shows from time to time. See the tabloid weeklies, such as the *Boston Phoenix,* for full listings of what's currently available, or contact the Department of Public Relations (tel. 266-5152) with your questions.

There's often an interesting exhibit in the lobby of the **Boston Architectural Center,** 320 Newbury St. (tel. 536-3170), at the corner of Hereford Street (Green Line to Auditorium). The show will be connected in some way with architecture, whether it be the life and work of Henry Mercer, the turn-of-the-century Pennsylvania tile maker, or a collection of neon signs from many cities and many decades. Hours are Monday through Thursday from 9am to 9pm, on Friday and Saturday to 5pm (on Sunday from 11am to 5pm only in the winter season). Shows are always free, and if you're strolling along this part of Newbury Street, at least take a look through the windows to see what's on.

MUSEUM OF SCIENCE

Nobody ever has a bad time when they visit Boston's famous Museum of Science, Science Park (tel. 523-6664), because there are so many things to see and do, and of such a variety, that each person's tastes and expectations can be gratified. Children are especially delighted here, for they can walk into a full-size model of the Apollo Command Module; they can play with a Wang computer, see themselves on closed-circuit TV, and push buttons to start dozens of various exhibits and demonstrations ranging from fluid dynamics to the human circulatory system. Stand next to a replica of America's first rocket launcher built by Robert Goddard of Auburn, Mass., in 1926; or walk around a tremendous replica of *Tyrannosaurus rex.* See how baseball pitchers throw a curve ball, and hear them explain their techniques; watch the counter on the World Population Meter click off another birth every second or so; or learn how to make herbal textile dyes from common plants and weeds. Special exhibits include the Hayden Planetarium with celestial shows on various themes daily. The Museum of Science costs $6 for adults, $4 for children or senior citizens. There is an extra charge for the planetarium (buy your ticket early for this, when you enter the museum), and for the exciting OMNIMAX theater. Hours September through April are Saturday through Thursday from 9am to 5pm, on Friday to 9pm. Hours May 1 through Labor Day are Monday through Thursday from 9am to 5pm, on Friday to 9pm, on Saturday to 5pm, and on Sunday from 10am to 5pm. During school months, the museum is open on Monday holidays and vacation weeks. Parking in the museum's own garage costs several dollars. Besides the rooftop Skyline Cafeteria, there's a Friendly's snack shop within the museum.

To get to the Museum of Science, take the Green Line toward Lechmere to the Science Park Station.

THE KENNEDY LIBRARY

The nation's memorial to JFK is the museum at the **John F. Kennedy Library.** This dramatic chalk-white building, designed by the distinguished architect I. M. Pei, sits on a peninsula on Dorchester Bay. The landscaping of Cape Cod roses, sea grass, and weeping willows serves to harmonize the building with the peninsula, harbor islands, and sea. The library features an exhibition that is introduced by a 30-minute movie on the late president's life. Then, arranged in chronological order, it displays JFK memorabilia from his christening dress, *PT-109* uniform, and flight jacket worn when president, to papers relating to the Bay of Pigs and Cuban Missile Crisis. There is a re-creation of the Oval Office as it was when he was president, and his desk and rocking chair. The library is open daily from 9am to 5pm except Thanksgiving, Christmas, and New Year's Day. Admission costs $3.50 for adults and $2.00 for seniors; those under 16 get in free. Take the MBTA Red Line to JFK/U Mass Station. For additional information, contact the John F. Kennedy Library at Columbia Point, Dorchester, MA 02125 (tel. 617/929-4523).

OTHER MUSEUMS

Boston has a score of other museums, each very rich in its presentations, and the best of these are outlined below:

Boston Children's Museum

Children's Museum is located at Museum Wharf, 300 Congress St. (tel. 426-8855), on Boston's waterfront near the Boston Tea Party ship, a short walk from Faneuil Hall Marketplace and South Station. The museum, an old brick-and-timber warehouse, is a kid's delight, for this is where the whole idea of "hands-on" exhibits began. Kids from preschool age to early adolescence can clamber through the two-story "Climbing Sculpture," explore Japanese culture in Japanese House, discover the life of 50 years ago in "Ahead to the Past," or take a video tour of Boston's ethnic neighborhoods.

The museum is open every day in July and August, till Labor Day; it's closed on Monday at other times of the year. Hours are 10am to 5pm, on Friday till 9pm. Admission is $6 for adults, $5 for children 2 to 15 and for seniors. On Friday from 5 to 9pm you can get in for only $1. Going by subway, take the Red Line to South Station, and follow the signs to Museum Wharf.

The Computer Museum

"What?" you may say, "Computers aren't old enough to have a museum!" But they are. The calculating and computing devices on display at the Computer Museum on Museum Wharf (tel. 423-6758 for information from the Talking Computer, or 426-2800 for a human) go back centuries. It seems that we've always had a passion for number-crunching, but have been unable fully to realize that passion until today. The abacus has been used in China for a millennium; Scottish mathematician John Napier (1550–1617), inventor of the logarithm, came up with a calculator called "Napier's Bones"; French army officer Amedee Mannheim invented the slide rule in 1850. In 1893, in Zurich, a "direct-multiplying machine" called The Millionaire came on the market, and sold 4,655 units in the years following.

It was World War II and the Atomic Age that began the rush to truly awesome computing power. Nowadays the Whirlwind computer (1951) looks like a dinosaur: hundreds of vacuum tubes, electrical consumption of 150,000 watts, and less computing power than an Apple II. The first fully transistorized machine, the TX-O (1956) required a full-time staff of top-level scientists just to turn it on and get it ready to compute. But it was a mere calculator compared to the 20-ton monster known as SAGE, built for the U.S. Air Force in the 1960s.

Besides the historical exhibits, the museum has 60 hands-on, interactive exhibits. You can do everything from designing a car on a graphics terminal to flying an airplane, launching a rocket, or haggling over the price of strawberries with a computerized "vendor." Perhaps most fascinating of all is the Walk-Through Computer, a gigantic working personal computer you can use by trying out its 25-foot-long keyboard; results are displayed on a 108-square-foot monitor. Walk through the computer, past the giant chips, to find out how it all works.

The Computer Museum is right next door to the Children's Museum, and just across Fort Point Channel from the Boston Tea Party Ship. Take the subway (Red Line to South Station), or drive, and visit from 10am to 5pm any day in summer (till 9pm on Friday); closed Monday in winter. Admission costs $6 for adults, $5 for students and seniors, half price for all after 5pm on Friday. Children under five get in for free.

The Boston Athenaeum

Tucked away atop Beacon Hill, facing the State House, is the Boston Athenaeum, 10½ Beacon St., off Boston Common (tel. 227-0270), an independent research library founded in 1807. The Athenaeum's collections are strong in the history and literature of Boston and New England; its picture and sculpture collections were once, de facto, Boston's premier art museum. This grand old Boston institution is owned by 1,049 "Proprietors" who can pass right of ownership by heredity, and its neoclassical 19th-century reading rooms are used by members, their guests, and other approved researchers (you must have references). You can visit the Athenaeum's second-floor gallery to view the current exhibition, or call and reserve a place on a guided tour (Tuesday and Thursday at 3pm) of the building. Hours are 9am to 5pm Monday through Friday (also 9am to 4pm on Saturday from October through May). Nearest subway station is Park Street.

Black Heritage Trail

You can take a Black Heritage Trail walking tour. Pick up a free walking-tour folder at the National Park Service Visitor Center, 15 State St.

NEW ENGLAND AQUARIUM

It seems fitting that a sea-conscious city such as Boston should have a major aquarium, and it has exactly that in the New England Aquarium (tel. 742-8870), on Central Wharf off Atlantic Avenue and two blocks from Faneuil Hall Market in the newly redeveloped waterfront area (look for the twin Harbor Towers apartment buildings, or take the Blue Line to Aquarium Station). Pride of the aquarium is the largest cylindrical, glass-enclosed saltwater tank in the world, and this and other exhibit tanks are stocked with over 600 species of marine life, from electric eels to sharks. In the ship *Discovery,* moored next door, dolphin shows are put on daily for aquarium visitors (call for current show times). The variety of fishes is truly astounding, and the shapes, colors, and forms that evolution and adaptation have produced in these creatures really give one a sense of the richness of the marine environment. The price of admission covers all exhibits, including the dolphin shows, plus daily films, multimedia presentations, and audio tours on aquatic subjects; it's $7 for adults, $3.50 for children 4 through 15. For senior citizens, servicemen, and college students with IDs, it's $5. On Friday from 4 to 8pm the charge is $1 off regular admission for everyone. Hours are Monday through Thursday from 9am to 6pm, on Friday to 8pm, on weekends to 7pm, but these may change a bit from season to season.

ARNOLD ARBORETUM

Ever since this 265-acre park was given to the city by Harvard, Bostonians have been going here to enjoy the peacefulness of the park and the more than 14,000 trees, plants, and shrubs from various parts of the world that make up the Arboretum's "living collection." Spring is a fine time to catch the first blossoms like the lilacs, early summer brings the rhododendrons, and all through the warm months the scents here will bring back any nose dulled by the city air.

The Arnold Arboretum of Harvard University, designed by Charles Sprague Sargent and Frederick Law Olmsted, is maintained jointly by Boston's parks department and Harvard, which uses it as an open-air classroom in botany. It's open to all and sundry from sunrise to sunset every day, free of charge. You can get there easily by taking the Orange Line to Forest Hills, or the Green Line to Arborway (the Orange Line's probably faster). For 24-hour recorded information, call 524-1717.

THE CHRISTIAN SCIENCE CHURCH CENTER

In 1866 a devout New England woman experienced quick recovery from a severe accident, attributing her cure to a glimpse of God's healing power as taught and lived by Jesus. Thereafter Mary Baker Eddy devoted the remainder of her long life (1821–1910) to better understanding, practicing, and teaching Christian healing; to founding the Church of Christ, Scientist; and establishing the church's periodicals, including the renowned international daily newspaper, the *Christian Science Monitor*.

Today the Christian Science religion has branch churches in some 68 countries with headquarters in Boston, site of the denomination's Mother Church, built in 1894. Next to the church stands the Christian Science Publishing Society, home of the *Monitor* and other Christian Science publications. Two new church office buildings and the Sunday School complete the Church Center. The whole complex, near Symphony Hall at the intersection of Huntington and Massachusetts Avenues (MBTA: Auditorium or Symphony), is a new Boston landmark, and it's right between two other landmarks, Symphony Hall and the Prudential Center. Tours are arranged for free, or you can visit the various buildings on your own: the Mother Church is open Monday through Saturday from 9:30am to 3:30pm, on Sunday from 11:15am to 2pm. The Publishing Society building is open Monday through Friday from 8am to 4pm, on Saturday and holidays from 9am to 4pm, on Sunday from noon to 4:45pm; and tours are given weekdays from 9:30am to 3:30pm (the tour takes 45 minutes). During the winter (November to April) the hours are slightly shortened. For exact times and tours call 450-2000. Free parking is available while visiting the Church Center.

The main points of interest are the plaza and reflecting pool, the exterior of the Mother Church and its grand extension where services are held, and the Publishing Society's Mapparium and elegant Reading Room. You can take a tour, which lasts 15 to 25 minutes, through the Mother Church, or just take the elevator up to see the auditorium. This huge chamber is the main inner space of the church, which is built on the plan of a Byzantine church with its great dome and two semidomes.

The church's newest addition is a multimedia Bible Exhibit, located in the Colonnade Building, displaying rare Bibles and a giant Plexiglas map. This is open Monday through Saturday from 10am to 5pm and on Sunday from 11:15am to 5pm (closed Tuesday).

---

6. Shopping

Like New York, Washington, and other great American cities, Boston has its special places to buy things, whether you're in the market for the mundane or the exotic. Here are some of the prime locales for getting rid of money.

DOWNTOWN CROSSING

The two Boston giants are **Jordan Marsh Company** and **Filene's,** located cheek-by-jowl in the downtown pedestrian shopping district on Washington Street (Red Line or Orange Line to Washington) called Downtown Crossing. Jordan's is a large department store with a vast assortment of items for sale, everything from baubles to bar stools. "Jordan's Great Basement Store" is admittedly great in terms of size, but it is outdone in popularity by neighboring Filene's Basement, which has become a New England legend. Stories circulate about women changing clothes right between the dress racks to try things on, of the crowds one must fight, of the "automatic reduction" policy, which dictates that if an item is not sold in a certain amount of time, it is simply given away just to get rid of it.

Well, the basement has become a bit more refined now that it's famous, and the prices in many cases are similar to those in any of the big new suburban discount stores. As for the automatic reductions, they're still in operation; but few items reach the date when they're given away, and if they do it's usually because they're too torn or ugly or useless to be bought, and even so they're given away to charity (Goodwill Industries, for example) as a tax write-off, and not to you. But the basement is still busy, often crowded, and it's because people know that there's a *good chance* they'll run into something that suits them at a very good price. Don't "go to Filene's Basement to buy a pair of shoes," but rather go dig around in the shoe bins and see what there is in your size, and at a good price—you may find something that it makes good sense to buy. And look through the other clothes departments, accessory counters, and various sections—a $400 outfit with a marked-down $40 price tag could very well be waiting there for you.

Surplus merchandise from famous stores such as Lou Lattimer's in Houston and Saks in New York comes frequently to Filene's Basement, with such classy labels as I. Magnin and Yves Saint Laurent. Don't be disappointed if you don't find anything. Come back in a few days, for the stock moves incredibly fast and new shipments arrive daily.

Also here at Downtown Crossing is **Lafayette Place,** a vast shopping mall with a central courtyard for sipping and dining, a 500-room hotel, and hundreds of shops.

Washington Street, the pedestrian thoroughfare of Downtown Crossing, has its own lineup of shops. Across from Filene's, at 333 and 387 Washington St., for instance, are entrances to the **Jeweler's Building,** a warren of little shops in a homely building. The building may not look like much, but the display cases in each shop are laden with fortunes in gold, diamonds, rubies, and emeralds. If you're at all interested in jewelry, take a stroll through here. Prices can be very good.

FANEUIL HALL MARKETPLACE

The Faneuil Hall Marketplace is a whole complex of buildings including **Faneuil Hall** and **Quincy Market,** flanked by the **North and South Markets** on either side.

Quincy Market is the centerpiece of this imaginative and fantastically successful redevelopment venture by the Rouse company with the guidance of Cambridge architect Benjamin Thompson. For years the area was a rundown waterfront slum, with only the 19th-century-style butchers' shops and provisioners to provide life. The early plan was to have the buildings razed to the ground and replaced with a modern shopping center, but architect Thompson changed the thinking to conservation, and the result is a beauty. Behind Faneuil Hall, the market is busy with crowds of customers from sunrise to sundown every day of the week. A granite block pavement is spread between Faneuil Hall and the market's pillared classic Greek facade, and, inside, the long main hall stretches for a city block on two floors. Downstairs the shops sell food, from a carry-out snack to a full picnic-style meal, to a pound of Camembert for the kitchen at home. On a recent stroll through Quincy Market I noted the following items for sale (partial list): a dozen kinds of bagels right out of the oven on the premises, an infinite array of deli sandwiches, southern fried chicken, shish kebab, subgum chow mein, Baby Watson cheesecake, German blutwurst, French brie, Châteauneuf-du-Pape, live lobsters, mixed nuts, cold cuts (domestic and imported), rumpsteak, fresh doughnuts, and, at the clam bar, half a dozen cherrystone clams opened and ready to eat. The wings of the market are of glass, and shelter restaurants, drinking places, and singles' hangouts patronized by the good-looking and well-to-do from the business, financial, and government offices nearby. In the basement are various shops selling fish, meat, health foods, imported delicacies. On the second floor the emphasis is on crafts and exotic imports—rugs from Persia, jewelry from India, baskets from China and Mexico. There's a fine flower shop in a very handsome all-glass building in front, on the granite pavement, and benches set out under the trees between the market and the adjoining buildings.

About the best purchase you can make here at Faneuil Hall Marketplace is tickets to the theater, concerts, ballet, shows, and so on. **Bostix** (tel. 723-5181) in a kiosk right next to Faneuil Hall itself, sells half-price seats for today's performances, and this is the only place in the city where you can buy them. Plan your nightlife while you're here, rather than coming all the way back. Cash only for same-day, half-price seats—that's the policy.

Street buskers and musicians are always on hand to entertain in the market promenades, and a genial mounted police officer draws scores of children, all wanting to pat his mount's nose. The whole complex is an all-year, day-and-night carnival you shouldn't miss, open for free. For restaurant details, see the restaurant section, above. To get to Faneuil Hall Marketplace, take the Green or Blue Line to Government Center, or the Blue or Red Line to State Street.

NEWBURY STREET

Boston's famous street of boutiques, galleries, and cafés runs from fashion to funk. It starts at the intersection of Arlington and Newbury, right next to Burberrys' and the Ritz-Carlton Hotel, and the shoppers' and strollers' delights continue for half a dozen blocks. Shops sell everything from the sublime (and expensive) to the ridiculous (and expensive); galleries can be chic or somewhat traditional. Cafés are good and bad, expensive and cheap, and all possible permutations of those four qualities. Serious shoppers and gallery goers should pick up two useful brochures, available at information booths (City Hall, Boston Common, Boston Public Library) entitled *The Newbury Street League Map,* which gives a list of most of the shops and some of the cafés along the street, their specialties, addresses, and phone numbers; and *Map of the Newbury Street Art Galleries,* which gives brief descriptions of the 30 galleries on the street, times of operation, special services, and so forth.

Newbury Street starts at the Ritz, and the shops in the first two blocks are, naturally, the most expensive. Furs, jewelry, art objects, and the like predominate. **Emmanuel Church,** just down from the Ritz in the same block, lends a cool note of English Gothic and ivy to the polished-brass-and-marble of some of the shops. By the way, the church sponsors a variety of musical and theatrical programs—jazz, chamber music, choral recitals, puppet shows—and advertises current offerings on a wooden signboard in the side doorway.

Streets in the Back Bay were laid out in a grid and the cross streets that run north-south were given names with initial letters running from A to H—Arlington, Berkeley, Clarendon, Dartmouth, and so on—so it's easy to know how far you are from the start of Newbury Street at Arlington Street. The second cross street, then, is Berkeley, and in the block between Berkeley and Clarendon is still more Gothic church architecture, this time in the form of the **Church of the Covenant** (Presbyterian), a bit plainer than the nearby Emmanuel. Organ recitals are held regularly at the Church of the Covenant, and usually a sign in the glass case will give the time: "Tuesday at 12:15," or whatever's current when you pass by. Two of the most famous stores on Newbury Street are located in this area, **Brooks Brothers** for men's wear, and **Bonwit Teller's** (in the old Boston Museum of Natural History Building) for women's fashions. **F.A.O. Schwarz,** the famous New York toy store, has two branches in Boston, at 40 Newbury and also in the Prudential Center.

COPLEY PLACE

Just off Copley Square is the vast new Copley Place, an ultramodern shopping, dining, lodging, and entertainment complex. **Neiman-Marcus** is the big store here, but there are dozens of shops as well. Ralph Lauren, Williams-Sonoma, Saint Laurent Rive Gauche, Jaeger, Gucci, and Godiva, among others, all have outlets. Hours are normally 10am to 9pm Monday through Friday, to 7pm on Saturday, and noon to 5pm on Sunday. The hotels in the complex are the Boston Marriott Copley Place and the Westin Hotel, Copley Place.

---

7. Nightlife

Forget everything you've ever heard about things being "banned in Boston," for at night in this big city it seems as though anything goes. The opportunities for evening activities are bewildering in their variety, and because of all the students in town, nightlife is very active, available, and—in many cases—not all that expensive. This section will give you some idea of what's going on, with details on a selection of the better things to see and do.

Bostonians have been known to call their city "The Athens of America"—they did this even before the city had a sizable Greek population. The reason, of course, is Boston's lively cultural and artistic life. It could fairly be said that on any given day of the year one could take a pick of a dozen or more lectures, concerts, or dance and theater offerings, and at least a few of these would be free of charge.

The best way to find out what's on tonight is to look in the listings: *Boston By-Week* (a brochure arts schedule at information booths, hotel desks, and depots), or the tabloid "alternative" weekly newspapers: the *Boston Phoenix* is most easily available. Each one has an arts and entertainment section with reviews and advertisements for the current hot topics, and also a listings portion (classifieds and notices in the back of the arts section), which gives the latest information on the club and coffeehouse scene, poetry readings, and so forth. Look under headings such as "Music," "Lectures," "Theater," "Poetry," and "Lounges." When in session (fall and spring semesters), Harvard publishes its own *Gazette,* available for free from the Harvard University Information Office, Holyoke Center, Harvard Square. The paper includes listings of a great many films, lectures, discussions, gallery shows, plays, and concerts taking place at Harvard, many of which are open to the general public. The other great universities in the area also publish similar calendars, yours for the asking.

NIGHTCLUBS AND SINGLES' BARS

The Boston area has over 75 colleges and universities, which give downtown nightlife a particularly lively character; a lot of graduates get to like the town so much they settle down here, and so Boston's crew of "young professionals" is also very large and very conspicuous in the clubs.

The Department of Commerce says that Boston is the most expensive city in the country except for Anchorage, and yet a night on the town won't kill your budget: drinks are mostly $4 to $6; beer or a glass of wine, $3 to $4.

Boston is covered with clubs, from the North End waterfront to Kenmore Square, but if I were asked to choose the top ones, here's what I'd pick:

The **Top of the Hub Lounge** (tel. 536-1775) is at the top of the lofty Prudential Tower in Prudential Center (subway: Green Line to Auditorium or Prudential). The view is panoramic, breathtaking, wonderful. The combo is cool, as are the drinks, as are the patrons. If you don't succeed in meeting someone interesting here, no matter—the view is worth it. Dinner is served in the adjoining Top of the Hub restaurant, for about $35 to $50 per person, tax, tip, and wine included.

The **Profiles Café** and **Box Seat Lounge** (tel. 267-6059) are at the top of the Howard Johnson Hotel at 575 Commonwealth Ave., just past Kenmore Square going west (MBTA: Green Line "Boston College" cars to the Kenmore Square stop). The hotel is no skyscraper, but still the views of the Charles River, and of the lights and activity in Kenmore Square, are entertaining enough to keep you interested when you've stopped dancing. Live music nightly, some of the best in town.

The music at **Friday's**, 26 Exeter St. (tel. 266-9040), is recorded, but the people are very much alive and sociable. You can have a full meal here, a sandwich, or just a drink in the sumptuous Victorian atmosphere. The routine is to cluster at the small bar under the glass canopy—which will be pretty crowded—and when you inevitably bump into someone interesting, move on to one of the small tables in the dusky interior. Friday's stays open till midnight weeknights, till 1am on Friday and Saturday.

Boston's all-time success story, the **Faneuil Hall Marketplace** (MBTA: Green Line or Blue Line to Government Center) is a riot of activity morning, afternoon, and evening, with buskers and street musicians outside (in good weather), and a host of clubs and restaurants. For happy hour, you can't beat the crowd that gathers at the **Piano Bar at Lily's** (tel. 227-4242), in the Quincy Market Building: beautiful, young, well dressed, smooth, and with some money to burn. Sometimes it's hard to find a place at the bar or at one of the tables, but then again, asking to share a table is the perfect ice-breaker. Happy hour (5 to 7pm) and after is the time when Lily's is most closely packed, with a piano player to provide accompaniment for the social action.

Daisy Buchanan's, 240a Newbury St. (tel. 247-8516), at Fairfield (MBTA: Green Line to Copley or Auditorium), is a favorite with the professional sports set and young Newbury Street sophisticates, making for an interesting mixture in the closely packed room. The music is recorded, the action is live. Drinks and light meals.

OPERA AND SYMPHONY

Although Boston does not have a proper opera house, the indefatigable Sarah Caldwell arranges for her **Opera Company of Boston** to perform in a downtown theater, and she and her company have gained fame nationwide for their ability to overcome all sorts of obstacles and stage memorable performances. Big-city opera companies are undergoing a period of great instability, mostly financial, and so I will not predict that you'll be able to see this-or-that opera in this-or-that hall; rather, call the Opera Company of Boston, 539 Washington St. (tel. 426-5300), to see what's up, or watch for the ads in the newspapers. Seats may be expensive, but usually there are cut-price student tickets for sale within two weeks of any performance; get to the office the first day they go on sale, and be prepared to wait in line.

· Often the Metropolitan Opera Company comes up from New York for several performances; watch the newspapers for an announcement.

Boston's universities have been known to put on operas. Again, watch for such special one-time events in the newspaper listings.

Among the most successful opera seasons in Boston is that of the **Boston Concert Opera** (tel. 536-1166). Performances are held during the traditional opera season in Symphony Hall. Though the old favorites appear on the program, there are many lesser-known and rarely performed works—a real treat for true opera fans. Last-minute seats at moderate prices are often available. Note that this is "concert" opera: no sets, no costumes, but excellent conductor, soloists, chorus, and orchestra who give you a superb opera experience at an unbeatable price.

Boston Symphony Orchestra

The **Boston Symphony Orchestra** preserves a reputation for excellence and innovation that it has had for over a century. The formal symphony season runs from October through April, with performances in Symphony Hall (tel. 266-1492). The hall was designed (1900) by McKim, Mead, and White, who carried out one of the earliest-known scientific acoustical studies for such a structure, and their careful work has been an outstanding success for nearly a century.

Symphony Hall is at 310 Massachusetts Avenue, corner of Huntington Avenue. To get there by subway, take the Green Line (Brigham Circle, also called the "E" train) to Symphony; you can also take any other Green Line train to Auditorium, turn left as you leave the station, and walk down Mass. Ave. Bus no. 1 ("Dudley") runs from Harvard Square down Mass. Ave. and right by Symphony Hall.

For the latest information on current symphony programs, call 617/266-2378 (that's 617/C-O-N-C-E-R-T). Symphony tickets range in price from $20 to $50, depending upon the seat. Normal ticket sales are at the Symphony Hall Box Office, open from 10am to 6pm Monday through Saturday, and 1pm through 6pm on Sunday, and also during concerts through the first intermission. To reserve seats and order tickets by phone, call Symphony Charge at 617/266-1200; there's a handling fee of $2 per ticket ordered by phone. To order tickets by mail, send your payment and a stamped, self-addressed envelope to Symphony Hall Box Office, 301 Massachusetts Avenue, Boston, MA 02115. You can pay for tickets by credit card, check, or cash.

Low-Cost Symphony Tickets: There are ways to enjoy the Boston Symphony Orchestra without paying full price: rush seats, open rehearsals, and "extras."

A limited number of tickets for each BSO concert (Tuesday evening, Friday matinee, and Saturday evening) are held back, to be sold only on the day of the concert, one to a customer, in the Massachusetts Avenue lobby of Symphony Hall. These **rush seats** go on sale at 9am on Friday, 5pm on Tuesday and Saturday, and cost a mere $8 each. You must buy them in person, not by phone or mail.

Open rehearsals are held on eight Wednesday evenings during the symphony season at 7:30pm, and are almost better than concerts because they're preceded by a half-hour lecture on the evening's program. Doors open at 6:15pm, the lecture begins at 6:30pm, and the music starts at 7:30pm. The "rehearsal" is not a stop-and-go process, but rather more like a dress rehearsal, almost the same as a full-fledged concert, but tickets are considerably cheaper.

If you can't get rush seats, and can't make an open rehearsal, you can fish for **extras** by loitering outside the door of Symphony Hall on the night of the concert and try to buy any tickets that others have bought in advance, but that they can't use. Announce yourself and your intention by saying, "I'll buy any extra tickets . . . any extra tickets?" The price you pay depends upon your ability to haggle. Offer half price, and work from there.

The Boston Pops

Many members of the BSO stay on for the **Boston Pops,** which runs from early May through mid-July. At Pops, the music is just that: the most popular and lighter pieces in the symphonic repertoire performed in a café atmosphere. The floor in Symphony Hall is cleared of seats, and café tables and chairs are brought in, the hall is festooned with boughs and garlands of flowers, and champagne and hors d'oeuvres are served at the tables. The program is always a full and varied one, with a major work and lots of "Pops Extras," unlisted numbers thrown in for fun, many of them catchy orchestral arrangements of current hit tunes. Since the Pops season is also graduation time at many of Boston's colleges and universities, many Pops performances are heavily subscribed by college groups. Call Symphony Hall for general information at 617/266-1492; for the latest program information, call 617/266-2378.

For tickets, the rules are similar to those for buying symphony tickets (see above). Pops concert ticket prices range from $10 to $30.

An easier way to spend an "Evening at Pops" is by going early to one of the several summer concerts given for free by the Boston Pops in the Hatch Memorial

Shell, on the Charles River Esplanade (Red Line to Charles Station). The finale to the Esplanade season is the traditional Fourth of July performance, which always ends with Tchaikovsky's *1812* Overture, accompanied by a battery of cannons and followed by a mammoth display of fireworks over the river.

Tanglewood

After Pops season, the indefatigable members of the orchestra move out to the Berkshire hills in western Massachusetts for the Tanglewood Music Festival in Lenox, Mass. The Tanglewood season runs from July through August to Labor Day weekend. Chamber music concerts, recitals, and full symphony concerts fill each week, and a jazz festival ends the season on Labor Day weekend. Again, these performances are very heavily attended, and it's best to go early to get a good seat (you can sit inside the "Music Shed" or on the lawn outside, depending on how much you want to spend for a ticket); even more important than going early to the concert is to get a room reservation nearby, unless you plan to drive out and back (over three hours one way) the same day.

Special excursions to Tanglewood concerts are offered by various tour companies, including, in New York City, Biss Tours (tel. 718/426-4000), Casser Tours (tel. 212/840-6500), and Parker Tours (tel. 718/459-6565). From Boston, K & L Tours (tel. 617/267-1905) will take you there, or you can catch a bus run by Peter Pan Bus Lines (tel. 617/426-7838), described in the beginning of this chapter.

For more information on Tanglewood, refer to the section on "The Berkshires" in chapter IX.

Other Concerts

Two well-known music schools offer frequent concerts by students, faculty, and visiting groups of performers. The **New England Conservatory of Music,** 30 Gainsborough St. (tel. 262-1120, ext. 257), has frequent concerts, many of them free, in its performance halls, which include Jordon Hall. The conservatory is located one block from Symphony Hall, on Gainsborough Street at Huntington Avenue, close to the Boston YMCA and Northeastern University (Green Line's "Arborway" or "Northeastern U" cars to Symphony Station, or to the first stop above ground; or take bus no. 39, "Forest Hills," from Copley Square and Back Bay). A monthly calendar of events is available on request.

The other school is the **Berklee College of Music** (tel. 266-7455 for a recorded schedule, or 266-1400 for a human being), which has a Recital Hall at 1140 Boylston St. for small ensembles, and the Berklee Performance Center at 136 Massachusetts Ave. (near the corner of Massachusetts Avenue and Boylston Street) for larger groups. There's also the Berklee Concert Pavilion, an urban amphitheater, for outdoors events. Take the Green Line's "Boston College," "Cleveland Circle," or "Riverside" cars to Auditorium Station for both places. Both halls are fairly near the Prudential Center.

Few Boston institutions predate the venerable **Handel and Haydn Society,** which has been giving choral concerts in Boston since 1815. The society's season runs year round, with a Symphony Hall Series, a Chamber Series, a North Shore Series, and a Summer Series. The society, older even than the Boston Symphony Orchestra, has a closely guarded reputation for high excellence in its performances. For information on its concerts, call the Handel and Haydn Society, 295 Huntington Ave. (tel. 266-3605).

Concert Music Cruises

Young Bostonians are crazy for both boats and serious music, and a firm called **Water Music, Inc.,** 12 Arrow St., Cambridge (tel. 876-7777), has put the two together to make the "Concert Cruise." Twice each evening boats leave for a twilight tour of Boston Harbor and Massachusetts Bay, with its own prominent local or national musical group on board. Cruises operate in summer only, and the musical group is different each week. Food such as quiches, pâté, salads, and sandwiches can be purchased on board, as can wine, beer, and cocktails. Call for current schedules, musical programs, prices, and boarding information.

Cheap Seats

An outfit called **Bostix** (tel. 723-5181 for a recording) sells all kinds of tickets to all sorts of events in Boston and beyond. Buy a ticket to almost anything in eastern Massachusetts here. You'll pay the regular price plus a small service charge. This is a useful service.

But the real excitement at Bostix is the sale of tickets at half price on the day of performance. Theater, concerts, shows, and so on are put on a "daily list" of half-price offerings, and you must stop by the Bostix kiosk next to Faneuil Hall in Faneuil Hall Marketplace (subway to Government Center, Green Line or Blue Line) to read the list—they won't give it to you over the telephone. For same-day, half-price seats you must pay in cash, no refunds or exchanges; for advance bookings you may pay with a check drawn on a Massachusetts bank. No credit cards are accepted at all.

JAZZ, FOLK, AND ROCK

Modern music is all over Boston, but except for a few clubs downtown and a few coffeehouses in Cambridge, performers do a gig here or there and then disappear. The very big names usually play in the **Wang Center for the Performing Arts,** 270 Tremont (tel. 482-9393; Green Line to Boylston or Orange Line to New England Medical Center); in the **Hynes Convention Center** (tel. 262-8000) at the Prudential Center (Green Line to Auditorium); in the **Boston Garden** (tel. 227-3200), below North Station (Green Line to North Station); or in one of the university halls.

The Jazzboat

Besides operating a concert music cruise, **Water Music, Inc.** (tel. 876-7777), has come up with weekly cruises featuring jazz musicians ("the Jazzboat") and various other groups from swing bands to a Caribbean steel band. Call for the latest information, and then get your tickets by mail from Water Music, Inc., 12 Arrow St., Cambridge, MA 02138, or pick them up from one of the outlets they'll tell you about.

THEATER

Boston's taste in theater runs the gamut from previews of Broadway musicals to the most experimental of experimental. The offering is so rich and varied it would be impossible in this small space even to give an idea of the range available: groups will pop up here and there, struggle to survive, and in the meantime put on fine performances, and then fail financially and disperse, having left many theatergoers with a lasting impression. I would stress that people interested in the theater should not limit themselves to the possibilities outlined below, but should take the trouble to seek out the new groups performing in odd places, for they're often at the frontier.

Nevertheless, if you have only a little time to spend in Boston and you'd like to take in a play or a musical, here are some hints:

The **Next Move Theater,** 1 Boylston Pl. (tel. 423-5572), is perhaps the city's most interesting and talented theater group. For all its technical excellence, it's a homey sort of place where the actors stand near the door as you enter and as you leave, greeting the audience and exchanging comments on the plays. Boylston Place is a tiny alley off Boylston Street, midway between Tremont and Charles Streets, across from Boston Common. By subway, take the Green Line to Boylston.

The old-line theaters with musicals and plays slated for Broadway are all downtown near the Green Line's Boylston Station: the **Colonial Theater,** 106 Boylston St. right near the station (tel. 426-9366); the **Shubert Theater,** 265 Tremont St. (tel. 426-4520), and the **Wilbur Theater,** 246 Tremont St. (tel. 423-4008), both two blocks south along Tremont Street from the Boylston Station.

Good drama is the rule at the **Charles Playhouse,** 74 Warrenton St. (tel. 426-6912), right down behind the Shubert and Wilbur Theaters and the Tremont

House Hotel (Green Line to Boylston; Warrenton is parallel to Tremont one block west, but it's only a block long). Comedians perform nightly in the **Comedy Connection;** and the **Charles Cabaret,** in the same building, has set the record for the longest run of *Shear Madness.*

Besides these, the universities have a great many drama offerings, usually at fairly low prices; and during the summer the city of Boston and other organizations sponsor outdoor performances in City Hall Plaza, other public squares, and along the Charles River Esplanade. (See also the section on **Cambridge.**)

DANCE

Dance is not quite as prominent in Boston's arts scene as, say, theater or music, but the energetic **Boston Ballet Company** (tel. 964-4070), is active all year. In spring, fall, and winter there is the regular ballet season at the Wang Center, 270 Tremont St.; in summer the troupe seems to be everywhere, putting on performances in the city's squares and parks, and along the riverbank. Watch for notices and times in the papers, then go to the box office of the Wang Center Monday through Saturday from 10am to 6pm to buy tickets ($11 to $47), or call Ticketmaster (tel. 617/787-8000) between 9am and 9pm, any day.

CINEMA

Movies are a big part of Boston's nighttime entertainment picture, and the hot-topic big releases are always crowded during the first few weeks. But besides major releases, silent movies, golden oldies, and bestsellers of the recent past are always available. Prices range from $7 per seat to free admission.

The local listings will let you know what's on tonight. What you may find of help is directions on how to get to the principal movie theaters. Remember to check out Cambridge movies as well, listed separately in the Cambridge section. Here are the prime movie houses in Boston:

Beacon Hill, 1 Beacon St., at Tremont St. (tel. 723-8110), near King's Chapel and the Parker House Hotel; Green or Red Lines to Park Street, or Green or Blue Lines to Government Center.

Charles, 195a Cambridge St. (tel. 227-1330), next to the Holiday Inn near the corner of Cambridge and Blossom Street; Green Line to Government Center, or Red Line to Charles.

Cheri, 50 Dalton St. (tel. 536-2870), next to Hynes Convention Center in the Prudential Center complex; Green Line's "Boston College," "Cleveland Circle," or "Riverside" cars to Auditorium, turn left out of the station, left again down Boylston, and look right.

Cinema 57, 200 Stuart St. (tel. 482-1222), in the tall 57 Park Plaza Hotel-Howard Johnson, in Park Square; Green Line to Boylston Station, then walk along the edge of the Common on Boylston Street to the intersection with Charles Street and turn left—it's right in front of you in the middle distance.

Coolidge Corner, 290 Harvard St., in suburban Brookline (tel. 734-2500); take the Green Line's "Cleveland Circle" car along Beacon Street to the junction with Harvard Street, called Coolidge Corner.

Copley Place, 100 Huntington Ave. (tel. 266-1300), in the new Copley Place complex next to Copley Square and the Prudential Center. Take a Green Line subway car to Copley or Prudential.

Nickelodeon Cinemas, 606 Commonwealth Ave. near Kenmore Square (tel. 424-1500), is actually slightly off Commonwealth at 34 Cummington St., behind Boston University's School of Public Communications, but you'll see the cinema's big sign as you walk west along Commonwealth from Kenmore Square.

Paris Cinema, 841 Boylston St. (tel. 267-8181), very near Prudential Center; Green Line to Copley, Auditorium, or Prudential.

The **Opera House** (tel. 426-5300) has two entrances: 163 Tremont St. (Green Line to Boylston, and the Tremont entrance is across the street from the subway station, a few doors down), or 539 Washington St. (Red or Orange Line to Washington, enter two blocks down on the right across from Lafayette Place).

Wang Center for the Performing Arts, 270 Tremont St. (tel. 482-9393), near Stuart Street in the Theater District; this is often booked with theater, dance, and concerts, but it does have several subscription film series; Green Line to Boylston, then south (away from the Common) on Tremont Street for two blocks, and the Wang Center is on the left.

Museum of Fine Arts, 465 Huntington Ave., has many film programs, with screenings most Thursday and Friday evenings. Call 267-9300, extension 306, for details, times, and prices.

Free Movies

Lots of films are shown for free in Boston, or very nearly for free—the college film series at many Boston colleges often charge as little as $1 for admission. Newspaper listings may or may not have information about college film series, and indeed the movie to be shown, place of screening, and even date and time may change without notice except for a few mimeographed flyers stuck up here and there on the campus. Still, try calling one of the college switchboards and asking about "the film series." For Harvard, check the *Gazette,* a weekly information sheet about the university available for free in the University Information Office, Holyoke Center, Harvard Square.

More dependable and predictable than the college film series are the films shown fairly regularly by these institutions, all for free:

Boston Public Library (tel. 536-5400), various films shown in the lecture hall and at the library's branches throughout the city. Take the Green Line to Copley.

Institute of Contemporary Art, 955 Boylston St. (tel. 266-5151), showing various films usually having to do with modern art or artists; see "Other Galleries" for transportation details.

SPORTS

Especially in summer, Boston is alive with outdoor activities: the Charles River is dotted with sailboats every day the breeze comes up, joggers and bikers huff and puff along the Esplanade, the roar of the Red Sox fans rises from Fenway Park. Every autumn, tickets to the Harvard-Yale game are grabbed up like passes into heaven, and while the aristocrats are urging Harvard to fight fiercely, the Boston Bruins and their opponents for the day are probably doing just that with their hockey sticks. Hockey is such a part of Boston's cold-weather life that in winter you may see a lot of kids with schoolbooks in their hands, but you'll see a lot more with hockey sticks. Here's a rundown on the major sports; parking is tough to find and expensive on game nights.

Baseball

The **Red Sox** play at Fenway Park (Green Line's "Riverside" car to Fenway Station, then follow the crowd!), and if you buy your tickets a few days before the game, you can get them at the nearest ticket agency (Ticketron, Bostix, and the like). Call 267-2525 for Red Sox information.

Basketball

The famous **Boston Celtics** play in Boston Garden (Green Line to North Station), a large hall that has nothing to do with Boston's Public Garden. Call 523-6050 for the latest info.

Football

The **New England Patriots,** affectionately called "The Pats" in these "pahts," play at Schaefer Stadium, Rte. 1 in Foxboro, Mass., some 30 miles southwest of Boston. Several Boston bus companies run special buses to the games; try calling Bonanza (tel. 423-5810) or Peter Pan (tel. 482-6620). For information on Patriots games, call 262-1776.

Hockey

The famed **Boston Bruins** battle it out with all comers at Boston Garden (same as basketball, above), and tickets are often sold out very early. Catch 'em when they take on Montréal and you've got a spectacle. Call 227-3200 for information.

THE COMBAT ZONE

Police hate it, politicians want to get rid of it, some citizens revel in it—the several blocks of Washington Street between West Street and Stuart Street (Green Line to Boylston or Orange Line to Essex) are perhaps the most "un-Boston-like" part of Boston. No grand old traditions are here except that of "the oldest profession"; no lofty artistry unless one can call nude dancing art. The Combat Zone, as it is known to all, is Boston's tenderloin: several blocks of prime downtown real estate full of strip shows, "naked college girl revues," porno films, and generally sleazy diversions.

Despite its sinister name and gamy appearance, the Combat Zone is not a wildly dangerous place to stroll through, and many of the bars and clubs and movie houses are safe enough to enter if you follow a few simple rules. First, don't go late at night; things are hopping by early evening, and you might as well see this part of the world around 8 or 8:30pm, rather than later. It's brightly lit and there are lots of police around. Second, don't go alone; anything's better than being a loner, whether you go with a date, a threesome, or a small group. In most places women are as welcome as men. Third, watch your wallet or purse. And finally, if you want to try out a place, go by gut feeling: some places are fairly attractive and seem safe enough; others look pretty bad, with all sorts of types hanging around. Walk around for a while until you find an acceptable place. And if all this seems terrifying, remember that the people who own the Combat Zone places are interested in selling you movie tickets and drinks, not in ripping you off so you never come back again; they'd rather not have any trouble that'll bring the police.

ACROSS THE CHARLES

1. CAMBRIDGE
2. LEXINGTON
3. CONCORD

As Paul Revere sped through the countryside along another road, William Dawes made a famous midnight ride that took him from the banks of the Charles through the communities of Cambridge (once called Newtown), Lexington, and Concord. Boston's expansion, like America's, was westward toward the mountains, and these important communities west of the city were large enough to play a significant role in the Revolution.

Today the cities of Cambridge, Lexington, and Concord are linked by Battle Road, a designation given by the National Park Service, which harks back to that historic day when Revere and Dawes rode out, followed by troops of redcoats. The story of Battle Road and the events of that day in 1775 is clearly told in the exhibits at Minuteman National Historic Park in Lexington and Concord, but before looking at revolutionary history, let's take a look at the home city of Harvard College, which is much older than the Revolution.

1. Cambridge

Cambridge means Harvard to most visitors who come to Boston, and although Harvard is not the only thing in the city of Cambridge (MIT's there too, after all), it is certainly the city's most important institution. Harvard Square, at the intersection of Massachusetts Avenue and John F. Kennedy Street (formerly called Boylston Street), is a crossroads that teems with evidence of a hundred life-styles, from the stuffily academic to the loosest of dropouts.

Cambridge has its own collection of hotels, restaurants, and sights to see, examined below. The MBTA's Red Line subway connects Harvard Square to Park Street Station on Boston Common. Service is the fastest, most frequent, and most comfortable in the system, and the journey normally takes about 15 minutes from turnstile to turnstile. Going from Harvard Square into Boston, take any "Inbound" train; all trains stop at Park Street Station. From Boston to Harvard Square, take trains marked "Alewife" or "Harvard."

Those staying in Boston's Back Bay section might find it easier to walk to Massachusetts Avenue and catch a no. 1 bus ("Harvard-Dudley"), which goes past MIT, through Central Square directly to Harvard Square, the last stop.

INFORMATION

There's an information kiosk right in the center of Harvard Square maintained and staffed by **Cambridge Discovery, Inc.** (tel. 617/497-1630), open Monday through Saturday from 9am to 6pm and on Sunday from 1 to 5pm. Walking tours of Old Cambridge leave from the kiosk four times daily between late June and Labor Day; call for details.

WHERE TO STAY

Guidelines for Cambridge hotels are similar to those mentioned for Boston. There is no reason why you shouldn't plan to stay in Cambridge during the length of your Boston visit. Remember to consider your means of transportation when you choose a hotel in Cambridge.

Remember also that bed-and-breakfast organizations serving the Boston area serve Cambridge, too. See the Boston hotel section for details.

The most dramatic hotel in town is the Aztec-pyramid **Hyatt Regency Cambridge,** 575 Memorial Dr., Cambridge, MA 02139 (tel. 617/492-1234, or toll free 800/233-1234). True to the Hyatt design tradition, it has a grand interior space rising from ground floor to top floor, planted with trees and hanging vines and surrounded with mezzanine walkways to the guest rooms. Of the several restaurants in the hotel, Jonah's Seafood Café is on the mezzanine one flight up from ground level, and diners thus can enjoy the atmosphere of the central space. The Pallysadoe Bar, just off this mezzanine, has a good view of the Charles River, as does Sally Ling's, the fancy oriental restaurant. Take one of the crystal-shaped glass elevators that slide up the wall to reach the Spinnaker Italian restaurant on the top floor. Open for lunch and dinner, the restaurant affords a panoramic view of Boston, Cambridge, and the Charles. Once you're seated, take in the view at once, because the entire dining area is on a revolving disc, which moves very slowly so that the perspective is always changing. Rooms cost $200 to $231 single, $220 to $242 double, but the weekend rate can be as low as $110, tax included. Other special services include a health club, a children's playground, and a free shuttle van to Harvard Square and downtown Boston.

Newest of Harvard Square hotels is the luxurious **Charles Hotel at Harvard Square,** in the complex called Charles Square off Mount Auburn Street and Brattle Square, only steps from Harvard Square (tel. 617/864-1200), 1 Bennett St. at Eliot St., Cambridge, MA 02138. The Charles is independently run, beautifully decorated, and luxuriously furnished, with 300 guest rooms fully equipped: cable color TV, refrigerated bar, two telephones, and 24-hour room service. As you might expect, the hotel has its own indoor swimming pool, sauna, whirlpool, and exercise room. The restaurant, called Rarities, is elegant, epicurean, and pricey. The Regattabar is among the Boston area's best jazz clubs, with top-name artists. Prices are $186 to $246 single or double. On weekends you can get a room (double or single) for $135, valet parking included.

The **Guest Quarters Suite Hotel,** 400 Soldiers' Field Rd., Boston, MA 02134 (tel. 617/783-0090, or toll free 800/424-2900), is a good choice if you're in search of more space and convenience for the same money. Though the address is Boston, this 15-story, 310-room building is actually at least as close to Harvard Square and MIT as it is to Boston University and downtown. Each suite consists of a bedroom with king-size bed, color TV, AM-FM radio, writing desk and telephone, full bath, refrigerator and wet bar, living room with full-size sofa bed, another color TV, dining table, and yet another phone. Weekend guests enjoy free continental breakfast and a manager's reception with hors d'oeuvres and discounted drinks, and free van shuttle service to Cambridge and Boston. Scullers, the hotel's jazz club, is one of the city's best. So what's the price? Not bad at all: $186 to $230 weekdays, $110 on Friday and Saturday; parking on weekends costs $7.50.

The **Howard Johnson Hotel,** 777 Memorial Dr., Cambridge, MA 02139 (tel. 617/492-7777, or toll free 800/654-2000), is a 14-story, 205-room establishment. Here, the floor your room is on determines its price, since the higher rooms have better views; some rooms have small balconies. Views are of Boston and the Charles, straight across the Charles, up the Charles River to Harvard (this is the prettiest view, in my opinion), and a city view of Cambridge. Prices are $88 to $143 single, $105 to $182 double. Reserve a week in advance for a weekend date and you can sometimes get a room for $80. The hotel has a year-round swimming pool, color TV, free parking, a restaurant and bar, and a pleasant brick-and-dark-wood interior. Harvard special events (freshmen registration, Harvard-Yale game, homecoming, graduation, and the like) can fill the hotel, and rooms should be reserved well in advance. Car or taxi must be used to get to and from Harvard Square or downtown Boston.

The **Harvard Square Inn,** 110 Mount Auburn St., Cambridge, MA 02138 (tel. 617/864-5200), is right in the midst of Harvard Square. Actually a motel, it has air conditioning, ice machine, vending machines, and free continental breakfast served in the lobby. Parking is free, and a parking place—any parking place—near Harvard Square is a very good thing to have. Rooms are modern, all with TV, and are rented for $103 single, $114 double, $125 triple, $135 for four; children under 16 stay free. Some rooms have views of Brattle and Harvard Squares.

At 1234 Soldiers' Field Rd., Boston (Brighton), MA 02135 (tel. 617/254-1234), is the local **Ramada Inn.** For $94 to $104 single, $105 to $136 double, midweek, you get a small swimming pool (open from Memorial Day to Labor Day) and a large restaurant, besides a selection of air-conditioned rooms with color TV and views of the river and the steeples and cupolas of Harvard in the middle distance. In fact, room prices are computed on the basis of the view, the front river-view rooms on the higher floors of the building being the most expensive. Children under 18 stay for free. On weekends, if the hotel is not busy, the price for a room may be as low as $76.

Daystop, 1800 Soldiers' Field Rd., Boston (Brighton), MA 02135 (tel. 617/254-0200), formerly the Charles River Motel but now a unit of the Days Inn chain, is not in Cambridge, strictly speaking, but it offers advantages to visitors to Cambridge who have their own cars. Larger-than-average recently refurbished rooms, buses to Cambridge and downtown Boston, and lots of free parking are among the advantages. Prices are $78 single, $88 double, tax included, for an air-conditioned room with color TV and bath; children under 12 stay free. The motel has no pool or restaurant, but there are several restaurants within walking distance. If you're driving, get to the south bank of the Charles River and go west to Soldiers' Field Road, which is the continuation of Storrow Drive. Follow signs to Newton, dip down for an underpass, and then a mile or so later look to your left for the pillared southern mansion–style facade of the red-brick motel. You can get to the motel by bus from Central Square (subway Red Line to Central) in Cambridge: take a no. 64 ("Oak Square") bus. Although Daystop is several miles from Harvard Square, Soldiers' Field Road allows you to speed to the center of town in only ten minutes.

A renovated hotel not far from Harvard Square is the **Sheraton Commander,** 16 Garden St., Cambridge, MA 02238 (tel. 617/547-4800, or toll free 800/325-3535). Garden Street runs from Harvard Square past Cambridge Common to Radcliffe, and the Commander is just about equidistant (a ten-minute walk) from either campus. The decor in the public rooms tends to the high-brow colonial—the "commander" for whom the hotel was named is George Washington, and a bronze statue of General Washington stands in the entry garden, to the right of the doors. Rooms cost $155 to $195 for one, $166 to $205 for two; children under 18 stay for free. Although there is free parking at the hotel, the lot is small and you may have to leave your keys at the desk so the doorman can jockey the cars around to best advantage.

The **Quality Inn of Cambridge,** 1651 Massachusetts Ave., Cambridge, MA

02139 (tel. 617/491-1000), is a 15-minute walk from Harvard Square along busy Massachusetts Avenue. It is functional, even comfortable, with a small swimming pool for the warm months, a homey restaurant off the lobby, and, of course, free parking. The 134 guest rooms come with color cable TV including free HBO movies. If you stay here, you can walk to the subway and be in downtown Boston within 30 minutes from when you close the door of your room. In summer, singles cost $82 to $105 and doubles are $90 to $116. Many rooms have two double beds; some have queen and king beds, which is useful because kids under 16 stay for free.

WHERE TO DINE

Cambridge, in its woolly way, is even more cosmopolitan than Boston, and this is well demonstrated in its restaurants. Cannelloni to couscous, wonton to weisswurst, Cambridge has it. Some of the best places to have a good, inexpensive lunch or a light supper are Cambridge's coffeehouses, almost all of which serve food as well as coffee, tea, and hot chocolate. And finally, there are the ice cream shops of Harvard Square, worthy of a list unto themselves.

The Top Restaurants

The **Bennett St. Café** in the Charles Hotel, in the Charles Square complex just out of Brattle Square (tel. 864-1200), is among the area's most attractive and interesting restaurants. In fair weather you can dine outdoors in the court; otherwise, the indoor dining room is plush and attractive. The selection of luncheon salads, sandwiches, and light entrees (the menu changes constantly) is among the finest and most interesting I've seen among Harvard Square's plethora of upscale dining places. Expect to pay about $15 to $20 total for lunch, and that includes a drink or glass of wine. At dinner you can spend twice that much. The café is open for breakfast, Sunday brunch, lunch, and dinner every day.

In the top price range, first place goes to **Harvest**, 44 Brattle St. (tel. 492-1115), hidden away down the tunnel that penetrates the four-story glass building that houses Crate and Barrel on Brattle Street. The restaurant's location allows it to have the most pleasant outdoor luncheon area in all Cambridge. Open for lunch and dinner every day from 11:30am to 2:30pm and 6 to 10pm, until 10:30pm on weekends (Sunday brunch from 11am to 3pm), Harvest offers meticulously prepared dishes: at lunch, a four-liver pâté to start, then venison stroganoff, and for dessert a chocolate marquise, for example. For dinner you might have Creole okra gumbo or a game terrine, a grilled pharaoh quail salad, and a main course of sautéed rock shrimp and sea scallops served with garlic fettucine, fennel, and plum tomato. The price-conscious will be able to dine well for $20 at lunch, for $40 or so in the evening: the menu in the section called Ben's Corner is less expensive than the main dining room, but equally interesting. Sunday brunch is fancy and satisfying.

About ten blocks north of Harvard Square, **Matsu-ya**, 1790 Massachusetts Ave. (tel. 491-5091), serves very tasty Japanese and Korean food. Sit at a comfy booth or at one of several low Japanese-style tables on a raised platform, take in the traditional but subdued decor, and enjoy. If you like steak tartare, you'll love yukhae, morsels of choice raw beef flavored with sesame seeds and oil. More familiar dishes, such as pork sukiyaki, are prepared right at your table and cooked to your specifications (nothing theatrical about this, no flaming braziers and such, and the food is served exactly when it is *à point*). A filling and very delicious meal for two, tax and tip included, may come to $20 per person. Matsu-ya is open for dinner every evening from 5 to 10pm, to 11pm on Friday and Saturday; wine and beer are served.

Favorite Cambridge Hangouts

The **Border Café**, 32 Church St. (tel. 864-6100), is a mock-stark Mexican cantina with rough wood tables and naive murals of favorite Mexican bottles, but also a chic black-clad hostess to seat you (she'd never survive in a real cantina). The café is popular partly because of its tongue-in-cheek decor, but more because the food is surprisingly inexpensive. The cuisine here borrows from Mexican, Cajun, fajita, and mesquite-grill cooking, and you'll love it. Not only that, but you can have a sandwich and Corona (beer) for as little as $6 or $8, or more elaborate and delicious plates of shrimp, fajitas (shredded fried meat or chicken), or blackened redfish, and end up paying only $16 to $20 for a meal, with drinks, tax, and tip included. The Border Café is open daily for lunch and dinner.

The wurst restaurant in Harvard Square is, of course, the **Wursthaus**, at 4 John F. Kennedy St., right in Harvard Square (tel. 491-7110). A long bar and several rooms of booths and tables provide a nearly German atmosphere, and prices for the wursts (knackwurst, bratwurst, Bauernwurst), sauerbraten, schnitzel, pig's knuckles and sauerkraut, are moderate, mostly in the $8 to $12 range, and that includes sauerkraut, black bread, and butter. Hearty sandwiches are only half that much. World travelers craving the exotic beer of some far-off land will probably find it here, for the Wursthaus tries hard to include on its "beerlist" just about every foreign beer you've ever heard of and dozens you never knew existed; they're priced from $3 to $8 a bottle. Breakfast is served from 7:30 to 11am (9am to 2pm on Saturday and Sunday); lunch is from 11am to 3pm, dinner from 4 to 9pm every day but Sunday, when the dinner menu is offered all day, from 11:30am on.

Every college freshman reads about Grendel, the dragon that threatens the hero of the ancient English epic *Beowulf*, but anyone in Harvard Square—freshman or not—can frequent **Grendel's Den**, 89 Winthrop St. (tel. 491-1160), a restaurant noted for its reasonable prices and large portions. Grendel's is behind a tiny patch of grass off John F. Kennedy Street at Mount Auburn Street, one block south of Harvard Square toward the Charles River: a huge sign on the roof leads the way. The cellar of the red-brick building is the bar, furnished with a fireplace for cold winter nights, and dark-wood tables. Upstairs is the restaurant, with two fireplaces and a glassed-in terrace overlooking busy John F. Kennedy Street. The menu tells of international specialties such as spinach pie, fettuccine, chicken curry, shish kebab, quiche, omelets, burgers, and sandwiches priced from $4 to $18. There's a good salad bar. Alcoholic beverages are served. As for the desserts, they're a list in themselves, but suffice it to say that they include chocolate fondue. Grendel's is open every day for lunch and dinner.

Among Cambridge's newer hangouts is the **Cottonwood Café**, 1815 Massachusetts Ave. (tel. 661-7440), in the renovated Sears, Roebuck building at Porter Square (take the Red Line subway in the direction of Alewife, one stop from Harvard Square). The Cottonwood is upscale Mexican, a cozy, attractive place with an inventive menu that might best be described as "New Latin American Cuisine:" although Mexican-inspired, the dishes are original creations. Many are pretty spicy, so ask. Authentic, carefully chosen crafts enliven the decor. Prices are moderate at lunch, about $12 to $16 per person, and quite a bit more expensive at dinner. They're open every day from 11:45am to 3:30pm for lunch and 5:45pm to 10pm (till 11pm on Friday and Saturday) for dinner.

Iruña, entered by a passageway between 54 and 56 John F. Kennedy St. (tel. 868-5633), is Harvard Square's best-kept secret. Though it's been here for years, only locals know about Iruña's good, hearty Spanish food, low prices, and pretty outdoor patio in the rear (summer only). Come for lunch and you can have soup, carne guisada (chunks of beef in a sauce of wine, mushrooms, and carrots), and salad for less than $12, tax and tip included! Arroz con pollo (chicken and rice) is the same price. You can spend even less by ordering only the main course. Prices at dinner are similarly pleasant. Wine and beer are served. Iruña is open for lunch from noon to 2pm Monday through Friday for dinner from 6 to 9pm Monday through Friday, and from 1:30 to 10pm on Saturday; closed Sunday.

Dolphin Seafood, on Massachusetts Avenue between Remington and Trowbridge Streets (tel. 354-9332), near where Massachusetts Avenue intersects Mount Auburn Street, is only six blocks east of the square. Upstairs in a split-level complex of shops, the Dolphin is decorated in plain and functional fashions, with the seafood being given all the attention. A big plate of steamers (steamed clams) with butter makes a substantial appetizer. Fried squid is a specialty (the chef is Portuguese), but there are always alternatives such as bluefish and whatever else is fresh that day, with potato, salad, rolls, and butter included. If you're lobster-happy, order twin lobsters with steamers or mussels. A whole dinner might cost $15 to $20 here, lunch even less. Wine and beer are served at reasonable prices. The Dolphin is good, and thus it's busy—go for an early or late lunch or dinner till 10pm.

Budget Meals

Many places in Harvard Square serve hamburgers and other sandwiches, but undoubtedly the best value-for-money is to be had at **Elsie's,** 71a Mount Auburn St. (tel. 864-0461), corner of Holyoke, a block from the square. Elsie's is nothing fancy, but the prices, for quantity and quality received, have never been rivaled in Harvard Square. The mainstay is the roast beef special sandwich, which comes with Bermuda onion and "Elsie's Special Russian Dressing,"; the turkey deluxe, the Elsieburger (a double hamburger), and the thick-cut Rumanian pastrami-filled Landsman are other features, each for only $3.25 to $4.75.

Taking its name from Harvard's famous Yenching Library, the **Yenching Restaurant,** 1326 Massachusetts Ave., at the corner of Massachusetts Avenue and Holyoke Street (tel. 547-1130), has the fastest Chinese food in the square. Furnishings are simple but bright and tasteful, and the food is authentic and good. When unsure, ask the waiter how a certain dish is prepared so as to avoid such surprises as too much garlic or red pepper. Most of the surprises here are pleasant, however, like the price of the daily luncheon buffet—only about $7—which attracts a large crowd about 12:15 each afternoon. Soup is brought to you after you're seated, then you attack the buffet whenever you like. The dinner menu is long but not encyclopedic, offering Szechuan shredded pork, Mandarin sweet-and-sour fish, and a whole Peking duck (order in advance). The average evening meal might come to $16 to $20. Service is quick and attentive. The Yenching is open for lunch and dinner every day, but the special luncheon buffet is served Monday through Saturday till 2:30pm only.

The half-dozen restaurants in the **Harvard Square Marketplace,** a sort of mall bounded by Kennedy, Mount Auburn, and Dunster Streets, are all moderate to inexpensive in price. Souper Salad is an attractive lunch or light-supper place, with interesting spaces in which to sit, an upbeat menu, and prices to suit any appetite or budget. Nearby is Baby Watson, noted above all for its desserts. Baby Watson cheesecake is Boston's best known.

COFFEEHOUSES

An intellectual center will have its coffeehouses, dedicated to serving that beverage which stimulates thought and aids conversation. Harvard Square has a good selection of coffeehouses, all of which serve light meals, desserts, ice cream, and beverages besides coffee. Each draws a special clientele, and you can spend a very pleasant day or two hopping from one to another of these, testing them out to find the one that suits you best. Here is a rundown of the best places:

It is generally agreed that the finest and most delicious coffee in Harvard Square —and the widest selection—is to be had at the **Coffee Connection,** 36 John F. Kennedy St., in the Harvard Square Marketplace, at the corner of Kennedy and Mount Auburn Streets, one block from the MBTA station. Although light meals are served here, such as a breakfast of fresh-squeezed juice, croissant, and coffee ($3.90), or lunch/supper dishes of quiche, salad, soup, yogurt, and the like, the star of the show is the coffee. The different characteristics of the various brews are described in the menu. Note that some coffees are very strong and hearty, others are smooth and mild—but the flavor in both is well rounded and delicious. The cheapest way to have good coffee here is to order the coffee of the day, at $1.25; cappuccino and other coffee specialty drinks go up to $3.50. Black and herbal teas are also available. Surroundings here are modern and attractive, light and airy, with a raised sitting area and a nearby counter where coffee beans and teas can be bought in bulk to take home. By the way, there's an entrance to the building at the corner of Dunster and Mount Auburn Streets as well.

Harvard Square's most obvious café is **Au Bon Pain,** 1360 Massachusetts Ave. (tel. 491-1523), in the Holyoke Center building next to the Cambridge Savings

Bank. In summer the little square in front of the café is filled with tables and chairs; in winter you can see all the tasty croissants, baguette sandwiches, and pastries through the huge plate-glass windows. Buy your breakfast, lunch, or supper at the counter, and then find an unoccupied table. Croissants cost $1.25 (plain) to $3 (ham and cheese). Sandwiches such as roast beef or brie cost under $5.

A coffeehouse in the square that features live entertainment is **Passim,** 47 Palmer St. (an alley running between the two buildings of the Harvard Coop). You can stop into Passim for a cup of coffee (varieties priced from $1.25 to $3), pie, cake, or a cheese sampler as a light lunch for about $8. Spend some time at the small gallery, which displays the work of local artists, or look for a bauble among the glass cases of interesting objets d'art from all over the world that are on sale here. But the big attraction at Passim is undoubtedly the evening performances by folk, blues, and jazz musicians of greater or lesser fame. Passim opens for business at noon, and shows begin somewhere around 7:30pm. Call 492-7679 for more information.

The crowd at **Algiers,** 40 Brattle St., in the complex of shops called Truc under the Brattle Theater, are usually lively and unorthodox, bright-eyed and interesting. The two subterranean rooms are often full, and when the weather's nice there's service at a tiny outdoor area along a passage at the side of the theater. Many people come just for coffee and conversation, or to meet new people. Lunches tend toward the Arabic, of course: a selection of sandwiches made with flat Arab bread is offered at $4 to $6 apiece, and there are soups, iced drinks, and desserts as well. Coffee costs $1.50 (espresso) to $2.10 (mocha espresso with whipped cream), and is served from 8am to 12:30am. The morning hours make Algiers the place to come for a midmorning cup of coffee and a break to read the newspaper or to plan the day's activities. Enter either by a door and stairway to the left of the Brattle Theater entrance or through the theater entrance itself: from the vestibule of the theater, another stairway descends to the Truc complex, and the Algiers.

It is said that Longfellow, who lived only six blocks away, wrote his famous poem about a Cambridge blacksmith whose shop was on Brattle Street: "Under the spreading chestnut tree/The village smithy stands/The smith, a mighty man is he,/With large and sinewy hands." The spot the smithy occupied is now taken by the **Blacksmith House,** 56 Brattle St., a café and bakery. In summer the large terrace in front of the house is set with tables; in winter coffee lovers have to settle for a nice upstairs room in the house, furnished with small wood tables and spindle-back chairs. Coffee costs 90¢ (free refill), but the stars of the show are the German- and Austrian-style pastries such as Wiener torte, Sachertorte, Mozart torte, Linzer torte, apple torte, each one $3.25 a slice. Other types of kuchen, and also brioche and croissants, are made daily too. The Blacksmith House does as big a business selling cakes and pastries to go as it does selling coffee to stay.

Harvard Square's woolliest of intellectual coffeehouses is the **Café Pamplona,** at 12 Bow St., five short blocks east from the MBTA station along Massachusetts Avenue. Nothing disturbs the current of conversation here, for there's no telephone, no music, no live entertainment. Various kinds of coffee are served ($1 to $3), from the inexpensive espresso to the mocha, a rich coffee-and-chocolate topped with real whipped cream. Most coffees start from a very dark–roast bean, and are therefore quite strong. From 11am to 3pm, gazpacho, toasted sandwiches, and other light lunch items are prepared, and in summer the tiny terrace beside the Pamplona's entrance stairway is furnished with tables, chairs, and umbrellas (the indoor café is in a basement). In winter the atmosphere is that of a group of high-brow troglodytes, and invariably the table next to yours will be occupied by someone writing a poem, or music, or translating some abstruse language. The Pamplona is tiny, and you may have to wait for a seat. It's open from 11am (from 2pm on Sunday) to midnight or 1am.

ICE CREAM

From a short study of Harvard Square shops, it might appear that the two most valued commodities hereabouts are the photocopy and the ice-cream cone. Ice cream, at $1.65 to $2.50 for a "small" (actually, huge) cone, is almost a cult object in Cambridge, and the virtues of the various shops and their selections of flavors are a frequent topic of debate, and even fierce loyalty. The eating of ice cream is by no means limited to the summer months, and in fact only one or two people thought it unusual that cones should be seen along Massachusetts Avenue during the bitter days of the winter of 1976–77. Herewith, a guide for the discriminating connoisseur:

Once upon a time, a local fellow decided to open an ice-cream parlor that served only ice cream made from cream and things like vanilla beans, fruits, and other natural ingredients. He set up shop in Somerville, and the lines of passionate devotees soon stretched around the block.

That's the legend behind the legendary Steve Herrell, founder of Steve's Ice Cream. He later sold the business and retired to the mountains for a breather, but then returned to franchise a new line of stores called **Herrell's,** with one at 15 Dunster St. (tel. 497-2179), along similar lines. Just around the corner from the Cambridge Savings Bank in Harvard Square, Herrell's is the ultimate of Harvard Square ice-cream shops. It's located in a former bank building, and you can devour your cone or dish in the vault, now walled with mirrors. Flavors change somewhat from day to day, and all cost the same. Take special note of Chocolate Pudding, a supercharged chocolate ice cream that leaves chocoholics in ecstasy. There's also their own frozen yogurt, made right here, and "No-Moo," a nondairy ice cream, as well as Vitari, another ice-cream alternative. Herrell's is open until 1am on Friday and Saturday during the summer months.

As for **Steve's Ice Cream,** at 31 Church St. (tel. 497-1067), it is now famous from coast to coast, still producing top-quality treats, still attracting hordes of faithful devotees. The Harvard Square location has been added to the original shop at 191 Elm St. (Davis Square) in neighboring Somerville. The solution to unhappiness on any hot summer day is a cone from Steve's; winter days too, for that matter.

Baskin-Robbins Ice Cream Store, 1230 Massachusetts Ave., corner of Bow Street, several blocks east along Massachusetts Avenue from Harvard Square proper, sells good ice cream in 31 flavors, plus frozen yogurt cones. They'll make you an ice-cream cake, sundae, shake, banana split, freeze, or ice-cream sandwich if you like. anytime from 11am to 1am.

WHAT TO SEE AND DO

Harvard Square is the heartbeat of Cambridge, a place where all styles of life commingle in a wild, busy carnival atmosphere. When you arrive at Harvard subway station on your Red Line train from Boston, you'll walk up the station's dingy stairs and out into a funky and fertile world right at the center of America's most staid and most prestigious institution of higher learning.

Harvard

The first college founded in the British colonies, Harvard was established in 1636 by the Great and General Court of Massachusetts Bay, the colonists' assembly. John Harvard, a clergyman, gave his library and a sum of money to the fledgling college, a generous gesture that has earned for his name worldwide fame. From that early beginning Harvard College grew into Harvard University, a huge educational establishment with an endowment of over $4.2 billion.

The university sponsors tours of its most historic sections during the summer, and during the school year when school is in session (that is, no tours during Christmas recess, spring vacation, etc.). Most of the tours depart from the **Harvard University Information Center,** 1350 Massachusetts Ave., in the Holyoke Center building, the tallest building in the square. During the months when school is in session, tours depart Monday to Friday at 11am and 3pm from Byerly Hall, across Garden Street from Cambridge Common, in the Radcliffe Yard. Additionally, both the University Admissions Office and Information Center conduct tours daily. Saturday tours leave from the Information Center at 2pm. Summer tours are at 10am and 2pm Monday through Saturday, all from the Information Center. The tours last about one hour and are free.

Harvard University Museums of Natural History

On Oxford Street, this is the largest and most varied of the museums at Harvard. To get there, ask your way to the Science Center and Memorial Hall, then walk between these buildings to get to Oxford Street; walk north on Oxford, and the third building on your right is the **University Museum** (tel. 495-1910), open from 9am to 4:30pm Monday through Saturday, and 1 to 4:30pm on Sunday. Admission costs $3 for adults, $2 for seniors and students, $1 for kids 5 to 15 years old.

Actually, the huge and rambling University Museum building houses four museums in one. Here are the high points of each:

Botanical Museum: The world-famous collection of glass flowers is the big attraction here. The incredibly delicate and detailed glass replicas of flowers that grow all over the world were made in the days before color photography allowed a botanist to make teaching aids easily and cheaply with only a camera. The variety of "flowers" on view and the craftsmanship that it took to make them are truly amazing.

The Botanical Museum has other displays and dioramas on the stair landing as you enter the University Museum. These change from time to time, but may include such things as an exhibit of cross-breeding in the cultivation of corn, or the various narcotic substances used by primitive peoples in different parts of the world.

Museum of Comparative Zoology: Despite its forbidding name, this museum is a favorite with children, for it's loaded with stuffed animals of all kinds, from a tiny hummingbird to a towering giraffe. Sharks, ostriches, hippopotamuses and zebras abound, as do the exotic beasts from exotic places: tapirs, lemurs, quetzals, and aardvarks. The museum is a product of the 19th-century rage for natural history, which sent Harvard men all over the world in search of specimens to use in scientific teaching. Don't miss the full-size whale skeletons, in the same high-ceilinged room that houses the giraffe.

Peabody Museum of Archeology and Ethnology: The collections here were gathered by adventurers, explorers, archeologists, and scholars. The museum's strong suit is the indigenous peoples of North America; its great hall of the North American Indian reopened in 1990 after having been closed for ten years. The Mayan civilization is particularly well represented, with statues (authentic as well as fiberglass copies), wall-size photographs of jungle scenes, copies of the giant stelae and zoomorphs from Quirigua, Guatemala, and Copan, Honduras, gold jewelry, and household artifacts. Notes and extracts from diaries posted here and there give you an idea of what it was like being one of the first archeologists to discover and study these fascinating works of art.

Other exhibits cover the tribal art of Oceania, and 19th-century photographs and objects from Japan. The Peabody Museum Shop is one of Cambridge's most fascinating places. Handcrafts and folk art from all over the world are on display and on sale, at reasonable prices.

Geological and Mineralogical Museum: This museum houses an internationally important collection of rocks, minerals, ores, and meteorites. Exhibits include an unusually comprehensive systematic mineral collection, minerals from New England, gems, and meteorites.

Harvard Art Museums

Harvard University has three major art museums: the Busch-Reisinger, the Fogg, and the Arthur M. Sackler. All three are on Quincy Street. All are open from 10am to 5pm every day except Monday; closed on Monday and major holidays. If you visit the museums on Saturday morning, admission is free. Otherwise you pay $3 ($1.50 for students and seniors) for a ticket that admits you to all three museums on that day. Kids up to 18 get in anytime for free. You can get recorded information on current offerings by dialing 495-9400.

The **Busch-Reisinger Museum** (tel. 495-9400) of central and northern Euro-

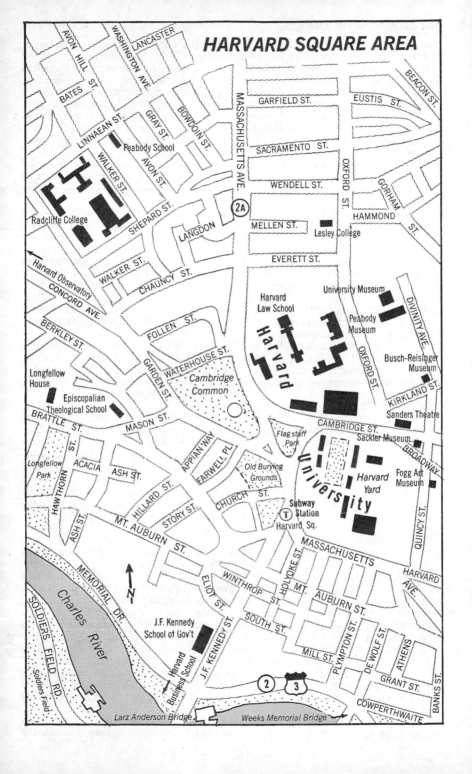

pean art used to be housed in Adolphus Busch Hall, a little Teutonic gem of a building complete with clock tower, just north of Memorial Hall, at the corner of Quincy and Kirkland Streets. However, as of this writing a brand-new museum, Berner Otto Hall, is being constructed adjoining the Fogg Art Museum (see below), with completion foreseen by 1992. Adolphus Busch Hall is open occasionally while it undergoes restoration. It continues as a gallery for medieval sculpture, plaster casts, and architectural fragments. The museum's famous Flentrop organ will remain in the building's Romanesque Hall, as will the full-size replica of the "Golden Gate," or main portal, of the cathedral of Freiburg, but the collections of the Busch-Reisinger Museum will be moved to the new building.

While the new museum building is under construction, major works from the Busch-Reisinger collection will be on view in a special gallery in the Fogg. Go here to see the museum's famous works by Kokoschka, Klimt, Kandinsky, Klee, Max Beckmann, and others.

The **Fogg Art Museum** ranks as one of the more important collections of painting and sculpture in the Boston area. Founded in 1891, the Fogg has long served as the center of art study at Harvard. The Fogg is on Quincy Street between Harvard Street and Broadway, east of Harvard Yard. As you enter, the mood for your visit to the galleries is set by the interior court, copied in Italian travertine from an Italian building. Sometimes exhibits are set up in the court; during the academic year concerts are given here most Tuesday afternoons—ask at the desk for a schedule. The museum's permanent collections include a fine collection of English silver, drawings, photographs; Italian, Dutch, and American art; and 19th- and 20th-century Parisian art. Shows of other works from the museum's holdings are set up periodically, and are very well done.

The **Arthur M. Sackler Museum** is Harvard's newest art museum, opened late in 1985. Housed here are the university's collections of ancient, Oriental, and Islamic art, including the world's most extensive collection of ancient Chinese jades, plus important collections of Persian miniatures and Japanese prints.

A Walking Tour

The Cambridge Historical Commission and Cambridge Discovery sponsor walking tours of Old Cambridge four times daily from late June through Labor Day. Call **Cambridge Discovery** (tel. 491-6278) for details. If you'd rather do the tour on your own, pick up a copy of the fine little brochure called the "Old Cambridge Walking Guide" ($1). The brochure has a map and a description of the 30 sights and buildings to be seen along the walk, each marked with a sign giving the place's name and the number corresponding to it in the brochure. You could walk through the tour route in about an hour if you didn't stop to look closely at any one place, but it's best to plan at least a few hours, for you'll want to visit some of the buildings.

The Longfellow House

Those interested in 19th-century Cambridge will want to see this house at 105 Brattle St., which is now a National Historic Site (open from 10am to 4:30pm daily; $3 admission; kids 16 and under, free). Although the house was built by one Major John Vassall in 1759, and was for a time Washington's headquarters (he and Martha celebrated their 17th wedding anniversary here), most of the furnishings are left from the time of Henry Wadsworth Longfellow, who lived here for 45 years. Mrs. Andrew Craigie took in boarders (mostly Harvard professors), and Longfellow was one, starting in 1837. Soon after he and Fanny Appleton were married, Fanny's father bought the house for the young married couple, and the poet lived here until his death in 1882. Virtually all of his belongings and furnishings are still here, as he left them when he died, for the house was occupied by his descendants until the early 1970s. It's an elegant and beautiful house, and yet still warm and homey, a treat to walk through. The National Park Service guides who take you through are friendly and knowledgeable.

Longfellow House sponsors concerts every two weeks on Sunday afternoons in summer, on the lawn, free, and open to the public. Other special events include the

February birthday anniversary celebration, and the Christmas open house. For exact information on dates, times, and programs, call 876-4491.

Theater

The touchstone of theater in Cambridge is Harvard's **Loeb Drama Center**, 64 Brattle St., corner of Hilliard (tel. 547-8300), home of the American Repertory Theater. This resident professional company performs a variety of works year round in a rotating repertory. For six weeks in the autumn and spring, the ART steps aside as Harvard/Radcliffe undergraduates take the stage.

The **Tufts Arena Theater** (tel. 381-3493), on the Tufts University campus in Medford, has lots and lots of plays both winter and summer. From Harvard Square, take a no. 96 ("Medford Square") bus, and get off at Talbot Avenue; walk up Talbot about a block, and the theater is on the left, behind the chemistry building.

The other outstanding college theater in the area is not really in either Cambridge or Boston. It's the **Spingold Theater** (tel. 894-4343), on the campus of Brandeis University in suburban Waltham. It's best to have a car for this one, since it's a long haul by public transport unless you catch the MBTA Commuter Rail train from North Station in Boston or Porter Square in Cambridge to Roberts Station/ Brandeis University.

Cinema

Although Boston has a lively movie nightlife, Cambridge has its own group of theaters, many of which tend to be slightly more "far out" than some of the mass-market houses downtown. If you're staying in Boston but want to go to a cinema in Cambridge, the Red Line to Central (for Central Square) or Harvard (for Harvard Square) will take you within an easy walk of the house you're looking for. Here are Cambridge's major film houses:

Brattle Theater, 40 Brattle St. (tel. 876-6837), one longish block from the Harvard subway station, specializes in nostalgia and American and foreign classics.

Central, 425 Massachusetts Ave. near Central Square (tel. 864-0426), features a mixed bag for the MIT clientele so near at hand.

Janus, 57 John F. Kennedy St. (tel. 661-3737), two blocks from the Harvard subway station down toward the river, usually has one of the hotter big films of the season, playing to a packed house until it gives out (the film, not the house).

Harvard Square, 10 Church St. (tel. 864-4580), is right in the square. The most popular films with the college crowd that have been released in the past few years are repeated at intervals of a few weeks; this is where you go to see it if you missed it two or three years ago, or didn't want to pay the high price when it was a hit. Seats are low-priced, especially before 6pm (call for exact times). There are also two other auditoriums for first-run showings.

Free Films: Get hold of a copy of the Harvard *Gazette* (free) from the Harvard University Information Office (tel. 495-1000), Holyoke Center, just across the street from the subway station in Harvard Square. The *Gazette,* published only when Harvard is in its fall and spring semesters, lists all the university activities, including quite a few films for free or for a very low price.

Jazz Clubs

The big names show up in the plush atmosphere of the **Regattabar** at the Charles Hotel (tel. 864-1200), in the complex called Charles Square, off Eliot and Mount Auburn Streets just steps from Harvard Square. The club has hosted Stephane Grappelli, Ahmad Jamal, the Ritz, and many other big names, at prices ranging from $15 to $30, parking in the hotel's garage included. You can book through CONCERTIX (tel. 617/876-7777) for an additional fee. Warning: the big names produce big crowds, and if you don't reserve seats in advance, you may have to wait in line for standing-room-only tickets—and you may not even get those.

2. Lexington

Lexington was the home of the first minutemen to die from British bullets in the Revolutionary War. Although they were not the first Americans to die for their country (victims of the Boston Massacre hold that honor), nor even the first to offer spirited resistance as the minutemen of Concord did, the eight minutemen who fell on Lexington Green served their country well. For without the battle at Lexington, the Concord minutemen might not have been determined to offer strong resistance to the British force.

Americans in the colonies had always had virtually total control over their own destinies, and so when the government in London tried to levy taxes of which the colonists did not approve, their anger was aroused. To show who was boss, the government sent troops from England and quartered them in the homes of the colonists, further stirring up their anger. As it looked more and more likely that a head-on collision might occur, the colonists, led by Samuel Adams and John Hancock, began stockpiling arms and ammunition, especially cannons. Hearing rumors of these stockpiles, General Gage, the British commander in Boston, prepared to send out a body of troops to scour the countryside and destroy the stockpiles so as to nip any armed resistance to London in the bud. But the colonists' spy network found out about the plan, and as the troops mustered late at night in preparation for the expedition, Paul Revere and William Dawes galloped through the darkness to alert the patriots.

The "alarm system" was so efficient that the Lexington minutemen, led by Captain John Parker, turned out shortly after Revere arrived at midnight, but there were no British troops in sight. The patriots returned home or retired to the Buckman Tavern near Lexington Green, ready to appear again the minute they heard the sound of the drum.

About daybreak the British column finally arrived in Lexington, and the 100-or-so minutemen drew themselves up in soldierly order on the Green. Nobody knew what would happen. The Minutemen knew only that a much larger force of some 600 soldiers was coming to search their homes, and although it would have been folly to try to stop them, they could still show that they didn't like it and perhaps worry the British a little. The British soldiers knew only that men with rifles were waiting in a position of defiance to keep the soldiers from doing their duty. When the forces finally came face to face at Lexington Green, officers on both sides seemed to think it would be just as well if everybody kept calm—everybody had a lot to lose—and not a shot was fired. Captain Parker, perhaps fearing capture of his men, ordered them to disperse peaceably; but this only encouraged the British to try and round them up, and some of the soldiers took after the minutemen. Somehow the running added a sense of alarm to the situation, and a shot rang out. Whether it was a patriot defending himself and his friends, or a British soldier "out to get the rebels" and excited by the chase, the identity of the man who fired the first shot is still a mystery. But other shots followed, of course, and soon eight minutemen lay dead, and ten others were wounded.

The "battle" was more like a troop riot, and once the British officers regained control of their troops, they started marching them out of town. The minutemen took their wounded to Buckman Tavern to treat them. It all took less than a half hour. Word was rushed to Concord, where minutemen assembled for the later events of the day, knowing that they might be the next martyrs.

GETTING THERE

The National Park Service has organized most of the interesting historical sites in Lexington and Concord into **Minuteman National Historical Park,** and those with their own car can pick up the Park Service's *Minute Man* brochure, which has a sketch map of Battle Road and most of the sights to see. Coming from Boston in a car, take U.S. 3 to Mass. 2, then a road with two route numbers, 4/225, into the center of Lexington. An alternative route subject to tolls is the Mass. Pike west to Rte. 128, exiting at Exit 44, "Bedford Street," for Lexington.

Public transportation to Lexington is good, but note that it is not possible to go directly from Lexington to Concord by public transportation. To Lexington, the easiest way is bus no. 528, "Hanscom Field–Harvard," which leaves Harvard Square on the 45-minute ride every hour during the day, every half hour during rush periods (no night or Sunday service). An alternative route is a commuter train from North Station to Waltham (every 20 minutes during rush hours, every 1¼ hours during the day, every hour in the evening, every two hours or more on weekends), and then bus no. 525, "Lexington-Waltham," to your destination—buses run every hour during the day (no evening or Sunday service).

WHERE TO STAY

Although Lexington will most likely be a day trip for you, here is a lodging suggestion in case your itinerary indicates a night in the minutemen's town.

Whether driving or busing, the **Battle Green Motor Inn** is a convenient place to stay, only a few blocks from Lexington Green at 1720 Massachusetts Ave., Lexington, MA 02173 (tel. 617/862-6100, or toll free 800/343-0235, 800/322-1066 in Massachusetts). The 96 units here are modern and comfortable, grouped around a long central court dotted with young trees and potted plants. Rooms have color TV, HBO, and air conditioning, and you can park your car in a covered lot free of charge. Rates are $62 to $65 for a double or queen-size bed (one or two persons), $71 for two beds. From the inn you can easily walk to the Green and to all the historic sites.

WHERE TO DINE

Lexington has a small selection of restaurants, many good for breakfast or a sandwich. **Brigham's,** about three blocks from the Green on Massachusetts Avenue in the main shopping district, is the local incarnation of the chain that has stores all over Boston and Cambridge. Ice cream, breakfasts, and sandwiches are their forte; any of these will be in the $3 to $5 range. **Baskin-Robbins,** an ice cream and sandwich place, has similar values.

The best value in a full restaurant is, believe it or not, Chinese. It's the **Peking Garden,** 27 Waltham St., several doors down from the intersection of Massachusetts Avenue and Waltham Street (tel. 617/862-1051), again right in the main shopping district. The cuisine is Mandarin and Szechuan; the hours are Sunday through Thursday from 11:30am to 9:30pm, on Friday and Saturday to 10:30pm; and the special bonus is the Chinese buffet served Monday through Thursday evening from 6 to 9pm—all you can eat for $10.50 (children under 10, $6), and the food is delicious and varied. Two or more can order the Special House Dinner at other times ($14 per person), and receive a varied and bounteous selection of dishes. Besides the evening buffet, the Peking Garden hosts a luncheon buffet Monday through Friday from 11:30am to 2:30pm—all you can eat for an astoundingly low $5.25. Wine, beer, and drinks are served. Special Mandarin dim sum is served every Saturday and Sunday from 11:30am to 2pm.

WHAT TO SEE

When you approach Battle Green and come up to the Minuteman statue (erected in 1900), you'll feel the great historic significance of the spot. Battle Green is really where it all began: the ivy-covered monument on the southwest part of the Green marks the burial spot of seven of the eight minutemen killed on the memorable day, April 19, 1775. The boulder that sits incongruously on the soft grass of the Green marks the place where the minutemen drew up in a double rank to face the British grenadiers.

The Lexington Village Green looked much different then than it does today. The meetinghouse, or town church, was located near where the Minuteman statue

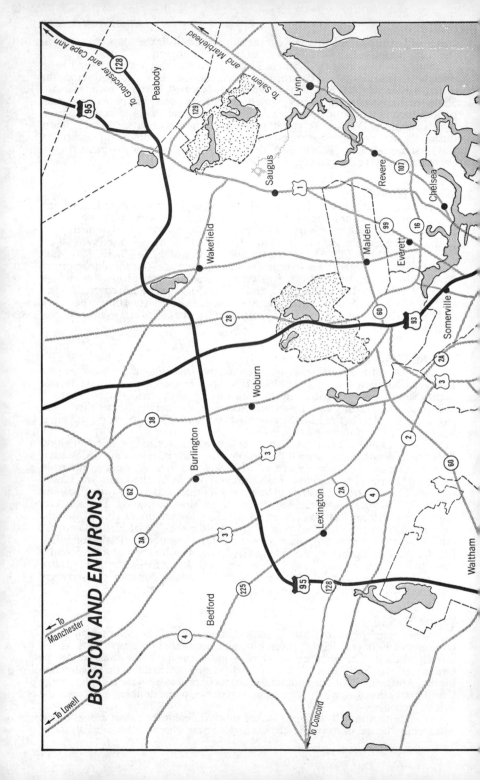

BOSTON AND ENVIRONS

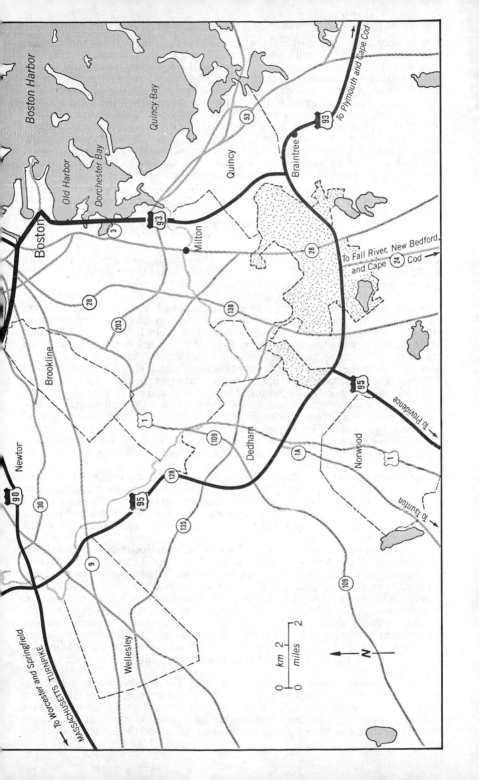

stands; since it was mid-April, and the Green was in the center of town traffic, it may have been pretty muddy rather than "green." The best time to visit Lexington's historic sights is, of course, on April 19, when the townfolk reenact the famous confrontation with festivities, musketry drill, and fife-and-drum corps. But any day after April 19, until the end of October, will do instead. Note that most of the happenings and places mentioned below are closed between November 1 and April 18.

First thing to do is to go to the **Chamber of Commerce Visitors' Center,** 1875 Massachusetts Ave. (tel. 617/862-1450), just off the Green near the Minuteman statue and next door to Buckman Tavern. Here, every day between the hours of 9am and 5pm (10am and 4pm in winter), you can pick up a sketch map of the town, and brochures and information on the sights. More important, you can inspect the diorama, or scale model, of the Battle Green and the events of April 19, 1775: the minutemen in their farmers' clothes scattering before the long files of crack troops dressed in brilliant colors. The diorama is well worth seeing (it's free, too); historical accounts and explanations of the battle accompany the display.

Besides the Battle Green, several early buildings figured significantly in the battle, and they are today maintained by the Lexington Historical Society, P.O. Box 514, Lexington, MA 02173 (tel. 617/861-0928). All three are open mid-April through October 31, and each tour costs $2.50 for adults, 50¢ for children 6 to 16 (children under 6 enter for free); an adult combination ticket good for all three houses is on sale at Buckman Tavern gift shop for $5.

Of the houses, **Buckman Tavern** (1709) is the most important. Here, in the taproom, many of the minutemen waited out the time between that first midnight call to muster and the final arrival of the British forces at daybreak. After the battle, the wounded were brought here and laid out on the tables for treatment. The tours are given by young ladies well versed in their subject, which not only encompasses the events of the battle, but ranges much more widely, covering a great number of topics on life in the colonies at the time of the Revolution. They'll tell you about the construction of the tavern; about the people who came there to stay, or to have a drink, or for a reception or tea; what and how they ate and drank, how they cooked, slept, and kept warm in unheated rooms. The tavern has an excellent collection of utensils, tools, and implements from the period, "time- and labor-saving devices" that show a good deal of Yankee ingenuity. The tour is well worth the price of admission. The tavern is located opposite the Common, has a gift shop, and is open from 10am to 5pm daily except Sunday, when the hours are 1 to 5pm; in high summer, the hours are extended to 8pm.

The **Munroe Tavern** (1695) was to the British what Buckman Tavern was to the Colonials: a headquarters and a place to care for the wounded after the battle. Today it's furnished with antiques and battle mementos, and is open to the public on the same basis as Buckman Tavern. It's a walk (or a short drive) from Battle Green, about seven blocks southeast along Massachusetts Avenue, at no. 1332; the tavern will be on your right.

The third significant house is the **Hancock-Clarke House** (1698), which was the parsonage of the Reverend Jonas Clarke at the time of the battle, and it was with Clarke that John Hancock and Sam Adams, the two "rabble-rousers" most wanted by the British authorities, hid themselves during the uncertain days before the battle. Clarke's house was the first place Paul Revere headed for when he heard of the British plan to march out into the countryside. Revere actually came to Clarke's house twice to warn Adams and Hancock: on April 15, just after hearing that the British were about to do something, and again on April 18, the night the British troops moved out. Hancock-Clarke House is open at the same times and with the same admission fees as Buckman Tavern. It's located at 36 Hancock St., only about a block north of Battle Green.

Several other sights in Lexington are worth a look. Gravestone-rubbers will want to head for **Ye Olde Burying Ground,** just off Battle Green by the church, on its western side. The oldest stone dates from 1690. Another way to get into the spirit of the day of battle is to visit **Cary Memorial Hall,** several blocks southeast of the Green along Massachusetts Avenue, between the town offices and the police station. Here you can see Sandham's famous painting *The Battle of Lexington,* and also statues of John Hancock and Samuel Adams.

Lexington has an ultramodern gallery for historical displays of Americana, the **Museum of Our National Heritage.** Built by the Scottish Rite Masons in 1975, there are four galleries exhibiting photograph collections, documents, artifacts, and works of art and industry. Lectures and films are scheduled frequently as well. A recently installed exhibit entitled "Let It Begin Here: Lexington and the Revolution," explains the town's crucial role in the American quest for independence. Call for details of current exhibits. The museum is at 33 Marrett Rd. (tel. 617/861-6559), near the intersection of Rtes. 2A and 4/225, a short way from the center of Lexington on the road to Boston. It's open Monday through Saturday from 10am to 5pm, on Sunday from noon to 5pm. Admission and parking are free.

---

3. Concord

Concord today is a Boston suburb. It is a beautiful town filled with tall, old trees, graceful houses and mansions, and a rich history that goes beyond the events of the Revolution. Besides the historical sites encompassed by Minuteman National Historical Park, Concord offers a look at the lives and times of America's great 19th-century writers and philosophers: Emerson, Thoreau, Hawthorne, and Louisa May and Bronson Alcott.

GETTING THERE

Those with their own cars should come via Lexington along Rte. 2A, following the signs reading "Battle Road." Along this route passed the British troops going out to Concord to search for arms stockpiled illegally by the colonials. A Visitors' Center has been set up a short distance past the intersection of Rtes. 2A and 128, and this is the place to get a map and brochure of Battle Road.

By public transportation, there's no way to go along Battle Road unless you're in a sight-seeing tour bus. But train service between Boston and Concord is quite good.

By Train

On weekdays, 20 trains a day leave Boston's North Station for the 40-minute trip to Concord; on Saturday there are 12 trains, and on Sunday, 8. The train can also be boarded at Porter Square in Cambridge (go north on Massachusetts Avenue from Harvard Square for about a mile, and the station is next to the shopping center, under the iron bridge). Call 617/722-3200 for the latest detailed schedule information. The train arrives at Concord's Depot, which is about five blocks from Monument Square.

WHERE TO STAY

What there is to see in Concord can be seen in a day, but the town is very fine, and you may want to spend the night.

The nicest place to stay is the **Hawthorne Inn,** 462 Lexington Rd., Concord, MA 01742 (tel. 508/369-5610), directly across the road from "The Wayside," Nathaniel Hawthorne's house. The location, although a mile or two from the town center, is convenient to Orchard House, the Alcotts' home, as well. Single rooms cost $82 to $104, and doubles are $104 to $165, tax and continental breakfast (with home-baked goods and fresh fruit) included. An extra person costs $21. The inn has pleasant gardens with a tiny fountain, and rooms decorated with period pieces, antique beds, original works of art, and nice homey touches like hooked rugs. Only seven rooms here, so reserve early.

Right on the town green in Concord is the **Colonial Inn,** 48 Monument Square, Concord, MA 01742 (tel. 508/369-9200). Although the main building of the inn dates back to 1716, and is therefore a smallish, colonial-size hostelry, several new and modern additions have been unobtrusively added, giving the inn a total of 60 rooms. Only 12 original rooms are available to guests, and these are the ones most in demand. If you call or write ahead for reservations, you might ask for one of these, and the manager will do his best to put you in one, but he cannot guarantee any given room to any given guest. Rooms in the main inn, mostly with bath, cost $106 to $132 single or double; in the Prescott Wing, where rooms have bath and individually controlled air conditioning, prices are $121 to $148 single or double for some rooms, more for a suite with parlor. A special weekend rate is sometimes offered. Housekeeping rooms are also available should you be planning to stay a while.

WHERE TO DINE

Everybody can find a suitable place to have a meal in Concord, no matter what his or her budget.

For my taste, the nicest place to dine in Concord is at **A Different Drummer,** 86 Thoreau St. (tel. 508/369-8700), upstairs in the Concord train depot, about five blocks from the town green (Monument Square). The decor is modern, Scandinavian inspired, with primary colors matched by plain white, and accents in smooth-finished wood and rough boards. Lunch is always a good value, while dinner is more elegant and moderately expensive. The daily luncheon specials might include chicken teriyaki, oysters Rockefeller, or lemon chicken. At dinner, feast on freshly shucked clams or oysters for an appetizer, then have chicken Amaretto, veal with prosciutto in a marsala sauce, or bay scallops in white wine with leeks and tomatoes. With dessert, coffee, wine, tax, and tip, a four-course dinner will be about $25 or $30 per person; a good lunch can be had for only $10 or $12. A Different Drummer is open every day in summer for lunch (11:30am to 3pm) and dinner (5 to 9:30pm). On Sunday, brunch replaces lunch, and dinner is served from 4:30 to 8:30pm.

WHAT TO SEE

Begin your walk around Concord at the town green, officially called Monument Square, complete with obelisk inscribed "Faithful Unto Death." The little church facing Main Street, **St. Bernard's** (Roman Catholic), is particularly pretty when seen from a short distance down Main Street. Of the other buildings on the green, the most historically noteworthy is the **Wright Tavern,** which, being right on the road from Boston, was one of the first places the British stopped to search for arms. Several shops and firms' offices are located in the tavern today, and you're welcome to walk in and look around during business hours. The **Concord Chamber of Commerce** (tel. 508/369-3120) operates an information booth on Heywood Street, one long block southeast of Monument Square, just off Rte. 2A, the road to Lexington and Cambridge. It's open on weekends, mid-April through May, and every day from June through October, from 9am to 4:30pm. They have brochures and maps. Also, you can ask questions at the front desk of the Colonial Inn on Monument Square.

Minuteman National Historic Park

The park encompasses many of the most important sites having to do with the first Revolutionary War battle at Concord. There's a Visitors Center located in the Buttrick Mansion, north of the center of Concord, on the other side of North Bridge. A large parking lot near North Bridge is often full during the summer, and if you have a good parking spot in town, and a few extra minutes, walk the half mile to the bridge and admire Concord's lovely old houses as you go.

After the events in Lexington, the British officers headed their men quickly off to Concord, afraid—no, certain—that since shots had been fired and men killed, there'd be a great deal more trouble coming. Of course, the minutemen in Concord knew of the Lexington battle shortly after it happened and long before the British troops arrived at 7am. The minutemen kept an eye on the British as they entered the town, waiting for whatever was to happen. When a force of regulars was sent to stand guard over Concord's North Bridge, the minutemen retreated before them, crossing the bridge and taking up a position on a hilltop nearby, where they awaited reinforcements from nearby towns.

Meanwhile, in Concord a polite and not-too-thorough search was being carried out; some arms were found, in particular a number of gun carriages, which were brought out and burned. The minutemen saw the smoke, assumed the British were burning the town, and began to advance in revenge. The regulars retreated across the bridge and began firing at the minutemen, who fired back and pursued them until they fled. It was here at the North Bridge, then, that the minutemen fired the "shot heard 'round the world."

Soon afterward the British troops began the return to Boston, but minutemen kept up a constant sniper fire on them all the way back to Boston, which enraged the regulars and goaded them to murder some of the innocent persons they met along the way of their march. The bitterness left on both sides by the events of April 19, 1775, would soon bring war to all the British colonies in North America.

Walk across the placid Concord River on the Old North Bridge (a modern reproduction of the kind of bridge that spanned the river in colonial times), and it is easy to imagine, even to half see, the way things happened on the day of the battle. At the far (western) end of the bridge is Daniel Chester French's famous Minuteman statue, the pediment inscribed with Emerson's famous poem. On the near (east) side of the bridge, take a look also at the plaque on the stone wall commemorating the British soldiers who died in the Revolutionary War.

The Old Manse

After visiting the bridge and the Visitor Center on the far side, turn back toward town. Right next to North Bridge, slightly nearer to the center of town, is the Old Manse (tel. 508/369-3909), Concord's most famous house. It was built in 1769 by the Reverend William Emerson and was lived in by his descendants for 169 years, except for a three-year period when young Nathaniel Hawthorne and his bride, Sophia, lived here. Hawthorne's residence here gave him material for several later stories. The house today is filled with the spirit and the mementoes of their short stay, and those of the Emerson clan. Admission—$3 for adults, $2.50 for seniors, $1.50 for ages 6 to 16—includes a guided tour. The Old Manse is open June 1 to October 31 every day except Tuesday and Wednesday from 10am to 4:30pm (on Sunday and holidays from 1 to 4:30pm). Open weekends only, mid-April to June.

Transcendentalist Associations

Concord was the center of a philosophical and social movement that, although small in scope, had important effects on American thought and literature. Emerson, Thoreau, Bronson Alcott, and others were all friends living in Concord from about 1836 to 1860. They were aware of the philosophical upheaval going on in Europe at this time, and were encouraged to break away from the Unitarianism that had been their belief. Although they never published a manifesto detailing their beliefs, their creed at this time was that each person has a part of God within himself, and by being sensitive to the dictates of that part, can do what is good and right. Nature had a large share in this belief as well, for the Transcendentalists thought true harmony in life could only be achieved by communing closely with nature and coming to understand it. This, perhaps, was the basis for Thoreau's period of retreat at Walden Pond.

The transcendentalists got together and tried out their beliefs by buying a farm and living with nature there (1841–47). The Brook Farm experiment, although it failed, has been an example down to our own times. (The farm was in West Roxbury, now a posh suburb of Boston.) Hawthorne lived on Brook Farm for a while, and he and his friend Herman Melville were both affected by transcendentalism.

The best way to learn about the transcendentalist movement is to read Ralph Waldo Emerson's works. While you're here in Concord, you can visit his house and those in which other adherents of the movement lived, and also go out to Walden Pond and see the place where Thoreau's famous cabin stood. Here, then, are the sights of transcendentalist Concord:

On your way back from the Old Manse, by Old North Bridge, take a detour up the hill, east off Monument Street before you reach the town green, to get to **Sleepy Hollow Cemetery.** Author's Ridge, on top of the hill, has the graves of Hawthorne, Thoreau, the Alcotts, and Emerson. Emerson's grave, you'll notice, is marked by a great uncarved boulder, very natural and without religious symbolism.

Starting from the town green, most of the transcendentalists' homes are east along the Lexington Road (Rte. 2A); Thoreau sites and memorabilia are, appropriately, off by themselves, in another direction.

The **House of Ralph Waldo Emerson,** 28 Cambridge Turnpike, is at the intersection of Lexington Road and Cambridge Turnpike, a ten-minute walk from the green. The house was a center for meetings of Emerson and his friends, and still contains original furniture and Emerson's memorabilia. It's open Thursday through Saturday from 10am to 4:30pm, on Sunday from from 2 to 4:30pm, from mid-April through October. Cost is $3 for adults, $1.50 for children 6 to 17 (children under 6, free).

Across the street from Emerson's house is the **Concord Museum** (tel. 508/369-9609), which transports the visitor back in time to the early 17th century, when the town of Concord was founded. The museum contains numerous period rooms and galleries, and vividly depicts the growth and evolution of Concord. The collections of documented decorative arts and domestic artifacts were either owned by Concord-area residents or made by Concord-area artisans.

Permanent exhibits include the lantern that hung in the spire of the Old North Church in Boston on the night of Revere's famous ride, Ralph Waldo Emerson's study, Henry David Thoreau's belongings used at Walden Pond, and a collection of early powderhorns including the one worn by the model for Daniel Chester French's Minuteman statue at the Old North Bridge. There are changing exhibitions in the French gallery throughout the year.

The museum is open weekdays and Saturday from 10am to 4:30pm, and on Sunday from 1 to 4:30pm (closed all of January). A guided tour lasts about 45 minutes; you can wander around on your own if you like. Admission is $5 for adults, $4 for seniors 65 and older, $3 for students, and $2 for children 15 and under.

Continuing east along the Lexington Road, a short drive will bring you to **Orchard House** (tel. 508/369-4118), home of the Alcotts during the period 1858 to 1877. Bronson Alcott, while he started life as an itinerant gizmo salesman, had as his life's passion the reform of traditional education methods. His open and natural approach to education was not appreciated in cosmopolitan centers like Boston, but was perfectly congenial to transcendentalist Concord. Here he was ultimately commissioned as superintendent of schools, and he opened a "School of Philosophy" in a building in his backyard. The house itself is a must for anyone, especially a child who has read Louisa May Alcott's *Little Women.* It's open April through September 15 from 10am to 4:30pm (on Sunday, holidays, and from September 16 through October, from 1 to 4:30pm); in March and November it's open on weekends from 1 to 4:30pm; closed December through February. Admission (and the requisite tour) costs $4 for adults, $3 for senior citizens, and $2 for kids.

The **Wayside,** 455 Lexington Rd. (tel. 508/369-6975), a mile east of Monument Square and just a few steps east of Orchard House, is actually the house described by Louisa May Alcott in her famous book, although today most of the furnishings are those of Margaret Sidney, who wrote *Five Little Peppers.* Hawthorne also lived here. There's a free audiovisual program, and several exhibits dealing with the house's famous former residents. A 30-minute guided tour costs $1 for adults, but is free to those 16 or under. You can visit the house from mid-April through October, Friday through Tuesday (not on Wednesday or Thursday) from 9:30am to 5:30pm; the last tour starts at 5pm, and tours are limited to ten persons.

Sights dealing with Thoreau's life are west and south of Concord's town green. The **Thoreau Lyceum** (tel. 508/369-5912) is a Thoreau "learning center," which includes a library, museum with artifacts dealing with his life, and a replica of Thoreau's Walden cabin. There is also a bookstore carrying old as well as new books by or about Thoreau. It's at 156 Belknap (pronounced *bell*-nap) St., and is open Monday through Saturday from 10am to 5pm, from 2 to 5pm on Sunday; closed on national holidays (and on Mondays, January through March). Admission is $2.50 for adults, $1 for students, and 50¢ for those in Grades 1 through 8.

You can visit **Walden Pond,** where Thoreau had his hut from 1845 to 1847, by driving out Walden Street (Rte. 126), which leaves the center of Concord from Main Street near the Green. After crossing Rte. 2, look for signs on the right not far from the intersection; park and walk to the site of his hut, marked by a pile of stones. The path circling the lake provides an interesting and refreshing walk; fires and alcoholic beverages are not permitted at any time. The main parking lot by the public beach costs several dollars per carload in summer; the beach itself is free.

In a Canoe on the Concord River

After you've taken the standard walking tour of Concord, see the town again, adventurously, by renting a canoe for a paddle up the Concord River. The **South Bridge Boat House** (tel. 508/369-9438), west of the center of town at 496–502 Main St. (Rte. 62), will rent you a canoe for $6 per hour, $26 per day on weekdays, or $8 per hour, $35 per day on weekends (students get lower rates). In two hours or so you should be able to make your way down to Concord North Bridge and back, depending on the strength of your paddling arms. The grand houses and gardens that grace the riverbanks alternate with patches of field and wild shrubbery to make a serene and lovely landscape. The boat house is open from the beginning of April into November until the first snowstorm.

You've heard of Concord grapes, a variety developed here by Ephraim Bull and now used to make grape juice, jelly, and sweet wines. You might think the **Nashoba Valley Winery,** 100 Wattaquadoc Hill Rd., Bolton, MA 01740 (tel. 508/779-5521), only a dozen miles west of Concord, would use Concord grapes. But you're in for a delightful surprise. Nashoba pursues the old New England tradition of making delicious wines from fruits other than grapes: apples, peaches, pears, blueberries, cranberries. They've taken this art one step further, and now make premium varietal dry table wines from fruit. I can attest that the wines are intriguing, satisfying, and delightful. The tart, dry Cranberry-Apple goes especially well with Thanksgiving turkey, and the After Dinner Peach has an exquisite sweet-dryness like good sauterne. Clear your palate and drop in for a free tasting any day of the week, until 6pm. Winery tours are conducted on Friday, Saturday, and Sunday from 11am to 5:30pm. Leave time for a self-guided walking tour through the orchards, with a picnic at one of the tables, all of which enjoy fine country views. June through October, come out and "pick-your-own" fruit.

To get there, take Rte. 62 west from Concord through Maynard to Stow, then Rte. 117 west to Bolton, just west of I-495 (exit 27). Take Rte. 117 west to the blinking yellow light in the center of Bolton. Turn left onto Wattaquadoc Hill Road; the winery is a quarter of a mile up the hill, on the left-hand side.

A Side Trip to Longfellow's Wayside Inn

Thirteen miles along the Sudbury Road (which starts from Main Street in Concord) and U.S. 20 West will bring you to the Wayside Inn (1700), South Sudbury, MA 01776 (tel. 508/443-8846). The inn was made famous by Longfellow's poems telling *Tales from a Wayside Inn,* and now boasts of being the oldest operating inn in the country. Bought by Henry Ford in the early 1920s, it is now a private, nonprofit operation, and all proceeds from the guest rooms and restaurant are put toward its upkeep and restoration. The inn has ten rooms with bath and air conditioning (but no radio or TV), eight twins and two doubles, which rent for $70 single, $86 double. Rooms 1 through 8 are of modern construction and traditional decor; rooms 9 and 10 are in the old, original part of the inn, and are very quaint. These two are the most in demand, particularly from April to December. Should you want to stay at the inn, it's wise to make reservations as far in advance as possible, even a month or two; but if you can't make them, call up in any case and see what vacancies they might have.

There was a fire in the inn around 1955 and it was heavily damaged (as you can see in the old kitchen), but restoration work was done well and the rooms are worth seeing even if you don't plan to stay for the night. A short tour of the inn is available for $1 per person, for free if you drop in for a meal. Lunch is served from 11:30am to 3pm; dinner, from 5:30 to 9pm; Sunday dinner, from noon to 8pm.

Besides the inn itself, you should explore the grounds and surroundings: the beautiful formal garden near the inn, the reconstructed barn across the road, and the **Grist Mill,** a short (15-minute) walk away, farther down the road. The Grist Mill, a pretty and romantic stone building, is a replica of the mills that used to dot the New England rivers and streams. It is in a beautiful spot, with a copse of pines nearby, and although it's not 100% authentic (the mill wheel is made of heavy-gauge steel), it is worth a look and a walk around. The flour ground here is used in the Wayside Inn's kitchens, and is for sale at the inn's shop. By the way, the Martha-Mary Chapel, on the road between the inn and the Grist Mill, is a typically New England meeting-house that Ford had built to be rented out for weddings. The chapel and the Wayside Inn are very popular with wedding parties and honeymooners.

THE MASSACHUSETTS NORTH SHORE

North of Boston are many of the towns that brought great wealth to the Massachusetts Bay area in the 18th and 19th centuries. Ships from these Essex County towns would sail to China and Africa, and return several years later with cargoes so rich that everyone involved in the voyage became wealthy overnight.

The gracious houses and public buildings constructed during this era are still here to be seen, and Salem's museums hold a treasure of mementos and artifacts from the maritime boom. Marblehead and Rockport are still important as yacht harbors and excursion points, but all three towns now make their living primarily from the land: as "bedroom" communities for Boston, and as vacation stops for Bostonians and those who come from farther away.

TELEPHONE NOTES

All the North Shore towns covered in this chapter, including Salem, Gloucester, Rockport, and all of Cape Ann, *except Marblehead,* use the 508 area code. Marblehead is part of the Greater Boston calling area, and uses the Greater Boston area code, 617.

1. Salem

Think of Salem, think of witches. Although the fame of Salem's witch trials has spread around the world, the town's place in New England history comes from its maritime industries—shipbuilding, warehousing, chandlery, and trade. In the late 1700s, ships from Salem sailed the world, many dealing in trade from the Orient, especially spices, silks, and other luxury goods. The wealth of the Indies brought great prosperity to the town, enabling its citizens to build and decorate fine mansions and impressive museums.

As for the witches, it has never been proved that there were any in Salem! The witch-hunt took place in only one year (1692), and the score of people executed met that fate because they would *not* admit to being witches—many of the less courageous "admitted" being witches so that they wouldn't be executed. The whole witch-calling affair reached the point of absurdity and then it fizzled out. Salem would like to forget it all, no doubt, but the rest of the world enjoys remembering this bizarre episode.

Salem today is a pretty town, with many of its old houses (dating back to the 1600s) and 19th-century mansions intact and in good repair. Part of the downtown section has been restored and closed to traffic as a fine pedestrian mall, and more restoration work is in progress. The **Peabody Museum,** the **Custom House** (National Maritime Historic Site), and the **Essex Institute** have brilliant displays of Salem's (and America's) maritime history. And painters, writers, and patrons add an active artistic element to this very cultured city, well worth a day trip.

GETTING THERE

Driving, the best way to Salem (and neighboring Marblehead) is to take the Mystic River Bridge (also called Tobin Bridge) and U.S. 1; when it intersects with Rte. 16, follow 16 toward Revere Bridge and Rte. 1A. Route 1A North becomes Lafayette Street in Salem. (For Marblehead, take Rte. 129 off 1A in Swampscott, and follow it right into Old Town, Marblehead.)

Note: It's only fair to warn you that street and highway signs on the North Shore seem to be particularly bad. Routes are filled with turns, and signs are confusing or missing—you will probably find yourself lost more than once. Resign yourself to stopping and asking the way, not once but several times.

By Bus

Salem is served by MBTA bus no. 450, which leaves from the parking garage next to Haymarket subway station in Boston; the trip, under good traffic conditions, takes 40 minutes. Buses leave every 15 minutes during rush hours, every hour during the day Monday through Saturday, every 90 minutes on Sunday.

By Train

Commuter trains run from Boston's North Station to Salem, Beverly, Gloucester, and Rockport. The trip to Salem takes about 30 minutes; trains run about every 20 minutes during rush hours, every half-hour during the day, every hour at night and on weekends. Call toll free 800/392-6099 for schedules.

Tourist Information

The **Salem Chamber of Commerce,** 32 Derby Square (tel. 508/744-0004), maintains several information booths around the city. The main one is in Riley Plaza, near the station for commuter trains from Boston, open Monday through Saturday from 9am to 5pm, on Sunday from noon to 5pm. The National Park Service maintains a **visitor information center** in the Central Wharf Warehouse on Derby Wharf, in the Salem Maritime National Historic Site. The center is open every day from 10am to 4:30pm. Derby Wharf is just east of Pickering Wharf.

WHERE TO STAY

Luckily for travelers wanting to spend a night in Salem, there are several excellent, moderately priced hotels right in the center of town.

Hotels and Inns

The **Salem Inn,** 7 Summer St., Salem, MA 01970 (tel. 508/741-0680 or toll free 800/446-2995), near the intersection with Essex Street, is only a half block from the Witch House and two blocks from the Peabody Museum. It's a lovely old restored brick mansion with 23 large, beautiful, and comfortable rooms. Rates are $88 to $105 double, or $105 to $110 for a two-room suite with kitchenette, tax included; an extra person pays $11 per night; children pay $8. Rooms have queen- or king-size beds, fireplaces, and telephones. The price differential for rooms depends on plumbing: All rooms have private bathrooms, but the baths for the less expensive rooms are across the hallway from the rooms themselves.

The **Hawthorne Hotel,** "on the Common," 18 Washington Square West, Salem, MA 01970 (tel. 508/744-4080 or toll free 800/833-2008), at the corner of Essex Street and Hawthorne Boulevard, is easy walking distance to all the sights in town. It's a good-size hotel, restored with lots of fine wood paneling, brass chandeliers, and new paint. The lobby and public rooms (including the Tavern and the restaurant, called Nathaniel's) use these elements to achieve a simple but very elegant atmosphere; it's echoed in the rooms with the use of smaller brass chandeliers and wingback chairs. Otherwise, the rooms are modern and decorated in solid colors. Rates are moderate: $87 to $154 single or double, suites for $204, tax included; $22 for each additional person; children under 12 free in their parents' room. In the restaurant (open for breakfast, lunch, and dinner daily), a good luncheon costs $8 to $12, dinner about $30 to $40. The hotel serves traditional Sunday brunch until 2:30pm; there's live entertainment in the Tavern Wednesday through Saturday from 9pm.

Guesthouses

Salem also has several guesthouses charging somewhat less than the inns, but without the inns' central location.

The **Coach House Inn,** 284 Lafayette St., Salem, MA 01970 (tel. 508/744-4092), a 10-minute walk from the center of town, is a large Victorian house built in 1879 by E. Augustus Emmerton, sea captain, merchant, and banker. The Victorian decor (some rooms even have antique fireplaces) has been updated with private bathrooms and color televisions; several rooms have kitchenettes. Doubles range from $66 to $94; the higher prices are for rooms with baths. Continental breakfast is included in the rates.

Those who are traveling in a group of four or six will find the **Stephen Daniels House,** 1 Daniels St., Salem, MA 01970 (tel. 508/744-5709), especially ideal. Smaller parties will enjoy its comforts as well. The house was built in 1667, with a wing added in 1756. It is owned today by Katherine Gill, who has furnished it with antiques of the period and virtually turned it into a time machine which takes you back to the Salem of witch-hunting and sea-captain days. Canopied four-poster beds, walk-in fireplaces hung with pots and kettles, low-beamed ceilings, and a delightful little terrace garden make it a real showpiece. Prices for the rooms are $66 to $88 single, $92 to $100 double, or $146 for four (if you show Mrs. Gill this guidebook). All rooms have private baths, and Continental breakfast is included. Be sure to call or write ahead for reservations.

WHERE TO DINE

Salem has lots of interesting restaurants, large and small. The **Lyceum,** 43 Church St. (tel. 508/745-7665), near the corner of Church and Washington Sts., was once at the center of the city's cultural life, and Alexander Graham Bell, who once lived in Salem, gave the first public demonstration of the telephone in its halls. Today the Lyceum is an attractive restaurant–bar and grill. The menu is heavy with local seafood, plus grilled meats and poultry. Dinner will cost $28 to $40 per person. Sunday brunch (11am to 3pm) is a buffet with its own special menu. In good weather, find your way to the terrace out back in the courtyard.

For Waterfront Dining

The **Chase House,** on Pickering Wharf (tel. 508/744-0000), offers lunch and dinner from 11:30am to 11pm Wednesday through Saturday, and until 10pm Sunday through Tuesday, in summer. All the air-conditioned dining rooms share a nautical motif and a view of the waterfront activity; a nice protected outdoor deck is good for cocktails and light meals. Seafood is the heavy on the Chase's menu, as one might expect. At lunch a filet of fish is $8, and you will spend $12 to $15 for the full meal. Dinner is fancier, and the oysters, scallops, lobster, and varieties of fish will probably tempt you to spend $20 to $28 per person. Kids and seniors get a price cut on some items.

WHAT TO SEE

A number of houses in Salem from the 1600s have been preserved, and are open to public view. But before you visit them, go to the **Salem Witch Museum,** 19½ Washington Square North (tel. 508/744-1692), next to Salem Common at the intersection of Brown Street and Hawthorne Boulevard. The museum's Gothic, church-like building houses an audio-visual re-creation of the witchcraft trials of 1692 using life-size figures, a sound track, and special lighting. It's open every day from 10am to 5pm (to 7pm in July and August). Admission is $3.50 for adults, $2 for students aged 6 to 14, free for kids 5 and under. Shows begin every half-hour.

17th-Century Houses

Visit one or more of the 17th-century houses, as you have the time, to see what life was like in one of the earliest towns in the United States.

Witch House (tel. 508/744-0180), the home of Magistrate Jonathan Corwin, one of the judges in the witch trials, stands at 310½ Essex St., corner of Essex and North Sts. Preliminary examinations of those accused of witchcraft were held in the house, which is now nicely restored. You can visit from mid-March through November, any day from 10am to 4:30pm (until 6pm July through Labor Day). Adults pay $3, children aged 5 to 16 $1.50.

The **House of the Seven Gables,** 54 Turner St. (tel. 508/744-0991), which served as the setting for Nathaniel Hawthorne's novel of the same name, is the centerpiece of a historic site with period gardens on Salem Harbor. The four sites—House of the Seven Gables (1668), Hooper-Hathaway House (1682), Hawthorne's birthplace (c. 1750), and Retire Becket House (1655)—are open July 1 through Labor Day from 9:30am to 5:30pm. Guided tours of the Gables and Hawthorne's birthplace cost $6 for adults, $2.50 for those 6 to 17 years old. During the rest of the year you can visit the House of the Seven Gables from 10am to 4:30pm daily (the Garden Coffee Shop is open from May to October). Parking is free.

For a look at 17th-century Salem, tour **Pioneer Village: Salem in 1630,** Forest River Park, off West Street (tel. 508/745-0525 or 744-1233), a "living history museum" built in 1930 and recently restored. Costumed "interpreters" will guide you through the village, past dug-out houses, wigwams, thatched cottages, and the governor's house, through gardens such as the colonists might have cultivated and past species of animals that they may have raised. Demonstrations of yarn spinning, building, and open-hearth cooking are here to see; you can even learn how to use a matchlock musket. Pioneer Village, adjacent to a beach and picnic area, is open from late May through October, Monday through Saturday from 10am to 5pm, Sunday from 1 to 5pm. Admission is $3.50 for adults, $2.50 for children. Discount tickets are on sale at the House of the Seven Gables.

The Essex Institute

The Essex Institute is a museum and historical society dedicated to the preservation, study, and exhibition of historical works and artifacts dealing with Essex County. The collection of artifacts ranges from rare early newspapers to entire houses, restored and furnished with authentic antiques. Just about anyone who comes to Salem finds something of interest here: The historian of American trade and culture uses the library, nautical buffs want to see the relics of the China trade, those interested in architecture and decoration take the tour through one or more of the institute's half-dozen Salem houses which date as far back as 1684. Children are fascinated by the unique collection of dolls, doll furniture, and toys from earlier times.

There's a lot more here than one can see on a day trip to Salem, but an hour spent in one of the institute's 13 buildings, particularly in the main building at 132–134 Essex St. (tel. 508/744-3390) and the adjoining houses, is a must for any Salem visitor. Here is a list of some of the special collections you can look over: clocks, ceramics, military uniforms and weapons, dolls and toys, glassware, buttons, silver and pewter, lamps and lanterns, sculpture, tools, costumes from earlier centuries, and bits and pieces from the China trade, as well as a very good collection of Massachusetts works of art including paintings and furniture. Several galleries and exhibition rooms have changing shows, so the return visitor should check to see what's new.

The Essex Institute is open in winter on Tuesday through Saturday from 9am to 5pm (November 1 to May 31), on Sunday and holidays from 1 to 5pm. From June 1 to October 31 the institute is open on Monday also. Admission for adults to the museum and library is $3, and $2 to each of the institute's houses; children from 6 to 16 get into the museum for $1.50 and into the houses for $1, seniors for a slight discount. A combination ticket, good for all the buildings, can be bought at $5 for adults, $4 for seniors, $2.50 for children.

Peabody Museum

When a group of Salem sea captains and world travelers formed the East India Marine Society in 1799, their charter included provisions for "a museum in which to house the natural and artificial curiosities" brought back from their worldwide travels. This was the genesis of the Peabody Museum, America's oldest museum in continuous operation.

In 1824 the society and its collections moved to grand new headquarters in East India Marine Hall. Since then, five annexes have been added. The most recent, the highly acclaimed Asian Export Art Wing, is dedicated to decorative art pieces made in Asia for western use from the 14th to 19th centuries.

The museum's other major collections are in New England maritime history; the practical arts and crafts of the East Asian, Pacific Islands, and Native American peoples; and the natural history of Essex County. Maritime collections include portraits of captains, pictures of ships, scale models, figureheads, old navigation instruments and tools, scrimshaw, prints, and gear from the whaling era, plus porcelain, paintings, furniture, and silver from Salem's China trade. There's even a reproduction of the saloon (main cabin) of America's first oceangoing yacht, *Cleopatra's Barge,* built in 1816 by a member of the East India Marine Society. The Ethnology Department has superb collections of objects from everyday life in primitive Polynesia, Micronesia, and Melanesia. A similar collection from preindustrial Japan is rated the best in the world.

The Peabody charges adults $5 for admission, half price for children 6 to 16, $4 for seniors and students with an ID card. It's open daily from 10am to 5pm (Thursday evening till 9pm), on Sunday from noon to 5pm, with a free guided tour at 2pm daily. Look for the Peabody on the Essex Street pedestrian mall, at the corner of New Liberty Street.

Salem Maritime National Historic Site

In 1937 the National Park Service took over the **Custom House** (tel. 508/744-4323), where Nathaniel Hawthorne once worked, and nearby Derby Wharf, one of the city's busiest trade centers, as a basis for the Maritime Site. First thing to do is to pick up free copies of the National Park Service's materials about the site, which have a sketch map and directory of the buildings as well as short histories of the prominent Derby merchant family and of the adventures of several famous Salem vessels, both merchantmen and privateers. These accounts are very well written, and are just the thing to get you in the mood for a tour of the Custom House, wharves, and warehouses. The Custom House is open from 8:30am to 5pm every day (except Thanksgiving, Christmas, and New Year's Day). Admission is free.

The National Park Service guides are very well informed, as usual, and daily in July and August will take you on a tour back to the Bonded Warehouse to show you what cargoes were like and how they were handled, measured, and weighed. **Derby House,** built for the shipping magnate Elias Derby by his father, Capt. Richard Derby, in 1762, is shown by a free guided tour April through December between 11am and 1pm. The West India Goods Store, right next to Derby House, is again open for business and selling teas, coffee (beans and brew), spices, and other treasures from the East.

For the Children

Something for the children? Follow Derby Street out of the center of town northeast to **Salem Willows Amusement Park.** If you are pressed for time, take the **Salem Trolley,** a re-created old-time vehicle which makes tours of the town and stops at Salem Willows every day between 10am and 4pm on the half hour. Tours leave from Riley Plaza; you can buy tickets on board the trolley.

Another sure favorite with kids, and even more elaborate than the Salem Witch Museum, is the **Witch Dungeon,** 16 Lynde St., near Washington Street (tel. 744-9812), just half a block from the western end of East India Marine Mall. Reenactments of a witch trial, a re-created dungeon, and a replica of Old Salem Village are among the exhibits. It's open daily from 10am to 5pm.

---

2. Marblehead

What Salem was to merchantmen a century ago, Marblehead is to yachts today. Summer and winter, the beautiful, perfectly sheltered harbor is full of white boats bobbing on the water, or in drydock, or heading out to sea. But it's not only yachters who come to Marblehead. This is without doubt one of the prettiest and best-kept towns in the country, and people love to come up from Boston on the weekend just to walk the streets and window-shop, or have a bowl of chowder in one of several good restaurants. They also come for a look at *The Spirit of '76,* the famous painting made even more famous during the Bicentennial celebrations, which is hung in Abbot Hall, Marblehead's Town Hall. If you plan to go to Salem, make the detour to Marblehead for at least an hour or two, or for a meal or even overnight.

GETTING THERE

The trip by bus between Marblehead and Boston means a transfer at Lynn. The commuter trains between Boston and Salem (see section 1, on Salem) stop at Lynn, and buses 441 and 442 run between Marblehead and Lynn's Central Square about every half hour during rush hours, every hour other times, but note that only bus 442 runs in the evening and on Sunday. The trip between Lynn and Marblehead takes about 25 minutes.

WHERE TO STAY

Should you really want to get into the spirit and soul of this beautiful seacoast town, you'll have to spend the night. Possibilities are limited, but very attractive. I suggest that you try to plan your visit for a weekday, and that you call ahead for reservations, especially in July and August.

The foremost place to stay is the **Harbor Light Inn,** 58 Washington St., Marblehead, MA 01945 (tel. 617/631-2186), between Pearl and Pickett streets, an 18th-century Marblehead house right in the center of the Historic District. The house is pretty from the outside, but even better inside. Each of the ten guest rooms has either a four-poster or a canopy queen-size bed; some have views of the harbor, some have television sets. One room has its own large private deck with a fine view, others have working fireplaces, and all have antique furniture and modern private baths. The three suites are large, with canopy bed, fireplace, and Jacuzzi. Prices range from $75 to $110, with suites renting for $135 to $160, plus tax. Free morning coffee is included. There's a beautiful formal parlor, and an observation deck on the roof. Here you're only steps from shopping and two blocks from the waterfront. To find the inn, drive along Washington Street all the way into the historic district, until you see the yellow Old Town Hall perched on its own little "island" in the middle of the road. Just behind the town hall is the corner of State Street, and just beyond that, on Washington, is the inn.

Another of Marblehead's good places to stay is the **Pleasant Manor Inn,** 264 Pleasant St. (Rte. 114), Marblehead, MA 01945 (tel. 617/631-5843). This grand Victorian mansion has been converted into a charming inn with 14 high-ceilinged guest rooms, a nice lawn, lots of parking, and a tennis court for guests. Several rooms are furnished with four-poster beds and dark-wood trim, and many have air-conditioners and beautiful decorative marble fireplaces; all have private baths and coffee makers, and there's a hall refrigerator for beverages. Rooms do not have TVs, but the antique charm makes up for this. Rates are $61 single, $75 double; an extended Continental breakfast is included. Dick and Takami Phelan, who keep the inn, will be glad to show you the third-floor room where aviatrix Amelia Earhart slept when she visited Marblehead.

The recommendable guesthouse on the waterfront is **The Nautilus,** 68 Front St., Marblehead, MA 01945 (tel. 617/631-1703), run by Ethel Dermody. This small Marblehead house is in great demand because of its waterfront location, so it's advisable to call ahead for reservations, particularly on weekends in summer. Rooms are cozy and homey, and cost $50 single, $66 double, tax included; a cot for an additional person costs $9. Bathrooms are not in the rooms but nearby, and a small fridge is in the hall for guests' use. One or two rooms have sea views. Parking is a problem downtown, but Mrs. Dermody will recommend places without danger of towing or tickets. The Nautilus is right across the street from the Driftwood Restaurant, which is by the municipal parking lot on the water at the end of State Street.

WHERE TO DINE

Marblehead is not particularly rich in good dining places, but you will certainly find a tasty and enjoyable meal here, perhaps even with a view of the harbor.

Without a doubt, Marblehead's most popular place to dine is **Rosalie's,** 18 Sewall St. (tel. 617/631-5353), at the corner of School Street, directly behind the National Grand Bank and not far from the Talbots clothing store and the YMCA. Enter the front door of the unprepossessing three-story brick factory building and climb the stairs to the small bar. Behind the bar booths is a large, high-ceilinged dining room where polite and friendly waiters glide professionally among the small tables. The decorations are eclectic, from 19th-century touches to Roman columns, but the overall effect is upbeat and elegant. There's another dining room at the top of the stairs, with its own kitchen visible at the back, and yet another one in the basement; but the maître d' is near the bar, so go there first. The menu changes daily, but always has various antipasti such as snails and garlic butter in mushroom caps, or shrimp with prosciutto in a mustard-butter sauce. Then comes the pasta (made here): lobster ravioli, canneloni, and fettuccine pomodoro. Main-course dishes include veal, chicken, and shrimp prepared in interesting ways. There's pollo francesca, sautéed chicken breast in a light egg batter, with mushrooms in Grand Marnier; veal marinara with eggplant, prosciutto, and mozzarella; and seafood posillipo of shrimp, mussels, Littleneck clams, and fish poached in marinara-clam sauce, on linguine. Dinner, served daily from 5:30pm, costs $30 to $40 per person, tax, tip, and wine included; on Sunday there's brunch from 10:30am to 2:30pm.

About the largest and most elaborate of Marblehead's restaurants is **The Landing,** on Clark's Landing off Front Street, down on the water (tel. 617/631-1878). Here you'll find an English-style pub, and dining rooms with a view of yacht-filled Marblehead Harbor. Catering to the boating crowd—which includes early-morning amateur scallop and lobster hunters—the Landing is open for lunch and dinner, every day. Come for a simple lunch of fish and chips ($8), or something fancier. At dinnertime there's mesquite-smoked duck, lobsters cooked with Pernod, and mahi-mahi fish; full dinners cost from $30 to $45 per person, all included. The setting, a semiformal dining room right over the water, is excellent. The Landing's Pub section, popular with the younger boating set, offers burgers and beer.

The literary-minded who have a free hour in Marblehead in the evening spend it at the **King's Rook,** a very European-style coffeehouse and wine bar at 12 State St., not far from the intersection with Washington (tel. 617/631-9838). Coffee is in the $1 to $3 range, depending on the type, of course, and the atmosphere—provided by captain's chairs, small wood-plank tables, low-beamed ceiling, tin lamps, and watercolors on the walls—is yours at no extra charge. Beers (imported and domestic), wines by the glass, sandwiches, and a long list of desserts are also served. Many couples find it a romantic place.

The **Driftwood Restaurant,** 63 Front St. (tel. 617/631-1145), next to the Municipal Parking Lot near the intersection of State and Front streets, on the water, is right out of a storybook about hearty New England fishermen and boatbuilders. Its barn-red clapboard exterior is matched inside with red-and-white-checked tablecloths and a long lunch counter. At 5:30am, when it opens, the fishermen troop in for coffee, eggs, and ham, and for talk of the day's weather and prospects for the catch; later in the day they may return for a bowl of chowder or a portion of "fried dough," a Driftwood specialty served with butter and maple syrup. Breakfast, clam chowder, sandwiches, and fish or seafood plates are the hot items here, priced from $3.50 to $7. The Driftwood's a piece of the real Marblehead.

Note: Although the Driftwood opens very early in the morning, it closes for the day around 5pm in summer, 2pm in winter.

WHAT TO SEE AND DO
Walking around, window-shopping, and admiring the buildings and the rugged coast are the best things to do in Marblehead's Old Town section. Here are some landmarks to seek out as you go.

Abbot Hall (tel. 617/631-4056) dominates the town from a hilltop, readily visible as you ride into Marblehead—you can hardly miss its brick clock tower. Go to the hall and ask the way to the Selectmen's Meeting Room (town council) to find that marvelous patriotic painting *The Spirit of '76.* While you're there, take a look at the deed by which the Indians transferred ownership of the land to the European newcomers in 1684. Abbot Hall is open year round during business hours; in summer it stays open till 9pm on Tuesday and Thursday, 9am to 6pm on Saturday, and 11am to 6pm on Sunday and holidays. It's closed on weekends from November to the end of May.

Down in the center of Old Town, near the intersection of Washington and Hooper streets, are two old Marblehead mansions open to the public for a fee. The **Jeremiah Lee Mansion** (tel. 617/631-1069), owned by the Marblehead Historical Society, was built by a wealthy maritime merchant and furnished with the best things money could buy in 1768—before the Revolution. The style is Georgian, of course, and the period furnishings—including hand-painted wallpaper and paneling—are from all over the world. Admission charge is $3 for adults, half price for children, $2 for seniors; it's open for visits from mid-May to mid-October, Monday through Saturday from 10am to 4pm.

The **King Hooper Mansion,** 8 Hooper St. (tel. 617/631-2608), more or less across the street from the Lee Mansion, is a smaller house and older—built in 1728, with a Georgian extension added in 1747. Now owned by the Marblehead Arts Association, it offers tours of four floors for $1 per person (no charge to visit exhibits in the gallery and the ballroom) and is open from 1 to 4pm every day but Monday. Art exhibits change each month.

After a walk in the "downtown" part of Old Town, make your way down to the waterfront and **Crocker Park,** on a hill at the western end of Front Street. Relax on one of the benches and admire the panoramic view of the harbor and the town. Bring a sandwich, or buy one in the Sandwich Shop, and have a picnic here. The view is unforgettable.

From Crocker Park walk east along Front Street, past its little restaurants, boatyards, and houses built on the rocks, to **Fort Sewall.** The fort is an earthwork fortification built in the 1600s and "modernized" in the late 1700s to include barracks and half-buried buildings, which still remain. The fort is right at the mouth of the harbor, and offers a commanding view of the water and of Marblehead Neck, at the other side of the harbor's mouth, dominated by a light. This is another good picnic place, especially for those with children, who will love playing within the fort with little risk of falling into the water.

When you're ready to leave Fort Sewall, walk back along Front Street, turn right on Franklin, then right again on Orne Street to get to **Fountain Park** and **Old Burial Hill,** where the town's first church meetinghouse was built (it's gone now) and where ancient gravestones mark the places of many of Marblehead's earliest inhabitants and Revolutionary War dead. Orne Street east of Fountain Park leads to the beach.

---

3. Introducing Cape Ann

When Bostonians tell you they're taking a trip to the Cape, they mean they're heading south to Cape Cod. But there is another cape that attracts weekend and summer visitors from the metropolis: Cape Ann, just over an hour's drive or train ride north of the city.

Though few out-of-towners are familiar with Cape Ann, many have heard of Gloucester and Rockport, the picturesque seaport towns with a fascinating, almost legendary, history of struggle and communion with the sea. Gloucester and Rockport both lie on Cape Ann, Cape Cod's less dramatic cousin to the north.

If you look closely at the map, you'll notice that Cape Ann is in fact an island connected by bridges to the mainland, as is Cape Cod (since construction of the Cape Cod Canal). The bays, inlets, harbors, and coves of Cape Ann lend a variety to the landscape and shoreline which has long attracted vacationers, especially in the summertime.

GETTING THERE

For a visit to Cape Ann, I'd suggest you tour by private car, using Rockport as your base. The drive up the coast from Salem is of exceptional beauty. Don't worry, though, if you have no car. There's train service to Gloucester and Rockport, and CATA, the Cape Ann Transportation Authority (tel. 508/283-7916), runs local buses among the towns and villages.

By Car

I'll describe the coastal road, Rte. 127, from Salem through Beverly, Magnolia, Gloucester, and Rockport. Starting from Marblehead, you must first go via Rte. 114 to Salem. Leaving from Boston and heading directly for Cape Ann, you'll save time by taking Interstate 93 north to I-95/Rte. 128. Follow I-95 North/Rte. 128 east, and when the highway divides, stay on Rte. 128 (I-95 will head north, toward Maine). For the coastal drive, follow Rte. 128 until you see signs for **Manchester.** This town is right on the water, and on the coast road, Rte. 127. Head for Manchester.

If you stay on Rte. 128, it will deposit you, quickly, right in downtown Gloucester. Between Gloucester and Rockport are two loop roads. Route 127 takes you to Rockport through the middle of Cape Ann, then loops around the northern and western shores to return to Gloucester. Route 127A, on the other hand, takes you up the eastern shore of the cape before reaching Rockport. If you get lost, don't worry. In a short while some loop will bring you back to one or the other town.

By Train

Boston's **MBTA** trains (tel. 617/722-3200), operated by the Boston and Maine Corporation, leave the downtown North Station 12 times a day (eight a day on weekends) for Manchester, Harbor Station, Gloucester, and Rockport. The ride takes about 1¼ hours to Rockport. Children's, seniors', and family fares can save you money, as can travel during off-peak hours (basically, that's before 4:30pm from Boston, and after 8am from Rockport, on weekdays; all weekend trains are off-peak).

ALONG THE COAST

Manchester is a tidy little North Shore town peopled by old New England types and many professionals who commute into Boston by train. Should you visit during the summer, you can take advantage of **Singing Beach,** half a mile from the train station (center of town) along Beach Street. If you drive, you'll have to pay a parking fee. If you walk, you swim for free. **White Beach,** off Ocean Street, has the same arrangement and the same facilities: bathhouse and snack bar.

MAGNOLIA

A drive 3 miles northeast of Manchester along Rte. 127 brings you to Magnolia. Once a humble fishing village, Magnolia is now a lush and wealthy town. Lavish "summer cottages" built by the rich during the 19th century have been insulated, and heating installed, so that they can be used as year-round principal residences. The scenery is wonderful.

The town center is quite pretty, and less than a mile past it lie two natural features you may want to inspect: **Rafe's Chasm,** a dramatic cleft in the shoreline rock, is just opposite the reef of **Norman's Woe,** which figured in Longfellow's poem "The Wreck of the Hesperus." Should you want to spend some time in this lovely setting, there's a good place to stay the night.

The **White House,** 18 Norman Ave., Magnolia, MA 01930 (tel. 508/525-3642), is a fine old Magnolia Victorian house with an unobtrusive residential wing attached. In the house are six charming rooms, three with private bath; in the wing are ten motel-style rooms with complete facilities: private bath, TV set, air conditioning. Guests receive passes for the use of a private beach; Rafe's Chasm, Norman's Woe, and Hammond Castle (see below) are all close by. Right across Rte. 127 is Lexington Avenue, a short and interesting street of shops, ice cream parlors, and small café-restaurants. Rooms at the White House cost $77 to $88 double in high season, continental breakfast included.

Hammond Castle Museum

Just outside Magnolia along Rte. 127, signs will point to the right, down Hesperus Avenue, to the Hammond Castle Museum, 80 Hesperus Ave. (tel. 508/283-2080 for a recording; 283-7673 for a person). The castle-mansion was built by inventor, electrical engineer, and collector Dr. John Hays Hammond, Jr. (1888–1965), whose creations included radio remote control, and aspects of radar and sonar, including torpedo guidance systems. Despite his name and his interest in things electric, J.H. Hammond, Jr., was not related to Laurens Hammond, inventor of the electric organ.

The castle builder's father, John Hays Hammond (1855–1936), was a mining engineer who helped Cecil Rhodes open up South Africa's hugely rich gold mines. He took part in the Boer War, was captured, ransomed, and returned to the United States.

His son grew up in a cosmopolitan and wealthy household, and did a lot of traveling himself, as you will see from exhibits in the castle. The younger Hammond grew rich on government defense contracts and the proceeds from his inventions, became a director of RCA, and spent his wealth on his obsession: European history. His castle is built in four sections, each made to epitomize a distinct period of European architecture. The Great Hall is Romanesque, the interior courtyard is fitted out as a medieval town square, and the living quarters are Gothic and Renaissance French. The guide who takes you on the obligatory 45-minute tour will explain Dr. Hammond's passion for collecting, and his macabre sense of humor. You come away from the tour marveling at the house's lovely setting, amused by its half-treasure-chest, half-gimcrack planning and construction, and puzzled by Hammond's genius, romanticism, and sheer weirdness. In any case, you don't want to miss it.

While you're waiting for the tour, you can explore the Tower Galleries, with various exhibits and artifacts, and you can pick up a flyer listing the museum's many concerts, lectures, and special programs. There are recitals on the Great Hall's fabulous 8,200-pipe organ, which got a brand-new console in 1987. Other concerts have included Scott Joplin rags, chamber music, and guitar music. There are special theme evenings as well.

Hammond Castle Museum is open daily from 10am to 4pm (till 9pm on

Wednesday in July and August—that's for the candlelight tour). Admission costs $4 for adults, $3.50 for seniors, $2.50 for children aged 6 through 12.

4. Gloucester

After Hammond Castle, it's only 3 miles to Gloucester along Rte. 127. Hesperus Avenue rejoins the highway and takes you into town through West Gloucester and across the little drawbridge. Just before the drawbridge, however, you may want to stop for some . . .

TOURIST INFORMATION

The **Cape Ann Chamber of Commerce** (tel. 508/283-1601) provides information at two locations. The downtown headquarters at 33 Commercial St., Gloucester, MA 01930, has a spacious information center furnishing maps, brochures, special-events bulletins, listings of accommodations, rest rooms, and a rack of restaurant menus. Not far from the statue of the Gloucester Fisherman, across the drawbridge, at the intersection of Rtes. 127 and 133, is their little **tourist information booth**. Guides at either of these locations will be happy to provide information on any town on Cape Ann.

GLOUCESTER'S HISTORY

The Pilgrims founded Plymouth in 1620, and three years later fishermen founded Gloucester. The marvelous natural harbor and the plentiful fishing grounds made that early settlement a fisherman's paradise. Almost four centuries later, it still is.

Gloucester prides itself on being the birthplace of the schooner (1713). At one time it was an important shipbuilding town. Like many others on the New England coast, it profited from the wealth of forests inland, the plentiful fish, and the richness of trade. Over the years Gloucester lost so many of its sons to the ravages of the sea that the town thought it fitting to set up a memorial to them. The **Gloucester Fisherman** (also known as "The Man at the Wheel") is one of New England's most famous statues, with a plaque that reads "They That Go Down to the Sea in Ships, 1623–1923."

The sea is still Gloucester's provider, and the "fishing boats out of Gloucester" still head for open water early each morning. You'll see some of these sturdy little boats, festooned with all sorts of nets and rigging, down in the harbor. Fish-packing plants at quayside process the catch as soon as it's brought in.

Another maritime industry has become important in recent years: whale-watch tours (see below). You might want to take yours from here.

WHERE TO STAY

First choice, without a doubt, is the **Twin Light Manor,** Atlantic Road, Gloucester, MA 01930 (tel. 508/283-7500, or call Best Western toll free 800/528-1234). Atlantic Road is the shore road on the eastern side of the East Gloucester peninsula, and forms part of the ring road around the peninsula. Twin Light Manor is a complex of buildings centered on an attractive English Tudor mansion, set on a highland overlooking the ocean from 7 acres of well-kept grounds. Six buildings hold the 63 guest rooms, which come in all shapes and sizes. The most delightful ones are in the ivy-covered, granite, stucco, and half-timbered mansion with its gracious large public rooms, big fireplaces, dark wood, and even a Victorian billiards room. All guest rooms have modern private bath, climate control, direct-dial telephone, and color television. The vast original manor bedrooms each have a king-size bed or two double beds, and some have fireplaces; they go for $165 in high season. The smaller "guest" bedrooms have king-size beds and rent for $148 double in high season. The other buildings have modern motel-style rooms, most with either king-size beds or two double beds, all with ocean views, and many with private balconies overlooking the grounds and the sea. Rates range from $132 to $165 in high summer. Tax is included in these prices.

The numerous facilities include the living room, where movies are shown frequently on wide-screen TV, the dining room, two swimming pools (one heated), and badminton, volleyball, croquet, and shuffleboard courts. As guests at the manor, you can take a harbor cruise, or play 18 holes at the Bass Rocks Golf Club, at no extra charge. Twin Light is the perfect place to get away from it all.

If you plan to stay at least a week, try the **Blue Shutters Inn,** 1 Nautilus Rd., Gloucester, MA 01930 (tel. 508/281-2706). This big white house with blue shutters is right in the curve of the road, only a block off Alternate Rte. 127, and just a few steps from Good Harbor Beach. Many of its guest rooms have beach and ocean views. Decorations are homey, neat, and comfortable. The inn has guest rooms with shared or private bath, as well as beach apartments capable of lodging four people and completely equipped with linens, kitchen utensils, barbecue grills, and TV sets. For a guest room with shared bath, the rate for two is $70 per night; with a private bath, it's $107 per night. Continental breakfast is included. The Blue Shutters is open from May through October.

Up the hill behind the Blue Shutters is **Gray Manor,** 14 Atlantic Rd. (Bass Rocks), East Gloucester, MA 01930 (tel. 508/283-5409). Robert and Madeline Gray have converted a nice big summer house to a guesthouse only a few minutes' walk from Good Harbor Beach. Guest rooms have private baths, air conditioning, refrigerators, and color cable TV; some even have their own decks. Rates here are $55 to $60 double per day in the summer, tax included. May through late June, lower off-season rates are in effect. Several efficiency apartments rent by the week ($400) in summer, by the day ($50) off-season. Gray Manor closes for the winter.

WHERE TO DINE

Gloucester is plentiful in restaurants, most specializing in seafood, of course. Those who do not care for seafood can rest assured that any seafood restaurant always has a few meat, chicken, or vegetarian dishes to satisfy their unmaritime appetites.

Gloucester's fanciest and best is the **White Rainbow Restaurant,** 65 W. Main St. (tel. 508/281-0017), in the basement of a 19th-century brick office building (go by the street numbers, as the sign is small and difficult to spot). There are two places to dine here: the formal dining room and the less formal café. Both have dusky brick walls, low lights, and modern paintings. Waiters and waitresses are in black and white, friendly but professional, and after you've been seated they will take your order for an opener like lobster stew, grilled shrimp, or baked Brie; then you can go on to roast duck, tournedos of beef, or a grilled prime veal chop. Desserts are heavily biased in favor of chocolate. The wine list gives you plenty of room for making your selection, and bottles are just slightly higher than the moderate range. Dinner is the only meal served, from 5:30 to 9:30pm Tuesday through Friday, and Sunday; on Saturday, hours are 6 to 10pm. You can expect to spend about $35 to $50 per person here. It's a good idea to call for reservations.

For seafood in an informal atmosphere, at moderate prices, right next to the water, I'd head for the **Harbor Deck Restaurant,** 17 Rogers St. (tel. 508/281-4811), in the same building as the Imperial Marina Chinese restaurant, and right next door to Captain Courageous, another seafood place. Choose a table in the light and airy room with large windows or on the outside deck looking out over the docks and the boats. Chairs and tables of bright wood add a cheery note. The menu lists American and Italian dishes, many based on the seafood that comes in on the boats right next door. There's shrimp primavera, a baked sea scallop casserole, lobster tortellini Alfredo, and the interesting seafood chicken (chicken breast stuffed with crab meat and scallops, topped with hollandaise sauce). As always in seafood restaurants, the freshest items are the daily specials listed on the blackboard menu. House wines are on order by the carafe or the glass; there's a full bar. Come for lunch ($15 to $18) any day from 11:30am to 3pm, for dinner ($26 to $38) from 4 to 9pm; on Sunday, brunch is served from 11:30am to 3pm, dinner from 11:30am to 9pm.

Gloucester has a good Chinese restaurant, the **Imperial Marina,** 17 Rogers St. (tel. 508/281-6573), serving lunch and dinner every day from 11:30am to 9:30pm (till 10:30pm on weekends). Service is fast and attentive, cocktails are served, and prices are moderate. The hot-and-sour soup is very hot and very good, the beef with mushrooms delightful. You can expect to spend $6 to $8 per person for lunch or $15 to $20 for dinner. Liquor is served.

Among my favorite dining places in Gloucester is **The Gull,** 75 Essex Ave. (tel. 508/283-6565), at the Cape Ann Marina on Rte. 133, a mile or so from the center of town right next to where the Yankee Whale Watch boats depart. The Gull is a big, friendly, fairly simple but attractive restaurant overlooking the Annisquam River, usually packed with boaters, whale watchers, families, couples, and sailors. All three meals are served; the restaurant opens at 5:30am and closes at 9pm. Seafood is the forte here, and you can have the huge, succulent lobster sandwich or a full clambake with steamers, corn on the cob, coleslaw, and a lobster, or settle for fish and chips. The Gull has a bar and serves alcoholic beverages. Lunch or dinner can cost from $12 to $22 per person, slightly more if you order a full lobster dinner.

Halibut Point is the name of a state park near Rockport, and also of a restaurant at 289 Main St. (tel. 508/281-1900) in Gloucester, not far from the A&P supermarket. The atmosphere is of a friendly neighborhood pub, not fancy but fun. The menu is short and to the point, with sandwiches, salads, burgers, and several popular seafood items, but the blackboard always bears interesting special dishes. Swordfish for lunch should be under $10. The soup-and-sandwich special, with a mug of beer, is even less. Open every day for lunch and dinner till midnight.

WHAT TO SEE AND DO

Signs direct motorists along Gloucester's **Scenic Tour,** covering the Harbor Cove, Inner Harbor, and Fish Pier, as well as to the famous statue of the Gloucester Fisherman by Leonard Craske.

If you're lucky enough to be in Gloucester late in June, ask about the **Festival of St. Peter,** the high point of which is the Blessing of the Fleet. Several hundred boats make up Gloucester's important fishing fleet, and the blessing pays tribute to them.

A great "summer cottage" turned museum, **Beauport,** the Sleeper-McCann House, is at 75 Eastern Point Blvd. (tel. 508/283-0800), on Eastern Point, the peninsula across the bay from downtown Gloucester. The house, now under the care of the Society for the Preservation of New England Antiquities, was built by Henry Davis Sleeper, a prominent interior decorator and antiquarian of the 1920s. Sleeper worked for 27 years to make Beauport a showplace. It still is. You can take the hourlong tour Monday through Friday, May 15 to October 15, from 10am to 4pm; also on weekends from mid-September through mid-October, 1 to 4pm. Admission costs $5 per adult, $2.50 for children 6 to 12, $4.50 for seniors.

On your excursion down to Beauport, you'll want to stroll through East Gloucester's **Rocky Neck Art Colony.** The winding streets offer interesting glimpses of the harbor, and every other house seems to be an artist's studio. You'll see signs asking you to park *before* you enter the narrow streets. Take advantage of the lot next to the signs.

Beaches

Gloucester's favored place for a hot summer afternoon is **Good Harbor Beach** in East Gloucester, on Rte. 127A toward Rockport. It may be crowded if the day is really hot, and parking will be tight. Alternatives are **Long Beach** and **Pebble Beach,** just a bit farther along 127A, within the boundaries of Rockport. **Wingaersheek Beach** is on Ipswich Bay to the northwest (head back down Rte. 128 south and watch for signs). **Coffin Beach** is just northwest of Wingaersheek.

Whale-Watch Cruises

Motoring out to hunt for whales with camera and binoculars is a favorite New England sport, and Gloucester has its share of good whale-watch cruise boats. Cruises usually last between 4 and 5 hours, and thus take up a full morning or afternoon. Bring warm clothing, even on a warm day, because the maritime breezes out on the water will make the ambient temperature at least 10 degrees cooler than on land, and the wind-chill factor might make it feel even colder. Also remember your sunglasses to ward off the glare from the water; and sunscreen, because that same glare, combined with the bright sun, can really give you a burn. Wear rubber-soled shoes if you have them. You can buy soft drinks and snacks on board.

Once out on the water, keep your eyes peeled for humpback whales, 30-ton creatures usually about 50 feet long which seem to love their briny habitat, breeching and playing for hours, accompanying themselves with their own curious songs. A cousin of the humpback is the finback, about twice as heavy and up to 80 feet long, making it second in size to the great blue whale. Long and slender, it's a super-fast swimmer, propelling its great bulk through the deep at speeds of 20 knots or even more. The minke whale is "small," weighing only 11 tons, and growing to 30 feet in length. Minke whales have a well-developed sense of curiosity, and may snoop around your boat just to see what's up. In addition, you may see right whales, dolphins, pilot whales, seals, sharks, and seabirds such as petrels, shearwaters, gannets, and gulls.

Capt. Fred Douglass and his sons pioneered whale-watch cruises out of Gloucester with their Daunty Fleet of boats, and now they operate **Cape Ann Whale Watch** (tel. 508/283-5110), with daily departures at 8am and 1:30pm from Rose's Wharf, at 415 Main St., across from the Old Colony gas station. On Saturday and Sunday evenings during July and August there are additional sunset whale-watch cruises departing at 6pm, returning at 10pm, with a cash bar on board. A research naturalist accompanies every cruise. Whale sightings are guaranteed (Capt. Douglass has had a 98% record during the past 5 years); if you don't see a whale, you'll receive a free pass for a future cruise. Reservations are requested, and tickets can be purchased from the ticket office on Rose's Wharf daily from 7am to 6pm. Daytime cruises cost $20 for adults, $10 for children under 16, $13 for seniors over 60.

Seven Seas Whale Watch, Seven Seas Wharf (tel. 508/283-1776), operates daily cruises at similar prices. Continental breakfast is available on board ship. In high summer, there are also sunset cruises with entertainment.

---

5. Rockport

North of Gloucester is the small seacoast town of Rockport, famed as an artists' colony and, well, just as a very picturesque place. Winslow Homer, Childe Hassam, and Fitz Hugh Lane came here to paint the fishermen working on their vessels and the quarrymen cutting and moving granite.

It's been a long time since Rockport was a village of hearty, independent fishermen and their wives, living by their daily struggle with the sea, and today you're likely to see ten times as many day-trippers as you are to see colorful village types. But the Rockport Art Association is active—the town is dotted with galleries holding paintings and crafts both pleasing and awkward, and amateur daubers test their skill at capturing daily life all over town. The Rockport Art Association's headquarters is also the venue for musical performances during the month-long annual Rockport Chamber Music Festival.

Rockport's newfound popularity means that there are lots of good places to stay and to dine, and if you decide to remain overnight here, you'll notice that as the evening wears on, the streets become calmer and the village resumes something of its slow, antique pace.

ORIENTATION

Parking conditions downtown are sure to be very tight any time in summer, so, if you drive, find a nice back street, or use the town-supported parking lot on the outskirts rather than getting snarled in the press of traffic downtown. The town lots charge several dollars per day for parking, but offer a free shuttle bus from the lot to downtown Rockport. This isn't a bad deal, considering the gasoline and frustration you'll waste trying to find a legal spot to park downtown.

If you arrive in Rockport by train, you'll be happy to know that the central area, with most of the inns, is only a few minutes' walk from the station.

INFORMATION

The **Rockport Chamber of Commerce** (tel. 508/546-6575) maintains an information booth on Upper Main Street (Rte. 127) on the outskirts of town, coming from Gloucester. In season, you'll get help finding a room for the night—if there's a room available. Stop at the booth for this free service.

WHERE TO STAY

Though Rockport has several motels, most of its guest beds are in old houses, and that's part of the town's considerable charm. Here's the rundown on Rockport's hostelries—first the inns and guesthouses, then a motel or two. Note that many of these establishments do not accept credit cards. Ask about payment when you make reservations, or when you register.

Inns in Town

For my money, Rockport's finest place to stay is the **Addison Choate Inn,** 49 Broadway, Rockport, MA 01966 (tel. 508/546-7543). Rooms in the tidy old house (built in 1851) have been meticulously restored, and are equally well maintained. There's a feeling of authenticity bred of fine taste; nothing in the decor is overdone, but neither is it spare. It is not "chock full of antiques"; it's tastefully furnished with them. With your room ($91 to $96 double, private bath, tax included) you get continental breakfast and use of a pretty swimming pool. There is also a three-person suite for $121 and a stable house for $110 for two. The center of town is within easy walking distance.

The **Linden Tree Inn,** 26 King St., Rockport, MA 01966 (tel. 508/546-2494), is a tidy inn on a quiet street, run by friendly innkeepers Larry and Penny Olson. The yard is shaded by an enormous old linden tree, as you'd expect. The inn has 18 rooms in various sizes and styles, priced from $77 to $93 double, with freshly baked continental breakfast included. Some rooms can take a folding bed ($11) as well; all rooms in the main house have private bath; half have air conditioning. The two rooms in the annex share a bath. There's even a single room for $55. This is a nice place—homey, convenient, and friendly.

The **Inn on Cove Hill,** 37 Mount Pleasant St., Rockport, MA 01966 (tel. 508/546-2701), is only a few steps from the center of town on Rte. 127A. The charming house was built in 1791 with the proceeds (so they say) from cashing in some pirate gold found on Cape Ann. Today the house is as neat as a pin, old-fashioned in feel but modern in comforts. The double rooms have television sets, private baths, and prices from $49 to $96. Continental breakfast, served to your room or by the garden if you like, is included in the rates, and I've included the tax. No smoking is allowed in the inn.

For many years now the **Peg Leg Inn,** 2 King St., Rockport, MA 01966 (tel. 508/546-2352), has been a haven for visitors to Rockport, and the original inn has now expanded to include five buildings with 33 rooms altogether, many with views of the water. The decor varies from room to room and building to building, but as the houses of the inn are a century or two old, emphasis is on Early American, with such modern luxuries as private bath and TV added. The rooms are kept as neat as the white clapboard houses they're in, and cost $71 to $105 double (three rooms are priced at $60 double) in high season, mid-June through October; off-season, the rates are lower. The difference in price depends on the size of the room, and the view it has of the water. Continental breakfast is included in the rates; the inn's full-service restaurant is next door. The Peg Leg Inn is a short walk from the center of town, but the location makes it a good deal quieter than most in-town lodgings. If you approach Rockport along the inland Rte. 127, you can reach the inn by turning left onto Railroad Ave. at the five-road intersection, then take the first right onto King Street. The inn is closed from late November through mid-February.

Lantana House, 22 Broadway, Rockport, MA 01966 (tel. 508/546-3535), is close to the center of town and moderately priced. It offers efficiency apartments as well as guest rooms. Doubles go for $55 to $70, continental breakfast included.

On the Outskirts

The **Yankee Clipper Inn,** P.O. Box 2399, 96 Granite St., Rockport, MA 01966 (tel. 508/546-3407; fax 508/546-9730), is on Rte. 127 toward Pigeon Cove, on the outskirts of town. Two of the inn's three buildings occupy a waterfront site with excellent views; the third is a fine old house designed by none other than Charles Bulfinch, architect of the Massachusetts State House in Boston and (in part) of the Capitol in Washington. Grounds include several shady nooks, and a heated saltwater swimming pool. Most rooms are rented with breakfast and dinner in summer; so a double room with sea view and meals, tax and 15% service charge included, can cost anywhere from $185 to $256 total per day for two people. At the Bulfinch House, however, up the hill a bit and across the road, the only meal you absolutely must take is breakfast, so rates are lower: $117 to $129 double, all in. Midweek packages can bring down the price if you can avoid weekends. The oceanfront dining room is open to the public.

Among the best things about the **Ralph Waldo Emerson Inn,** Pigeon Cove, Rockport, MA 01966 (tel. 508/546-6321), is its location: a block in from the road, on a bluff overlooking the sea. The grand white inn actually did host Emerson at one time. Since then a new section has been added (1912), but the porch is still fine for sitting and taking in the view. The gracious and airy public rooms hold lots of good paintings. For fun, there's a heated saltwater pool, whirlpool bath, sauna, and recreation room. A room in summer costs $60 to $116 single, $87 to $123 double, tax included; if you'd like breakfast and dinner, add about $25 per person. To get to the inn, follow Rte. 127 north and west from Rockport center for 2 miles.

North and west of Pigeon Cove is Folly Cove, on the way to Annisquam, just past the road to Halibut Point. It's here you'll find the **Old Farm Inn,** 291 Granite St., Rockport, MA 01966 (tel. 508/546-3237). It may be old but it is kept pretty as a picture. Set on 5 acres of grounds very near Halibut Point State Park, the farmhouse has four guest rooms, and there are another four rooms in the barn guesthouse. All have private bath, television, and such country touches as rustic antiques and homey quilts. Rooms cost $75 to $97 double, tax included; the highest-priced is a two-room suite, which sleeps four; Continental breakfast is included. Off-season, rates come down $11 per room.

Motels

The **Captain's Bounty Motor Inn,** 1 Beach St. (P.O. Box 430), Rockport, MA 01966 (tel. 508/546-9557), is right on the beach near the center of town, with 24 modern rooms and efficiencies facing the sea, on two levels. In season, rates for the double rooms are $87; for the efficiencies, $90 to $105.

For a modern motel on the outskirts, try the **Sandy Bay Motor Inn** (tel. 508/546-7155), on the road into town (the official address is 173 Main St., Rockport, MA 01966). The modern, colorful rooms here, equipped with color TV, air conditioning, and all the luxury features, are only the beginning of the story. Besides these, the motel has an indoor swimming pool, a whirlpool bath, saunas, tennis courts, and Michael's Restaurant. Rates are $90 to $101 per room from late June through Labor Day, $64 to $82 from Labor Day through October, and $53 to $70 from November through the end of March. It's a good idea to make reservations in the busy summer months.

WHERE TO DINE

The first thing you should know is that Rockport is a *dry town*. No liquor, wine, or beer is served in its restaurants or sold in its inns or shops. You can drink in

Rockport if you BYO, and the restaurants will provide setups, corkscrews, ice buckets, and the like. But you must plan ahead and buy your booze in Gloucester, or in Lanesville, on Rte. 127 west of Rockport.

This all came about in 1856 when one Hannah Jumper, an outspoken leader of the temperance movement in Rockport, led a raid on the town's liquor supplies. In the four preceding years, sale of ardent spirits in Rockport had more than doubled, and many a fisherman and quarry worker spent wages on rum which should have gone for family needs.

The town's Fourth of July bash in 1856 had gotten out of hand as usual, and on July 8, Hannah and other good citizens went to work. Casks and bottles stored in shops and warehouses—and even private homes—were breached and broken, and though some people cried "Foul!" most people supported this radical solution. Hannah's early-morning direct action changed the history of Rockport, and it has been dry, by the active consent of a majority of its citizens, ever since.

Bearskin Neck, the center of Rockport's tourist industry, has numerous restaurants. One is named **The Hannah Jumper,** on Tuna Wharf, Bearskin Neck (tel. 508/546-3600). Its sign bears a huge axe—in gold leaf, no less—such as Hannah used to break casks during her noble endeavors to rid the town of Demon Rum. Though you can't get a glass of wine here, you can bring your own, and get a table with one of the best views of the harbor, especially good at sunset. Come for a lunch of sandwiches, chowder, salads, or seafood plates, or return in the evening for dinner. The chef offers baby gulf shrimp, fried for just a few seconds to retain the delicate flavor; and chicken Kiev, the breast wrapped around a luscious stuffing of butter and flavorings. Of course, there's boiled lobster. The dinner bill, not including your BYO drinks, will be about $18 to $22 per person. You can sit in the narrow dining room with its simulated rough-board walls, brick floor, and hanging ferns, or out on the shaded Harbor Deck, with the best harbor view of all. The restaurant is open every day from Memorial Day to Labor Day from 11:30am to 8:30pm. In the spring and fall it's open every day for lunch only.

Out at the end of Bearskin Neck where the cars turn around is **My Place-by-the-Sea,** 68 Bearskin Neck (tel. 508/546-9667), a typical cedar-shingled building with several tiny dining rooms, a shaded patio, and wooden decks right down among the granite riprap overlooking the north bay. The blackboard is the menu here, and it changes daily, featuring the cuisine of chef-owner Charles Kreis. Lunch and dinner often depend on what's fresh in the way of seafood. Last time I visited, it was oysters Rockefeller, stuffed wolf fish, and halibut baked in lime and butter. Also offered were prime rib of beef, steak au poivre, and chicken marsala for the landlubbers. My Place has the nicest homey "feel" of any Rockport restaurant. It's open for lunch (about $7 to $10) and dinner ($15 to $25) daily from May through late fall, from noon to 9:30pm.

Just want a bowl of chowder? The place to go is the **Portside Chowder House,** Bearskin Neck (tel. 508/546-7045), to the left off the main street on the Neck, a tiny hole-in-the-wall of a place with low ceilings, narrow passageways, and a few tables with partial views of the water. Chowder made from various seafoods is the specialty here, and it comes by the cup, the bowl, or the quart. Salads of lobster and crab, and fish sandwiches are served, and there are also a few beefy items from the grill. A quick and hearty lunch should cost something like $6 to $10 per person, all in. The Chowder House is open daily in summer from 11am to 8pm, in September and October to 4pm, in winter for lunch on weekends only.

The **Blacksmith Shop Restaurant,** 23 Mount Pleasant St. (tel. 508/546-6301), just off Dock Square, has something that Bearskin Neck restaurants don't have: lots of space. And yet the views of the harbor and of Motif No. 1 from the Blacksmith Shop are as good as any in town, and better than most. There is so much space here that you enter through various old-time kitchen exhibits and memorabilia, then step down into the spacious waterside dining rooms to order from a menu heavy in seafood and traditional American favorites. Long hours are another advantage here, for the restaurant is open daily from 11am to 10pm. You can expect to pay anywhere from $22 to $38 per person for dinner.

Ellen's Harborside, a tiny, crowded but pleasant place just off Dock Square on T-Wharf (tel. 508/546-2512), specializes in budget seafood and homemade desserts, and packs 'em in every night of the summer. Ellen's is especially popular with thrifty seniors, who like the freshness of the seafood, the hardworking waitresses, and the delicious and abundant desserts. The dining room and lunch counter are simple and functional, and the hours of service are long enough to please anyone: Ellen's opens for breakfast at 5:30am and closes when things calm down after dinner. One person can have a full three-course seafood repast here for as little as $12 or $15, or a simpler seafood special for a mere $5.95. No credit cards are accepted.

One more popular Rockport restaurant is on Main Street, up the hill from Dock Square. For many years the standby in Rockport for dining has been **Oleana-by-the-Sea,** 27 Main St. (tel. 508/546-2049), not far from the center of town. With a tinge of Norwegian atmosphere, Oleana emphasizes the seafood of the area. The decor is simple but attractive, as though the decorators wanted you to concentrate on the views of the Atlantic to be had from most of the tables. The soup is homemade, and is quite good; seafood entrees generally run about $10 to $16, but the daily special will always save you money, and may be haddock in a cheese sauce, with potato and vegetable for about $10 or $12. For dessert, a Norwegian pastry with strawberries and custard is a good choice. Oleana is open April through November: in June, July, and August the restaurant's in service seven days a week from 11:30am to 8pm.

On the Outskirts

Let's face it: when you're on Cape Ann, you should order fresh seafood. If you wander out of town by bike or car, you'll find it at every turn.

Just down the hill from the Old Farm Inn on Rte. 127 in Folly Cove is the **Lobster Pool** (tel. 508/546-7808), known locally as Tommy's. The food is simple and good, the surroundings spare but cheery. Order a lobster roll of solid lobster meat (Tommy's doesn't use celery as filler). Portions are gargantuan, and it's not unusual for two semihungry people to share, say, one bowl of chowder and one clam plate, which comes with french fries and coleslaw. Total cost, with soft drinks, is less than $10 per person. You can get your food to take out, if you like.

WHAT TO DO

First thing every visitor does after arriving in Rockport is to take a stroll down **Bearskin Neck,** the narrow peninsula jutting into the water off Dock Square, the town's main square. Here you'll find lots of quaint shops and art galleries to draw your attention, and many good views of the water and of the town.

Other strolls in town are also rewarding, and local brochures will urge you to take a photograph of the red fisherman's shack called "Motif No. 1," apparently named for its popularity among the first picture painters who moved to Rockport. Actually it should now be named "Motif No. 2," as the original shack was swept away in the great storm of 1978 and a new one was built from scratch. In the interest of originality, I suggest that you try to be the first person to have visited Rockport *without* seeing this unimportant landmark. Take my word for it, the thing is now famous because it's famous.

Rather, spend your time looking at the local granite. It was cut at the town's Swan Quarry (now flooded), and shipped out, giving the town its name. Curbstones, markers, pavements, foundations, piers, even whole buildings were made of the durable stone during the town's quarrying heyday. Now, if "Motif No. 1" were a fisherman's shanty made of granite, that would be something to see!

For swimming, walk along Beach Street north to Front Beach and Back Beach, or wander (in your car or on your bike) north along the coast to **Pigeon Cove,** about 2 miles north (a half-hour walk).

You can go farther than Pigeon Cove by car or bike. In fact, you can make a loop of Cape Ann on Rte. 127 via Pigeon Cove, Folly Cove, Plum Cove, Annisquam, and Lobster Cove, ending in Gloucester.

If you love chamber music, plan your visit to coincide with the **Rockport**

Chamber Music Festival. Recitals are given Thursday through Sunday from early June to early July. For exact dates and details, call 508/546-7391.

Halibut Point

Head north out of Rockport on Rte. 127, toward Lanesville and Annisquam, and after a few miles you'll see a sign pointing off to the right (north) to **Halibut Point State Park,** just before the Old Farm Inn. Drive to the parking lot, leave your car, and then follow the path through the forest for 10 minutes, and you will come to an old granite quarry, now flooded with water. The park interpretive center, still being furnished at this writing, is in the building that dominates the quarry. Exhibits demonstrate the flora and fauna of the reservation, and how granite quarrying contributed to the culture and economy of the region. A weird World War II concrete observation tower has been grafted onto the building, a typical clapboard Cape Ann house. From the tower during the war, sharp eyes kept a lookout against enemy submarines. The entrance fee is $5.

Continue along the path to reach the Observation Point atop a cliff of granite quarry rubble. Far beneath, the Atlantic's waves roll in and crash on the smoothed granite bedrock below. You can make your way down to the water. Some people go swimming here, although it's not an ideal spot: The water is always chilly, the rocks difficult and slippery, the waves sometimes perilous.

Castle Hill

Not far from Rockport is Castle Hill, the fabulous hilltop mansion built by Richard Teller Crane, Jr., who made a fortune in plumbing and bathroom fixtures early in this century. The house, in a style from the time of King Charles II, is surrounded by extensive gardens and deer parks. You can take a tour of the house and grounds on certain Fridays and Saturdays during the summer; or you can visit for a crafts fair, concert, or theater performance and get a look at the estate that way. First thing to do is to find out what's scheduled, by contacting the Castle Hill Foundation, P.O. Box 283, Ipswich, MA 01938 (tel. 508/356-4070).

. . . AND THE SOUTH SHORE

1. PLYMOUTH
2. NEW BEDFORD
3. FALL RIVER

Of the many communities on the South Shore of Massachusetts Bay, Plymouth is easily the most famous. Crowds of visitors make the pilgrimage every summer to see one of the places where this country began. Due south of Boston on Buzzards Bay is New Bedford, one of the region's best-known towns during the whaling era, home of Melville's Captain Ahab of *Moby Dick* fame. The whaling museum and the ferry to Martha's Vineyard are the big attractions in New Bedford today. And in Fall River, on the border with Rhode Island, battleships and submarines are waiting to be visited and toured by nautical buffs, while everybody else goes shopping.

All of the South Shore towns covered in this chapter, including Plymouth, New Bedford, and Fall River, use the 508 telephone area code.

---

1. Plymouth

Plymouth is famous because of a small and rather unimpressive boulder. But when visitors come to Plymouth Rock, they are coming not because the rock is much to look at—its only notable features are a crack and the date "1620" engraved on it—but because Plymouth, as the landing place of the Pilgrims, is a symbol for the ideal of religious freedom and the quest for a better life.

Besides the Rock, which will take you about 5 minutes to inspect, Plymouth has lots of other sights and exhibits dealing with Pilgrim and Early American history: a collection of historic houses, a full-size replica of the Pilgrim ship *Mayflower*, an authentic re-creation of an entire Pilgrim village complete with living inhabitants, a wax museum, and still more. Many people make Plymouth a day trip, stopping here on their way from Boston to the Cape or vice versa, but should you want to stay overnight in the Pilgrims' town, there are several attractive lodging possibilities.

GETTING THERE
Plymouth is served from Boston and Hyannis by buses of the **Plymouth & Brockton (P&B) Street Railway Company** (tel. 617/773-9400, or toll free in Mass. 800/328-9997). About two dozen buses a day run in each direction between Plymouth and downtown Boston and/or Logan Airport; about the same number of buses run from Hyannis to Plymouth and back. In Boston, buses leave from

Greyhound at 10 St. James Ave. (tel. 617/423-5810) or from the **Peter Pan (Trailways)** bus terminal, 555 Atlantic Ave. (tel. 617/482-5510), either across the street from South Station or from the bus stops alongside South Station. Buses serving Logan Airport pick up and take on passengers at all airline terminals. In Hyannis the P&B terminal (tel. 508/775-5524) is at 17 Elm St. In Plymouth, the P&B Terminal is in the Industrial Park Road, Rte. 3, Exit 7, North Plymouth (tel. 508/746-0378), but buses stop downtown in Plymouth as well. The express trip between Boston and Plymouth takes 45 minutes; the local route, stopping in downtown Plymouth and at Plimoth Plantation, takes 1½ hours. From Plymouth to Hyannis is a 40-minute ride.

INFORMATION
The town of Plymouth maintains an **information booth** (tel. 508/746-4779) and **accommodations service** on North Park Avenue. Samoset Street (Rte. 44) is the road you take east from the highway (Rte. 3), and Samoset turns into North Park after you cross Court Street (Rte. 3A). Look for the booth on your right just as the road jogs to the right. The guides will help you find a room if you don't have a reservation or if you'd like to see what's available. They also have a current list of events and attractions for the area.
There is a **Regional Information Complex for Visitors** on Rte. 3 at Exit 5. For information, call 508/746-3377.

WHERE TO STAY
Most of your choices are among Plymouth's good selection of motels. But there are alternatives.

Guesthouses
You can find a room in a private home in Plymouth, "America's Home Town." Prices will be about $40 to $50 single, $50 to $75 double. Breakfast is included, of course.
Be Our Guest, P.O. Box 1333, Plymouth, MA 02360 (tel. 617/837-9867), will find you a room in or near Plymouth, Boston, and Cape Cod.
Call and see if there's a room at **Hall's Bed & Breakfast,** 3 Sagamore St., Plymouth, MA 02360 (tel. 508/746-2835), then head south along the waterfront from Plymouth Rock until you see the town green on your right. Turn up North Green Street, continue on Jefferson to Sagamore, and turn right. You'll see the Halls' tidy white clapboard house perched on the hillside at no. 3. There are two rooms here, sharing a bath, for $55 per room.
A new B&B to try is **Two-Sixty-Four Sandwich Street,** 264 Sandwich St., Plymouth, MA 02360 (tel. 508/747-5490). The proprietor, Julie Beach, charges $55 for a single room, $72 for a double with shared bath, or $77 for a double with private bath. Full breakfast is included, served until 10am. The house is some distance from the center of town, but only a mile from Exit 5 and very convenient to Rte. 3.

Motels
Right downtown are two motels with similar names and identical management, the **Governor Bradford** (tel. 508/746-6200), right on the waterfront street, and the **Governor Carver** (tel. 508/746-7100), on Summer Street at Town Square, Plymouth, MA 02360. Both are about the same distance—two blocks—from Plymouth Rock. The Governor Bradford has a little fish-shaped outdoor pool and two tiers of modern rooms, each with individual heat/air-conditioning units, two double beds, TV, and coffee makers. The Governor Carver is a three-story inn with a pool, 82 rooms, all with two double beds, and the other features of the Bradford, plus a restaurant and lounge. Rates at the two inns are similar and change depending on the view from your room. In season, rooms go for $97 to $128 single or double. Substantial reductions are offered outside the high summer months. Children under 14 stay in their parents' room for free. Package plans are available.

One of the better bargains is to be found at the **Cold Spring Motel,** 188 Court St. (which is Rte. 3A), Plymouth, MA 02360 (tel. 508/746-2222). Although a bit out of the center of town—it's about a half mile to the Rock—the surroundings of grass lawns and large trees make up for the small distance. Some 31 rooms and cottages, many paneled in pine, are for rent. All have air conditioning, electric heat, color TV, and parking at the door. A picnic area is provided for guests' use. The motel has no restaurant, but there's one almost across the street in the small shopping plaza. The rate structure at present is quite complex because of the several types of accommodations (rooms with double beds, cottages with two bedrooms sleeping four). In high season double rates are $56 to $72; two-bedroom cottages, $78; $5 for each extra person, $5 extra per cot. In April, May, and October, prices are $10 less. Note that the Cold Spring Motel *closes* in winter; exact dates vary from year to year.

The tiny **Blue Anchor Motel,** 7 Lincoln St., Plymouth, MA 02360 (tel. 508/746-9551), has only four units; thus there's a good chance it'll be full in busy periods, but it's worth considering because the motel is on a quiet street next to Plymouth's town hall and only a short walk from the center of town. It's very much a ma-and-pa place, informal and friendly, with comfy rooms renting for $55 to $66, depending on the unit and the number in your party. Rates are about $5 less per room off-season. From the center of town, go south on Sandwich Street from the post office. The third street on the left is Lincoln.

Down near Plimoth Plantation, 2½ miles south of the center of Plymouth, is the **Pilgrim Sands Motel,** 150 Warren Ave. (Rte. 3A), Plymouth, MA 02360 (tel. 508/747-0900). The bonus here, besides proximity to the plantation, is the private beach, which you'd normally enjoy for $3 weekdays, $5 weekends; it's free for motel guests. There's an indoor–outdoor pool and spa as well, and all the modern amenities, including air-conditioned rooms and all-tile bathrooms; some rooms have refrigerators. After a day's walking in the sun it's great to take a swim and then sit looking out to sea, before going to bed to be lulled asleep by the sound of the surf. All rooms have two double or queen-size beds and cost $86 to $108 mid-June to Labor Day, $53 to $90 off-season, tax included; the higher rates are for oceanfront rooms. The Sands is open year round.

WHERE TO DINE

Plymouth has a number of snack places, sandwich shops, and restaurants, and although it's not noted for a wide range of culinary styles, the town will be able to fill your needs.

Among Plymouth's most popular restaurants is **Station One,** 51 Main St., at Middle Street (tel. 508/746-6001), in the commercial center of town, up the hill from the waterfront, open daily from 11:30am to 9:30pm (10:30pm on weekends). Station One started life as the town's Central Fire House in 1904, but has been utterly transformed into an elegant space paneled with mahogany and glistening with brass and crystal. Have lunch, dinner, or Sunday brunch either inside or on the patio out front. The menu is exhaustive, with something for any mood or taste, from crab bisque to ziti with chicken and broccoli. Prices are moderate: about $14 to $18 for lunch, $30 to $40 per person for a good dinner. Liquor is served.

For my money, the best way to sample Plymouth's seafood is to pick up lunch from one of the self-service places on the waterfront. You'll see them crowded together near Mayflower Seafood on the Town Wharf: Wood's, Souza's, the Lobster Hut.

My choice is the **Lobster Hut,** on the Town Wharf (tel. 508/746-2270). Open every day from 11am to 9pm, the Lobster Hut serves up steaming bowls of clam chowder, lobster bisque, fried clams, fish and chips, and lobsters, plus wine and beer (with your meal only). Order a huge portion of fish and chips, or fried clams, and with a soft drink you'll pay less than $10. Dine inside, or at one of the picnic tables overlooking the bay.

Just south of the turnoff to Plimoth Plantation, on Warren Avenue (Rte. 3A), is **Bert's Restaurant** (tel. 508/746-3422). Air conditioning keeps you cool and the view of the ocean, plus a decor accented with various pieces of ships' paraphernalia, makes you think (almost) that you're out to sea. The menu features seafood but offers chicken and beef as well. Most entrées are in the range of $13 to $18, and full dinners (with appetizer, vegetable and potato, salad, dessert, and coffee) cost a few dollars more. Bert's is open for lunch and dinner daily, from 11:30am to 10pm.

WHAT TO SEE

Sightseeing in Plymouth means Pilgrim lore: what the early settlers looked like, how they dressed, how they lived from day to day. The many exhibits here make it possible to get a very clear picture of what arrival in America meant to these pioneers.

Plymouth Rock

From anywhere in Plymouth, road signs or the fingers of residents will guide you to the Rock on the waterfront.

Plymouth Rock is an American icon, a symbol of intrepid discovery, liberty, and freedom of conscience. The stone itself is granite, probably from a formation known as the Dedham granite, formed 680 million years ago (give or take a few million years). The Rock was picked up from this formation at a spot south or west of Boston and transported by a glacier to Plymouth about 20,000 years ago. The spot it left was somewhere in the *terrane* (specific geologic area) called Atlantica, which surrounds Boston.

Geologists who study plate tectonics say that many millions of years ago there was a huge continent called Pangaea which split into eastern and western parts, the eastern becoming Europe and Africa, the western part North America. The Dedham granite is found mostly in Africa, so it is surprising to consider that Plymouth Rock came over from another continent just as the Pilgrims did, only millions of years before.

When the Pilgrims arrived, they may or may not have stepped on the Rock. If they did, they never mention it in their letters and written accounts. In any case, the Rock was much larger in 1620, but erosion by sea and wind has reduced it to a mere fraction of its former self. Nature did havoc to the Rock, but humans did worse, chipping off small pieces for patriotic souvenirs, taking large pieces to put on display to build patriotic fervor, even using it as part of a wharf at one time. In 1774, 20 yoke of oxen came to move the Rock, and it split in the process. Half of the Rock was put on display at Pilgrim Hall from 1834 to 1867, but was then brought back here. In November 1989, the Rock was repaired and strengthened to withstand the blows from the sea and the laserlike gazes of a million affectionate visitors.

Today the Rock is sheltered by a monumental enclosure, designed by McKim, Mead & White and built in 1921, which stands in **Plymouth Rock State Park** (tel. 508/866-2580).

Just as the Rock marks the beginning of the Pilgrims' adventure in America, so it can serve as the beginning point for your tour of Plymouth. After your look at it, head for the attractions nearby.

Right next to Plymouth Rock is a replica of the sort of house the Pilgrims first built in the New World. Though there's not much to the interior, you can best imagine what it'd be like to live in so tiny a house by stepping inside. Remember that in the 1600s people were not as tall as average Americans today.

The Mayflower

The fact that the Pilgrims suffered to get to America will be brought home more forcefully when you tour the *Mayflower II* (tel. 508/746-1622), a replica of the original ship built in England in 1955 and sailed across the Atlantic to Plymouth in 1957. How, you are sure to ask yourself, was it possible for 102 people—even small ones—to fit themselves and all their baggage for setting up a new town into the tiny rooms and onto the tiny decks of this little ship? And how could they stay on it for 2½ months? The only answer that comes to mind is "by courage and dedication," and it's for that the Pilgrims are admired and remembered. Guides on the *Mayflower II* will tell you about the boat's workings and will answer questions; display panels on the dock and an excellent leaflet given to you as you enter will explain other details of nautical lore.

Mayflower II is only a few steps from Plymouth Rock, and is open April through November from 9am to 5pm; in the busiest months of July and August the ship stays open until 6:30pm every night. Admission is $5.50 for adults, $3.75 for children 5 to 12 (under 5, free); this includes free parking, a visit to the ship, an audiovisual show at the theater, and indoor exhibits on early Pilgrim life. A museum shop, restaurant, and picnic area are here as well. A special combination ticket ($15 for adults, $10 for children 5 to 12; under 5, free) admits you to the *Mayflower II* and to Plimoth Plantation.

Pilgrim Hall

Seeing how the Pilgrims lived in the earliest period of America's colonization is what Plymouth is all about. You can see exhibits like *Mayflower II* and the early huts to give you an idea, or you can see the actual Pilgrim furniture and huge oil paintings featured in Pilgrim Hall, 75 Court St. (tel. 508/746-1620), at the corner of Chilton and Court. (Court Street, Main Street, and Sandwich Street are all different names for different sections of the same street.) The oldest historical museum in continuous service in the United States, Pilgrim Hall was built in 1824 to house artifacts the Pilgrims used, a library for research into Plymouth's early history, and galleries for the monumental paintings depicting important events in Pilgrim history. In the Lower Hall, the slide show puts the Pilgrim experience into the perspective of the times, surrounded by the exceptional furniture of Brewster and Bradford and the rest, and the arms and armor they brought with them. In the Main Hall above are the paintings, the relic of a 17th-century transatlantic ship, and the magnificent pewter, delftware, and woodenware the Pilgrims and their descendants treasured, along with the tools and cookware of the Indians who lived beside the Pilgrims. Many of the items identified as *Mayflower* cargo, such as the wicker cradle of the first English child born in New England, are on display. Pilgrim Hall is open from 9:30am to 4:30pm every day, all year, and costs $4 for adults, $3.50 for seniors and students, and $1.50 for children 6 to 15.

Plymouth National Wax Museum

Even more lifelike than Pilgrim Hall's paintings are the tableaux at the Plymouth National Wax Museum, 16 Carver St. (tel. 508/746-6468), at the top of the hill across the street from Plymouth Rock. The hill is Cole's Hill, where the first Pilgrim cemetery was established and where the first victims of the frigid New England winter were laid to rest. The museum's scenes trace the history of the Pilgrims from persecution in England through the move to Holland to the trip across the Atlantic and the foundation of the settlement at Plymouth. Soundtracks add to the vividness of the scenes. The Wax Museum is open from 9am to 5pm in spring, summer, and fall; admission is $5 for adults, half price for children.

Plimoth Plantation

Most lifelike of all the representations of early colonial life is Plimoth Plantation (tel. 508/746-1622), a "living history museum of 17th-century Plymouth," a Pilgrim village as it may have looked in 1627.

Historical research was done to determine every aspect of the village: The small houses have thatched roofs and kitchen gardens and are surrounded by a fortification (palisade). The people moving about in period dress, known as Plimoth Plantation "interpreters," make the daily activities of a different era comprehensible today. The women may be seen grinding corn, baking bread in an outdoor clay oven, or cooking on open hearths, the men tending the fields or hewing logs to make planks. Even the animals here have been bred to resemble those of the 1600s! There is also Hobbamock's Homesite, a settlement offering demonstrations of how the Wampanoag Indians lived in 1627.

Plimoth Plantation is a nonprofit educational institution, open April through November from 9am to 5pm every day; tickets are sold until 4pm (it's hardly worth entering if you have less than an hour to look around). Admission costs $12 for adults, $8 for children 5 to 12 (under 5, free), but this includes free parking, audio-visual shows at the theater, indoor exhibits on early life, and access to the museum shop and bookstore, restaurants, and a picnic area. Combination tickets allow you to see both Plimoth Plantation and *Mayflower II* at a discount.

The Forefathers' Monument

The National Monument to the Forefathers (tel. 508/746-1790) is the sort of grand statue-and-pedestal one would expect to see on a central boulevard in a world capital, but instead it stands in a small park on Allerton Street, off Samoset (U.S. 44) near the junction with Rte. 3A—follow the signs on the road. First proposed in 1820, the monument was designed by Hammet Billings of Boston in 1855 and dedicated in 1889.

The composition is figurative, with a great granite statue of Faith surrounded by smaller figures of Liberty (with Peace and Tyranny Overthrown), Law (with Justice and Mercy), Education (with Wisdom and Youth), and Morality holding the Decalogue (Ten Commandments) in the left hand and the scroll of Revelation in the right. Between the statues, bas-reliefs remember the most significant events of Pilgrim history: the departure from Delft Harbor in the Netherlands, the signing of the Mayflower Compact at Provincetown, the landing at Plymouth Rock, and the treaty with Massasoit, Sachem of the Wampanoags.

The monument, 81 feet high, is impressive, and it's interesting to speculate about the times and people's thoughts through its history: when it was planned (only 44 years after the signing of the Declaration of Independence), when the cornerstone was laid (1859, on the eve of the Civil War), and when it was dedicated (a year after invention of the Kodak box camera and the electric motor). The view from the little park, by the way, is very fine; a small cast-iron outline map near the base of the monument traces the outline of Cape Cod, which you can see on a clear day.

Plymouth's Old Houses

One of the antique houses in town of particular interest is the **Richard Sparrow House,** 42 Summer St., overlooking Town Brook Park (tel. 508/747-1240). Built in 1640, it's the oldest house in Plymouth; in 1990 it celebrated its 350th anniversary. It's open from late May to Thanksgiving, daily except Wednesday from 10am to 5pm; donation requested. There is also a craft gallery with pottery made on the premises; the gallery stays open through Christmas, so you can pick up some Plymouth crafts as holiday presents.

The **Howland House, 33** Sandwich St. (tel. 508/746-9590), dates from 1667, and is the only Plymouth house still standing which was known to have been occupied by Pilgrims. The parents of Jabez Howland, builder of the house, came over on the *Mayflower,* and it's presumed that they spent their last years with their son. Hours are 10am to 5pm (noon to 5pm on Sunday), late May through mid-October. Admission costs $2.50 for adults, 50¢ for children.

Hand-hewn beams in the **Harlow Old Fort House,** 119 Sandwich St. (tel. 508/746-9697), are from the Pilgrims' log fort on Burial Hill. Built in 1677, the house is now occupied by costumed guides who demonstrate 17th-century crafts and conduct tours. It's open weekends in June, 10am to 5pm; late June through early September, Wednesday through Sunday; early September through mid-October, Tuesday through Thursday. Admission costs $2.50 for adults, 50¢ for children.

The **Spooner House,** 27 North St. (tel. 508/746-9697), was built in 1749, and used to be the home of the Spooner family, famous through the Plymouth Cordage Company as the world's largest maker of rope and twine. James Spooner, last of the family to live here, died in 1954. It's open weekends noon to 5pm during June; Thursday through Saturday 10am to 5pm and Sunday noon to 5pm during July and August; Tuesday and Wednesday 10am to 5pm from September through mid-October. Adults pay $2.50; children, 50¢.

A handsome Federal-style structure is the **Antiquarian House,** 126 Water St.

(tel. 508/746-9697), built by a wealthy shipowner in 1809 and furnished with precious objects brought home by his ships. The fully equipped 19th-century kitchen is a treat. Hours are 10am to 5pm daily from late June to early September, weekends in June, and from mid-September to mid-October. Admission costs $2.50 for adults, 50¢ for children under 16 (under 6, free).

The **Mayflower Society Museum**, 4 Winslow St. (tel. 508/746-2590), was once the elegant home of Edward Winslow. Part of the house was built in 1754, and the other part in 1898. Besides the furnishings, a primary attraction is a daring, flying staircase which looks as though it really should fall down, but doesn't. It's double the size it was in 1754. The formal gardens are nice as well. The museum is open daily from July through early September from 10am to 5pm, plus Fridays and weekends in June and till mid-October. It's open Thanksgiving weekend as well. Admission costs $2.50 for adults, 25¢ for kids.

Pilgrim Progress

At 5pm on Friday in August a group of Plymouth citizens dressed as Pilgrims honor the memory of their ancestors by re-creating the procession to church. The number of persons, their sexes, and ages have been matched to the small group of Pilgrims who survived the first winter in the New World. When you see the procession you may be amazed at the small size of the group that started it all.

Cranberry World

Why do Americans have turkey with cranberry sauce for Thanksgiving? Because both are indigenous to New England. The Pilgrims found both turkeys and cranberries in abundance when they arrived, and made a fitting feast. Cranberry harvesting and processing is still a big industry in and around Plymouth, on Cape Cod, and on the islands. You can learn all about these tart, juicy berries, the bogs where they are grown, and the products made from them, by visiting Cranberry World Visitors Center, 225 Water St. (tel. 508/747-1000 or 747-2350), operated by Ocean Spray Cranberries, Inc. Admission is free, and you can sample free cranberry refreshments as well. From April 1 to November 30, hours are 9:30am to 5pm daily, till 9pm on weekdays in July and August.

2. New Bedford

New Bedford, like Fall River, owed part of its living to textiles, but its fame rests on its history as a whaling port. Herman Melville set his American classic, *Moby Dick,* in New Bedford as the logical spot to begin a whaling epic, and so it was. During the heyday of whale-oil lamps, New Bedford had about 400 ships out scouting the seas for the monster denizens. A ship might be at sea for several years, and when it returned to port it could have thousands of barrels of whale oil in its hold. The story of what whaling was all about—how the ships were manned and equipped, how the search went, how the men pursued and killed the whale, and then butchered and rendered it to make the oil—is all told in New Bedford's famous **Whaling Museum** on Johnny Cake Hill.

Today New Bedford's historic waterfront downtown section is undergoing extensive renovation and restoration. A pedestrian shopping mall complete with trees, benches, and music in the air—called **Melville Mall,** appropriately—has been completed and it does much for the town. East of the mall, going down to the water's edge, the **Custom House** and many merchants' buildings are being restored, cobbled streets are being uncovered or restored, and the center of the city is taking on an appearance much like it had during its 19th-century heyday.

INFORMATION

Right in the middle of the restoration area is the Bristol County Development Council's **Tourist Information Office,** 70 N. 2nd St., New Bedford, MA 02741 (tel. 508/997-1250); signs throughout town point the way. The office is open from 9am to 5pm Monday through Friday (Memorial Day weekend through Labor Day, also open on Saturday from 9am to 5pm and 1 to 5pm on Sunday), and is very helpful with maps, brochures, and touring suggestions.

Second Street is actually very important to visitors. Besides the Bristol County Development Council right next to the big parking garage, there is another source of information, the **City of New Bedford Visitors Center,** 47 N. 2nd St., New Bedford, MA 02741 (tel. 508/991-6200), open from 9am to 5pm Monday through Saturday and 10am to 3pm on Sunday. The center is in a restored brick commercial building which now also houses numerous shops and eateries. Twice daily in summer, the center sponsors hour-long walking tours ($1 donation requested).

In the same building at 47 N. 2nd St. are the offices of Pineapple Hospitality (see below under "Where to Stay").

Note that if you come to 2nd Street for information, you might want to plan a visit to the New Bedford Glass Museum at the same time, as it's right in between the two information offices.

WHERE TO STAY

New Bedford has its own bed-and-breakfast referral service. **Pineapple Hospitality,** P.O. Box F821, New Bedford, MA 02742-0821 (tel. 508/990-1696), will take your reservation and provide details on a local B&B any time from 9am to 5pm Monday through Friday. Actually the service has listings for B&Bs throughout New England, but your most immediate need is here, now, in New Bedford. Room prices range from $40 to $95 single, $48 to $145 double (quite a range!). Many of the homes participating in the service welcome young children. Why the pineapple, you ask? In New Bedford's nautical heyday, ships would bring this tropical delicacy back home at the end of a voyage. A pineapple set out in front of the house meant the occupants were at home, receiving visitors, and celebrating the success of the voyage.

There are several comfortable motels on I-195 west of downtown New Bedford. In the city proper is the **Durant Sail Loft Inn,** 1 Merrill's Wharf, New Bedford, MA 02740 (tel. 508/999-2700), right in the waterfront district, which is half commercial and half industrial. The inn is in a fine old granite countinghouse, now refurbished with 16 simple rooms which rent for $64 with double bed or twin beds and $97 for a suite, tax included. The inn has its own restaurant called Portofino. Getting there can be tricky. First find Union Street. Go south on Union, cross the expressway, and turn right just before the gates of the New Bedford State Pier (don't enter the pier area). The inn is a short distance along this road, on the left.

WHERE TO DINE

The most convenient eatery is **Johnny Cakes Restaurant,** 1 Johnny Cake Hill (tel. 508/993-3326), just to the left of the Seamen's Bethel and only a few steps from the Whaling Museum. There's a light, cheery upstairs dining room or a sunny patio, and a menu of interesting lighter fare including seafood pie, vegetable stir-fry, various burgers, and a roast turkey sandwich. Lunch here should cost less than $12, all in. Hours are Tuesday through Saturday from 8am to 3pm.

WHAT TO SEE

You've come to see whaling memorabilia, of which New Bedford has lots. But there are other things to see as well, including the local glass museum and a museum dedicated to firefighting.

The Whaling Museum

At 18 Johnny Cake Hill in the heart of the Historic Waterfront District, the **New Bedford Whaling Museum** (tel. 508/997-0046) is a complex of seven buildings which form the block between William and Union streets. It's open from 9am to 5pm Monday through Saturday and 1 to 5pm on Sunday. Admission costs $3.50 for adults, $3 for seniors, $2.50 for kids 6 to 14. The museum is dedicated to the history of New Bedford, with particular emphasis on the story of whaling in the age of sail.

The first exhibit to confront you is the largest ship model in the world: a replica of the bark *Lagoda* made to exactly one half the ship's original size. Rigging, tryworks, whaleboats, and other equipment are all in place, and you can walk about the model at will. On the wall of the *Lagoda* room is a 100-foot-long mural showing various types of whales. The family who owned and operated the *Lagoda* donated the model, and the building to house it, to the museum. Around the walls of the museum are old photographs and drawings explaining the whaling industry, and many other rooms in the museum hold collections of other whaling lore: cooperage and chandlery; records of the countinghouse, brokerage, banking, and insurance; and articles of glass, china, and pewter manufactured in the New Bedford area, or made by leading citizens. A gallery exhibits dozens of paintings done on whaling themes.

Perhaps the most beautiful exhibit besides the *Lagoda* is the scrimshaw, the delicate, intricate articles of carved whalebone and tooth which the whalesmen made to while away the long hours at sea. The artistry displayed is almost breathtaking, and the ingenuity very revealing of quick and sensitive minds. It wouldn't be far wrong to say that without understanding whaling, one couldn't understand 19th-century New England; and the place to find out about whaling is certainly New Bedford.

Seamen's Bethel

Across the street from the Whaling Museum is the Seamen's Bethel (tel. 508/992-3295), a chapel constructed in 1832 "for the moral improvement of sailors," and immortalized in *Moby Dick*. With a gratefully appreciated donation you can explore the Bethel. And several blocks away, at Pleasant and William, the **Public Library** has displays of whaling books and pamphlets. Open from 9am to 9pm daily, May 1 through Columbus Day only.

New Bedford Glass Museum

The city of New Bedford has been producing glass continuously longer than any other town in New England, and an outstanding collection of its glass products is housed in a fine Federal mansion (1821) at 50 N. Second St. (tel. 508/994-0115). The museum's collection of almost 2,000 objects includes many items of porcelain and silver, as well as drawings and paintings related to the crafting of glass. The museum costs $2 for adults, $1.50 for seniors, and 50¢ for children 6 to 12, and is open Monday through Saturday from 10am to 4pm.

New Bedford Fire Museum

Anyone interested in the history of firefighting in America will want to take a look at the New Bedford Fire Museum, Bedford Street at 6th Street (tel. 508/992-2162). The museum's beginnings date back to 1890, and it is situated appropriately next to New Bedford's Fire Station No. 4, a building that dates from 1867 and is still in active use. Come from 9am to 5pm any day in summer to see the restored antique fire trucks and other firefighting equipment, displays of old uniforms, working models of pumps and fire poles, and other memorabilia. Admission costs $2 for adults, half price for children.

Rotch-Jones-Duff House and Garden

A beautiful example of Greek Revival architecture as practiced by New Bedford's wealthy whaling merchants, the **Rotch-Jones-Duff House,** 396 County St. (tel. 508/997-1401), was designed in 1834 by Richard Upjohn, founder of the American Institute of Architects. The historic house museum and period gardens (including a wildflower walk) are open to the public from 11am to 4pm Tuesday through Friday (on Saturday as well in June, July, and August). Admission costs $4 for adults, half price for children.

The Ferry to Martha's Vineyard

M. V. *Schamonchi,* operated by Cape Island Express Lines, Inc., P.O. Box J-4095, New Bedford, MA 02741 (tel. 508/997-1688), carries passengers (no cars) from New Bedford to the town of Vineyard Haven on the island of Martha's Vineyard three or four times daily in summer for $8 one way, $14 round trip for adults; for kids under 12, $4.50 one way, $7 round trip. Call for up-to-date schedules and information (in Vineyard Haven, call 508/693-2088).

---

3. Fall River

In the mid-19th century Fall River was a boom textile town. Because of its natural harbor, ample waterpower, and a moist climate ideal for working thread, it became a world textile-weaving center. Huge mills made from blocks of the local granite were built everywhere, making an awesome scene of industry and wealth. But in the 20th century the textile business began moving to the south, and Fall River's industry foundered.

Prosperity has returned to Fall River, and now many of the impressive granite mills produce finished apparel; others turn out rubber products, foods, and paper. The town's new Government Center, built on the airspace over I-195, is a symbol of Fall River's resurgence, and adds its impressive appearance to that of the great mills.

WHAT TO SEE

Most people pass through Fall River on their way from Providence to Cape Cod or from Boston to Newport, and when they do, the sight they stop to see is **Battleship Cove** (tel. 508/678-1100), permanent berth of a number of impressive craft. The U.S.S. *Joseph P. Kennedy, Jr.,* a World War II destroyer, is here, as is a wooden PT boat, and also the submarine U.S.S. *Lionfish.* But the star of the exhibit is the mighty U.S.S. *Massachusetts,* the battleship berthed here as a memorial to Massachusetts men and women who were killed in World War II. In the Fall River Heritage State Park Visitor Center are local history exhibits. From I-195, follow the signs for Battleship Cove (sometimes just the silhouette of the battleship is on the sign). The exhibits are open May to October, every day from 9am to 5pm; November through April, every day to 4:30pm. You can tour both above and below decks on all the ships. For lunch, have a meal or a snack in the wardroom of the U.S.S. *Massachusetts.* Other facilities at Battleship Cove, under the impressive I-195 bridge, are a snack bar, a tourist information office with free hotel reservation assistance service, and rest rooms.

The **Marine Museum at Fall River,** 70 Water St., (tel. 508/674-3533), past the battleship and the State Pier, on the left, has a number of fascinating shipping exhibits. Certainly the most popular is the 1-ton, 28-foot-long scale model of the *Titanic,* created in 1952 for Twentieth-Century-Fox's movie about the *Titanic* tragedy. Other beautiful ship's models and maritime artifacts detail the history of the Fall River Line, which ran luxury steamers between Fall River and New York from 1847 to 1937. Yet another exhibit follows the history of steam power at sea. Nautical buffs from around the world, many of them famous collectors, have donated exhibits to the museum, which is open Monday through Friday from 9am to 4:30pm, Saturday and Sunday from 10am to 5pm. Admission costs $3 for adults, $2 for kids 6 to 14.

SHOPPING

Fall River is a mecca for those who love factory-outlet shopping, because the revival of apparel manufacture here has led to the opening of dozens of huge factory-outlet stores. Billboards on I-195 trumpet that it is the "largest factory-outlet center in New England!" Signs lead you off the highway to the "Heart of Fall River's Factory-Outlet District," with over 90 outlet stores. If you follow the signs, will you really save money? Yes, a definitive yes!

I'm a skeptical shopper, and not a particularly enthusiastic one, but when I went to check out this factory-outlet district, even I was impressed. I ended up buying shirts, underwear, belts, and other items at very, very good prices. Quality can be either tops, or just under, or factory seconds, or worse. But in the store where I bought, quality was clearly marked, and prices were excellent on all of the different grades.

What can you find here? When it comes to clothing, *everything!* Shoes, sweaters, raincoats, accessories, designer labels, coats, handbags, jewelry, children's clothing, cosmetics, luggage. Branch out a bit and you'll find kitchenware, gifts, furniture, braided rugs, curtains, crystal, candy and nuts, greeting cards and giftwrap, toys, towels, linens, baskets, brass—even wallpaper. This is definitely a town in which you can shop till you drop.

A NOTE ON LIZZIE

Fall River's other claim to fame is the celebrated Lizzie Borden murder trial in 1892, in which Lizzie, a young Fall River girl, was tried for chopping up her parents with an axe: it's good to remember that the poor girl was acquitted. The guilty party was never found.

CAPE COD

Cape Cod is a world of its own. This 70-mile-long arm of sand curled into the Atlantic was formed by glacial action and was given its name by an early (1602) visitor to the New World, Bartholomew Gosnold. The Pilgrims landed in the New World at Provincetown and drew up the Mayflower Compact before heading on to the mainland at what would become Plymouth.

Strictly speaking, Cape Cod is an island separated from the rest of Massachusetts by the Cape Cod Canal, a deep waterway built from north to south across the base of the Cape in the early part of this century. Two graceful bridges span the canal —one at Bourne to the south (Rte. 28), one at Sagamore to the north (Rte. 6)—and both are very busy in the warm months. Just before crossing either bridge, look for the little information sheds established by the Cape Cod Chamber of Commerce, open from 9am to 7pm every day during the summer. Maps, booklets, motel brochures, and tabloid newspaper "current listings" are all yours for free, and if you need a room reservation, you'll get help.

The telephone area code for Cape Cod is **508.**

1. Getting There

Cape Cod was once a seafarers' domain, and although it's still possible to get there by boat, the rail, bus, air, and road routes make it easy to get there any way you choose.

BY CAR

Coming from New York and Providence, take I-195 to Rte. 28 South and cross the Bourne Bridge if you're heading for Falmouth and Woods Hole; if you're going to Sandwich, Hyannis, or other Cape points, don't take the Bourne Bridge, but take U.S. 6 East just before the Bourne Bridge, and this will take you to the Sagamore Bridge, where you cross the canal. Coming from Boston, the Southeast Expressway (I-93) will take you right to Rte. 3, which goes straight to the Sagamore Bridge. If you're on your way to Falmouth and Woods Hole, stay on I-93 past the intersection with Rte. 3 and take Exit 66 for Rte. 24 South. This beautiful superhighway changes numbers and becomes Rte. 23, then Rte. 28, before taking you right over the Bourne Bridge.

BY RAIL

Cape Cod's first crowds of summer visitors came via rail from New York and Boston, and now you can come the same way.

Amtrak (tel. toll free 800/368-8725) in recent years has operated weekend service from New York City, Providence, and Boston to Hyannis, with trains departing New York on Friday and Saturday, and returning from Hyannis on Saturday and Sunday. One-way fare is currently $48. The railroad has arranged with Plymouth & Brockton Street Railway Company for dedicated connecting bus service from Hyannis to Chatham, Dennisport, Eastham, Harwich, Orleans, South Yarmouth, Wellfleet, and Provincetown, which means that you can buy an Amtrak ticket in New York City for the trip all the way to the tip of the Cape. The service is funded in part by the Commonwealth of Massachusetts. Such special contracts are subject to governmental budgetary ups and downs, so you should definitely call Amtrak to see if the service is still running when you want it.

BY BUS

Bus service to the Cape from New York, Providence, and Boston is good, fast, and frequent. Here are the details.

From New York: Bonanza (Greyhound/Trailways ticket counter in Port Authority terminal; tel. 212/564-8484 or 212/594-2000) runs buses via two routes, along the coast or via Waterbury and Hartford. In high summer there are five buses a day from New York all the way to Provincetown at the tip of the Cape, and a good number of other buses going as far as Hyannis, where you can transfer for other points.

From Providence/Newport: From Providence, catch the Bonanza bus (about six a day) to Hyannis, or the two a day going to Provincetown. The trip takes less than 2 hours to Hyannis. Bonanza's headquarters are at P.O. Box 1116, Annex Station, Providence, RI 02901 (tel. 401/751-8800).

From Boston: Plymouth & Brockton Street Railway Company has buses which leave from the Greyhound Terminal (tel. 617/423-5810) and the South Station (Amtrak) Terminal (tel. 617/749-5067). The trip to Hyannis takes 1½ hours.

South Shore & Cape Cod Limo Service (tel. toll free 800/343-7540) makes four trips a day between Boston's Logan International Airport and Hyannis, with stops at Sagamore, Plymouth, and three other points. Reservations are strongly advised.

BY AIR

Business Express (tel. 203/222-1000 or toll free 800/345-3400), a Delta Connection carrier, provides service from Bridgeport, Conn., to Martha's Vineyard and Nantucket; also to Baltimore, Boston, Hyannis, New York (La Guardia), Philadelphia, and White Plains (N.Y.).

BY BOAT

Bay State Provincetown Steamship Company (tel. 617/723-7800 in Boston) operates the M.V. *Provincetown II* on a run from Boston to P-town every day from late May through July and August until Labor Day; there's one daily sailing leaving Boston's Commonwealth Pier at 9:30am, arriving P-town at about 12:30pm, and returning from P-town (at 3:30pm) to Boston (arriving about 6:30pm). A round-trip ticket for an adult costs $25, or $18 for seniors and kids under 12; the one-way fare is $15; for seniors and kids, $13.

TRANSPORTATION ON THE CAPE

Route 6, the Mid-Cape Highway, is the fastest way to travel from the "Upper Cape" (the part you first come to by land) to the "Lower Cape" (the narrow portion north of Orleans to Provincetown). But Rte. 6 is not necessarily the prettiest way to go; if you have the time, travel one of the smaller, scenic roads instead.

Bus transportation on the Cape is provided by **Plymouth & Brockton Street Railway Company,** Elm & Centre streets, Hyannis (tel. 508/775-5524). You can take a Plymouth & Brockton bus from Hyannis to Provincetown via Orleans, Eastham, and Wellfleet.

Transportation to the islands of Martha's Vineyard and Nantucket is covered in the sections on Woods Hole and Hyannis.

ROOM RESERVATIONS

Bed & Breakfast Cape Cod, P.O. Box 341, West Hyannisport, MA 02672 (tel. 508/775-2772), will find you a room on Cape Cod in one of 60 historic inns and host homes for $44 to $66 single, $50 to $203 double, breakfast included. Write in plenty of time, and you'll be sent a free catalog listing homes and inns that might interest you.

---

2. Falmouth and Woods Hole

Falmouth is a pretty town which has grown rapidly in recent years but which has managed to preserve a lot of the charm of a rural New England town. A city park next to the library, a well-preserved Village Green, and magnificent tall trees along Main Street make the downtown section attractive, and manicured lawns and white clapboard houses dress up the side streets. The town has a few pleasant historical inns, several good beaches, and daily ships to Martha's Vineyard.

A few miles past Falmouth to the south is Woods Hole, home of world-famous Woods Hole Oceanographic Institute; car-ferries depart from Woods Hole for Martha's Vineyard several times daily in summer.

TOURIST INFORMATION

The **Falmouth Chamber of Commerce,** P.O. Box 582, Falmouth, MA 02541 (tel. toll free 800/526-8532), operates an Information Office downtown off Main Street in the Lawrence Academy building. Look for a short street called Academy Lane. If the chamber can't answer your question, it's probably not about Falmouth.

WHERE TO STAY

Falmouth has dozens of motels, mostly expensive and somewhat sterile, though modern and comfortable. For the true flavor of Falmouth, however, I'd recommend the moderately priced small inns and guesthouses. I've included descriptions of the best of the larger places as well. During off-season, when inquiring about room prices, be sure to ask about reductions for stays of a few days or more. A room costing $60 for one night may well cost $55 per night if you stay two or three days.

Guesthouses and Inns

Falmouth is rich in guesthouses, which is not surprising. The way to spend a week or two by the sea, at moderate cost, is to rent a room in a private home. Lots of houses in **Falmouth Heights,** southeast of the center of Falmouth proper, are devoted to renting rooms for about $40 to $50 double, with a shared bathroom. If you specifically request it, your room may have a view of the sea. You should also be aware that this is the most boisterous section of town. But before describing the guesthouses, I should tell you about two charming inns right downtown near Falmouth Green.

DOWNTOWN A few steps from the Falmouth Historical Society is the **Palmer House Inn,** 81 Palmer Ave., Falmouth, MA 02540 (tel. 508/548-1230), very near the green and the center of town. The innkeepers, Bud Peacock and Phyllis Niemi-Peacock, have decorated each of the eight guest rooms in this turn-of-the-century Victorian house with antiques and authentic period pieces, and each room has a private bath. The Peacocks serve a wonderful fancy breakfast (cheese blintz with blueberry compote, Finnish pancake and strawberry soup), which is included in the room price of $93 double on weekdays, $100 double, per night, on weekends; tax is included in these prices. If the perfect location doesn't get you, the stained glass, wicker, and doilies will.

Mostly Hall, 27 W. Main St., Falmouth, MA 02540 (tel. 508/548-3786), is only steps from Falmouth Green and the beginning of the bicycle path to Woods Hole. The plantation-style house was built in 1849 as a wedding present for the New Orleans bride of Capt. Albert Nye. These days you can stay in any of six guest rooms for $83 to $105 double with private bath; rates include a full breakfast, the use of bicycles, and the inevitable tax. For getting the real flavor of Falmouth, Mostly Hall can't be beat.

ALONG GRAND AVENUE The guesthouses on Grand Avenue in Falmouth Heights differ only slightly from one another in price, accommodations, sea views, and charm. During the summer season your selection may well have to be made on the basis of availability.

Head down Falmouth Heights Road, which skirts the eastern side of Falmouth Harbor, and soon you'll see Grand Avenue bearing off to the right. It then makes a loop south and east, running along Falmouth Heights Beach before heading back to rejoin Falmouth Heights Road. Heading in this direction, house numbers go in descending order.

Bud and Phyllis Peacock of the Palmer House also own **Peacock's Inn on the Sound,** 313 Grand Ave. (P.O. Box 201), Falmouth, MA 02541 (tel. 508/457-9666). This waterfront B&B has ten recently renovated guest rooms with private baths done in a country-cozy decor, a picture window in each room; many rooms have hardwood floors, and two have fireplaces. Fresh-baked breads and pastries are served for breakfast, which is included in the rates: $82 to $100 double per day, tax included, on weekends in the summer. Reductions are offered midweek and off-season; the inn is open all year.

The **Grafton Inn,** 261 Grand Ave. South, Falmouth Heights, MA 02540 (tel. 508/540-8688), is right across the street from the main beach area, with snack stands and restaurants located conveniently nearby. All 11 rooms have private baths and rent for $72 to $94 double, year round. Rates include a fine buffet breakfast, an enclosed porch, sufficient parking, and a very comfortable, simple atmosphere. No smoking, no children, and no pets.

The **Gladstone Inn,** 219 Grand Ave. South, Falmouth Heights, MA 02540 (tel. 508/548-9851), owned by Jim and Gayle Carroll, is at the corner of Montgomery Avenue, across the street from the beach. A glassed-in veranda shares the sea view, and this is where you have your buffet breakfast or cool afternoon drink. All rooms share baths; singles go for $31 and doubles run $53, tax included. The newly renovated apartment over the garage behind the house rents for $75. The house is open from mid-May through mid-October.

OUT OF THE CENTER Located on Jones Road at the corner of Gifford Street are the venerable red farmhouse, barn, and sheds that make up the **Coonamessett Inn**

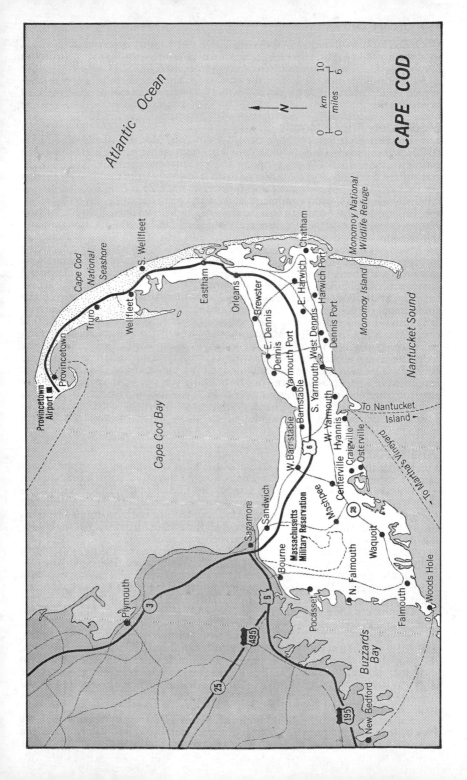

CAPE COD

Atlantic Ocean

Cape Cod National Seashore

Provincetown
Provincetown Airport

Truro

S. Wellfleet

Wellfleet

Eastham

Orleans

Brewster

E. Dennis

Dennis

E. Harwich

Harwich Port

Dennis Port

Chatham

Yarmouth Port

Barnstable

W. Barnstable

S. Yarmouth West Dennis

W. Yarmouth

Hyannis

Centerville

Craigville

Osterville

To Nantucket Island

Monomoy National Wildlife Refuge

Monomoy Island

Nantucket Sound

Cape Cod Bay

Sandwich

Mashpee

Massachusetts Military Reservation

28

Waquoit

To Martha's Vineyard

Sagamore

Bourne

6

Pocasset

N. Falmouth

Woods Hole

Falmouth

Plymouth

3

495

25

195

New Bedford

Buzzards Bay

N

km   10
         6
miles
0   0

6

(P.O. Box 707), Falmouth, MA 02540 (tel. 508/548-2300). After swiftly checking in at the hotellike lobby, two people can move right into a sitting-room/bedroom combo for $127, a living-room/two-bedroom combo for $143, or a cottage for $154. Prices drop roughly 30% in the off-season. The rear of the property is landscaped beautifully, sloping gently down to a lake where a gaggle of geese make its home.

Moderately Priced Motels

The **Elm Arch Inn,** off Main Street, Falmouth, MA 02540 (tel. 508/548-0133), was originally a private house, but it has been taking paying guests for over a century—more than 60 years under the present management. The location couldn't be better: right in the center of town, a few steps from the library park, and yet back off Main Street in peace and quiet. The inn's 24 rooms are furnished in colonial-style pieces, many handmade, and are just plain charming. Several have private baths; others have running water and share a bath down the hall. In Richardson House, the addition to the inn, there are private baths and air conditioning throughout. Rooms with a double or twin beds and bath cost $55 to $66 in season, $50 off-season, tax in. Rooms with running water cost $44. No meals are served, but the inn offers free coffee in the mornings, in season. Although you're a 15-minute walk from the beach here, the inn has its own small pool, bordered by a lush lawn and large trees, and a big screened patio for summer evenings.

The **Shore Way Acres Motel** is more a resort than a motel, with two pools (indoor and outdoor), extensive grounds covered in lush grass, flowers, and trees. It's midway between downtown and the beach on Shore Street (tel. 508/540-3000 or toll free 800/352-7100 in Massachusetts)—you'll first come across its centerpiece, the stately old white clapboard lodge, dripping with wisteria. Behind the lodge are several attractive buildings with rooms and the glassed-in pool building. Saunas and an exercise room are included among the facilities. The rates here are somewhat of a tangle, and depend on the building you stay in, the time of year you stay, the length of your stay, the number of beds you use, and whether or not your room has kitchen facilities. In general, double rooms with bath cost $83 to $138. In season and on holidays, the minimum reservation period on weekends is three nights.

WHERE TO DINE

Falmouth is not a culinary mecca, although it does have a few quite decent eateries, some good for breakfast or a light lunch, others for a more formal dinner. The **Town House Restaurant,** 275 Main St. (tel. 508/548-0285), across the street from the town library, has been serving for more than 40 years. One of the first things you'll notice as you enter is the wood wainscoting and barn boards that dress the walls, and the liberal use of brick that gives the restaurant a rustic but warm feeling. At lunchtime there's a soup-and-sandwich special: a bowl of the soup of the day plus a choice sandwich for under $5. In the evening, the Mariner Platter (sole, clams, scallops, shrimp, and onion rings) is $13. Broiled seafood and fresh boiled live lobsters are also offered. Be sure to inspect the seascape in watercolor painted by a local artist. Note that the Town House is open from late May to late October *only;* hours are weekdays from 7:30am to 10pm, weekends from 11:30am to 10pm.

Domingo's Olde Restaurant, on Rte. 28A, West Falmouth (tel. 508/540-0575), serves excellent, moderately priced seafood (with Italian overtones) in an unassuming converted old home. Choose from lobster, swordfish, seafood kabob, and veal marsala. I had bouillabaisse chock-full of shrimp, haddock, oysters, scallops, and mussels, a side order of garlic bread, and a simple dessert for $28 (tax and tip included), but that's about as high as it goes, unless you order lobster. Check the daily specials for the freshest fish. Give Domingo's a day's notice to prepare a special request for you. The restaurant is open every day from 4 to 11pm; make reservations to be on the safe side.

For an earthy-crunchy, healthful lunch (from 11:30am to 3pm any day), try **Peach Tree Circle,** on Old Palmer Avenue (tel. 508/548-2354). Take the

Sippiwissett exit of Rte. 28 and keep to the left; it's worth the 2-mile drive from the Village Green. In addition to selling flowers, fruit, cheeses, and other picnic fixings, Peach Tree also serves fish chowder for $3.75 a cup, broccoli quiche for $3.50, and full chef's salads for $6. Enjoy a relaxing lunch out on the platform porch under the shade of old trees or inside amid natural-stained paneling.

For quick and surprisingly light fried seafood, go where the locals go year round: **McMenamy's Fried Seafood,** on busy Rte. 28 heading toward Hyannis (tel. 508/540-2115). Eat on picnic tables behind the restaurant, inside with noisy families, or take lunch to the beach. For $5.50 try the fish 'n' chips or splurge by these standards and get a shrimp or clam plate for $8.50. For an authentic taste, add a dash of vinegar to the chips.

Falmouth's finest place to dine from late May through mid-September is undoubtedly the **Regatta** (tel. 508/548-5400), at the southern end of Scranton Avenue, overlooking the mouth of Falmouth's long harbor. Open only for dinner every evening from 5:30 to about 10pm, the Regatta offers classic French and American cuisine. You'll want to be dressed neatly, if informally, and you should bring $50 per person to dine, wine included. Start with Chesapeake Bay soft-shell crab pancetta, or grilled shrimp with three-mustard sauce; then proceed to the palette of two fish, each with its own sauce, or boneless rack of lamb en chemise with sauce Cabernet, and finish up with the chocolate seduction cake and raspberry sauce. Call for reservations.

On the same wavelength is the **Coonamessett Inn** dining room, on Jones Road at the corner of Gifford Street (tel. 508/548-2300), with casual elegance, traditional New England cuisine, and service that's attentive yet not overbearing. Start with chilled oysters on the half shell or the popular quahog chowder, proceed to a delightful seafood Newburg in casserole, save room for a side of homemade fresh pasta of the day, and then linger over coffee and the inn's deservedly famous Indian pudding. Expect to spend $38 (for one), including tax and tip, for that particular combination.

The dining room is open for lunch from 11:30am to 2:30pm Monday to Saturday, noon to 3pm Sunday; for dinner from 5:30 to 9pm nightly. Eli's, a more casual alternative, serves the dining-room lunch menu throughout the day; try a chicken club ($7) or shrimp scampi ($12). Before you leave check out the *Legend of the Mermaid* paintings that hang in the dining room.

WHAT TO SEE

Falmouth is a very pretty town, and walks through the beaches, the older sections of town, and along the Village Green are a must. For a detailed map, or for other information, send for the 68-page brochure from the **Falmouth Chamber of Commerce,** P.O. Box 582, Falmouth, MA 02541 (tel. toll free 800/526-8532).

The **Falmouth Historical Society** has interesting displays pertaining to Falmouth's history in its lovely old mansion, the Julia Wood House, at 55/65 Palmer Avenue (tel. 508/548-4857), just off the Village Green. For the price of admission you also get to see the adjacent Hallett Barn, with displays of early tools and farm implements, and the Historical Society's shop, as well as Conant House, next door, with more historical collections. The Katharine Lee Bates Room holds memorabilia of Falmouth's poet, who wrote the words to "America the Beautiful." The cordial staff at the Historical Society will be sure to point out that the white Congregational church on the green is equipped with a bell cast by Paul Revere. The museums are open Monday through Friday from 2 to 5pm, mid-June through mid-September. Admission costs $2 for adults, 50¢ for children.

One of America's—and the world's—most exciting experiments in ecological living is being carried out at the **New Alchemy Institute,** 237 Hatchville Rd., in Hatchville (East Falmouth), MA 02536 (tel. 508/564-6301). The latest, or sometimes the most ancient, cultivation methods are being researched and adapted to fit the world of the future. The success that the New Alchemists have had in growing nutritious vegetables and fruits year round, using solar energy, without chemical fertilizers or pesticides, is amazing. You have to see it all to believe it, and you can do it by dropping in any Wednesday through Sunday from mid-June through mid-September, for a guided tour at 1pm. Self-guided tours are possible daily year round. There is also a garden stand selling organically grown produce.

WHAT TO DO

A prime Falmouth activity is to rent bicycles and take the **bike path** down to Woods Hole (see below). The Bikeways Committee of the Falmouth Chamber of Commerce publishes a pamphlet-map showing bike routes and beaches, and giving the addresses of shops that rent bicycles. Ask at the Information Office mentioned above, or call the chamber toll free at 800/526-8532. By biking to a beach you avoid paying the several dollars for parking, and you can put the money saved toward the rental fee.

Besides bike trips down to Woods Hole, Falmouth's greatest outdoor attraction is its coastline. The **Town Beach** is down at the end of Shore Street (best to walk, as parking can be a problem). The water can be very chilly except in July and August, but otherwise the beach is fine, with a view of Martha's Vineyard in the distance.

Reputedly the best beach in the area is called **Old Silver Beach,** several miles to the northwest of downtown Falmouth. If you have a bike, that's the way to go even though it's a distance, because it will cost you $6 to park when you get to Old Silver. In a way the parking fee is not so bad, for it helps the town keep the beach clean. A headland and several jetties set the beach off into sections; the town runs a **clam bar** which sells sandwiches, fried clams, and soft drinks, and offers changing rooms. The crowd at Old Silver is spirited, young, and sun-hungry.

The town of Falmouth sponsors free **band concerts** down at the Falmouth Marina on Thursday evenings during the months of July and August. Try to make it to at least one concert; it's a real old-time event.

Falmouth also has its own summer theater, the **Falmouth Playhouse** (tel. 508/563-5922), with a playbill of musicals which begins in June and goes right through October. The playhouse has its own restaurant and lounge, and you get a cut on dinner-and-theater deals. Theater tickets cost $12 to $13 on Wednesday through Friday and Sunday, $14 to $16 on Saturday. Those with children will want to call and find out what's playing on the Children's Theater bill (Monday mornings and afternoons) as well, where all tickets cost $4.

ACROSS TO MARTHA'S VINEYARD

Falmouth's own *Island Queen,* Falmouth Heights Road (tel. 508/548-4800), built 1974 and operated by Island Commuter Corp., carries passengers and bicycles only (no cars) from Falmouth Harbor to Oak Bluffs on the island. The ferry does not operate year round, but sails two times a day in each direction during early June and mid-September (four times a day on weekends), and seven times a day in each direction from mid-June through the first week in September. Adults pay $8 round trip ($5 one way); children under 13 pay $4 round trip. Bicycles are taken at a charge of $5 round trip. The voyage takes about a half hour, and is usually quite smooth and comfortable. A refreshment bar on board serves snacks, sandwiches, soft drinks, beer, and cocktails. There is even a moonlight cruise on Thursday evenings in July and August.

For car-ferries to the islands, you'll have to go to Woods Hole or Hyannis (see those sections for full particulars).

WOODS HOLE

When Emperor Hirohito of Japan visited the United States in 1976, the only scientific center he wanted to visit was Woods Hole. Being a marine biologist himself, he was interested in seeing one of the world's great centers for the study of sea life, especially the Marine Biological Laboratory. Besides the laboratory, Woods Hole is home to the Woods Hole Oceanographic Institute (WHOI), the Northeast Fisheries Center of the National Marine Fisheries Service, and the U.S. Geological Survey's Branch of Atlantic Geology. Marine science is the lifeblood of the town, for the scientific buildings take up most of the space at the tip of a tiny peninsula, leaving room for only a few streets of fine old houses, a few small boatyards, a restaurant or two, and the car-ferry docks to Martha's Vineyard and Nantucket islands.

The Oceanographic Institute has no exhibits open to the public, but the U.S. Department of Commerce's National Marine Fisheries Service maintains an **aquarium** (tel. 548-5123), on Water Street (the town's main street) down at the end of the peninsula. Follow Water Street through the town; just after it turns right, the aquarium is on your left. It's open mid-June to mid-September from 10am to 4pm daily; from 9am to 4pm the rest of the year; admission is free.

Where to Stay

Staying overnight in Woods Hole is not particularly cheap, although it can be very pleasant. The **Sands of Time Motor Inn,** P.O. Box 106, Woods Hole, MA 02543 (tel. 508/548-6300), just out of town on the road to Falmouth, has a fine view of the harbor and is only a short walk from the ferry docks. Rooms are in a modern motel unit and a grand Victorian house, both overlooking the harbor. A small garden and swimming pool are fitted into the hillside between the two. Rooms have air conditioning, private bath, color TV, and two double beds. Those in the motel are modern and comfortable; the ones in the house have nice old touches like crystal doorknobs, fireplaces, bright new paint, and sparkling bathrooms. A grandfather clock inhabits the pretty entranceway. Prices are $93 to $115 double, tax included, during the busy summer months. Children under 18 pay half price. Off-season rates are lower.

A few doors down from the motel you'll find eight more distinctive rooms and a cottage at the **Grey Whale Inn,** 565 Woods Hole Rd., Woods Hole, MA 02543 (tel. 508/548-7692). Two attic rooms share a bath, but the rest have private baths. Antique beds, immaculate rooms, a lovely view of Little Harbor, and complimentary bikes are included in the high-season room rate of $94 to $105 double. The inn is a half mile from the dock, but the owners have been known to drive guests who have too much luggage to manage on their own.

Where to Dine

A few restaurants near the ferry docks specialize in big, rich seafood dinners at substantial prices—just what you don't want before taking a boat ride if there's any chance the water may be a bit rough. Instead, I recommend a light lunch at the **Fishmonger's Café,** on Woods Hole's main street just before the little bridge, on the left (official address, 56 Water St.; no phone). Lunch and dinner specials are written on the blackboard and sandwiches are available any time. There are also many burgers and vegetarian entrees from which to choose. Fish and chips is $10; a good clam chowder is $3.25 a cup, $4.25 a bowl. Wine and beer are served with meals. The atmosphere is rustic, with rough wood tables, board floors, and sea breezes wafting in through the windows. Heavily patronized by local people and visitors to the institute, the café may echo with Japanese or Spanish as foreign biologists discuss their countries' marine problems and opportunities. Service is fast (there's a take-out window too), which is what you need if you have to catch a ferry. The Fishmonger's Café is open from 7am to 11pm every day except Tuesday, when it opens at 11:30am.

CAR FERRY TO THE ISLANDS

The **Woods Hole, Martha's Vineyard and Nantucket Steamship Authority,** P.O. Box 284, Woods Hole, MA 02543 (tel. 508/540-2022), operates car-carrying ferries between the points listed in its name, and also Hyannis. Schedules change several times a year, so it's best to call in advance for full current information. In fact, if you plan to ship your car, you must have a car reservation. You can get one by calling the number above. Ferries from Woods Hole to Vineyard Haven or Oak Bluffs on Martha's Vineyard leave about 6 times a day in winter, 14 times a day in summer, on the 45-minute trip. Fares are $8 round trip for adults, half price for kids 5 to 12, free for kids under 5. Bikes go for $2.75 one way. Autos cost $30 one way in season. You can't get from Woods Hole or Falmouth to Nantucket, but you can from Hyannis (see section 4 below).

Parking Fees at the Docks: If you don't plan to ferry your car over, and you don't ride a bike or take the bus to Woods Hole, figure on paying $7 to park your car for each *calendar* day ($14 if you leave your car overnight). It is virtually impossible to find a free, legal parking place in Woods Hole in summer or for overnight unless you stay at a motel and use its lot. The Steamship Authority has a dockside lot charging these fees, and also two large lots in Falmouth (if one is full you'll be directed to the other), with free shuttle-bus service to the Woods Hole docks. In late July and all of August the dockside lot is almost always full, so you'll save yourself some time by planning to park in a Falmouth lot. The Woods Hole ferry docks are served by Plymouth & Brockton Street Railway buses to Boston and by Bonanza lines to Providence and New York.

Important note: Although bus schedules leaving Woods Hole are designed to work in conjunction with ferry arrivals, connections are not guaranteed because weather can make the ferry late, and *the bus does not wait.* Do not take the last ferry of the day from the islands to Woods Hole (or to Hyannis) and count on getting the last bus out—you may in fact be able to do it, but it's not dependable. Take an earlier ferry.

---

3. Sandwich

Sandwich calls itself "the oldest town on the Cape" (incorporated 1639), and it is certainly one of the most beautiful and serene. Much of the vacation traffic to the Cape rushes past it on the way to Provincetown, leaving Sandwich to those few who appreciate it. The town holds its appeal both winter and summer, for although it has beaches, its antique stores and gracious old houses also draw visitors. Other attractions are Heritage Plantation, Dexter's Mill, and the Sandwich Glass Museum, which holds a fine collection of the interesting glassware once made here.

WHERE TO STAY

Sandwich has a good selection of guesthouses. The prime bed-and-breakfast place has a perfect name: the **Summer House,** 158 Old Main St., Sandwich, MA 02563 (tel. 508/888-4991). Built around 1835 in the Greek Revival style popular at that time, the entire whimsical front of the house is set aside for guests. One double room, on the first floor, has a private bath ($66 to $77 double); the four bedrooms on the second floor share two baths ($55 to $66 double). Continental breakfast and English-style afternoon tea are included in these prices, as is the lodging tax. You'll enjoy the porch, lawn, patio, and garden here.

The **Captain Ezra Nye House,** 152 Main St., Sandwich, MA 02563 (tel. 508/888-6142 or toll free 800/388-2278), is a lovely little place with six bedrooms, two of which share a bath and rent for $55 to $66 double, while the rooms with private bath rent for $72 to $83 double in the summer season, tax included. From November to Memorial Day, rates drop $11 or so. Choose your bedroom according to color preference—green, yellow, blue, or a calico mix—and admire the hand-stenciling upstairs on the floors and walls. An expanded continental breakfast is included in the rates.

The **Isaiah Jones Homestead,** 165 Main St., Sandwich, MA 02563 (tel. 508/888-9115), is a small bed-and-breakfast operated by the Catania family. The four rooms, all with private bath (one has a whirlpool), have a rather formal feel to them, but not uncomfortably so. Plush carpeting, chintz fabrics, alcove sitting areas, triple sheeting on the beds, and fresh flowers are all the norm here. A candlelit continental breakfast set at one long table and afternoon tea are included in the room rates of $88 to $121 double. Off-season, when Cape Cod is pleasantly devoid of traffic snarls, rates are $15 less per room.

WHERE TO DINE

Those watching their budgets and yet possessed of a great hunger will want to know about the **Sagamore Inn** (tel. 508/888-9707), on the Sandwich–Sagamore line on Rte. 6A (the green-and-white inn is just past the Sagamore Bridge, before the town of Sandwich). The decor is not fancy: wooden booths, a stamped-tin ceiling. The waitresses are all hometown women, the clientele are local families, and the food is hearty, savory, and delicious, with huge portions and low prices. The cook's inspiration is Italian cuisine; you can find spaghetti dishes for $7.25 to $12.50, seafood for $9.95 to $15.50, sandwiches for $1.95 to $9.50, and such treats as a medium-size antipasto plate for $5. Everyone here is friendly and pleasant, and out to make you happy. Open from 11:30am to 9pm Friday through Sunday, 4 to 9pm on Monday, Wednesday, and Thursday in season.

Those who are not watching their budgets but who still value their dollar will want to know about the Conservatory at the **Daniel Webster Inn,** 149 Main St. (tel. 508/888-3622), right in the middle of town. The dining room here is run by a family with a long history of restaurant success; all three meals are served. The Conservatory is a grand solarium with high ceilings, views of the grounds, potted indoor trees, servers in period costume, and a bounteous menu, with lots of beef and seafood choices. A full dinner costs $25 to $35 per person, but there's often an early-evening special (you must be seated by 4:45pm) offering a full dinner with drink, tax, and tip for under $18.

WHAT TO SEE

Sandwich is an old-fashioned town true to its traditions, a very pleasant place to live or visit. A walk downtown will give you clues to its character right away: backyard shops for artisans working in wood, leather, wrought iron, clay, or oil-on-canvas; graceful church steeples; small, well-groomed parks; comely old houses, many with the date of construction posted over the front door.

Sooner or later your walk will bring you by **Yesteryear's Doll and Miniature Museum** at Main and River streets, in what was once the First Parish Meetinghouse (tel. 508/888-1711). Literally hundreds of fascinating antique dolls, dollhouses, and toys as well as many other domestic articles are on display, and exhibits change from time to time. The museum is nonprofit, but charges admission to defray expenses: $2.50 per adult, $1.50 per child under 12, $2 for seniors. It's open mid-May through late October, Monday to Saturday from 10am to 4pm.

From Yesteryear's it's a short walk to the **Dexter Mill,** at the end of a lovely mill pond (complete with ducks), and next to a cool, splashing mill race and an old pump. The mill (1654) was fully restored in 1961, and is not just a picturesque attraction, although you can go in (daily from 10am to 5pm till Labor Day) and see the wooden mechanisms at work. The mill actually grinds corn, and you can buy bags of fresh meal the same day it's ground. Admission is $1.25 for adults, 75¢ for children 12 to 16.

Across from Sandwich's Greek Revival town hall on Rte. 130 is the **Sandwich Glass Museum** (tel. 508/888-0251), open daily from 9:30am to 4:30pm April 1 through October 31, shorter hours in winter (closed January). Admission is $2.50 for adults and 50¢ for children between 6 and 12; special group rates and a year-round schedule are available. Sandwich was a major glass-producing town from 1825 to 1888, and although it specialized in the new process of pressing glass in a mold, it also produced blown, cut, etched, and enameled works as well. A brilliant collection of this American glassware is on display, and dioramas, videos, and pictures show how it was made. Glassmakers' tools and other articles of Sandwich memorabilia are also part of the museum's collection. The glass museum is the only one of its kind on the Cape. Special exhibits are installed each year.

Perhaps the most famous local attraction is the **Heritage Plantation of Sandwich** (tel. 508/888-3300), a mile from town on Grove Street. Another of the museums in which New England abounds, Heritage Plantation does not specialize in any one era but has exhibits from all periods of American history. The automobile collection, 34 cars dating from 1899 to 1936, is one of the most popular sights in town.

Another collection features firearms and military miniatures, and still others show American crafts and the tools used to perform them. The buildings and grounds of the plantation are an attraction in themselves: all are reproductions of early-style buildings set in gardens and nature areas covering 76 acres. The plantation is open daily from 10am to 5pm mid-May through the end of October, and one ticket ($7 for adults, $6 for seniors, $3 for kids; 5 and under, free) admits a visitor to the grounds, all exhibits, and any of the periodically scheduled shows, concerts, and other activities.

Sandwich has several old houses open to the public for a fee. The best known is **Hoxie House,** on Rte. 130 along the shore of Shawme Pond (the mill pond). The house dates from the end of the 1600s, and has been restored and furnished with articles of that period. The house is open from 10am to 5pm Monday through Saturday, 1 to 5pm on Sunday, from mid-June through September. You can buy a $2 combination ticket good for admission here and at the Dexter Mill.

The town's beaches include **Town Beach,** the most westerly, and then, in order heading east, **Spring Hill Beach, East Sandwich Beach,** and over the line in Barnstable, **Sandy Neck Beach.** They all have toilets and places to park, and the bay side of the Cape has generally warmer swimming than the ocean side. Look for signs to the beaches on the side roads left (north) off Rte. 6A between Sandwich and Barnstable.

---

4. Hyannis

Hyannis gained national fame during the presidency of John F. Kennedy because of his summer home in nearby Hyannisport. Some of the town's growth and perhaps a good portion of its honky-tonk dates from that time, and although curious or devoted fans of the late president still stop to look at the town or to visit its memorial to JFK, the attractions in Hyannis these days are commercial. Should you need the services of an airline or a department store, supermarket, or foreign auto parts warehouse while on the Cape, Hyannis is the place to come. If you don't need these things, there are many nicer places on the Cape to spend precious vacation time.

TRANSPORTATION

Specifics on schedules and routes are given above in this chapter's first section, "Getting There." Here's what you'll want to know about Hyannis's facilities.

Airport

The airport is right in town, a short taxi ride from the bus stations or downtown. Several companies offer small planes for charter.

Bus Stations

Greyhound/Bonanza and **Plymouth & Brockton buses** all use the same terminal at Elm and Centre streets (tel. 508/775-5524). **Cape Cod Bus Lines** has its main terminal in Falmouth, and uses the Plymouth & Brockton terminal in Hyannis for its trips to Yarmouth, Dennis, Brewster, Orleans, Eastham, Wellfleet, Truro, and Provincetown. **Peter Pan Bus Lines,** which has routes from Hyannis to Amherst, Northampton, Holyoke, Springfield, and Worcester (daily in the summer but only on Friday and Sunday off-season), also uses the Plymouth & Brockton terminal.

Boat Docks

Hyannis has two main docks, at the foot of Ocean Street for fishing and cruise vessels, and at the foot of Pleasant Street for the passenger and car-ferries to Nantucket on the Steamship Authority's boats (tel. 508/771-4000). The docks are about five blocks from the bus stations. (Many buses connecting with ferries take passengers right to the dock.)

WHERE TO STAY

A choice area of motels and guesthouses is down Sea Street, off Main Street south toward Keyes Memorial Beach. One such place is just off Sea Street on Gosnold Street. The **Captain Gosnold Village,** P.O. Box 544, Hyannis, MA 02601 (tel. 508/775-9111), is a collection of different types of housing units spread through large and well-kept lawns and copses of trees. Guests have the use of a heated pool, children's playground, shuffleboard, and picnic tables. From late June until Labor Day, motel rooms cost $86 (suitable for two, three, or four people); efficiencies are $93; and a one-bedroom cottage is $108 (other cottages higher); $10 for an extra person. Also, discounts for longer stays (over a week) can save you money during off-season periods. Rooms are paneled, carpeted, and equipped with a refrigerator, TV, and coffee maker, and all have private bath. The beach is a 10-minute walk away.

The **Sea Breeze Inn,** 397 Sea St., Hyannis, MA 02601 (tel. 508/771-7213), is very close to Sea Street Beach, and has 13 rooms and one efficiency cottage equipped with TV, private tile baths, and (in a few rooms) a view of the ocean. Rates vary with the size of the room, number of beds, and similar features, but a normal double costs $60 to $88 in season; breakfast is included.

Sea Street has at least six guesthouses, varying from those with very simple rooms only to those offering a bit of atmosphere and service. The **Sea Witch Inn,** 363 Sea St., Hyannis, MA 02601 (tel.508/771-4261 or 775-3608), is one such guesthouse on the street, about equidistant from Main Street and Keyes Beach. The lawn is large and lush, shade trees rise here and there, and the inn is painted an appropriately nautical blue and white. Rooms here cost $33 to $71 per day for two people; most are in the $33 to $50 range. If you rent by the week or in months other than July and August, there's a reduction. For longer stays, the Sea Witch has a studio apartment and a cottage for rent by the week, and simple apartments in the barn meant for college students working on the Cape in summer.

What's in a name? Well, Mary and Clark Boydston, innkeepers at the turn-of-the-century bed-and-breakfast named **Elegance by the Sea,** 162 Sea St., Hyannis, MA 02601 (tel. 508/775-3595), would certainly answer "everything" to that question. With only six guest rooms in this huge Victorian house, bedrooms, common rooms, and even bathrooms are quite spacious. Upstairs are pineapple-post beds, other period antiques, and black-and-white-tiled floors in the old-fashioned bathroom. Rooms rent for $71 to $88 double with private bath, tax in; the room downstairs has a working fireplace. The price includes a hearty breakfast; theme weekends are hosted throughout the year. If you come during the holidays, you'll be in for special treats. The inn accepts children of 16 years and older.

One of my favorites is the **Inn on Sea Street,** at 358 Sea St., Hyannis, MA 02601 (tel. 508/775-8030). It's another small, elegant Victorian house, with flair and without pretense. Everything feels crisp, bright, neat, and useful. On the low end of the price scale are three rooms with shared baths ($60 to $70 double); one of them, a white and wicker room, was fashioned from the sun porch. Several rooms have canopy beds. The three highest-priced rooms ($88 to $93 double) have private baths, though for one of these access is down a private set of stairs. (It's unique and fun if you're in the mood.) Five small antique tables with lace cloths comprise the dining room, where a delicious breakfast of fruit, eggs, cheese, cake, granola, and the usual hot drinks is served. You can often make a reservation for only one night here, even at busy times; it's worth a try.

Bouchard's Tourist Homes and Apartments and Cottages, 83 School St., Hyannis, MA 02601 (tel. 508/775-0912), has several buildings and therefore a larger number of rooms at tourist-home prices, plus some apartments for long-term stays. Lowest price is for a room with running water which shares a tub-and-shower bathroom with one other room; cost is $24 single. For $39 two people can have a room with twin beds, running water, cable TV, and shared bath; air conditioning costs $5 more. For $60 there are rooms with cable color TV, air conditioning, twin beds, private tub-and-shower bath, even a private entrance. A suite of two adjoining rooms and bath sleeps four and rents for $104, good for families. Off-season rates for the rooms (after Labor Day until the last week in June) can go as low as $33 to $44 a day double. Tax is included in all these rates. Celina Bouchard has been running this place since 1935, and she'll charge you only $4 to keep your car here if you're heading to the islands.

WHERE TO DINE

Hyannis has a good number of restaurants, most of them serving the same things in the same surroundings at the same prices (with food of the same quality). All the national chains, from Burger King to Howard Johnson's, have representatives here, and while serviceable, these places are hardly atmospheric. If you've just landed in Hyannis from New York and you want to dive into New England's gustatory pleasures right away, seek out the following:

Follow your nose and the locals' toes to Hyannis's value-for-money eatery: **Up the Creek**, on Old Colony Road (tel. 508/771-7866). Turn left off Sea Street onto Gosnold Street and then take the first left (you can't miss the jammed parking lot). It's open for lunch weekdays and Saturdays from 11:30am to 2:30pm, brunch on Sunday (quite a bargain at $7.50), and dinner every night from 5 to 10pm. Reservations are recommended. Expect a cozy, tasteful, dark interior. Try a fish, chicken, or sirloin lunch for $5 to $6. For dinner choose chicken Simone at $9.50 or a light sole Florentine at $9 or the special seafood strudel (lobster, shrimp, scallops, crab, and cheese wrapped in pastry) at $8.

In the mood to go where the pretty people go? Then head to the **Roadhouse Café**, 488 South St., right off Main (tel.508/775-2386). It's as good for afternoon cocktails as it is for a romantic dinner. The mood is evoked by hanging plants, a wraparound glassed-in porch with tables for two or four, lanterns on the stained-wood exterior, and blue awnings. But what about the food? Well, it's heavy on Italian favorites, with some good New England standard dishes too. At lunch, have soup and a sandwich for under $10. For dinner, check the blackboard for daily specials, or order from the menu: fettuccine primavera, baked stuffed Cape scallops, beef burgundy, veal marsala, or chicken parmesan, followed by a portion of some delightful dessert made right in the restaurant. You can expect to spend about $25 to $30 per person at dinner, wine, tax, and tip included. The Roadhouse is open seven days a week from 11:30am to 10pm; Sunday brunch is served from 10am to 3pm.

Right on Main Street, at no. 415, in the center of the shopping district, is the **Asa Bearse House Restaurant** (tel. 508/771-4131). The house's big old porch is a favorite Hyannis spot for cocktails; the crowd usually moves to the front-lawn terrace if the weather's fine. The luncheon menu lists lots of sandwiches, but the special lunch-of-the-day—something like a quiche or fish dinner—is only $8, including salad and rolls. At dinner the menu turns exotic, to escargots, and familiar, to steaks; dinner costs about $35 to $45. Open daily from 11:30am to 10pm for food, till 1am for drinks in season. The 1840 barn in back, opened in 1981, is quite handsome.

Harvard Square's **Wursthaus** (tel. 508/771-5000) has a branch in Hyannis, in the Cape Cod Mall. Boasting the "world's largest selection of foreign beers," the Wursthaus is the place to find Mexican Dos Equis and Israeli Gold Star as well as Löwenbräu and Beck's. A long list of sandwiches ($3 to $6), salad plates, side orders, and desserts keeps the light-lunch and late-night crowds happy; for hungrier diners there steaks ($8 to $14) and moderately priced fish. The Wursthaus specializes in Bavarian-style food and is open for lunch and then until midnight daily.

WHAT TO SEE

Many visitors to Hyannis stop to see the memorial to President Kennedy, a stone structure bearing the presidential seal and a small fountain, on Ocean Street right along the water. Hyannisport and the **"Kennedy compound,"** noted in news stories while the late president vacationed here, are not far from the monument. None of the buildings is open to the public.

Also along Ocean Street are **Kalmus Park** and **Veteran's Park,** with their respective beaches, bathhouses, and snack bars. Go down to the south end of Sea Street for none other than **Sea Street Beach.** Besides swimming facilities, Sea Street Beach has a little platform on top of a dune from which you can take a look at the sweep of the beach.

Big-name stars and bands are booked into the **Cape Cod Melody Tent,** at the West Main Street Rotary in Hyannis (tel. 508/775-9100). The season goes from late June through Labor Day, and runs the gamut—from Bob Hope and Tony Bennett all the way to Crystal Gayle. Tickets are priced differently depending on the show, but most run in the $18 to $35 range, with selected Tuesday and Thursday matinees and weeknight performances. Children's shows are Wednesday mornings at 11am. Tickets can be charged by calling the box office.

FERRIES TO THE ISLANDS

Two firms operate ferries to the islands of Martha's Vineyard and Nantucket from Hyannis, each sailing from a different dock. Here are the details.

Woods Hole, Martha's Vineyard, and Nantucket Steamship Authority (tel. 508/540-2022 for car reservations) runs car and passenger ferries from Hyannis's Pleasant Street docks (follow the signs in town). No direct service is run between Hyannis and Martha's Vineyard by this firm—you have to go via Nantucket or, preferably, direct from Woods Hole to Martha's Vineyard. The Steamship Authority's boats run six times daily to Nantucket in summer, less frequently off-season; the trip takes less than 2½ hours and costs $9 for adults, half fare for kids 5 to 12, one way. Car-ferry space must be reserved in advance; in high summer it costs $71 to ship a car one way from Hyannis to Nantucket. In high summer, one passengers-only boat is run in each direction daily between Martha's Vineyard and Nantucket, taking about 2 hours and costing $9 per adult (kids pay half fare). The ferries are large, comfortable, and equipped with lunch counters and bars. Note that if you park in the dockside lots you'll have to pay $7 per calendar day for the privilege, and that you should arrive at the lot 45 minutes prior to the ferry's departure time.

Special note: When returning to Hyannis from Nantucket, don't plan on taking the last ferry of the day and meeting the bus to Boston or New York, for the ferries are often delayed and *the bus does not wait.* To be safe, catch a ferry well ahead of the last bus trip scheduled from Hyannis. If you find yourself in a jam because of ferry mixups, you can always take another line (see below) or fly.

The **Hy-Line** (tel. 508/778-2600) has several swift (2-hour) passenger-only boats which depart from Hyannis's Ocean Street docks for Nantucket or Martha's Vineyard; fare is $10 for an adult, half price for a child, to either island. Although no cars are carried on the Hy-Line's boats, you can take your bicycle over for $4 one way. These boats operate May through October only. By the way, if you sign up for a same-day round trip, you'll have to decide which boat you plan to return on, and your ticket will be stamped with the boat's departure time. Reservations are accepted with an additional nominal charge (tel. 508/778-2602). Otherwise, parking is $6 to $8 per calendar day.

---

5. Barnstable, Yarmouth, and Dennis

The stretch of Rte. 6A between Sandwich and Dennis is a lush panorama of bogs and marshes, distant views of dunes and the sea, birds calling and fluttering, the winding road dotted with antique shops, craft shops, art galleries, and other businesses including lots and lots of real estate offices. The road leads through the villages of Barnstable, Cummaquid, Yarmouthport, Yarmouth, and Dennis before heading eastward to Brewster.

Visitors may be surprised to know that Barnstable, the largest incorporated town on the Cape, actually includes within its boundaries the busy commercial center of Hyannis, its airport, and several small historic villages on the wide salt marshes along the shores of Cape Cod Bay. The village of Barnstable proper is little more than a namesake for the much larger township.

Yarmouth is also a town with two natures. In the north, along Rte. 6A, it is hamlets of dignified old houses shaded by beautiful lofty trees. In the south, along Rte. 28, it is gaudy motels built chock-a-block along the crowded beaches. The town of Dennis is much like Yarmouth. Here, it is claimed, the commercial cranberry-harvesting industry began, and salt works flourished for a period.

BARNSTABLE

As you wend your way eastward along Rte. 6A, the village of Barnstable offers several good choices for lodging. In Barnstable, as well as Yarmouthport, Rte. 6A becomes Main Street, also called the Old King's Highway.

Where to Stay

Though it only has four rooms (all with working fireplaces and private baths), the **Charles Hinckey House,** Old Kings Highway (P.O. Box 723), Barnstable Village, MA 02630 (tel. 508/362-9924), is very special and welcoming. This Federal colonial house is a historic landmark and has been painstakingly renovated. Flowers from the profuse bank of wildflower gardens fill the interior. The innkeepers keep their distance, but will spoil you if you give them half a chance. Rooms rent for $120 to $153, and include the lodging tax and a beautifully presented full breakfast.

A stay at **Ashley Manor,** 3660 Old Kings Hwy. (P.O. Box 856), Barnstable, MA 02630 (tel. 508/362-8044), is a lesson in leisurely living. Innkeepers Donald and Fay Bain will encourage you to linger over afternoon cocktails, evening conversations, and a full breakfast on the backyard brick terrace, enjoying the inn's 2-acre grounds. The six spacious suites and guest rooms in the main manor house (all with private bath, Oriental carpets, and antiques, and all but one with a working fireplace) are priced from $110 to $181 per room. A more private cottage with a freestanding fireplace and efficiency kitchen rents for $142 per night, or $900 per week. Ashley Manor has its own new tennis court. Children 14 and older are welcome at the inn.

Also on Old Kings Highway is **Beechwood,** 2839 Main St., Barnstable, MA 02630 (tel. 508/362-6618). This Victorian house takes its name from the big old beech trees that shade the veranda. Don't let the staid parlor mislead you; it's not at all in keeping with the light and airy guest rooms. Period antiques, colored glass, marble-topped dressers, unique bathrooms, and tall shuttered windows make this place special. The garret room in the attic is very private and has angled walls and eaves. A room with breakfast costs from $105 to $148, tax included.

YARMOUTHPORT

Yarmouthport has several fine inns and guesthouses, with good variety in prices and accommodations. It's a nice place to spend the night. Here's a description of the places as you'll encounter them going from west to east through the town on Rte. 6A.

Where to Stay

Yarmouth's best inns are actually bed-and-breakfast houses. The **Wedgewood Inn,** 83 Main St., Yarmouthport, MA 02675 (tel. 508/362-5157), is a gracious and comfortable place to relax. It's a charming inn with period (1812) wallpaper, pencil-post beds, quilts, Oriental rugs, wide-board floors, and working fireplaces. Each of the six spacious rooms has a private bath; two have private screened porches. Doubles cost $105 to $160 (20% less in the off-season), and a full breakfast is, of course, included.

Atop Liberty Hill, set back from Rte. 6A at the corner of Willow Street, is **Liberty Hill Inn,** 77 Main St., Yarmouthport, MA 02675 (tel. 508/362-3976). The classical pillars are a giveaway: Greek Revival architecture, built in 1825. The Liberty Hill is perhaps Yarmouthport's best bargain: You get a double room (private bath) in the lovely house furnished with authentic Early American pieces, a full breakfast, and a convenient location for $93 to $110 in season, tax in. Innkeepers Beth and Jack Flanagan see to it that your stay is an enjoyable one. You save money if you come in spring or fall, especially on a weekday.

Despite its name, the **One Centre Street Inn** (tel. 508/362-8910) is on Old King's Highway. But the entrance is around to the side, on Centre Street, right in the middle of Yarmouthport. For simple good taste, the inn is first choice in this town. Innkeepers Stefanie and Bill Wright have five guest rooms; baths are private or semi-private; full breakfast is included in the price: $55 to $93, tax included. This is my favorite sort of hostelry: small, congenial, thoughtfully and finely furnished with taste but without pretension, walking distance to the activities of the town, friendly owners. Need I say more?

Where to Eat

The **Cranberry Moose**, 45 Main St., Yarmouthport, MA 02675 (tel. 508/362-3501), is one of the best restaurants on Cape Cod and the prices reflect the cuisine. The four white dining rooms are simple but elegant, with oak chairs and tables dotted with roses and carnations. Start with a goat cheese tart topped with thin slices of apples and move on to roast duck with a papaya and raspberry sauce. Save room for a rich crème brûlée with a carmelized sugar topping. For $35 to $40 per person (including tax and tip but no beverage) these artful presentations can be yours from 5:30 to 10pm nightly in summer and Thursday to Monday from mid-October through mid-May.

What to See and Do

Across the street from the Old Yarmouth Inn is the **Parnassus Book Store,** in a building which started life as a church and later became the local incarnation of the A&P grocery chain. No charge for browsing.

Just down Rte. 6A from the inn, a minute's walk east, is the U.S. Post Office, and behind it are the **Nature Trails** of the Historical Society of Old Yarmouth. The trails are open during daylight hours seven days a week year round; 50¢ admission for adults, 25¢ for children. Note that these are not formal "botanical gardens," but rather trails through particularly beautiful wild areas of Yarmouth's land and marshes. Local flowers and trees, plants, and geological features are on view, and maps and trail booklets available at the gatehouse where you pay admission will tell you all about what there is to see.

Near the Botanic Trails is the **Bangs Hallet House** (tel. 508/362-3021), built by a captain in the China trade. The house's history is as interesting as its Greek Revival façade. The devoted caretaker will fill you in on the confusing chronicle of the house's various owners and reconstructions. The house is open June 1 through Labor Day from 2 to 4pm Wednesday to Friday and Sunday. Admission is $1 for adults, 25¢ for children. At other times of the year, call for an appointment to see it.

The **Winslow Crocker House** (tel. 508/227-3956), owned and maintained by the Society for the Preservation of New England Antiquities, is open June through mid-October on Tuesday, Thursday, Saturday, and Sunday from noon to 5pm. Admission is $2.50 for adults, $1.25 for children 5 to 12 years old. The rooms in this Georgian house are furnished with 17th- to 19th-century collections.

By law, **Grey's Beach** is free and open to the public, as terms of the bequest that gave it to the town of Yarmouth. It's at the end of Centre Street (turn north off Rte. 6A), and as you go down to the beach, note the cemetery on your left with graves dating from 1639. Picnic tables, toilets, nice lawns, and parking facilities are all available at the beach; a wooden walkway stretches a good distance out across the marshes, and is pleasant to stroll along even if you don't feel like a swim.

DENNIS

As you enter the center of Dennis, start looking for a cemetery and a white church, and as you come to them look for Old Bass River Road. Turn right onto this road and follow signs for eight-tenths of a mile to the **Scargo Hill Tower.** Park at the base of this stone structure surrounded by oak and pine, and climb the iron staircase inside to the top (not far) for a view that will tell you what the Cape is all about. On a clear day you can easily see Provincetown, the white blade of the Cape beaches cutting the deep blue of Cape Cod Bay. The Cape itself appears as a huge green scimitar, a sea of green trees with little white or silver-gray shingled houses poking through here and there. At the foot of the hill that holds the tower is Scargo Lake, and west is the outline of Barnstable Harbor. The tower was given to the town of Dennis in 1929 by the Tobey family, who had had ancestors living in Dennis since 1678. Follow the same road back to Rte. 6A.

More pretty scenes, including those cranberry bogs and salt marshes, await you in Dennis. If you get off of Rte. 6A to wander and explore, expect to get lost. This is a confusing, if beautiful, place. For instance, though the village of East Dennis is actually east of Dennis, the village of South Dennis is due north of West Dennis, and these two are due south of East Dennis . . . got it?

Where to Stay
The **Isaiah Hall B&B Inn,** 152 Whig St., Dennis, MA 02638 (tel. 508/385-9928 or toll fre 800/736-0160), is a gem of a bed-and-breakfast run by Marie and Dick Brophy. Good old-fashioned, homespun country comforts prevail in this 1857 Greek Revival farmhouse. The newly converted barn, with cathedral ceiling and white wicker, sports rooms with small balconies. The living room, dining room, and quilted guest rooms in the main house are filled with solid antiques and are very unpretentious. The house abuts a cranberry bog, is a 10-minute walk to Corporation Beach, and is right behind the Cape Playhouse. Rates are quite reasonable in the summer season: $46 to $82 for one, $53 to $93 for two, tax in; the lower rates are for rooms which share baths. Rates are somewhat less off-season.

Located across from Scargo Lake, the **Four Chimneys Inn,** 946 Main St. (Rte. 6A), Dennis, MA 02638 (tel. 508/385-6317), has some of the most spacious guest rooms on the entire Cape. Ceilings are high, floors painted, and common rooms (one with a VCR, one with a fireplace) relaxing. Seven of the nine impeccable rooms in this Victorian house have private bath; continental breakfast is served in the dining room, near the fireplace. Rates, for one or two people, are reasonable at $55 to $77 for a shared bath and $86 to $99 for a private. Off-season they drop $5 to $20 per room; an additional person is charged $15 per night.

What to Do
The **Cape Playhouse,** on Rte. 6A in Dennis (tel. 508/385-3911), is the place to go on the Cape if you want to see a famous actor or actress in a well-known play. The plays (and actors) usually change every week, so call to see what's current. The season runs from early July through Labor Day, with performances each evening (except Sunday) at 8:30pm, plus matinees on Wednesday and Thursday at 2:30pm. Tickets are priced from $17 to $25. The playhouse has its own restaurant, open for lunch on matinee days, dinner, Sunday brunch, and after-theater snacks. Also here is the **Cape Cinema,** designed after the Congregational church in Centerville, home of the first-run movies and of a mammoth, 6,400-square-foot mural of the heavens by Rockwell Kent.

---

6. Brewster

Brewster is another of the picturesque little towns along Rte. 6A. A country store, several fine churches, and a Town Hall make it look like many other pleasant Cape towns, but Brewster's different in the number of noteworthy museums and exhibitions situated in the town or nearby. It also has one of the best French restaurants on the East Coast.

WHERE TO STAY
The **Old Sea Pines Inn,** 2553 Main St., Brewster, MA 02631 (tel. 508/896-6114), is a pleasant surprise. Built in 1907 as the Sea Pines School of Charm and Personality for Young Women, it retains its turn-of-the-century grace beneath the shade of several old oaks. The spacious, comfortable common rooms have hard-

wood floors and a working fireplace, and the wraparound porch is furnished with green cane rockers. Of the 14 rooms, the five smaller ones share baths and rent for only $44, single or double. Rooms with private bath cost from $66 to $99; the highest-priced room comes with a fireplace and four-poster bed. The family suite costs $104 for four people; the suite with a fireplace can accommodate two, three, or four people; it's priced at $137 for two with a bottle of champagne included; each extra person pays $18. Off-season rates (November through May) are about 12% to 15% lower. A full breakfast is included in the price.

Just west of the intersection of Rtes. 6A and 124 South in Brewster is the **Old Manse Inn,** 1861 Main St. (P.O. Box 839), Brewster, MA 02631 (tel. 508/896-3149), a lovely old white building surrounded by tall trees. Like so many other gracious Brewster houses, this one was built in the early 1800s by a captain in the China trade, one William Knowles. The nine guest rooms, all with private bath, rent for $88 to $97 double during the high season (July and August), $71 to $80 in spring and fall, $65 to $71 in winter, tax and breakfast included. For a room with fireplace, add $16.50. If you just want to relax and not wander out for meals, dinner is served (by reservation) on Friday, Saturday, and Sunday evenings in the inn's cozy sunroom or dining room. Children 6 and older are welcome.

WHERE TO DINE

Chef-owner Robert Rabin's **Chillingsworth,** on Rte. 6A in Brewster (tel. 508/896-3640), is one of the loveliest restaurants on the Cape. The fare is French nouvelle cuisine; the atmosphere is a delightful blend of modern and traditional, cozy and spacious. If you have a special celebration for a party of two to four, request the separate "library room." There are two seatings for the seven-course dinner: 6 to 6:30pm and then again at 9 to 9:30pm. An evening for two will cost close to $100, everything included. Lunch is a good deal, costing $15 to $20 per person, all in. From late June through early September, lunch is served daily except Monday and Tuesday, dinner is served daily except Monday; in the off-season (Memorial Day weekend to late June, and mid-September through November), lunch and dinner are served Friday and Saturday, only brunch on Sunday, and the restaurant is closed Monday through Thursday. Reservations are a must.

David and Vernon Smith's **Brewster Fish House,** also on Rte. 6A in Brewster (tel. 508/896-7867), is a nice place for an informal, leisurely lunch or dinner. The menu is simple and to the point: good fresh seafood, and lots of it. Tables are covered in linen, and servings are generous. Luncheon chowder and salad are yours for less than $4, a char-broiled chicken breast sandwich for only slightly more. You can tuck into a grilled seafood brochette or swordfish steak for under $10. Main courses at dinner range from $11 to $17, full meals from $18 to $30. It's open mid-April to mid-November, seven days a week during high summer season, for lunch from 11:30am to 3pm, dinner from 5pm on, but you can always get a filling bowl of soup here between meals.

WHAT TO SEE

Brewster is proud of its **Old Grist Mill and Herring Run** at the Stoney Brook Mill Sites, on Stony Brook Road near the intersection with Satucket and Run Hill roads. The waterwheel, still in good working order, powers the grinding machinery inside the mill. You can watch the whole process at work, and buy freshly ground cornmeal, from 2 to 5pm on Wednesday, Friday, and Saturday afternoons in July and August. Upstairs there's a small museum with artifacts from the "Factory Village" which occupied this site over 100 years ago.

The mill is now part of a park owned by the town of Brewster. Wander around the millpond, certainly one of the most romantic and picturesque locales on all of Cape Cod. If your visit falls during mid-April to early May, watch for the run of **alewives** (herring) which surges upstream from the ocean to freshwater spawning grounds.

The **Cape Cod Aquarium,** 281 Main St. (tel. 508/385-9252 or toll free 800/367-6372), is right on Rte. 6A in West Brewster. It's open year round from 9am to

5pm and features a crew of dolphins as well as horseshoe crabs, loggerhead turtles, moray eels, otters, sea lions, and any number of different fish. There are three large buildings and several outside pools set in a tree-filled park. Seal and sea lion performances are given every day, usually at 10am, noon, 2pm, and 4pm, but call to confirm these times. Admission costs $7 for adults, $4.50 for children 5 to 11, free to kids under 5. The aquarium is a nonprofit educational institution.

The **New England Fire and History Museum,** on Rte. 6A in Brewster (tel. 508/896-5711), has one of the world's largest (35 engines) and most varied collections of early firefighting equipment and memorabilia, plus gardens both herbaceous and ceremonial, and a picnic area. Firefighting paraphernalia dates as far back as the 18th century and includes the world's only known 1929 Mercedes-Benz fire truck. Other exhibits include the Arthur Fiedler memorabilia collection, a historic apothecary, and a blacksmith shop. Guided tours are given; related movies are shown. The museum is open daily from Memorial Day weekend to mid-September, then on weekends only until Columbus Day (mid-October). Hours are 10am to 4pm weekdays, noon to 4pm weekends. The entrance fee is $4.50 for adults, $2.50 for children ages 5 to 12, free for kids 4 and under.

Those interested in Cape Cod's flora, fauna, and ecology will want to visit the **Cape Cod Museum of Natural History,** on Rte. 6A (tel. 508/896-3867), open from 9:30am to 4:30pm Monday through Saturday (plus 12:30 to 4:30pm on Sunday during the summer). Closed Sunday and Monday from mid-October through April. The museum organization was founded in 1954 to preserve the wildlife and plant life in the area around Stony Brook and its marshes, to study this land, and to teach others about it. Nature walks, a lecture program, and children's classes are held the year round. Adults pay $2.50 and children 6 to 14 pay $1.50; kids under 6 are free.

---

7. Chatham

Chatham was once the railhead for Cape Cod, and the trains that brought vacationers in and took fish, salt, and shoes out also brought the opportunity for wealth. Chatham is therefore a graceful community with many big old houses and inns, an easy pace, friendly people, and pleasant vistas all around.

During the summer season, there's an **information booth** on Main Street in the center of town (tel. 508/945-0342). It's run by citizens who know the town inside and out, and offers brochures on places to stay, copies of menus from local restaurants, and information on activities. Public rest rooms are next door, in the rear of the Town Hall.

WHERE TO STAY

Chatham seems to have at least one kind of every accommodation imaginable, so you should have little trouble finding a place you'll like by skimming down this list:

A Resort Hotel

The **Chatham Bars Inn,** at the corner of Chatham Bars Avenue and Shore Road, Chatham, MA 02633 (tel. 508/945-0096 or toll free 800/527-4884), is a true bit of old Chatham, a huge, rambling, gracious resort complex with 26 attractive cottages (no kitchens) on the property. Approach the inn by the motor entrance, bear to the right, and you'll enter the parlor, with its high-arched ceiling, lots of windows looking onto a shady veranda, and wicker furniture for cool sitting on warm summer days. The lobby is also grand, large, and spacious, and a stairway out the front door tumbles down the hillside to the road and beyond it to the inn's private beach. Swimming at the beach or in the inn's own outdoor heated pool, tennis on five outdoor courts, and golf on the inn's own nine-hole course are other services offered. The staff is large, friendly, well trained, and soft-spoken. Of course, proper dress is required in the cocktail lounge and in the main dining room in the evening: jacket and tie for men; summer cottons or cocktail dress for women. Breakfast and dinner are included in these high-season rates: $316 to $473 per couple per day, tax and service included, for a double with bath. If these figures look high, remember that, on the average, a luxury inn or motel room costs around $100, plus two breakfasts and two good dinners, which often brings a normal vacation day's expenses to around $240 per couple daily. The Chatham Bars Inn is a bit of history brought up to modern standards of comfort and service, and I doubt that you'll be disappointed here.

Inns

For my money, Chatham's most perfectly charming inn is Cathy and Dave Eakin's **Captain's House Inn,** 371 Old Harbor Rd., Chatham, MA 02633 (tel. 508/945-0127). Located a half mile from the center of town on Rte. 28 going toward Orleans, the Captain's House has plenty of space for green lawns and flower gardens. It was in fact built by Capt. Hiram Harding in 1839, with various additions later. The 14 guest rooms all have private bath and period furnishings, which include some wing chairs, canopy beds, and braided rugs. Three rooms have fireplaces. The Cottage and the Carriage House have three bedrooms each—the best choice for large families or small groups. Rooms cost $120 to $170 single or double in summer, Continental breakfast and tax included. This place is very nice indeed.

The **Queen Anne Inn,** 70 Queen Anne Rd., Chatham, MA 02633 (tel. 508/945-0394 or toll free 800/545-4667), is just a few blocks from the center of Chatham, and has been a favorite hostelry here for well over a century. The graceful, shingled, gabled inn is authentic 19th-century Cape Cod, but with many of the amenities of a resort hotel: restaurant, tennis courts (with a resident pro for lessons and clinics), bicycles, an indoor spa, boats for waterskiing, and excursions to Monomoy Island to see the seals, shore birds, and deer. Guenther Weinkopf, the innkeeper, is also a licensed boat captain, so the excursions are easy and reliable. Rooms, many with fireplaces, private balconies (some look onto the Oyster Pond), and whirlpool baths (but no TVs), are priced from $134 to $233 double, Continental breakfast included. Elegant dinners are available at the inn's Earl of Chatham restaurant.

The **Chatham Wayside Inn,** 512 Main St., Chatham, MA 02633 (tel. 508/945-1800), is also owned by Guenther Weinkopf of the Queen Anne Inn. His extensive renovations have brought this old 19th-century hostelry up to—and beyond—current standards for comfort and charm. The guest rooms are located in the cottages surrounding the inn; decor is Early American, but the bathrooms are modern, and all rooms have phone and TV. The inn's dining room, called Sam Bellamy's Tavern, specializes in seafood and pub grub; in the fine summer weather, the Bandstand Café takes over the large porch overlooking Main Street. There's a swimming pool too. You won't find an inn more centrally located than the Wayside, right next to Kate Gould Park (where the band concerts are held in summer). The rate is $137 double in summer, tax included.

In a town of sea captains' houses, the **Cyrus Kent House Inn,** 63 Cross St., at Kent Place, Chatham, MA 02633 (tel. 508/945-9104), certainly stands out as a gem. It's not as old as many, dating "only" from 1877. But it was built by boatwrights from ship timber brought from Maine, and has been finely restored. Unencumbered by tons of Victoriana, the Kent House has an airy, sunny quality about it, and innkeeper Richard Morris makes the most of it with a simple, tasteful decor. Each of the eight guest rooms has a private bath, and rents in high season for $108 double, Continental breakfast and tax included. Here you're a mere block from the center of Chatham's historic district, and a short walk from the excellent beaches.

A few minutes' walk from downtown is the **Cranberry Inn at Chatham,** 359 Main St., Chatham, MA 02633 (tel. 508/945-9232 or toll free 800/332-4667), operated by Richard Morris and Peggy DeHan, who also run the Cyrus Kent House. The Cranberry Inn is a Chatham landmark, having stood here since 1830.

Its 19th-century guests might still feel at home by the fireplace in the restaurant, or among the antique and reproduction furnishings of the guest rooms, but modern travelers appreciate the air conditioning, private baths, color TV, and telephones. The rate in summer is $108 single or double, tax included. Off-season it's $86 per room. The Cranberry Inn is open from April to December; children 12 or older are welcome.

Another inn downtown is the **Chatham Town House,** 11 Library Lane, off Main Street, Chatham, MA 02633 (tel. 508/945-2180 or toll free 800/242-2180; fax 508/945-3900). There are 24 rooms here with private bath, plus a six-room lodge and several cottages. All the rooms are decorated differently, but with taste and thoughtfulness, even to using hand-hooked rugs rather than wall-to-wall carpeting so that the beautiful old floors can be seen. All have air conditioning, refrigerators, cable color TV, and individual thermostats. Besides its center-of-town location, the inn boasts a new swimming pool and spa, and the Two Turtles restaurant serves breakfast and dinner. Innkeepers Russell and Svea Peterson set rates of $126 to $192 for a double with bath, including tax, in summer. An extra person costs $25. You can get a Scandinavian breakfast at the inn for $7 if you wish.

The Gray family's **Bradford Inn and Motel,** 26 Cross St., Chatham, MA 02633 (tel. 508/945-1030 or toll free 800/562-4667; fax 508/945-9652), is right at the center of town. This extremely neat and tidy complex has 25 guest rooms (11 in a motel annex), an outdoor heated swimming pool, a patio, and flowers everywhere. Rooms and suites come with a basket of amenities, cable color TV, private bath, air conditioning, and full breakfast; some have refrigerators and kitchen facilities. Prices are $121 to $181 double in high season; add $27 for each extra person in a room. This should be your first motel choice in Chatham. It also now serves lunch and Sunday brunch.

Right next door to the Bradford is the **Mulberry Inn,** 44 Cross St. (P.O. Box 212), Chatham, MA 02633 (tel. 508/945-2020), also managed by the Gray family. They've restored this historic house with turn-of-the-century furnishings, including canopy beds, and have added new private bathrooms, color cable TVs, and air conditioning, making the house a thoroughly delightful place to stay. The rate is $159 double, tax and full New England breakfast included, in summer; reductions are offered off-season, as are single rates.

A Guesthouse

A nice cozy guesthouse out toward the water and also only a few minutes' walk from the center of town and a shopping center is the **Bow Roof House,** 59 Queen Anne Rd., Chatham, MA 02633 (tel. 508/945-1346), run by the Mazulis family. The main house is that of an old sea captain, and many rooms still have the fireplaces (not working now) that were installed to keep out the chill of those winter blasts that roll in off the water. A large living room with rough-timbered ceiling and large fireplace is here for guests' use, and just through the door from it is a terrace with tables and umbrellas for a glass of wine (BYO) or tea in the evening. Rooms, based on three or more nights, cost about $42 to $48 double with private bath and continental breakfast. If you go in summer, the bank in front of the house will be a riot of wildflowers, and the two yuccas by the door may be in bloom.

Motels

Accessible only by car is the **Pleasant Bay Village Resort Motel,** P.O. Box 772, Chatham, MA 02633 (tel. 508/945-1133), on Rte. 28 several miles north of town in the section called Chathamport. The motel is about as pleasant as you'll find, located on 6 acres of very carefully kept grounds, with evergreen hedges, trees, bushes, and cascades of roses along the front rail fence. The motel's buildings are scattered through the grounds, and there's a heated pool, shuffleboard, and Ping-Pong, besides just lounging in the sun, to keep you occupied. The motel has a breakfast room (light lunches served as well). Rooms are modern with air conditioning, private baths, wall-to-wall carpeting, and cable color TV (28 channels), and most have two double beds. In season (last week in June to Labor Day), motel rooms cost $93 for one double bed, $126 to $170 for rooms with two double beds of ever-increasing size and luxury; tax is included in these prices.

Close to the downtown area without being right smack in the center is **The Moorings,** 326 Main St., Chatham, MA 02633 (tel. 508/945-0848). This grand old Chatham house has a carriage (or coach) house with a motel annex, efficiency apartments, and cottages. The complex once belonged to a retired admiral, and now serves well as a hostelry, owned by Jan and Earl Rush. Furnishings and styles of rooms vary with the building you stay in: The guesthouse is traditional Victorian, the motel annex is modern but decorated in colonial style. Prices vary as well. The rooms on the upper floor of the carriage house cost $77 to $93, those in the guesthouse and motel are $93 to $115, including continental breakfast.

WHERE TO DINE

Chatham has a good assortment of restaurants in different price ranges, each with its own ambience. It's easy to find one you like.

Best place to dine is at **Christian's,** 443 Main St. (tel. 508/945-3362). Lodged in an old Chatham house, Christian's has a cocktail bar and light menu served upstairs on a pretty deck (open at 4pm), and several dining rooms within the house itself. The dinner menu is original: crab buerrecks (flaky pastry filled with crabmeat and a bit of curry), seafood mélange (lobster, shrimps, and scallops), or filet mignon prepared any of three ways. Dinner is served from 5pm every day in summer. Downstairs, expect to pay between $28 and $40 per person, all in; upstairs the menu can feed you well for only $10 to $15 per person. In the summer there's entertainment nightly; in spring and fall the music is on weekends only.

The **Impudent Oyster,** on Chatham Bars Avenue just off Main Street (tel. 508/945-3545), has a long and eclectic menu perfect for those afternoons and evenings when you don't know what sort of cuisine to choose. Chinese, French, Italian, and Mexican-style dishes, each with a different local touch; sandwiches and elegant main courses; seafood and meats—all share the menu. The oysters, by the way, are freshly shucked. Plan to spend $30 to $40 per person for a nice dinner with wine. For lunch, anything on the menu can be yours for under $10. Dress neatly, but not formally, and call for dinner reservations. Hours are 11:30am to 10pm Monday through Saturday, noon to 10pm Sunday in summer.

The young and golden and the young and hip have dinner at the **Chatham Squire Restaurant,** near the intersection of Main and Chatham Bars Avenue (tel. 508/945-0945), open every day from 11:30am to 11pm. The tavern in the room to the left is semifunky, with license plates from all the states and many foreign countries nailed to huge, rough ceiling beams; the dining room to the right is nicely furnished with Pennsylvania Dutch-style wooden tables. It's a big place, attractive and well tended, and with an interesting menu: For lunch perhaps a "crock o' chowder" with crackers ($3.50) or a salad plate ($5 to $8); at dinnertime try any of the fresh fish specials. Dinner will cost $25 to $30 per person; no reservations taken.

If you don't mind driving 10 minutes from the center of town, head out to **Sea in the Rough,** on Rte. 28 in the direction of Harwich (tel. 508/945-1700). It's a good, hearty, informal, family place with red vinyl chairs, basic service, and generous servings. In nice weather, sit outside on the side patio under the shade of umbrellas. Open April through October, seven days a week from 11:30am to 10pm (high season only); the entire menu is available all day. Dinner specials on the blackboard start at 5pm and might be fresh salmon or tuna, or any number of chicken dishes, from $11 to $17. Regular seafood and steak entrees cost $7 to $11.

Cafés

The **Garden Café** (tel. 508/945-4081) is in the Swinging Basket Mall, a small collection of shops at the intersection of Chatham Bars Avenue and Main Street. Set near numerous fascinating browsing places, the café is a fine place for a sip, a snack, or a supper (11:30am to 4pm weekdays, to 8pm on weekends, mid-June through August). For instance, the ploughman's lunch of cheeses, fresh fruit, and French bread costs $8; soups, salads, sandwiches, and wine and beer are served as well.

This season the place for ice cream seems to be **Cookie Manor,** 499 Main St. (tel. 508/945-1152). Don't let the noisy kids outside keep you away. Baked sweets, 18 flavors of ice cream, and "the best sandwiches in the state, no matter what state you're in" know no age limit. Whether you choose a breakfast snack, baked ham sandwich ($3), or cookiewich (any two cookies with a scoop of ice cream in between; $2), you can be confident it's done with expertise here. Open daily Memorial Day through Labor Day from 8am to 10pm, until 5pm the rest of the year.

Nearby in Harwich Port

Café Elizabeth, 31 Sea St., Harwich Port (tel. 508/432-1147), is 6 miles from Chatham, south off Rte. 28. The atmosphere is that of an auberge, a French country inn. The owner, Marguerite, will greet you with a French accent and show you to a table in one of the small, cozy dining rooms. As for the food, well, try this: as an appetizer, shrimp quickly sautéed in butter, cayenne pepper, and fresh gound pepper, then flambéed with cognac. As a main course, try an assortment of four medallions: shrimp with sauce Bonifacio, veal with wild mushrooms, lamb with fresh tarragon, filet with bearnaise; as dessert, a special chocolate truffle. If you prefer a strawbery tarte, I'd suggest you put your name on one when you walk past the dessert tray; they seem to disappear rapidly. Expect to spend $40 to $50 per person for dinner. Hours are 6 to 9pm daily.

WHAT TO SEE

There's quite a lot to see and do in this venerable New England town.

The Light and the Fish Pier

The Light is the first place to go in Chatham. Go east on Main Street and turn right (south) on Shore Road to the Light. The lighthouse is right next to the Coast Guard Station; on the other side of the street is a place to park while you look at the view through some pay telescopes, and down below, a fine beach. The first light was erected on this point of land in 1808, and the present lighthouse dates from 1878, just over a century ago.

The view is very pleasant, looking out to sea across Nauset Beach (the sand bar, actually a peninsula, you see out in the water). The cool sea breeze in summer and the nautical blast in winter make it incredible to think that Rome is at almost exactly the same latitude (but 4,200 miles away) as Chatham. To get to the Fish Pier, take Main Street east to Shore Street, then go left (north). The pier is operated by the town for licensed Chatham fishermen. Chatham is very proud of its fishing fleet of small boats, which the townpeople boast brings in the freshest fish around. The boast has some truth to it, for the use of little boats means that the catch must be brought home every day; larger boats often stay out to sea for several days, refrigerating their catch on board.

The time to go down to the pier is between 3 and 6pm (aim for 4). You'll see the fleet come in and unload, and you can buy the day's catch right after it comes off the boat. Those who like to do it themselves can rent a boat at Fish Pier for a day's hunting for bass, bluefish, and tuna out at sea.

Beaches

The town of Chatham has public beaches ($5 a day, $20 a week, $40 the season) at **Oyster Pond,** only a few blocks from the center of town south on State Harbor Road from Main Street; and a bit farther out at **Harding's Beach**—follow Main Street (Rte. 28) west from the center of town for about 2 miles, and turn left (south) on Barn Hill Road to Harding's Beach Road. Lifeguards and toilets are at both beaches, but no bathhouses.

The Bird and Wildlife Sanctuary

Chatham is a particularly good place for seeing birds, for **Monomoy Island,** south of the town, has been a National Wilderness Area since 1970. Over 300 different species of birds have been spotted on Monomoy. May is the best time to see birds in their mating plumage, and starting in late July many birds begin to be seen in winter plumage. The only way to get to Monomoy is by boat from Chatham. Full details on current offerings are available from the town's information booth on Main Street (tel. 508/945-0342). For wildlife tour information, call 508/349-2615.

Band Concerts

One of the nicest things about Chatham in July and August is the schedule of band concerts (every Friday evening at 8pm) in **Kate Gould Park,** just past the Wayside Inn on Main Street. Everybody comes to the concerts, and on a typical Friday evening the crowd may reach into the thousands. Most of the musicians in the town band are year-round residents of Chatham who live and work in the town and enjoy providing a little free entertainment for their fellow citizens and visitors once a week.

Theater

The **Monomoy Theater,** 776 Main Street, not far west of the intersection with Old Harbor Road (tel. 508/945-1589), is the summer-stock operation of Ohio University, and offers a different play each week during July and August. Performances are given Tuesday through Saturday (curtain rises at 8:30pm), and the current play is advertised on flyers around town and in the local newspapers. Season tickets are available, should you be spending the summer in Chatham.

Historical Sites

Chatham has its share of antique buildings open to the public, each highlighting a separate part of the town's interesting past. The **Atwood House and Museums** are run by the Chatham Historical Society (tel. 508/945-2493) and feature over 2,000 exhibits, including an outstanding shell collection, a good number of pieces of Sandwich glass, and a crewel bedspread which took townspeople six years to make. Also on display at the house is a set of French lighthouse lenses used in the Chatham Light from 1923 until recently. Atwood House is open Monday, Wednesday, and Friday mid-June to mid-September from 2 to 5pm, except holidays. Admission is $1 for adults, 50¢ for students, free for children accompanied by adults.

Chatham's **Railroad Museum** is located in the old station on Depot Road (take Old Harbor Road north off Main Street, and Depot Street is a short distance up on the left). The station was built in 1887 by the Chatham Railroad Company, and turned into a museum in 1960. Among the railroading exhibits is a real caboose, once used by the New York Central until that company gave it to the museum. The museum is open Monday through Friday from 1:30 to 4:30pm during late June, July, August, and early September. It's staffed with townspeople who act as volunteer guides, and admission is free.

Chatham also has an old **Grist Mill** open to the public daily except Tuesday, July and August only. Entrance is free, but donations are accepted. Sometimes corn is ground between the mill's stones if the wind is sufficient. To find it, take Cross Street south off Main Street to Shattuck Place, which winds down to the mill.

---

8. Orleans and Eastham

Orleans owes its name and its fame to French connections. Known as Nauset since its earliest settlement in 1644, the town was renamed Orleans in 1797 when it was separated from neighboring Eastham and incorporated. The Duke of Orléans had made a visit to Cape Cod, and the townspeople chose the name in the French nobleman's honor.

Orleans's other French connection was as close as can be without moving continents. In 1879 Orleans was physically connectd by underwater telegraph cable with the town of Brest in France, almost 4,000 miles away. You can still see the telegraph station where the cable came ashore before continuing overland to New York.

In its day Orleans has made its living through fishing and shellfishing, clothing manufacture, agriculture, and the production of salt from seawater, not to mention trade in contraband. During the Revolutionary War, Orleans sent men and supplies to aid the colonial forces. In the War of 1812, the town refused to pay $1,000 "protection money" demanded by the British enemy. A landing force was sent ashore from H.M.S. *Newcastle,* and the town militia quickly convinced the Redcoats that it was probably a good idea to return to the ship, which they did. Needless to say, Orleans kept its $1,000. When a German submarine broke the surface off Nauset Beach during World War I, the townspeople again demonstrated their coolness in the face of danger. The sub released a few torpedos at some coal barges, and everybody turned out to watch the show.

Today Orleans is known as the midpoint between the Cape Cod Canal and Provincetown, a good place to stop for a meal or a night's rest.

WHERE TO STAY IN ORLEANS

You really have quite a choice of places to stay in Orleans, as motels and inns are the town's business.

Inns and Guesthouses

The **Nauset House Inn,** P.O. Box 774, East Orleans, MA 02643 (tel. 508/255-2195), is actually in East Orleans, nearer to the beach than to the Mid-Cape Highway. Once you get on Beach Road in East Orleans, you'll come to the inn on the right-hand side as you head east. The setting is bucolic and relaxing, the inn nestled into lush surroundings, yet only a short distance from the beach. The 14 rooms range from $50 to $105 single or double (tax included); the higher-priced rooms offer a balcony or sitting area or private bath. Full breakfasts are served every morning, to guests only, at an extra charge. This is Orleans's most charming place to stay.

The **Ship's Knees Inn,** Beach Rd., P.O. Box 756, East Orleans, MA 02643 (tel. 508/255-1312), is a restored 160-year-old sea captain's house a mere 10-minute walk away from Nauset Beach. The inn has 19 rooms done in a colonial decor, some with water views, and with either private or shared baths; the nearby Cove House has more rooms, each with private bath, color cable TV, and water view. Two rental cottages here are right at the water's edge, with private baths and color cable TV. A tennis court and swimming pool are on the grounds, and Continental breakfast is included in the rates, which range from $55 to $83 for a room with shared bath or $99 to $110 with private bath, tax included, in summer. Donna Anderson is the genial owner.

Though it's a bit off the beaten path, I still recommend Carolyn and Dick Smith's **Whalewalk Inn,** 220 Bridge Rd., Eastham, MA 02642 (tel. 508/255-0617), for those who want solitude after suntanning. From the traffic rotary in Orleans, take the street marked for Rock Harbor, then turn right onto Bridge Road. On 3½ acres, this restored 1830s whaling master's home offers a nice blend of modern updates and old-fashioned hospitality. Choose your double room with bath from among those in the inn proper ($99 to $148), the barn ($165), the guesthouse ($99 to $165), or the saltbox studio cottage ($148); all are different and appealing in their own ways. A full breakfast comes with your room.

Motels

The **Orleans Holiday Motel** is on Rte. 6A, Orleans, MA 02653 (tel. 508/255-1514 or toll free 800/451-1833, 800/451-1818 in Massachusetts), just past the intersection of Rtes. 6A and 28 as you're driving northeast. The Orleans Holiday has contemporary motel rooms, all with tile bath and shower, cable color TV, air conditioning, picture windows, and a balcony-walkway. There's a fine large pool surrounded by lounge chairs and equipped with a slide and a backyard garden and picnic area. Most rooms have two double beds and rent for $84 to $98 double, $12 for an extra person, from late June through Labor Day. Several rooms in the unit behind Nick's Family Pub (open for breakfast, lunch, dinner, cocktails, and entertainment) are larger than normal, newer, and a bit more luxurious.

Another motel near the intersection of 6A and 28 is **The Cove,** on Rte. 28 (P.O. Box 279), Orleans, MA 02653 (tel. 508/255-1203 or toll free 800/343-2233; 800/322-2205 in Massachusetts). The rooms here are modern and sound-proof (not that there's all that much noise in The Cove's area), the layout of the motel is quite beautiful, and it has its own heated pool. The rooms, which come with color cable TV, and queen- or king-size beds, rent for $98 to $175 double in high summer, depending on whether you want one room, a two-room efficiency, or a water view. All rooms are air-conditioned.

WHERE TO DINE
Kadee's Lobster & Clam Bar (tel. 508/255-6184) is right next to the East Orleans Fish Market on Beach Road, and indeed these two establishments share the same telephone and management. That should tell you the fish, lobsters, and clams are fresh and moderately priced. What's left to say is that you dine in attractive rustic rooms or under a colorful umbrella on the pretty deck; or you dine wherever you like, having bought your chowder, fried fish, or boiled lobsters from the take-out window. The take-out is marvelously inexpensive, of course. But the dining room and deck are delightful: Have kale soup, corn on the cob, steamers, or fish, or order the Blue Plate Lobster Special ($14.50), with a 1¼-pound lobster and trimmings. To find Kadee's, follow Beach Road east toward East Orleans, and watch for it on the left-hand side of the road. It's open from 11:30am to 9:30pm every day.

Something less formal? The **Lobster Claw** (tel. 508/255-1800), right next to the Pancake Maid near the Orleans Holiday Motel on Rte. 6A, is open for lunch and dinner from April to October. Fish nets cover the restaurant's ceiling, and sea-blue booths and natural wood tables and chairs crowd the floor. Upstairs is a lounge and raw bar. The menus are in the shape of lobster claws (why not?), and they list fish and seafood plates priced at $9 to $16, lobsters for about $15 to $20 (in season), and daily specials such as soft-shell crabs with french fries and coleslaw for $12. There's a special children's menu. The Lobster Claw is not very far from the big Orleans traffic circle, and is thus a good place to stop if you're just passing through. Open every day, April through November, from 11:30am to 9pm.

Serving creative cuisine in more eclectic surroundings is **The Arbor,** on Rte. 28 in Orleans (tel. 508/255-4847). This place combines just the right ingredients to make a person relax. Perhaps it's the yellow toy truck and the antique tins, or maybe it's the sincere service. At any rate, for starters you'll get an extensive assortment of vegetables, dips, and crackers, followed by homemade biscuits. Proceed to a main course of veal, beef, fowl, or fish. In the adjacent Binnacle Tavern, fare is less formal and more family-oriented, and includes rich and elaborate pizzas. If you dine before 6:25pm and pay cash, your dinner will cost 20% less. The Arbor is open from 5 to 10pm (the Binnacle Tavern stays open until 11:30pm) every night from May through October; hours are shorter during the winter.

Captain Cass, in Rock Harbor, just north of Orleans off Rte. 6A (no phone), is a basic New England diner, right on the harbor with colorful buoys hanging outside. The food is simple but good, and reliable; lobsters ($17 to $20) and lobster rolls ($9) are the appropriate house specialties. The atmosphere is pleasant and informal, a favorite with locals. Lunch is served from 11am to 2pm; dinner, from 5 to 9pm. In the summer, there is generally a 15- to 20-minute wait at dinner; no alcoholic beverages are served.

WHAT TO SEE AND DO
Orleans has a rare sight: a museum in the building erected to house the Americancan terminus of a transatlantic cable from Brest, France. Laid in 1879, the cable came to Orleans in 1891, and the **French Cable Station Museum** remains much as it was when the cable was still in use. Among other important messages, the cable transmitted word of Lindbergh's arrival in Paris, and remained in use until 1959. Today the museum is open in July and August Tuesday through Saturday from 2 to 4pm, at $2 for adults, $1 for children 7 to 17 (7 and under free). It's located at Rte 28 and Cove Road.

Several good beaches are a short distance from Orleans. Remember that Atlantic-side beaches will invariably be cooler for swimming than the beaches on Cape Cod Bay.

Nauset Beach, a stretch of sand 10 miles long, is a town beach of Orleans and therefore is subject to a $5 daily parking fee ($10 on weekends and holidays); the use of bathhouse and other facilities is included. Permits for a week or more are also available at reduced prices. The surfing's not bad at Nauset, and a section of the beach is reserved for that activity.

Skaket Beach, on Cape Cod Bay, has less surf, but warmer water and a gently sloping beach. It's operated by the town, with lifeguards, parking places, and a bathhouse, and there's a $5 charge.

Pilgrim Lake is a freshwater swimming spot run by the town. A sand beach runs into the clear water, and a lifeguard is on duty during the summer season. No charge for use of the facilities.

A short detour to **Fort Point** off Rte. 6A will reveal a breathtaking view of the surrounding marshlands. There are also some nice trails you can take down to the Nauset Marsh.

Eastham

Eastham's main attraction is the Salt Pond Visitor Center of the Cape Cod National Seashore (see below). Right across the street from the center is the quaint and attractive **Eastham Historical Society Museum.** Look for the curious gateway, made from the jawbones of a huge whale. The museum, once a schoolhouse, dates from 1869.

Just south of the Salt Pond Visitor Center on U.S. 6 is the oldest windmill on Cape Cod (1793), a favorite place to stop and take a photo. From the windmill, take a side trip west to **First Encounter Beach,** where the Pilgrims first met the Indian inhabitants of the Cape back in 1620. A plaque on a boulder up the hill just north of the parking lot commemorates the meeting, which apparently was anything but cordial. You can visit the boulder plaque for free, but if you want to park and use the beach during the summer, you'll have to pay the town's beach-use parking fee ($5 daily, $10 weekly).

---

9. Cape Cod National Seashore

To preserve intact the particular wild beauty of Cape Cod, Congress established the Cape Cod National Seashore in 1961. It's administered by the National Park Service and includes something less than 27,000 acres of beach, dunes, marsh, forest, and glacial ponds. Acquisition of land is still going on, and therefore much private property is found in and around the Seashore. Within the Seashore, which stretches for 50 miles from the southern tip of Nauset Beach all the way to Provincetown, there are four developed areas for visitors.

NAUSET AREA

The **Salt Pond Visitor Center** is at Eastham on U.S. 6, and it's here you'll find interpretive exhibits and pamphlets, guide leaflets to the nature trails, an 8pm evening program, rest rooms, picnic areas, and **Coast Guard Beach** and **Nauset Light Beach,** open for swimming. Parking is $3 at Nauset Light, but you must take a $3 shuttle bus to the Coast Guard Beach, as parking is not allowed there. Several bicycle and bridle trails lead from the Visitor Center to the beaches through the pretty woods, marshes, and dunes. Be sure to enter the Visitor Center building and take in the picture-postcard view of Salt Pond, below.

MARCONI STATION AREA

The Seashore's headquarters is here near Wellfleet, and also an interpretive shelter at the site of Marconi's wireless station, the first in the United States; a nature trail; and Marconi Beach, open for swimming (parking is $3). The Great Island Trail is in a separate area southwest of the town of Wellfleet.

PILGRIM HEIGHTS AREA

Between North Truro and Provincetown, this area includes an interpretive shelter dealing with the Pilgrims and the Indians, nature trails, a picnic area, and, nearby, Head of the Meadow Beach, open for swimming.

You'll also see signs pointing the way to Highland Light, with its picturesque lighthouse and ocean observation point. On a nearby hill are several radar installations which look surprisingly like enormous golf balls. And then there's a golf course, right below.

PROVINCE LANDS AREA

A Visitor Center outside Provincetown on Race Point Road provides information and exhibits dealing with the Seashore and its natural treasures, with a schedule of programs at the amphitheater in the evening. Two beaches, a picnic area, a nature trail, and a bicycle trail are here as well. Parking costs $3 at Race Point and Herring Cove.

---

10. Wellfleet

Cooking lobsters and corn on the cob at a beach picnic, meeting friends downtown at the lunch counter for a midmorning's lazy second cup of coffee, running errands barefoot or in rubber thongs—if you've enjoyed that sort of an easy summer atmosphere, Wellfleet will bring it back to you. Although a number of motels on U.S. 6 take in travelers heading for Provincetown, Wellfleet is mostly a town of "steadies," people who come every summer for all summer. But it does have a few inns and restaurants worth a look should you find it good to stop here.

WHERE TO STAY

Not far from the center of Wellfleet is the **Holden Inn,** P.O. Box 816, Wellfleet, MA 02667 (tel. 508/349-3450), open mid-April to Columbus Day. The inn consists of three buildings of very nicely kept rooms, all different, some with water views, and with double or twin beds. One room, for instance, is paneled all in cedar, and is very handsome. No meals are served, and rates vary with the plumbing: Doubles with shared bath are $55; doubles with private bath are $66. Several of the rooms are furnished with some antique pieces. To find the Holden Inn, from Rte. 6 take a left at the Wellfleet Center sign, another left at the sign to the pier; the inn is on the right.

WHERE TO DINE

The **Wellfleet Oyster House** (tel. 508/349-2134) takes its name and its menu from the renowned Wellfleet oyster. It's just off Rte. 6 on East Main Street, the road into town, overlooking a small pond. The restaurant is in an early Cape house (built 1750) with wide-board floors and old paintings on the walls. Have oysters as an appetizer, or as a main course, broiled, in a stew, casino, or Rockefeller. The menu lists a dozen other seafood items, including curries, paella, shrimp, sole, and lobster. For meat eaters, there's prime rib, sirloin, and steak tartare. Most main courses are priced from $13 to $20, and since each includes relish tray, salad, vegetable, potato or rice, garlic bread, and coffee or tea, the main-course price is virtually the dinner price (add 5.7% tax plus tip and cost of drinks). The restaurant is open from 6 to 10pm March through November (off-season, weekends only).

Try a restaurant called **Cielo** (pronounced "chello"), on East Main Street across from the Oyster House (tel. 508/349-2108), for a unique, romantic, five-course, evening-long dinner extravaganza. The two owners do it all: from gingerly cleaning fresh green beans to serving each course to washing the dishes afterward. As you can imagine, the set menu changes daily (if you're a vegetarian, don't dine there on a night beef is served), Tuesday through Saturday, Memorial Day through Columbus Day. The set menu is about $40 per person. A sample evening's fare includes salad; pasta with a fresh, cool tomato-and-basil sauce; plum bisque; marinated and broiled boneless leg of lamb; rice and fresh vegetables; and an almond tart with apricot glaze. The glass-covered terrace which is the dining room overlooks Wellfleet Marsh and seats 16 or so; the sole 8pm seating is by reservation only.

For fine New American cuisine, **Aesop's Tables,** on Main Street (tel. 508/349-6450), is the place to go. Once the summer mansion of a Massachusetts governor, it now has six welcoming dining rooms, all busy on any summer night, so call for reservations. You might start dinner with poached medallions of scallop mousse wrapped in salmon filet, or a salad of exotic greens and sun-dried tomatoes, then go on to herb-roasted duck with brandy walnut sauce and cranberry-orange relish, grilled paillards of veal, or any of the daily seafood specials. There's always a vegetarian dish offered as well. Finish with Aesop's trademarked Death by Chocolate dessert, and watch your diet pass away happily. Expect a full dinner to cost $35 to $45 per person with wine, tax, and tip. The second-floor lounge is an enjoyable place for a pre- or post-prandial drink (you can take dessert here too).

Down by the town dock is **Captain Higgins' Seafood Restaurant** (tel. 508/349-6027), with views of the pier and the harbor. In season, hours are noon to 9:30pm, and when last I visited, a daily evening special of Wellfleet bluefish was less than $13; many main courses are even cheaper. With a half dozen Wellfleet oysters on the half shell and a bottle of wine, two people can dine here for $55, tax and tip included. There is a children's menu.

The **Bayside Lobster Hutt** (tel. 508/349-6333) is hardly an exotic place—unless you come from far away. Wellfleet regulars and visitors come into this old oyster shack for a summer picnic-style self-service dinner consisting of live boiled lobster—you pick 'em from the tanks—corn on the cob, steamed clams, and the like. A 1½-pound lobster, easily a plentiful meal for one person, with corn, costs less than $15. The huge plate of fried clams costs less than $10, and the fish and chips plate is even cheaper. Informal, fun, and good food. The Lobster Hutt, on Commercial Street, on the way to the town dock, is open for dinner daily from Memorial Day through September, 5 to 10:30pm, and for lunch starting at noon in July and August. Bring your own wine or beer.

Wellfleet's best place for a quick breakfast, good lunch, or inexpensive and tasty dinner is **The Lighthouse** (tel. 508/349-3681), on Main Street right in the center of town. It's Wellfleet's hometown eatery, and everybody meets everybody else here during the day, for brunch or for a cocktail out on the screened-in deck. The atmosphere is very informal, the service by young local women quick and friendly. For breakfast, French toast, juice, and coffee is $3.75; at lunch, sandwiches such as turkey club or clam rolls are offered. Complete seafood dinners in the evening (till 9:30pm) run $14 to $17; if you want the main-course plate only, it's a few dollars less. There's a good menu of light suppers as well. When you're searching for the Lighthouse, look for the little model of its namesake over the front door.

WHAT TO SEE

As most of Wellfleet's crowd is permanent for the summer, not as many things are available for the transient visitor. Note the town clock in the steeple of the First Congregational Church, which, Wellfleetans proudly say, is the only church clock in the world that rings ship's time. The beaches are mostly reserved for permanent or all-summer residents (you need two different permits to swim there, and if you're passing through it's not worth getting them), but **White Crest Beach** and **Cahoon's Hollow Beach,** off U.S. 6 on the Atlantic coast, are open to day visitors for $10. And you can always go south on U.S. 6 a short distance from Wellfleet and turn left (east) to the **Marconi Beach** in the National Seashore. At the beach is an ocean overlook and an interpretive shelter explaining the activities of the Marconi Wireless Station, the first in the United States, which was on this site. The Atlantic White Cedar Swamp nature trail starts from here as well.

The Massachusetts Audubon Society operates the **Wellfleet Bay Wildlife Sanctuary,** P.O. Box 236, South Wellfleet, MA 02663 (tel. 508/349-2615), 700 acres of woods and marshland which you can see on your own or by guided tour. The sanctuary is open all year long and interpretive walks are given in summer. There are also birding tours to Monomoy National Wildlife Refuge. The charge is $3 for adults, $2 for children. A natural history day camp for children operates in July and August, with trips and tours on and off the property. From July through September there's a field school for adults too.

A STOP IN TRURO

If you want to head straight to the beach, but you're starving from the long drive and don't want to deal with traffic in P-town, turn off Rte. 6A into downtown Truro for a quick stop. **Jams, Inc.** (tel. 508/349-1616), in addition to carrying standard grocery items, stocks an impressive assortment of pâtés, spreads, meats, cheeses, breads, imported crackers, and the like (even an authentic baklava). It's open long hours during high season.

---

11. Provincetown

Provincetown is separated from the rest of the Cape by sand, forest, and marsh, and thus has something of an island ambience, a feeling accentuated by the town's compact size. Out of season, the inhabitants are mostly fishermen, descendants of hardy Portuguese sailors who came here for the whaling trade a century ago. In season Provincetown is a carnival constantly alive with all sorts of people from all around: New York, Boston, Montréal, Québec, and also Podunk. Artists and writers, the successful and the hopeful, college sophomores and sophisticates, dowagers and down-at-heelers all mix and mingle in the evening along P-town's narrow streets. The town is at the same time quaint and sophisticated, elegant and tawdry, depending on where you look and how you see.

Of all things, the most important when planning a visit to P-town in late July and August is to *have a room reservation without fail.* It is just not possible to find a room in Provincetown for the six weeks of hectic high season unless you reserve ahead. If you have no reservation, it's best to plan to stay in Orleans or Wellfleet, or along U.S. 6 some distance from P-town, and to drive up for the day.

Gay and Straight in P-town: Like San Francisco and Key West, Provincetown hosts a large gay community on vacation during the summer. The great majority of establishments—hotels, inns, guesthouses, restaurants, cafés, bars, and nightclubs —welcome all customers regardless of sexual orientation, regardless of whether the proprietor is gay or straight. But in a few places you'll definitely feel out of place if your sexual preference doesn't match that of the proprietor and the majority of customers.

GETTING THERE

You can get to Provincetown by car, by bus direct from New York, Hartford, Providence, points in between, by sea, and by air. Here's the rundown.

By Car

U.S. 6 is divided highway all the way to P-town, where it ends and brings you face to face with a parking problem. *Don't* try to park in the center of town. Get a space in one of the municipal lots (follow the signs) if you can.

By Bus

In summer, **Bonanza Bus Lines** will take you to Hyannis from New York (Port Authority Terminal, Greyhound counter; tel. 212/564-8484) or from Providence (Bonanza Terminal; tel. 401/751-8800 or 331-7500). In Hyannis, transfer to **Plymouth & Brockton** bus (tel. 508/775-5524). The trip takes 8 hours from New

York, 3¼ hours from Providence. Bonanza also runs buses from Albany and Springfield, Mass., to Hyannis, where you connect for P-town. In Hartford the terminal is at Union Station (tel. 203/547-1500). Plymouth & Brockton runs four buses daily in summer from Boston to Provincetown. Connections are arranged for buses coming from Montréal via Boston to the Cape (two buses daily in summer, with additional services on weekends). Note that the bus will drop you off near or right at your hotel, if it's out of the center of town, if you ask the driver to do so. This is a normal service, so feel free to ask.

By Sea

You can take a delightful cruise to Provincetown aboard the M.V. *Provincetown II,* operated by **Bay State Provincetown Cruises,** 66 Long Wharf, Boston, MA 02110 (tel. 617/723-7800). The 3-hour cruise costs $15 one way ($13 for seniors and children under 12), or $25 round trip ($18 for seniors and kids) if you make the round trip all in one day. The ship leaves from Boston's Commonwealth Pier: Take the T (subway) Blue Line to Aquarium Station, or the Red Line to South Station, and then cross the Fort Point Channel. Ask for Northern Avenue, and walk southeast along it for a few blocks; Commonwealth Pier will be on your left. The walk from either subway stop takes about 15 minutes.

Here's the schedule: Leave Commonwealth Pier at 9:30am, arrive at P-town's MacMillan Wharf right in the middle of town at 12:30pm. The return trip leaves MacMillan Wharf at 3:30pm to arrive at Commonwealth Pier by 6:30pm. Breakfast, lunch, snacks, cocktails, and refreshments are on sale aboard; a band provides music, and the captain describes the landmarks and sights in passing. The 1,100-passenger, 195-foot *Provincetown II* has three decks providing open, covered, and enclosed seating areas.

By the way, MacMillan Wharf is where intercity buses begin and end their runs, and where the Provincetown Chamber of Commerce operates its information office.

By Air

PacAir (tel. toll free 800/359-7221) operates about seven daily flights by small Piper aircraft between Boston's Logan International Airport and Provincetown, a trip of less than half an hour.

INFORMATION

The **Provincetown Chamber of Commerce** operates an information office (tel. 508/487-3424) at 307 Commercial St. on MacMillan Wharf. Boats from Boston arrive at this wharf, and the chamber's office is also the stop for intercity buses from New York, Providence, and Boston. Bus and boat schedules are posted here. You can also get information on the new shuttle bus (50¢ for senior citizens, $1 for everyone else) that takes you to different points in P-town.

WHERE TO STAY

Provincetown's streets are lined with guesthouses and inns and motels, and in the six weeks from mid-July to Labor Day every room in every one will be rented. Outside of that time you have a chance of finding a room by arriving in town by late morning or early afternoon. A special note is in order concerning credit cards. Demand for services is so great here that very many hotels and restaurants *do not accept credit cards.* As they get all the business they want anyway, they choose not to bother with the extra expense, delay, and paperwork that cards entail. Also, most lodging places require some minimum stay during the peak season period, usually from three or four days (at least, on weekends) to a full week. And you won't be able to fudge it: You'll probably have to pay the full amount for your stay when you check in.

When you set out to hunt for accommodations, or to find your reserved room, remember that P-town is about 3 miles long from one end of Commercial Street (the main street) to the other.

P-town's ZIP Code is 02657, for reservations by mail.

West End Guesthouses and Inns

The quaint, picturesque character of Provincetown is best expressed in its small inns and guesthouses. The West End—west of MacMillan Wharf, that is—has the richest concentration of guesthouses. Many are really inns, carefully restored with lots of guest rooms, some luxury features, and moderate to high prices. Others are mom-and-pop establishments, simple and unpretentious, at very reasonable bargain rates. First I'll describe the nicer places, and then the West End bargain finds.

MODERATELY PRICED ROOMS   Start your room search by walking west along Commercial Street from MacMillan Wharf, with the street numbers descending as you go west.

The **Anchor Inn** is a gracious, expansive turn-of-the-century house at 175 Commercial St. (tel. 508/487-0432). As with most inns and guesthouses in P-town, every room is different, although most have a deck, balcony, or porch, and many have a sea view. Room size, view, and deck determine room price, and the date of your visit is an important factor as well. From late May through mid-September, expect to pay $93 to $116 for a double room, tax included. (During July Fourth and Labor Day weekends there's a seven-day minimum stay and a $10-per-room surcharge in effect.)

The **Captain and His Ship** (tel. 508/487-1850) sounds like the title of a Cape Cod novel, but in fact it's a handsome guesthouse at 164 Commercial St., corner of Central Street, just far enough from the heart of town to keep the noise level low. Provincetown's shipboard tidiness characterizes the house, its eight guest rooms, and its small front lawn complete with bench. Each room is different, furnished with fascinating Victoriana, and each has a different price: With private bath, rooms are $93 to $104; with shared bath, the double rooms are $66; tax is included. The more expensive ones are those with water views, of course. Reductions of $15 to $20 are in effect any time except mid-June through mid-September (the house is open all year); in high season, minimum stays of four to seven nights are required if your visit includes a weekend or part of one.

Along Commercial Street, as you come to the Coast Guard Station on your left, note that Commercial Street bears left around the station. If you keep going straight you'll be on Tremont Street.

Past the Coast Guard Station, at 96 Commercial St., is the **Captain Lysander Inn** (tel. 508/487-2253). The ancestral home of Dr. Vannevar Bush, it was built by Capt. Lysander Paine in 1852. The rooms feature a blend of antique and traditional-style furnishings. Rooms with private bath are $76 and those with shared baths are $70; the efficiency is $88. Each additional person pays $10 a day. Rates are about $10 to $15 less off-season. Enjoy a complimentary continental breakfast in the front parlor, or outside on the spacious front deck or sun porch. Parking is free. There is a four-night minimum over holidays and a three-night minimum for weekends.

Bright, cheerful, comfortable, and well equipped—that describes the **1807 House,** 54 Commercial St. (tel. 508/487-2173). The cedar-shingled main house faces the street, and behind it are several other buildings which hold rooms, studios, and apartments. Names say it all: the Master's Suite, the Artist's Studio, the Cottage Garden Apartment, the Cottage Studio Apartment, the Red Room, the Beige Room, and more. Each is tastefully and attractively done, many have kitchens, and all share the quiet location, free parking, and grassy lawns. The owners will be happy to describe each room for you, and will quote prices such as $50 single, $60 to $86 double—high-season rates. In fall, winter, and spring, prices are about $15 lower. Three-day minimum stays are required on Memorial, July Fourth, and Labor Day weekends.

The **Masthead,** 31–41 Commercial St. (tel. 508/487-0523), lists cottages, apartments, and motel rooms among its accommodations, but you must see the place to appreciate it. All these overnight possibilities are contained in a collection of cozy little cottages which look across flawless green lawn to a private boardwalk, a beach, and the water. Write for the descriptions of the 21 types of accommodations, from modern rooms through efficiency studios to cottages for up to seven people. In high season (July through Labor Day), the cottages, suites, and efficiencies are rented by the week, anywhere from $919 to $1,422 for two people; a few motel rooms rent by the day for $64 to $147. Mid-September rates are a few dollars less, but off-season rates (late September to early June) are substantially lower. If you can't find the sort of room you want at the Masthead, you're probably looking for a tent.

BUDGET-PRICED ROOMS Now let's do that same walk westward from MacMillan Wharf, this time looking for the lowest-priced rooms in P-town. While not fancy, these rooms are always comfortable, though few have private bath.

Helen Valentine is the proprietor of **Valentine House,** 88 Commercial St. (tel. 508/487-0839), a very tidy guesthouse with its own parking facilities and rooms that rent in summer for $33 single, $44 double with shared bath, $55 double with private bath. Off-season prices are $5 lower per room. Quiet and fairly convenient—it's an excellent place to stay.

Corea's Guest House (tel. 508/487-0274) is at 5 Cottage St., off Commercial right behind Valentine House. It's a comfy, homey place, rather than classy or chic, with prices that are appealing: $33 single, $42 for two in a double bed, $52 for two in twin beds.

Nearby is the **O'Donnell Guest House,** 6 Atwood Ave., a little alley off Commercial (tel. 508/487-0103). John and Marian O'Donnell rent rooms which share a bath for $55 (twin or double bed) or $39 (single), plus a cottage (weekly for $440). It has a nice lawn, set back from the street, and free parking.

Tremont Street is parallel to Commercial Street and one block inland. (In fact, if Commercial Street didn't jog around the Coast Guard Station, Tremont Street would be the natural continuation of Commercial—see the map.) **Bob White's Rooms and Cottages,** 21 Tremont St. (tel. 508/487-0482), is operated by Ethel White, who will show you a twin-bedded room with a TV, sharing a bath, for $42 or a room with private bath and color TV for $48; the cottage goes for $52 per day, double.

East End Guesthouses and Inns

The eastern reaches of Provincetown, along Commercial Street, Bradford Street, and the small cross streets between them, hold dozens of small inns and a few guesthouses. Generally speaking, these are more expensive than the majority of West End places. The location is roughly the same in terms of convenience. You may encounter a bit more noise here, though. Look your room over with this in mind.

The **Bradford Gardens Inn,** 178 Bradford St. near the corner of Miller Hill Road (tel. 508/487-1616), is certainly one of Provincetown's most charming and serene places to stay. Every room in the century-and-a-half-old inn is different, and each has a name rather than a number. In season, standard double rooms, with private bath and color TV, are $109; six double rooms have fireplaces as well, and these rent for $124. An extra person pays $15 sharing a room. Alternative arrangements include two apartments, a Swiss-chalet-type cottage, and a six- to eight-person lodge ($148 double, $15 for each additional person). Rates include a big breakfast and (for rooms with facilities to use it) firewood as well. And speaking of gardens, the Bradford has 'em, spreading around the house, set with benches, chairs, and even a garden swing.

The **White Horse Inn,** 500 Commercial St. (tel. 508/487-1790), is a neat and tidy place painted white, with blue shutters and a bright-yellow door. Inside, lots of quaint old pieces picked up in the area were used in decoration to keep the period feeling (the house is at least two centuries old), and every room seems to contain at least five original paintings. The beach is right across the street (guests have beach rights), and for after-swim, the inn's backyard lawn chairs hit the spot. Doubles with

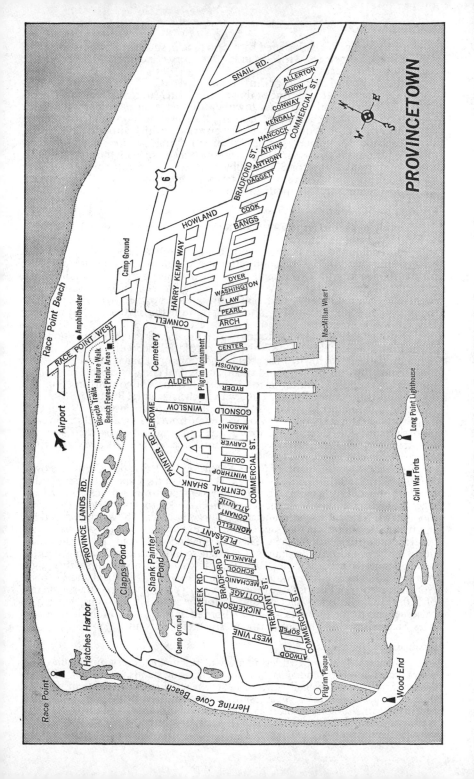

PROVINCETOWN

private bath go for $77; with shared bath, $66 to $71; studio apartments cost $715 weekly; single rooms are $33 to $38; and an extra person is charged $15. Off-season, the rates go down; just ask.

Asheton House, 3 Cook St., Provincetown, MA 02657 (tel. 508/487-9966), just off Commercial Street, is one of those immaculately restored, beautifully decorated guesthouses found in Provincetown. Each of the seven guest rooms is unique: One has a four-poster bed; another has a fireplace, dressing room, and private bath; yet another has a canopied bed. There's an apartment with bedroom, living room, and kitchen too. The smallest, simplest room with double bed and shared bath rents for $50; most others go for $66 to $77, although the suite (with the fireplace) costs $99. The apartment rents for $757 double per week, $11 per day or $77 per week for an additional person. All these prices are for summer, and all include the tax. Fall, winter, and spring prices are about 25% lower.

Motels

A nicely kept motel is the **Cape Colony Inn,** at 280 Bradford St. (tel. 508/487-1755). Here, besides clean and well-kept modern rooms, you have a big heated pool, volleyball, badminton, shuffleboard, and a coffee shop. The Cape Colony has a policy of accepting reservations for a minimum of two nights (three on holidays). Rates for the rooms, all with two double beds (or one queen-size), air conditioning, phone, refrigerator, and color TV, are $76 to $98 for two. There is a suite of two rooms and three double beds, with one bathroom to serve the two rooms, for $122 for up to four people. These in-season rates apply from the last week in July to Labor Day. Off-season, from April to closing, rates are lower.

The **Shamrock Motel & Cottages** is at 49 Bradford St., at the intersection with Shank Painter Road (tel. 508/487-1133). A cute little place with a swimming pool right near the center of town, it has accommodations of all different varieties: motel rooms, motel apartments large and small, and several cottages capable of sleeping from two to five people. The motel rooms have tile baths, wall-to-wall carpeting, and TV. The apartments are efficiency units with kitchen facilities. Rooms are $99 double in the high summer season, $66 off-season; motel apartments cost $99 for two, $7 per person extra for two to five; cottages range from $82 for a small studio capable of sleeping two or three, to $93 for a deluxe cottage which sleeps five. These rates are cut by 40% off-season, and weekly rates both in season and out give you in effect one free night every week you stay.

The **Moors Motel,** Bradford Street Extension (P.O. Box 661), Provincetown, MA 02657 (tel. 508/487-1342), is right at the tip of the Cape, at the very end of Bradford Street. It is, therefore, a bit out of the center of town, but this has its advantages. For one, the motel's 32 modern, bath-equipped rooms overlook the scenic moors of the National Seashore, and are very near the beach. The weathered wood of this two-decker motel is in the Cape Cod style, and on the second floor a walkway is good for sitting to look at the view. There's a small pool and color TV for those who tire of the view, and a good restaurant (Portuguese and American food) and cocktail lounge connected with the motel. Rates vary almost by the month, but at their highest they're $83 to $97 for two, going down to $44 to $51 in April and October. Note that every room sleeps three people (the third person pays an extra-person rate of $10). The higher prices in every case are for the second-floor rooms, which have balconies and the best views. Continental breakfast is included in the high-season rates. Stays of seven days in high season receive a 10% discount.

WHERE TO DINE

Provincetown has a bewildering array of restaurants, everything from classy places with sommeliers and an ocean view to hot-dog stands with a view of Commercial Street. Some general rules: All P-town restaurants specialize in seafood, often prepared Portuguese style. Most restaurants on the seaward side of Commercial Street, with sea views, are more expensive than those on the landward side. If this is your first experience dining on clams, oysters, or lobster, be sure to read "A Real New England Clambake" in Chapter I.

First I'll describe P-town's best all-round good, moderately priced establishments in the middle of town. Then I'll go on to some special, or elegant, or out-of-the-way places you might want to try.

Moderately Priced Restaurants

The **Grand Central Café** (tel. 508/487-9116) boasts that it was established in 1968. That might not seem a long run when compared with Boston's century-old Durgin-Park, but for Provincetown it's an eon. Why so long-lived? Because it's got the formula down: good food at moderate prices in attractive, cozy, even romantic surroundings. Stained-glass lamps, wrought-iron fancywork, plants everywhere, a variety of small dining rooms, and an outdoor garden provide the atmosphere, and the sea provides the main courses. Swordfish, lobster, fresh salmon, and scampi are at the high end ($16 to $24) along with the steaks and prime rib, but you can get sole Florentine or bluefish for $14, and that includes rice, potato or vegetable, salad, bread, and butter. There is a 10% discount on all dinners before 7pm. Wine and cocktails are served. Note that a 15% service charge will be added to your bill, so there's no need to tip. The café is at 5 Masonic Pl. (a little street that starts between 216 and 218 Commercial St.), open from Memorial Day to late September for dinner: early, leisurely, and late-night (till midnight).

Front Street, 230 Commercial St. (tel. 508/487-9715), is a very popular place for dinner these days. Through a trellis walkway and down into the basement of a 140-year-old house, you'll find entrees of duck, lamb, calamari, and soft-shell crab with tricolor pasta on the menu, each for about $16 or $18. Atmosphere is typical Cape Cod, with lots of wood and beams overhead. Call for reservations; there's service until 10:30pm. A complete dinner for two will cost $60 to $75.

Let's conjure up a mood now. It's the evening of a fine, adventurous day, and you want to have a good dinner at some small, very intimate candlelit spot with particularly interesting and delicious food at moderate prices. The place is **Sal's Place,** 99 Commercial St. past the Coast Guard Station in the West End (tel. 508/487-1279). The day to go is any day of the week in summer; the time is 6 to 10pm. The food is Italian, and all cooked to order. Tiny wooden tables, chianti bottles hanging from the ceiling, and a small dining room both simple and romantic; there is also a new, larger room on the water, and outdoor dining. Specialties are brodetto (served on Friday); Wellfleet mussels, shrimp, clams, and fish in a wine broth; and bistecca alla pizzaiola, prime-rib eye steak with mushrooms and olives in a red-wine marinara sauce. On Tuesday several special veal dishes are featured. Appetizers, main courses, coffees, and wine for two at Sal's will bring the tab to about $50 or $60, all included. Call ahead for reservations. Sal's has been here since 1963.

Out of Town, On the Moors

The **Moors Restaurant** (tel. 508/487-0840) is at the end of Bradford Street Extension, at the junction with Rte. 6A, on the moors. The dining rooms are positively fraught with nautical paraphernalia—on the walls, on the ceiling, adorning the bar. Lunch and dinner are served April through October, and the cuisine is Provincetown seafood with Portuguese accents. At lunchtime you can eat for as little as $7.50 if you can be contented with a linguica roll (a mildly spicy Portuguese sausage in pastry) and a beer; or you can spend a few dollars more for sea-clam pie or something like broiled Cape scallops. Dinnertime main courses generally cost $13 to $17, but for the same price you can order the daily special dinner, which includes soup, salad, and coffee. Besides the standard fresh fish and lobster casserole, you might find carangueijo vieira a moda de peniche (scallops and crabmeat in a casserole, made with wine, brandy, and tomato sauce). There's live entertainment most evenings in the Smugglers' Lounge.

The **Red Inn,** 15 Commercial St. (tel. 508/487-0050), is almost at the western end of the street, the town, and indeed the Cape. Perched on a grassy rise, it overlooks the harbor and takes full advantage of the view. A quaint old red Cape building, the Red Inn serves all three meals every day of the year in its quiet location. The dining rooms are refined but not stuffy, with high-backed captain's chairs and nicely set tables. The menu is short, specializing in traditional dishes: broiled scallops, baked scrod, roast duckling, pork, lamb, and beef. The bill will come to $25 to $35 per person, all in. Lighter fare is available in the tavern.

Outdoor Cafés

Want to sit at an outdoor café? The most obvious place to go is the **Café Blasé,** 328 Commercial St. (tel. 508/487-9465), just east of the center of town. Lots of tables shaded by umbrellas sit out in a courtyard surrounded by flower boxes. Should you want solid sustenance, try a portion of quiche Lorraine, mushroom and spinach, or crab, a huge salad, a Mexican snack, or the Blazing Blasé Burger made with fresh mushrooms, grilled cheese, and bacon. It'll cost well under $10. The array of drinks offered is nothing short of astounding, with nonalcoholic specialties such as piña colada, orzata, grenadine, coco rico, guava and mango nectar. Imported and domestic beer, wine by the glass, half liter, or liter, or by the bottle satisfy stronger thirsts. The café is open for breakfast, lunch, cocktails, afternoon espresso, and dinner.

Another place to while away the day is the **Euro Island Grill,** 258 Commercial St. (tel. 508/497-2505), next to the Provincetown town hall. The outdoor café really does have a European ambience; breakfast, lunch, and supper (grilled burgers, pizza, a raw bar) are served. At 7pm the indoor restaurant opens, with dining in a former church. The Euro is open from Memorial Day through late October.

For Breakfast

Fresh coffee in the morning, yes, but also fresh bread and rolls: Find the **Portuguese Bakery,** right down by MacMillan Wharf at 299 Commercial St.—follow the coffee and fresh-bread smells. Not only is breakfast the freshest here, it's the cheapest. Put it together yourself, take it out to the wharf to consume, and you can do it for $2.50 easily.

For a big breakfast on the quieter end of town, try **Pearl's Café,** 401½ Commercial St. (tel. 508/487-2114). The place itself is actually bustling; it's usually packed from 8am to noon. Pearl's serves a tasty granola concoction for $3, and a three-egg omelet with your choice of almost anything on it for $3.75.

For a Quick Fix

A real institution in P-town for do-it-yourself lunch or quick dinner is the **Cheese Market,** 225 Commercial St. (tel. 508/487-3032), offering a multitude of different sandwiches, both hot and cold, soups and salads from $3 to $5. Open from 9am to 11pm daily from Memorial Day through October and until 7pm the rest of the year.

WHAT TO SEE AND DO

Provincetown's an interesting small town to browse around. Although people watching could keep you amused for days, here are some of P-town's other highlights. *Provincetown* magazine hits the streets every Thursday; it's free and will have plenty of suggestions for things to do.

Pilgrim Monument and Provincetown Museum

For a general view, the **Pilgrim Monument** and **Provincetown Museum,** on Town Hill off Winslow Street (tel. 508/487-1310), give you the best view of the town in both its physical and historical aspects. Both attractions are open during the same hours, and you pay one fee for the two: $3 per adult, $1 per child 4 through 12. The museum is an interesting potpourri of old firefighting gear, costumes, a whaling ship captain's quarters on board, primitive portraits, World War I mementos, arctic lore, and a sequence of displays on the activities of the Pilgrims in Provincetown, for this is the first place they touched land in the New World. After seeing these you can continue with the Wedgwood, model of a Thai temple, antique dolls, and other arcana. Then head for the tower.

The Pilgrim Monument is copied from the Torre del Mangia in Siena, Italy, and is all granite and 252½ feet high. The cornerstone was laid in 1907 with President Teddy Roosevelt in attendance, and the structure was completed three years later, when President Taft did the dedicating. You may think that there's an elevator in it. Well, there's not, and you'll have to c-l-i-m-b to the top, the equivalent of going up the steps in a 20-story building, to see the view. Most of the climb is on a ramp, not steps, and you can take your time and read the commemorative plaques from New England cities, towns, and civic groups which line the granite walls. The view is worth the climb: Provincetown and all Cape Cod spread out like the maps you've been following.

Both the monument and the museum are open at 9am. Tower climbing stops a half hour before closing, so get there before 4:30pm. From July through Labor Day, hours are extended to 9pm.

A Walk Around Town

Drop in at the chamber of commerce's information office down by the town wharf and pick up the Provincetown Historical Society's pamphlet (25¢), which tells you all the historic sights and houses in P-town. Check out the Pilgrims' first landing place, the monument commemorating the signing of the Mayflower Compact (America's first democratic "constitution"), and the 12-room Seth Nickerson House, the oldest dwelling in town (1746), at 72 Commercial St., open June through October from 10am to 5pm daily; $2 for adults, 50¢ for kids. The house is now the home of artist-photographer John W. Gregory and his wife, who will be happy to show you around and explain how it was built by a shipwright from heavy oak posts and beams salvaged from shipwrecks.

The **Provincetown Heritage Museum**—actually the municipal museum—at Commercial and Center streets (tel. 508/487-0666), preserves the town's heritage in its wide-ranging displays. Relics of the fishing industry, Victoriana, and many other items capture Provincetown's history. Especially exciting for children are the antique fire engine, and the *Rose Dorothea,* the world's largest half-scale fishing schooner model. The museum is open from 10am to 6pm daily from mid-June through mid-October. Adults pay $2; children under 12 are free.

Galleries, Cinemas, and Theater

Latest schedules are published in the local sheet, the *Provincetown Advocate.* Galleries dot the downtown streets, often open until late in the evening. The **Provincetown Playhouse** (tel. 508/487-0955) is active all summer. Call for current information. The **New Art Cinema** (tel. 508/487-9222), across from the post office downtown at 212 Commercial St., plays both foreign and domestic first-run films. It's the newest cinema in P-town, blissfully air-conditioned. The **Metro Cinema** is right next to the Town Hall at Commercial and Ryder streets.

Other Activities

Arnold's, at 329 Commercial St. (tel. 508/487-0855), and **Nelson's,** on Race Point Road (tel. 508/487-0034), rent **bicycles,** and you can use them in town or on the bike trails in the National Seashore. Drop in at the Seashore's Province Lands Visitor Center for a free guide pamphlet to the trails.

The **Provincetown Horse and Carriage Co.,** 27 W. Vine St. (tel. 508/487-1112), will rent you a riding horse for $20 per hour.

Several companies will take you through the dunes in a four-wheel-drive vehicle on a daylight or sunset tour for a reasonable price. Call **Drifting Sands Dune Tours** (tel. 508/349-9231) in North Truro for a reservation, or **Art's Sand Dune Taxi Tours,** at the corner of Standish and Commercial streets (tel. 508/487-1950).

What about a sail on a schooner? Several boats make 2-hour **cruises** through the waters around the tip of the Cape, giving you a very different view of the land and water. Try the *Hindu* (tel. 508/487-0659), or the *Olad* (tel. 508/487-9308); both have sunset cruises. It's best to reserve in advance. The price, like that for all the other activities here, is very reasonable, and won't set you back by even the price of a good dinner. Those who want more action on their cruise can go out with one of the two daily deep-sea fishing voyages that leave from MacMillan Wharf; whale-watching boats also leave from here, especially from mid-April to mid-June.

Should you want to do nothing more active than sit, you can have a local artist do your portrait in pastels while you're sitting. Shops are along Commercial Street and inside Whalers' Wharf near the town wharf (MacMillan Wharf), and prices start at $70 for a front view, $40 for the side, $40 and $20 if it's to be charcoal; frames and glass are extra and cost $35 and up. The portrait can be done, framed, and wrapped to take home in a surprisingly short time.

But biking, schooner sails, deep-sea fishing, and portrait sitting can't equal the sense of freedom you get if you sail your own boat out onto Cape Cod Bay. You don't have to own a boat, of course, because Provincetown has **Flyer's Boat Rental,** 131A Commercial St. (tel. 508/487-0898), behind Gallerani's restaurant. Little Sunfish, larger (18- to 20-foot) sailboats, dinghies with outboard motors, and dinghies with just a pair of oars are all for rent. Flyer's will even teach you how to sail if you don't already know.

Whale Watching

Believe me, it's a great thrill when you see one of the monster denizens break the surface, spout, sport, and play. You can sight whales from the Coast Guard Station on Race Point Beach, and just with the naked eye you'll see their spouting and their backs roll. But to see them up close is something else, and for that you need to sign up for a whale-watching cruise. Several boats leave on morning and afternoon runs, and give you several hours in which to find and watch the whales. Call the **Dolphin Fleet** (tel. 508/255-3857 or toll free 800/826-9300), which by the way has a 99.7% sighting record; or **Portuguese Princess Excursions** (tel. 508/487-2651 or toll free 800/442-3188); or **Whale's Tales Tours** (tel. 508/497-2980 or toll free 800/942-5376); or the **Ranger V** (tel. 508/487-1582 or 487-3322, or toll free 800/992-9333) for times, prices, and reservations. Boats leave from MacMillan Wharf and charge about $20 per person. By the way, the whales—which seem to perform expressly for the appreciative crowds on the boats—enjoy the trip as much as you do.

NIGHTLIFE

No one who visits Provincetown spends an evening without at least a few minutes' stroll along Commercial Street, for the main drag is P-town's greatest free entertainment thrill, a circus in a straight line. But to get away from it all, try one of these things-to-do:

Lounges: After the dinner hour, many Provincetown restaurants will have entertainment in their lounges, perhaps a guitarist or pianist, even a violinist. Drop in at any one you see open in late evening, and see what's on. **Ciro and Sal's,** 41 Kiley Court (in the 400 block of Commercial Street), is a popular place; so are the **Terrace,** at the corner of Bradford and Standish streets, and the bar at the **Mews Restaurant,** 359 Commercial St.

Clubs: The Crown Club & Dance Bar, 247 Commercial St., is a veritable entertainment supermarket, with a disco at the rear of the parking lot named the Backroom; the front room (Lobby Bar) on Commercial Street has live entertainment.

Speaking of revues, the **Madeira Room,** at 336 Commercial St. (tel. 508/487-0319), always has something going, usually on the decent side of raunchy, most often very funny. Pass by for a look at the signboard.

MARTHA'S VINEYARD AND NANTUCKET

Martha's Vineyard and Nantucket are among the eastern seaboard's most attractive and visited resorts. There's something special about vacationing on an island, a particular feeling of isolation, of being apart from the schedules and worries of city life, and this is truly relaxing and therapeutic. Here is a detailed description of Massachusetts retreats in the Atlantic.

The telephone area code for both islands is 508.

MARTHA'S VINEYARD

To Bostonians and denizens of Cape Cod, it is simply "the Vineyard"; sometimes you'll see the name given as Martha's Vineyard Island, just so visitors know they're in a special place out to sea. The island got its odd name in the early 1600s, when mariner and explorer Bartholomew Gosnold stopped here. It's said he found wild grapes, and it's thought he had a daughter named Martha. *Voilà!* Today the island actually has a commercial vineyard and a winery producing fine vintages which you can sample and buy. But more of that later.

The Vineyard is not really a part of Cape Cod, and does not look upon itself as such. Vineyard residents are proud that the island is the County of Dukes County, not part of some mainland county, and they guard the anachronistic redundancy of that title very closely. For a long time the Vineyard had its own representative in the General Court (state legislature), and when redistricting made the island a part of the Cape Cod legislative district, the islanders threatened to secede from Massachusetts and become part of another state, one that would allow them their own representative.

Islanders get their exceptional sense of independence from a history of struggle with and mastery of the sea, from the days when whaling brought great wealth to an otherwise poor island. And just about the time the whaling industry declined, the tourist industry began, and Martha's Vineyard found its place in the modern world. Today the big ferries that ply the waters of Vineyard Sound are packed with visitors every day in summer, and also are very crowded on weekends in spring and fall.

A WARNING ABOUT RESERVATIONS

In high summer—July and August—you need reservations for everything: space for your car on the ferry, or for a rental car on the island, or for a hotel room, or for a weekend mainland-to-island flight. You can't reserve passenger space on the ferry, so the thing to do is get to the docks 15 or 20 minutes early, buy your ticket, and get in line. If the ferry's passenger capacity is reached, the remaining passengers in the line will have to wait for the next boat. If you don't have a room reservation in an island hotel, there's a direct-line telephone in the Steamship Authority ticket office in Woods Hole for island hotels; you'll have to wait in line to use it. On weekends in high season, chances of finding a room are not good; on weekdays you may find a room for a few nights because of a cancellation, or a gap between reservations. If all else fails, plan to visit the island for the day, returning to the mainland in the evening.

GETTING THERE

For ferries to Martha's Vineyard, see the information in the sections on Woods Hole, Falmouth, Hyannis (all in Chapter VII), and New Bedford (in Chapter VI). One ferry a day, between mid-June and mid-September, runs between the islands of Martha's Vineyard and Nantucket. Contact the **Hy-Line** ferry company (tel. 508/778-2600). When taking a ferry, note which island port—Oak Bluffs or Vineyard Haven—the ferry operates from or to.

Several regional and commuter airlines serve the islands. For details, see the beginning of Chapter VII, "Cape Cod."

GETTING AROUND THE ISLAND

There are lots of ways to get around: rental cars (which are best reserved in advance), buses, bikes, or motorbikes. Taxi service is also readily available.

Car Rentals

The big names are here: **Hertz** (tel. 508/627-4728) in Edgartown (closed Sunday) and at the airport (tel. 508/693-2402, open daily); **Budget** (tel. 508/693-1911) in Oak Bluffs and Vineyard Haven; and **National** (tel. 508/693-6454) at the airport and in Oak Bluffs (tel. 508/693-4059).

If these places produce no results or if you'd rather rent from a small local firm, try **Adventure Rentals** of Martha's Vineyard (tel. 508/693-1959 and also a direct line from the Woods Hole Ferry Terminal), which specializes in offbeat equipment such as dune buggies, vans, mopeds, four-wheel-drive vehicles, and trucks, but it does rent cars as well. Other firms are **Atlantic Auto Rentals** (tel. 508/693-0480) in Vineyard Haven and **All-Island Rent-a-Car** (tel. 508/693-6868) at the airport. Or try **Vineyard Rent-a-Car** (tel. 508/693-9780) on Water Street in Vineyard Haven.

Bikes and Motorbikes

Rental agencies abound, and you can barely descend from the ferry without coming across one. Prices are all competitive, and a three-speed bicycle should cost in the range of $8 to $12 for a day's rental (plus a $10 deposit); motorbikes and mopeds are a good deal more, in the range of $37 to $47, and entail greater responsibility, possible destination limitations, and more chance of breakdowns. I think the island and the bicycle were made for each other, and islanders have even helped this relationship along: There's a fine bike path between Oak Bluffs and Edgartown, right along the beaches. No need to reserve bikes in advance, for there are always plenty to go around.

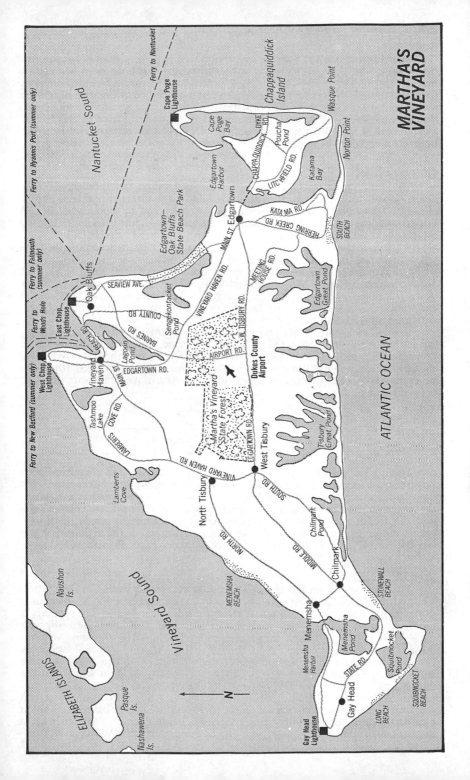

MARTHA'S VINEYARD

Bus

Island Transport Bus Service (tel. 693-0058) operates school-bus-type vehicles between the Vineyard's various settlements every half hour or so, with stops near the various ferry docks. (Trips to Gay Head from Vineyard Haven are much less frequent, though.) Prices vary according to distance traveled; round-trip tickets are always sold at a discount over the normal two-single-trip fare, so ask for a round trip if that's what suits your needs. The cheapest fare is Vineyard Haven to Oak Bluffs, and fares can be several dollars for longer trips. Don't plan on being in a hurry, as the buses frequently run behind schedule.

ORIENTATION

The island's three principal towns are **Vineyard Haven,** the commercial center where many of the mainland ferries dock; **Oak Bluffs,** a Victorian resort community of ornate "gingerbread" houses, a marina, and several grand old wooden hotels; and **Edgartown,** the county seat and main tourist attraction—clearly the prettiest town on the island. The more rural, less populated area is referred to as **Up Island;** these are the towns in the southwestern third of the island. I'll list the recommended hotels, restaurants, and things to do by town.

The **Martha's Vineyard Chamber of Commerce,** Beach Road (P.O. Box 1698), Vineyard Haven, MA 02568 (tel. 508/693-0085), is located a few doors down from the Tisbury Inn off Main Street. The chamber publishes a very helpful and complete visitor's guide, as well as a list of summer events, and can also help you with long-term accommodations.

You will undoubtedly learn it for yourself when you disembark from the boat, but let me be the first one to tell you. The best value on the Vineyard is a $1.75 homemade ice cream cone at **Mad Martha's.** Prime locales in Vineyard Haven, Oak Bluffs, and Edgartown will assure that no matter where you are, a Mad Martha's will never be very far. Keep your eyes peeled for the wild antique ambulance that zips between stores.

---

1. Vineyard Haven

Though the island's most popular vacation location is and always has been Edgartown, Vineyard Haven has been growing in popularity as a place to stay and to dine. Inns and motels are opening downtown, and guesthouses are springing up on the outskirts. The dining situation is both helped and hurt by Vineyard Haven's status as a "dry" town. You don't have the convenience of ordering wine with dinner, but if you remember to bring your own from Edgartown or the mainland, you'll save the normal (substantial) restaurant markup on beverages. Plan ahead and save.

WHERE TO STAY

The location of John and Mary Clarke's **Lothrop Merry House,** at Owen Park, Vineyard Haven, MA 02568 (tel. 508/693-1646), makes it special. The lawn slopes gently down to a little beach on the quiet side of the harbor. The property is protected on both sides; it's a 3-minute walk along the shoreline right to the boat dock. And if that's not enough, the sunrise sends reflections from the bay waters into most of the seven guest rooms. The ambience in this 18th-century house is country comfortable, with braided rugs and uneven door frames. Doubles with private baths and working fireplaces on the first floor rent for $148 to $159 in season; smaller doubles, two of which have harbor views, all share baths on the second floor, and rent for $97 to $108 in summer, tax included. You can while away the morning with the complimentary breakfast served on the patio overlooking the harbor. Ask about a sail on the innkeepers' 54-foot alden ketch *Laissez Faire.* There's also a canoe and a Sunfish (small sailboat) for guests' use. The Lothrop Merry House is open all year.

The **Captain Dexter House of Vineyard Haven,** 100 Main St., Vineyard Haven, MA 02568 (tel. 508/693-6564), is one of those rare finds: meticulously restored and exquisitely furnished in the colonial period, yet surprisingly unpretentious. Each of the eight rooms (one is actually a suite) has a private bath, and some have working fireplaces and four-poster beds with white lace canopies. From the fresh flowers to the fresh-squeezed orange juice served with the "expanded" continental breakfast, you'll notice attention to detail which makes this one of the loveliest inns on the island. A bed and breakfast costs $132 to $192 double in the summer, $55 to $80 less per room in the winter. If you're walking from the boat, it's two blocks away; if you have a car, there is private parking behind the house.

The **Vineyard Harbor Motel,** P.O. Box 1609, Vineyard Haven, MA 02568 (tel. 508/693-3334), near the edge of town on the coast road to Oak Bluffs, is modern and comfortable, with cable color TV, wall-to-wall carpeting, air conditioning, and a refrigerator in each room; some rooms have kitchen facilities as well, and many have a fine ocean view. In-season rates are $88 to $105 double; the higher prices are for rooms with a harbor view or a kitchen. A two-room apartment costs $110 for two people, and the penthouse, complete with view, waterbed, and private deck, is $121; tax is included. An extra person pays $10 per day.

WHERE TO DINE

The finest place to dine in town, and one of the more expensive, is the **Black Dog Tavern** (tel. 508/693-9223), at the water end of Beach Street, right down next to the yacht marina. Its location and good food bring in the yachting crowd, and this keeps the quality high. A large screened porch overlooking the harbor and marina is the choice place to sit, and you must come early to get a seat there. No reservations are accepted, so get there by about 6pm for dinner. I had island steamers, sautéed scallops primavera, and fresh-baked apple pie for dessert, and with coffee, tax, and tip the total was $35. The Black Dog is open May through October seven days a week from 6:30am to 11am, 11:30am to 2:30pm, and 5 to 10pm. In the off-season it's closed Monday and Tuesday. Bring your own wine or beer, as Vineyard Haven is a dry town.

Walk up the street from the ferry, turn right, and soon you'll see the cobble-studded porch of **Le Grenier** on Main Street (tel. 508/693-4906). The menu, as you might guess, tends to classical French, but stresses local ingredients. Dinner (served nightly from 6 to 10pm) will cost between $25 and $30. Try the stuffed mushrooms to start and the shrimp Pernod flambé with cream sauce for a main course.

In the Tisbury Inn on Main Street is the **Tisbury Inn Café** (tel. 508/693-3416), where the specialty is New American cuisine with Cajun accents. The scrod jambalaya, for example, is a unique blending of New England and New Orleans. Dinner here goes for about $30; you bring your own wine.

Not quite a mile out on State Road toward Gay Head is **Louis' Tisbury Café & Take-Out,** 102 State Rd. (tel. 508/693-3255). The name of the game here is pasta, great homemade pasta. Might I suggest a hot and spicy linguine shrimp diavolo for $17 or perhaps linguine with salmon, bluefish, scallops, and shrimp for $14. (Knock $2 off if you want it as an appetizer; everything on the menu is also available for take-out.) A low-key, casual atmosphere reigns here. Expect to wait if you don't arrive before 7pm; no reservations are taken. There's a terrific following among the locals—Louis' really packs 'em in here. The café is open Monday to Saturday from 11:30am to 9pm; Sunday from 4 to 9pm.

WHAT TO SEE

The Dukes County Historical Society (tel. 508/627-4441) owns the historic **Jiran Luce House** on Beach Road, now a museum of Vineyard history, and opens it to the public from mid-June through mid-September. Admission costs $2 for adults, 50¢ for children under 16. The museum is open from 10am to 4:30pm Tuesday through Saturday.

2. Oak Bluffs

It's odd that Oak Bluff, which began as a tent camp for summer meetings of the Methodist Church, should be one of the two "wet" towns on Martha's Vineyard, but so it is. Although the camp meetings are still the most important part of the summer's activities here (your hotel will have a schedule), many other nighttime pleasures are available as well, including movies, penny arcades, and an antique merry-go-round called "The Flying Horses." During the daytime, stroll straight in from the ferry docks and along the shores of the marina for a view of the fantastically ornate Victorian "gingerbread houses." As you continue farther into the settlement, the houses become even more wildly decorated.

WHERE TO STAY

The **Attleboro House,** at 11 Lake Ave. (P.O. Box 1564), Oak Bluffs, MA 02557 (tel. 508/693-4346), is in that marvelous row of gingerbread houses, next to the old Wesley Hotel (below), which faces the sheltered harbor. If you arrive by Hy-Line boat, you'll be able to spot Attleboro House even before you debark. The wide verandas are well furnished with rockers and fine views. Many rooms have porches overlooking the harbor. The eight rooms are spartan but tidy, and fully in the spirit of Oak Bluffs; in fact, the house is on land owned by the Methodist Campmeeting Association, so guests must agree to refrain from "rude or loud behavior." Only a few rooms have washbasins; none has private bath; and though there are plenty of clean sheets and towels, maid service is strictly do-it-yourself. Single rooms cost $41; doubles are $55 to $77. Here, and at the Wesley, you're living right within Oak Bluffs' history.

You'll never see so much oak under one roof as at **The Oak House,** on Seaview Avenue, Oak Bluffs, MA 02557 (tel. 508/693-4187), overlooking the water; oak ceilings, oak floors, oak paneling, oak furniture, and oak bannisters. The living and dining rooms are dark and rich in contrast to the white, glass-enclosed sun porch. All ten bedrooms in this Victorian house have private bathrooms; three have private balconies; two are suites. Rooms rent for $105 to $154, more for the suites. There is a three-night minimum stay on summer weekends. In the spring and fall prices drop by 25%.

With 82 rooms, the **Wesley Hotel,** 1 Lake Ave. (P.O. Box 2370), Oak Bluffs, MA 02557 (tel. 508/693-6611), dominates the lodging market in town. From the Steamship Authority docks, walk straight inland toward the marina; the Wesley is a few blocks down on the left. This big, rambling wooden place has recently experienced a make-over. The lobby is country formal and the hallways are papered with a pretty floral design. The rooms, while not in keeping with the gracious common area, are still clean and boast standard motel furnishings; most have televisions. A big plus here is the harbor view from the old-time rocking chairs on the wraparound porch. Rates are $110 to $132 for a double with private bath, $55 for a double with a bath in the hall, $148 for a suite with private bath. An extra adult pays $22 in the summer but only half that in the spring and fall.

The people who own the Black Dog Tavern in Vineyard Haven also run the **Admiral Benbow Inn,** 520 New York Ave. (P.O. Box 2488), Oak Bluffs, MA 02557 (tel. 508/693-6825), a short distance out of the center of town. Rooms in this graceful old Victorian house topped by an observatory all have private baths and period furnishings, and go for $83 to $137 double, tax and continental breakfast included.

WHERE TO DINE

For some reason Vineyard Haven has a good number of good restaurants, and Edgartown has its share, but in Oak Bluffs the fare is less than inspired. Of course, resort towns always present problems to the visitor in search of a fine dinner: The crowds must be fed, and customers will continue to come whether the food is great or not, because they must eat. But you won't go to bed without your dinner (be it fashionable or filling) in Oak Bluffs.

The place that packs 'em in is **Giordano's**, at the corner of Circuit and Lake avenues (tel. 508/693-0184). The large, modern, brightly lit dining room is full every night of high summer with the hungry and the thrifty filling themselves with the inexpensive Italian cuisine that's been offered here since 1930. Elegant it's not, and although it's a bit noisy, the service is efficient, the food is filling, and the price is reasonable; a full dinner special with chowder, potato, vegetable, coffee, and dessert can cost $9.50 (entree of veal cutlet or $12 sirloin steak). The à la carte items are also reasonably priced; the pizzas and spaghettis are in the $5 to $8 range. Cocktails, house wines sold by the half liter and liter, and bottled wines are available. There may well be a line of the value-minded waiting to get in, so it's good to arrive early. Open daily from 11:30am to 11:30pm.

For delicious breakfasts or lunchtime salads, soup, and sandwiches you can't beat **Linda Jean's** on Circuit Avenue (tel. 508/693-4093). It's nothing fancy, but is always full of folks who appreciate an honest meal at an honest price. Try L.J.'s omelet of three eggs, ham, tomato, broccoli, mushrooms, and cheese, plus home fries, toast, juice, and coffee for $5.50. At lunch order a bowl of tasty chowder for $2.50; a bacon cheeseburger goes for $3.15. The seafood platter of clams, scallops, shrimp, and haddock tops the menu at $11. Don't forget to leave room for a hefty slab of pie à la mode.

Very trendy and very upscale, that's the **Oyster Bar,** 162 Circuit Ave. (tel. 508/693-3300). The solitary strip of hot-pink neon, high on the back wall, sets the tone. General decor is pink and gray with soft lighting; the ceiling is high (it's tin, so the noise level is a bit high too), and the Doric pillars are mahogany painted to look like marble. The dinner menu (as well as the wine and dessert menu) is quite extensive: Oysters galore from the raw bar or as a cooked appetizer, striped bass or mahi-mahi, and a Belgian chocolate pâté with white and dark chocolate sauces will run you about $45 to $50 per person with tax and tip. Dinner (6 to 10pm) is served seven days a week from June through September, closed Monday and Tuesday in May and October. Reservations are advisable.

The **Ocean View** restaurant, a block from the northern end of the harbor on Chapman Avenue (tel. 508/693-2207), has a simple and basic New England dinner menu. A 10-ounce New York sirloin will run you $15, and a baked scrod topped with Ritz cracker crumbs will cost you $12. The salad bar comes with the entree, but cooked vegetables are served à la carte. Check the board for fresh daily specials. This is a real neighborhood place, hardly intimate dining, but the food is certainly well prepared; ask to be seated to the left of the front entrance (it's less noisy). Open for dinner only from 6 to 10pm.

---

3. Edgartown

Undoubtedly the prettiest and most picturesque town on the island, Edgartown is the place most people want to stay when they come to Martha's Vineyard, so the selection of rooms is fairly good. Whether your taste calls for a resort hotel with golf course, a modern motel with a sea view, or a colonial inn, Edgartown has what you want.

Besides being the residential center of the island, Edgartown has many good restaurants, most of the island's finer shops and art galleries, and street after street of attractive houses. Many of the houses were built by whaling captains with the profits of their voyages, and these same profits provided the funds to build the Methodist church (1843) on Main Street. In more recent times, Edgartown came to national prominence as the place where the movie *Jaws* and its first sequel were filmed, and many island residents made the daily stroll down to the harbor to look at the small mechanical shark in its special rack, covered by a canvas tarpaulin.

WHERE TO STAY

Edgartown has a place for any taste. Here's the rundown.

Inns Downtown

For many years visitors to Martha's Vineyard have been staying at the **Daggett House,** on North Water Street at Daggett Street (P.O. Box 1333), Edgartown, MA 02539 (tel. 508/627-4600). The rooms are tastefully furnished with numerous antique pieces; several are of very good size and some have good water views—the larger rooms and those with views are the more expensive ones. All rooms have king-size, queen-size canopy or four-posters, double, or twin beds, and private bath; some rooms, good for groups of friends or large families, are arranged in suites. There are even lodgings with kitchen facilities, and a garden cottage with three double rooms down by the water. Prices for the 25 rooms in three different houses are $121 to $247 in summer, $93 to $203 in spring and autumn, even lower in winter; tax is included. Continental breakfast is part of the room rate, and a full country breakfast is offered at additional cost. The main house has its own dock, and a Chimney Room (circa 1660) said to have been Edgartown's oldest tavern, now used as a dining room (ask to be shown the secret staircase). The Cap'n Warren House is across the street, and is equally nice, and guests at either house may use the lawns and beach.

Edgartown's most charming and elegant hostelry is the **Charlotte Inn,** South Summer Street (P.O. Box 1056), Edgartown, MA 02539 (tel. 508/627-4751), a unique complex combining the services of an inn, a fine art gallery, and a very good French restaurant called L'Etoile. Rooms here are all given a personal touch with furnishings—some fine English antiques—selected by the owners. The best way to select a room is to see several, although this is often difficult, as many are sure to be occupied. The rates are in keeping with the elegant atmosphere: Doubles run $192 to $384 in season (mid-June to mid-October); rates go down to $93 to $384 double during the winter. Continental breakfast is included every day but Sunday. Even if you decide not to stay at the Charlotte Inn, stroll by some evening to admire the graceful house and the very good gallery, and perhaps enjoy the garden-terrace dining at L'Etoile.

The **Edgartown Inn,** North Water Street (P.O. Box 1211), Edgartown, MA 02539 (tel. 508/627-4794), has been hosting famous guests for well over a century, including the likes of Daniel Webster, Nathaniel Hawthorne (who wrote *Twice Told Tales* here), and John F. Kennedy (during his days in the Senate). The inn is thus a place of contrasts: In the rooms, 19th-century decor competes with the modern tile baths, and in the parlor, a portrait of Hawthorne hangs glowering at the color TV. There are 12 rooms in the inn proper, which cost $88 to $160 from late May to October 1, $55 to $105 in the off-season. In season, the main inn may not take reservations of less than three days.

Rooms in the Captain's Quarters out back do not have private bath, and rent for $59 in season; also, several rooms in the old barn attached to the inn are rented for $77 to $110. The Edgartown Inn serves country breakfasts in its quaint, cozy breakfast room, old-fashioned and neat as a pin: a deer head, a fine ship's model, and the only "colonial" ceiling fans I've ever seen add to the decor. Whether a guest at the inn or not, you can have the full breakfast here for $6, or a continental breakfast of homemade cakes and breads baked every day for $3.75.

The **Colonial Inn,** 38 N. Water St. (P.O. Box 68), Edgartown, MA 02539 (tel. 508/627-4711), looks like Edgartown's answer to the huge rambling Victorian hotels of Oak Bluffs and elsewhere, although to keep with tradition on North Water Street, this one is covered in cedar "shakes" (shingles), and many windows have shutters like those of the sea captains' houses. The advantages at the Colonial, besides its central location, recent renovations, restaurant, shops, and sea views (from six rooms), are its large number of rooms (42, all with private bath) and varied rates. Double rooms with harbor views are the most expensive at $181, but if you choose a double without the view (which you can enjoy from the grounds), the price drops to $110 to $174, continental breakfast and tax included. Children under 12 stay for free; an extra person pays $17 year round. Off-season room rates are $35 to $60 less per room. The Colonial has its own restaurant and pub, and is open from mid-April to mid-December.

Inns on the Outskirts

As Edgartown is not that big a place, the outskirts in this case are only a few blocks from the center. The inns below are on the way into town from Oak Bluffs, on Main Street near Cannonball Park.

The **Point Way Inn,** on Main Street at the corner of Pease's Point Way (P.O. Box 128), Edgartown, MA 02539 (tel. 508/627-8633), was once a 14-room whaling captain's house, but has been converted to a cozy, charming 15-room inn with a satisfying variety of accommodations. You'll know it's nice as you walk through the garden, past the gazebo and croquet lawn, and into the house, which has a real family feel to it. There are small rooms, large rooms, 11 rooms with fireplace or deck, even a luxury two-room suite, all with private bath. Prices are $83 to $225 double, continental breakfast and tax included. The inn is open all year.

Very near the junction of Main Street and Pease's Point Way is the **Shiverick Inn,** P.O. Box 640, Edgartown, MA 02539 (tel. 508/627-3797), run by innkeepers Claire and Juan del Real. You'll spot the huge, substantial white house with mansard roof and rooftop observatory easily. Go in the mahogany front door, straight through the house, and out to a charming little patio garden. The interior is rich in period pieces; the bedrooms have private baths and appropriately sumptuous and frilly Victorian decor. Rooms cost $165 to $220 double per night, continental breakfast and tax included. With fireplace and sitting room, suites, which sleep three, cost $265 double.

The **Governor Bradford Inn,** 128 Main St., Edgartown, MA 02539 (tel. 508/ 627-9510), is a handsome white clapboard New England Gothic house with high-peaked roofs and bright windows. The atmosphere in the common rooms is one of restrained elegance rather than frilliness—a very satisfying feeling. Many of the 16 rooms have televisions; all have private baths. Rates include continental breakfast and afternoon tea: $105 to $214 double in summer, $66 to $170 double off-season.

The **Jonathan Munroe House,** P.O. Box 1165, Edgartown, MA 02539 (tel. 508/627-5536), is at 100 Main St., not too far from the center of town. It's a house converted to receive guests, which is exactly what it does, placing them in quaint and homey rooms, nicely done, and charging $93 from the end of May to September. The six rooms share two upstairs baths. Guests share the use of a refrigerator; tea and coffee are offered free all day. Call for reservations.

WHERE TO DINE

Edgartown—and the island in general—can boast a large number of eateries, plain and fancy. I couldn't possibly list them all in the limited space here, and in fact an all-inclusive list would be more bewildering than helpful. Although I can heartily recommend the establishments below as delivering good value for the money, you will no doubt want to do some exploration of your own.

Of Edgartown's restaurants, one of the most elegant and congenial is certainly **L'Étoile** (tel. 508/627-5187), in the garden and glassed-in terrace of the Charlotte Inn on South Summer Street. The white tables and chairs set out among the trees, vines, and flowers on a patio surrounded by trelliswork provide the perfect place for a warm-weather evening's repast; in bad weather the terrace room is just as good, with lots of windows and skylights. The menu reads like a list of ambrosias: roasted French pheasant with a sauce of oysters, mushrooms, warmed figs, thyme, and cognac; rack of lamb with warm goat cheese, balsamic vinaigrette, and herbed vegetable julienne; grilled swordfish steak with a trio of American caviars, champagne, and chive beurre blanc. Seven nights a week, dinner (6:30 to 9:45pm) is set at $50 or so, plus tax; Sunday brunch (10:30am to 12:30pm), equally scrumptious-sounding, is about $25. Closed New Year's Day through Valentine's Day.

Edgartown is one of the Vineyard's two "wet" towns, so you can order wine to accompany your meal. Call for reservations, and ask what the day's special will be.

After years of being Edgartown's prime fish market, **Lawry's,** on Main Street out of town toward Oak Bluffs (tel. 508/627-8857), added a modern dining room and became one of Edgartown's prime seafood restaurants as well. Formica tables and red padded benches make the atmosphere bright but simple, and though the restaurant serves sandwiches, the seafood is the thing. I recently filled myself with steamed clams (a huge portion that was sufficient for two), then a portion of broiled bluefish and one of fish-and-chips. The main courses came with coleslaw, potato, rolls, and butter, and the total bill was $20, tax, tip, and a glass of beer included. All of Lawry's food can be taken out too. Lunch is served every day but Sunday from 11:30am to 2pm; dinner is served nightly from 5 to 9pm.

The **Seafood Shanty,** on Dock Street at Kelley Street (tel. 508/627-8622), is a favorite with the younger crowd because of its atmosphere and its very reasonable seafood prices—not to mention a fine harbor view. At lunch (11:30am to 3pm), something such as a seafood Newburgh crêpe is $11, but the fish-of-the-day is even less, and sandwiches a lot less. At dinner, fish main courses run $16 to $18; or you can have a steak, or chicken, or a huge salad if you prefer. Dinner is served daily from 5:30 to 10:30pm seven days a week from Memorial Day through October.

Martha's Restaurant, across the street from Edgartown's Town Hall on Main Street (tel. 508/627-8316), has one dining room downstairs, another upstairs near the raw bar; this dining room spills onto an open terrace overlooking Main Street. The menu is interesting and varied, with everything from bluefish through fettuccine and Mexican dishes to sushi. Sunday brunch is a tradition. Prices are not bad, with many dinner entrees selling for $13 to $24, which means a full dinner with wine will cost anywhere from $22 to $45.

---

4. Up Island

The best place to get away from the crowds and to begin to feel the serenity of island living is to spend time "up island"—in the towns and areas around West Tisbury, Chilmark, Menemsha, and Gay Head. The scenery here resembles parts of the English countryside; you'll find stone walls, forested roads, and plenty of space.

WHERE TO STAY

Captain Flanders' House, North Road (P.O. Box 384), Chilmark, MA 02535 (tel. 508/645-3123), enjoys 60 acres of rolling pastures and secluded woodlands; the 18th-century house also overlooks aptly named Bliss Pond. This renovated farmhouse built in the late 1700s offers six guest rooms in the main house, a separate two-room suite with a fireplace, and a four-bedroom rental house. A single with shared bath is $55 in summer; a double with shared bath is $94; a double with private bath is $116, tax, beach pass, and continental breakfast included. Off-season rates are considerably lower.

At the other end of the spectrum is the **Beach Plum Inn and Restaurant,** North Road (P.O. Box 98), Menemsha, MA 02552 (tel. 508/645-9454). Perfectly kept formal gardens pave the way to a gracious, plush living room with matching floral furniture. For the ambitious, there is a pond stocked with bass and perch, as well as a tennis court. Chaise longues on the shady lawn or the private ocean beach will satisfy other ambitions. The guest rooms, located in the main house, private cottages, or farmhouse, range in price from $264 to $313 per couple with a full breakfast, late afternoon cocktails plus hors d'oeuvres, and a full dinner included. The restaurant is renowned (see below), so you'll enjoy having your meals here.

WHERE TO DINE

The restaurant at the **Beach Plum Inn,** Menemsha (tel. 508/645-9454), is unique on the island because dinners are cooked to order. You choose from five or six entree selections in advance. The fixed price is $45 per person, slightly more for lobster. Nouvelle New England cuisine is served every night during high season.

Two possible, good options are roast duck with a honey-curry sauce and filet mignon with a béarnaise sauce.

There's no better seafood platter (baked, broiled, or fried) on the island than at **Homeport,** Menemsha Harbor (tel. 508/645-2679). It's not an intimate place, but the sunset from here will bring out the romantic in anyone. At first, the main course price of $25 for swordfish or $21 for Vineyard scallops seems high, but further inspection tells you that the price includes an appetizer of your choice, salad, beverage, and dessert. Expect to spend $45 to $50 for two; bring your own wine. Call for reservations, for sure. Open nightly from 5pm.

5. What to See and Do on Martha's Vineyard

The most delightful thing about Martha's Vineyard is that it is its own entertainment, and one can often be fully satisfied just strolling along past picket-fence houses, swimming at the many beaches, or biking past the marshes, forests, and island heath. But should you wish a little directed, purposeful activity, you will not be at a loss. First thing to do is to find out what's on currently in the way of festivities and special events. There's an **information desk** in the Steamship Authority's dockside ticket office in Woods Hole, so you can find out some things even before getting to the island. But once on the Vineyard, pick up a copy of *This Week on Martha's Vineyard* (a pull-out section of the paper). Here you'll discover a list of the church-sponsored white elephant sales, musical concerts (many free), lectures, dances, movies, tournaments (kite flying, fishing, table tennis), community sings, and the like. Two other free papers, *Island Light* and *Vineyard Summer,* can be picked up in most shops. The island's most important to-do is the annual **Regatta and Around-the-Island Race,** held on a weekend in late July (hotels are extra-full then).

TOURS

The **Gay Head Sightseeing Company** (tel. 508/693-1555) operates daily sightseeing bus tours of the island, including the Vineyard's six towns and two villages, the sea captains' houses (from the outside), and even a stop at the multicolored cliffs at Gay Head. The trip takes about 2 hours, covers 56 miles, and costs $8 for adults, half price for children. Tours leave the ferry wharves after the arrival of the ship, and tickets may be purchased on board the ship or on the sightseeing bus.

THE THOMAS COOKE HOUSE

The Dukes County Historical Society (tel. 508/627-4441), at the corner of Cooke and School streets in Edgartown, operates the island's most interesting museum in the former Thomas Cooke House (1760s). All the artifacts in the refurnished house came from Vineyard houses, including scrimshaw, china, glass, paintings, and nautical paraphernalia. In other buildings on the grounds, various types of boats that played a part in the island's history can be seen, and there's a special tower to hold the Paris-made lens (1854) that revolved in the Gay Head lighthouse from 1856 to 1952. A guided tour of the museum costs $2 for adults, 50¢ for children under 16. From mid-June to mid-September the museum is open from 10am to 4:30pm daily except Sunday and Monday; in off-season, visits to its nearby library can be made on Wednesday, Thursday, and Friday from 1 to 4pm, on Saturday from 10am.

THE STATE LOBSTER HATCHERY

The Massachusetts State Lobster Hatchery and Research Station (tel. 508/693-0060) is just outside Vineyard Haven on the road to Oak Bluffs, and is open

Monday through Friday from 1 to 3pm, free of charge. Here thousands of tiny lobsters are raised on pieces of shrimp meat to keep them from devouring one another until they are judged capable of fending for themselves in the chilly waters of the Atlantic. This is the oldest operating lobster hatchery in the world, and a fascinating stop for anyone interested in the life and times of New England's tastiest crustacean.

A VINEYARD ON THE VINEYARD

Martha's Vineyard has its own real vineyard, and you can visit it. **Chicama Vineyards** (tel. 508/693-0309) is southwest of Vineyard Haven off State Road on Stoney Hill Road, in West Tisbury. The 33 acres are planted in vinifera varieties such as Cabernet, Chardonnay, Chenin Blanc, Pinot Noir, Riesling, and Zinfandel. The vineyard has been in operation since 1971. Visit daily May through September 11am to 5pm, Sunday from 1 to 5pm. Closed on July 4 and Labor Day.

BEACHES AND BIKE TRIPS

The **State Beach** on the road between Oak Bluffs and Edgartown is probably the first beach you'll see. It's a fine long stretch of white sand, free and open to the public, with parking along the road. South of Edgartown the **County Beach at Katama Bay**, also called **South Beach**, has surf swimming, and is likewise free. The three major towns all have town beaches open to everyone, but the smaller towns and villages reserve their beaches for local property owners, or charge a beach-use fee.

Bicycle riding is fun anywhere on the island as the hills are few and gently sloped, but it's particularly good on the bike path between Oak Bluffs and Edgartown, and on the island of Chappaquiddick, reached by ferry (a 5-minute trip) from the docks in Edgartown. Wildlife preserves are dotted about Martha's Vineyard, particularly on Chappaquiddick and at Menemsha, Felix Neck, and Cedar Tree Neck. The excursion to the strikingly beautiful cliffs at Gay Head is a must, but you'll need a bit of stamina for this trip on a bike, and should devote most of a day to it.

You can, of course, drive or take a tour to the **Gay Head Cliffs,** which is Martha's Vineyard's top "excursion." Don't expect a dramatic, towering wall of land staunchly resisting the thundering waves: The cliffs are dramatic only when set against the more-or-less level terrain of the island. But the cliffs and their colors are pretty, and Gay Head is the perfect goal for what would otherwise be an aimless meander. You can view the cliffs for free (although you must pay to use the nearby public toilets).

In **Menemsha Harbor** there isn't exactly anything "to do" except stroll and loll away a couple hours. When you see this place, you'll wish you'd never used the word "picturesque" before. It's an authentic, small, working harbor, complete with seagulls, fishing nets, and aged bottles of whisky in the windows of boathouses. Turn right off South Road in Chilmark at Beetlebung Corner; the harbor is a mile or so down the way. If you arrive hungry, try a lobster roll for $7 at the **Galley** (tel. 645-9819), a little snack shack with shaded picnic tables right on the edge of the harbor.

SAILING, CRUISING, AND SUCH

The Harborside Inn, on Lower Main Street (tel. 508/627-4321), will rent you a 15-foot Boston Whaler with a 25-hp outboard motor for $125 per day or a 17-foot Daysailer for $75 for 4 hours. The boatyard is open from 8:30am to 5pm daily. If you don't understand the lingo or the techniques and can't tell a sheet from a painter, you can even buy lessons.

An even grander way to sail the seas is aboard the clipper schooner *Shenandoah* out of Vineyard Haven, commanded by Capt. Robert Douglas for the Coastwise Packet Company (tel. 508/693-1699). The *Shenandoah* is no small boat, measuring 108 feet along the rail, and was built at South Bristol, Me., in 1964. Going all out at better than 12 knots, the *Shenandoah* has all nine sails gusting in a classic square topsail rig. For $600 per person, you can sail aboard the ship for a week—adventure, food, and lodging all included Cruises start every Monday morning, mid-June through September, from the Union Street Wharf. Call for particulars and reservations.

---

6. Nantucket

The Vineyard's island sister, Nantucket, is even more of an oceangoing grande dame. More difficult of access (at least in terms of time and price), Nantucket draws an elite crowd. But the crowd is no smaller even though it's elite; prepare for your visit in advance, in high season, by booking reservations.

To its year-round inhabitants Nantucket is not just another resort island off Cape Cod, but a special seagoing world of its own. All the brochures and booklets handed out on the island seem to bear the legend "Thirty Miles at Sea." With its history of whaling, its choppy Indian name, and its people's reputation for hardiness, you might expect to find clusters of peasant dwellings and strong-armed shipwrights making rough island boats, but in fact the opposite is true: Nantucket's Main Street is lined with gracious buildings and towering elms, and the rest of the town boasts street after street of charming and dignified houses from the 18th and 19th centuries. This is to be expected when you think of the money that whaling brought to Nantucket. Before the oil sheiks there were the whale-oil magnates, for whale oil fired the lamps of all New England, whalebone provided the stays for the corsets then in style, and ambergris was the base for perfume, a luxury item.

In 1659 the first colonists came ashore to settle the island, already inhabited by four tribes of Indians. The Jethro Coffin House, the first fine house to be built, went up in 1686, almost 20 years after the first whale had been claimed off Nantucket's shores. By the time of the Revolution, Nantucket was already wealthy from the whale-oil trade and contributed greatly to the Revolutionary cause, losing over 100 whaling ships and 2,000 Nantucketers in the war. Before the island could recover fully, the War of 1812 again interfered with its prosperity. In another 50 years the age of the sail-rigged whaling ship was at an end, but the same device which put an end to that era—the steamship—brought the beginning of a new era for Nantucket as a vacation destination. In summer, the cobblestones of Main Street are worn down by visitors from Boston, New York, and even farther away, and in winter the islanders go about their business getting ready for the next summer season.

GETTING THERE

Ferryboats carrying both cars and passengers run to Nantucket from Hyannis, Martha's Vineyard, and Woods Hole in summer. (See those sections in Chapter VII for details.)

By Air

Flights to Nantucket are operated by several national carriers and by various local air services. Except at the evening rush hour, or on weekends, you should be able to show up at Hyannis's Barnstable Municipal Airport or New Bedford Municipal Airport, buy a ticket, and be in the air, bound for Nantucket, within a half hour, even without advance reservations.

By the way, parking at the New Bedford airport is free of charge.

Business Express, a Delta Connection carrier, operates flights to Nantucket from New York (La Guardia) and Boston (Logan), with connections from many cities in the region, including points as far away as Albany, Baltimore, Burlington, Vt., Montréal, Philadelphia, Presque Isle, Me., Toronto, and Washington, D.C. For reservations and information, call toll free 800/345-3400.

Cape Cod Air, Chatham Municipal Airport, Chatham, MA. (tel. toll free 800/553-2376), provides air-charter service from Chatham to Nantucket (20 minutes one way), or indeed to any point within flying distance.

Coastal Air Services, with offices at Groton–New London Airport, Groton, CT 06340 (tel. 203/448-1001), at Nantucket Memorial Airport (tel. 508/228-

3350), and at Martha's Vineyard Airport (tel. 508/693-5942), provides air-charter and aircraft rentals. If you don't want to charter the entire plane, you can join an "Open Charter" with a few other people who want to fly to the same point at the same time.

Continental Express, a commuter operation of Continental Airlines (tel. toll free 800/525-0280), flies sturdy DC-3 and smaller craft on routes to Nantucket from Boston, Hyannis, Martha's Vineyard, New Bedford, and Provincetown.

Express Airlines (tel. 508/999-3231 or toll free 800/852-2332 in Massachusetts) flies a shuttle service in small planes between New Bedford and Nantucket, departing every 2 hours from 8:30am to 6:30pm from New Bedford, 7:30am to 7:30pm from Nantucket. The trip takes slightly over a half hour.

Nantucket Airlines, at Nantucket Memorial Airport (tel. 508/790-0300 or 228-6234, or toll free in Massachusetts 800/635-8787), flies daily shuttle service between Nantucket and Hyannis, departing about a dozen times a day from each place.

Nantucket Memorial Airport

Nantucket's one and only airport has a restaurant and bar called the Compass Rose, a gift shop, a photocopy machine, vending machines for soft drinks, and car-rental desks (Budget, Hertz, National). Note that during the summer there may not be any cars available for those who have not reserved them in advance. The airport is about 3 miles from the center of Nantucket town, about 5½ miles from 'Sconset.

GETTING AROUND

Nantucket's a small place without the need of a large bus service, but **Nantucket and 'Sconset Bus Line, Inc.** (tel. 508/228-0420 or 228-3118), runs several buses five times daily in summer between Nantucket and 'Sconset; there's one bus a day to Wauwinet, to Jetties Beach (leaves every 30 minutes or so), and to other, more distant beaches. Buy tickets, get information, and board the bus at the stop on South Water Street at Chestnut Street, opposite the firehouse.

Taxis abound and their rates are $3 for one person within town limits, $1 for each additional person; between airport and town, $5 for one person, $1 for each additional person. Rates are higher at night. Other rates are established for trips to the beaches and sights, and are posted in the cab.

Bicycles and **mopeds** are for rent at over a half dozen shops in town. Rates for a bicycle are $8 to $12 a day, $24 to $36 for a moped, and these vehicles do well on this small island (except on the cobblestones of Main Street!). The 7-mile trip to 'Sconset on a bike path takes less than an hour—less than a half hour if you push it. Incidentally, almost any taxi driver will be glad to give you a tour of the island, with rates depending on how much ground you want to cover and time you want to spend.

INFORMATION AND RESERVATIONS

The **Nantucket Chamber of Commerce** (tel. 508/228-1700) and its Public Relations Committee have done a lot to organize the tourist industry on the island, and information about rooms, tours, and sights is surprisingly easy to get. The **Nantucket Information Bureau,** 25 Federal St. (tel. 508/228-0925), is the place to go for a free copy of the *Nantucket Vacation Guide,* a summertime ads-and-information booklet; you'll also get help finding a room for that day if you haven't already reserved one. But note that the bureau *does not make advance reservations for you*—you must do that directly with the establishment concerned. The bureau is not far from Main Street and the ferry docks, and it's open from 9am until the evening hours (usually 6pm) during the summer (10am to 4pm on Sunday), shorter hours off-season.

Reserve in Advance for Summer!

Rooms may be hard to find in July and August unless you reserve well in advance, and while you will have a chance of finding a room for a day or two during the week, on weekends it's sometimes impossible. If you plan to try to find a last-minute room in those two months, arrive on the island early in the day—fly over and beat the ferryboat crowds—and go straight to the town information booth and ask what's available in town.

Useful Facts

Nantucket Cottage Hospital, at South Prospect Street and Vesper Lane (tel. 508/228-1200), is a modern, accredited facility. You can contact the **Massachusetts State Police** at their office on North Liberty Street (tel. 508/228-0706), and the **Nantucket Town Police** on East Chestnut Street (tel. 508/228-1212). The **emergency number** for police, firefighters, and ambulance service is 911.

Nantucket is well organized and governed, and local residents have various regulations which they want visitors to observe, such as not wearing bathing suits on Main Street, obeying all traffic rules when riding a bicycle, and not camping—whether in a vehicle or a tent or under the stars—anywhere on the island.

WHERE TO STAY

Nantucket Island harbors nearly 100 places to stay, but the real character of the place is best captured in the old whaling merchants' and ship captains' houses converted to inns and guesthouses. Many of these are carefully restored, luxuriously appointed, and staffed with professionals; others are run by one person or a couple and are modest but warm and friendly.

Notes on Reservations

Although some lodging establishments on Nantucket stay open all year, many operate only between May and October. Any place will give you an off-season discount on room rates if you come in spring or autumn, although the dates vary from one place to the next. In high season (roughly mid-June to mid-September), you'll certainly have to send a substantial deposit to hold your room reservation. Minimum-stay requirements may be imposed during the high season as well. Some lodging and dining places may not accept credit cards.

Here, then, are Nantucket's best guesthouses and inns, followed by a few recommendations for hotels.

The Top Inns

The **Jared Coffin House,** 29 Broad St., Nantucket, MA 02554 (tel. 508/228-2405), was the first three-story mansion to be built on the island. Its builder, a wealthy shipowner, put up the impressive Federal-style brick house in 1845, just before deciding to move to Boston. He and his family lived in the house for a matter of months, after which it became, and still is, a hotel.

Since its conversion to a hotel in 1846, additions have been built, and neighboring houses bought and converted to lodgings, so that the hotel now has 58 rooms in six different structures priced from $72 to $82 single, $121 to $192 double. In the Jared Coffin House proper are nine guest rooms with double or twin beds; the Eben Allen wing of the building has 16 rooms with single, twin, or double beds. The neighboring Swain House, dating from the 1700s, has three rooms, each with a queen-size canopy bed. Similar beds are in the six rooms of the Federal-style Henry Coffin House (1821), and also in the 12 rooms of the Greek Revival Harrison Gray House (1842). The Daniel Webster House (1964) is a recent building in a Federal-inspired style, with 12 canopy-bedrooms and a conference room. No matter which building you choose, you will enjoy the elegant public rooms of the several buildings, and the hotel's two restaurants (see below).

Harbor House, P.O. Box 1048, Nantucket, MA 02554 (tel. 508/228-1500 for information, 228-5500 for reservations), is a modern hotel that looks just like a small group of old Nantucket houses. Set on a private street amid groves of shade trees, the nine buildings of the Harbor House give you a choice between staying in the Townhouse, with six smaller dwellings holding a total of 57 large and luxurious rooms, or in the main hotel, its neighboring Garden Cottage, or the Springfield House. All rooms are modern and have every comfort, despite the Federal-inspired decor designed to harmonize with their location on Nantucket. The Townhouse rooms have twin double beds, and cost $247 double in high season; rooms in the main hotel have twin beds, two double beds, one queen- or one king-size bed, and cost $160 to $192 double. An additional person in a room pays $15.

Guests at the Harbor House can enjoy the outdoor swimming pool, with its own bar, and the hotel's main dining room, named The Hearth. There's a cocktail lounge as well. The location is good—walking distance from the center of town, and not far from Children's Beach and Brant Point.

The inn at **Seven Sea Street,** Nantucket, MA 02554 (tel. 508/228-3577), operated by Matthew and Mary Parker, is among Nantucket's best small lodging places. Though built fairly recently, it follows the canon of post-and-beam construction, and is furnished in colonial style, so that you will feel Nantucket all around you. The eight guest rooms have queen-size canopy beds, exposed beams, and lots of colonial touches, but also cable color TV sets, small refrigerators, and of course, modern private baths. The theme of modern comforts in colonial atmosphere continues in the public spaces. You can relax in a full-size, heated whirlpool bath, and then sit by the fireplace or go up to the widow's walk to take in the view. The location, just a few blocks from Steamboat Wharf and the center of town, couldn't be better. Rates include a good continental breakfast (served in bed if you wish), and range from $94 to $170 double, depending on when you visit. Two-room suites for two people cost $121 to $220; an extra person in a room pays $16.50. Tax is included in these prices. Sea Street is only one block long, running between North Water Street and South Beach Street. By the way, the Parkers are the publishers of *Nantucket Journal* magazine.

The Better Inns and Guesthouses

Nantucket is rich in charming small inns and guesthouses. Sometimes it's difficult to know whether a place should be called an inn or a guesthouse. I think of an inn as providing more services, such as meals and cocktails, and having more spacious public rooms and gardens. A guesthouse is more like someone's home, perhaps not as fancy as an inn, with few services but with a warm, family atmosphere. I'll start by describing some of the better inns, and then some more inns and guesthouses.

A trio of inns under the same management offers typical and charming Nantucket accommodations at moderate prices. The **Great Harbor Inn,** 31 India St., Nantucket, MA 02554 (tel. 508/228-6609), is an 18th-century sea captain's home now restored and furnished in 19th-century style with handmade patchwork quilts and four-poster or canopy beds. All rooms have 20th-century facilities, including private bath and color cable TV. You can have continental breakfast (included in the room price) served in your room, or in the parlor, or on the pretty terrace. Rates in high season are $110 to $159 double, tax included. The inn, about a 5-minute walk from the town center, is open all year.

A close relation is the **Brass Lantern Inn,** 11 N. Water St., Nantucket, MA 02554 (tel. 508/228-4064), only a few blocks from downtown on North Water Street. Here again there is a nice old Nantucket house, but besides the traditional rooms the inn has a more modern annex with larger and lighter rooms that still carry 19th-century touches in their decor. You can have breakfast in your room, on the patio, or in a small grassy yard. The Brass Lantern is open all year, charging $88 to $154 double in high summer, continental breakfast and tax included. Afternoon hors d'oeuvres are served as well. The inn is open from April to December.

Fair Gardens, 27 Fair St., Nantucket, MA 02554 (tel. 508/228-4258), is the description as well as the name of the third member of the trio, located in a quiet residential neighborhood. Behind the house is an English-style garden, complete with a Shakespearean herb plot, carefully tended flowers and lawns, and a patio for breakfast or an afternoon's cup of tea. The ten rooms are unique, and all have private

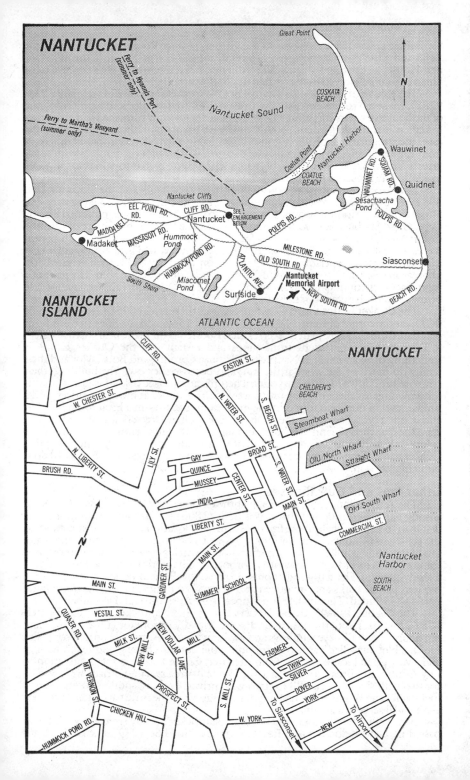

bath; there are two deluxe rooms in the Garden House. Rooms are priced between $105 and $148 double, with prices lower in the old house, higher in the new Garden House; an extra person pays $22. All rates include breakfast with freshly baked bread or muffins, served in the garden in good weather.

The **House of Orange,** 25 Orange St., Nantucket, MA 02554 (tel. 508/228-9287), has seven rooms decorated with an artist's eye for color and harmony—one of the house's owners is a painter. The rooms are as lovingly furnished and as carefully kept as is the little garden. Some rooms have fireplaces, although, as is often the case, local regulations prohibit guests from using them. Every room is different, from the small single with semiprivate bath at $45 through the doubles with semi-private bath at $77 to $88. A double room with private bath is tops in price, at $105 to $121. The House of Orange is open year round.

Fair Street has its share of houses built by ship captains, but the **Ships Inn** (tel. 508/228-0040) is more a mansion than a house, its three stories looking over Fair Street from a position just opposite the Episcopal church. It was built in 1812 by Capt. Obed Starbuck and occupies the site that once held the birthplace of Lucretia Coffin Mott, the abolitionist and suffragist. The rooms are furnished with period pieces and all, except two small singles, have private bath. Those little singles cost $55. Otherwise, one person pays $99 for a room; two pay $111, with private bath. Off-season (November through mid-June), rates go down about 30%. The price of a room includes continental breakfast in season. The Captain's Table restaurant (see below) is in the basement of the Ships Inn.

The **Quaker House Inn,** 5 Chestnut St., Nantucket, MA 02554 (tel. 508/228-0400), at the corner of Centre Street, was built in 1847, and the huge tree out front may date from the same year, or even earlier. Located right in the heart of the Historic District, just a few steps from shops and restaurants, the Quaker House is something of an anomaly in Nantucket. Because Caroline and Bob Taylor and their family do much of the work at the inn, and because they own the building, their costs are kept down, and so are yours. Their restaurant (see below) is justly famous for providing excellent dinners in attractive surroundings at moderate prices, and a similar level of quality is found in the inn's eight guest rooms. Each room is different: in one a brass bed, in another a carved four-poster. Dressers and wardrobes also echo the era when the inn was built, and tab curtains are a reminder of even earlier colonial days. Rooms are simple, but comfy and attractive, as befits an inn with a Quaker name. Each has private bath and queen-size bed. Rates are $85 to $110 double in high season.

Other Inns and Guesthouses

The **Anchor Inn,** 66 Centre St., Nantucket, MA 02554 (tel. 508/228-0072), is aptly named, considering that it was built (1806) by Archaelus Hammond, the first man to strike a whale in the Pacific Ocean. The location is good: close enough to the center to be convenient, far enough away to be quiet. Pass through the white picket fence and you'll find a sea captain's house which preserves many of its original features, from its old random-width floorboards to its working fireplaces. Outside is a shady garden. The ten guest rooms preserve the Federal period style, but have modern private baths and are priced at $94 to $126 double in season, continental breakfast included. The Anchor Inn is open from April through December.

The **"While Away" Guest House,** 4 Gay St., Nantucket, MA 02554 (tel. 508/228-1102), is of the old-time school: a friendly proprietor (Elise Link), a fine old house with bull's-eye windows and a widow's walk. A friendly proprietor (Elise Link), a blossom-filled garden surrounding the house, a baby grand piano within, and a very good location across from the Jared Coffin House at the intersection of Gay, Centre, and Broad streets make the While Away a real find. Prices are low: $77 for two with shared bath, $88 for two with private bath, in spotless rooms. When looking for the While Away, try to spot the flagpole in the little park right next door —that will serve as a landmark.

After only a bit of wandering through Nantucket's shady streets, you will have passed **Le Languedoc Inn and Restaurant,** 24 Broad St. (P.O. Box 1829), Nan-

tucket, MA 02554 (tel. 508/228-2552 or 228-4682). No doubt you'll have no-
ticed the attractive restaurant; but it's not readily apparent that there are several nice
guest rooms upstairs, and even more (and better) in nearby houses. In Le Languedoc proper are two tidy, homey rooms which share one bathroom, priced at $93
double; and one room with private bath, going for $110. Rooms at the 3 Hussey
Street Guest House (tel. 508/228-4682 or 228-4298) are similar in comfort and
price, with most sharing baths in this nice mid-19th-century building. However,
accommodations at the Grey Lady Apartments (same phones) have been renovated
and modernized, while keeping or adding many artistic and historical features.
Rooms at the Grey Lady are light, attractive, and simple, each with one or two softly
pretty modern paintings, and for contrast, one or two pieces of antique furniture,
resulting in congenial decor without sensory overload. Each room has a modern private bath, and one room has a private deck, another a kitchenette with utensils. All
guests get to use the common living room, which has a color TV and refrigerator. A
double with bath costs $115; with bath and kitchenette, $137; a suite for four with
bath and kitchenette goes for $187 in high season.

The **Chestnut House,** 3 Chestnut St., Nantucket, MA 02554 (tel. 508/228-
0049), between Centre and Federal, is Jeannette and Jerry Carl's home, which they
open to visitors. There's a common room with television available to all guests.
Rooms are furnished in the style of Nantucket's heyday, one with canopy bed,
quilts, and interesting old pieces. All rooms have private baths, and cost $99 double;
suites cost $152 double. A connecting cottage sleeps four, has a private bath, and
costs $165. These prices are for the high summer season, when a three-night mini-
mum stay is required. The location, next to the Quaker House Inn on quiet
Chestnut Street, is right in the middle of town.

A 10- or 15-minute walk northwest of the center of town is Cliff Road, so
named because it follows the top of a ridge and offers fine views of the sea to several
of its well-situated houses. It's in this quiet residential neighborhood that you'll find
the **Century House,** 10 Cliff Rd., Nantucket, MA 02554 (tel. 508/228-0530), run
by Jean Heron and Gerry Connick. The late Federal building has a wraparound
porch, a 19th-century parlor, and a custom of late-afternoon tea (which may also be
early-evening cocktail setups). Furnishings follow the rules of Laura Ashley designs
and canopy beds, and the double rooms have either private bath ($93 to $159) or
shared bath ($82 to $105). The largest room, with a king-size bed, costs $116 to
$159. These prices include continental breakfast and snacks at tea/cocktail time.
Jean and Gerry also rent quaint cottages in 'Sconset and on the harbor.

Cliff Lodge, 9 Cliff Rd., Nantucket, MA 02554 (tel. 508/228-9480), has that
marvelous Cliff Road view from its widow's walk, and many other views from its 12
guest rooms and two patios. Built in 1771, the house has recently been redecorated
in period style. All rooms have private baths, telephones, and TV sets, and some have
king-size beds and fireplaces. Freshly made continental breakfast, use of the pantry,
refrigerator, and kitchen utensils, and towels for the beach are all included in the
room prices of $55 to $66 single, $99 to $154 double. An apartment rents for $154
to $210 per night, $1,375 per week in high season. Other apartments are available at
Cliff Lodge's sister facility, called Still Dock.

The **Periwinkle Guest House** is very close to the Whaling Museum, at 7–9 N.
Water St., Nantucket, MA 02554 (tel. 508/228-9267). A nice old Nantucket house
run by Sara Schlosser-O'Reilly, the Periwinkle has 18 rooms of various shapes, sizes,
sleeping capacities, and bath facilities: Doubles with private bath are $110 to $176
daily; singles, doubles, or twins with shared bath are $77 to $93. A few single rooms
with shared bath are priced at $39 to $44. Continental breakfast and tax are included in all rates. The Periwinkle—the name is that of a spiral-shaped saltwater
snail—is open all year, and rates are 25% to 50% lower off-season.

The **Bartlett House,** 14 Gardner St. (P.O. Box 218), Nantucket, MA 02554
(tel. 508/228-1139), prides itself not merely on the attractiveness of the 150-year-
old house and the coziness of its rooms, but on the quietness of its clientele. Only
five rooms are for rent, at $66 to $110 per night, single or double, with a three-night
minimum stay. Off-season rates are $5 to $15 lower. Two of the rooms share a bath-

room; all the others have private facilities, although one room's shower is down the hall. Bartlett House has no living room for guests' use, but the garden is most people's first choice of a place to relax in any case. Room prices are among the best in town, and the silence, as they say, is golden.

The **House of the Seven Gables,** 32 Cliff Rd., Nantucket, MA 02554 (tel. 508/228-4706), was once the Victorian annex to an even larger old Victorian seaside hotel. Actually, "Seven Gables and a Tower" would be an even more accurate description of this good example of Victorian architectural enthusiasm. As it's not one of those small and quaint Nantucket houses, it has more rooms to offer—ten in all, with nine bathrooms. Continental breakfast is served year round and rates run from $83 to $143 for a room with double bed and semiprivate bath, or a room with double bed and private bath, or a triple with private bath. Mid-September to mid-June these rates drop by about a third. The location is a 10-minute walk from Main Street, not as close to town as some other houses; but the area is a quiet residential one.

The **Cliff House,** 34 Cliff Rd., Nantucket, MA 02554 (tel. 508/228-2154 or 969-8293), was built as a cottage annex to the Seacliff Hotel, one of Nantucket's landmark Victorian resorts. The Seacliff is gone, but the Cliff House continues to lodge guests in its seven rooms (five with private baths). Four of the rooms have brass beds, another has a queen-size mahogany canopy bed, all have the appropriate Victorian furnishings, and several have views of the sea. A fancy continental breakfast is served outside each morning, if the weather permits, and it often does. Rates in high season are $62 for a single room with shared bath, and $119 for a double with private bath.

Hotels

Nantucket still has a few of the rambling old Victorian wooden hotels which used to be found throughout New England, and indeed throughout North America, but which have been disappearing quickly since the advent of the automobile and the motel. Although there are a few motels on the island too, I'll describe an older hotel that offers accommodations more in keeping with the island's traditions, at prices that are undeniably good value for the money.

The **Folger Hotel,** at the corner of Cliff Road and Easton Street, (P.O. Box 628), Nantucket, MA 02554 (tel. 508/228-0313), is just such an old rambling hotel, set on sunny lawns, well kept, and now easily informal, though in earlier times everyone had to dress for dinner. Open only from mid-May to mid-October, the Folger charges $47 for a single room without private bath, $94 to $105 for a similar double; rooms with private bath cost $71 single, $106 to $116 double. In the annex, called the Captain's Corners (open April through December), rooms are $44 for a single with semiprivate bath, $74 to $84 for a similar double-bedded room; doubles with bath are $96 to $99. The hotel's restaurant, called the Whale, provides breakfast (included in the room price), and dinner too.

Budget Guesthouses

Almost all of Nantucket's budget guesthouses charge the same rates: $65 to $83 for a double room that shares a bath; $83 to $93 for a double with private bath. When you call for reservations, find out if breakfast is included, and if it's rolls and coffee or bacon and eggs. Ask if the room has a view, or is especially large. Every room is different, and you must know these things to get the most for your money.

The **Hungry Whale,** 8 Derrymore Rd., Nantucket, MA 02554 (tel. 508/228-0793), is exceptional in several ways. Mrs. Johnson, the smiling owner, charges several dollars less than most other houses, and includes a hearty breakfast to boot! The location is off North Liberty Avenue.

The **Nesbitt Inn,** 21 Broad St., Nantucket, MA 02554 (tel. 508/228-0156), despite its appellation and downtown location, is one of the island's lodging bargains, a nice big mansard-roofed Victorian house (1872) three blocks from the wharf, charging guesthouse prices for its ten double and three single rooms with shared baths. All rooms have sinks, so you need walk down the hall only for toilet or shower; many rooms have original Victorian furnishings, including brass beds and marble-topped tables. Guests have use of a refrigerator, and of the common rooms with fireplace. The innkeepers, Dolly and Nobby Noblit, are the third generation of a Nantucket innkeeping family which has been welcoming guests here since 1914.

The **Ivy Lodge & Cottages,** 2 Chester St., Nantucket, MA 02554 (tel. 508/228-0305 or toll free 800/626-8825), at North Water Street, is a homey, tidy place far enough from downtown to have reasonable prices, and close enough to be very handy.

WHERE TO DINE

For a seafood lover, Nantucket is a dream come true. Look at it this way: All the dining places are surrounded by waters full of fish, lobsters, crabs, clams, scallops, and squid! But visitors do not live by seafood alone. Island restaurants offer many wonderful meat and fowl dishes as well as the occasional vegetarian platter. The range of cuisines includes French, Italian, New England, and New American, with the occasional Mexican entree. On weekends in July and August dinner reservations are advisable at the restaurant of your choice; otherwise, you may end up dining somewhere else—just as good perhaps, but not the place you had in mind.

I'll start by describing the best restaurants in Nantucket Town, then some of the good, dependable places there, and finally the dining opportunities in the village of 'Sconset.

Nantucket's Top Restaurants

Among Nantucket's most pleasant dining places is **Le Languedoc,** 24 Broad St. (tel. 508/228-2552), just up from Steamboat Wharf near the Jared Coffin House. In good weather, most diners choose the umbrella-shaded tables in the pretty patio beside the house, though there are several simple but pleasant, small, airy dining rooms on the main floor of the inn. Le Languedoc offers very good French and New American cuisine in attractive presentations, with cheerful and attentive service. Figure $50 per person for dinner (the only meal served), because you may want to try a glass or two of some interesting vintage available from the wine bar.

Obadiah's Native Seafood, 2 India St. (tel. 508/228-4430), near Federal, specializes in just that, and you can start your meal here with quahog pie (clams, salt pork, potatoes, and onions in a pastry shell) or scallop chowder, then go on to any of 20 main courses, including all the fresh seasonal fish and dishes like baked yellow tail sole stuffed with lobster scallops. A full dinner might cost $30 to $40 per person. Dining areas include the cozy main room in the cellar of the building and the cool, shady patio behind it. Lunch and dinner are served every day, and on Sunday there's brunch from 11:30 am to 3pm. The restaurant is open from mid-June through mid-October.

The famous Jared Coffin House at 29 Broad St. (tel. 508/228-2400), corner of Centre, has two restaurants worthy of consideration. First of these is **Jared's,** the main dining room. The menu lists such elegant and delectable items as sesame chicken and grilled duck. Service and surroundings here are more old-worldly, and prices for a full dinner range from $40 to $50 per person, all included.

Jared's informal counterpart is the **Tap Room,** a 19th-century tavern with a wonderful verdant terrace shaded by lofty elms. The food is heartier and more traditional here, from baked sole Florentine to sirloin steak. Prices are lower, about $30 for dinner. Note that all three meals are served here daily (breakfast is on from 8 to 11am), and that there is entertainment most evenings in summer.

For northern Italian cuisine in the grand manner, head for **De Marco,** 9 India St. (tel. 508/228-1836), near Centre Street. The downstairs rooms of this old Nantucket house are furnished as simple but elegant dining rooms offering, among other treats, linguine con vongole al pesto (the ever popular pasta with Littleneck clams and basil-garlic sauce). A substantial part of the treat comes from the fact that all the pasta, baked goods, and desserts consumed in the restaurant are made right here, fresh daily. Seafood is prominent on the menu, but so are the classics, such as veal medallions and rack of lamb. If you have a light supper of an appetizer, a pasta plate, a dessert, and wine, with tax and tip your bill might come to $40. For a full dinner in the grand manner of Italian dining, figure $65 to $70 per person, all in. De Marco is open every day for dinner only from 6 to 10:30pm.

The **Company of the Cauldron,** 7 India St. (tel. 508/228-4016), serves only dinner, at one or two sittings (usually 7 and 9:15pm)—and you *must* have a reservation. The menu is completely table d'hôte, and fixed price: You have no choice, although if you've called for reservations (as you must), it's presumed you've asked what will be served—perhaps homemade fettuccine tossed with eggplant, capers, and olives, followed by an apple-and-watercress salad, and then medallions of veal rolled with spinach and mozzarella, served with a parfait of pimentos. In all, two dining together can expect to pay about $110 to $120 with wine, tax, and tip all in. The dining room is small, with kitchen and wine racks in the rear. A harpist plays at dinner. An antique-fancier's collection of old tubs, buckets, and cauldrons serves to show off a cascade of flowers. As you walk to the restaurant, don't look for a sign, but rather for the old copper tub (cauldron?) hanging above the entrance: that *is* the sign.

Good Moderately Priced Restaurants

First place in this category must go to the **Quaker House Restaurant,** 31 Centre St. (tel. 508/228-9156), at the corner of Chestnut Street. Lunch is not served, but come for breakfast (8 to 11:30am), or drop in any evening for dinner (6 to 9 pm). The charming dining rooms have fireplaces, lace curtains, crisp tablecloths, antique accent pieces, and candlelight in the evening. At breakfast, try the baked apple pancakes, baked German pancakes, waffles or pancakes made with blueberries or pecans, fresh vegetable omelets, and fresh-squeezed orange juice. At dinnertime, order one of the seven main courses—such as filet of sole, shrimp scampi, Bombay chicken, or beef burgundy—and you get Nantucket clam chowder, Portuguese bread and butter, a tossed garden salad, and a choice of dessert all included in the price. And the price, for Nantucket, is truly surprising, as the most expensive dinner costs $25, plus drink, tax, and tip. Many dinners are priced at only $15. Beer and wine by the glass, carafe, or bottle are available at moderate prices. Note that the Quaker House has room for only 40 diners at a time, and does not accept reservations, so arrive early in order to be assured of finding a table.

If you make your way to **Vincent's Restaurant,** right across the street from the police station at 21 S. Water St. (tel. 508/228-0189), you'll find unpretentious food at prices that are very moderate for Nantucket, and have been since 1954, when the present family management took over. The tourist-special plate of fish and chips is generous, and costs about $9 with a drink. A bowl of chowder and a fish filet sandwich costs even less and Italian dishes such as chicken cacciatore, eggplant parmigiana, pizza, and calzones cost $7 to $12. In good weather, you can even dine on a small outdoor terrace, or just have one of Vincent's delicious lobster rolls and a beer there. The vanilla custard ice cream is homemade. Vincent's has a full liquor license, and is open for breakfast, lunch, and dinner seven days a week. This is Nantucket's dependable old standard, worthy of your patronage.

During your shopping stroll on Old South Wharf, you can stop for a bite at the **Morning Glory Café** (tel. 508/228-2212), down near the water end of the wharf. Tables are set out on a brick patio beneath an awning. All three meals are served: breakfast omelets, french toast, and pancakes from 7 to 11:30am; luncheon seafood chowder, sandwiches, salads, and pasta plates from 12:15 to 3pm. Dinner (6 to 10pm) is fancier, but prices are still moderate and service is informal because all the utensils and plates here, except for the wine glasses, are disposable (the location on the wharf doesn't permit the café to have a dishwasher). Cuisine is Italian, with spaghetti Sicilian style, fettuccine with fresh tomato and basil, or with shrimp and scallops, and penne rigate (tube pasta with sweet Italian sausage). Expect to spend $10 to $15 at lunch, $25 to $30 at dinner.

The **Captain's Table,** in the basement of the Ships Inn on Fair Street (tel. 508/228-0040), offers entrees like lamb chops and Nantucket scallops for about $16 to $20. For dessert try chocolate mousse or cranberry sherbet with cassis. And don't let the "basement" dining room worry you. It is a supremely warm and cheerful place, with old oil paintings adding grace and beauty to the light-colored walls. You can have a drink with your meal, or in the Dory Bar. The restaurant is open every day from 7am to 10:30pm.

The **Mad Hatter Restaurant,** 72 Easton St. (tel. 508/228-9667), at South Beach Street, is a popular spot with people who own summer houses on Nantucket. Looking somewhat like a summer house itself, the restaurant is set in a green lawn, with shade trees and a small secluded patio café on the Easton Street side. Owners Jeanne and Richard Diamond have decorated the dining room in coral and green hues, and the ambience is that of an informal but proper yacht club. The dinner menu lists fettuccine Alfredo, baked stuffed shrimp, canneloni, and grilled salmon, as well as several meat and chicken dishes. The extensive wine list includes numerous American vintages. At dinnertime, a full meal, with wine, tax, and tip included, runs something like $25 to $35, but there is also a pub menu (4 to 9pm) featuring sandwiches, pasta, soup, hamburgers, and salads, at considerably lower prices. The Mad Hatter is open daily mid-April through December for lunch from 11:30am to 2:30 pm, for dinner from 5:30 to 9pm; Sunday brunch is served from 11am to 2pm.

At **The Tavern,** on Straight Wharf at Harbor Square (tel. 508/228-1226), open daily, right by the marina, you may eat at tables set out in the picturesque brick-paved square, or on a second-floor balcony overlooking the marina and the activity on the street, or even in a little flèche-topped gazebo in the cobbled square. Drinks are served, as are salads, hamburgers, and sandwiches ($7 to $10) at lunch; dinner-time is 6 to 10pm, and then you can get fish and chips, scampi, or a London broil for $14 to $20. The food is okay here, but the situation is even better.

The **Gaslight Theatre Café,** on North Union Street just off Main Street (tel. 508/228-4479), is on the terrace of the Gaslight Theatre. The tiny patio is usually crowded with tables of diners having breakfast (8 to 11am), lunch (11:30am to 4pm), or dinner (5 to 10pm), perhaps before attending the show, or perhaps just because of the excellent people-watching possibilities. Burgers, seafood kabobs, and fancier items such as grilled tuna steaks are offered. Lunch might set you back $8 to $12, dinner $15 to $25.

For Breakfast

The **Dory Restaurant,** 10 India St. (no phone), just off Centre Street, serves breakfast, brunch, and light lunches only, from 6am to 1pm daily. As the house special, breakfast is fine here, with a good selection of omelets, crêpes, croissants, pancakes, and bacon-and-egg dishes. Sandwiches and burgers are added for lunch. Eat here, in true American lunch-counter atmosphere, or take out. You can spend anything from $3 to $6 at the Dory.

For Sandwiches

I'd recommend that everyone pick up a mammoth sandwich from **Henry's Sandwiches,** on Steamboat Wharf (tel. 508/228-0123), before getting on the boat. Henry's huge sandwiches are made in the best Italian sub/grinder/hoagie/po'boy tradition, and cost about $3 or $4. Soft drinks are available, and everything can be wrapped to go or consumed post-haste at small tables on the premises. Remember Henry's if you're planning a picnic, or are down to your last $3 plus your ticket home.

Dining in 'Sconset

Almost everyone who gets to Nantucket for a few days has a chance to ride a bike to 'Sconset on the other side of the island. You can go for dinner to the **Chanti-cleer Inn** (tel. 508/257-6231), which is noted for its elegant French cuisine and for the charm of its dining area, which at lunchtime in the summer is a courtyard surrounded by rose-covered trellises under which tables are set. For dinner there are three lovely indoor rooms. Dinner prices are not low: the fixed-price menu is $50, plus wine, tax, and tip. Order á la carte to get whole sea bass grilled with roasted peppers or Nantucket bay scallops in a Madeira sauce. There's a bar and lounge called the Grill Room. This is 'Sconset's most elegant spot, and a meal here becomes a nice memory.

Right by the flagpole at the Siasconset traffic circle is **Claudette's** food-catering shop (tel. 508/257-6622), where you can sit at a tiny table on the wood deck and watch the easy activity of the square while drinking coffee, tea, or lemonade. Meanwhile, Claudette will be making you a delicious box lunch for your picnic or bike trip for $5; clam bakes are a specialty.

'Sconset's all-purpose eating place is the **'Sconset Café**, Post Office Square (tel. 508/257-4008), open daily in summer for breakfast, lunch, and dinner. This light, pleasant eatery has pastel walls hung with local artists' works, and a tempting array of edibles such as breakfast pancakes made with blueberries and cranberries ($4.25), and a soup-and-salad special at lunch ($6). The fare at dinnertime (6 to 9:30pm) is fancier, including homemade pastas, confit of duck, and fresh grilled seafood. Expect to pay $23 to $28 for a complete dinner.

Just around the corner from the post office is the **Siasconset Market,** at which you can choose the makings of a sandwich or picnic lunch, and the clerk will put it all together for you so that all you have to do is the eating.

WHAT TO SEE AND DO

Once on Nantucket, you'll find that your activity schedule will take care of itself. In good weather everyone takes off to the beaches, by taxi, bus, or bike. For variety, the island offers tennis, golf, horseback riding, movies, antique stores, and art galleries. Sports fishermen should wander down to **Straight Wharf** to talk to one of the charter boat captains about a day's run for bluefish or striped bass. Those who just like being in a boat can rent a sailboat and take sailing lessons at one of the establishments on **Washington Street Extension** or **Steamboat Wharf.** The island's information office on Federal Street will be able to help you out with details.

Museums

The **Maria Mitchell Science Center** (tel. 508/228-0898 or 228-9198) is a group of buildings organized and maintained in honor of Nantucket's foremost astronomer, Maria Mitchell (1818–1889). Born on Nantucket of an astronomer father and teacher-librarian mother, Mitchell became interested in the stars at an early age. Out here on Nantucket, away from the pollution and haze of cities, she studied the heavens, and in 1847 discovered a hitherto uncharted comet. Her scientific feat earned her a gold medal from the king of Denmark and membership in the American Academy of Arts and Sciences (the only woman so honored at the time), and led to a distinguished career as a professor at Vassar College.

Founded in 1902, the Nantucket Maria Mitchell Association seeks to preserve a fitting memorial to the island's famous astronomer, and to make available science facilities to residents and visitors. The Science Center consists of astronomical observatories, with lectures on Monday at 8pm and stellar observations on Wednesday at 9pm if the sky is clear; the Hinchman House at 7 Milk St., with its Museum of Natural Science, Thursday-evening (8pm) lectures, birdwatching, wildflower and nature walks, and children's nature classes; the Mitchell House at 1 Vestal St., birthplace of Maria Mitchell, with wildflower and herb gardens; the Science Library at 2 Vestal St.; and the aquarium at 28 Washington St. The museums are free to members of the association; admission costs $3 for adults, $1 per child for nonmembers. Check with the center for current activity schedules.

Nantucket's history can keep you occupied for days as well. To run the gamut, buy a special visitor's pass ($5) to the 11 buildings filled with the exhibits of the **Nantucket Historical Association** on Union Street (tel. 508/228-1894). Association buildings include the famous Whaling Museum, The Thomas Macy Warehouse (Nantucket history museum), the oldest house on the island, and a windmill built in 1746 and still functioning. Individual admissions to all buildings would cost much more, and the pass gives you the advantage of being able to browse in a museum for a while, go to the beach, and return to another museum later in the afternoon. You can get your pass at the Whaling Museum on Broad Street, or at any of the other association buildings.

Tours

Tour buses of the various companies will meet your ferryboat at Steamboat Wharf or Straight Wharf, ready to take you on a 1¼-hour tour of the island. There's no better way to get your bearings, and the short time spent will help you better organize the few precious days you'll have on the island.

Nantucket Island Tours, with offices on Straight Wharf (tel. 508/228-0334), offers six island tours daily in summer, charging $9 per adult, $4 for a child.

Barrett's Tours, 20 Federal St. (tel. 508/228-0174), the island's Gray Line company, operates six daily tours running on several different routes between Nantucket Town and 'Sconset. The 1½-hour tour, the shortest, costs $7.50 for adults, $4.50 for children. Senior citizens get discounts on all tours departing from Barrett's office. Barrett's also operates a **surfside beach bus,** running to and from the downtown office to the beach six times daily.

Walking Tours of the Town

The Nantucket Historical Association, mentioned above, also publishes a number of detailed **walking-tour brochures,** available from the association's museum shop.

The Historical Association also sponsors a 1½-hour tour through the best of Nantucket's art and architecture. The tour begins at 8:30am Tuesday through Saturday, and departs the Thomas Macy Warehouse on Straight Wharf. Cost is $6 per person. Call 508/228-1894 Monday through Friday from 8am to 5pm for a reservation, as the tour is limited to 15 people.

Music

In the past few years Nantucket has supported chamber music concerts at various times, particularly in the weeks of high summer. Ask at the Information Bureau, or look for notices of upcoming events.

Also, visiting and local bands often give free concerts in the gazebo near Straight Wharf (at the foot of Main Street). The *Weekly Vacation Guides,* available at the Information Bureau, will have listings of times and programs. There is also summer theater at the Folger Hotel.

'Sconset

The village of Siasconset is called nothing but 'Sconset by islanders—the contracted name is hallowed by tradition. The village consists of Post Office Square, a roundabout from which you can see the tennis courts, post office, Sconset Café, Claudette's, and various houses. To the right of Claudette's is the road to the beach, only 100 yards away.

The rest of 'Sconset is residential, with many typical Nantucket houses, but also a few streets of small, low-roofed bungalows that sit squarely as though avoiding the violence of winter storms.

Though there are several daily buses to 'Sconset, in my opinion the best way to go is by bicycle along the bike path from Nantucket Town. The journey from the center of Nantucket Town to the center of 'Sconset is 7½ miles. If you make the trip in late July or early August, watch for the carpet of low-bush blueberries. Maybe you'll be in luck and find the bushes full of tangy fruit, yours for the picking.

Once in 'Sconset, have something to eat, go to the beach, take a walk or bike ride around, and in the evening drop in at the Siasconset Casino (on the opposite side of the tennis courts from Post Office Square) for a movie or a show. Just across the street from the casino is the Chanticleer Inn, founded in 1909, and still 'Sconset's prime spot for elegant dining (see above for details).

CENTRAL AND WESTERN MASSACHUSETTS

West of Boston spreads a landscape familiar to the early pioneers, a beautiful land of clear lakes and glacial ponds, cool forests and massive granite outcrops. Farming, forestry, and light industry occupy the people of central and western Massachusetts, not to mention the textile and paper mills dotted along its many rivers. Amid this bucolic scenery you'll also find several of America's finest colleges, posh 19th-century mountain resorts, and New England's premier summer music festival.

Wealthy vacationers of the 19th century who loved the sea would get away to Newport, Cape Cod, or Bar Harbor; those who loved the mountains would head for Saratoga Springs, N.Y., or for the storybook New England towns scattered through the low mountains known as the Berkshires in western Massachusetts. The grand residences and hotels of the wealthy remain in Stockbridge, Lenox, Williamstown, and other Berkshire communities, adding to the romance and interest of the area and serving a new purpose as hostelries for the new wave of vacationers. Today the lure of the Berkshires is enhanced by one of the country's major summer musical events, the Berkshire Music Festival at Tanglewood, near Lenox; another Berkshire town draws crowds because of its beauty and its educational opportunities, for Williamstown in the northern Berkshires has been the seat of Williams College since the school was chartered in 1785. Whatever your reason for going, you can't fail to enjoy the lush countryside, the picturesque towns with rows of fine houses, and the acres of manicured greenery.

The telephone area code for central Massachusetts is 508, for western Massachusetts, 413.

---

1. Getting There

BY CAR

From New York City, the Taconic State Parkway provides a very pleasant route to the Berkshires; from other points I-90 (the Massachusetts Turnpike) and I-91 can be used as the fastest routes to the area. There's convenient public transport as well.

BY BUS

Greyhound (tel. 617/423-5810 in Boston or toll free 800/237-8211) provides direct service between Boston and Albany via Worcester, Sturbridge, Springfield, Lee, Lenox, and Pittsfield, Mass., with several buses a day. In addition, there is direct Toronto–New York service with stop in Albany, where transfer can be made to a Lenox-bound bus.

Vermont Transit (tel. 617/423-5810 in Boston) operates buses between Montréal and New York City, stopping in Albany at the Greyhound terminal, where transfer can be made for the trip to Lenox. There are also direct buses between Montréal and Pittsfield, Mass., passing through Williamstown; in Pittsfield the transfer can be made for Lenox.

Englander Coach Lines (tel. 617/423-5810), operating from the Greyhound terminal in Boston, has several buses a day between Boston and Albany, stopping in Pittsfield; connecting services are also run between Boston and Providence.

Bonanza Bus Lines (tel. 212/971-6363 in New York City 617/423-5810 in Boston, or toll free 800/556-3815) has direct Providence–Albany service, with stops in Pittsfield, Lenox, and Lee, and also direct buses between New York City and Great Barrington, Stockbridge, Lee, Lenox, and Pittsfield. There is direct service from Boston's Greyhound terminal to Springfield, Pittsfield, Greenfield, North Adams, and Williamstown.

Peter Pan Bus Lines (tel. 617/426-7838 in Boston or 413/781-3320 in Springfield), which operates from its terminal near Boston's South Station, provides service from Boston to Amherst, Northampton, Holyoke, South Hadley, Worcester, and Springfield, Mass., and thence to Pittsfield, Lee, and Lenox.

By taking a Greyhound bus from Hartford or New York City to Springfield, you can connect with the Bonanza or Peter Pan buses to reach just about anywhere in western Massachusetts.

Local buses connect Berkshire County towns and resorts with one another.

BY RAIL

Amtrak's *Lakeshore Limited* runs daily between New York/Boston and Chicago, one section leaving Boston (South Station) in midafternoon and another leaving New York City in early evening. The two sections link up in Albany-Rensselaer and continue on to Chicago. The section from Boston passes through Worcester and Springfield, and then Pittsfield, Mass., in the evening. The *Adirondack*, traveling between Montréal and New York City (Grand Central Terminal), passes through Albany-Rensselaer as well. From that point, arrangements have to be made to get to your destination by bus.

In addition, Amtrak's Inland Route trains traveling between Boston and New York pass through Wellesley, Framingham, Worcester, and Springfield, Mass., as well as Hartford and New Haven, Conn. There are at least two trains daily on this route. Call Amtrak toll free 800/872-7245; in New York, 212/582-6875; in Boston, 617/482-3660.

---

2. Worcester

Massachusetts' second-largest city has much to recommend it, and only one serious drawback (which is not its own fault): Worcester is only an hour's drive west of Boston. What this means is that people consider Boston as the Massachusetts metropolis, and simply forget about her sister city so close at hand.

Worcester's claims to fame are considerable: It is the home of American Antiquarian Society (founded in 1812), of the famed Worcester Art Museum, and of the Higgins Armory Museum. If you're searching for documents dating from America's early years, Edward Hicks's famous painting *The Peaceable Kingdom,* or rare suits of medieval armor, you've come to the right place.

PLANNING YOUR VISIT

What I'd suggest is this: Get to Worcester, take a turn through the center of town, stopping at the fine Town Common and impressive City Hall, and perhaps at the modern shopping, dining, and entertainment complex called the Galleria; then admire the massive auditorium named Mechanics Hall, 321 Main St., as you make your way to the Worcester Art Museum. Spend the morning at the museum and nearby sights, perhaps have a bite of lunch in the museum's nice café (see below), go on to the Higgins Armory, then head for Sturbridge (18 miles) to spend the night. Don't plan this tour for a Monday, as all of Worcester's museums are closed on that day.

SEEING THE SIGHTS

What you will see of Worcester is very pleasant. There are spacious parks and gardens, several academic institutions of note (Clark University, College of the Holy Cross, and Worcester Polytechnic Institute), and many attractive buildings. Such beauty must be paid for, and Worcester bought its share by being a very active manufacturing center during the mid-1800s. This city was the birthplace of ingenious machines which were the first to weave carpets, fold envelopes, and turn irregular shapes on a lathe. You can still see many of the old mill buildings in town. Some have been converted to office or retail centers, others lie abandoned, and many are still turning out products: men's and boys' clothing, raincoats, sportswear, winter coats, shoes, and dozens of other items. Worcester kept its spirit of Yankee ingenuity right into the 20th century. Dr. Robert Goddard, the father of modern rocketry, was a Worcester native.

Most of Worcester's products can be bought at a discount in the **factory outlets** sprinkled across the city—you'll see them. **Spag's,** at 193 Boston Turnpike (Rte. 9) in neighboring Shrewsbury, could be considered the L.L. Bean of discount houses. Vast quantities of discount merchandise are trucked in and sold out each day to a horde of loyal customers.

Worcester Art Museum

Worcester's famous art museum, at 55 Salisbury St., off Park Avenue and Main Street (tel. 508/799-4406), will surprise you. It's one of those smaller museums with an amazingly comprehensive collection, studded with masterpieces. Besides Hicks's *Peaceable Kingdom,* you'll see Paul Gauguin's famous *St. Bartholomew,* Rembrandt's *Brooding Woman,* and Mary Cassatt's *Woman Bathing.* The collection ranges from ancient Chinese, Egyptian, and Sumerian objects through Roman statuary and mosaics, Pre-Columbian artifacts, Japanese *ukiyo-e* prints and European paintings by the great masters, to American primitives and works by the great American painters.

Hours are Tuesday through Friday from 10am to 4pm, on Saturday to 5pm, and on Sunday from 1 to 5pm; closed Monday (also New Year's Day, Independence Day, Thanksgiving, and Christmas). Admission is free on Saturday from 10am to noon (courtesy of Shaw's Supermarkets); otherwise, it is $3.50 for adults, $2 for students and senior citizens, free for youths under 18. The museum has a pleasant **café** serving an interesting menu of soups, salads, and sandwiches (including its own oven-roasted beef). There's a daily quiche or omelet special, a daily main course plate, and a children's menu, as well as lots of desserts. Wine and beer are served. Lunch can cost as little as $4 or as much as $12 per person. The café is open Tuesday through Saturday from 11:30am to 2pm for luncheon, to 3pm for desserts and beverages.

Worcester Historical Society
At 30 Elm St., just around the corner from the art museum, is the Worcester Historical Society (tel. 508/753-8278), with a library and galleries dedicated to the town's history and lore. You can visit Tuesday through Saturday from 10am to 4pm, Sunday from 1 to 4pm, for a voluntary contribution.

American Antiquarian Society
At 185 Salisbury St., only a few blocks from the art museum, the American Antiquarian Society (tel. 508/755-5221), is a research library of American printed materials dating from 1640 to 1877. The priceless archives are open only to scholars, but you can view displays of many documents important to American history Monday through Friday from 9am to 5pm. Free tours are given Wednesday at 2pm.

Higgins Armory Museum
That Worcester should have one of the world's great collections of medieval armor is not as odd as it may seem. The ingenious Yankees who lived here in the 1800s were fascinated by machinery, and thus deeply involved with metallurgy. John Woodman Higgins wanted to know how medieval armorers made such excellent steel, so he collected their work. Now over 100 magnificent suits, true works of art, are arranged in the museum, many in the Great Hall. You'll even see armor made for kids, and for dogs. Among the museum's most popular exhibits is the Quest Gallery, with hands-on exhibits, including replica armor and "castle clothing" you can try on for size. Hours are Tuesday through Friday from 9am to 4pm, on weekends from noon to 4pm; open Monday from 9am to 4pm in July and August; the museum is closed on legal holidays. There's an admission fee of $4 for adults and $2.75 for senior citizens and children 5 to 12. The Higgins Armory Museum is at 100 Barber Ave., off West Boylston Street (Rte. 12; tel. 508/853-6015).

3. Sturbridge

The creators of Old Sturbridge Village couldn't have chosen a better spot for their "living museum." It's set in the beautiful hills of east-central Massachusetts right where the Massachusetts Turnpike (I-90) intersects with I-84, a major route to Hartford and New York City. Most people who tour New England would pass this junction sometime. Anyone who passes should certainly stop to see Old Sturbridge Village, and perhaps to spend the night. Take Exit 9 from the Massachusetts Turnpike, and Exit 2 from I-84, to U.S. Route 20 West.

WHERE TO STAY
Because of Old Sturbridge Village, and because the village of Sturbridge is very near the intersection of two major interstate highways, motels abound in this town

and nearby. Trade is brisk in summer, even brisker during the autumn foliage season, and briskest of all during the three annual Brimfield Flea Market weekends. Nearby Brimfield, 8 miles west of Sturbridge on U.S. 20, is a normally sleepy place which springs to life in early May, mid-July, and mid-September. As Brimfield has few hotels and motels itself, those in Sturbridge—and even in Springfield, 35 miles away—are filled to overflowing. If you come at flea market time, have ironclad reservations. The flea markets are in May, July, and September.

During the normally slow months of January through March, several Sturbridge inns and motels band together to offer attractive discount "Winter Weekend" package plans. For details, contact the Publick House (described below).

You should note that the village of Sturbridge, a bona fide Massachusetts colonial-era town, and Old Sturbridge Village, a "living museum," are actually two different places in the same general area. They're only about a mile apart, but the village of Sturbridge's Town Common, or center, is on Rte. 131, while the entrance to Old Sturbridge Village is on Rte. 20.

With hotels, motels, and inns in the Berkshires packed to capacity on summer weekends, some visitors and music lovers actually plan to stay as far east as Sturbridge, where rooms are plentiful. With Sturbridge as a base, a tour through the Berkshires, including a stop at Tanglewood, can be a day's outing.

Inns and Guesthouses

The **Publick House on the Common,** P.O. Box 187, Sturbridge, MA 01566-0187 (tel. 508/347-3313), is a local institution. Founded in 1771 by Col. Ebenezer Crafts, the Publick House occupies the original building plus several large (but tasteful) additions, mostly furnished for dining. The inn has 17 guest rooms, including several suites for three or four people. All rooms and suites have private bath, air conditioning, and direct-dial phone. In the adjoining Chamberlain House are four suites with queen-size beds, color TV, air conditioning, direct-dial phone, and living-room area; each suite accommodates up to four people. Double rooms cost $76 to $120; suites are $109 to $153 for two, tax included.

The Publick House people also operate the **Colonel Ebenezer Crafts Inn,** Fiske Hill, Sturbridge, MA 01566 (tel. 508/347-3313), at the summit of Fiske Hill. The fine old house was built by David Fiske in 1786, and later converted to an inn. It's gracious, filled with antiques, and small, taking only about 20 people at one time. Rates are good for what you get: continental breakfast, a morning newspaper, and later on afternoon tea and sherry; and at bedtime you'll enter your room to find sweets by your bed. It's all included in the rates: $99 to $110 for a double room with private bath; a suite capable of sleeping four people costs $115 to $148. All the rooms are air-conditioned, and while they don't have TV, there's one in the library you can watch.

About 25 miles northwest of Sturbridge, at the junction of Rtes. 9 and 32, is the town of Ware, and the **Wildwood Inn,** 121 Church St., Ware, MA 01082 (tel. 413/967-7798). If you're headed for Amherst and would rather travel the scenic back roads than the turnpike, you'll find a friendly welcome here. Double rooms with shared baths and lovely handmade quilts are priced from $41 to $73, full breakfast included.

Motels

Prime among Sturbridge's modern hostelries and right across from Old Sturbridge Village is the **Sheraton Inn and Conference Center,** U.S. 20, Sturbridge, MA 01566 (tel. 508/347-7393 or toll free 800/325-3535). This lavish 241-room spread on the shores of Cedar Lake has its own tennis and racquetball courts, health clubs, indoor swimming pool, and miniature golf course. Decor in the plush guest rooms is, of course, colonial. "Heritage Row," a special group of VIP rooms, has its own private lounge and concierge services. Regular rooms go for $98 to $148 single, $109 to $148 double, tax in. Weekend packages that include some meals are available.

The **Old Sturbridge Village Motor Lodge,** Rte. 20 West, Sturbridge, MA

01566 (tel. 508/347-3327), right next to Old Sturbridge Village, is owned by the Village. Guest rooms are clustered in a variety of buildings designed along colonial lines and positioned as though in an Early American village. All 60 accommodations are modern, full-comfort rooms with TV, air conditioning, telephone, and private bath. The rooms in the Oliver Wight House, (1789), a Revolutionary-era 10-room inn right next door, have a bit more character. The modern rooms in the "village" rent for $83 double; rooms in the Wight House and Dennison Cottage suites cost $104; each additional person pays $5 and children 12 and under stay free in their parents' room. Tax is included.

The **Sturbridge Coach Motor Lodge,** 408 Main St., Sturbridge, MA 01566 (tel. 508/347-7327), is on U.S. 20 almost opposite the entrance to Old Sturbridge, up on the hill. Although it's obviously a modern two-floor luxury motel, the inspiration for both design and decor is colonial. There's nothing colonial about the swimming pool, though, or the rooms, each equipped with color cable TV, air conditioning, and private bath with separate dressing room area. Rates in summer are $62 to $75 for two in a double bed, $66 to $81 for two in two beds.

The **Sturbridge Motor Inn,** P.O. Box 185, Sturbridge, MA 01566 (tel. 508/347-3391) is on the service road parallel to I-84 a quarter mile north of I-84. (Take Exit 2 to Rte. 131.) With 34 rooms, the inn offers air conditioning, color TV, telephone, and an interesting swimming pool nestled among the pines. High-season prices (May through October) are $55 to $72, single or double. Each additional person pays $6.

Right near the intersection of Rtes. 15, 20, and 131 is the **Days Inn at Sturbridge,** P.O. Box 206, Sturbridge, MA 01566 (tel. 508/347-9000), a modern and attractive two- and three-floor brick and wood motel with a swimming pool. All 100 rooms have air conditioning and color TV. Convenient, attractive, and comfortable, the rooms cost $77 single, $82 double in summer, continental breakfast included. From October to April rates are a few dollars more.

WHERE TO DINE

Sturbridge abounds in fast-food joints and snack shops, both for the hungry Old Sturbridge Village visitors and for highway passersby. But good places for a full meal do exist.

The **Publick House** (tel. 508/347-3313), mentioned above, is a Sturbridge favorite, located right on the Town Common on Rte. 131. It's big: The several dining rooms can handle a large number of diners at once, yet the scale of an old New England inn has not been lost. The lunch menu lists a few sandwiches, but concentrates on hot main courses or cold meat or salad plates. Omelets, chicken, and broiled fish are all priced about $10 to $15, but the price includes vegetable, potato, assorted relishes, and a bakery basket filled with freshly baked bread and rolls. Dinner is fancier, with main-course prices about $16 to $20; steaks are a few dollars higher. But for such a price you get almost a full meal, with all the extras that are given with a comparable luncheon plate plus salad. The Publick House's wine list is fairly short, diverse, and moderate-to-expensively priced.

The fare at the **Oxhead Tavern,** off U.S. 20 near the Sheraton Inn and Conference Center (tel. 508/347-9994), is designed with transients in mind. It's not an elegant restaurant, and doesn't try to be, but it succeeds beautifully in being a roadside tavern. Furnished in rustic colonial, it has an old-fashioned pub bar at one end, a big stone fireplace at the other. The menu is well suited to what a roadhouse must provide: various meals at any time of day or evening. The fare includes New York sirloin for $14 and various meat and fish dishes for $9 to $12; lots of sandwiches are cheaper ($5 to $7) and equally filling. Open from 11am to 11pm Monday through Saturday and noon to 11pm on Sunday.

A Sturbridge Institution

Rom's (tel. 508/347-3349), the Italian-American restaurant on Rte. 131 across from the shopping plaza, is an all-American success story. Started as a roadside sandwich-and-seafood stand, Rom's now seats up to 700 people in attractive, air-conditioned surroundings. What packs 'em in is Rom's unbeatable formula: good, plentiful food in pleasant dining rooms at low prices. A lunch of soup, broiled halibut steak, potato, vegetable, and cole slaw costs less than $10; a four-course dinner need cost only $10 to $15, complete. The menu features Italian dishes, steaks, seafood, and traditional meals. Service is seven days a week from 11am to 9pm, on Saturday to 10pm.

The original dairy bar/lunchstand is still here, by the way. Food to go, including Italian dishes, is even lower in price.

WHAT TO SEE

Besides the obvious headline attraction in Sturbridge, you might want to have a picnic in **Wells State Park,** a few miles north of Sturbridge (take U.S. 20 east, then Rte. 49 north and follow the signs). Swimming and camping are available here as well.

Don't miss the chance to pore over trash and treasures at the **Brimfield Flea Market,** held three times a year (see the introduction to this section for details). If Brimfield is not in session, you can still do some browsing in the many shops on U.S. 20 west of Old Sturbridge Village.

Old Sturbridge Village

Old Sturbridge Village (tel. 508/347-3362) is one of the first of America's outdoor museums. It's a re-creation of a New England town of the early 1800s, but it's a re-creation formed with the artifacts: Buildings and tools, machines and methods of work were all collected and brought together in this beautiful part of the Massachusetts hinterland so that Americans could see whence their ancestors had come. Like Plimoth Plantation and Mystic Seaport, Old Sturbridge Village is peopled with authentically dressed "interpreters," folks who perform the tasks of the village's daily life, and explain to visitors how things are done and how things are made. Plan at least a few hours, or perhaps a full day, to get into village life.

The admission fee of $14 per adult, $6 per youth from 6 to 15 (children under 6 get in for free), entitles you to a map/guide to exhibits in the Village, and readmission the following day at no extra charge. The Village is open throughout the year, closing only on Christmas, New Year's Day, and Monday from November through April. Hours are 9am to 5pm May through October and 10am to 4pm Tuesday through Sunday from November through April. Within the Village are several varied places to eat: a bake shop, the Pantry (serving soft drinks), a cafeteria, and the Tavern, which serves full meals, cocktails, and—from late May to late October—a luncheon buffet.

St. Anne Shrine

Those interested in Russian icons will want to stop at the St. Anne Shrine, a mile west of Old Sturbridge Village along U.S. 20, in Fiskdale (tel. 508/347-7338). As you drive through Fiskdale, watch for a sign on the right, just before the junction with Rte. 148, and turn right on Church Street up the steep hill.

The icons were collected by Msgr. Pie Neveu, an Assumptionist bishop who served in Russia from 1906 to 1936, and by other Assumptionist fathers who served as chaplains at the U.S. Embassy between 1934 and 1941. The collection of 60 treasured icons is rare, as they can no longer be exported from the Soviet Union.

The exhibit, in a new building, is open every day from about 9am to 6pm. Admission is free, but donations are accepted.

4. Deerfield, Amherst, and Northampton

The Connecticut River cuts through western Massachusetts on its way through Hartford and Essex to Long Island Sound. In colonial times the river provided easy and cheap transport from the interior to the bustling markets of New York and Philadelphia. Today the river valley serves as pathway for Interstate 91, the modern equivalent of the ancient waterway.

Because of this easy access, pioneer farmers and settlers poured into Massachusetts' portion of the Connecticut River Valley very early in colonial times. The alluvial riverbed soil is rich, and English settlers were farming at Springfield as early as 1636. Remote from the colonial power centers, they suffered from attacks by the French and their Indian allies.

This early settlement gained the region its modern name: the Pioneer Valley. Although it is still a rich farming region, other interests now predominate: Springfield's industrial career started with the construction of an armory there in 1777, and Holyoke and Hadley benefited from abundant waterpower and fostered a paper industry. But to most of the world the towns of Amherst, Northampton, and South Hadley are famous for education. Here in this pastoral setting are five famous colleges—Amherst College, Smith College, Mount Holyoke College, Hampshire College, and the University of Massachusetts—and several smaller institutions. To the north, Old Deerfield is one of the most gracious, best-preserved colonial and Federal towns in the country.

INFORMATION

The region has an area organization, the **Greater Springfield Convention and Visitors Bureau,** 56 Dwight St., Springfield, MA 01103 (tel. 413/787-1548). In addition, each town's chamber of commerce sponsors a visitor information office. In **Amherst,** there's an information booth right on the Town Common across the street from the bus depot, or you can look to the Amherst Chamber of Commerce, 51 E. Pleasant St., Amherst, MA 01002 (tel. 413/549-7555). For **Northampton** information, try the Greater Northampton Chamber of Commerce, on State Street (tel. 413/584-1900). In **South Hadley,** the chamber is at 362 N. Main St. (tel. 413/532-6451).

WHERE TO STAY

Accommodation in the area is very much geared to college life. Most visitors come on college business, and when big college events such as homecomings, graduations, and major football matches draw big crowds, rooms are scarce throughout the area. Try to plan and to reserve well in advance if you think you'll arrive in a busy time.

In Amherst

Every college town has its college inn, usually a gracious old place with a refined atmosphere and very comfortable—often plush—accommodations. Amherst is no exception, for right on the Town Common stands the **Lord Jeffrey Inn,** 30 Boltwood Ave., Amherst, MA 01002 (tel. 413/253-2576). Named for Lord Jeffrey Amherst, the Lord Jeff is cozy, colonial, and collegiate, but with all the conveniences: cable color TV, direct-dial phone, individual heating and air conditioning, and, of course, private bathroom. A tavern and dining room can provide food and refreshment from morning to night. In summer, the Lord Jeff charges $88 to $110 for a single room and $121 to $132 for a suite.

From the Town Common, head out North Pleasant Street and soon you'll see the **University Motor Lodge** at 345 N. Pleasant St., Amherst, MA 01002 (tel. 413/256-8111), on the right-hand side. Up on the hillside above the road, this is an attractive neocolonial place which charges $55 to $82 single, $66 to $82 double, for its newly renovated, fully equipped (right down to coffee in the room) motel rooms. The location is good, as you can walk in 10 minutes either to Amherst or to the University of Massachusetts.

"U. Mass." has its own major lodging facility for out-of-towners. Within the modern tower named the Murray D. Lincoln Campus Center is the **Campus Center Hotel** (tel. 413/549-6000), with over 100 rooms. Besides the standard luxuries such as air conditioning, color TV, telephone, and private bath, most rooms have wonderful, panoramic views of the campus, the town, and the surrounding farmland. Prices are $60 single, $70 double, $82 triple, tax included; suites are also available. To find the Campus Center, head north on North Pleasant Street, enter the U. Mass. campus, and follow signs to Campus Center Parking, an underground lot right next to the Campus Center.

Northampton Road is the highway (Rte. 9) between Amherst and Northampton. The road starts at the southern end of the Town Common, and exactly 1 mile later, after crossing the Amherst town line, it enters a commercial zone. A bit farther along Rte. 9 toward Northampton is the local **Howard Johnson Lodge,** 401 Russell St., Hadley, MA 01035 (tel. 413/586-0114 or toll free 800/654-2000). Although it's very close to Amherst—only a few miles from the Town Common—its mail address is Hadley. Rooms are of the high Hojo standard, some with cathedral ceilings and balconies, and in addition the lodge has a nice big outdoor pool and lots of deck chairs for sunning. All 59 rooms are newly renovated, have two double beds, and rent for $66 single, $76 to $94 double, tax included. VIP, handicapped, nonsmoking, and adjoining family rooms are also available. Children under 18 can stay in their parents' room for free.

In Deerfield, Buckland, and Ashfield

Deerfield, the 18th-century village that's virtually a museum, has an inn. Buckland, the picture-perfect New England village with the church, library, historical society, and beautiful 18th-century houses facing the village green, has a fine bed-and-breakfast which just happens to be one of those houses on the green. Ashfield is yet another beautiful village, a leisurely 40-minute drive from Amherst or Northampton, in the foothills of the Berkshires.

Built in 1884, and modernized in 1981 after a fire, the **Deerfield Inn,** The Street, Deerfield, MA 01342 (tel. 413/774-5587), now has 23 rooms which were inspired by the 18th-century, shall we say, but constructed with 20th-century materials and comforts. All the rooms have private bath and air conditioning, and they have been decorated with period pieces and good replicas to put you in the mood of two centuries ago. The inn has a good restaurant, coffee shop, bar, and lounge; on the very fine front porch rocking chairs are all set to take in the view of The Street with its 12 museum houses. The inn is open all year (except for several days at Christmas), and charges $139 single or double with breakfast, $215 with breakfast and dinner; service charge and tax are included in these rates. Jane and Karl Sabo are your innkeepers here.

In Buckland, on the green, stands the **1797 House,** Charlemont Road, Buckland, MA 01338 (tel. 413/625-2975), run by a very hospitable lady named Janet Turley. The house (built guess when?) has three immaculate guest rooms with private baths and down quilts, and also numerous fireplaces, a screened porch for warm-weather breakfast or relaxation, and interesting nooks and corners. Included in the price of your room is a full country breakfast of juice, fruit, eggs, breakfast meats, french toast, and a hot beverage. Rates are $60 single, $77 double, tax included. Buckland is a few miles southwest of Shelburne Falls, just off Rte. 112. The inn is closed in November and December.

In Ashfield, overlooking Ashfield Lake, is the **Ashfield Inn,** Main Street (P.O. Box 129), Ashfield, MA 01330 (tel. 413/628-4571). The eight guest rooms that share four bathrooms in this Georgian mansion are all quite large and furnished to convey the elegance of the early 1900s. There's a living room (with a fireplace) in which to socialize, books to read, and VCR and TV to watch; there are tree swings and huge porches to enjoy the outdoors. Rates ($60 to $83 single, $83 to $104 double) include an expanded continental breakfast during the week and a full breakfast on the weekends. If the inn is not full, the innkeepers will make every effort to give you a private bathroom at no additional charge.

In Northampton

Closest thing in Northampton to the traditional college inn is the **Autumn Inn,** 259 Elm St., Northampton, MA 01060 (tel. 413/584-7660). From the street you see an attractive brick house, but behind the house are comfortable motel units and a small, pretty swimming pool. Special attention is given to good-quality furnishings and equipment here; a lounge and dining room provide sustenance. Prices in summer are $57 to $68 single, $75 to $90 double, $12 for an extra person; children under 6, $6. Here on Elm Street (Route 9), you're right across the street from Smith College.

At the corner of Main and King streets, the grand **Hotel Northampton,** 36 King Street, Northampton, MA 01061 (tel. 413/584-3100) is the most prominent place to stay in town. After undergoing a substantial period of renovation, the rooms and suites have been furnished with classic pieces and Laura Ashley fabrics. Room rates are $77 single, $86 to $98 double, $125 for a suite. The various eateries within are popular meeting places for Northampton's young and old alike. Wiggins Tavern is a dark, colonial restaurant serving traditional American fare. The Coolidge Park Café dishes up lighter items and drinks; customers spill out onto the patio for dining in warmer months.

Budget Motels Farther Out

In the vicinity of Northampton are two members of the Susse Chalet budget motel chain that offer exceptional value. In the city of Holyoke on U.S. 5, there's a **Susse Chalet Inn,** 1515 Northampton St., Holyoke, MA 01040 (tel. 413/536-1980, or toll free 800/258-1980, 800/572-1880 in New Hampshire). Look for the Susse Chalet on the right-hand side as you head south from Northampton, behind a Howard Johnson's restaurant. Susse Chalet Inn rooms are comfortably furnished with all the usual services, yet they cost a lot less than "standard" motel rooms: to $47 single, $49 to $52 double. By the way, the exit to take from I-91 for this Susse Chalet Inn is Exit 17 or 17A.

At Chicopee, near Massachusetts Turnpike Exit 6, is a **Susse Chalet Motor Lodge,** Burnett Road, Chicopee, MA 01020 (tel. 413/592-5141 or toll free 800/258-1980, 800/572-1880 in New Hampshire). Susse Chalet Motor Lodges, almost as comfortable as the chain's inns, are a few dollars lower in price—and they still have all the conveniences, including TV, air conditioning, ice machine, coin-op laundry, direct-dial phone, even a swimming pool.

WHERE TO DINE

The area has a number of good restaurants. Here are my favorites.

In Amherst

Among the longtime favorites is **Judie's,** 51 N. Pleasant St. (tel. 253-3491), right on the main street in the center of town. The eclectic menu has something for everyone, from seafoods to salads, from quiche to beef. For lunch I had a cup of shrimp bisque, then a hamburger with cheddar, bacon, and onions, and with a soft drink the total bill, tax and tip included, was less than $10. Many people come just for a light meal of soup and a popover with apple butter (a specialty) for $5.50. Main courses at dinner cost between $10 and $15. You dine in one of several small, attractive dining rooms in this converted house or on the glassed-in streetside porch. Go early to get a porch table for lunch. Judie's opens at 11:30am every day, and closes at 11pm (at midnight on Friday and Saturday). Liquor is served.

The **Lord Jeffrey Inn,** 30 Boltwood Ave. (tel. 253-2576), offers elegant colonial-style dining, serving breakfast (7:30 to 9:30am), lunch (noon to 2pm), and dinner (6 to 9pm), plus Sunday brunch (11:30 am to 2:30pm). Expect to spend $20 to $30 per person for a full dinner, less for a hearty lunch.

The **Top of the Campus Restaurant and Lounge** (tel. 545-0636), is in a unique position atop the Murray D. Lincoln Campus Center of the University of Massachusetts. Here the formula is decent food at decent prices, with that panoramic view as a bonus. Note the hours, though: Lunch is served Monday through Friday from 11:30am to 2pm; dinner is Tuesday through Saturday from 5 to 9pm. When college is not in session, more limited hours apply.

Bonducci's Café, 63 S. Pleasant St. (tel. 256-1390), right across from the little information kiosk on the green, opens at 7am (at 8am on Saturday and 9am on

Sunday), and stays open till 11pm weeknights, 11:30pm weekends. This is the place for morning croissant and coffee ($1.75), a bowl of soup and sandwich ($5), or a pick-me-up any time of day. In good weather, sidewalk tables authenticate its college-town-café atmosphere. Bonducci's is also convenient if you're waiting for a bus.

In Northampton

Not your average Chinese restaurant, **Sze's** (tel. 586-5708) on Main Street serves gourmet meals in a contemporary, stylish, and open (and thus rather noisy) dining room. All the old standbys are here—sweet-and-sour chicken, moo-shu pork, beef with pea pods—but they're done with flair. More exotic dishes include sesame game hen with a Szechuan sauce and General Tso's chicken, cooked in a spicy sauce with green and red peppers. Check the blackboard for daily specials; my favorite is the crispy orange chicken. Dishes fall between $6 and $14, but a full meal can be kept to $12 per person. Lunch is served Monday through Saturday from 11:30 am to 3pm; dinner from 3pm to 9:15pm (till 10:45pm on weekends). The Sunday brunch from 11:30am to 3pm is always a good value, and the lounge is a nice place for a before- or after-dinner drink.

The place for breakfast and lunch (and I do mean breakfast *and* lunch—some devotees come with the newspaper at breakfast, do some shopping, and return for lunch) is **Curtis and Schwartz,** 116 Main Street (tel. 586-3278). There's much to love about this place: pecan waffles with fresh fruit, crème fraîche, and real maple syrup ($5.75), summer squash ravioli in a parmesan cream sauce ($5.50), and a cheesy herb omelet ($4) served with a warm scone. Curtis greets and seats customers and Schwartz cooks. In a town with many breakfast places, this one reigns. There's always a line, but the wait never seems too long.

Good Mexican and Southwestern cooking in Northampton? You bet, at **La Cazuela,** 7 Old South St. (tel. 586-0400), off Main Street. The dining room accented with regional artwork is pleasant, but in the warmer months if the mosquitos aren't too fierce, I prefer eating outside on the terrace. A complimentary basket of corn chips and salsa was hastily dispatched before I settled into pollo verde, a breast of chicken baked with mild green chiles, cheese, tomatoes, and cilantro for $10. Portions of food and drink are generous; a frosty margarita costs $3.50. La Cazuela (it means "earthen cooking pot") is open for brunch on Saturday and Sunday from 11am to 3pm; daily for dinner 5 to 9pm, until 10pm on Saturday and Sunday. Buen provecho!

On Northampton's main street is **Paul and Elizabeth's** (tel. 584-4832), a natural-foods restaurant. The main entrance is at 150 Main St., with a second entrance on Old South Street above Herrell's Ice Cream. In the pleasant dining room you'll see a cross-section of Northampton society dining on fresh fish, salads, tempura, fresh-baked breads, and desserts. Prices are quite moderate. For the fish lunch of the day, with salad, rice, and tea, you can get away for under $10. Wine and beer are served. Hours are 11:30am to 9:15pm (to 9:30pm on Friday and Saturday); closed Sunday.

The **Iron Horse Music Hall,** 20 Center St. (tel. 584-0610), is just a few steps off Main Street right downtown. It's the real thing: a converted storefront with newspaper readers, poets and proto-poets, and a full schedule of entertainment in the evenings, from the best in the Northeast to nationally known folk, jazz, rock, and blues artists. Drop by, pick up a schedule, and have one of a dozen coffees, or one of 52 beers. Full breakfasts, cheese boards, Greek salads, quiche, chocolate desserts, and fully licensed liquor bar are available from 8am to midnight daily (from 9am on weekends).

WHAT TO SEE

You'll want to take a tour of **Amherst College,** founded in 1821. The information booth on the Town Common in Amherst can furnish you with a handy map and guide. The college is all around you. Want more information? Contact Amherst College, Converse Hall (tel. 413/542-2000).

The sprawling campus of the **University of Massachusetts** takes more time to see, but there is a free PVTA bus line you can use, and an excellent campus map. Ask at the information booth on the Common, or at the information desk in the Campus Center (east end of second floor concourse; tel. 413/545-0111). U. Mass., by the way, was founded in 1863 as Massachusetts Agricultural College. Present enrollment on the Amherst campus is about 24,000—compare that to Amherst College's 1,500.

The roads between Amherst, Northampton, and South Hadley form a triangle and are some of the prettiest in the area. Rte. 116 between Amherst and South Hadley passes **Hampshire College,** the newest and most unconventional of the area's colleges. Farther along the road you may want to stop at **Atkins Fruit Bowl** (tel. 253-9528). Cider, pumpkins, apple picking, maple sugar products, and locally grown produce are all here. Atkins has grown so large from its humble beginnings as a farm stand that it now stays open daily, year round. Continuing along, you'll climb into the tiny Holyoke Mountain Range, the only range of mountains that runs east to west. Well-marked hiking trails lead in from the visitors center here. Once over "the notch," you'll coast down toward South Hadley.

Mount Holyoke College in South Hadley bears the distinction of being the country's oldest women's college, founded in 1837. The lovely campus was originally designed by Frederick Law Olmsted, who fashioned so many beautiful parks and forests during the 19th century. The campus now boasts a $9-million sports complex, an equestrian center, a Japanese teahouse and meditation garden, and a unique handcrafted classical organ (one of the last designed by Charles B. Fisk) in the chapel. The College Art Museum is open year round to campus visitors, and the Summer Theater offers plays in a tent on the green Tuesday through Saturday nights. The enrollment at Mount Holyoke is about 1,900 women. For a campus tour, call 413/538-2023.

On the way from South Hadley to Northampton on Rte. 47 (a gorgeous drive especially in the spring and fall), take a detour to **Skinner State Park** at the top of Mt. Holyoke (the mountain, not the college). On a clear day from the Summit House you'll have a great view of the winding Connecticut River, the fertile valley's patchwork of farmland, church and college steeples, and distant mountain ranges.

Also worthy of a stroll is the pretty campus of **Smith College** in Northampton, founded in 1871. You can arrange for a tour of the campus by contacting the Office of Admission, Garrison Hall, Northampton, MA 01063 (tel. 413/585-2500). But the handy campus guide folder available at the college switchboard in College Hall, and from the Office of Admission, may well satisfy your needs. Smith's enrollment is about 2,700 women.

For a closer look at the Connecticut River, climb aboard the *Quinnetukut II* riverboat for a 12-mile, 1½-hour interpretive **boat cruise.** Geology, ecology, and history of the river are the featured subjects, but the scenery alone is worth the fee: $6 per adult ($5 for seniors), $2.50 per child 14 and under. To check prices and schedules, call 413/659-3714. Call to make reservations so that you're sure to get the cruise you want. Buy your tickets at the Northfield Mountain Recreation and Environmental Center, on Rte. 63 to the north of Rte. 2, due east of Greenfield (take I-91 north to Exit 27, then Rte. 2 east, then Rte. 63 north).

OLD DEERFIELD

About 15 miles north of Northampton and Amherst on Rtes. 5 and 10 is **Historic Deerfield,** P.O. Box 321, Deerfield, MA 01342 (tel. 413/774-5581), a wide street lined with well-preserved 18th-century houses. Unlike Old Sturbridge Village or Mystic Seaport. Deerfield lets you walk its streets for free and admire the nice old buildings and the setting; there is an admission charge (for 2-day entry) to all houses. Each of the houses has a guide or two who will give a 30-minute tour. Adults pay $7.50, children 6 to 17 pay $4. You can visit every day of the year (except Thanksgiving, Christmas Eve, and Christmas Day) from 9:30am to 4:30pm. The information desk at the museum across from the Deerfield Inn has maps, brochures, information, and a short audiovisual show which gives you an overview of the Village.

The **Wright House** (1824), beautiful in itself, holds collections of Chippendale and Federal furniture, American paintings, and Chinese export porcelain.

The **Flynt Textile Museum** (1872) houses a large collection of textiles, costumes, and needlework from America, England, and continental Europe.

The **Henry N. Flynt Silver and Metalwork Collection** (1814) holds the museum's collection of silver, pewter, and other base metals.

Allen House (1720) is furnished with items made in Boston and the Connecticut River Valley.

Stebbins House (1799–1810) is a wealthy landowner's residence, with the rich period furnishings you might expect such a grandee to have.

Barnard Tavern (1740–95) is a favorite with children because some of its rooms have exhibits that are okay to touch.

Wells-Thorn House (1717–51) has a series of period rooms extending from the frontier to the Federal periods.

Dwight House (1725) was actually built in Springfield, and moved to Deerfield in 1950. Local furniture and a period doctor's office are the attractions.

The **Sheldon-Hawks House** (1743) was home for the same family during two centuries. Rich Deerfield farmers, the Sheldons were able to buy the best available at the time.

Ashley House (1730) was the minister's residence in old times, and by the look of it, this wasn't such a bad life.

One of the most fascinating exhibits is the **Ebenezer Hinsdale Williams House** (1816), which is open to view as a restoration-in-progress. The tour fills you in on the technical and historical work being done to re-create the house as it may have been between 1816 and 1838.

Besides the exhibits of Historic Deerfield, you should see the **Memorial Hall Museum,** at the corner of Memorial Street and U.S. 5 and 10 (tel. 413/774-7476), open every day May through October from 10am to 4:30pm (from 12:30 to 4:30pm on weekends). Admission costs $2.50 for adults, $1.50 for students, 75¢ for children 6 to 12.

Memorial Hall (1798) was the original home of famed Deerfield Academy, still one of New England's most prestigious private schools. Less than a century after its construction, the building became a historical museum of Pocumtuck Valley life, both Indian and Puritan. Local furniture, pewter, tools, textiles, decoration, and Indian artifacts, arranged in period rooms, make up the collection. There are special collections for carved and painted chests, local embroidery, musical instruments, and glass-plate photographs (1880–1920) by the Allen sisters, Deerfield's talented early photographers.

But no exhibit brings life in Old Deerfield closer than the **Indian House Door.** Deerfield suffered two Indian massacres in its early days, and numerous other battles. On February 29, 1704, during the French and Indian War, the Sheldon House (now gone) was attacked, its door suffering chops and bashes. The attackers finally hacked a hole in the center, through which they got at the inhabitants. The door is pretty dramatic.

5. Springfield

Springfield is Massachusetts' third-largest city, with a solid place in American history and life. The Springfield Armory produced weapons for use by American troops in the War of 1812, and Union soldiers in the Civil War used the famous Springfield rifle. The armory was a virtual cornucopia of small arms, many of which you can still see in its museum.

Yankee ingenuity and technical prowess were lavished on weapons, yes, but on other things as well. The monkey wrench was invented here, as were steel-bladed ice skates and the first American planetarium.

Elegant as these things may be, they were not Springfield's finest products. This honor is reserved for the Duryea and the Rolls-Royce. The Duryea brothers, Charles and Frank, built the first practical internal-combustion engine automobile (1894) on the top floor of the building at 41 Taylor St. And for a short time in the 1930s the world's most elegant auto, the Rolls-Royce, was assembled here in Springfield.

Among all its inventions, only one has brought real world fame to Springfield: basketball. Yes, this is the place where, in 1891, Dr. James Naismith, a physical education instructor at Springfield's YMCA college, originated the game. The city has a suitable memorial, the Basketball Hall of Fame, a new structure (1985) that's fascinating and fun even if you're not sports-minded.

SEEING SPRINGFIELD

Located at the junction of I-90 (Mass. Turnpike) and I-91, Springfield is a city most people know only through the car window. Even though you're headed for somewhere else, spend a few hours here. Exit from I-91 at State Street, go to Main Street and you'll find Court Square, Springfield's heart, surrounded by fine buildings, including Symphony Hall, the First Congregational Church (1819), and the granite Hampden County Superior Courthouse, modeled somewhat on Venice's Palazzo Vecchio by H. H. Richardson. The statue in the square is of William Pynchon, who led the group of Puritans who settled here in 1636, and incorporated the town five years later.

Museum Quadrangle

Just northeast of Court Square is the **Springfield Library** (tel. 413/739-3871), at the Quadrangle, corner of State and Chestnut streets, open from noon to 5pm (closed Monday). Admission to the surrounding museums is free, though donations are accepted. Hours of operation are uncertain these days because of cutbacks in state funding. If you call ahead, you may find that the museums are open for longer hours than those noted below.

At the entrance to the Quadrangle, in Merrick Park, is Augustus St. Gaudens's statue called *The Puritan.*

The **George Walter Vincent Smith Art Museum** (tel. 413/733-4214) houses the collection of its eponymous founder, who amassed a packet manufacturing carriages, and then spent it on works of art, everything from Japanese armor to Islamic carpets. The armor collection is one of the finest outside the Orient, and the Chinese cloisonné is equally impressive. There are lacquer-work screens, textiles, ceramics, and a fine collection of 19th-century European and American paintings. The museum is open Thursday through Sunday from noon to 4pm.

The **Museum of Fine Arts** (tel. 413/732-6092) continues the theme in more than 20 galleries. Its collection is built on lesser masters, or lesser paintings of the great masters, but is a fine representation nonetheless. Pride of place—right above the main stairway—goes to Erastus Salisbury Field's *The Rise of the American Republic,* which can keep you busy for the better part of an hour. You'll see why. The Impressionist and Expressionist gallery includes a painting from Monet's *Haystacks* series, and works by Degas, Dufy, Gauguin, Pissarro, Renoir, Rouault, and Vlaminck. In the Contemporary gallery you'll find works by George Bellows, Lyonel Feininger, Georgia O'Keeffe, and Picasso, among others. Modern sculptures include some by Leonard Baskin and Richard Stankiewicz. The museum's hours are from noon to 4pm on Wednesday, Friday, Saturday, and Sunday.

Also in the Quadrangle is the **Springfield Science Museum** (tel. 733-1194), a good place to take the children. Besides the historic Seymour Planetarium, there's a multilevel African Hall with exhibits explaining that continent's diverse peoples, animals, and ecology. In the Dinosaur Hall, standing beneath the full-size replica of Tyrannosaurus Rex, you can learn what it feels like to be some creature's prospective lunch. In another exhibit, TAM (the Transparent Anatomical Mannikin) explains how her very visible and nicely illuminated organs and physical systems work. There's lots more. It costs several dollars to see one of the eight weekly planetarium shows, but admission to the museum itself is free. Hours are Thursday through Sunday from noon to 4pm.

The **Connecticut Valley Historical Museum** (tel. 413/732-3080) is devoted to the decorative and domestic arts of the Connecticut River Valley from 1636 to the present. Collections of furniture, pewter, and glass are enhanced by four period rooms: a 17th-century kitchen, a Federal-period dining room, and two rooms from an early 19th-century tavern. Hours are noon to 4pm Thursday through Sunday.

Springfield Armory

The Springfield Armory National Historic Site is on Federal Street at State Street, a 10-minute walk from Museum Quadrangle. This was the place where, from 1795 to 1968, a good proportion of our national defense budget was spent. Springfield Technical Community College now occupies the gun factories and officers' quarters, except for the **Small Arms Museum** (tel. 413/734-8551), open daily from 10am to 5pm, on Sunday from 1 to 5pm, for free.

There's an awful lot of firepower here, not just the Springfields and Garands that were made in the armory, but even some weapons dating from the 1600s, and lots of Remingtons, Colts, and Lugers. It is thought to be the world's largest such collection of weaponry, and is mighty impressive. Don't miss the Organ of Rifles.

Basketball Hall of Fame

This is where you have some fun. Get to Union Street, south of State Street, and head west, passing under I-91, and you'll come smack up against the Basketball Hall of Fame. Hours are 9am to 6pm daily July through Labor Day, 9am to 5pm the rest of the year. Admission costs $5 for adults, $3 for kids 9 to 15.

The Hall of Fame is no stuffy museum, but a very active place. The light, spacious structure is decorated with elements relating to the sport: One whole wall is made of those tiny strips of hardwood used on courts. Video displays abound, telling the history of the sport and recalling its most exciting games and players. In a stand-up cinema, you're surrounded by giant movie screens synchronized to make it seem as though you are right in the middle of the frenzied action on the court. In another exhibit, you step onto a conveyor belt from which you can shoot balls at baskets which vary in height and distance from you. At the end of the belt, try your skill at jumping to touch one of the tapes hanging from the ceiling, suspended at heights from 7 to 11 feet. You can see and do a lot here in less than an hour, but you could also spend an entire morning.

Indian Motorcycle Museum

Here's an odd one. Do you know Indian motorcycles, those early motorized two-wheelers? If you have any interest whatsoever in motorized transport, call 413/737-2624 or 732-6029 to make sure the Motorcycle Museum is open, then get on I-291 to the Page Boulevard exit, not far from the Mass. Pike interchange. Turn right (east) on Page Boulevard to an industrial complex and the small museum. If you're into motorized marvels at all, you've got to see this place. Admission is $2 for adults, $1 for children.

Starting on the second or third Wednesday in September, for about 12 days, West Springfield hosts New England's great state fair, **The Big E,** located on the grounds of the Eastern States Exposition (tel. 413/737-2443). There's an admission fee to the grounds, but lots to do once you're inside. Call for exact dates and ticket information. The fairgrounds are on Rte. 147, near the Westfield River.

---

6. The Berkshires: Lenox and Lee

In the 1700s, pioneers spreading through the lands west of Boston came to settle among the fertile fields of the Berkshires. At first the settlement at Lenox was called Yokuntown, after a local Indian chief, but the name was later changed to honor an English lord—Charles Lenox, Duke of Richmond—who was sympathetic to the American Revolutionary cause. Although small industries have at times appeared in the town, it has been predominantly rural and agricultural, and has remained unspoiled. In the 19th century business tycoons (including Andrew Carnegie) came to admire the tidy farms and streets of Lenox as the perfect place for a summer's retreat, and many of them bought up farms for this purpose. The houses are still standing for visitors to admire.

If Lenox is the dowager aunt, pristine and correct in her beauty, neighboring Lee is the boisterous 20th-century daughter, lively and more modern, somewhat careless of her beauty.

BERKSHIRE INFORMATION

Granddaddy of Berkshire informational founts is the **Berkshire Visitors Bureau,** Berkshire Common, Pittsfield, MA 01201 (tel. 413/443-9186 or toll free 800/237-5747 in New England except Massachusetts), which can provide you with information on all of Berkshire County, covering the entire western end of Massachusetts.

The **Northern Berkshire Chamber of Commerce** is at 69 Main St., North Adams, MA 01247 (tel. 413/663-3735).

In Lenox, apply to the **Lenox Chamber of Commerce,** Lenox Academy Building, Main Street (P.O. Box 646), Lenox, MA 01240 (tel. 413/637-3646).

In Lee, the local chamber of commerce maintains an **information booth** (tel. 413/243-0852) right on U.S. 20 (Main Street) in the center of town by the park (officially 10 Park Pl., Lee, MA 01238).

Berkshire Bed and Breakfast, P.O. Box 211, Williamsburg, MA 01096 (tel. 413/268-7244) publishes a directory of homes scattered throughout the Berkshires, the Pioneer Valley, and Sturbridge. Write for a copy or call between 9am and 6pm weekdays.

WHERE TO STAY

The overnight lodging situation in Lenox is not the best. Proprietors of inns and motels bemoan the short season and the incredible press of traffic on Tanglewood weekends, which thins out to less-than-capacity during the week. For most lodging places, rooms are in great demand. Some Tanglewood travelers stay as far east as Springfield, and drive to the concert, then back to Springfield. In any case, have reservations for weekends.

As you begin the task of making reservations, you will discover that many inns require a three-night minimum stay on weekends, and full payment in advance; some inns do not accept credit cards, but will take personal checks with proper identification. Children under the age of 8, or even 12, may not be accepted; pets, almost certainly not.

During the off-season, though, all that's missing from Lenox is Tanglewood and the crowds. The same gorgeous rooms are still here, but at a fraction of the price. More and more travelers are realizing this value and making the Berkshires a year-round destination.

Lenox's Inns

Of the Berkshire inns, none is more dignified or luxurious than **Wheatleigh,** West Hawthorne Road (P.O. Box 824), Lenox, MA 01240 (tel. 413/637-0610). Center of the vast estate is the tawny brick mansion in the style of a 16th-century Florentine villa which once belonged to the American-born Contessa de Heredia. The gracious turn-of-the-century, top-of-the-heap lifestyle has been preserved in the airy public rooms, the 17 porticoed and balconied guest rooms and suites, and the sweeping lawns. There are Tiffany windows, tennis courts, and beautiful views in this, the Berkshires' best. Breakfast and dinner are served. Rates (18% service charge and 5.7% tax included) range from $295 to $527 on weekends during summer and fall foliage, $136 to $341 midweek, and 50% less than that in winter. Full payment is required for a confirmed reservation. The restaurant compares New York's finest; dinner is served nightly except Monday. Don't miss the unrestored clock tower-

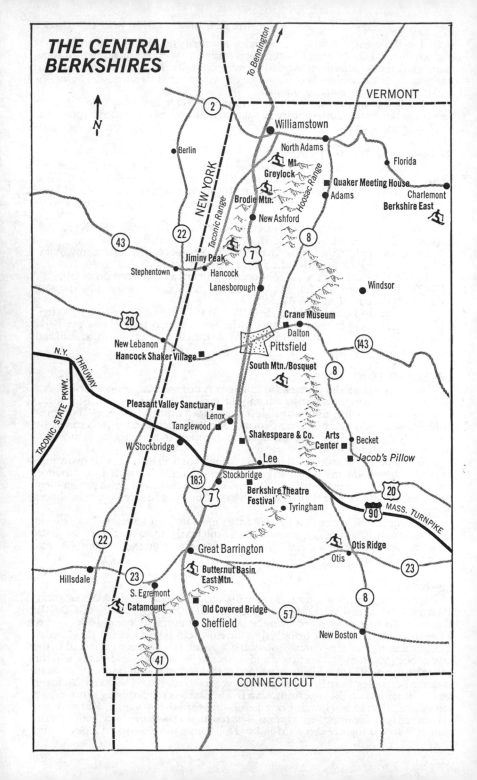

water tower-lookout down by the parking area. The contessa's poodles, all 20 of them, are buried nearby. To find Wheatleigh, start from the monument intersection in Lenox, go down the hill on Old Stockbridge Road, and turn right onto Hawthorne. At West Hawthorne Road, turn left and watch for signs.

Rather formal, the **Gateways Inn,** 71 Walker St., Lenox, MA 01240 (tel. 413/637-2532), is a fine place to stay, but an even finer place to dine. Quite near the center of Lenox, the Gateways is a grand old white mansion built by Harley Proctor of Proctor & Gamble in 1912. In-season summer and fall rates are $132 to $143 (weekdays) and $159 to $181 (weekends) for a double room with private bath and continental breakfast; from $236 to $325 for the cavernous Fiedler suite. With accommodations as large as these, it's no wonder the huge house boasts only eight rooms. During July and August there's a three-night minimum stay if you plan to visit from Thursday to Sunday. The main courses at dinner cost between $19.50 and $27.50 and may include medallions of beef or rack of lamb.

"Across the road from Tanglewood" is how the owners describe the **Apple Tree Inn and Restaurant,** 224 West St., Lenox, MA 01240 (tel. 413/637-1477). The name suits, for the century-old mansion is indeed in the midst of an apple orchard. Perched high on the hill directly opposite Tanglewood's West Street entrance, the gracious restaurant and public rooms, and many of the guest rooms, look out on a gorgeous panorama. Some rooms in the main house have a fireplace, most have private bath, all have air conditioning. There are also 20 modern rooms in the nearby guest lodge. The inn has its own heated swimming pool and clay tennis court, and in the summer and fall midweek charges $99 to $242 for a double room, more for suites.

The **Birchwood Inn,** 7 Hubbard St., Lenox, MA 01240 (tel. 413/637-2600), was built in the 1700s as a private home, was converted to a tavern for a few years, became a private home again, and since 1954 has been an inn. If an inn can feel as welcoming as a private home, this is it! Across from the Church on the Hill, overlooking the village, the Birchwood has nine double rooms (some with canopied beds), a two-room suite, and a carriage house with two efficiency apartments, all in a very fine and convenient location. Rates range from $101 to $186 double; continental breakfast is included.

Across Greenwood Street from the Church on the Hill is **Whistler's Inn,** 5 Greenwood St., Lenox, MA 01240 (tel. 413/637-0975), a half-timbered Tudor mansion built in 1820, now boasting 11 guest rooms (all with bath). Cozy, old worldly, and atmospheric, the house has seven fireplaces, seven acres of grounds, and a good location overlooking the village, just a short walk away. High-summer rates are $82 to $176 double, evening sherry and full breakfast included.

Right downtown in Lenox is the **Village Inn,** 16 Church St. (P.O. Box 1810), Lenox, MA 01240 (tel. 413/637-0020), a charming old landmark built in 1771 and furnished to match. All but two of the 29 rooms and suites have private bath, and prices range from $77 to $159 double in summer, tax included. The Harvest Restaurant serves brunch on Sunday and breakfast, afternoon tea, and full dinners nightly except Monday. There's also the congenial Village Tavern for drinks and light meals.

The **Garden Gables Inn** is very near the center of town at 141 Main St., Lenox, MA 01240 (tel. 413/637-0193), at the bottom of Church Hill down its own private road. The inn's name is appropriate, as you'll see when you drive or walk down the road through the gardens to the large white house with three sharply triangular gables set in its roof. The shape of the house gives you a clue that all the rooms are of different shapes and sizes, with lots of interesting nooks, crannies, and angles. All are furnished differently. Downstairs there are two cozy low-ceilinged living rooms with rows of books and fireplaces. Rooms are $77 to $143 in July and August, with a three-night minimum stay on weekends; the lowest price is for a midweek small room, and the highest price for just the opposite: a large room with private bath on a weekend. The inn has its own 72-foot swimming pool out back. Breakfast is included in the rates. Rates from November through May are dramatically lower. Guests are welcome year round.

Go down the hill from the monument intersection on Old Stockbridge Road, turn right onto Hawthorne Street, and at no. 15 is **Brook Farm Inn** (tel. 413/637-3013), about two blocks from the center of town. Brook Farm, run by Bob and Betty Jacob, has 12 guest rooms with private bath, a cozy, authentic Victorian atmosphere, a swimming pool, and prices of $69 to $143 double per night. The brochure claims "there's poetry here" and there sure is: Hundreds of volumes are carefully organized on shelves, renowned poets give readings, a poem-of-the-day is displayed, and guests, once they've learned to relax, have been known to spend an entire day pondering one or two poems. On a more somber note, there's that three-night minimum on summer weekends, as at most Lenox hostelries.

Walker House, 74 Walker St., Lenox, MA 01240 (tel. 413/637-1271), is right in the heart of town. Built in 1804, this spacious house has eight rooms, each with private bath, each named after a composer, some with fireplace, and many looking onto the three acres of lawn, gardens, and woods. Common rooms are decorated with modern art and attractive antiques, creating gracious eclectic spaces. Room prices of $114 to $162 double include breakfast, afternoon tea, and a small bottle of wine in your room.

Rookwood Inn, 19 Old Stockbridge Rd. (P.O. Box 1717), Lenox, MA 01240 (tel. 413/637-9750), is just a short walk down the hill from the monument intersection in Lenox. A charming Victorian place with a nice lawn and formal gardens, it can accommodate up to 35 guests in rooms with private bath. A full breakfast is included with rates of $110 to $154 double (tax included) on weekends in summer, depending on which room you choose. A few have a small screened-in porch, one has a multiwindowed turret. Spaces in this gracious turn-of-the-century "cottage" are larger than normal. The welcome from innkeepers Betsy and Tom Sherman is warm and friendly.

Built in 1885, **The Gables Inn,** 103 Walker St., Lenox, MA 01240 (tel. 413/637-3416), is a Queen Anne-style Berkshire "cottage." Once owned by the family of Edith Wharton's husband, this was her home for two years while she waited for her own cottage, the Mount, to be built. The present innkeepers have re-created the famous eight-sided library where Mrs. Wharton wrote many short stories. To surround yourself with all this grace and history (as well as a swimming pool and tennis court) will cost $93 to $156 single or double, breakfast included.

The **Candlelight Inn** (tel. 413/637-1555) is best known for its restaurant (described below), but there are eight rooms with private bath for rent in the big and graceful old house at 53 Walker St., corner of Church, Lenox, MA 01240. Off-season, the rooms go for $58 to $89, but in July, August, and October the prices rise to $88 to $198 double. The location is excellent. Call early for July, August, or October reservations.

The **Cliffwood Inn,** 25 Cliffwood St., Lenox, MA 01240 (tel. 413/637-3330), is a vast mansion set back from the street on its own crescent-shaped drive. As you pass through the curious split Dutch front door into the spacious foyer, you'll be surprised to learn there are only seven bedrooms (six with private bath, fireplace, and king-size bed) for rent—the huge place looks like it should hold many more. Evening wine and hors d'oeuvres and continental breakfast are included in the room price of $105 to $170 ($85 to $145 in winter) double. In 5 minutes you can walk into town from here.

A Lenox Guesthouse

The **Colonial Guest House,** 59 Walker St., Lenox, MA 01240 (tel. 413/637-0043), is right next door to the Candlelight Inn in downtown Lenox. A very fine old "summer cottage," it has spacious, airy rooms with simple, attractive furnishings which go with the house and its era. In fact it's the only Lenox summer cottage that hasn't been substantially altered by the addition of private bathrooms, bars, large kitchens, and other modern "improvements." The huge front porch, right in the center of town, is wonderful for people watching. Of the five rooms, two share an adjoining bathroom; the other three share baths in the hall. Prices are $88 double in summer. This place is really charming, but open only in July and August.

Inns in South Lee

The hamlet named South Lee is on Rte. 102, south of the Massachusetts Turnpike (I-90) and Lee proper. Right on Main Street and along a river bank is Charles Reynolds' elegant and authentic **Merrell Tavern Inn,** South Lee, MA 01260 (tel. 413/243-1794). Those two words describe it best, for this house, built in 1800, has been an inn since 1817. From 1947 to 1981 it belonged to the Society for the Preservation of New England Antiquities. Preservation of the inn's character, including a nonfunctioning but historic cagelike bar and authentic period furnishings, has obviously been paramount. In high season on weekends, prices (full breakfast included) are $72 to $143 per night; higher-priced rooms have fireplaces. During the week, prices drop to a very reasonable $72.

South Lee holds an inn famous for its cuisine as well as its rooms: the **Federal House,** Main Street, South Lee, MA 01260 (tel. 413/243-1824). Thomas O. Hurlbut had the brick Greek Revival mansion built in 1824 when he was head of the Owen and Hurlbut Paper Company here. Owned by the original family for 124 years, it was just recently converted to an inn. The seven guest rooms have many original Hurlbut touches and furnishings, but also modern private baths and air conditioning. Rates are $159 double in July and August, full breakfast included. Read on to find out about the restaurant.

Guesthouses in Lee

Lee has numerous guesthouses. They're not furnished in antiques like Lenox's inns and many don't have dining rooms, but they offer good lodging value in the Berkshires. Exactly what you pay depends on the particular room in the particular private home, but the price will easily be less than half that for a room in Lenox. As the rooms are scattered around town, the **Lee Chamber of Commerce** 10 Park Pl., Lee, MA 01238 (tel. 413/243-0852), handles reservations. An after-hours phone number is placed in the window of the information booth when it's closed.

A Motel

North of Lenox center on Rtes. 7 and 20 (same road) are numerous motels, extending all the way to Pittsfield. One of the closest to Lenox proper is also one of the least expensive. The **Susse Chalet Motor Lodge** (tel. 413/637-3560 or toll free 800/258-1980, 800/572-1880 in New Hampshire) has all the standard motel facilities in an attractive hillside location priced at $74 for one or two. These are midweek rates; weekend rates are substantially higher. It's the best value in the Berkshires, but you must reserve early. There is a two-night minimum stay during Tanglewood season.

WHERE TO DINE

Lenox is not covered with restaurants, as many of the classy places to eat are out in the countryside. But for a snack or a good dinner in town, try one of these.

Very successful is the **Church Street Café,** "an American bistro" at 69 Church St. (tel. 637-2745). Lunch, dinner, and Sunday brunch are served daily in the small, cozy dining rooms or out on the pleasant covered decks. Service is personal and informal, and prices are quite moderate for Lenox. I had baked native goat cheese with minced greens to start; then charcoal-grilled Jamaican chicken. A lemon-almond tart and espresso finished up, and the bill—including tax, tip, and a half bottle of the California house wine—was $34. The pasta is homemade here, and the country pâté too. Luncheon prices include $7 sandwiches and a few good southwestern items; dinner starts at $12.

Local restaurateur Jimmy De Mayo is at it again, this time with **Lenox 218** (tel. 637-4218) on Main Street slightly out of town. The exterior gives you no hints about the upscale, art deco interior. Chairs and tables are black, linens are gray in the evening, and the ceilings are high. As for the food, try appetizers of fried zucchini in a tomato-basil salsa or prosciutto and fresh fruit for lunch, followed by an all-meat pot pie or a California-style vegetable sandwich. Without a beverage lunch will cost $9 to $12, tax and tip included. Main courses at dinner run $13 (for fillet of scrod) to $19 (for French lamb chops grilled with mint conserve). The restaurant is open 11:30am to 2:30pm and 5 to 10pm every day.

The **Candlelight Inn,** 53 Walker St., at the corner of Church Street (tel. 637-1555), right near the center of town, is warm, friendly, and popular with locals and visitors alike. The menu lists a good number of appetizers and a selection of main courses, most of which are continental favorites like shrimp in a mustard-scampi sauce. Lunch at the Candlelight Inn is served daily from noon to 2:30pm in the summer only; dinner is every day from 6 to 9:30pm. You don't have to dress up, but you'll feel better if you do. Expect to make reservations and to spend $30 to $40 per person here.

For Breakfast

It's easy to find "kiwi-fruit this" and "shiitake-mushroom that" in Lenox, but where do you find breakfast eggs and bacon, hash browns, and fresh coffee at 7:30am, for $3.25? At **Cherry's,** 4 Franklin St., very near the town hall and police station, that's where. After 11:30am the menu switches to sandwiches and platters priced from $2 to $4. The eatery is run by the Desista School, and many of its students are employed here in the school's culinary training program.

Dinner in South Lee

The aforementioned **Federal House** on Rte. 102 in South Lee (tel. 243-1824) is among the Berkshires' more acclaimed restaurants. Elegantly set tables are arranged in the mansion's original dining room, front parlor, and billiards room. To get a table on Friday or Saturday evening you must reserve well in advance for one of the two seatings. The fare is continental and classic, with innovative touches: flounder stuffed with scallops, roast duckling with brandied plums, or perhaps thinly sliced veal sautéed in Grand Marnier. The bill at dinner will come to around $40 per person, perhaps more if you get extravagant with the wine list. No lunch is served, but there's brunch on Sunday, with a smoked salmon omelet ($10). Good!

WHAT TO DO

The number-one activity in Lenox is, of course, the **Tanglewood Music Festival,** the summer season of the Boston Symphony Orchestra. Since 1934 the concerts have been held in July and August on the grounds of a fine estate called Tanglewood, about a mile from the center of Lenox out in the Berkshire Hills. Over 50 concerts —by full orchestra, chamber groups, and soloists in recital—take place during the Tanglewood season, including the famous weekend BSO concerts. In addition to the seasoned musicians from the Boston Symphony, there are performances by the young and extremely promising musicians who attend the Tanglewood Music Center for study and advanced training. Maestro Seiji Ozawa, now music director of the BSO, was once among this young up-and-coming elite. On the Labor Day weekend there's a special Jazz at Tanglewood program featuring such jazz greats as Ray Charles, Betty Carter, the Dizzy Gillespie quintet, Ella Fitzgerald, and the Modern Jazz Quartet.

Programs of the concert series are available from the information booth in Lenox, or by mail from Symphony Hall, 301 Massachusetts Ave., Boston, MA 02115. For concert information, call the Tanglewood Concert Line (tel. 413/637-1666), July through August. For other information, call Symphony Hall (tel. 617/266-1492) until early June; from early June until the end of the season, call Tanglewood (tel. 413/637-1940).

Seats in the Music Shed ($12 to $60) are bought up early, but general admission tickets to the grounds ($8 or $9.50, depending upon the concert) are easy to find at Tanglewood. All tickets can be bought by phone through **TICKETMASTER** (tel. 617/787-8000 in Boston, 212/307-7171 in New York City, toll free 800/877-1414 elsewhere).

Special excursions to Tanglewood concerts are offered by various tour companies, including, in New York City, **Biss Tours** (tel. 718/426-4000), **Casser Tours** (tel. 212/840-6500), and **Parker Tours** (tel. 718/459-6565). From Boston, **K&L Tours** (tel. 617/267-1905) will take you there, or you can catch a bus run by Peter Pan Bus Lines (tel. 617/426-7838).

Tanglewood Tips

If you drive to Tanglewood for one of the BSO concerts, here are some tips to make things easier. First, expect heavy highway traffic. Plan to get to Tanglewood proper by 6pm or earlier (the concert begins at 8:30pm). Bring your picnic lunch— that's what everyone does, and that's why the parking lots fill up early, and that's why no one minds getting there 3 hours before the concert begins. Expect a tremendous jam of traffic when you leave at the end of the concert. The flood is ably directed by Tanglewood staff, but the exodus takes time nonetheless.

Other Concerts

Tanglewood has begun to sponsor a series of popular, folk, and rock concerts as well as the more lofty Tanglewood Music Festival series. When you call 413/637-1600, ask about what's coming up in the **Popular Artists' Series.**

South Mountain Concerts (tel. 413/442-2106), in nearby Pittsfield, specializes in chamber music, and concerts begin in August and last into October. South Mountain Concerts was started in 1918 in a lovely old hall located a mile south of Pittsfield on U.S. 7 and 20. For a printed schedule of concerts, drop a line to the South Mountain Association, P.O. Box 23, Pittsfield, MA 01202.

Shakespeare and Edith Wharton

What do the two have in common? **The Mount** (tel. 413/637-1899) is a house and gardens planned by the Pulitzer Prize–winning author. You can tour the house, and watch a salon drama based on Ms. Wharton's life and works, June through October, Tuesday through Friday from noon to 4pm, on weekends from 10am to 4pm.

On Tuesday through Sunday afternoons at 1 or 2pm and evenings at 8pm, an outdoor stage at the Mount is the setting for Shakespearean plays staged by **Shakespeare & Company,** Lenox, MA 01240 (tel. 413/637-1197; box office at 413/637-3353). Shakespeare in the open air on a warm summer evening is definitely among the finer things in life, let me tell you!

The Mount is located just south of Lenox, at the junction of Rtes. 7 and 7A.

Sightseeing in Lenox

Lenox is home to the **Berkshire Scenic Railway Museum** (tel. 637-2210), where you can find out about local railroad lore, poke around in a New Haven Railroad caboose, watch a complex model railroad run, and see railroading videos; there's a gift shop too. Nostalgic excursion trains used to run from the museum on a 15-mile route connecting Lenox, Lee, Stockbridge, and Great Barrington, but they've recently been discontinued, at least temporarily, in a dispute over use of the tracks. Drop by, or call, for latest information on the trains.

In Lenox proper, be sure to walk to the top of the hill on Main Street (U.S. 7), north of the center of town, to see the **Church on the Hill,** a very fine New England Congregational church building erected in 1805.

Otherwise, long walks or a drive around the "back streets" and lanes of Lenox can turn up unexpected sights: tremendous mansions, even small castles, nestled in fine parks and copses of trees, once occupied for a few months in summer by commercial and industrial magnates and their immediate families. Many of the mansions are still in private hands, enjoyed by an ever-widening circle of the descendants of the original builders. Most are not open to the public, so you must settle for tantalizing looks from the sidewalk.

For a beautiful hike through 1,000 acres of the Berkshire countryside, find your way to the **Pleasant Valley Sanctuary,** northwest of Lenox. Follow the signs, or take Rte. 7A north to West Dugway Road, then West Mountain Road. Pay the admission fee ($3 adults, $1 children 6 to 12) from dawn to dusk daily (closed Monday), and set out on the 7 miles of nature trails to explore native Berkshire flora and fauna.

Sightseeing in Lee

The most notable sight in Lee is not in Lee at all, but in the tiny neighboring village of Tyringham, 5 miles south of Lee along the Tyringham Road. It's the **Gingerbread House,** a curious thatched cottage built as a studio by sculptor Henry Hudson Kitson at the turn of the century. Kitson's most famous statue is the one of Captain Parker *(The Minute Man)* on Lexington Green. Now an art gallery, the Gingerbread House is open 10am to 5pm daily in the summer and fall. Admission is $2 for adults, 50¢ for children 6 to 12.

Jacob's Pillow Dance Festival

In Lee, a dilapidated barn served as the birthplace, in 1932, of a major American dance festival. Bought by Ted Shawn and renovated for performances, the barn and the festival grew larger and more important over the years, enlisting the talents of Alvin Ailey, Merce Cunningham, and similar lights.

The 10-week Jacob's Pillow season begins in late June and runs through August. For a season brochure, contact Jacob's Pillow Dance Festival, P.O. Box 287, Lee, MA 01238 (tel. 413/243-0745). The performance center is 8 miles east of downtown Lee, off U.S. 20. Performing groups change weekly and ticket prices range from $24 to $28.

---

7. Stockbridge

Any way you look at it, Stockbridge is a very beautiful town. Its wide Main Street is lined with grand houses and other buildings each set apart in its own lawns and gardens. Stately trees fill the skyline. Stockbridge is the center of many Berkshire activities, including the Berkshire Playhouse (details below) and also once the home of famed painter Norman Rockwell.

The town of **West Stockbridge** is a different municipality altogether, 4 miles west of Stockbridge and Lenox. The dilapidated town was bought up by developers some years ago and reconstructed, expanded, and spruced up as a real-life Disneyland for shoppers, browsers, and sightseers. Purists may say the town is now like a movie set, but most visitors enjoy their time here, meandering along the short streets, peering in windows and shops, having a meal or a cool refresher. It's all pretty commercial, it's true, but that's the attraction.

TOURIST INFORMATION

The Stockbridge Kiwanis Club maintains an **information booth** on Main Street right in the center of town. Guides will provide you with pamphlets and brochures, answer your questions, and even help you find an inexpensive room in a private home—but only if lodging conditions are tight. If the local motels are not full, they'll direct you to one of those, as the private-home rooms are more of an emergency measure.

WHERE TO STAY AND DINE

The **Red Lion Inn,** on Main Street in Stockbridge, MA 01262 (tel. 413/298-5545), is a town institution. The huge white frame hotel with a wide front porch was established as an inn in 1773. Always bustling with guests and diners in summer, the Red Lion charges its high-season rates on weekends from late May through October. Minimum weekend stay is two nights, at $86 (shared bath) or $118 to $144 (private bath) per night, double. On weekdays the rate drops to $68 or $89 to $107 for the same double with bath.

The Red Lion is also Stockbridge's premier place for dining. Besides the formal dining room, there's the Widow Bingham Tavern, a rough-hewn and woody place of colonial flavor. The Lion's Den, downstairs, is the cocktail lounge with a sandwich-and-salad menu. Plan to spend about $35 or $40 per person for a luxurious beef dinner in the dining room, about the same in the Widow Bingham Tavern. In summer there's dining in the pretty courtyard in back. By the way, the building dates from 1897, when it was constructed on the site of an earlier inn which was completely destroyed by fire.

In West Stockbridge

West Stockbridge harbors several establishments offering lodging and meals at lower rates than in Stockbridge proper. These are well worth a look.

So many places call themselves country inns these days, even though they have downtown locations, Muzak and cable color TV, bus tours, and whirlpools. The **Williamsville Inn** (tel. 413/274-6118) is a true country inn, however. It's out in the country, about 4 miles south of West Stockbridge on Rte. 41. Some of the 15 guest rooms have fireplaces, some have four-poster beds; all have private bath and fine old furnishings. Some are in the main house, while others are out back in a renovated barn and a cottage. The inn, built in 1797, has 10 acres of grounds, a swimming pool, clay tennis court, and woodland trails. The dining room is well known and well regarded. June through October, rooms cost $106 to $138 double, and a three-day minimum is applied on summer and holiday weekends. The address is simply Rte. 41, West Stockbridge, MA 01266.

Over in West Stockbridge for the day, one of the very best things you can do is have a meal at the **Truc Orient Express,** on Harris Street (tel. 232-4204). Light and airy, with wicker furniture, it is an exceptionally attractive place, and a welcome change from the antique-packed dining rooms hereabouts. The "Orient" in the name is Vietnam: appetizers on such as mien cua (crab and bean-thread soup) or ga nuong chanh (skewered lemon chicken) with a main course of sautéed squid with bamboo shoots or fresh flounder in a spicy sweet-and-sour sauce. For dessert, the customary lychee or not-so-customary flan finish up nicely. Such a dinner costs $16 to $25, and if you choose carefully you might even squeeze a glass of saké or plum wine into the price. There are lots of vegetarian dishes too. Open for lunch and dinner. Don't miss it.

WHAT TO SEE AND DO

Stockbridge is rich in historical and cultural attractions. You'll want to visit the **Norman Rockwell Museum,** in the Old Corner House (tel. 298-3822) in the center of Stockbridge, which has a large permanent collection of Norman Rockwell paintings. The famed American illustrator did many pictures for magazine covers and posters, and the originals of those paintings, or at least many of them, are housed in the Old Corner House. Admission is $5 for adults, $1 for children ages 5 to 16, and it's open from 10am to 5pm every day; closed last two weeks in January.

Two other old houses worth a visit are owned by the Trustees of Reservations (tel. 298-3239). **Mission House** (1739), on Main Street, built by the Rev. John Sergeant to carry out his Christian mission to the Stockbridge Indians. The house is a National Historic Landmark, and is furnished in American pieces all dating from 1740 or earlier. Guided tours are offered Memorial Day through Columbus Day, Tuesday through Sunday and holidays, from 11am to 4pm. Admission is $3.50 for adults, $1 for children 6 to 12.

Naumkeag, on Prospect Hill, was built by Stanford White for Joseph Choate, a New York City attorney, in 1886. Many of the sumptuous furnishings are still in place, and there are extensive formal gardens designed by Fletcher Steele and Miss Choate. Take Pine Street from the Red Lion Inn, then turn onto Prospect Street to reach Naumkeag. The palatial house is open Tuesday through Sunday and Monday holidays from 10am to 4:15pm, late May to early September. From early September to mid-October it's open weekends and Monday holidays only. Admission is $5 adults for house and garden, $3 adults for gardens only, and $1 for children 6 to 12.

Right near Naumkeag is another sumptuous estate reached by the same route via Pine Street and Prospect. From its beginning as an Indian mission in 1734, the estate atop Eden Hill in Stockbridge has seen many additions over the years. Having served as a mansion for the wealthy and as a private school, it is now a monastery for the **Marian Fathers,** and visitors are welcome to stroll the grounds and take in the impressive buildings and the views of the Berkshire Hills.

Chesterwood

Just a few miles from Stockbridge is Chesterwood (tel. 298-3579), the former summer estate of Daniel Chester French, sculptor of the statue of Lincoln that graces the Lincoln Memorial, and also of *The Minute Man* at Concord North Bridge. French (1850–1931) summered here from 1897 until 1931 and used the studio (built in 1898) near the house for his work. You can visit both the mansion and studio as well as an 1800s barn which has been converted to a gallery featuring exhibits on French's life and work. A lovely country gentleman's garden, a woodland walk laid out by French himself, a panoramic view of Monument Mountain, and a museum store are unexpected extras to a Chesterwood visit. Admission fees go toward the upkeep of the property, which is maintained by the National Trust for Historic Preservation. Adults pay $5; children 7 to 18 pay $1; children under 6 are admitted for free. Chesterwood is open daily from 10am to 5pm May through October. To get there, drive west on Rte. 102 from Stockbridge, and follow the signs.

Berkshire Theater Festival

In the **Berkshire Playhouse** (tel. 413/298-5536) and in a big red barn close by, the Berkshire Theater Festival hosts a series of performances now in its second half century. From late June through August, plays are staged Monday through Saturday evenings, and on Thursday and Saturday afternoons. The classic plays with name performers are in the playhouse proper. The Unicorn Theater Company puts on experimental and new plays in the barn, and throughout July and August special children's theater performances are held outside, under a tent, Thursday through Saturday at 11am.

Hancock Shaker Village

North of West Stockbridge a 9-mile drive along Rte. 41, then west on U.S. 20, will bring you to the outskirts of Pittsfield, Mass., and Hancock Shaker Village, one of the most fascinating sights in the Berkshires. Up until 1960, the village was home to members of a religious sect noted for their quiet, simple lives, hard work, and quality handcrafts.

"The United Society of Believers in Christ's Second Appearing" or "The Millennial Church," more readily known as the Shakers, was a movement begun in 1747 in England as an offshoot of Quakerism. It gained momentum when Ann Lee, "Mother Ann," proclaimed that she had received the "mother element" of the spirit of Christ. Imprisoned for her zeal, Mother Ann and eight followers immigrated to the American colony of New York and founded a settlement near Albany in 1774. By the time Mother Ann died in 1784, her followers were ready to spread out and found other Shaker communities based on the principles of communal possessions, celibacy, pacifism, open confession of sins, and equality of the sexes. The communities were organized into "families" of 30 to 90 people. Work was a consecrated act, reflected in the high quality of workmanship and design in Shaker furniture and crafts: In effect, every product was a prayer.

Shakers, named for the trembling that came upon them from their religious zeal, believed that God had both a male and female nature. The male was embodied in Jesus, the female in Mother Ann. Though converts devoted themselves and all their possessions to the community, they were free to leave at any time. Celibacy and the onslaught of the 20th century's complex lifestyle almost put an end to Shakerism after more than two centuries; there are only a handful of the faithful left now, living in small communities in Maine and New Hampshire.

One cannot help but admire a gentle fanaticism which feeds on kindliness and good hard work. Shaker products are still copied and admired, because these good people took daily tasks to the level of an art. Twenty of the original Shaker buildings at Hancock have been restored, furnished with artifacts of Shaker life, and staffed with men and women who can explain and demonstrate the Shakers and their lives to you. Hancock Shaker Village, P.O. Box 898, Pittsfield, MA 01202 (tel. 413/ 443-0188), is open late May through October from 9:30am to 5pm every day; 10am to 3pm during April, early May, and November. Admission is $8 per adult, $4 for children 6 to 12, $7.25 for seniors and students, $22 for a family (two adults and children under 18). Don't miss it.

Skiing

There are at least six well-known downhill ski areas in the Berkshires. Call to get information on ski conditions and year-round activities: **Butternut** (tel. 413/528-2000), **Bosquet** (tel. 413/442-8316), **Catamount** (tel. 413/582-1262), **Brodie** (tel. 413/443-4752), **Berkshire East** (tel. 413/339-6617), **Jiminy Peak** (tel. 413/738-5500), and **Otis Ridge** (tel. 413/269-4444).

---

8. Great Barrington and Egremont

Although it is certainly not a city, Great Barrington is the largest town in the southern Berkshires, a major crossroads and commercial center. Supplies and services that you might not find in Stockbridge or Lenox will be available here.

Great Barrington was an important town even before the Revolution. The citizenry, angered at Britain's denial of the colonials' rights, prevented the king's judges from convening in the courthouse here in 1774. In the 19th century Mr. and Mrs. Edward Searles became the town's benefactors, establishing many public buildings and constructing for themselves an immense mansion in a 100-acre park which nudges right into the center of town.

INFORMATION

There's a little information kiosk in the center of town, by the Berkshire Motor Inn and Searles' Castle, on Main Street. It's operated by the **Southern Berkshire Chamber of Commerce,** 362 Main St., Great Barrington, MA 01230 (tel. 413/ 528-1510). You'll get help finding a room if you need one. Donations are accepted to defray expenses.

WHERE TO STAY

A short ride from the center of Great Barrington on the way to South Egremont are two of the Berkshires' best lodging places.

Inns and Guesthouses

Jo and Ray Elling run **Elling's Guest House,** R.D. 3, Box 6, Great Barrington, MA 01230 (tel. 413/528-4103), which is a mile from the center of town southwest along Rte. 23. The house, which dates from 1746, is actually more like an inn. The six rooms are all pretty and quaint; those with private bath rent for $88, and those with shared bath for $72. An extra person in a room pays $15; no children under 12. The rates go down $10 to $15 in winter, but whatever the season, a good continental breakfast is included. No credit cards are accepted, by the way, and there is a two-night minimum stay on weekends in season. Quiet, friendly, reasonably priced, this is the best of the Berkshires.

A bit farther along the same road, 2½ miles from the center of town, is the **Seekonk Pines Inn,** 142 Seekonk Cross Rd., Great Barrington, MA 01230 (tel. 413/528-4192). As you come from town, look for it on the right-hand side, behind the pines. Linda and Chris Best are your hosts here, and their inn features a nice swimming pool, a garden from which they will sell you fresh produce, bicycles for rent, and a full breakfast; and in winter, a fireplace in the large living room, besides the cozy rooms. It's clean, neat rooms are decorated with antiques, old quilts, and Linda's watercolors, and moderately priced at $81 to $88 for a shared bath. For the suite with sitting area and room for four to sleep (perfect for a family or couple on a longer visit), and with private bath, the price for four is $140. An extra person pays $15. Discounts are given on stays of five days or more.

Motels

Besides these fine guesthouses, Great Barrington has motels. Numerous establishments are spread along U.S. 7 north of town, and one luxurious place is right in the center.

The **Berkshire Motor Inn,** at 372 Main St., Great Barrington, MA 02130 (tel. 413/528-3150), is right behind the town information booth and across the street from Searles Castle. The two-story building holds rooms with all comforts priced at $58 to $68 double Sunday through Thursday, $106 on Friday and Saturday in summer. An indoor pool, sauna, and central location are the bonuses.

If you have a car, try the **Lantern House Motel,** P.O. Box 97, Great Barrington, MA 01230 (tel. 413/528-2350), which is on U.S. 7 north of town, on the right. Accommodations are quite good (outdoor pool, room phone, AAA approval, and cable TV), and prices are moderate for the Berkshires in high season: $54 to $64 on weekdays, $79 to $92 on weekends.

An Inn in Egremont

The first thing you must know is that Egremont actually consists of two towns. North Egremont is a tiny place on Rte. 71, due west of Great Barrington. It has a country store, an inn-restaurant, and a few houses. South Egremont is a much bigger place, with several inns and restaurants, shops, and churches, and more antique dealers than you've ever seen in one place before. South Egremont, on Rtes. 23 and 41, is 4 miles southwest of Great Barrington.

A block off the highway in South Egremont (follow the signs) is the **Egremont Inn,** Old Sheffield Road, South Egremont, MA 01258 (tel. 413/528-2111), sometimes called the 1780 Egremont Inn. A stagecoach inn since the early days of the republic, the inn's 22 guest rooms now are fitted out with private baths and air conditioning, besides the period furnishings. A swimming pool and tennis courts provide entertainment the stagecoach never had. All of the village is within walking distance. Rooms are rented with continental breakfast and dinner included for $155 double on July and August weekends (two-night minimum). Monday through Wednesday you can rent a room with continental breakfast for $65 single, $90 double.

Staying in Sheffield

Five miles south of Great Barrington is the **Staveleigh House,** South Main Street, Sheffield, MA 01257 (tel. 413/229-2129). It's a homey bed-and-breakfast, run by two women who enjoy the slower pace of life in this quiet corner of the state. The mood is reflected in their comfortable living room and simple but lovely guest rooms. Antiques are used here, not doted over. The innkeepers enjoy chatting with the guests, suggesting outings, and making sure repeat guests aren't served the same breakfast twice. Doubles cost $66 to $93, singles $5 less. Only one room has a private bath.

WHERE TO EAT

In the center of town on Rtes. 23 and 41 is the **Old Mill** (tel. 528-1421), which in this case is indeed an old mill (1797) and blacksmith's shop. The rustic interior has been faithfully preserved, and rings to the conversation of diners every evening of the week. Much of the talk is of antiques, and the Old Mill menu sticks appropriately to the classics, though with original touches. Dinner with wine costs about $30 per person. Lunch is served on Saturday and Sunday.

D&J's American Grill, 11 Stockbridge Rd (tel. 528-3201), at the intersections of Rtes. 23 and 7 north, will serve you half a barbecued chicken for $7 or great barbecued ribs for $8 to $10. It's not fancy, but rather an authentic bit of the Berkshires urban landscape. D&J's is open from 11:30am to 9pm every day but Wednesday.

WHAT TO SEE AND DO

Great Barrington and south Egremont are the antiquer's towns par excellence. Everyone here, it seems, deals in antiques and old stuff. Browsing the shops is the daily passion, but several excursions out of town to nature spots provide an antidote to buy-and-sell.

Take U.S. 7 south from Great Barrington for about 10 miles, and turn onto Rte. 7A for Ashley Falls. Your destination, a mile from Ashley Falls along Rannpo and Weatogue roads, is **Bartholomew's Cobble,** bordering the Housatonic River. A "cobble" in this case is a high knoll of limestone, marble, or quartzite, 500 million years old, and covered with a rich and varied collection of native flora: trees, ferns, mosses, wildflowers. The nature reservation is owned by the Trustees of Reservations (tel. 229-8600), is open year round, and has 6 miles of hiking trails. A naturalist is on duty from mid-April to mid-October, Wednesday through Sunday from 9am to 5pm, to answer your questions and point out highlights.

Another pretty nature nook, good for a picnic, is **Bash Bish Falls,** 12 miles southwest of South Egremont, right on the New York state line. Take Rte. 41 south out of town, and turn right onto Mount Washington Road (signs for Catamount ski area). Follow signs to the falls, taking East Street, then West Street, and finally Bash Bish Falls Road, deep in the Mount Washington State Forest. You'll plunge into the valley carved by the Bash Bish Creek, and finally come to a parking area from which a steep trail leads to the falls. Stay on the road a bit farther and you'll come to another parking place, and an easier—but longer—trail. Stay on the road any longer and you'll end up in New York.

At the end of the trails, deep in the forest, is the 50-foot Bash Bish Falls, cascading into a chilly pool. A half hour's relaxation here on a hot summer's day is pretty close to Nirvana.

If mountain hiking is more to your taste, head north out of Great Barrington on U.S. 7, and after 4½ miles you'll see signs for **Monument Mountain.** There are two trails to the summit, one easier but slightly longer than the other. The hike to the top, a rest, and back down will take between 2 and 3 hours. The view at the summit is very fine.

---

9. Williamstown

The town was founded in 1753 as West Hoosuck, but its life and its name were soon affected by the career of one Ephraim Williams, Jr., a soldier in the British colonial army. Born in 1714, Williams surveyed several townships in these parts, then took command of fortifications which demarcated the frontier between the British and French North American empires. Among these defenses was Fort Massachusetts, which stood in North Adams.

Williams led a column of troops from Massachusetts toward the French positions on Lake George, and died in the fighting (1755). His will provided for the founding of a school in West Hoosuck, but only if the town took his name. It did, and Williams College enrolled its first students in 1793. The college now looks forward to celebrating its 200th anniversary in 1993.

Williams College, with an annual freshman class of 2,000, is the reason the town of 8,500 exists. It's a beautiful, delightful example of the New England rural college town.

GETTING THERE

You'll probably come to Williamstown by way of the Berkshires or southern Vermont. But if you are coming directly from Boston (145 miles) or New York City (165 miles), contact **Bonanza Bus Lines** (tel. toll-free 800/556-3815 or 617/423-5810 in Boston). You may have to change buses in Springfield or Pittsfield.

WHERE TO STAY

Far enough from Tanglewood to avoid the crush of its summer crowds, Williamstown is favored with a fine selection of small guesthouses and inns, two full-service hotels, and several moderately priced motels. You should have little trouble finding the sort of room you want in this charming Berkshire town, except when college events are in progress. Reserve early for dates in September (classes begin), October (foliage season), and early June (graduation).

Small Inns and Guesthouses

My favorite place in all Williamstown is the **River Bend Farm,** 643 Simonds Rd. (U.S. 7 North), Williamstown, MA 01267 (tel. 413/458-5504 or 458-3121), open April through November. This 1770 roadside inn and tavern-turned-farmhouse has been lovingly restored by Dave and Judy Loomis, who run it with an engaging low-key, unpretentious style that makes guests immediately feel at home. There are five rooms (sharing two baths) to rent at $53 double. True country-inn feeling is provided by the hosts' warm welcome, by the variety of interesting old furnishings at the inn, and by the bounteous, delicious breakfast included in the price. Go north on U.S. 7 a mile from Williamstown's information booth; turn left onto the private drive immediately after crossing a bridge over the river.

Dave and Judy Loomis also administer the **Field Farm Guest House,** 554 Sloan Rd., Williamstown, MA 01267 (tel. 413/458-3135), about 5 miles southwest of the information booth. A guesthouse in the country near historic Williamstown conjures images of a quaint Berkshire farmhouse or exuberant Victorian inn, so Field Farm comes as a surprise, almost as a shock. Set on 254 acres, the house was the country villa of Lawrence H. and Eleanore Bloedel, noted art collectors, who built it in 1948 in the clean, spare, understated style that came to dominate in the 1950s. Field Farm was bequeathed to the Trustees of Reservations in 1984. The five guest rooms share baths; four face the sunny lawns (one has its own deck), one faces the back. The huge, airy living room and dining room, the kitchen, tennis court, swimming pool, and hiking trails are yours to enjoy. Field Farm is open all year; a double room with breakfast costs $75.

Downtown next to the Williams Inn is **The House on Main Street,** 1120 Main St., Williamstown, MA 01267 (tel. 413/458-3031), a nice old Victorian house renovated by Henry Poses and opened as a bed-and-breakfast in the warm months. Two guest rooms have private bath, the other two share 1½ baths. Prices are $60 single (shared bath), $77 to $93 double, breakfast included. Call for advance reservations if you can.

Full-Service Hotels

The top-of-the-line hostelry in Williamstown is **The Orchards,** a mile east of the center of campus on Rte. 2, Williamstown, MA 01267 (tel. 413/458-9611 or toll-free 800/225-1517, 800/231-2344 in Massachusetts). Though a fairly simple modern stucco building on the outside, this 49-room inn's interior is an eclectic gallery of English antiques, Oriental carpets, and furnishings of classic design. The owners are especially proud of the 18th-century carved oak mantelpiece in the lounge, a nice little army of Victorian tin soldiers, and a fine collection of silver teapots. The courtyard has a quiet garden; there's also a swimming pool and exercise room. Standard guest rooms are nicely furnished in subdued colors, with thick carpets, his-and-hers washbasins, tub and shower trimmed in marble, and all the expected luxury-hotel touches. Superior rooms are larger, and some have a four-poster bed, fireplace, and little refrigerator. All rooms have one or two antique accent pieces (perhaps an armoire, desk, or dresser), and are priced from $140 to $200, single or double, tax included. The inn's dining room is the fanciest in town (details below).

The **Williams Inn,** at the junction of Rtes. 2 and 7, Williamstown, MA 01267 (tel. 413/458-9371; fax 413/458-2767), is the town's largest hostelry, with 100 rooms equipped with colonial-style furniture and the amenities expected in a comfortable full-service hotel. This is the town's "college hotel," a very comfortable place with a good dining room, a less formal tavern lounge, a heated indoor pool, men's and women's saunas, and a spa. You can walk to any point on campus from here. Rates are $83 to $99 single, $110 to $135 double, tax included, with junior suites costing a bit more. Children under 14 stay free in their parents' room; pets are welcome in first-floor rooms. November through March, prices are lower.

Motels

One motel is located within walking distance of anything on campus. Numerous others are along the highways (Rtes. 2W and 7) on the outskirts of town.

Very near the Williams Inn, and sharing its convenient location, is the **Northside Inn Motel**, 45 North St., Williamstown, MA 01267 (tel. 413/458-8107), on U.S. 7 just north of the information booth. This little two-story establishment has a small pool, and rooms equipped with air conditioning, ceramic tile bath, cable color TV, and telephone, priced at $53 double, tax included.

A Hikers' Lodge

The Appalachian Mountain Club operates **AMC Bascom Lodge**, P.O. Box 1652, Lanesboro, MA 01237 (tel. 413/743-1591; off season, call 603/466-2727) in the Mount Greylock State Reservation atop Massachusetts' highest peak. Bascom Lodge is one of those substantial, well-designed rustic hostelries built by the Civilian Conservation Corps in the 1930s; it's open from mid-May through late October. The simple accommodations here benefit from the mountain air and the closeness of the park's hiking trails, not to mention the panoramic views. Beds in the bunkroom, covered in snowy sheets and red wool blankets, cost $28 per adult, $15 per child under 10; the two private rooms go for $50 double. These nonmember rates are for Friday and Saturday from July on, and they include breakfast and taxes; prices are a few dollars lower on other days, and for AMC members. Simple but hearty, wholesome meals are served from an open kitchen in the spacious dining room overlooking the mountains; dinner costs less than $10. Call first, then write for reservations; the lodge is open from mid-May until late October.

WHERE TO DINE

You can easily find a good meal in town, and you may get entertainment as well. During the summer months when the Williamstown Theater Festival is in progress, cabaret troupes offer song-and-dance revues in some local restaurants after the curtain has fallen on festival's main evening performance. When you've exhausted all the dining possibilities in Williamstown, try one of the places in Bennington, Vt., a mere 13 miles to the north along U.S. 7 (see Chapter XIV).

Fancy Dinners

Williamstown's fanciest is the dining room of **The Orchards**, a mile east of the campus center on Rte. 2 (tel. 413/458-9611), open for all three meals every day. The inn's several small dining rooms, though of modern construction, gleam with dark-wood accents, mirrors, and brass candle lamp sconces. Potted plants and antiques lend an old-fashioned air. Chef Kevin Cook's interesting menu of comestibles combines traditional favorites with original creations. It changes daily, but recently he offered appetizers of smoked trout with Gribiche sauce, sautéed escargot with roasted red peppers, and grilled quail with wild mushrooms alongside shrimp cocktail, clam chowder, and lobster bisque. Main courses included grilled sirloin, poached salmon, and such intriguing dishes as braised pheasant and polenta with shiitake-rosemary demiglacé, or sautéed sweetbreads with crawfish Madeira demiglacé. The pastry cart is bounteous, as you might imagine. A five-course table d'hôte costs about $35 to $45 per person, wine, tax, and tip included; ordering à la carte adds perhaps $5 to your bill. On Sunday, come for brunch; any afternoon, come for tea in the parlor.

Another good dining choice lies 2 miles south of town along U.S. 7. The inn named **Le Jardin** (tel. 413/458-8032) is noted for excellent dinners graciously served in semiformal old-fashioned country inn dining rooms. Dinner is the only meal offered, and it's on from 5 to 10pm Monday through Saturday. Sunday brunch begins at 11:30am, and the dinner menu is served all day until 9pm. Expect to spend about $40 per person, all included.

Just 100 yards down the hill from the information booth, north on U.S. 7, is **Le Country,** 101 North St. (tel. 413/458-4000), a restaurant with a longstanding reputation for good, standard fare in pleasant surroundings. Rough boards accent the dining room's white walls, and hunting prints add a note of country gentry life. The menu is short and to the point, listing longtime favorites such as coquilles St-Jacques, chicken divan, filet mignon, coq au vin, and veal curry. Start with marinated herring or shrimp cocktail, and end with cheesecake, pecan pie, or baba au rhum, and your bill will come to $28 to $35 per person, plus the cost of your wine. The wine list, too, is short and to the point, with bottles well chosen and prices surprisingly moderate, about $10 to $20, with a few up to $35. Service is slow (you are warned on the menu) but competent and friendly. Come for lunch Tuesday through Friday, 11:30am to 1:30pm, or dinner Tuesday through Sunday from 5 to 9pm; closed Monday.

Moderately Priced Meals

For moderately priced meals in Williamstown you must seek out **Water Street** (Rte. 43), the town's small commercial district; turn south off Rte. 2 by the Methodist church in the midst of the campus.

A few short blocks down Water Street is the **River House,** 123 Water St. (tel. 413/458-4820), Williamstown's most popular downtown restaurant. The homey, rustic dining room is pleasant and informal, with a fireplace, soft candlelight, a long wine-and-spirits list, and a menu that pleases everyone. Have roast turkey, steak, an Italian specialty, or baked scrod for dinner, and you'll get a salad, fresh bread, and rice pilaf with it for something like $10 to $16. The Tavern Room opens at 4pm; dinner is served from 5 to 10pm Thursday through Saturday, sandwiches and late-night snacks are served from 10pm until midnight. The restaurant is closed Monday.

Only 100 yards farther down Water Street is **Hobson's Choice,** 159 Water St. (tel. 413/458-9101), a big house converted to a restaurant. Dining rooms are paneled in wide rough boards with country curtains at the windows and lots of hanging plants. The mood is light and informal, the menu familiar and reasonably priced. Order a steak, veal, chicken, or seafood for dinner, and you'll get good, solid, dependable cooking for less than $14 to $18 per person, all included. The wine list is simple but adequate. Lunch and dinner are served Monday through Friday from 11:30am to 9pm, till 10pm on Saturday; closed Sunday.

Lighter Fare

For a quick breakfast, sandwich, pizza, snack, or ice cream cone the place to go is **Spring Street,** one long block west of Water Street in the midst of the campus. This short commercial street is crowded with good places to find quick pick-me-ups, like the **Slippery Banana Deli** (tel. 413/458-4788), **Colonial Pizza** (tel. 458-8014), a bakery called the **Clarksburg Bread Co.** (tel. 458-2251), and **Goodies Café** (tel. 458-3916).

WHAT TO SEE

Stop by the information booth and pick up the brochure entitled "Williamstown: A Walk Along Main Street," which gives details on the interesting buildings lining Main Street (Rte. 2 East), many of them now part of Williams College.

For a small town in the Berkshires, Williamstown has a surprising number of cultural offerings. The **Sterling and Francine Clark Art Institute,** 225 South St. (tel. 413/458-9545), less than a mile south of the information booth, is perhaps the most famous. The institute's marvelous collections are the achievement of Robert Sterling Clark (1877–1956), a Yale engineer whose forebears had been successful in the glass and sewing machine industries. Clark began collecting works of art in Paris in 1912, married a French woman named Francine, and eventually housed his masterpieces in a classic white marble temple here in Williamstown.

The pristine original museum was greatly expanded in 1973, and now has strong collections of paintings by the Impressionists, their academic contemporaries in France, and the midcentury Barbizon artists, including Millet, Troyon, and Corot. Of the Americans, there are significant works by Cassatt, Homer, Remington, and Sargent. Earlier centuries are represented by well-chosen pieces of Piero della Francesca, Memling, Gossaert, Jacob van Ruisdael, Fragonard, Gainsborough, Turner, and Goya. There are some sculptures, including Degas' famous *Ballet Dancer Dressed,* as well as prints, drawings, and noteworthy collections of silver and porcelain.

Admission is free. The institute is open Tuesday through Sunday from 10am to 5pm but closed on New Year's Day, Thanksgiving, and Christmas. It's usually closed Monday, but is open on Memorial Day, Labor Day, and Columbus Day.

The **Williams College Museum of Art,** on Main Street between Spring and Water streets (tel. 413/597-2429), is in Lawrence Hall, the Greek Revival building with the rotunda. Call to ask about current exhibits, which are lively, timely, and well displayed in the museum's galleries and dramatic open spaces. Hours are Monday through Saturday from 10am to 5pm, Sunday from 1 to 5pm; admission is free.

No matter if the weather is clear or cloudy, stroll over to the **Milham Planetarium** (tel. 413/597-2188) in the Hopkins Observatory building on Main Street. The observatory itself is the oldest institution of its kind in the United States. Mid-June through mid-August on two evenings each week the planetarium has free celestial shows; from October through May, when college is in session, shows are on Friday evenings.

WHAT TO DO

The big draw from late June through the end of August is the **Williamstown Theater Festival,** Box 517, Williamstown, MA 01267 (tel. 413/597-3399 for information, 597-3400 for the box office). The **Main Stage** company puts on the principal production in the 500-seat Adams Memorial Theater on Main Street, and the smaller (96-seat) **Other Stage** next door is the scene for new works by both young and established playwrights. The festival's **Cabaret** performances take place at area restaurants. There are special Sunday dramatic events at the Clark Art Institute, and even an open-air Free Theatre literary adaptation staged at twilight in a meadow near the town (bring a picnic dinner). Until June 7, call the festival's New York number, 212/922-1130; after June 7, call the box office to charge tickets on your credit card.

The **Williams College Department of Music** arranges numerous concerts when college is in session. Call the Concertline at 413/597-3146 for information. In the summer, **Williamstown Chamber Concerts** (tel. 413/458-8273) organizes several chamber music performances at the Clark Art Institute.

Mount Greylock

Five miles east of Williamstown along Rte. 2, in North Adams, a road goes off to the right, climbing the slopes of Mt. Greylock (3,491 feet), the highest point in Massachusetts. If the weather is clear, drive the several miles to the top, where you'll find marvelous views, the AMC Bascom Lodge (see above under "Hotels"), and a curious, imposing 92-foot-high war memorial that was originally designed as a lighthouse. The memorial is open to the public.

Other roads approach the summit from the south, starting from U.S. 7 at New Ashford or Lanesboro.

While you're up here, explore some of the 40 miles of hiking trails (including part of the Appalachian Trail) which thread through the forest of the Mount Greylock State Reservation's 11,000 acres. Bascom Lodge will sell you a simple but satisfying and portable trail lunch for less than $3.

RHODE ISLAND

Just because Rhode Island is the smallest state in the union, many people assume that the variety of things to see and do in this corner of New England is limited. Not so. The state's beaches are famed throughout the region, sites and structures of historical importance abound, the cities are pleasant and of manageable size, and then there's Newport—a world apart. In fact, the only real effects the state's small size seem to have are to make the residents feel that they are a part of a very special place—which they are—and to make everything easily accessible to the visitor.

In the 1600s, when New England was being colonized by Europeans, the best solution to a community conflict was for the weaker of the conflicting parties to shove off into the wilderness and found and develop his own community. To save his skin and freely express his beliefs, Roger Williams left Puritan Salem in 1636 and came to Narragansett Bay, followed soon afterward by others who shared his views, or at least knew they would be allowed to disagree. Williams was ahead of the times in his political, religious, and ethical thinking, and his contribution to the American democratic tradition is very important: In his new community of Providence, citizens could think and say what they liked. In the years that followed the founding of Providence, Williams persuaded Parliament to include the settlements of Portsmouth and Newport on Rhode Island with his own Providence Plantation under the same charter—these towns had also been founded by dissenters who desired freedom of thought and speech—thus securing to the colony as a whole the right of absolute liberty in matters of belief. The official name of the state to this day remains "Rhode Island and Providence Plantations."

Today Rhode Island is a manufacturing center, a maritime state, with a lot of rich agricultural land and several industries of importance. But the summer vacationers who come to Rhode Island—beginning with the very wealthy socialites who started the custom in the 19th century—are also an important part of the economy, and the state government does a lot to see that "Little Rhodie" retains the lure it had for those discriminating types who built palatial mansions in Newport, Watch Hill, and other coastal towns.

INFORMATION

You can get Rhode Island tourist information toll free by calling 800/556-2484 from any state between Maine and Virginia. By the way, the room tax in

Rhode Island varies from only a few percent in Providence to a whopping 11% in Block Island and Watch Hill. The tax will be added to your hotel bill. The sales tax is 6%. The telephone area code for all of Rhode Island is **401.**

1. Providence

Providence is a pretty city. The downtown area is compact enough that a visitor can get off the train, or park the car, and walk to just about everything there is to see and do. The State Capitol, a pleasant and harmonious building of white Georgia marble, crowns a hilltop on the edge of the downtown section. College Hill rises from the east bank of the Providence River, which runs through downtown; Brown University, the Rhode Island School of Design, and a collection of exceptionally beautiful and interesting houses from the 17th, 18th, and 19th centuries give College Hill its character.

The city was founded in 1636 by Roger Williams (1603–83), who had been minister of the church at Salem, Mass., but whose freethinking religious ideas had made the General Court banish him from Massachusetts Bay. (He held that the Massachusetts Bay charter was not legal; that the Puritans should face the fact that they had really separated from the Church of England, whether they chose to admit it or not; and that in matters of conscience no civil authority had any power—no wonder the powers-that-be thought him a dangerous man!) Because of his own belief in free-thinking, he dedicated his new settlement of Providence to the proposition that all people should have freedom of conscience. A good number came from Massachusetts, and others came directly from England, to the new colony. Williams had bought the land for the town from the Narragansett Indians, and he remained on very good terms with them, even writing a book on their language which was published and sold in England.

Providence became the first colony to declare independence from England, in May 1776. After the Revolutionary War, it took over from Newport the position as the state's most important seaport. It's still an important port, and its industries of textiles, machine tools, rubber, jewelry, and boatbuilding also contribute to its prosperity.

GETTING THERE

Getting to Providence couldn't be easier, whether you're going by car or by public transport.

By Car

I-95 goes right through the center of Providence on its way between New York and Boston; right downtown I-195 branches off to go through Fall River (the turn-off for Newport), New Bedford, and then on to Cape Cod.

Note on Parking: Street parking in Providence is scarce, and meters are checked frequently. The center of town has lots of private pay lots, which it is best to use if you need to be downtown. Otherwise, park on a side street on College Hill, where there's plenty of shade and no time limit.

By Rail

The new, modern, white marble **Amtrak** railroad station (tel. 401/751-5416) in Providence is right at the base of the State Capitol's southwest lawn, a 5- or 10-minute walk from Kennedy Plaza. The old Union Station overlooking Kennedy Plaza is presently under restoration, but it will no longer be a railroad station. Ten trains a day in each direction pass through on their way between New York and Boston. Travel time from New York is less than 4 hours; from Boston, about 1 hour. You can, if you want, take an early-morning train from New York, get off in Providence and stroll around downtown and College Hill for several hours, have lunch, get back on the train, and be in Boston by four in the afternoon.

By Bus

The **Bonanza Bus Station** (tel. 401/751-8800) is a block from Kennedy Plaza. **Greyhound** uses this same terminal. Both run buses to Providence from New York City, Boston, Newport, Hartford, Cape Cod, Springfield (Mass.), and Albany. Travel time from New York is about 4 hours; from Boston it's 1 hour. A bus from Providence to Newport takes just over an hour; to Cape Cod (Hyannis) the trip takes 1½ hours.

By Air

Rhode Island is so compact that one airport handles all the important national flights: **T.F. Green State Airport** in Warwick, just a few miles south of Providence. From the airport you'll have to take a taxi to the center of Providence

TOURIST INFORMATION

The people to ask are at the **Greater Providence Convention and Visitors Bureau,** 30 Exchange Terrace, Providence, RI 02903 (tel. 401/274-1636). Drop by, or telephone them, with any of your questions about the city.

WHERE TO STAY

Most people who visit Providence stay in motels on the outskirts of town; these offer the best value and the greatest selection, although staying out of the center entails driving and parking problems. Providence does have a choice place to stay right downtown, plus a few of the familiar and comfortable chain hotels.

Providence has a 4% room tax which, when added to the 6% state sales tax, increases the price of any Providence hotel room by 10%.

College Hill

The **Old Court,** 144 Benefit St., Providence, RI 02903 (tel. 401/751-2002 or 351-0747), at the corner of North Court Street, is a handsome old three-story brick mansion only a short walk from downtown, on the slopes of College Hill. The house was built in 1863 as a rectory, but takes its name from the old Rhode Island Courthouse next door, which now houses the Rhode Island Historical Preservation Commission. The inn itself is a fine example of historic preservation: All of its Italianate features—12-foot ceilings, plaster moldings, crystal chandeliers, brass sconces, and ornately carved marble mantelpieces—are in place. Furnishings in the spacious, airy guest rooms are true to the period, with wallpapers sporting large flowered patterns, antique-style telephones, and old-fashioned alarm clocks. But the full tiled bath attached to each room (often installed in what was formerly a walk-in closet) is thoroughly modern in plumbing and fixtures. Some rooms have air conditioners. The prices for a double room, including breakfast served in the pretty ground-floor breakfast room, are $110 and $120. This place is very nicely done, and quite charming.

Downtown Hotels

Right on Kennedy Plaza in the center of Providence is the **Omni Biltmore Hotel,** Providence, RI 02903 (tel. 401/421-0700 or toll free 800/228-2121). The Biltmore was the most elegant hotel in Providence when it was built in 1922, and after a $14-million renovation, it's Providence's poshest place to stay once again. Of the 289 rooms and suites, 120 have their own lounge areas; 14 are designed especially for the handicapped. If you knew the Biltmore before, you'll hardly recognize it now, as much has been changed. The outstanding features of 1920s elegance have been carefully preserved, but even the façade has seen a change. Now a glass-enclosed elevator starts from the hotel lobby, penetrates the three-story-high lobby ceiling, and glides up the side of the 18-floor hotel to the top. Rooms at the Biltmore cost $132 to $165 single, $154 to $187 double, with the highest prices going for the luxurious rooms. Ask about reduced weekend rates.

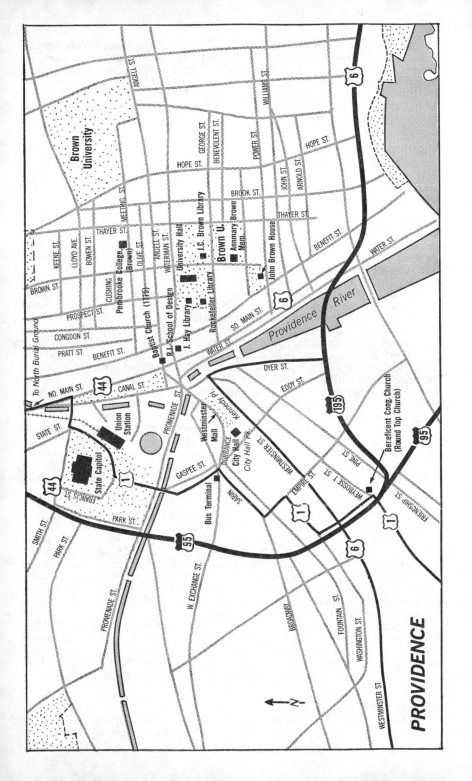

Another centrally located hotel is the downtown **Providence Holiday Inn,** at 21 Atwells Ave., Providence, RI 02903 (tel. 401/831-3900), right next to the Civic Center. The 13-story, handicapped-accessible hotel has 274 rooms, a restaurant, a lounge with live entertainment, and an indoor pool. The bus and train stations are less than half a mile away. Rooms cost $100 to $105 single, $111 to $117 double; in the higher-priced room (with two double beds), teenage children or younger can stay for free.

A Bed-and-Breakfast Service
Bed & Breakfast of Rhode Island, P.O. Box 3291, Newport, RI 02840 (tel. 401/941-0444), will find a room for you near Providence or any other Rhode Island town. Rates depend on the room, of course, but range from $45 to $90 single, $50 to $100 double.

On the Outskirts
Most of Providence's hotel capacity is on the outskirts of greater Providence, in the neighboring cities of Warwick near the airport to the south, Pawtucket to the north toward Boston on I-95, and Seekonk, Mass., on I-195, the road to Cape Cod. As most of these hotels and motels are right off the highway, it is a good idea to pick them according to your plans for *tomorrow:* If it's evening as you approach Providence, stay in Warwick and then see Providence the next day; if it's early in the day, tour through Providence and then head out I-95 to Pawtucket if your next stop is Boston, or I-195 to Seekonk if you're headed for Cape Cod. You can call for a reservation while you're seeing the sights in Providence.

Warwick has one of the five **Howard Johnson Motor Lodges** in the Providence area. This one is at 20 Jefferson Blvd., Warwick, RI 02888 (tel. 401/467-9800 or toll free 800/654-2000), which is at Exit 15 of I-95, near T. F. Green State Airport. There's a 24-hour restaurant, a lounge with entertainment, and a variety of package plans which can save you lots of money, particularly on weekends. Seniors get a discount; kids under 18 stay for free. Rates are $80 single, $91 double.

In Pawtucket your best bet is the local **Howard Johnson Motor Lodge,** a stone's throw off I-95 (Exit 27) at 2 George St., Pawtucket, RI 02860 (tel. 401/723-6700 or toll free 800/654-2000). The lodge charges $81 single, $92 double; an extra person is $10. Children under 18 can use their parents' room for free. The lodge has an indoor heated pool, a sauna, and an adjacent Hojo's restaurant open 24 hours a day.

In Seekonk, Mass., there are several good lodging possibilities. Note that you have a different telephone area code (508) to contend with if you're calling from Rhode Island. Take Exit 114A from I-195 for these.

One good bet is the **Howard Johnson Motor Lodge** in Seekonk at the intersection of I-195 and Rte. 114A, 821 Fall River Ave., Seekonk, MA 02771 (tel. 508/336-7800, or toll free 800/654-2000). Facilities and rates are very similar to those in the Pawtucket lodge mentioned above, but rooms with one bed (accommodating one or two people) are cheaper here: $70 single, $81 double. In the winter (November through April) special weekend package rates are offered. The lodge has no restaurant of its own, but there are several nearby.

There is also a **Ramada Inn** here, very close to the Howard Johnson at 940 Fall River Ave. (which is Rte. 114A), Seekonk, MA 02771 (tel. 508/336-7300 or toll free 800/228-2828). The Ramada is structured and priced very competitively, with pool, sauna, lounge with live entertainment, and a children's playground, all costing $94 single, $105 double; kids 18 and under stay free in the same room.

Budget Lodgings
A family-run set of motels in Seekonk, operated by the Darling family, are on U.S. 6 near the intersection of Alternate Rte. 114 (114-A), Seekonk, MA 02771.

The **Esquire** and **Town 'n' Country** motels are right across the highway from one another (tel. 508/336-9000) and share an outdoor pool, open during the warm months. Rooms are brightly painted and have individual air-conditioning units. The motels also share a putting green, coffee shop, and cocktail lounge, as well as Eileen Darling's Restaurant. Rates for the rooms are $49 for one double bed, $54 for two double beds—one of the better bargains in the area.

WHERE TO DINE
Providence's sophisticated university crowd generates a need for good restaurants, and Providence has plenty. Not all of them are up on College Hill, however.

Downtown Restaurants
"The best of Paris in the heart of Providence" are the words used to describe the **Pot au Feu,** 44 Custom House St. (tel. 273-8953), off Weybosset Street, not far from Providence's famous Arcade. Upstairs is the Salon, an elegant dining room with high ceilings, gold chandelier, tall windows, spotless linen napery, fresh flowers, glistening crystal, and hushed, professional service. A sumptuously long menu of French classics and nouvelle cuisine dishes includes salmon filet in lemon butter, poached in white wine with shallots, parsley, and essence of anchovies; and veal chops in a sauce of shiitake mushrooms, shallots, ginger, and heavy cream. You can order a main course either à la carte or prix fixe. The latter allows you to have appetizer, soup, salad, main course, dessert, and coffee for as little as $40 to $50 per person, tax, tip, and wine included. This is the perfect method if you are not ravenously hungry, for the prix fixe portions of soup, salad, and other courses are smaller than the normal à la carte portions.

Downstairs in Le Bistro, the menu is just as long, and almost as elegant, but cheaper. Dinner might cost $25 to $35 per person, all in.

Lunch is served in the Salon from 11:30am to 2pm Monday through Friday; dinner is on from 6 to 9pm. Tuesday through Thursday, till 10pm on Friday and Saturday. The Salon is closed Sunday and Monday, but Le Bistro is open and serving brunch, lunch, and dinner seven days a week.

On the ground floor of the Omni Biltmore Hotel on Kennedy Plaza is **Stanford's** (tel. 272-6581), named for Stanford White, the famed architect who designed the Rhode Island State Capitol, the Newport and Narragansett casinos, and the original Madison Square Garden. Stanford's is "an American Bar and Grille," but both its food and decor are quite eclectic. This is a place where you can truly take your choice: Dine in the modern café section, all bright colors, angles and split levels, openness and coziness; or in the more formal salon; or even in the bistrolike lounge which features live jazz Tuesday through Saturday. The long menu includes prime rib, many steaks, and jumbo shrimp. Expect to spend $15 to $30, all included, for lunch or dinner here. Stanford's is open for Sunday brunch and breakfast, lunch, cocktails, and dinner, every day of the week.

Light Lunch, Downtown
The place to go if you're just interested in an informal bite is the **Arcade,** 65 Weybosset St. (tel. 456-5403). This National Historic Landmark was built in 1828—a Greek Revival shopping arcade running between Weybosset and Westminster streets, with three stories of shops surmounted by a glass canopy. The Arcade's ground floor is nothing but food shops, including the following: the China Inn, specializing in Chinese food to eat here or take out; the Grand Central Café, serving hot and cold beverages and pastries; Hot Dogs & More; the Providence Cookie Co.; Periwinkles, which has a very full sandwich menu; Villa Pizza; the Grog Boy Bar for stronger stuff; Natural Sweetness, a vegetarian restaurant; Great Soups, which serves just that; the Ritz, serving Middle Eastern pocket bread sandwiches; Le

Greque, with a full menu of Greek dishes; Baby Watson, nationally famous for its cheesecake and other desserts; and Créme de la Créme, which may not have the right French accents, but has wonderful ice cream and candy nonetheless. It's difficult to spend more than $10 per person for lunch at the Arcade, and easy to fill up for $5 or $6

Up on College Hill

Providence consumes almost as much succulent seafood as Newport, and a lot of the best seafood in Providence disappears at **Bluepoint,** an oyster bar and restaurant at 99 N. Main St., corner of Elizabeth (tel. 272-6145), between Steeple and Meeting streets. The one-room restaurant, with the oyster-and-spirits bar on the right as you enter, is usually filled with a classy young clientele talking but mostly eating. The clam chowder comes Provençal (with tomatoes) or New England (with cream and potatoes) for $4.25. Oysters, a half dozen of any variety of your choice on the half shell, are $6.25 to $7.25. Littleneck and Cherrystone clams are a bit less. The list of main courses on the blackboard is very short because the daily specials are what most people order. The specials, whether they be squid, grilled prawns, swordfish, bluefish, or scallops, constitute the best and freshest seafood at the lowest price. Dinner will cost about $25 to $30 per person here, a bit more if you drink lots of wine or beer, a bit less if you order carefully. Bluepoint is an easy walk from downtown, and is open for dinner only, Sunday through Thursday from 6 to 11pm, to 11:30pm on Friday and Saturday; the bar is open from 5pm to 1am daily.

Another fine place for lunch or dinner is about 10 blocks from Brown University. **Rue de L'Espoir,** at 99 Hope St. (tel. 751-8890), takes its name from a French translation of the street it's on. Its menu is an international collection of fare light and hearty, *minceur* and *gourmande*. There are soups, salads, pastas, whole-wheat pizza, and main courses such as rack of lamb, filet mignon, and veal medallions. Note especially the menu of "small plates"—chicken and cashew spring rolls or petite ravioli is just the thing to order with a glass of wine for a light lunch or supper. Your bill can be anything from $7 to $40, depending on how hungry and thirsty you are. Rue de l'Espoir is open Tuesday through Sunday from 11:30am to 10:30pm; closed Monday.

WHAT TO SEE

Preservation and urban redevelopment have done much to make Providence a delightful place to walk in today. The most interesting districts are small enough that you can make your way around on foot. For an expert look at Providence's historical treasures, consider the following.

Walking Tours

The **Providence Preservation Society,** 21 Meeting St. (tel. 401/831-7440), offers two audio cassettes and seven self-guided walking-tour booklets of historical areas in the city. Areas include Benefit Street, with its restored 18th- and 19th-century houses, the downtown section with its 19th- and 20th-century architecture, the waterfront, Brown University, and three Victorian neighborhoods named Armory District, Elmwood, and Broadway. Rent a cassette for $3.50 or buy the booklets for 80¢ each at the society's headquarters, Monday through Friday from 9am to 5pm. In spring and fall, society members lead guided walking tours of these and other areas. Call for details.

Seeing Providence, Old and New

The place to start touring Providence is **Kennedy Plaza,** in the center of town. Shady trees and benches make the plaza an oasis in the middle of the city, and an equestrian statue of Gen. Ambrose Burnside, the Civil War officer whose long side whiskers were the first "sideburns," watches over the eastern end of the plaza. **City Hall** is at the other end, an agreeable Second Empire building completed in 1878 (go inside to see a wall display of other entries in the competition for the city hall design).

From Kennedy Plaza to College Hill

Go one block southeast from the plaza to reach the **Westminster Mall,** a six-block section of Westminster Street closed to vehicles. The mall is a pleasant place to sit and people-watch, or to stroll down. Just past its eastern end, at 130 Westminster St., is the **Arcade,** which looks like an imaginative bit of urban renewal, but is in fact the creation of Russell Warren and James Bucklin, who designed the building in 1827. For a century and a half some of Providence's better shops have operated in the Arcade. There are three levels of shops topped by a roof of glass panes; one modern addition to the Arcade is an elevator to take shoppers to the upper floors. Besides restaurants, the Arcade has stores selling antiques, jewelry, rare books, fine tobaccos, cosmetics, and other luxury items. Decorative cast-iron balustrades and stairways recall the Arcade's early 19th-century construction. Look at both façades—on Westminster Street and on Weybosset—which clearly show that each architect had his own idea of how the exterior should look. With two façades, each got his chance to do what he wanted.

Walk through the Arcade from Westminster Street to Weybosset Street, and turn right to get to Providence's historic **Round Top Church**—you'll see its golden dome in the distance. The church, officially known as the Beneficent Congregational Meetinghouse, got its name because of its dome, which is a departure from the usual New England church spire. Finished in 1810, it was influenced by the classical revival then going on in Europe. The interior is as pleasant to look at as the exterior: Besides the gracious New England meetinghouse furnishings, the Round Top Church has a crystal chandelier consisting of almost 6,000 pieces. (Enter by the door on the side, around to the right.)

Now head northeast down Weybosset, past the Arcade, to the intersection of this street with Westminster and Exchange. Here in front of the Hospital Trust Bank activities and shows are held during the warm months, perhaps a Boy Scouts' display of fancy marching or a small (but highly amplified) jazz combo giving a lunch-hour concert.

College Hill

Walk two more blocks east and you will cross the Providence River to the foot of **College Hill.** The hill is the prettiest section of the city, its streets lined with 18th- and 19th-century houses, most of which have been well preserved or restored and many of which bear plaques, put up by the Providence Preservation Society, giving the builder's name and the date of construction. At the bottom of College Hill, on South Main Street between Thomas and Waterman streets, take a stroll past the **First Baptist Meetinghouse.** Roger Williams founded the first Baptist congregation in the New World in 1638, but this building dates from 1775. The architect was Joseph Brown, and the steeple—designed from a plate in James Gibbs's *Book of Architecture* representing suggested steeples for St. Martin-in-the-Fields in London—rises to a height of 185 feet. It's one of the outstanding churches in New England, and a guide will take you through for free between the hours of 10am and 3pm Monday through Friday, 10am to noon on Saturday, and at noon on Sunday following the weekly church service. Between November and March the church is open daily, but guides are available only by appointment (tel. 751-2266). The front door of the church will probably be locked, so go around to the right to the side (office) door.

To the left of the church, at 7 Thomas St., is a fantastic old building with half-timbering and stucco bas-reliefs on its façade. This is **Sidney Burleigh's "Fleur de Lys" House,** built by this Providence artist in 1885 (the date is in the stucco). Thomas Street might be called "Artists' Row," because very near Burleigh's house is the Providence Art Club, at no. 11. Open from 10am to 4pm (3 to 5pm on Sunday), the club has changing shows exhibited in its galleries. The club also runs the Dodge House at 10 Thomas St., which has contemporary shows from September through May.

At the intersection of Waterman and Benefit streets, turn right and go south on Benefit for a block to the **Museum of Art, Rhode Island School of Design,** at 224 Benefit St. (tel. 331-3511, ext. 360). The museum is Providence's finest, and one of the best small museums in the country, with collections from Greece and Rome, China and Japan; paintings by Manet, Monet, Degas, Cézanne, and Matisse, as well as other masters; and a good collection of American painting, furniture, costumes, and modern works of art. Of the choicest pieces in this impressive collection, Rodin's famous statue of Balzac ranks high, as does Monet's *Bassin d'Argenteuil* and the collection of Townsend/Goddard furniture in Pendleton House, the museum's "American wing." You can see all this for $2 for adults, 50¢ for senior citizens and youths (5 to 18), free for small children. Admission is *free* on Saturday. The museum is always closed Monday.

Special Note: Museum hours are rather complicated. From mid-June through August, hours are noon to 5pm Wednesday through Saturday; the rest of the year, the museum is open on Tuesday, Wednesday, Friday, and Saturday from 10:30am to 5pm, on Thursday from noon to 8pm, and on Sunday from 2 to 5pm.

The **Rhode Island School of Design** or **RISD,** (known in Providence as *"riz-dee"*) is one of the country's best art, architecture, and design schools. Founded in 1877, it shares College Hill with Brown University (see below).

RISD has another attractive building besides its museum dedicated to the display of art. It's the **Woods-Gerry Mansion,** 62 Prospect St., which was built between 1860 and 1864 and now serves as RISD's administration building and gallery for students' works of art. Admission is free and the galleries are open Monday through Saturday from 11am to 4pm, on Sunday from 2 to 5pm (except in summer when they're open weekdays only; closed all of August). The big old brick-and-brownstone mansion is empty of its plush furnishings now, but parquet floors and gorgeous marble fireplaces give an idea of what it must have been like, and the high-ceilinged rooms with large windows provide perfect space for exhibiting students' efforts: Drawings, paintings, sculpture, or what-have-you, all guaranteed to be the most *avant* of the avant-garde. The grounds of the mansion are covered with grand shade trees and rhododendron bushes (which bloom in late June and early July), and dotted with pieces of sculpture and benches for a welcome rest. The museum is closed in August.

Another RISD building open to the public is the **Bayard Ewing Building,** 231 S. Main St., which houses RISD's architectural division. Exhibits here change frequently, and feature architectural and industrial design.

Also up here on College Hill is **Brown University** (tel. 863-1000), a member of the Ivy League and the seventh-oldest university in the country. Founded in 1764, Brown's first building was University Hall, used as a barracks for colonial and French soldiers during the American Revolution. It's now a National Historic Landmark. To get to it, walk up the hill (east) on Waterman Street, cross Prospect Street, and turn into the gates on your right. Do you want a full, free tour of the beautiful and historic campus? Find your way to the College Admission Office, one block from University Hall at the corner of Prospect and Angell streets. Tours depart from here at 10 and 11am, and 1, 3, and 4pm.

Prospect Street is so named because it passes near **Prospect Terrace** (go north a block from Woods-Gerry House to Cushing Street and turn left). From the Terrace, a small park, you can see downtown Providence and the State Capitol, along with a famous but—pardon me—rather wooden statue of the founder, Roger Williams. His grave is here as well. Trees have grown up below and block a bit of the perspective, but the view is still panoramic and impressive.

College Hill has lots of other places to see, including many historic houses. One of the fanciest is the **John Brown House,** 52 Power St. at Benefit Street (tel. 331-8575), a late-Georgian mansion constructed in 1786 and now owned and operated by the Rhode Island Historical Society. Proclaimed by John Quincy Adams to be "the most magnificent and elegant private mansion that I have seen on this continent," this restored house-museum reveals the prosperity of post-Revolutionary Providence and houses an outstanding collection of furnishings and decorative arts. John Brown was a merchant whose ships plied the seas both east and west out of Narragansett Bay and ultimately made him a wealthy man. The Brown family, by the way, had been prominent in Providence commerce and industry since the early 1700s. John's brother, Moses, joined with Samuel Slater to set up the first water-powered cotton spinning mill in America in 1790, now known as Slater Mill (see below). One of his nephews, Nicholas Brown, was a graduate of Rhode Island College, which was later renamed Brown College (and later, University) in his honor. John Brown House is open Tuesday through Saturday from 11am to 4pm, on Sunday from 1 to 4pm; closed holidays. Admission and guided tour costs $3.50 for adults, $2.50 for seniors and students. Combination tickets good for a visit to both the John Brown House and the Aldrich House (see below) are on sale as well.

The Rhode Island Historical Society also operates the **Museum of Rhode Island History** (tel. 331-8575), in the Aldrich House, a Federal-style mansion (1822) at 110 Benevolent St. The museum holds changing exhibitions highlighting various aspects of Rhode Island, its history, and its citizens. Hours are Monday through Saturday from 11am to 4pm, and on Sunday from 1 to 4pm; closed holidays. Adults pay $2 for admission; students and seniors pay $1; families pay a maximum of $5.

The State Capitol

Rhode Island government was conducted in the Old State House (1762), on North Main Street between North and South Court streets, from 1762 to 1895, when the new State Capitol building was dedicated. The Capitol is a pleasant sight, its tall dome floating over the Providence skyline, its white Georgia marble gleaming in the sun. Whether it is "the most beautiful in the country," as the state's tourist brochures claim, might be disputed by admirers of 49 other such capitols, but certainly it is one of the more beautiful. Enter by the portal on Smith Street (Rte. 44) to see display cases filled with battle flags from the state's proud military units which served in the Civil War, the Spanish-American War, and the world wars. Here also is a Civil War cannon that was hit right in the muzzle by another cannon's ball. When the crew tried to charge the cannon again, they put the powder and wad in but couldn't get the ball in; then they couldn't get the ball *out*. The gun was retired, but it was only in the 1960s, after the cannon had been in the Capitol for decades, that someone remembered the gunpowder charge! So after 100 years of being loaded and ready, the Civil War cannon was finally decharged. Beyond the cannon is the rich, gleaming marble interior and hallways decorated with paintings of the founding fathers of Rhode Island and Providence Plantation. Free tours of the capitol are offered on weekdays from 9am to 4:30pm (last tour at 3:30). It's worth seeing.

Sights on the Outskirts

Two more places to visit lie a few miles outside the center of town. **Roger Williams Park** is south of the city on Elmwood Avenue (Exit 17 from I-95) and boasts magnificently restored 19th-century Victorian buildings, the **Charles E. Smith Greenhouses,** a museum of natural history, zoo, and amusement area besides its 430 acres of beautifully kept lawns, copses, lakes, and paths. The park is open to the public for free, and special concerts and programs are scheduled throughout the summer—call 401/785-9450 for the latest information. The zoo, by the way, is open every day from 10am to 4pm.

Water-powered cotton and textile mills changed all of New England in the 19th century, and it all started in Pawtucket, a few miles from downtown Providence. In 1793 three enterprising men named Slater, Almy, and Brown set up the first water-powered cotton-spinning factory in America, on the Blackstone River. Today the early mills and the **Sylvanus Brown House** (1758), home of the skilled artisan, make up the **Slater Mill Historic Site.** The mills have many of their old machines in working order, such as the water wheel, shafts, and pulleys in **Wilkinson Mill** (1810), and you can see them in action. Earlier handcraft devices for doing the same jobs are also on display to show you what a breakthrough the machine-filled **Slater Mill** (1793) was. Besides the permanent exhibits, traveling and temporary displays are set up from time to time, and guided tours interpret the history of the textile industry and the impact of factories on working conditions. Admission is $3 for adults, $2 for children 6 through 14. Group rates are available. The site is open in summer, June 1 to Labor Day, Tuesday through Saturday from 10am to 5pm, on Sunday from 1 to 5pm; in spring and fall it's open on weekends from 1 to 5pm, but closed in January and February. Call 401/725-8638 for information. To get there, take I-95 north from Providence, get off at Exit 28, and turn left (under the highway) onto School Street. Cross the Blackstone River and turn right into Roosevelt Avenue; the site is on your right. From I-95 south take Exit 27 and follow signs to the mills.

---

2. Newport

Whatever glittering reports you've had of Newport, they're probably correct, because Newport is a fascinating, diverse place. Palatial mansions, the wealthy yachting set, major naval and Coast Guard installations, tennis tournaments, cocktails on marble terraces in the soft air of a summer's evening, or succulent seafood served in a waterfront restaurant—Newport is all of these.

Newport has enjoyed prominence during two periods in American history: In colonial times it was an important trade center, and so, like Salem, Mass., it has a lovely colonial section right downtown, much of which has been restored authentically in the styles of centuries ago; and in the mid-19th century it became a resort for the very wealthy, who built what are indeed palaces in another part of town. Newport preserves remembrances of this past while pursuing its future as one of New England's prime vacation destinations: People who own yachts and people who can only afford to look at yachts, people who play tennis and those who watch it, people who live in mansions and others who take guided tours through mansions—they all flock to Newport. Besides the visitors, Newport is home to tens of thousands of Rhode Islanders who take all the glamour and glitter for granted, and who live here year round.

Several things are important to remember when you're planning a visit to Newport. First, it is crowded in summer, particularly on weekends, and when the important tennis tournaments and yacht races are being held. Second, prices tend to go up on weekends and when the yachters are around. Third, Newport prides itself on having style, and many visitors will be dressed like movie stars; many restaurants, cocktail lounges, and hotels require "proper" dress at dinner, and perhaps even lunch: jacket, or jacket and tie for men, skirt and top or pants suit, or similar attire, for women.

HISTORY

Newport is at the southern tip of an island which the Indians called Aquidneck, and which the colonial settlers dubbed Rhode Island. Just as Providence was settled by Roger Williams, dissident from Salem, so Newport was founded by one William Coddington, who decided to strike out on his own from Providence in 1639. The new town soon became famous for shipbuilding, and as soon as the ships were built in sufficient numbers, for trade. The famous "triangle trade," from Newport to ports in the West Indies and Africa, would later bring great wealth to the town from the buying and selling of slaves, rum, molasses, and other goods. Because Providence and Newport were founded by dissidents, they became places of refuge for others wishing to worship as they pleased: Quakers from England, Jews from Portugal and Spain, and Baptists all came to Newport in the mid-1600s to find religious freedom. They brought talent and a gift for hard work, and the settlement prospered so that it became the colony's most important town, and one of the New World's busiest ports. The many beautiful colonial homes, the handsome Old Colony

House (center of government), Touro Synagogue, and other landmarks attest to the wealth and prosperity of Newport at the time.

During the American Revolution the British occupied the town and its excellent harbor, and held it for three years. A British frigate, H.M.S. *Rose,* did much to hinder the transport of supplies to the Americans, and spurred them to found the U.S. Navy in retaliation. Despite a French naval blockade and an American siege, the British held onto Newport until 1779, and after this interruption in its social and economic life, Newport never regained its status as Rhode Island's prime trade center.

Several decades later, however, it achieved prominence in another fashion. Drawn by the beautiful woods and dramatic coastline, wealthy merchants from New York and Philadelphia began to come to Newport to spend their summers. In the mid-1800s the first of Newport's famous mansions, Château-sur-Mer, was built, and others followed until Newport's Bellevue Avenue and Ocean Drive could boast the highest concentration of summer palaces—and they are *palaces*—anywhere in the world.

Today the city's symbol is the pineapple, a sign of welcome left from Newport's great commercial era when traders back from West Indies with this fruit would put a pineapple outside their warehouses to invite customers to come in and look over the stock. Newport is used to welcoming visitors, and with the hints and recommendations given below, you should have no trouble finding your way around and having a good time.

GETTING THERE
Newport is served by bus, boat, and air taxi service.

By Bus
Bonanza Bus Lines serves Newport, with a stop right downtown at Newport Gateway Center, 23 America's Cup Ave. (tel. 401/846-1820). Bonanza works in conjunction with Greyhound and the Rhode Island Public Transit Authority, and has frequent daily buses from Boston to Newport (2 hours), Providence to Newport (1 hour), and New York City to Newport (5½ hours).

By Boat
There are daily boats between Providence, Newport, and Block Island. (See Section 4 on Block Island for details.)

By Air
Several national and regional airlines fly into T. F. Green State Airport in Warwick, and from there you can take **Sakonnet Air Charter,** Newport State Airport, Middletown, RI 02840 (tel. 401/847-6948). Sakonnet will fly you one way in 10 minutes for $36. It also offers shuttle service from Newport to Boston, Nantucket, Martha's Vineyard, and Block Island.

From Newport State Airport you'll have to take a taxi into town.

GETTING YOUR BEARINGS
The island of Rhode Island has three main towns: Portsmouth in the north, Newport at the southern end, and Middletown in between. Newport and Middletown are so close that many visitors to Newport stay in motels in Middletown and then drive the mile or two into Newport to see the sights. The two most important streets in Newport are **Thames Street** (pronounced "thaymz," *not* "temz"), center of the colonial section, the wharves, and modern downtown; and **Bellevue Avenue,** parallel to Thames but south and east of it. Bellevue is the street with many of the old mansions on it. Maps and information are handed out by the **Newport County Chamber of Commerce** office, 10 America's Cup Ave. (P.O. Box 237TB), Newport, RI 02840 (tel. 401/847-1600). It's open from 9am to 5pm every day in summer; weekends in winter from 9am to 4pm. Get help here if you're stuck without a reservation and can't find a room. America's Cup Avenue is parallel to Thames

Street and runs right along the water downtown. If you'd like to be sent information on Newport, the chamber is ready to do so.

WHERE TO STAY

Newport has several large, comfortable hotels, a good number of charming small inns, and numerous bed-and-breakfast houses. In neighboring Middletown are many inexpensive motels, and more guesthouses. No matter what sort of accommodation you choose, it's a good idea to have reservations in advance, particularly in summer and especially on weekends. If you arrive in Newport on Friday from mid-July through Labor Day, you may well have to spend hours searching for that last hotel or inn room. On summer weekdays there may be more rooms, but you may not be able to find your preferred facilities and price unless you reserve in advance. I'll start by describing some of Newport's fine inns, which are moderate in price but high in comfort and good looks, then go on to guesthouses (almost as charming, but cheaper), and hotels and motels.

The **Newport Chamber of Commerce** (tel. 401/847-1600) has a nice long list of bed-and-breakfast guesthouses and small inns. Send for it if you have the time; pick one up when you arrive if you don't; or call and ask for help in locating a room. Remember that Rhode Island has a 6% sales tax, and that a 5% Newport room tax is also applied to prices in establishments with 10 or more rooms.

The **Newport Historic Inns**, P.O. Box 981, Newport, RI 02840 (tel. 401/846-7666), will send you a list of its dozen member establishments. You can call to find out where there are vacancies—but you'll have to contact the guesthouse directly to make reservations. Members of the association tend to be the larger establishments with, say, 6 to 16 rooms.

Newport's Inns

For the full Newport experience, stay in a mansion right on Bellevue Avenue. The **Wayside,** Bellevue Avenue, Newport, RI 02840 (tel. 401/847-0302), is just that: a fine, huge, somewhat austere 1890s house of tawny brick set back from the avenue with its own little driveway and porte cochère. The interior spaces are rich and elegant, but austere rather than fussy. The many parlors and bedrooms have been redone into comfortable accommodations with private baths which rent for $125 double. Continental breakfast is included in the rates. To find the Wayside, drive from the Newport Casino (International Tennis Hall of Fame) down Bellevue Avenue. Pass "The Elms" on the right, then the Oakwood Healthcare Center on the left. The next building on the left past the healthcare center is the Wayside. A small marble plaque with gilt letters, mounted on a post by the driveway, is the only marking.

The **Inn at Castle Hill,** Ocean Avenue, Newport, RI 02840 (tel. 401/849-3800), is a Newport favorite, a marvelous Victorian summer mansion perched on a hill at the southwestern tip of Rhode Island, overlooking Narragansett Bay. The house was built in 1874 for Alexander Agassiz (1835–1910), naturalist, industrialist, and great benefactor of Harvard. It has been authentically maintained and restored, and is a fine example of a wealthy family's Victorian summer cottage extravaganza: dark wood, ornate fireplaces, large-flower-pattern wallpaper (different in each room, of course), Oriental carpets, a sunny solarium—it's all here. Whether you stay at the inn or not, you can enjoy the house by coming for lunch or dinner (see below). If you choose to stay, one of the six double rooms with private bath in the inn costs $200 in high summer; the three doubles with shared bath are $89. Rooms with shower in the Harbor House, an unobtrusive motel-style structure next to the inn and just above the pebble beach, cost $128. Continental breakfast is included in all these rates. The inn also has a number of beach cottages capable of lodging two to four people. The cottages are rented by the week in summer, and are booked very far in advance.

The **Yankee Peddler Inn** has a very fine downtown location at 113 Touro St. (between Spring Street and Bellevue Avenue), Newport, RI 02840 (tel. 401/846-

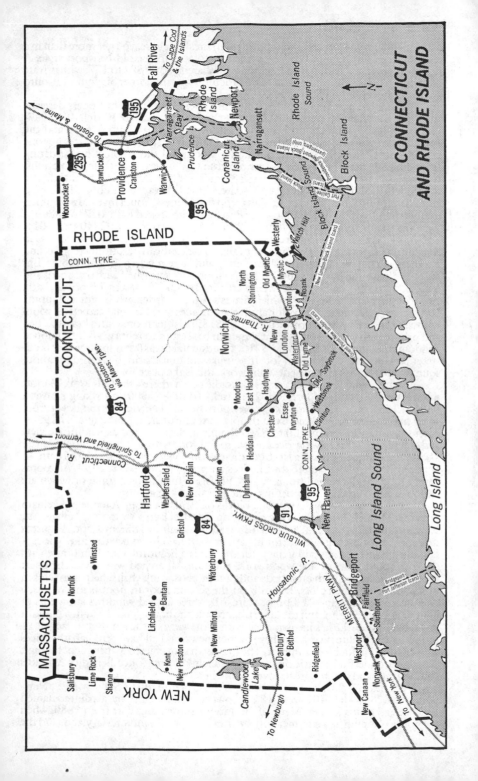

1323). Though you get bed and (continental) breakfast here, you get more than in a simple B&B: The Yankee Peddler is finely decorated in the old Newport style. A double room in the high summer season with shared bath is $72 to $77; with private bath, $94 to $105. Suites are more. Look for the inn at the corner of High and Touro streets in the center of Historic Hill.

"Where the past is present" is how innkeepers Rita and Sam Rogers describe their inn, the **Melville House,** 39 Clarke St., Newport, RI 02840 (tel. 401/847-0640). Only a few blocks up Historic Hill from America's Cup Avenue and the Brick Marketplace, on a quiet street, the inn couldn't be situated better. It is not one of Newport's Victorian palaces, but rather a beautiful old colonial house dating from about 1750. The owners have been true to the period in their decorations, which recall colonial and Early American times, yet have catered to guests' desires for modern facilities by installing up-to-date, if small, private bathrooms. The mood here is one of antiques, good taste, quiet, and friendliness. You'll love it. In summer, double rooms with private bath cost $88 to $99; with shared bath, $77 to $88.

The **Inn of Jonathan Bowen,** 29 Pelham St., Newport, RI 02840 (tel. 401/846-3324), is a nice old gambrel-roofed house only a half block off America's Cup Avenue up Historic Hill. The interior of the house has been beautifully redone, and is as neat as a pin, with wall-to-wall carpeting and large modern tile bathrooms. But true to its historical heritage, the inn's guest rooms are furnished with brass beds and old oak wardrobes and dressers. There are nine rooms in all, six with private bath, two that share a bath. Room 7, which shares a bath, is particularly bright and sunny. You'll enjoy relaxing in the parlor amid the antiques and Oriental carpets. A room with a queen-size bed and private bath costs $139; a larger room with a king-size bed and private bath costs $160. Recently the inn has begun to rent two fully equipped condominium units for $194 and $216. Continental breakfast is included, as is off-street parking in the inn's own lot. If you like antique charm, but can do without squeaky floorboards and ancient woodwork, this is the place for you.

For those who want to be very close to the beach, there's the **Cliff Walk Manor,** 82 Memorial Blvd., Newport, RI 02840 (tel. 401/847-1300), a striking mansion built in 1855 on a hill overlooking Newport Beach. The view of the beach from some of the guest rooms, and from the pleasant café deck, is panoramic. The guest rooms vary in price from $100 to $249 double in the summer, depending on view and amenities. At the lowest price are two rooms (one with an ocean view) that share a bath; at the highest price is a large oceanview room with its own whirlpool bath. In between, rooms with private bath and deck are priced from $139 to $194. All rooms have TV sets and air conditioning, and Victorian furnishings, some of which are antiques. And yes, Cliff Walk begins right in front of the manor.

Just slightly more than two long blocks off America's Cup Avenue, up Pelham Street on Historic Hill, stands the charming **Admiral Benbow Inn,** 93 Pelham St., Newport, RI 02840 (tel. 401/846-4256). It was built in 1855 by Capt. Augustus Littlefield to be used as a lodge for his guests, so it has always been an inn. The captain must have been a wealthy man, for the inn is a beautiful Victorian house with spacious rooms, lots of fine woodwork, and unusual arched windows. The guest rooms are furnished with brass beds and canopy beds, wing chairs, fireplaces (closed up), and pretty watercolors. Room 5 on the second floor in front is marvelous, a large space better termed a "junior suite." Its three arched windows allow lots of light to flood the room, and the large trees beside the house lend the light a pleasant green hue. Room 12 has its own deck with a fine view of the sea. But in fact all 14 rooms here are quite nice; some have harbor views, and all have private bath. Prices are $83 to $110 double in summer. The inn also has an efficiency apartment for rent. This is a wonderful inn in a quiet, shady neighborhood (once Benedict Arnold's family farm), and you're sure to love staying here.

Very near Cliff Walk and the beach is the **Cliffside Inn,** 2 Seaview Ave., Newport, RI 02840 (tel. 401/847-1811), owned at one time by a painter named Beatrice Pasatorius Turner. Many of the antique furnishings date from 1880, when the house was built as a summer cottage for Governor Swann of Maryland, and the

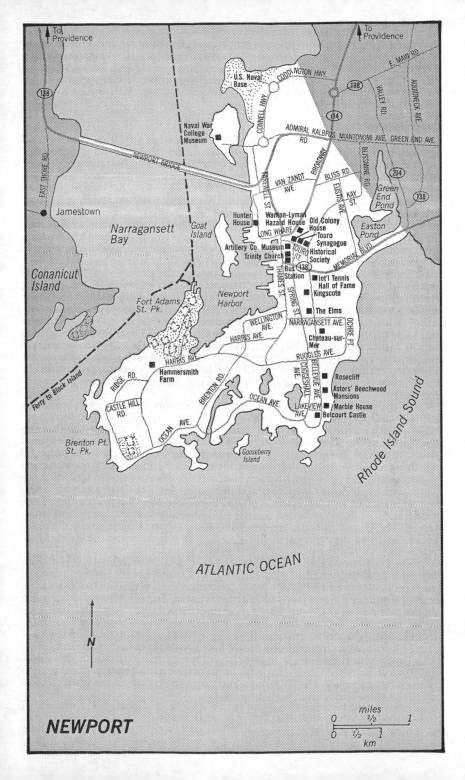

NEWPORT

inn exudes Victorian charm. Rooms have private shower and tub and rent for $89 to $111 in season (May through October). To get to the Cliffside, take America's Cup Avenue or Bellevue Avenue to Memorial Boulevard (Rte. 138A), follow Memorial east to Cliff Avenue, which is before you get to Newport Beach; turn right onto Cliff Avenue and go the two short blocks to Seaview Avenue. As you turn left onto Seaview, Cliffside is on your left.

Guesthouses

Many of the lodging establishments listed below are similar in ambience and facilities to the inns listed above. The distinction between inn and guesthouse is mine, and somewhat arbitrary. My feeling is that guesthouses have just a little more of the feeling you get when you stay in someone's home.

Ivy Lodge, 12 Clay St., Newport, RI 02840 (tel. 401/849-6865), is in the midst of the mansions, a block off Bellevue Avenue down Parker Avenue. Indeed, this huge, shingled summer cottage with its gables and chimneys, its curving veranda with wicker furniture, and its tidy carriage house can stand proudly even in such an elegant neighborhood. When you pass through the front door its elegance is even more pronounced, for there you are greeted by a lofty entrance hall done complétely in glowing, artfully carved woodwork which rises all the way up to the third-floor roof. Staircases cascade in front of you, and stained glass glows above. There's a fireplace, and to the right a reading room with etched-glass windows. To the left is the formal dining room, where a full buffet-style breakfast is served. Guest rooms are similarly ornate and authentic. The hosts, Ed and Mariann Moy, will welcome you, and then leave you pretty much to enjoy yourself as you please. Rooms with shared or private bath and continental breakfast are priced at $132 to $154 double in high season. Little extras include bicycles, coolers and beach chairs, and transportation to the airport. To find Ivy Lodge, drive along Bellevue Avenue and watch for the Oakwood Healthcare Center on the left; turn left onto Parker Avenue just before the center, then right onto Clay Street. Ivy Lodge is a short distance along, on the left-hand side.

Of the several guesthouses downtown in Newport, perhaps the most convenient is the **Queen Anne Inn,** at 16 Clarke St., Newport, RI 02840 (tel. 401/846-5676), which is a half block off Touro Street at Washington Square, two blocks from the harbor, in the Historic District. Peg McCabe, the affable owner of the Queen Anne, advertises that you can "park your car in our lot and walk to everything," which is true of everything downtown, and even of the mansions if you're a good walker. One of the old Victorian town houses (rather than a wooden summer mansion), the Queen Anne has a dozen rooms furnished in a cheerful way with lots of nice little antique touches. Prices at present are $72 to $94 double, and there's one single at $52; seven baths are shared. Complimentary continental breakfast is served. The Queen Anne has its own patio and garden. You can't miss the place: Headquarters of the Newport Artillery Company is right across the street. Open year round.

The **Covell House,** 43 Farewell St., Newport, RI 02840 (tel. 401/847-8872), was built in 1805, completely renovated in 1982, and has six antique-decorated guest rooms which rent for $76 to $104 double, depending on bath facilities and on season. Continental breakfast is included, of course. The neighborhood is a quiet, residential one, but you're still only a short walk from the bustling waterfront.

Hotels and Motels

Newport has several large downtown hotels with all the luxury services.

The **Sheraton Islander,** is on Goat Island, Newport, RI 02840 (tel. 401/849-2600 or toll free 800/325-3535), in the midst of the yachts, connected to the center of town by a causeway. The 200 rooms and suites come with all the amenities, and cost $168 to $218 double in high summer.

The **Newport Harbor Treadway Inn,** on America's Cup Avenue, Newport, RI 02840 (tel. 401/847-9000), has 133 rooms, all modern, some with fine sea views, all right in the very center of the action. Prices are $172 to $222 double in season.

Among Newport's newest hotels is the **Newport Marriott,** 25 America's Cup Avenue, at Long Wharf, Newport, RI 02840 (tel. 401/849-1000 or toll free 800/228-9290). The hotel's amenities include an indoor-outdoor swimming pool, racquetball courts, health club, and four dining and drinking places. Many of the very comfortable rooms have water views. Rates in high summer are $195 to $240 double.

Besides these downtown hotels, there are many motels on the outskirts, in Middletown, particularly along **West Main Road** (Rte. 114). Prices are lower, but so are quality, convenience, and ambience.

WHERE TO DINE

Dining in Newport is anything you want to make it, from a seaside clambake on paper plates to an elegant dinner with candlelight, soft music, and polished service. There are two things you should know about Newport dining, however. First, if you plan to dine in one of the better restaurants, you may have to meet the requirements of a dress code. Many restaurants ask that their patrons meet jacket-and-tie/skirt-and-sleeved-blouse formality. Second, call for reservations when you plan to dine at one of the better places. Some restaurants are booked solid a week in advance for dinner on Saturday evenings in July and August.

Newport's Best Restaurants

The **White Horse Tavern,** at the corner of Marlborough and Farewell streets (tel. 849-3600), boasts that it is America's oldest tavern building, and it is certainly a Newport institution, having served the hungry and thirsty since about 1687. One family, the Nichols, ran the tavern for almost two centuries. Rescued from a period of neglect by the Newport Preservation Society in the 1950s, it is again in private hands and in excellent condition.

The old tavern is authentic and totally charming, with large fireplaces, huge exposed beams, and old oil paintings. Staff are formal in black and white, soft classical music wafts through the air, and the menu lists dishes which are a fascinating blend of the old and new: Duck is served with a cranberry sauce, beef Wellington with sauce périgourdine (Périgord is a region of France where geese are force-fed to produce foie gras), and sautéed lobster. Appetizers include poached salmon, and snails sautéed with ham. Desserts are rich and delicious. Expect the dinner check to cost $50 to $70 per person here, tax, tip, and wine included. Lunch is served from noon to 3pm every day (on Sunday it's brunch); dinner is served daily from 6 to 10pm. Call for reservations, and arrive well dressed.

Of the waterfront redevelopment projects completed so far in Newport, the one at **Bannister's Wharf/Bowen's Wharf** is the most charming, and it has a selection of good restaurants. Bannister's Wharf is right next to the Treadway Inn, downtown on the waterfront, and would be West Pelham Street's extension if the wharf were still a street. Poshest place on this very posh wharf is the **Clarke Cooke House** (tel. 849-2900), which has one of the most interesting French menus in Newport (not all frogs' legs and escargots) and two very different dining rooms. To your left at the top of the short flight of steps is the Dining Room, a very authentic-looking colonial room with rugged ceiling beams (original to the house, which is colonial), wood chairs and tables, gleaming crystal stemware, and tuxedoed waiters. To the right as you enter is the Candy Store Café, a light, airy, and open room overlooking the wharf and the water—about as different from the dusky colonial room as can be. Plan on spending about $40 to $55 per person on a full dinner here (served from 6 to 10pm). In the café, a lunch or light supper will cost about $16.

The dining rooms at the **Inn at Castle Hill** (tel. 849-3800) are among Newport's most famous, partly for the cuisine, partly for the service, and partly for the marvelous ocean views. There are actually several dining rooms, and a wood-paneled bar with entertainment, on the ground floor of this imposing Victorian summer cottage on Ocean Drive (see above). One dining room is the solarium, all white; another is paneled in dark wood; yet another is lighter but still formal. Take your pick, then order lunch from among such dishes as chicken parmesan, stuffed sole Florentine, and a gargantuan club sandwich. The dinner menu is fancier, and more French, but stays in touch with traditional American tastes. Expect to spend $25 to $30 at lunchtime, twice that at dinner. Here are other details: Lunch is served Tuesday through Saturday, Memorial Day through October; Sunday brunch is served April through November; dinner is served Monday through Saturday, June through October, and on Thursday, Friday, and Saturday in April and May; in November, it depends. No meals are served December through March, except continental breakfast to inn guests. In the dining rooms, men must wear jackets, and women must be similarly formal; no denim is allowed.

Best-Value Restaurants

Newport's well-established restaurant is the **Black Pearl** (tel. 846-5264), on Bowen's Wharf right next to the Clarke Cooke House. For lunch and dinner, on weekdays and weekends, the Black Pearl is crowded with the blonde and beautiful, the tanned and handsome. There are actually four places to dine here. In the Commodore's Room, dinner is served from 6 to 10pm, and a jacket is required for men and similarly suitable dress for women. This is not the busiest of the Pearl's eating places, but rather a refuge from the busy places. Table settings are quietly elegant and include a candle lantern. The decor is subdued, quite unlike the overdone or garish atmosphere characteristic of many waterfront restaurants. The menu is classic French, with all the familiar dishes of that tradition, and a full meal will cost about $50 per person with wine. Next to the Commodore's Room is the Tavern, where a jacket is not required, and happy, hungry yachting types press in for a drink, a "Pearlburger," an omelet, or perhaps a daily special such as fresh bluefish with lemon-caper butter. Outdoors, next to the Black Pearl, is the outdoor bar, a sort of waterfront café, with white metal tables and chairs set out on a patch of white gravel, shaded by brightly colored umbrellas.

Also on Bowen's Wharf is **The Landing** (tel. 847-4514), which is the place to go if you like to sit by the water. There are lots of different places to do that here: upstairs on the awning-shaded decks (one of which is the bar), in the glassed-in dining rooms, or on the open-air patios. The mood is yachting-informal and nautical; the menu is straightforward, with fish and chips, sandwiches, and numerous more substantial seafood plates. The Landing is open for lunch and dinner daily, and you can expect to spend from $15 to $24 here. Look for the Landing just down from Checkers Café, the café-club attached to the Newport Harbor Treadway Inn.

Those in the mood for beef should head for the **Chart House,** on Bowen's Wharf (tel. 849-7555), which is open daily for dinner only. Modern and attractive, it has only indoor dining rooms, but you get good views of all the activity through large windows. Tables are made with laminated nautical charts, and the menu lists steaks, prime rib, chops, and seafood in the traditional American manner. The daily specials are somewhat more inventive and adventurous. You can expect to spend $30 to $40 for a full dinner here.

The **Café Zelda,** 528 Thames St., corner of Dean Avenue (tel. 849-4002), offers the simple elegance of a French café atmosphere, plain furnishings of high quality in good taste. The luncheon standards—salads, burgers, quiche—are good and moderately priced, but it's the daily special plates, many featuring crab, that draw the crowds. A bowl of clam chowder, the fish-of-the-day sautéed with almonds and wine, dessert, and a glass of wine could come to $25 or less. Dinner is served till 10pm, except Monday.

After a hot morning's sightseeing in Newport, the **Brick Alley Pub and Restaurant** (tel. 849-6334 or 849-8291) is just what you want: a cool, quiet place to sit down and have some refreshment. At 140 Thames St., it's right across the street from Brick Marketplace and right behind the block of shops housing the Newport Chamber of Commerce's information office. Walk up the passage beside the restaurant and you'll come to a shady courtyard with tables set out. The selection of sandwiches, burgers, salads, and omelets is enormous, all costing about $7 to $8 (for $5 more you can have soup and a trip to the salad bar). Open every day for lunch and dinner, the Brick Alley has indoor dining rooms as well.

Another good place for good, moderately priced fare is the **Rhumb Line,** 62 Bridge St. (tel. 849-6950), one block north of the Gateway Information Center in the Historic Point section. The menu here goes through the lighter selections and courses all the way to full-course dinners, and there's a full bar. Evenings on weekends live jazz draws a crowd. Expect to spend about $10 or $12 for lunch (served from 11:30am to 3pm and until 5pm on weekends), about $15 to $20 for dinner (from 5 to 10 or 11pm). Sunday brunch is served from 11:30am to 4pm. What's a rhumb line? It's a line on a map or chart showing a constant compass direction straight to the destination. The principal advantage of a rhumb line is that it maintains a true direction, as does this establishment as an eatery.

The Ark, 548 Thames St., at the corner of Memorial Boulevard (tel. 849-3808), is Newport's restaurant for any taste, at any time. It has a prime location at Newport's busiest street corner, and the management uses it well by providing good, dependable food and competent, friendly service, a vast variety of dishes, moderate prices, and a full day's serving schedule. A sign outside advertises "Breakfast, Lunch, Cream Teas, Dinner, Raw Bar, Pub, Café," and it's all true. For instance, you can start the day with an English breakfast of eggs on fried bread with fried tomatoes and mushrooms, sausage, bacon, and coffee or tea for less than $8, all in— and it's a huge meal. Breakfast is served in July and August from 7am to noon. Lunch and dinner are served every day from 11am to 11pm. Come back and lunch on anything from tortellini to shepherd's pie, then dine on pasta primavera, veal medallions with sweetbreads, or blackened bluefish. Sit in the enclosed sidewalk café, or the gold-walled bar, or the cozy tavern with quiet booths, or the upscale upstairs dining room. Dinner in any of the ground-floor rooms might cost $15 to $20; in the fancier upstairs dining room, it might be $25 to $40. The Ark is a Newport standard, and has been so for years, for good reasons.

Inexpensive Seafood

Newport has lots of places where you can get delicious seafood at very reasonable prices. Most of these are on upper Thames Street, across Memorial Boulevard from the center of town. Some restaurants allow you to bring your own wine or beer, which also helps to keep the price of a good seafood dinner in the reasonable range. You can pick up your favorite vintage or brew at **Thames Street Liquors,** 520 Thames St., or at one of several other stores in the area. The BYO restaurants can tell you how to find the nearest liquor store.

Dry Dock Seafood, 448 Thames St. (tel. 847-3974), seven very short blocks south of Memorial Boulevard on upper Thames Street, is an attractive, clean, and modern eatery with lots of bright, cheerful wood and tile, a lunch counter, and tables with bentwood chairs. Ceiling fans keep you cool, and hanging plants add a touch of greenery. Order New England clam chowder or clams casino, for starters, and then a sandwich of fish, meatballs, or chouriço (spicy Portuguese sausage) and peppers. Or you can order a main-course dinner such as fish and chips, or a fisherman's platter, or swordfish steak, or (as I did) broiled scallops. I got about a pound of succulent sea scallops perfectly broiled in a light coating of crumbs, with an immense mound of french fries and a paper thimble of coleslaw, for a mere $9.95. One of the things that keeps prices reasonable here is that you bring your own wine or beer. All in all, expect to spend as little as $6 or $8 for a cup of soup and a sandwich, or as much as $20 to $25 for a bowl of soup and a swordfish steak, tax and tip included. This place is great!

Shore dinners are an old New England custom. A shore dinner is a no-frills clambake, with clam chowder, steamed clams, boiled corn on the cob, steamed lobsters, and other simple but delicious dishes served on paper plates to diners seated at wooden picnic tables. Newport's most authentic shore dinner is served at the **Newport Shore Dinner Hall** in the Newport Harbor Marketplace, Waites Wharf, off upper Thames Street (tel. 848-5058). Here a large, open warehouse-type building has been nicely spruced up, painted, and hung with colorful flags. Pick up wine or beer on your way here, or decide on soft drinks with your dinner, then order any of the aforementioned items, or lobster rolls, clam rolls, mussels, hot dogs, french fries, or clam cakes. Fish and chips costs $8.50, a large steaming plate of mussels is $8, and a steamed lobster over a pound in weight goes for less than $13 (depending on the season). The view, through large, open doorways overlooking the bay, is among the best in Newport. The Shore Dinner Hall is operated by the S.S. *Newport* restaurant next door, and is open from 11am to 9pm every day (till 10pm Thursday through Sunday). There's plenty of free parking here. If you drive, turn right off Thames Street when you reach the high 400s of the street numbers; there's a small sign for the Shore Dinner Hall.

In the center of town is **Salas'**, 341 Thames St. (tel. 846-8772), on lower Thames, a half block past the post office. Salas' actually consists of three establishments in one: a fish market and raw bar (open from 11am to 1am), a brasserie (open for dinner from 5 to 10pm), and the dining room (open from 4 to 10pm for dinner). Lunch could be breaded, fried fish strips with french fries and coleslaw, or any of numerous daily special plates priced from $6 to $9. For dinner there are several set-price meals which offer good value, such as the No. 1 Clambake, a 1-pound lobster, clams, corn on the cob, sausage, clam broth, and so forth, for $22.

WHAT TO SEE

There is plenty to see in Newport, and therefore during the summer there are also plenty of people here to see it. Parking places are at a premium, although the situation is certainly not hopeless. But why bother? If you are among the readers of this book who live close enough to Newport to make it practicable, why not bring a bicycle, or rent one when you get here? You can't really see the mansions by car—you always have to keep moving (the car behind you will make sure you do)—and Newport is small enough so that even an out-of-shape biker can see the town without much of a strain.

Several shops in Newport rent bikes, both three-speed (which is all you'll need), and ten-speed, among them **10 Speed Spokes,** 18 Elm St. (tel. 847-5609), at America's Cup Avenue, down the street from the chamber of commerce. You can rent a three-speed for $10 per day.

Tours

The Newport Historical Society sponsors **walking tours** of historic Newport on Friday and Saturday from mid-June through September, departing at 10am from the society's headquarters at 82 Touro St. (tel. 846-0813). The cost for an adult is $4; children under 12 can come along for free.

Should you want to get the "lay of the land" before heading out to see individual sights, take a bus tour of the town, Ocean Drive, Bellevue Avenue, and other districts. You don't necessarily have to take a tour that stops and goes through a mansion, although those are offered as well. **Viking Tours,** in the Brick Marketplace (tel. 847-6921), will take you on a 22-mile Newport tour for $9 (kids, $4.50); throw in another few bucks to go through one mansion. Viking also has hour-long harbor tours, from Goat Island, for $5 (kids, $2.50).

Another way to tour Newport is via prerecorded taped commentary from **Art's Island Tours,** for rent at $7 through the chamber of commerce, 10 America's Cup Ave., right downtown on the water (tel. 847-1600). You put a deposit on the cassette player, take the map, and walk or ride along the mapped route while listening to the commentary.

The Mansions

Newport boasts mansions of two types these days: those that are now, in effect, museums and are open to the public, and those that are still private summer residences and are most emphatically *not* open to the public. Believe it or not, many of these palatial houses are indeed still privately owned and maintained and lived in. In fact, the wealthy people who live in Newport mansions are also responsible for opening others to the public, for it was through the efforts of the Preservation Society of Newport County, to which many of them belong, that the marvelous houses were preserved. To think that The Elms, perhaps the most graceful and charming of the mansions, was to be torn down to make way for a housing development until the Preservation Society bought it, is nothing short of astounding.

Not all the mansions that are open to the public are owned by the Preservation Society, however. Several notable houses are privately maintained and open to visitors on terms similar to those of the society houses. When visiting the mansions, remember these two rules of thumb: First, figure on at least an hour per house to take it all in; second, don't try to see more than three, or at the most four, houses in one day unless you have a tremendous capacity for absorbing glitter and magnificence. More than three or four tours in one day will leave you dizzy and exhausted. Also, try to visit the mansions on a weekday, when the crowds are smaller, saving Saturday and Sunday for Newport's other attractions. If you must go on Saturday, get there early.

PRESERVATION SOCIETY MANSIONS The **Preservation Society of Newport County,** 118 Mill St. (tel. 847-1000), maintains six Newport mansions, plus **Hunter House** (a colonial house built in 1748), and **Green Animals** (a topiary garden with 80 sculptured trees and shrubs, many in the shapes of animals, in Portsmouth to the north of Newport).

A combination ticket covering all of these attractions is available for $28 per adult, $9.50 per child 6 through 11. Tickets for individual mansions cost $5 and $6 ($3 and $3.50 for children), but since you'll probably be seeing more than one mansion, buy a "strip ticket" good for two mansions ($9.50), three ($14), four ($17), five ($20), six ($22), or seven mansions ($25). Children's prices are less than half of these. Tickets are on sale at any of the society's mansions. During the summer (May to October) the mansions are open every day from 10am to 5pm. In the spring, in April the four fanciest mansions are open every day; the rest are open on Saturday and Sunday at the same times. Note that from July to early September, The Breakers stays open from 9:30am until 6pm. During the winter, Marble House, The Elms, and Château-sur-Mer are open Saturday and Sunday from 10am to 4pm. The Breakers, Marble House, and Green Animals are decorated for the holiday season in December.

Admission to any mansion includes a very informative tour through the rooms, and the right to stroll about the grounds at your leisure. Tours are very frequent, and the guides are almost always charming and very well informed. Here is what you'll see.

The Breakers: Certainly the most grandiose of the mansions, and most popular with visitors, is The Breakers, an Italian Renaissance palace built for Cornelius Vanderbilt. It is nothing short of sumptuous, with lavish use of the finest marble. The marble columns in the two-story-high Great Hall have capitals carved of alabaster. Priceless tapestries, fine mosaic work, irreplaceable paintings, and ornate furniture testify to the wealth of The Breakers' owners and their desire to flaunt it. Hard to believe. The Breakers was built in only two years. It was designed by Richard Morris Hunt, who did a great many buildings in New England, especially in Newport.

Besides the mansion, there is a children's cottage on the grounds (included in the price of admission to the mansion).

The Elms: E. J. Berwind, son of a Philadelphia tradesman, got an appointment to the U.S. Naval Academy, and served in the Navy until mustered out with high rank because of an injury. He soon made it big in the coal business, and secured the contract to supply all U.S. Navy ships with coal. With the profits he built The Elms, perhaps the most gracious and pleasant of the Newport mansions. Although it is grand, it is also supremely harmonious, having been modeled on a château in France. The sunken formal garden at the far end of the spacious lawn was designed by a French landscape artist. The Elms is the masterpiece of Philadelphia architect Horace Trumbauer. It was threatened with destruction when a land development firm bought it and planned to build a housing project on the site, but was saved by the zoning laws and the Preservation Society. Few of the original furnishings are left, but the mansion has been furnished with pieces from museum collections and private lenders.

Château-sur-Mer: The first stone mansion to go up on Bellevue Avenue was Château-sur-Mer (1852), built as a home for William S. Wetmore of New York. Wetmore's son, who met Richard Morris Hunt while on a tour of Europe, was responsible for bringing the American-born architect to Newport to rebuild his mansion, and later the mansions of others. (The senior Wetmore had lived in the mansion 10 years before he died, and upon his death his son took it over.) The château is very rich Victorian Gothic, and to modern tastes it seems luxurious, but also dark and heavy. Château-sur-Mer has the feeling of being lived in and enjoyed—something that can't be said of some of the other mansions.

Marble House: Richard Morris Hunt threw himself into building this mansion for William K. Vanderbilt, finishing it in 1892. It was modeled on the palace at Versailles, and is therefore decorated pretty much in the style of Louis XIV, which was, well, pretty grandiose—you'll see! As in The Breakers, the furnishings in Marble House are all original to the building. Get ready to see the Gold Room, a ballroom decorated with a king's ransom in gold, and the kitchen and the fascinating Chinese teahouse.

Kingscote: Built in 1839, Kingscote is the type of "summer cottage" lived in by wealthy visitors to Newport before the great stone mansions were built. First built for G. N. Jones of Georgia by Richard Upjohn, it was later acquired by a merchant in the China trade called William H. King, who gave the house its name. Kingscote is coined from "dovecote," so, by analogy, it means "Mr. King's Cottage." A cottage it isn't, for no peasant lived here; but rather a man who appreciated Tiffany glass and a gorgeous dining room.

Rosecliff: Another famous New England architect, Stanford White, built Rosecliff in 1902 for Mrs. Hermann Oelrichs, whose father had made a fortune in the Comstock Lode of the California Gold Rush. The building is modeled on the Grand Trianon, the larger of the two châteaux in the park at Versailles, but was meant to be even more lavish in layout and decor. Its ballroom is the largest one in Newport, and the mansion is still used for summer entertainments, as it has been for most of this century.

OTHER MANSIONS Besides the mansions maintained by the Preservation Society, several others are open to the public. Grandest of these is **Belcourt Castle,** another creation of Richard Morris Hunt, done in 1891. Oliver Belmont and his wife, formerly Mrs. William Vanderbilt, had Hunt make them a castle in the style of Louis XIII (1610–43). Today the castle is filled with appropriate memorabilia: stained glass, armor, silver, carpets. It even boasts a golden coronation coach. Well-informed guides escort the visitor through the beautiful period rooms and explain the collection. Tea or coffee is then served. Belcourt Castle, on Bellevue Avenue, is open daily from 9am to 5pm from mid-June through October 29. Admission is $5 for adults, $2 for children 6 to 12, $4 for senior citizens; a family admission costs $12. Special parties are arranged by calling 401/846-0669.

Beechwood, the house of William B. Astor, was built at 580 Bellevue Ave. in 1856. It was the home of *the* Astors. The "tour" here is quite a different experience from what you'll find at any other Newport mansion. Here, Beechwood Theater Company actors and actresses play the parts (tongue in cheek) of characters who might have lived in such a summer cottage during Newport's gilded age. It's all done in fun and with spirit, and it gives you quite another view of Newport life. Admission—which in this case is to a show as much as to a house—costs $5.50, $4.25 for seniors. For hours, call 401/846-7288.

Richard Morris Hunt's **Ochre Court,** a mansion built for Ogden Goelet, is styled after a French château. You can visit the mansion any weekday from 9am to 4pm, and admission is free. The **Edward King House,** in Aquidneck Park (which is bounded by Bowery, Spring, William, and King streets) is now Newport's senior citizens' center. It was built in 1845 on the plan of an Italian villa. The architect was

Richard Upjohn. The King House is open weekdays from 9am to 4:30pm. Admission is free.

Want to visit a summer White House? **Hammersmith Farm,** on Ocean Drive (tel. 846-0420), was built by John W. Auchincloss in 1887 as his family's 28-room summer "cottage." Jacqueline Bouvier, daughter of Mrs. Hugh Auchincloss, became Mrs. John F. Kennedy, and after the Newport wedding the reception was held at Hammersmith Farm. President Kennedy and his wife enjoyed visiting the farm when they could find the time, and no wonder. Beautiful rolling lawns and gardens, nature paths and copses of trees—not to mention the lovely old house itself—make the farm a seaside paradise. Mrs. Auchincloss sold Hammersmith Farm mansion in 1977, and it is now open to the public with many of the original furnishings. Guided tours are given daily: mid-April through mid-November and for "Christmas in Newport" from 10am to 5pm, in summer till 7pm. The charge is $5 per adult, $2 per child.

Newport's Other Sights

The mansions are on everyone's list of things to see in Newport, but there are lots of other things to do as well. Here's a rundown on some other possibilities.

A WALK IN WASHINGTON SQUARE Right downtown between Thames and Spring streets, next to the new Brick Marketplace shopping mall, is Washington Square, the center of colonial Newport. At the western tip of the square is the **Brick Market,** a Newport landmark, built in 1762 and designed by Peter Harrison. (The name derives from its use as a market, and its brick construction—no bricks were sold!) Having served variously as a town hall, theater, and crafts center, as of this writing it is undergoing yet another metamorphosis to serve a new purpose. At the other end of the square from the Brick Market stands the **Old Colony House,** center of Newport governmental affairs for 160 years from its construction in 1739 until the Rhode Island General Assembly (which met in Newport in the summer) last used it in 1900. It was from the Colony (later State) House's balcony that the Declaration of Independence was read to Rhode Islanders. In the assembly room is Gilbert Stuart's famous portrait of George Washington. You can get a free tour of the building July through Labor Day from 9:30am to noon and 1 to 4pm on weekdays, 9:30am to noon on Saturday and Sunday.

HISTORIC HOUSES OF WORSHIP Because Rhode Island allowed so much religious freedom, many religious groups suffering persecution made their way here in early times. Thus Newport boasts a number of firsts. The **Touro Synagogue,** a half block from Washington Square up Touro Street, is the most famous early house of worship. Designed by Peter Harrison (it resembles in some ways his King's Chapel in Boston) and built in 1763, the temple was the spiritual center of Congregation Jeshuat Israel, an Orthodox Sephardic congregation. The synagogue and congregation prospered along with Newport; but after the British occupation of the town during the Revolutionary War, prosperity fled Newport and few of its erstwhile citizens returned. In the late 19th century Newport came to life again. The temple reopened in 1883, and has been used for services ever since.

Touro Synagogue (the name may come from a 19th-century benefactor, Abraham Touro, son of the rabbi who presided at the synagogue's dedication) is open to visitors from May to late June, Sunday through Friday from 1 to 3pm and from late June to early September Sunday through Friday from 10am to 5pm. During the winter months it's open on Sunday from 1 to 3pm, and by special arrangement (call 847-4794). On Friday nights and Saturday mornings you may come to attend services. Admission is free, though donations are accepted. During the summer, short tours are conducted. You can see a copy of George Washington's letter to the congregation, written while he was president in 1790.

The Newport Historical Society is housed today in another early house of worship, the **Seventh Day Baptist Meetinghouse** (1729), the first in America of that sect. The buildings are at 82 Touro St., a few steps from the Touro Synagogue;

they're open Tuesday through Friday from 9:30am to 4:30pm, on Saturday to noon. Take a look at the meetinghouse and its famed pulpit, and also at the society's museum, which houses paintings, furniture, china, silver, and marine artifacts.

The **Quaker Meetinghouse,** at the corner of Marlborough and Farewell streets, was built in 1699, but was greatly modified in the early 1700s and again in the early 1800s. The congregation, founded in 1657, is the oldest of the Society of Friends in this country. The meetinghouse has been restored to look as it did in the early 1800s. Admission is $2, and it's open from 10am to 5pm. Monday to Saturday from mid-June through August; other times by calling 846-0813 for an appointment.

Of course, Newport has a beautiful old pre-Revolutionary church, and this one, just restored, is a real gem. **Trinity Church** (1726), at the corner of Spring and Church streets (tel. 846-0660), was built from plans by Sir Christopher Wren, and still has the "bishop's miter" weathervane, as it did before the Revolution. The church is full of history: Bishop George Berkeley gave the organ (1733), Washington was known to have worshiped here (pew no. 81), and its famous three-decker "wineglass" pulpit is widely admired. You can get in to see the church Monday through Saturday from 10am to 4pm in summer (late June to Labor Day), the rest of the year on weekends from 1 to 4pm, or at Sunday services at 8and 10am. Other times, call 846-0660 and make an appointment. Donations are accepted.

OTHER ATTRACTIONS Army buffs will want to drop in at the **Artillery Company of Newport,** 23 Clarke St., a few steps from Washington Square. The company got its charter in 1741, and since that time, besides defending Newport, has been collecting military uniforms. You can see this great collection on display June through September, afternoons Tuesday through Sunday from 1 to 5pm. At other times of the year it's open Saturday and Sunday afternoons only. Children are admitted free; adults are asked to give a donation.

The **International Tennis Hall of Fame and Tennis Museum** is sure to be of interest to anyone obsessed with the game. It's in the Newport Casino building on Bellevue Avenue across from the shopping center. The casino (1880) is the perfect location for a tennis museum, as it was here that the first national tennis tournaments were held. Major professional tournaments are played here during June, July, and August. The museum has trophies, tennis fashions, and displays explaining the evolution of tennis equipment. The 13 grass courts (and 3 indoor courts) are open to the public for play, so bring your racquet and call 849-3990 to make arrangements. The Hall of Fame and Museum are open all year: daily from 10am to 5pm May through September, and October through April on weekdays from 11am to 4pm. Admission costs $4 for adults, $2.50 for seniors, and $2 for children 5 to 16.

Newport has a **Museum of Yachting** (tel. 847-1018), as you might imagine. It's in Fort Adams State Park on Ocean Avenue, a short drive along Ocean Avenue from the center of town. If you're at all interested in small wooden craft, boatbuilding, or yachting, you should make a visit. A new exhibit highlighting the single-handed sailor is on the second floor. Hours are 10am to 5pm daily, mid-May through October 31.

The **Newport Art Museum** (tel. 847-0179) has changing exhibits in a house (1862) designed by Richard Morris Hunt. Call for information on current shows, then visit between 10am and 5pm. Tuesday through Saturday, or 1 to 5pm on Sunday. Admission is $2 for adults, $1 for seniors, free for those 18 and under. It's located at 76 Bellevue Ave.

WHAT TO DO
Here are several absolute musts while you're in Newport.

Ocean Drive and Cliff Walk
Take a drive (or ride your bike, if you're in shape) along Newport's 10-mile **Ocean Drive.** The scenery is very beautiful, with low heath, evergreens, stretches of rugged coast, and several smooth, grassy lawns maintained as state parks. **Brenton**

Point State Park has parking, walking, and picnic areas, and there's a Public Fishing Area with parking nearby. Ocean Drive also gives you a look at some of the yachts sailing on Rhode Island Sound, and at the mansions dotted around the end of the island. For walkers, the pedestrian equivalent of Ocean Drive is **Cliff Walk,** a path which runs along the shore and along the edge of the "front yards" of the mansions on Bellevue Avenue. Official start of the hour-long walk is off Memorial Boulevard just before Newport Beach beneath the Cliff Walk Manor, but you can also get to the path by going east on one of the side streets off Bellevue Avenue. By the same token, you needn't take the entire walk, but can head back to Bellevue Avenue at various points along the way.

Fort Adams State Park

On a peninsula jutting into Newport Harbor, Fort Adams State Park (tel. 847-2400) offers several attractions. The park is open from 6am to 11pm daily all year, and picnic and fishing sites are open to all. The fort itself, named after President John Adams, is open for guided tours from 11:30am to 4:30pm. Wednesday through Sunday in the summer (for a fee). Boat-launching ramps, beach with lifeguard, picnic area, the Museum of Yachting (see above), and soccer fields.are among the services. The fort's defenses are some of the most impressive in the country—so impressive, in fact, that it rarely came under fire. Views of the town and the harbor from hills in the park are well worth the short climb.

Beaches

Newport's beaches are of two types, public (open to everyone for a fee), and private (open to members only, "Keep Out—This Means You!"). Bailey's Beach, at the southern end of Bellevue Avenue, is definitely very private, but **Newport Beach,** also called First Beach, is public and quite large. It's on the isthmus at the eastern reach of Memorial Boulevard. Second Beach is in Middletown, a bit farther along the same route where the street changes names to become Purgatory Road. Just around the corner from Second Beach is Third Beach, at the mouth of the Sakonnet River, facing east. It may be a bit chilly at any time except July and August.

Gooseberry Beach, on Ocean Drive, is an especially attractive beach, open to the public for a car-parking fee of $5 on weekdays, $1 for pedestrians and cyclists. It's framed by nice mansions on either side, and has interesting rock formations.

Jai Alai

An unusual spectator sport and game of chance in Newport is the fast-moving game of jai alai ("high lie"), familiar to those who have traveled to Latin America and Florida. Because of a change in the law, minors (12 years and older) are now allowed if accompanied by an adult. The season is May 1 to October 13. The Newport Fronton is at 150 Admiral Kalbfus Rd., near the Newport end of the Newport Bridge. Seats cost $3 to $5 and general admission (standing room) is $2, $4 for the lounge and restaurant. Betting is on which player or team will win, and is parimutuel as it is at horse and dog tracks. The game is fast and exciting, and the ball (harder than a golf ball) moves at murderous speeds approaching 188 miles an hour. If you've never seen it before (or bet before), you can get a brochure at the door explaining it all. For seat reservations, call 849-5000 in Rhode Island or toll free 800/556-6900 out-of-state. There are matinees Monday and Saturday, at which seniors are free; ladies, free Tuesday; closed Sunday. There's a moderately priced restaurant and a lounge which overlooks court action.

Festivals and Events

Newport seems to have a festival going, one or another, all summer long. For current information on exact dates and offerings, contact the **Newport County Chamber of Commerce,** P.O. Box 237, Newport, RI 02840 (tel. 401/847-1600). For the state's *Guide to Rhode Island,* write to Rhode Island Department of Economic Development, Tourist Promotion Division, One Weybosset Hill, Providence, RI

02903. This 50-page pamphlet has a complete list of Rhode Island events and festivals for the current year.

One of the world's great yachting races, the **America's Cup,** held every three years or so, took place in the waters off Newport until 1983. Newporters hope to have the Cup "back home" some time soon.

Here are the major festivals and approximate times.

Music Festivals: Perhaps the biggest annual event in the town, the **Newport Music Festival** attracts great crowds to the grand mansions for the many and varied concerts. There are performances morning, afternoon, and evening for two consecutive weekends and the weekdays in between in mid-July. As the capacity of all the mansions and halls is limited, it's best to order tickets—and to make reservations for a hotel room—in advance. Write to the Newport Music Festival, P.O. Box 3300, Newport, RI 02840 (tel. 401/846-1133). For a list of all the concerts and performers, and the prices of tickets (usually $18 to $25). You can order tickets by phone (tel. 401/849-0700) starting in June.

The **Jazz Festival** in Newport is held on a weekend late in August, in Fort Adams State Park. Each day from noon to 6:30pm, top-name stars perform. The Viking Hotel (tel. 401/847-8100) is usually festival headquarters, where you can buy your tickets (general admission only).

May Breakfasts: May is officially celebrated as Heritage Month in Rhode Island, as "Little Rhodie" was the first colony to declare independence from British rule (May 4, 1776). On May 1, or thereabouts, May Day Breakfasts are held by all sorts of church, civic, and fraternal organizations across the state, and the public is invited to most of them. These can be pretty lavish affairs, and you're sure to get your money's worth. Write to the Department of Economic Development (address above) for a full list of breakfasts throughout the state.

Outdoor Art Festival: The end of July, usually the last weekend, sees Newport's Outdoor Art Festival, when painters, sculptors, and craftspeople display their works downtown and in several parks throughout the city.

Fishing Tournaments: From June to October, tournaments are organized periodically to see who can make a record catch of one of the familiar fish in the waters off Newport. The chamber of commerce can tell you more.

Tennis: Championships are held at the Newport Casino (Tennis Hall of Fame) in July, hosting the top professional male stars. For tickets and information, contact the Hall of Fame, 194 Bellevue Ave., Newport, RI 02840 (tel. 401/849-3990).

3. Narragansett Bay

To get across Narragansett Bay from Newport, you will have to cross two bridges on Rte. 138: first, the Newport Bridge from Newport to Jamestown Island ($2, payable in both directions), and then the Jamestown Bridge from Jamestown Island to Saunderstown (free). The total fee, therefore, to cross from Newport to Saunderstown or vice versa is $2. From Saunderstown, head south on Rte. 1A (Alternate U.S. 1).

NARRAGANSETT PIER
Route 1A skirts the southwestern shore of Narragansett Bay passing through this famous Victorian resort town, which is also the main town on the peninsula here. Although not quite so famous now, the town is still popular for the same reasons as in an earlier age: beautiful sea views, a fine waterfront promenade, and gracious old Victorian houses.

Where to Stay
The **Summer House Inn,** 87 Narragansett Ave., Narragansett, RI 02882 (tel. 401/783-0123), is just that: a bed-and-breakfast inn in a big summer house with 20 guest rooms that share baths. You can have breakfast (included in the room price) on

the spacious porch while enjoying the mood of this charming bayside town. On weekends, a room costs $62 double with shared bath, or $86 double with private bath; midweek prices are lower. By the way, children are welcome at the Summer House, something that cannot be said for all bed-and-breakfast places.

What to See

Passing through Narragansett on Ocean Road, you'll drive right under the last standing remnant of Stanford White's mammoth Narragansett casino, **The Towers,** built in 1882. The town's chamber of commerce maintains a Tourist Information Office in the base of the seaward tower—park on either side of the underpass arch and walk to the door.

The main beach in Narragansett is north of these hotels and The Towers, about a half mile distant. The parking fee is your admission fee, as usual.

FROM SAUNDERSTOWN TO POINT JUDITH

As you drive south along U.S. 1A to Saunderstown, look for signs off to the right (west) that point the way to the **Gilbert Stuart birthplace.** Stuart (1755–1828) was America's most famous portrait painter after the Revolutionary era, and did no fewer than three portraits of George Washington from life, perhaps the most famous of which is the so-called *Athenaeum Head,* model for the portrait of Washington on the dollar bill. (Look for the original of this in the Museum of Fine Arts in Boston.) Stuart was the son of a snuff-maker. Judging from the house, his father had a comfortable living, and the son was able to go to London to study painting with Benjamin West. Period furnishings, waterwheel-powered snuff mill, and copies of Stuart's portraits adorn the house. Open daily except Friday from 11am to 5pm; closed in November through March. Admission is $1.50 for adults, 50¢ for children.

Ocean Road (U.S. 1A) also passes by the **Scarborough State Beach** facilities, very popular on hot summer days although never filled to capacity. Scarborough Beach, like all Rhode Island beaches, works on a system of parking/admission fees, charged *per car.*

Continuing along U.S. 1A south will bring you to Point Judith and the departure place for Block Island ferryboats.

Point Judith/Port Galilee

Jutting southeast into the Atlantic Ocean and dividing Block Island Sound from Rhode Island Sound is Point Judith. The peninsula of Narragansett's southern extremity offers several things to travelers: The car and passenger ferry docks for boats to Block Island, located at Port Galilee; camping and picnic facilities at Fishermen's Memorial State Park, only 2 miles from Port Galilee; and good sand beaches along the southern and eastern shores of the peninsula. Port Galilee exists for the ferries to Block Island, the Wheeler Memorial Beach, several small fisheries, and a Coast Guard station.

The Beach and the Ferry

First of all, be warned that Port Galilee has very few parking places on the street, and that these are usually taken up quickly by the people who work for the fishing companies. Parking for the beach is $2 a day ($3 on weekends and holidays) for Rhode Island residents, $4 a day ($6 on weekends and holidays) for out-of-state cars, but this includes the entry fee to the beach for everyone in your party, and is standard practice at all state beaches in Rhode Island. Whether you park next to George's of Galilee or at the large lots of the Wheeler Memorial Beach several hundred yards east, the rate and arrangement are the same.

For the ferry, parking fees are of the same order, and the lot is across the street and down a few yards from the ferry dock. Note that the restaurants and motel in Galilee have parking lots, but they also put out fierce signs that threaten to have your car towed if your intention is other than patronizing their establishments. It's best to take them at their word, especially if you're going away to Block Island for the day.

4. Block Island

In 1614 a man named Adriaen Block visited a small island off the coast of Rhode Island, but his visit did little more than give the island its name. Slightly over 20 years later a colonist was found in a boat near the island, presumed murdered by the local Pequot Indians, and this unhappy event precipitated a battle between Pequots and colonists which turned out to be very bloody.

A generation later, these events forgotten, settlers from the colony moved onto the island and the town of New Shoreham (incorporated in 1672) was built. For almost 200 years the people of Block Island lived their quiet lives, fishing in boats from the island's two natural harbors, growing what they could in the sandy and windswept soil. But in the mid-1800s the Age of Steam changed Block Island from a fishermen's outpost in the Atlantic to a summer excursion paradise, with regularly scheduled steamboats bringing residents of the sooty factory cities out for fresh air and bright sunshine. Late-19th-century frame hotels, huge and sprawling, went up to accommodate them, and the island's economy came to depend on tourism rather than fishing, and so it has remained. Most of the island's buildings—houses as well as hotels—date from the late 1800s or the turn of the century. The roads are rough and sandy (nobody has to be in a hurry to get quickly from one end of the island to the other—it's only 7 miles); the pace is very relaxed; and the citizens of New Shoreham, which takes up all of the island, have a strong sense of community.

GETTING THERE

During the summer season from late June to early September, Block Island is very accessible, whether you're touring New England by car or by public transport. During spring, autumn, and winter, there's limited service to the island.

By Air

New England Airlines, Block Island's own airline, will fly you over from the State Airport, Westerly, RI 02891, on any of 14 daily flights year round. The $30 flight one way ($52 round trip) takes 15 minutes. You must have reservations, so call 401/596-2460, or toll free 800/243-2460 outside Rhode Island. If you're on Block Island, dial 466-5881. The airport is on Airport Road, Westerly, off Rte. 78.

Action Airlines (tel. 203/448-1646 or 448-1710, or toll free 800/243-8623) will fly you to Block Island from Groton/New London, Conn., or Madison, Conn., or Teterboro, N.J.

For details on flying to Block Island from Westchester County, N.Y., call the charter company **Westchester Air, Inc.,** at 914/279-5800.

By Boat

Boats leave for Block Island from four ports during the summer.

FROM PORT GALILEE This is the port with the most frequent service, and there are at least six and at most nine daily sailings in each direction from mid-June to early September. The trip takes less than 1¼ hours and costs $6.10 per adult, one way, or $10 for a same-day round trip; children pay half price. It costs about $40 round trip for a car (driver not included), and you must have reservations in advance. The Port Galilee agent is the **Interstate Navigation Co.,** Galilee State Pier, Point Judith, RI 02882 (tel. 401/783-4613). Motorcycles and bikes are also carried. During spring, fall, and winter there are fewer trips: two daily in each direction in May and early June, and late September through October; in winter, there's one trip daily.

FROM NEW LONDON In summer (mid-June to early September) there's one trip daily (plus an additional Friday evening boat) in each direction between New London and Block Island, leaving New London mid morning, returning from Block Island midafternoon. The trip takes about 2 hours and costs $12 for adults ($16 for same-day round trip), and $8 for children over 5 ($10 for same-day round trip). A car costs $44 round trip. The fee for bikes is $6 round trip. The boat leaves from Ferry Street, about one-eighth of a mile from the railroad station. Advance reservations for cars is a must. For more information, contact the **Nelseco Navigation Co.,** P.O. Box 482, New London, CT 06320 (tel. 203/442-7891 or 442-9553 during business hours). By the way, ferries from New London arrive at Old Harbor on Block Island, and you may have to take a taxi to reach hotel and restaurant choices.

FROM PROVIDENCE The same people who operate the Port Galilee–Block Island ferry, the **Interstate Navigation Co.** (see above), run a daily passenger boat from Providence via Newport to Block Island. Departure from Providence's India Street dock is at 8:30am, from Newport's Fort Adams dock at 10:30am, arriving at Block Island around 12:30pm. The return trip leaves Block Island at 3:45pm, leaves Newport at 5:30pm, and arrives back in Providence at 7:45pm.

One-way fares between Providence and Block Island are $6 for an adult, $3.25 for a child. Bicycles and motorcycles can be transported, but no cars. Ask about special same-day round-trip fares.

FROM MONTAUK, L.I. Another point of departure for Block Island is Montauk, N.Y., at the southeastern tip of Long Island. From here, the **Viking Fishing Fleet** (tel. 516/668-5700) operates a daily passenger boat (no cars) to Block Island at 10am. The voyage takes 1½ hours, and same-day round-trip fare costs $25 for adults, $15 for kids ages 5 to 12.

MAIL/TELEPHONES

Block Island's ZIP Code is **02807;** the telephone area code is **401,** the exchange is **466.**

ARRIVING IN OLD HARBOR

The boat trip is pleasant enough, plenty of room to sun on the top-deck benches, a small bar and snack counter on board. As you approach Block Island, the character of the place becomes clear: dunes and white cliffs, low shrubs and grass with a few trees, ponds, and hillocks (highest point on the island is 211 feet above sea level). The big old hotels come right down to the harbor, most looking pretty weathered from the stiff breezes and salt air, not to mention the winter storms, that are the norm here. Several of the hotels have vans which will be waiting at the dock to pick up passengers who have reservations, or those who want a room but have not reserved.

WHERE TO STAY

Block Island is currently enjoying a tourist boom. Most of the large old Victorian hotels have been renovated and modernized, many small family guesthouses have been opened, and in general the lodging picture is good but pricey. Because demand for rooms is high, you should be sure to have reservations in advance during high season (from mid-July through Labor Day). You can save 10% to 20% on many lodging establishments by staying during the week (Monday through Thursday) instead of the weekend if your schedule allows for it.

Most hotels on Block Island serve breakfast to their guests at no additional charge. Breakfast may be anything from pastries and coffee to a full eat-all-you-can buffet. Also, all hotel prices are subject to the Rhode Island 11% sales plus room tax, and some hotels levy a service charge (usually 4% to 6%) in place of your tips to the staff. These extra costs have been included in the prices given below, unless otherwise noted.

Reservations, Deposits, Refunds

The following general guidelines for lodging policies during high summer may vary slightly from hotel to hotel. Often there is a requirement that you stay at least two or three nights, perhaps even a week. All hotels require that you send a deposit (or give your credit-card number) to secure your reservation. Deposit refund policies vary, but may be something like this: Your deposit will be returned, less a $10 to $25 processing fee, if you cancel more than 15 or 21 days prior to your planned arrival date. If you cancel closer to that date, your deposit may be refunded only if the hotel succeeds in renting your room to someone else. Most hotels require that you pay in full upon arrival for your reserved stay, by traveler's checks, credit card, or cash. Estimate the total cost of your stay, and make arrangements for payment.

Canceled Flights

Several hotels caution guests that bad weather such as fog or storms may affect flights and ferryboats to the island; usually the flights are what's canceled, and the ferries keep running. If you plan to fly, be aware that fog may cause cancellation of your flight, and you should plan your schedule so that in the event of fog you will still be able to catch a ferry and get to your hotel in time to claim your reserved room. If you don't make it, you will forfeit your deposit and your reservation.

Hotels

Without a doubt, Block Island's loveliest place to stay is the **Hotel Manisses,** Spring Street, Block Island, RI 02807 (tel. 401/466-2421 or 466-2063), operated by Block Island's premier hoteliers, the Abrams family. The Manisses was built in 1870 as a small Victorian resort hotel. Restored by the Abramses in 1972, it is at least as fine a hotel as it was 100 years ago—probably better. The large-pattern floral wallpaper, white wicker and wrought-iron furniture, beveled mirrors, heavily carved and marble-trimmed parlor pieces, even the bubbling garden fountain, recall the best of a more gracious time. The 17 guest rooms have double, queen-size, or king-size beds; some have whirlpool bath and little refrigerator, and all have private bath, telephone, and period furnishings. The hotel's dining room is the best on the island. Guest rooms at the Manisses, single or double, are priced at $153 to $295 in summer; these rates include 6% service charge, 11% tax, buffet breakfast, and afternoon wine and "nibbles". The Manisses is open April through late October, the dining room is open on weekends only from mid-April through late May, daily from late May through late October. (See my restaurant recommendations for details.) You'll love the Manisses.

Also operated by the Abramses is their original establishment, the **1661 Inn and Guest House,** Spring Street, Block Island, RI 02807 (tel. 401/466-2421 or 466-2063), just up the hill a short distance from the Manisses. A large white island house, the inn has been nicely adapted to hospitality, with many good-size guest rooms, pleasant public spaces, and decks with sweeping view of the Atlantic. As at the Manisses, guests at the 1661 Inn and its neighboring guesthouse (23 rooms in all) find all the little touches for which the Abramses are famous: a full buffet breakfast, beach towels, and a decanter of brandy and dish of hard candy in each room. Some rooms have private bath, refrigerator, and private deck with ocean view. Prices in high season are $99 to $156, single or double, for rooms without private bath; $148 to $290, single or double, for rooms with private bath; 6% service charge and 11% tax are included in these prices. The buffet breakfast, which by the way is the only meal served in the 1661 Inn's dining room, is included in the summer rates. For other meals, by reservation, you can stroll down the hill to the Manisses. The 1661 Inn closes from mid-November through March, but the guesthouse stays open year round.

The **Inn at Old Harbour,** P.O. Box 994, Block Island, RI 02807 (tel. 401/ 466-2212), stands on a rise overlooking the ferry docks. It's right on Water Street, Block Island's main street, and you'll spot it at once as you walk from the ferry to Water Street, turn left, and walk a half block. There, facing the statue of *Rebecca at the Well,* is this three-story gambrel-roofed Victorian inn dating from 1882. What was once the lobby is now occupied by shops, but the 10 guest rooms upstairs have all been totally renovated, fitted with modern fixtures and carpeting, and half have been equipped with private bathrooms. Each room is different, the decor being a blend of fresh decorator-modern style and Victorian accent pieces. The price for a room, single or double, is $126 to $148, continental breakfast included, during the summer. Prices are $20 less midweek. The inn has its own eating establishment, the Water Street Café, and a Ben & Jerry's Ice Cream Parlour.

The **Water Street Inn,** P.O. Box 580, Block Island, RI 02807 (tel. 401/466-2605), facing the ferry dock, is a blocky shingled building, just the opposite of Block Island's ornate Victorian gingerbread style. On the ground floor is the Monhegan Café. If you walk down the right side of the building, go through the door and up the stairs, you'll find new, neat, and clean rooms totally refurbished, and now boasting wall-to-wall carpeting, bamboo furniture, color TV, and private bath. The inn is a fine place to stay—cheery, comfortable, convenient, and well kept. Rooms with private bath and continental breakfast are priced at $122 to $144 double.

Just up Spring Street from the 1661 Inn is the **Spring House Hotel,** P.O. Box 902, Block Island, RI 02807 (tel. 401/466-5844 or toll free 800/234-9263), a grand old clapboard Victorian hotel perched atop a hill with a magnificent view. Chairs for sunning and sipping are set out on the lawn and along the long veranda. In the spacious lobby, the Victorian ambience has been maintained, but brightened up and made a bit more plush to satisfy modern tastes. The guest rooms have been completely rebuilt, and are now very much like rooms in a modern luxury hotel. There is a dark-wood furniture with gleaming brass trim, including four-poster beds. Most of the 36 rooms are designed as "studio suites," with a sitting room, a bedroom, and a modern bathroom, all with baseboard heat. Not all rooms have ocean views, so ask for one with a view if you prefer it. The price list here is somewhat confusing. The least expensive accommodation is a "deluxe studio suite with ocean view," for $172 double in high summer, full breakfast and happy-hour cocktails included. Most expensive accommodation is the "superior three-room suite with ocean view," at $222 double, $20 each additional adult. Note that the Spring House is both a hotel and a condominium, so your neighbors may be newcomers or condo owners. The Spring House's dining room is gracious, and appeals to an older clientele.

The **Surf Hotel,** Dodge Street, Block Island, RI 02807 (tel. 401/466-2241 or 466-5990), is another Victorian wood palace, rather homey as only a great Victorian wood palace can be homey: cranberry-glass hanging lamps, wicker furniture, a great ornate iron stove, and a grandfather clock in the parlor, colonial wallpaper prints in the rooms. A good number of the rooms have fine ocean views—the beach is just a few steps away down the hill—and the hotel is a mere block and a half from the Old Harbor ferry dock. All but three rooms do not have private bath, and during July and August reservations can be made by the week only. For a single with a shared bath, the price is $66 per day, $427 per week; for a double, $72 to $83 per day, $471 to $538 per week (twin beds or double bed); there's no discount for children except for infants. Meals at the Surf Hotel cost $6 for breakfast ($36 a week). Cooking and service are home-style.

The **Harborside Inn,** P.O. Box F, Block Island, RI 02807 (tel. 401/466-5504), directly facing the ferry dock, is something of a social center in Block Island. Its terraced patio restaurant-café, right on Water Street, is popular with young and old, hotel guests and day-trippers alike. When it rains, the Harborside's spacious indoor bar, done with nautical motifs, is lively and jolly. As for the inn and its 36 guest rooms, it's an unpretentious Victorian beach hotel in which yet another coat of paint keeps things looking good. The large, simple rooms are popular with younger people and with the family crowd because they are clean, presentable, and comfy, and located right in the midst of town. Doubles in summer, full breakfast included, cost $117 without private bath, $150 with private bath. An extra person in a room pays $20, and that price also includes a full breakfast.

The **National Hotel,** Water Street, (P.O. Box 189) Block Island, RI 02807 (tel. 401/466-2901 or toll-free 800/225-2449), is a Block Island landmark, built in 1888 and renovated a short time ago. The renovations included the provision of telephone, color TV, radio, alarm clock, and new private bath in all of the hotel's 45 rooms and suites. Each room also has several Victorian pieces as an echo of the hotel's golden age. Room prices in high summer season are $144 to $233 double; the standard oceanview room with a queen-size bed is $194. Children under 12 can share their parents' room at no extra charge. Continental breakfast is included in the price. The National appeals to an upbeat crowd, who like the Japanese steak house, the juke box, and the player piano.

Guesthouses

The **Blue Dory Inn,** Dodge Street (P.O. Box 488), Block Island, RI 02807 (tel. 401/466-2254), right next to the Surf Hotel and the National Hotel, is actually a guesthouse and several cottages perched right at the tip of Crescent Beach. The main building has 10 guest rooms, all with private bath and Victorian furnishings, and also a living room and a kitchen, which serves as the breakfast room. The Cottage can sleep up to six, has kitchen facilities, and is perfect for a family or for two couples traveling together; it's priced at $281 (for four) per night. The Doll House ($155 double per night) is a one-room house good for couples who get along very well (it's tiny), and the Tea House ($195 per night) sleeps two, and has its own kitchen, plus a porch overlooking the beach and the sea. In the inn proper, double rooms with private bath cost $139 to $183 per night in summer. All these prices include 4% service charge, 11% tax, and continental breakfast.

The **Seacrest Inn,** High Street, Block Island, RI 02807 (tel. 401/466-2882), just a few steps from the statue of *Rebecca at the Well,* was renovated in 1982, and now holds very comfy, modern guest rooms with private bath which rent for $94 to $117 double in high summer. The inn has rooms for up to four people, renting for $138 (for four) per night. Free coffee, tea, cocoa, orange juice, and danish are available to inn guests each morning, and if I were you, I'd take a cup outside and sit in the cute little Victorian gazebo. The Seacrest is a family-owned and -operated inn which provides pleasant, comfortable lodging at moderate prices, with a smile and an honest welcome. It also has its own bicycle-rental shop, so you can be easily equipped for touring the island.

Lovers of family guesthouses will want to check out the **Gables Inn,** on Dodge Street (P.O. Box 516), Block Island, RI 02807 (tel. 401/466-2213), just around the corner from the Surf Hotel and behind the old National Hotel. The Gables is a traditional Block Island house converted to a guesthouse, and with its companion, the Gables II, it has a good variety of accommodations. Single rooms are $50 daily; doubles are $73 to $100. Most of the rooms don't have running water, but there are bathrooms nearby. There are also efficiency apartments for $688 to $821 per week. The Gables has several advantages over other places on the island: Its prices are low, it is open spring and fall, free coffee and tea are available throughout the day, and guests have the use of barbecues and picnic tables.

In New Harbor at 1 Ocean Ave., one of the first hotels you'll see is the **Narragansett Inn,** New Harbor (P.O. Box 186), Block Island, RI 02807 (tel. 401/466-2626). The big advantages here are convenience to the New Harbor docks, and rooms that are a minute's run across the lawn to the beach. The inn itself is a Victorian three-story house with several new additions. Prices are $105 to $139 double, depending on whether there is a private bath. The rates for the 54 rooms include breakfast. The inn is open from mid-June through mid-September.

WHERE TO DINE

I'm happy to say that there is good food on Block Island even though there are not all that many restaurants. You probably will have had breakfast at your hotel, so here are recommendations on where to have lunch and dinner.

As with lodging, the best place for dining is the **Hotel Manisses,** on Spring Street (tel. 466-2836). You can have dinner in the hotel's cozy dining room, or out on the awning-shaded deck by the bubbling fountain. Light fare is served from 3 to 6pm, and dinner is on from 6pm till 10:30pm. Dinner might be two tournedos of beef with a sauce of two mustards, or quail, or bouillabaisse. The chef does not probe the exotic too deeply here, but neither does he ever bore your palate. Expect to spend $40 to $50 per person, all in, for dinner. In high season, especially on weekends, call ahead for reservations, as the Manisses is small, and it does have the best situation and cuisine on the island.

Block Island's most popular luncheon spot is definitely the front terrace café of the **Harborside Inn,** on Water Street facing the ferry dock (tel. 466-5504). Take in the sun, or duck beneath one of the shady café table umbrellas, and order something simple such as a hamburger or club sandwich, or something fancier, like baked stuffed clams, broiled scallops, or sirloin steak. Wine, beer, and cocktails are served, and lunch with a beer might cost $10 to $20. At dinnertime, the fare is somewhat fancier but similar; and prices are still reasonable. Open daily.

WHAT TO DO

Most people coming to Block Island are looking for an easy schedule, quiet relaxation, time at the beach, bicycle trips, and seafood dinners. The island has a movie theater and a number of cocktail lounges, mostly in the hotels. A few small art galleries and craft shops are good for a browse. But beaching and bicycling are the two main activities.

Beaches

You can't miss **Crescent Beach,** to your right as you approach Old Harbor on the ferry. It stretches from the ferry dock for several miles north to the cliffs of Clay Head. It's simply beautiful, although the water is a bit brisk this far out in the Atlantic (it's warmest in late July and August, of course). Crescent Beach is divided into the State Beach, with a bathhouse, which is the section nearest the ferry dock, and Scotch Beach, which is the section farther north. Other beaches are over in the New Harbor area, several small ones on Great Salt Pond, and Charleston Beach facing west on the Atlantic.

Bicycle Touring

Block Island is too small to handle many cars, so most visitors get around by bicycle. Rental places abound and rates are not expensive, about $5 per day for a three-speed, $10 for a ten-speed. The rental shop at the **Seacrest Inn,** High Street (tel. 466-2882), has good equipment and helpful personnel.

Mopeds are available for rent as well, but many local residents—especially those who belong to the medical rescue squad—advise visitors to rent a bike rather than a moped. If you are not an experienced motorcyclist, it's best to heed their advice. The medics respond to some six dozen moped accidents annually, some of them serious injuries. You'll get along better with the Block Islanders if you rent a bicycle.

A suitable Block Islandish goal for your bicycle outing is **Mohegan Bluffs,** and the nearby **Southeast Lighthouse,** about 1½ miles due south of town. Head out of town on Spring Street, until it becomes Southeast Light Road, which traces the heights of the bluffs.

About 2½ miles farther along, on Cherry Hill Road, lies **Rodman's Hollow,** a glacial ravine that's now protected as a wildlife refuge. Bring your binoculars if you plan to explore it.

Three miles north of town, on the eastern shore off Corn Neck Road, is the **Clayhead Nature Trail,** as well as a network of other trails on private land once known as the Maze. Take the nature trail east to the shore (less than a mile), then north all the way to Sandy Point, where you'll see the **North Lighthouse** and also **Settler's Rock.** The granite lighthouse, now being considered for restoration, dates from 1867 and is no longer in use. Settler's Rock monument, erected in 1911, marks the spot where the island's first English settlers landed in 1661.

Only about a mile northwest of town along Ocean Road and West Side Road is the island's **cemetery,** with headstones dating from the 1600s and 1700s. It's a pretty spot, and interesting to anyone intrigued with Block Island's history.

Fishing

Several marinas on the island have fishing boats for hire, and surfcasting for striped bass and other delicacies is popular. Even if you're alone, the marina hands may be able to get together a party to go out, thereby reducing your costs greatly. For details, drop by any one of the marinas. All the boat-rental and sport-fishing businesses operate out of the New Harbor.

What Not to Do

Block Island and the town of New Shoreham are really one and the same, so the local government of the island is the town council. On the island the town's ordinances are the law, and these prohibit camping (except Scout groups and the like), sleeping overnight in cars or on beaches, riding motorcycles on the beaches, and shellfishing without a license.

---

5. Watch Hill

Rhode Island is known for its beaches, and some of the finest are along the state's southwestern shore: wonderful Native American names such as Misquamicut, Weekapaug, and Quonochontaug identify the built-up areas along the strand. The buildings are usually private homes, or snack bars and restaurants, and much of the waterfront land is privately owned and fiercely guarded. But the state beaches dotted along the shore are open to all at a fee of $2 per car with Rhode Island plates, $4 per car with out-of-state plates during the week, a dollar more on weekends and holidays.

As a base for your day at the beach, you could choose no better place than Watch Hill, an old and genteel town at the end of a peninsula between the Atlantic Ocean and the Pawcatuck River. Watch Hill is a sort of Newport-in-miniature, with stately old homes (grand, but not palatial), yachts in the harbor (expensive, but not priceless), and a gentility still strongly felt if slightly faded. It's a quiet town, with fewer than a half dozen places to put up for a night or a week, unless, of course, you own a summer home.

WHERE TO STAY

Of Watch Hill's lodging places, the most comfortable and pleasant by far is the **Inn at Watch Hill,** Bay Street, Watch Hill, RI 02891 (tel 401/596-0665). Don't expect a great old Victorian palace, for the inn here is actually a suite of motel-style rooms perched above a block of shops on the main street. You enter by going around to the rear and up the hill, where there is a large parking lot and a little office cabin. After check-in, you proceed along a wooden walkway to your room. Rooms 1 through 12 have the best harbor views; Rooms 14 and 15 have some water views; Rooms 16 and 17 see a bit of the harbor, but mostly shops. The view from all is interesting and attractive. The rooms themselves are very good, new, neat, and tidy, each with a little refrigerator, microwave oven, and small table for breakfast or snacks; all rooms have separate kitchen sink. White brick walls, natural-wood floors, and sliding glass doors opening onto little balconies overlooking the town make the rooms quite charming; and full private bath, air conditioning, and TV add to the comforts. High-season summer prices are $158 to $187 double, depending on the size and comforts of the room, and whether you rent on a weekday or on the more expensive weekend. Weekly rentals offer reductions of 8% to 20%. An extra person pays $24 per night, but there's no charge for children, except if you need a cot or a crib. Call for reservations early, as this is the village's prime hostelry and it fills up early. Open May through October.

If you're pressed for lodgings, you might want to take a look at the **Harbour House,** on Bay Street, Watch Hill, RI 02891 (tel. 401/348-8998). Apartments, rooms, and suites rent for $67 to $72 double, but are often booked in advance by the week. Another possibility is **Hartley's Guest House,** Larkin Road, Watch Hill, RI 02891 (tel. 401/348-8253), up behind the Inn at Watch Hill, with simple, homey rooms renting for $61 to $72. Only one of the 10 rooms has a private bath.

WHERE TO DINE

The most amusing place to dine in this pretty village is the **Olympia Tea Room,** Bay Street (tel. 348-8211), in a row of shops at the center of town, across from the little park and the police kiosk. The Olympia is an authentic early 20th-century seaside-resort soda-fountain café, with black-and-white checkerboard floor tiles, well-used wooden booths, a few sidewalk tables, and waitresses in black dresses with white aprons. The atmosphere is refreshingly real, not "re-created." As for the food, there's plenty of it, and it's more up to date: sautéed shrimp with feta cheese, clam stew, chicken fajitas with hot tortillas and guacamole, bouillabaisse, and of course, lots of seafood, from clams and sausages on linguine to boiled lobster. Lunch, served daily from noon to 5pm, might cost you $7 to $15. Dinner checks are usually $16 to $25, if you have a good, full meal. Breakfast is served daily as well. The Olympia is a wonderful bit of old New England, lovingly preserved for us all to enjoy.

WHAT TO DO

In Watch Hill, you spend time at the beach, you stroll along Bay Street and go window-shopping, you buy ice cream cones early and often.

Children will jump at the chance to ride (50¢) on the **1883 Carousel** at the end of Bay Street, one of the oldest merry-go-rounds in the nation.

In the little park across Bay Street from the Olympia Tea Room is a **statue of Ninigret,** Great Sachem of the Narragansett Indians, a noble man and friend of the local English colonists. The statue was erected in 1914.

Watch Hill is a place to start a romance, or to pursue one; to read and relax, or swim strenuously all day—to do as you please. There are no crowds, no neon signs, no plastic "lifestyles." Watch Hill is a bit of fading glory, which, luckily for those who go there, the rest of the world has already passed by.

CONNECTICUT

Connecticut's landscape is sprinkled liberally with lakes, rivers, and streams. But the state's namesake is the mighty Connecticut River, which springs from the Connecticut Lakes in northern New Hampshire, flows southward forming the boundary between New Hampshire and Vermont, cuts through Massachusetts and Connecticut, finally to empty into Long Island Sound. The great river is navigable as far north as Hartford, a significant fact that was not lost on the region's Native American inhabitants. They were the ones who gave it the name *Quinnehtukqut,* "the long tidal river."

Later inhabitants pasted different labels on the land. "The Nutmeg State" used to be a popular nickname, coming from the time when itinerant peddlers sold nutmeg from door to door. As often as not, the "nutmegs" were cleverly carved balls of wood. By the time a customer discovered the fakery, the peddler was gone.

For obvious reasons, the people of Connecticut prefer the moniker "Constitution State," which reminds one and all that Connecticut was the first American colony to have a written constitution.

Almost three-quarters of the territory in Connecticut is woodland, and drives along the back roads through these forests reveal rich fields of corn, grain, vegetables, and tobacco. But the state's wealth comes not from agriculture, or from tourism, but rather from insurance and manufacturing. The capital city of Hartford is laden with tremendous buildings which are headquarters for dozens of insurance companies. As for manufacturing, Charles Goodyear, Eli Whitney, Seth Thomas, and Mr. Fuller of Fuller Brush fame were all Connecticut Yankees. In the old days the state's production of buttons, pins, doodads, and kitchenwares gave rise to the breed of men known as Yankee peddlers, who traveled from town to town in horse and buggy, spreading the products of Connecticut's industry far and wide. Today the state's industries are a bit different: Sikorsky makes helicopters, General Dynamics makes atomic submarines, and the rubber companies turn out tires and products such as Naugahyde, the synthetic leather named after the Connecticut town of Naugatuck where it's made.

Although Connecticut has many historic houses and lovely New England villages, the places which are popular with tourists are mostly along the coast: New Haven, home of Yale University; Essex, a fine old town at the mouth of the Connecticut River; Groton and New London, submarine capital of the world; and of course Mystic Seaport, the exciting and attractive re-creation of an old Connecticut maritime village. Hartford, although not what one would think of as a tourist mecca, is a pretty and interesting city well worth a short visit. Besides the attractions of the city itself, it can be used as a base for excursions into the lush farm and woodlands of Litchfield County, in the northwest corner of the state among the Litchfield Hills, Connecticut's "Berkshires."

The telephone area code for all Connecticut is **203**.
The state tax on rooms and meals is **8%**.

GETTING THERE

The capital and the southern coastal region are well served by public transport, most of which goes through or originates in the metropolis of New York.

By Air

The state is served by **Bradley International Airport** in Windsor Locks, 12 miles north of Hartford. There's direct one-plane service between Bradley and over 60 other North American airports, operated by Eastern, United, TWA, Delta, American, and USAir. Buses leave the terminal for downtown Hartford and for Springfield, Mass., periodically, and limousines shuttle from Bradley to most cities in Connecticut. By the way, the Connecticut Aeronautical Historical Association operates the **New England Air Museum** (tel. 203/623-3305) at the airport, with over 70 aircraft, plus engines, accessories, and memorabilia, on display. The collection is open to visitors all year from 10am to 5pm every day. Admission for adults is $5; children 6 to 11, $2; children under 6, free.

By Rail

Amtrak runs trains daily from New York to Boston along both the coastal route (via New Haven, Old Saybrook, New London, Mystic, and Providence) and the inland route (via Hartford, Windsor Locks, and Springfield). Stopovers are allowed at no extra charge on most trains, so if you buy a ticket from New York to Boston, the stops in New Haven, New London, and Mystic, or New Haven and Hartford, need cost no more. It is usually possible to catch a train from New York in the morning, be in Mystic by noon, tour the Seaport thoroughly, catch another train around 5pm, arrive in Providence by about 6pm and Boston by 8pm. The trip from New York to Hartford takes less than 3 hours; to New Haven, about 1½ hours; to New London, about 2¾ hours; to Mystic, about 3 hours.

Besides the Amtrak trains, there are frequent commuter runs operated on the Connecticut Department of Transportation's New Haven Line by **Metro North**. These trains depart New York's Grand Central Terminal hourly from about 7am until after midnight on weekdays, with even more frequent runs during rush hours. Service on Saturday, Sunday, and holidays is almost as frequent, with trains at least every 2 hours. The trip by Metro North takes 1 hour and 40 minutes. For exact schedule information, call toll free in Connecticut 800/223-6052 or in New York City 212/532-4900. The big advantages of the Metro North trains over Amtrak on the trip to New Haven are the convenience of Grand Central Terminal—midtown, right beneath the Pan Am Building—and the great frequency of trains.

By Bus

Greyhound, Bonanza, and **Vermont Transit** all operate daily buses between New York City, New Haven, and Hartford. The trip to Hartford takes about 3 to 4¾ hours, depending on the line and the number of stops en route. Greyhound and Bonanza have services between New York and New London, and on to Providence and Cape Cod. The trip from New York City to New London takes about 3 or 3½ hours, depending on stops. It's difficult to take a bus to Mystic Seaport—the train's the best way to get there.

From Hartford, Bonanza has buses to Providence and Hyannis; Vermont Transit operates buses to Vermont, New Hampshire, Montréal, and Québec City. All the large lines have buses between Hartford and Boston. In Hartford, the bus stations and the railroad station are all within a block of one another close to downtown. The terminal for Greyhound, Vermont Transit, and Bonanza is at 409 Church St. (tel. 203/547-1500).

---

1. Ridgefield

Connecticut's extreme southwest corner is a busy maze of light industry, highways, and bedroom communities serving the metropolis of New York. But only a short drive to the north of the bustle along U.S. 7 lies Ridgefield, as tranquil and beautiful a town as one can find. Stately old trees shade the grassy lawns along its quiet streets, and huge old houses are well sited among the gentle rises and hollows of its topography.

To reach Ridgefield by car from the north, leave I-84 at Exit 3 near Danbury, and head south on U.S. 7. Coming from the south, leave I-95 or the Merritt Parkway near Norwalk, exiting to U.S. 7 North. From the west, you can exit from I-684 (the New York Thruway) at Katonah and head east on N.Y. 35, which becomes Conn. 35 at the state line, then leads straight into Ridgefield.

WHERE TO STAY AND EAT

Ridgefield has several gracious old inns. The grandest is the **West Lane Inn,** 22 West Lane, Ridgefield, CT 06877 (tel. 203/438-7323), set back from the street on a large lawn. Though the management advertises "colonial elegance," in fact the building dates not from colonial times but from the early 1800s, and was completely renovated as recently as 1978. You enter the fine old house to find a world of gleaming wood paneling, thick carpeting, wingback chairs, fine old fireplaces, and a hushed quiet. In the guest rooms, furnishings are classic and comfortable, and facilities are right up to date. You'll find air conditioning, color TV, radio, and telephone in each room, as well as a modern private bath. Rooms come with either one or two queen-size beds, and several have working fireplaces. Continental breakfast, including fresh-squeezed orange juice, muffins, and pastries, is included in the room prices of $108 single, $130 double, plus tax. Other services provided by the inn include babysitting, bicycle rental, laundry, and dry cleaning.

As for meals, the West Lane Inn serves light fare "from the pantry," such as sandwiches, desserts, and cold platters, from noon till evening in the breakfast room or on the long, spacious front veranda furnished in wicker.

You'll find more formal, elegant dining next door at the **Inn at Ridgefield** (tel. 203/438-8282). The restaurant's entryway is paneled in ends from old whisky and wine crates, each printed with the shipper's trade name. Inside, a grand piano dominates the plush, understated dining room where waiters in black and white glide from table to table. One can start with a pâté aux trois poissons (pâté made from three different "fish": salmon, sole, and lobster), flavored with fresh basil, and then go on to a sliced breast of duck in a sweet-and-sour sauce with green peppercorns. With pastry, and tea or coffee, this table d'hôte dinner is priced at $40; add the costs of wine, tax, and tip to get the final bill, which might be about $60. An à la carte dinner would cost more, but would also be well worth the money spent.

Another of Ridgefield's fine inns is the **Elms Inn,** 500 Main St., Ridgefield, CT 06877 (tel. 203/438-2541). It is in fact a colonial inn, having been built as a private residence in 1760, and converted to an inn in 1799. Since that year it has been an inn continuously, operated during almost two centuries by only five different families. Though colonial in decor, inn accommodations are quite modern in amenities and comforts, including private bath, color TV, and telephone. Prices for double rooms range from $101 for a double bed, to $107 for twin double beds or a four-poster, to $130 for suites. Single travelers pay $10 less per room.

The restaurant is justly famous, as owners Robert and Violet Scala have mixed French, Italian, and New American cuisines on the long menu. Veal is a highlight, of course. Expect to pay about $50 for a good, full dinner with wine, tax, and tip.

An inn outside Ridgefield draws a loyal and appreciative clientele who love its situation off the main road, among the trees, right by a pretty little pond. It's called **Stonehenge,** on Stonehenge Road, off U.S. 7 (P.O. Box 667), Ridgefield, CT 06877 (tel. 203/438-6511). Don't expect a rocky, turreted castle. Rather, Stonehenge is a large, newly rebuilt farmhouse with six rooms in the main inn, filled with plush carpeting, some king-size beds, floral wallpapers, and brightly tiled private baths. In a nearby guesthouse and cottages are four more suites and six rooms. Furnishings in these are a mixture of antique pieces for proper ambience, and modern conveniences (color TV, telephone, air conditioning) for comfort. The quiet of the country is yours for $105 to $170 double, more for one of the two suites. This includes a continental breakfast, which is brought to your room with the morning paper.

The dining room is justly famous as one of Connecticut's finest. The cuisine is French, sophisticated, artistic, sometimes rich, and always of a high order. Dinner is served nightly from 6 to 9:30pm; expect to spend $55 per person, all in. The price for Sunday brunch is fixed at $25 per person.

WHAT TO SEE

Ridgefield's history dates from colonial times, when the town was a way station on the carriage road from New York to Boston. Carriage passengers need inns for sustenance and lodging, and Ridgefield provided them. One such inn is the **Keeler Tavern,** 132 Main St. (tel. 438-5485), at the junction of Rtes. 33 and 35. The tavern is now a museum, open (except January) on Wednesday, Saturday, and Sunday from 1 to 4pm (last tour leaves at 3:20pm). Pay the admission fee of $3 per adult, $2 per senior citizen, $1 per child, and guides in colonial garb will take you through the historic (1733) building with its late 18th-century furnishings, pointing out the tap room, guest quarters, dining room, kitchen, and parlor. Despite the careful preservation and reconstruction of the tavern's early life, its most famous feature was added by accident. During the Battle of Ridgefield (1777) in the Revolutionary War, a British cannon sent a ball right into the Keelers' wall, where it remains to this day.

There is more to see in Ridgefield than cannonballs, however. The **Aldrich Museum of Contemporary Art,** 258 Main St. (tel. 203/438-4519), hosts changing exhibits of work by modern artists, even though the museum building itself is classic Ridgefield, having been built in 1783. The museum's sculpture garden is a fine place for a stroll or a few precious moments of peace, quiet, and beauty. Concerts, films, and lectures are offered from time to time. Plan your visit for Friday from 2:30 to 4:30pm; or on Saturday and Sunday from 1 to 5pm; closed Monday through Thursday. Adults pay $2; seniors and children, half price.

2. New Haven

This is a town of spires and steeples, of Gothic towers and steel-and-glass towers, very much of the present and very much of the past. Although New Haven was founded in 1638, the crucial year in its history was 1718, when Connecticut's "Collegiate School" for the training of young men for the ministry decided to make its permanent and perpetual home in New Haven, ignoring the suits and blandishments of the other notable towns of Hartford and Saybrook. Perhaps the college came to New Haven because a local man offered a good deal of financial assistance, and in fact it was for this assistance that the school's name was changed to honor Elihu Yale.

New Haven has never been the same. Although today it is a town of business and industry—small arms, the telephone company, the county government—it is still more than anything the town where Yale is, and the presence of the great university dominates New Haven's social and cultural life.

INFORMATION

The **New Haven Convention & Visitors Bureau** maintains a year-round information center right in the heart of town on the green at 900 Chapel St., Suite 344 (tel. 203/787-8367), open Monday through Friday from 9am to 4pm. There's another information center off I-95 at Long Wharf Exit 4b, open from mid-April to mid-October. At no cost guides will answer questions and give maps of the bus routes and streets, suggested walking tours, the city's attractions, and current material on recreational, educational, cultural, and special events in the area.

WHERE TO STAY

New Haven is short on those cozy, charming lodging places (inns and bed-and-breakfasts) which are found so densely scattered throughout the rest of New England. Most of the city's lodgings are to be found in modern hotels downtown, and motels on the outskirts.

Downtown Hotels

The prime downtown location is that held by the **Park Plaza Hotel,** 155 Temple St., New Haven, CT 06511 (tel. 203/772-1700), in the shopping and office complex facing the green. The Park Plaza has all those nice big-hotel services, such as an outdoor swimming pool, rooftop restaurant, lounge with entertainment, and comfortable guest rooms with private bath, cable color TV, and air conditioning. Rates for this convenient location are quite reasonable, at $97 single, $112 double.

The **Colony Inn,** 1157 Chapel St., New Haven, CT 06511 (tel. 203/776-1234), on Chapel between Park and York, is known to Yalies and their parents as a comfortable and convenient place to stay during campus visits. It's located just a block from the Yale Rep Theater and the Yale Art Gallery, and only 3½ blocks west of the green, so you can't go wrong. The spacious rooms in this modern five-story building are done in contemporary style with colonial accents and reproduction pieces. All the comforts are here: free cable TV movies in your room, as well as telephone, air conditioning, and turn-down service. Other hotel services include indoor parking, a restaurant, and a lounge with live entertainment. Single travelers pay $90 to $96; two people pay $105 to $110; and an extra person pays $10. Suites are $150 to $400.

The **Holiday Inn-Downtown** is at 30 Whalley Ave., New Haven, CT 06511 (tel. 203/777-6221 or toll free 800/465-4329), very near Yale and only a 5-minute walk from the center of town. The 160 rooms here are all equipped with color TV and cost $89 to $96 single, $99 to $126 double. Teenage children can stay free with their parents. The hotel has its own Café Sandalwood restaurant and lounge, with foods from all over the world.

The downtown **Howard Johnson Motor Lodge–Long Wharf** is at 400 Sargent Dr., New Haven, CT 06511 (tel. 203/562-1111 or toll free 800/654-2000), near Long Wharf. Take Exit 46 from I-95. At this very comfortable, hotellike lodge, you're very close to the Long Wharf Theater and not far from the center of town. Some of the rooms have king-size beds. Prices are $88 to $94 single, $98 to $106 double; an extra person pays $10, but kids under 18 stay free with their parents. Higher rates apply at graduation time. Senior citizens get a 15% discount.

The marvelous old **Hotel Duncan,** 1151 Chapel St., New Haven, CT 06511 New Haven (tel. 203/787-1273), boasts that it is "New Haven's oldest established hotel," and it is certainly well established, having stood solidly on Chapel Street between Park and York for almost a century. To enter its Romanesque portal is to step back in time, right into a set for a black-and-white movie from the 1940s or 1950s. The Duncan's advantages are its location, just four blocks west of the green, and even fewer blocks from the Yale campus; its prices, which are $44 single, $60 double

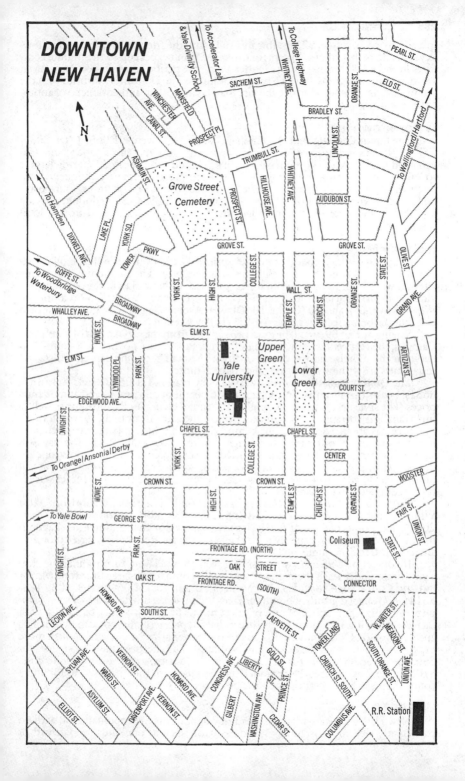

in a room or $54 single, $72 double in a suite; and the friendly, unpretentious, low-key staff and management. Except for cable TV, don't expect up-to-the-minute comforts in these 100 rooms, for the Duncan is a true period piece. Expect basic, even worn, accommodations, but also basic cleanliness. The Duncan is a favorite with the young and the artistic, who love the fact that it is an honest, authentic echo of another time.

A Downtown Inn

The **Inn at Chapel West,** 1201 Chapel St., New Haven, CT 06511 (tel. 203/777-1201), is a well-located Victorian clapboard house that fills a gap in New Haven's lodging market. The ten rooms are elegant and sophisticated, catering largely to Yale parents, alumni, and dignitaries. All the rooms are, of course, uniquely decorated with a designer's flare: touches of lace, mahogany, brass fixtures, four-poster beds, and down pillows. Prices for all this luxury are $146 to $204 double; cots are available. A light breakfast is included; the innkeeper has it catered from a local restaurant.

Highway Motels

Your best bet for a good, moderately priced motel room is the cluster of hostelries near New Haven on the Wilbur Cross Parkway. The parkway is the scenic alternative to I-95. Passing several miles northeast of New Haven, the parkway provides access to the city at its Exits 57 (Conn. 34, Derby Avenue), 59 (Conn. 63, Whalley Avenue), and 60 (Conn. 10, Dixwell Avenue). Motels are grouped at each exit, but the best selection is at Exit 59, Whalley Avenue.

Staying at Exit 59, you'll be exactly 3½ miles from the greensward of Yale's Old Campus, the very center of the city. The "Amity Road" bus, no. B-1, will shuttle you between the motels and the center of town. A small shopping center and several restaurants are within walking distance of each motel.

The **Quality Inn,** 100 Pond Lily Ave., New Haven, CT 06525 (tel. 203/387-6651), boasts that it can accommodate 1,086 people at one time—and at moderate prices. The style here is what you might call "motel Georgian," handsome as well as functional. As you approach the motel (follow the signs from Exit 59), you'll think the place has about 18 rooms. But behind the main building (which is where you register) are several other large buildings boasting 125 rooms in all. You pay $68 single, $80 double (as always, tax included) to stay here. Swimming pools (one indoors), putting green, saunas, whirlpool baths, exercise room, and restaurant are all on site. The Quality Inn was once the city's prime place to stay. The motel was recently completely refurbished.

Farther north, at Exit 61 North (Exit 62 South) is a **Howard Johnson,** 2260 Whitney Ave., Hamden, CT 06518 (tel. 203/288-3831 or toll free 800/654-2000). The bonus here, as at many large nationally franchised motels, is that children up to 17 years old can stay with their parents for free. Rooms have color TV, and cost $60 to $65 single, $69 to $73 double.

If you get off I-95 at Exit 55 coming from New Haven, turn right at the stop sign to pass underneath the highway and you'll come to the large **Branford Motor Inn and Conference Facilities,** 375 Main St., Branford, CT 06405 (tel. 203/488-8314). A U-shaped group of buildings faces U.S. 1 across a wide swath of lawn complete with swimming pool. Scores of guest rooms fill the two-story buildings, with each room having air conditioning, direct-dial telephone, coffee pot, cable color TV, and Home Box Office movies. Rooms in the newer annex are several dollars more expensive than those in the older main buildings. The cheapest single room goes for $50, the cheapest double for $61. The most luxurious, expensive minisuite costs $108. Note that children 18 or under stay for free with their parents. You'll find a coffee shop and restaurant right on the premises.

WHERE TO DINE

New Haven's restaurants are spread throughout the metropolitan area, with no particularly rich concentration right downtown such as one finds in Hartford or

Boston. But if you are selective, it is not difficult to find the meal you're looking for, at the price you want to pay, within walking distance of the green. Part of the problem is that many New Havenites who enjoy dining out belong to private clubs (the famed Mory's is one of these), and thus tend not to patronize restaurants that are open to the general public.

Restaurants Near the Green

The chic brasserie and bar near the green is **Bruxelles,** 220 College St. (tel. 777-7752), at the corner of Crown Street, a block west of the green. Black bentwood chairs and tables are the main feature of the simple but elegant decor here. To the left as you enter is the well-stocked bar; to the right, the dining rooms, and huge vertical grills with spits loaded with chickens, ducks, and whole roasts of pork and beef. At dinner you can start with something like goat cheese on an herbed tomato, then order Texas barbecue chicken, or roast tuna steak au poivre, or roast duck with peach-raspberry sauce. There is good luncheon fare as well, but don't miss a roast in the evening. Dinner might cost $25 to $35, including a glass or two of some premium vintage or brew from the well-selected wine and beer lists. Bruxelles is open Sunday through Thursday from 11:30am to 11:30pm, on Friday and Saturday till 1:30am, which makes it good for an after-theater drink and snack.

Perfect for elegant picnic supplies, that's **Soirée,** 230 College St. (tel. 562-0821), between Chapel and Crown streets, a half block west of the green, and virtually next door to the Palace Theater. In this group of shops established in an old townhouse you can buy potato-leek soup, chicken salad, asparagus spears with wild-mushroom cream sauce, lobster salad, French cheeses and breads, and sandwiches. You can have it all packed up to go, or you can sit at one of the little tables inside, or out front by the sidewalk, and dig in. You can easily spend $6 to $11 per person for restaurant-class fare. But for a main course such as grilled salmon or a braised lamb shank with goat cheese expect to pay upward of $20. The fancy desserts here are beautiful! The café is open every day from 11am to 3pm and Tuesday to Thursday from 5 to 8pm, from 5 to 9pm on Friday and Saturday. The shops are open every day, throughout the day.

Book lovers (and there are plenty of them in New Haven) congregate at the **Atticus Bookstore-Café,** 1082 Chapel St. (tel. 776-4040), right next to the entrance to the Yale Center for British Art. Sip tea and consume pastry while scanning the shelves from the comfort of your table, or browse through the store accompanied by the heavenly smell of coffee brewing. Come in the morning for croissants and coffee, in the afternoon for cakes and tea. Either repast might cost about $5, but perhaps you should add in the price of the book you'll discover, and buy. The store is open Monday through Friday from 8am to midnight, on Saturday from 9am to midnight, and on Sunday from 9am to 9pm.

An old standby for lunch or supper is the **Foundry Café,** 104 Audubon St. (tel. 776-5144), near the corner of Whitney Avenue and Audubon. The Foundry was just that, a machine foundry building, until it was recycled into a bookstore, shops, and the café. The one small café room has a bar/lunch counter, a blackboard menu, and some beautiful old inlaid-wood chess tables as dining tables. Lunch and dinner are served Monday through Saturday from 11:30am to midnight. Fare is simple but tasty: a selection of sandwiches for $3 to $5, a seafood-salad platter for $8, cheesecake for less than $3. In the evening the Foundry Café is a bar and nightclub. Happy hour, when the snacks are free, is every weekday evening from 4 to 7pm, and there's entertainment (usually jazz) on Wednesday through Sunday evenings.

It's an audacious claim to say that **Louis' Lunch,** 261 Crown St. (tel. 562-5507), at the corner of College Street, was the "purveyor of the first hamburger in the U.S.A.," but so it is. Louis' started in 1900, serving the first thinly sliced steak sandwich, and then developed the vertically grilled ground-beef sandwich. The beef is still ground fresh daily and grilled in the original antique vertical grills. Served on toast with tomato and onion, the hamburger ($1.90) is also available as a cheeseburger (introduced in 1931) for no extra charge. Threatened by downtown redevelopment some years ago, Louis' was rescued by faithful fans who saw to it that the brick structure was picked up and moved safely to its present location. Many—from all over the world—donated bricks for use in resettlement.

Louis' caters faithfully to New Haven's weekday lunch crowd from 9am to 11am and from 11:30am to 4:30pm; closed weekends. Coffee and soft drinks are available.

Restaurants near Wooster Square

About six blocks east of the green along Chapel Street lies Wooster Square, a lovely green park surrounded by some of this city's most interesting old houses. In this area, Chapel Street and Wooster Street (parallel, one block south) hold many restaurant choices, many of them featuring Italian cuisine.

My favorite here is **Tony & Lucille's Little Italy,** 150 Wooster St. (tel. 787-1621), near Crown and Chestnut streets. It's actually a restaurant in two locations. At Wooster and Crown is a modern building meant to resemble an Italian villa inside, with a skylit courtyard and arcade that are sunny and cheery, but at the same time air-conditioned. An antique espresso machine shines gloriously beneath one arcade. Tables are clothed in red-and-white checks, waiters wear black and white, and the menu is pure Italian. I had a huge bowl of zuppa di mussels and clams on a bed of linguine—I couldn't finish it—with a salad that was in fact a small antipasto. With bread and butter, coffee, tax, and tip, I paid $16 at lunch. At dinner, top prices are for the fancy cuts of veal, but there are many pasta choices such as fettuccine and linguine, and some seafood dishes, so you can spend anywhere from $25 to $35 for a full meal.

The restaurant's other location, called the Annex, a block east at the corner of Wooster and Chestnut streets, is a cozy storefront bistro serving simpler fare such as calzones for $4 to $6.

Hours for Tony & Lucille's are Tuesday through Thursday from noon to 10pm, on Friday to 11pm, on Saturday from 3 to 11pm, and on Sunday from 3 to 10pm; closed Monday.

For pizza, New Haven's favorite is **Frank Pepe's,** on Wooster Street at Crown (tel. 865-5762), two storefronts in which you will find bare wooden booths, brick walls, little in the way of atmosphere, but fantastic pizza. People line up in front of the restaurant to receive the hot pizzas that issue from the huge ovens in the back. The assortment is bewildering, ranging from a small grated-cheese pizza for $4 to large pies at $12; large ones with chicken or fresh clams cost more, up to $16. Pepe's is open Monday, Wednesday, and Thursday from 4 to 10:30pm, Friday and Saturday from 11:30am to midnight, and Sunday from 2:30 to 10:30pm; closed Tuesday.

WHAT TO SEE

The churches on the green have illustrious heritages of design, for Gothic-style **Trinity Church** is said to have been modeled somewhat on England's York Minster; **Center Church** and **United Church** are both said to have sprung from early plans for London's famous St. Martin's-in-the-Fields. Center Church, in Georgian style, is particularly interesting. It was built on an old burying ground, and today has a crypt underneath where you can see over 100 of the early gravestones. Guided tours of the church are offered Tuesday through Sunday.

Three blocks northeast of the green is **Grove Street Cemetery,** a beautiful parklike sward, fitting final resting place for such eminent New Haven citizens as Eli Whitney, Noah Webster, and Charles Goodyear.

Yale University

New Haven's prime attraction is Yale, almost three centuries old, founded in 1701 and moved to New Haven in 1716. Daily, Yale sponsors free guided tours of the campus (tel. 432-2300) weekdays at 10:30am and 2pm, weekends at 1:30pm.

Tours start at 344 College Street across from the green, at a place called Phelps Gateway (look for the inscription "Lux et Veritas"), where the university has its information office.

Yale's campus recalls England's Oxford, for it's much more American Collegiate Gothic than, say, Harvard, which is mostly Georgian and colonial in style. Yale's got lots of open, grassy courts, and fleched towers. Centerpiece of this English Gothic world is **Harkness Tower,** inscribed with the famous motto that has for generations admonished Yale students to move ever upward: "For God, For Country, and For Yale." Harkness Tower has a carillon, which is played daily throughout the academic year. You can also see the art galleries, the Beinecke Rare Book Library, the Georgian-style Connecticut Hall, and the Gothic-style Sterling Memorial Library.

The Peabody Museum

Yale's Peabody Museum of Natural History (tel. 432-5050 or 432-5799) has one of those fine, turn-of-the-century collections assembled when American scientists were venturing into all the corners of the world to bring back specimens of terra, flora, and fauna for study and observation by university students. Dinosaur fossils, dioramas featuring North American animals in their habitats, exhibits on human origins and cultures, invertebrate life, meteorites, and minerals are all on display, although what the museum can show is only a fraction of its vast holdings. Besides the permanent exhibits, the museum sponsors special events, lectures, and films. Admission is $2 per adult, $1.50 per senior, $1 per child 5 to 15 (under 5, free); if you enter Monday through Friday from 3 to 5pm, admission is free. The museum, at 170 Whitney Ave., corner of Sachem, is open from 10am to 5pm. Monday through Saturday, from noon to 5pm on Sunday and holidays.

Galleries

Opened on the campus in April 1977 is the **Yale Center for British Art,** 1080 Chapel St. near the corner of High Street (tel. 432-2800). The center has a fine collection of works by British artists, and also features special exhibitions, lectures, films, and concerts. Check *New Haven Info* or the *New Haven Register* listings for current offerings. You can see what the center has to offer from 10am to 5pm. Tuesday through Saturday, from 2 to 5pm on Sunday; closed Monday. Admission is free.

Yale's major art collection is in the **Yale University Art Gallery,** on Chapel Street between High and York. The oldest university art museum in North America, the Yale Gallery is justifiably proud of its Garvan Collection of American furniture and silver. Anyone interested in 18th-century American silver has got to see the Garvan—it's the best in the world. Along with Van Gogh's masterpiece *The Night Café,* there are paintings by Rubens, Hals, Manet, Picasso, and others. The university's collections form a substantial holding of European, African, Pre-Columbian, American, Ancient, and Asian art on view Tuesday through Saturday from 10am to 5pm, on Sunday from 2 to 5pm; closed Monday. There are also Thursday-evening hours from 5 to 8pm during the academic year. Lectures, concerts, films, and special exhibits are always on when the university is in session; see the listings for current events.

Performing Arts

Because of Yale, New Haven has a rich cultural life in music, dance, and drama. Each academic year sees concerts and performances by over a dozen excellent groups, including the New Haven Symphony Orchestra, the Yale Concert Band, Yale Glee Club, Yale Jazz Ensemble, the Bach Society, the New Haven Civic Orchestra, and the Community Choir. The Yale Repertory Theater and the Long Wharf Theater (a proving-ground for New York–bound plays) get very good reviews each season, as does the Connecticut Ballet Company. New Haven also plays host to visits from the Boston Symphony Orchestra, major concert and popular performers, and groups. Several buildings in and around the campus are foci for these events. The listings recommended above have full information on the current season's performances. Most will be within a few blocks of the green. **Long Wharf** is a bit farther out, next to Howard Johnson's, in the wholesale market at 222 Sargent Dr. (Connecticut Turnpike Exit 46; tel. 787-4282).

Downtown theaters include the **Shubert** (tel. 624-1825) and the **Palace** (tel. 624-8497), across from one another on College Street between Chapel and Crown, a half block south of the green behind the Taft Apartments. The **Yale Rep** (tel. 432-1234) is in a former church building on Chapel Street, corner of York, two blocks west of the green.

Nightlife Notes

New Haven must retain its dignity as the seat of Yale University. But that doesn't mean things are dead at night. Try the **Foundry Café,** mentioned above, for live music.

Boppers, at the corner of College and Crown streets (tel. 562-1957), is a re-created 1950s diner, complete with half the body of a '56 Buick Special. Though you can dine here on burgers and pizza, the attraction is the fifties music (recorded) for dancing.

3. Connecticut River Valley

Strictly speaking, the Connecticut River Valley extends all the way from Long Island South to northern New Hampshire. It's the lower valley that we're interested in, though. Besides being particularly beautiful, the last 100 or so miles of the river's course have figured prominently in Connecticut history. The small towns retain the charm of a bygone era, and the river's banks are scattered with state parks and forests.

From New Haven, it's about 30 miles along I-95 to the mouth of the river. About midway you pass **Hammonassett Beach State Park,** which has facilities for camping and picnicking, hiking trails, and a fine beach for boating, swimming, and scuba diving.

Before reaching the river's edge, the highway passes Westbrook, where there's a nice inn, and then Old Saybrook, a town with picturesque views. On the east bank of the river is Old Lyme, with several fine inns. Heading northwest up the river on Rte. 9 brings you to Essex, perhaps the busiest and most charming river town, with one of Connecticut's most acclaimed inns. Ivoryton, to the west, also has several fine inns, and an old steam railroad. Due north of Ivoryton lies Chester, a charming village with good possibilities for dining and lodging, and just across the river from it, by an antique car-ferry, is Hadlyme, with its own hilltop castle. North of Hadlyme, on the same (east) bank of the river is East Haddam, home of the famous Goodspeed Opera House, and several good inns. All of this is yours in a distance of 20 miles, from Westbrook to East Haddam.

WESTBROOK

In 1850, Capt. Elbert Stannard built a gracious mansion in Westbrook for his retirement years after a long career of commanding trading ships in the Orient. His home is now the **Captain Stannard House,** 138 S. Main St., Westbrook, CT 06498 (tel. 203/399-7565), a lovely old inn and antiques shop. The house has been carefully restored and maintained; the guest rooms are filled with nice old pieces of brass, wicker, and oak, including brass and four-poster beds, handmade textiles and crafts, and equipped with modern bathrooms and climate control. There's the antiques shop for browsing, a lounge with TV, and a refrigerator with ice and soft drinks. The innkeepers, Ray and Elaine Grandmaison, are out to make your stay here an enjoyable and memorable one. Prices for the six guest rooms are $73 to $84 during the high summer season; the room with the canopy bed goes for $73 double. A light breakfast is included in these rates. To find the inn, take Exit 65 from I-95, to U.S. 1 East, then immediately left onto South Main Street. Follow this street to its end, where you'll see the grand house with a fan window above the door and a cupola perched on top.

OLD SAYBROOK

Old Saybrook is the gateway to scenic Saybrook Point, with its two lighthouses. If you have time for a pretty drive, come up from Westbrook on U.S. 1 East, then follow Rte. 154 through Knollwood, Fenwick (where Katharine Hepburn lives), and Saybrook Point to Old Saybrook. To cross the river to Old Lyme, you will have to leave all this tranquillity and climb back onto I-95 eastbound.

OLD LYME

This village is a painter's paradise, and has been so for quite a while. During the early years of this century, Miss Florence Griswold opened the doors of her mansion on Lyme Street to painters, mostly American Impressionists, whom she admired, including Charles Ebert, Childe Hassam, Willard Metcalfe, Henry Ward Ranger, and Guy and Carleston Wiggins. Painters being painters, no matter how talented, they were sometimes unable to scrape together the month's rent for a room in the mansion, so instead they did what they could: They painted the door panels of the house with scenes from around Old Lyme. The house is now a museum, and one of your prime reasons for stopping here. The other reason is that Old Lyme has several fine inns, good for lodging and for dining.

Inns

The village's prime hostelry is the gracious and elegant **Old Lyme Inn,** Lyme St., P.O. Box 787, Old Lyme, CT 06371 (tel. 203/434-2600), a fine mansion dating from the 1850s. Innkeeper Diana Field Atwood has found period furnishings from many New England locales with which to do the rooms, so you'll find canopy beds, marble-topped dressers and vanities, and antique mirrors. Nine of the guest rooms are in the new (1985) North Wing, which is designed to harmonize with the original mansion and other structures on historic Lyme Street. North Wing rooms are preferable because of their better size and quiet, though the five rooms in the original mansion are certainly charming. All rooms have air conditioning, private bath, telephone, and clock radio, and rent for $102 to $135 double. A continental breakfast is included in the rates.

The Old Lyme Inn's dining room is open daily except Monday for lunch from noon to 2pm, on Sunday from noon to 4pm; for dinner from 6 to 9pm, on Sunday from 4 to 9pm. Tapestries, gleaming silver, and a formal atmosphere greet you in the high-ceilinged dining room, renowned for its fine cuisine, especially local seafood and veal. There is also a less formal grill room, open Tuesday through Friday and Sunday.

Bob and Penny Nelson's **Bee and Thistle Inn,** 100 Lyme St., Old Lyme, CT 06371 (tel. 203/434-1667), dates from colonial times (1756), with many later additions. Its situation, on its own estate of more than five shady acres bordering the Lieutenant River, is superb. The 11 guest rooms have furnishings reflecting the inn's long history—canopy, four-poster, or spool beds with handmade quilts and afghans, washstands, wing chairs—but also private baths in most cases. The price for a room is $85 to $125 double. The dining room is open for lunch and dinner as well. Fare at lunch can be simple as a sandwich, but there are always daily-special plates which are more elaborate. Dinner is full course, emphasizing seafood and game in elegant and ingenious preparations. The dining room is closed on Tuesday.

Museums

The **Florence Griswold Museum,** the late-Georgian mansion at 96 Lyme St. (tel. 434-5542), was built in 1817 and is home to the Lyme Historical Society. Visit the first-floor rooms where Miss Florence's artist guests used to paint. Upstairs are galleries concentrating on the works of this "Lyme School" of American Impressionism, and on changing exhibits, including New England furnishings and decorative arts. Hours June through October are Tuesday through Saturday from 10am to 5pm, on Sunday from 1 to 5pm (closed Monday); and November through

May, Wednesday through Sunday from 1 to 5pm. Admission costs $2 for adults, and children under 12 can enter for free.

Lyme Street has a wealth of cultural offerings. The **Lyme Academy of Fine Arts,** 84 Lyme St. (tel 434-5232), housed in another gracious building dating from 1817, has changing exhibits of painters and sculptors. Hours are 9am to 4:30pm Monday through Friday, or by appointment.

The **Lyme Art Association,** 70 Lyme St. (tel. 434-7802), has five major shows each summer, and asks only for a donation to see them. Call for news of the current exhibition, and viewing hours.

ESSEX

This was a shipbuilding and sea captain's town, founded in 1648. At first life in Essex was centered on farming, but within 100 years the shipbuilding industry grew and brought Essex much greater prosperity. The early name, by the way, was the Indian one of Potapaug, which served to identify the town until well into the 19th century.

Today Essex is one of the most picturesque towns in Connecticut, its old houses well kept, its boatyards and marina bobbing with sleek yachts and power boats.

Where to Stay and Eat

The fine old **Griswold Inn,** Main Street, Essex, CT 06426 (tel. 203/767-1776), is famous throughout Connecticut for its location, food, and lodging. The rooms are quaint and old-fashioned, with low ceilings and exposed rough-hewn rafters, hooked rugs on the floors, perhaps a marble-topped vanity or a similar piece in one corner. All the rooms are air-conditioned, and all have private bath. Price for the rooms: $84 double (both double beds and twins are available). Price for the six suites with fireplaces: $102 to $178 double. Continental breakfast is included in the rates. Note that in summer it may be necessary to reserve a weekend date two months in advance, so call or write to the inn.

The Griswold's several dining rooms are well done and interesting. At lunch, have the Griswold's own brand of sausages for $6, or a sandwich for about the same. Luncheon plates are only $1 more. Dinner specialties are hearty, with seafood and steaks for $14 to $20. The wine list is quite good, the beer both domestic and imported, and one of the drafts is the English lager named Courage.

The Griswold is known for its Sunday "Hunt Breakfasts," when for $12 (11am to 2:30pm) you can help yourself to unlimited amounts of eggs, bacon, and ham, sausage, grits, fried potatoes, kippers, chicken, lamb kidneys, creamed chipped beef, smelts, or whatever else is offered for the day. For children 6 and under, breakfast is on the house.

One of the most elegant and delightful dining places in all southern Connecticut is a few minutes from Essex in nearby Ivoryton. It's the **Copper Beech Inn,** described a few paragraphs below—read on.

What to See and Do

From Essex Square (the intersection of Main, North Main, South Main, and Pratt streets), walk down Main Street past the Griswold Inn to the riverside end, known as the Foot of Main, where you'll come across the **Connecticut River Museum** (tel. 767-8269), a dockhouse for steamboats built in 1878 and recently restored. Ship's models, paintings, photographs, and other exhibits recall life on the Connecticut River in years gone by. Kids will love the replica of the nation's first submarine, the *Turtle,* constructed in 1775. The museum is open year round, Tuesday through Sunday from 10am to 5pm. Admission costs $3. Call to verify winter hours.

Walk up Pratt Street for a look at the old houses, and then from Essex Square, take a drive out North Main Street to view the fine old mansions. This quick tour leaves out lots of interesting side streets, corners, and crannies of Essex, and if you have the time, you could do worse than to poke around town, turning up quaint vignettes and fine river views. To see the inside of an old Essex house, go to the **Pratt House** at 19 West Ave. (tel. 767-0861), west out of Essex Square on Methodist Hill, toward the highway. Now owned by the Society for the Preservation of New England Antiquities, the house is a center-chimney colonial with an outstanding collection of American furnishings from earliest colonial times up through the last century. Except for a special exhibit at Christmastime, it's open from 1 to 4pm only on Friday, Saturday, and Sunday from June through September. Admission costs $3 for adults, $2 for seniors, free for children under 12.

IVORYTON

Ivoryton is a part of Essex for municipal government purposes, but it has a character and history of its own. The name came from the ivory industry set up here by the Comstock family, and many of the ivory keys for America's pianos and organs were made here. The ivory industry is gone, but the company that makes Witch Hazel, that soothing and astringent distillate, is still going strong on the Essex/Ivoryton boundary.

Inns

The reason to go to Ivoryton is to dine at the **Copper Beech Inn,** Main Street, Ivoryton, CT 06442 (tel. 203/767-0330). The inn was built as the home of a prosperous ivory merchant, and is now one of New England's most gracious places to dine: tables have fresh flowers and a full French service in silver. The Comstock Room has fine dark-wood paneling; the garden porch is mostly windows and plants, with a floor of quarry tiles and a unique pineapple chandelier. Behind the inn is the Greenhouse, a real one set with wicker chairs and small tables, and it's here that cocktails are served. The menu for dinner is among the best in New England: boned breast of pheasant, grilled shrimp and scallops with a sauce of sun-dried tomatoes, filet of beef Wellington with sauce périgourdine—and it goes on to 13 items, none common, all interesting. Entrees are mostly $22 to $25, with some less, some more. Appetizers such as clams roasted with garlic butter and Pernod, topped with hazelnuts, cost $8 to $13. Desserts (about $6) include the Copper Beech Inn's famed chocolate crêpes filled with chocolate mousse.

Dinner is served at the Copper Beech from 6 to 8:30pm Tuesday through Thursday, to 9:30pm on Friday and Saturday; Sunday dinner is from 1 to 8pm. The Copper Beech also has 13 fine guest rooms with air conditioning and private bath for $103 to $167 double, continental breakfast included.

Also on Main Street is the **Ivoryton Inn,** Ivoryton, CT 06442 (tel. 203/767-0422). Once the favorite of ivory traders visiting the town, it's now a favorite with vacationers. You'll recognize the gray clapboard building with orange awnings a half mile west of the Copper Beech Inn, and just a few minutes' walk from the Ivoryton Playhouse. The 30 rooms here are quite simple and homey, but comfortable and sufficient, with private bath (except for two rooms). The price includes continental breakfast: $68 to $98 double. On the ground floor of the inn is the tavern, a world of mellow wood and Windsor chairs, and the fairly formal restaurant.

The Valley Railroad

On the way from Essex to Ivoryton, the road (Railroad Avenue) passes the station of the Valley Railroad (tel. 203/767-0103). You can ride the old steam train 5 miles upriver to Chester and back. At Deep River Station, if you wish, you can get off the train and onto the riverboat *Becky Thatcher* to motor farther upriver past Gillette Castle (see below). Trains leave four times a day in fall, two times a day during spring, and several times every day beginning at 10:30am in summer; they connect with the boat for a 2-hour combination trip. The train ride alone costs $8 for adults, $4 for children under 11; with a 1 hour cruise, the prices are $10 and $5. Call for the latest information on schedules and fares.

CHESTER

The picture-perfect little Connecticut riverside village of Chester is nestled in the valley of the Pattaconk Brook. Its buildings are of white clapboard, yellow brick, or somber granite, its fences of fieldstone. Little shops line the short main street, along with the general store, the post office, and the library. It is charming, scenic, small, and wealthy.

Indian deeds to the land once known as the district of Pattaconk date from the 1660s. Colonial settlers moved to the district from Saybrook in the early 1700s, and by 1836 the town was incorporated as Chester. During the colonial period Chester was an industrial town, with a gristmill and a sawmill, and shipyards. The ferry service across the Connecticut River to Hadlyme was inaugurated in 1769, and continues to this day.

There is little to do in Chester except to enjoy the place itself, to stroll its main street, to ride or walk through the surrounding countryside, to dine in one of its few restaurants, and to stay the night in its excellent inn.

The Inn

The **Inn at Chester,** 318 W. Main St., Chester, CT 06412 (tel. 203/526-4961), is the town's prime place to stay. It is not right in the village proper, but almost 5 miles from the center. Follow Rte. 148 west from Rte. 9, and you'll find the inn just this side of the Killingham town line. Its full name is "The Inn at Chester at the John B. Parmalee House," and it is in fact a miniresort of lush landscaped lawns and gardens with the clapboard farmhouse built during the Revolutionary War (1776–78) at its center. State forests adjoin the inn's land, providing nature trails for walks and lakes for swimming or ice skating. The original farmhouse now serves as the inn's dining room, for elegant and fancy cuisine in an appropriate setting. The other inn buildings are modern, but inspired by the Parmalee house, with natural wood, brick, and fieldstone used throughout. The 48 guest rooms are furnished with a double, a queen-size, or twin beds, and cost $104 to $116, single or double. Each comfortable, modern room has a private bath, air conditioning, and TV set, but also fresh flowers, antiques, replicas, and Oriental carpets to maintain the ambience of a country inn. It's a beautiful place in a fine setting, often selected by small business and social groups for country retreats.

Restaurants

Downtown Chester's prime dining spot is the **Restaurant du Village,** on the main street (tel. 526-5301), a former shop with a simple, even plain decor of white walls, white tablecloths, and fresh flowers. The food's the thing here, and the French country-inn menu includes among the appetizers various French soups, and also saucisson à l'ail (French garlic sausage), smoked salmon, terrines, and the traditional escargots. Main courses range from the delicate trout poached in Riesling, through duck with pistachios, to a braised shoulder of lamb with garlic and vegetables. In season (autumn) there's fresh game. Dinner, which might cost $40 to $50 per person, is served Wednesday through Sunday from 5:30 to 9pm. The restaurant is closed on Monday from Labor Day to Memorial Day (that is, in fall, winter, and spring).

A few doors down the main street is the **Pattaconk Inn** (tel. 526-9285), a good local eatery featuring lots of seafood, including shore dinners, twin lobsters, baked scrod, and filet of sole, but also Rhode Island duckling. A full dinner should cost $20 to $30 here. Lunch is served every day, and dinner is served every day but Monday.

Going on a picnic? Right next door to the Pattaconk Inn is the **Chester Bread Works,** a bakery providing fresh baked goods and soups for picnics.

HADLYME

If you're driving, the most enjoyable way to get from Chester to Hadlyme is to take the old **Chester–Hadlyme ferry,** which takes cars ($1 for car and driver) as well as pedestrians (25¢) at prices more antique than the fairly modern boat which makes the run. Although the boat is new, the history of the ferry run at this point goes back to 1769, when one Jonathan Warner would drag you across the river for a small fee. Today the ferry is run by the State of Connecticut, and it operates April 1 through November 30 from 7am to 6:45pm every day. The trip across the river is made right in the shadow of Gillette Castle, and takes about 5 minutes, not counting the short waiting time.

Gillette Castle State Park

Shortly after the turn of the century, an actor named William Gillette realized a lifelong dream by building himself a castle to live in. His stage career, including a very successful period in the role of Sherlock Holmes, had brought him the wealth he needed, and so in 1914 he started. Over five years and a million dollars later, the result was a strange-looking mansion of fieldstone named "The Seventh Sister," complete with a commanding view of the Connecticut River and its own 3-mile-long excursion railroad. Inside the castle, on River Road in East Haddam (tel. 526-2336), Gillette gave vent to his passion for detail and exotica, bringing furnishings from around the world and specifying in great detail the form that was to be given to the intricately carved oak trim and the ingenious wooden door latches. Today William Gillette's fantasy house is known as Gillette Castle, and it's a state park open to all and sundry. The narrow-gauge railroad is gone, but forest paths, picnic tables, and river vista spots have replaced it. Tours of the house itself are given daily Memorial Day to Columbus Day, and weekends through mid-December, from 10am to 4pm, at a charge of $1 (children under 12, 50¢). Gillette Castle is either Connecticut's most distinguished medieval castle or the largest backyard barbecue ever constructed—you decide.

EAST HADDAM

From Hadlyme, drive northwest a few miles to East Haddam, where you'll come face to face with the wonderful old Goodspeed Opera House.

Goodspeed Opera House

The Goodspeed Opera House is a riverside Victorian gem built in 1876 and now carefully restored to serve as a venue for American musical theater. The setting by the river and bridge is so picturesque that it's worth the ride just to see the exterior, but if you have the time, take a tour of the interior. It's on view Monday and Saturday, July 7 through August 27, and Saturday only, September 8 through October 6, from 1 to 3pm; $1.50 for adults, 50¢ for kids. Best of all, see a play; the specialty is the revival of early musicals and the production of new works. Twelve Goodspeed shows have moved to Broadway. Three musicals are offered each season beginning in mid-April and continuing through mid-December with performances every day but Monday and Tuesday, and a matinee on Wednesday. Tickets cost $25.50 to $26.50 Friday through Sunday, $1 less on other days. For the latest information and ticket reservations, call 203/873-8668.

River Cruises

Across the river from East Haddam in the village of Haddam is the office of **Camelot Cruises, Inc.,** 1 Marine Park, Haddam, CT 06438 (tel. 203/345-4505). From March through Christmas, you can board the M.V. *Camelot* for a luncheon or dinner cruise along the placid river. There's no better way to enjoy the scenery, and you get a meal and live entertainment to boot. This is fairly formal dining, and you are expected to dress "appropriately"—suits or sport jackets for men, a dress, skirt and blouse, or a nice slacks outfit for women.

Cruises depart rain or shine. The luncheon cruise boards at Haddam at 11:30am and departs daily at noon, returning at 2:30pm; in October, November, and December, luncheon cruises are operated only on Saturday and Sunday. The evening dinner cruise boards at 6:30pm and departs Wednesday through Saturday at 7pm, returning at 10pm; in October, November, and December, cruises are on Friday and Saturday only. The price, meal (but not tax and tips) included, is $20.75 per person for the luncheon cruise, $34.75 for the dinner cruise; $23.75 for the Sunday Brunch Cruise. Children under 12 pay half price on either cruise.

4. New London and Groton

Visitors to these navy towns are usually here to see the U.S. Coast Guard Academy, or the navy submarine base at Groton. But there are other things to see and do as well. New London has a state park and a beachfront amusement park, as well as car-ferry services to Block Island, R.I., Fishers Island, N.Y., and Orient Point, Long Island, N.Y. Groton has Fort Griswold State Park.

The big draw in this region is, of course, Mystic Seaport. Many visitors choose to stay near Mystic, and tour New London and Groton on a day trip. However, there are some lodging possibilities in New London, Groton, and the nearby towns of Niantic and East Lyme, to the west.

WHERE TO STAY

Lodging establishments in this area consist almost exclusively of highway motels. Many are geared to the tourist trade rather than to the business or armed forces traveler.

Motels in Niantic

Just off I-95, Exit 74, at the intersection with Rte. 161, north of the town of Niantic, is a collection of motels with similar facilities and fairly low prices.

The local incarnation of **Howard Johnson,** P.O. Box 185, East Lyme, CT 06333 (tel. 203/739-6921 or toll free 800/654-2000), is a pretty good bargain at $60 to $85 single, $70 to $90 double, or for a family (in the higher-priced rooms) during the summer season (late June through Labor Day); April, May, the greater part of June, and September, rates are 20% lower. Two saunas, an indoor pool, and color TV in the rooms make it a fairly plush place for a reasonable price. Kids under 18 stay free, and there's a senior-citizen discount.

Motels in Groton

The **Windsor Motel,** 345 Gold Star Hwy., Groton, CT 06340 (tel. 203/445-7474), at the Rte. 184 exit from I-95, has a good choice of accommodations—some especially good for families—at reasonable prices. Of the 58 motel rooms, 33 come with complete kitchens; all have TV, refrigerator, and air conditioning. The price structure is to your advantage: Use only one double bed and you pay only $48 to $58; use both double beds and the price is $60 to $70. Children of any age, when traveling with a parent, stay free, so the two-bed price is what a family of four would pay! All these prices are substantially lower off-season, or for longer stays (a week or more).

WHAT TO SEE IN NEW LONDON

The major tourist attraction in New London is the **U.S. Coast Guard Academy,** on Mogehan Avenue, New London, CT 06320 (tel. 203/444-8270), which opens its campus to visitors from 9am to 5pm. Admission is free. Start your tour of the grounds at the Visitors Pavilion (open from 9am to 5pm from May 1 through October). A special treat here is a visit to the Coast Guard's training barque, *Eagle,* generally in port at the academy in April and May (open to visitors on Friday, Saturday, and Sunday from noon to 5pm when in port). If you miss the *Eagle,* perhaps you can catch the colorful dress review of the Corps of Cadets, usually held (weather permitting) in April, May, September, and October. For times and dates, contact the Public Affairs Office at the above number.

Ferry to the Islands

New London is a major ferryboat port, with frequent summer sailings to Block Island, R.I., and Fishers Island and Orient Point, N.Y., on the tip of Long Island.

BLOCK ISLAND   See the Block Island section of Chapter X for full details. The pier in

New London is north of the railroad station (tel. 203/442-7891 or 442-9553). Follow the red-and-white signs to the dock.

FISHERS ISLAND Daily ferries go to this New York island a few miles off the Connecticut coast, departing from the dock on State Street. For fares and schedules, call 203/443-6851.

ORIENT POINT, LONG ISLAND The dock is on Ferry Street; details from the Cross Sound Ferry Service are available by calling 203/443-5281, 444-0783, 444-0482, or 443-5035; for reservations from Orient Point, call 516/323-2415, 323-2695, 323-2525, or 323-2743. Cars are carried ($26, several dollars less Tuesday through Thursday), and reservations for the 1½-hour cruise (adults, $8 one way, $12 round trip; kids, half price) are a must in high summer.

Ocean Beach Park

New London's major beach-and-amusement complex is at Ocean Beach Park, near Harkness Memorial State Park south of the city (Exit 75-76 from I-95; tel. 447-3031). Besides the beach, a boardwalk allows strolling to check out other members of the swimsuit set, miniature golf will test your reflexes, amusement rides provide a cheap thrill, and an Olympic-size pool is provided for diving and freshwater swimming. If amusement parks and commercial beaches are your thing, this is one of the best on the coast.

WHAT TO SEE IN GROTON

Groton, "The Submarine Capital of the World," makes its living from General Dynamics' Electric Boat Division and from Pfizer pharmaceuticals, besides the naval facilities at the submarine base. A warning is in order: Rush-hour traffic (8 to 9am and 5 to 6pm) in the Groton/New London area is extremely heavy, especially along I-95 and its feeder roads. Make your getaway before 5pm, or stay and have dinner till the roads empty out.

No one comes to Groton to see anything but submarines, and there are plenty to see. Your tour here should be an auto cruise along **Submarine Drive,** the waterfront road along the eastern bank of the Thames River named Thames Street south of I-95 and Military Highway to the north. Take Exit 85 from I-95, and follow Bridge Street to Thames Street.

Near the point where Bridge Street runs into Thames, just south of the Gold Star (I-95) Bridge, is the **U.S.S.** *Flasher* **National Submarine Monument.** The conning tower of this World War II Angler-class sub has been established here as a memorial to the American submarine sailors who lost their lives during that war. The *Flasher* sank more than 100,000 tons of enemy shipping during the war, and its crew members were repeatedly cited by the President for their services.

South of the monument a short drive is the **U.S.S.** *Croaker* **Submarine Memorial** (tel. 203/448-1616), a World War II submarine built by the Electric Boat Company of Groton and commissioned in April of 1944. After service in the Pacific, at the end of the war the *Croaker* came back to Groton, and the sub is now moored next to its "birthplace" and is open to the public. You can visit the control room, the torpedo rooms, the conning tower, and the engine rooms. Admission to the sub costs $3 for adults, half price for children 12 and under, $2 for seniors. Members of the armed forces in uniform are admitted for free. Visit any day from 9am to 4:30pm (to 3pm in winter).

While you're down in Groton, see the **Fort Griswold State Park** (tel. 445-1729), at Monument and Park streets (Monument runs parallel to Thames Street). The heroic, tragic story of the American force which defended the fort in 1781 against the British is told in the museum, open from Memorial Day to Columbus Day. The Memorial Tower (view from the top) was erected for the courageous defenders who fought until overpowered and then perished in the massacre by the victorious British. The state park is open all year, and both the park and the museum are free of charge.

North of the Gold Star (I-95) Bridge, Submarine Drive continues along the Military Highway. Near the entrance to the U.S. Navy's Groton Submarine Base (Exit 86 from I-95) is the **U.S.S. Nautilus National Memorial** (tel. 449-3174 or toll free 800/343-0079), and the Submarine Force Library and Museum, featuring the world's first nuclear-powered submarine. Launched in Groton in January 1954, the *Nautilus* saw its finest hour when it passed beneath the ice cap at the geographic North Pole in 1958, the first ship ever to reach that geographically significant spot. Decommissioned after 25 years of service in 1980, the sub is now open for free to visitors daily (except Tuesday) from 9am to 5pm, till 3:30pm in winter (mid-October through mid-April). Note that the sub is closed for a week in March, June, September, and December, and on Thanksgiving, Christmas, and New Year's Day. Displays in the library and museum chronicle the history of the U.S. submarine force since the Revolutionary War. You can peer into working periscopes, inspect miniature submarines, wonder at the Revolutionary War–era *Turtle*, all at no charge.

---

5. Mystic and Stonington

Connecticut's maritime life, past and present, is all on view in the area comprising the open-air museum called Mystic Seaport, and the pretty old seaside town of Stonington. Mystic Seaport is one of the top tourist attractions in New England, drawing very large crowds every day of the summer. The huge open-air "museum" is big enough to handle the crowds, but the capacity of nearby motels is not—the motels are packed in July and August, and guests must prepay their entire stay.

You can avoid the hotel crush altogether by taking an Amtrak train through this area and getting off for the day at Mystic, where a bus will take you from the station to Mystic Seaport. After your day roaming around the ships, old buildings, and exhibits, board an afternoon train to Providence or Boston (or New Haven, or New York). There's no extra charge for the stopover if you buy a through ticket, and you obviate the need for a room.

INFORMATION

Each of the towns listed below has its own information booths and offices, which I'll mention as we go along. For general inquiries your best bet is the **Mystic and Shoreline Visitors Information Center,** Olde Mistick Village, Mystic, CT 06355 (tel. 203/536-1641). Olde Mistick Village is the new colonial-style shopping complex just south of I-95 on Rte. 27, very near Mystic Seaport. The information center is in Building 1, and is open Monday through Friday from 9:30am to 5:30pm, to 6pm on Saturday, and on Sunday from 10am to 5pm.

WHERE TO STAY

During much of the year, and especially in high summer, Mystic is crowded with visitors who've come to tour famous Mystic Seaport. Though there are lots of lodging places, most will be full in July and August, so advance reservations are good to have.

Lodgings in Mystic proper are mostly hotels and motels, with a few guesthouses. In the nearby quiet village of Noank, a few miles south and east along Rte. 215, are some quiet inns. And in the delightful village of Stonington, about 5 miles east of Mystic along U.S. 1 and U.S. 1A, are several bed-and-breakfast houses.

Mystic's Hotels and Motels

One of Mystic's longtime favorites is the expansive **Inn at Mystic,** at the junction of Rtes. 1 and 27, Mystic, CT 06335 (tel. 203/536-9604). This large complex has several different classes of accommodation in separate buildings, all set atop a hill overlooking the water. As you drive up, you first approach the tidy motel units in several large buildings. The office is here, and also the Flood-Tide Restaurant. Motel rooms are modern, clean, and attractive, with some colonial reproductions to put you in the proper mood for visiting old Mystic. All have television, air conditioning, and private bath, and are priced at $103 to $140 during high summer. Above the motel along a drive shaded by large trees is the inn, a fine old mansion at the summit of the hill. Green lawns complete with miniature waterfall surround the house, which has a number of fine guest rooms decorated with period furniture and replicas, and renting for $178 to $200 double, including private bath. The inn's wide veranda is a favored place to sit and take in the view. Beyond the inn is the Gatehouse, a smaller building, also very pretty. The inn has its own boat dock, tennis court, swimming pool and hot spa, and walking trail. Children can share their parents' room at no extra charge; a third or fourth adult in a room pays $10. This is a dependable favorite, and worthy of your consideration.

The **Mystic Hilton**, Coogan Boulevard, Mystic, CT 06355 (tel. 203/572-0731 or toll free 800/445-8667), across from the Mystic Marinelife Aquarium and Olde Mistick Village, is just off I-95 at Exit 90. All the modern conveniences, comforts, and luxuries are here, in the 184 guest rooms, in the indoor swimming pool, and in The Moorings (the hotel restaurant) and Soundings (its lounge). The price for a room is $92 to $157 single, $112 to $177 double, but you should definitely ask about the package plans, which can be very attractive. Also, note that there is no charge for children, regardless of age, when they occupy the same room as their parents.

The cluster of motels at Exit 90, the Rte. 27 interchange on I-95, includes several branches of big chains, and several local establishments.

Best buy here is the **Howard Johnson**, P.O. Box 159, Mystic, CT 06355 (tel. 203/536-2654 or toll free 800/654-2000), where, besides their standard rooms with cable color TV, you can enjoy an indoor pool, sauna, and a lounge with wide-screen cable TV as well as live entertainment (although presumably not at the same time). Children up to 18 can stay free. Prices depend on when you go: off-season rates are lower, but mid-June through September, rates are $90 single, $100 double. For a deluxe room with whirlpool, during this same time, rates are $100 single, $122 double. An extra person pays $10.

At the 150-room **Ramada Inn**, I-95 at Rte. 27, Mystic, CT 06355 (tel. 203/536-4281 or toll free 800/228-2828), the facilities include a restaurant, sauna, indoor pool, live entertainment, and a playground too. The year-round rates are $125 single or double.

The **Taber Inn and Guest House**, 29 Williams Ave., on U.S. 1 east of Mystic, CT 06355 (tel. 203/536-4904), is more than a motel: Besides its very tidy motel rooms, it can rent you a room in a restored inn (1829), a restored farmhouse, a two-bedroom cottage, two-bedroom town houses, or an efficiency apartment. All rooms have private bath, cable color TV, phone, and air conditioning. In high summer, rooms go for $100 double in the motel, about $15 less in the inn and farmhouse, about double that in the town houses, free coffee included.

Only a few car lengths north of I-95 at Exit 90 is the **Days Inn**, Rte. 27, Mystic, CT 06355 (tel. 203/572-0574 or toll free 800/325-2525). The pleasant new two-story motel has 122 simple but clean rooms, each with two double beds, cable color TV, wall-to-wall carpeting, direct-dial telephone, and air conditioning. Though prices are $80 to $88 single, $92 to $99 double, extra services such as a restaurant open for all three meals, an outdoor swimming pool, nonsmoking rooms, cots, cribs, and elevator service are standard.

Guesthouses

Mystic has only a few guesthouses, but there may be more in the future, and the information center may be able to provide you with more names.

The **Harbour Inne & Cottage**, Edgemont Street (Rte. 1, Box 398), Mystic, CT 06355 (tel. 203/572-9253), is right next to the water in a part of town that is part residential and part industrial, but clean and quiet. The two small buildings of bright natural cedar, once a fisherman's house, are neat as a pin. In the guesthouse, the rooms are cozy and cheerful with that same honey-colored wood, private bath with shower stall, TV set, and air conditioning. In the cottage next door are one bedroom, a kitchen and bath, and sofas that convert to beds so that the place can sleep up to six people. Rooms in the guesthouse cost $49 to $70 double; the cottage rents for $119 to $162 per night. Charley Lecouras, Jr., the smiling owner, will rent you a canoe or rowboat, and you can set out for a cruise right from the inn's own dock. To find it, first make your way to Mystic's Amtrak station. Take the dead-end street to the right of the station, then turn right onto Edgemont Street, also a dead end; the guesthouse is down a ways, on the left.

Comolli's Guest House, 36 Bruggeman Pl., Mystic, CT 06355 (tel. 203/536-8723), is a tidy white house in a residential neighborhood very near Mystic Seaport, where your homey room has its own color television. Room prices range from $50 to $85, depending on the room, the privacy of the bath, and the season. Call Dorothy M. Comolli for reservations. Bruggeman Place is off Rte. 27 near Mystic Seaport, and the guesthouse is at the top of the hill, on the right-hand side.

An Inn in Noank

The **Palmer Inn,** 25 Church St., Noank, CT 06340 (tel. 203/572-9000), was once the home of local shipyard owners, who had the house built by their shipbuilding craftsmen. Approach the house through the high surrounding hedges, and through the lofty portico, and you enter a place of large spaces, fine materials, and careful detail work, though sparsely furnished with an eclectic assortment of pieces. On the second floor, Donald and Patricia Cornish rent four rooms with bath, named Oak, Mahogany, and Master, after themes in their decor or earlier function, for $124 to $162 double. On the third floor are the Brass, Balcony, and Wicker rooms, which rent for $124 to $141 double, with private bath. Rates include a continental breakfast, and the innkeepers note that the inn does not accommodate children under 16 or pets. To find the inn, drive southwest from Mystic along Rte. 215. Turn left onto Noank village's main street, then left again onto Church Street. The village is so small that you can't possibly get lost for very long.

Bed-and-Breakfast in Stonington

The village of Stonington is 5 miles east of Mystic, on the water. It's a pretty, traditional New England seacoast village, just the place to stay if you want to escape the crowded highways and modern motels. Stonington's bed-and-breakfast guesthouse list is beginning to grow. If you can't get a room at the following places, drop by the **State of Connecticut Tourism Division Information Center** off I-95 southbound at North Stonington for help.

Farnan House, 10 McGrath Court, Stonington, CT 06378 (tel. 203/535-0634), is a large, nice old Stonington house which takes in travelers for the night. Originally a colonial homestead, it is now a guesthouse hosted by a nice lady, Ann Farnan. She has four guest rooms, one with a private half-bath ($70); the others share a bath ($68). Continental breakfast, served in the big country kitchen, is included.

Lasbury's, 24 Orchard St., Stonington, CT 06378 (tel. 203/535-2681), bills itself as "a quiet guesthouse" in the village of Stonington. Double rooms cost $87, and continental breakfast is included. To find Lasbury's, head into the village on Water Street, turn left onto Church Street, then left again onto Orchard.

WHERE TO DINE

The great number of Mystic's restaurants—and there are many of them—are connected to the many hotels and motels. There are exceptions, however. One quite good restaurant is on the grounds of Mystic Seaport, just outside the admission ticket office. Other good places to dine are in the town of Mystic, south of Mystic Seaport. Still better places to dine are found in Noank and Stonington. Here they all are.

At Mystic Seaport

The **Seamen's Inne,** 65 Greenmanville Ave. (tel. 536-9649), is right next to the main entrance to Mystic Seaport. The attractive building is actually three restaurants in one: a bar with long hours for refreshments and snacks, an informal room for sandwiches and lighter meals, and a full-fledged dining room for hearty dinners. Price depends upon where and what you eat, and can be anywhere from $10 to $40 per person.

The town of Mystic has several restaurants worthy of consideration. Head south on Rte. 27, then right onto Main Street, to reach the center of town. The restaurants are located in the commercial district, on the far side of the quaint old bascule bridge.

The Landing, 73 Steamboat Wharf (tel. 572-0549), behind some of Main Street's shops, has two nice dining areas. Downstairs is an informal dining room with lots of wood and nice views of the water through small windows. Upstairs is a café-restaurant with a bar—a tavern ambience—with small tables and views of the water. The long, eclectic menu lists onion soup next to buffalo wings and blackened swordfish steak, and is sure to have something for everyone. A full lunch need cost only $15; a full dinner, $18 to $28. Come to dine any day from 11am to 9pm (till 10pm on Friday and Saturday).

Giaco's Ships Lantern Restaurant, 21 W. Main St. (tel. 536-9821), always has an interesting blackboard menu out on the sidewalk. Last time I was there it listed fresh mako shark, fresh tuna steak, and a shore dinner featuring a 1-pound lobster with a pound of steamed clams, each priced at about $16. Nautical flotsam, jetsam, and memorabilia decorate the dining room, seafood fills the menu (along with prime rib and Italian specialties), and the dining hours are long, from 10:30am until 11pm every day.

Looking for just a sandwich, a salad, or dessert? Head for the **2 Sisters Deli,** 4 Pearl St. (tel. 536-1244), just off Main. The sandwiches are fresh, and the menu is very long, listing 42 sandwiches, plus various soups, bagels, salads, salad plates, cakes, pies, brownies, and cookies. Come for breakfast, lunch, picnic, or an early supper, any day.

Lobsters in Noank

Here is something you *have* to do. If you love seafood, if you love shore dinners, if you love the real New England, follow Rte. 215 south to the village of Noank, go left on Main Street, then right on Pearl Street. Stop at the Universal Package Store here (open Monday through Saturday until 8pm) to pick up wine or beer if you like, then continue along Pearl Street until you spot, on the left-hand side, **Abbott's Lobster in the Rough** (tel. 536-7719). Here you will find a parking lot, a large restaurant, and numerous seaside picnic tables. Approach the cashier's window and order what you like: clam chowder, steamed clams or mussels, oysters, shrimp in the shell, steamed lobster, a lobster or crab roll, cheesecake, carrot cake, and a soft drink (unless you prefer that wine or beer you brought). Pay the tab (about $14 to $25 per person), then take a table and wait for your number to be called. When it is, you get to enjoy some of the finest seafood in the region. It's not fancy, but it's fantastically delicious. The lobsters at Abbott's are steamed (the way I do them), not boiled, and I can personally attest to the difference. A steamed lobster is sweeter and more tender. Abbott's handy tabloid-newspaper-style menu bears full directions on how to eat a lobster. Besides, when lobster is this good, you learn fast. Abbott's is open every day, late April until Labor Day, from noon to 9pm and Labor Day till mid-October Friday through Sunday from 10am to 7pm.

Stonington Restaurants

Drive or walk down Stonington's main street, named Water Street, and you will pass several interesting restaurants. The best are all the way down on the southern part of the street near Cannon Square.

The **Harborview Restaurant,** 66 Water St., Cannon Square (tel. 535-2720), is among the best restaurants in the region. As you enter from Water Street, the dark-ish, cozy bar is to your right, and it features a special menu of lighter fare for lunches, snacks, and suppers. In the dining rooms, the atmosphere is nautical, with lots of ocean views, bentwood, and low lamps, but the service is polished and professional as well as friendly. The menu here is French and fairly classical, with appetizers such as brie en croûte (baked in puff pastry), French onion soup, and smoked salmon. Your main course might be beef tournedos with peppercorns, or escalope niçoise (veal cutlet with artichoke hearts, tomato, capers, and vermouth butter). There's plenty of seafood featured, of course. Come any day for lunch (11:30am to 4pm) or supper in the bar, or brunch on Sunday from 11am to 4pm, and plan to spend about $15. For dinner (5 to 10pm any day), expect to pay $30 to $40 per person, all in.

Behind the Harborview is its sister restaurant, the **Skipper's Dock,** 66 Water St. (tel. 535-2000), right by the docks and meant to be convenient to the yacht crews who tie up nearby. Open daily from 11:30am till late in the evening, the restaurant has nice waterside decks set with dining tables, as well as two indoor dining rooms fitted out with bentwood furniture. The air smells of the sea, the landward wall of the restaurant is hung with hundreds of salvaged lobster buoys, and the sound of bellbuoys wafts easily on the air. The menu here is simple: seafood, with the requisite token offerings of chicken and steak. Have a big bowl of steamed clams, or linguine with shrimp and clams, or broiled scallops, or an entire clambake with steamed lob-ster. Lunch, served from 11:30am to 4pm, can be yours for about $15; dinner, with drinks, tax, and tip, will cost $18 to $30.

Right in the center of Stonington's commercial district is **Noah's,** 115 Water St. (tel. 535-3925), an informal restaurant of two rooms with tin ceilings, booths sporting nice etched glass, and wood tables draped with cloths. Prints and paintings ornament the walls, and Noah's has a feeling of the authentically old-fashioned. You can come for breakfast from 7 to 11am (till noon on Sunday), when a tuck-in of the standard fare of eggs, pancakes, and muffins will be yours for $5 or less; or come for lunch, with a varied menu of light meals served from 11:15am (12:30pm on Sun-day) to 2:30pm; or for dinner, when you can order seafood, filet mignon, or pork chops, and get vegetable, potato, salad, bread, and butter with your main course for $12 to $18 complete. Dinner is served from 6 to 9pm (till 9:30pm on Friday and Saturday). Noah's accepts no credit cards, and is closed on Monday.

WHAT TO SEE

The big draw here is, of course, Mystic Seaport Museum, but the area has other sights as well, including the Mystic Marinelife Aquarium, the shops in Olde Mistick Village, the Denison Nature Center, and the charming town of Stonington.

Mystic Seaport Museum

Mystic Seaport Museum (tel. 203/572-0711) is impressive. One could return again and again to see the various indoor exhibits, walk through the preserved 19th-century town, or climb aboard one of the venerable sailing ships moored and pre-served here. (Foremost among these is the *Charles W. Morgan,* the last wooden whaling ship in the United States). Although it is technically a nonprofit museum, there is much more life to it than just rows of glass cases housing exhibits. You will see scrimshaw, old tools, watches, clocks, chronometers, navigational instruments, and so on, but most of your time will be taken walking through the village and watching the interpreters (staff) do their jobs and explain what they're doing. You will see a half dozen crew members high in the rigging of the square-rigged ship *Joseph Conrad,* furling a sail in time to a chantey they sing, with one rope supporting all of them high above the deck.

Mystic Seaport Museum is open every day of the year except Christmas Day. May through October, hours of admission are 9am to 5pm, and the grounds close at 6pm. November through April, hours are 9am to 4pm, and you must be off the grounds by 4pm. In winter, interpreted exhibits and craft demonstrations don't begin until 10am. Admission costs $13 for adults, $6.75 for children 5 through 12. Museum members and children under 5 are admitted for free.

Remember that the crowds are heavy in summer—although the museum seems large enough to absorb them all without too much crowding—and that traffic on the mile-long road from I-95 to Mystic Seaport may be pokey. At Mystic Seaport there's quite a lot of free parking.

Mystic Seaport Museum began in 1929 as the Marine Historical Association, founded by three citizens of Mystic who were interested in preserving aspects and objects from the town's maritime past. The site of the museum is the former shipyard of George Greenman and Company, which built wooden clipper ships in the 19th century.

To get the feel of the place, the management recommends that you stay at least 3 or 4 hours; if you've arrived late in the day, you can buy a ticket and have it validated for the next day as well. With your ticket you'll be given a very handsome map of the village and its exhibits, plus a list of the daily events, from special lectures to sea chantey sings. Look at the list to get an idea of what'll be in action for the hours you're in the village. The museum can be divided basically into three areas: the exhibits of various boats, instruments, figureheads, and the like, mostly near the Seamen's Inne entrance gate; the restored village and waterfront area; and the shipyard at the southern end of the grounds where the seaport cares for its ships.

The **Coastal Life Area** is the official name of Mystic's old-time seaside village at the northern reaches of the museum, near the Seamen's Inne. The village includes the shops of a shipsmith, shipcarver, and printer, a cooperage, model shop, bank, shipping office, grocery, hardware store, chapel, schoolhouse, pharmacy, rope walk, clock and nautical instrument shop, mast hoop shop, ship's chandlery, and tavern.

Indoor exhibits are housed in several buildings. In the three-story Stillman Building are ship's models, paintings, scrimshaw, and an exhibit which traces the history of New England's maritime towns from their beginnings in the 1600s through their golden age in the 1800s. The Mallory Building is devoted to exhibits explaining the Victorian-era shipping business of the Mallory family, and also shipbuilding in Mystic. In the Wendell Building are collections of figureheads and other nautical wood carvings. Changing exhibits of paintings, prints, and other artifacts are the specialty of the R. J. Schaefer Building.

Children are fascinated by the **Children's Museum,** a replica of the captain's quarters on a late 19th-century ship. Here the captain and his family would live, and kids can climb into the bunk, look through the porthole, and examine the toys and games used by seafaring children to ward off the boredom of a long sea voyage a hundred years ago.

The museum's shipyard is in the southern section. Today, the museum's **collection of old ships** includes the *Charles W. Morgan* (1841), the full-rigged training ship *Joseph Conrad* (1882), and the fishing schooner *L.A. Dunton* (1921). It also owns a steamboat called the *Sabino* (1908), which once plied the waters off Casco Bay in Maine, but which now takes museum visitors on half-hour cruises on the Mystic River from mid-May to mid-October, for a small fee. In addition, the museum has a collection of 300 small craft, many of which can be seen in the Small Boat Exhibit and the North Boat Shed.

Besides these exhibits, the museum can boast of the **Henry B. duPont Preservation Shipyard,** fully equipped and staffed to perform repairs and to preserve wooden vessels; and the **Seaport Planetarium,** where shows explain the significance of stars in the night sky, and the importance of celestial navigation.

Mystic Marinelife Aquarium

Near Exit 90 off I-95, on Coogan Boulevard, is the Mystic Marinelife Aquarium (tel. 536-3323), with 48 living maritime exhibits and over 6,000 sea creatures in the main aquarium. Marine mammal demonstrations, held every hour on the half hour, feature Atlantic bottle-nosed dolphins, California sea lions, and beluga whales in the marine theater. An outdoor exhibit area called Seal Island lets you watch five species of seals and sea lions sport and play in re-creations of their natural habitat. There's a penguin exhibit as well. Admission hours are from 9am to 5:30pm (but you can stay until 7pm) daily in July and August, till 4:30pm (but you can stay until 6pm) the rest of the year. Admission costs $7.50 for adults, $4.50 for children ages 5 to 17.

Denison Homestead

On Pequotsepos Road is the Denison Homestead (tel. 536-9248), a restored 1717 house which has belonged to one family for 11 generations (open mid-May to mid-October from 1 to 5pm daily except Monday; adults pay $2; kids, 75¢). Nearby is the **Denison Pequotsepos Nature Center** (tel. 536-1216), a 125-acre wildlife sanctuary with exhibits explaining the flora and fauna, and several miles of trails for nature walks. It's open April through October, Monday through Saturday from 9am to 5pm, on Sunday from 1 to 5pm; November through March, Tuesday through Saturday from 10am to 4pm, on Sunday from 1 to 4pm; closed Monday in winter. Adults pay $1; children 6 to 12, half price.

Stonington Sights

As you drive into Stonington, you will cross a bridge over the railroad tracks, turn left, and proceed down Water Street, the town's main street. Water Street holds many boutiques, antiques shops, restaurants, and real estate offices. Beyond this commercial area is a residential one, ending in **Cannon Square.** The square is small, with two 18-pound cannons used in repelling a naval attack mounted by five English ships on August 10, 1814, during the War of 1812. The pretty square is surrounded by a neoclassical bank building, a fine old granite house, and several houses in Federal style.

Beyond Cannon Square, continue south along Water Street to visit the **Old Lighthouse Museum,** at 7 Water St. (tel. 535-1440), a fine old granite structure which was the first government lighthouse in Connecticut. Inside are displays of maritime gear from the days of wooden whaling and fishing craft, swords, firearms (some made right here in Stonington), local stoneware, toys, decoys, and 19th-century portraits. There's a special room for children's exhibits. The museum is open from May through October, daily except Monday from 11am to 4:30pm. Adults pay $2 admission; children 6 to 12 pay half price.

6. Hartford

Hartford is Connecticut's capital, a fairly small (pop. 150,000) and manageable city with an admirable range of attractive architectural styles and a businesslike spirit. It is and has been a city with a good amount of wealth, much of it generated by the tens of thousands of workers who sit in the thousands of offices of Hartford's great insurance companies and banks. Insurance companies seem to have a penchant for expressing their wealth and prestige through skyscrapers: the Prudential Tower in Chicago, the John Hancock Tower in Boston, and others. Hartford has four dozen insurance companies, and therefore lots of skyscrapers. The downtown area has been given a new attractiveness by redevelopment, which has left most of the buildings of great historical value intact.

The city was founded by Rev. Thomas Hooker, who left Newtown (Cambridge, Mass.) on foot with a band of followers in 1636 after a dispute with another clergyman over the strict rules that governed the colony of Massachusetts Bay. In 1639 Hooker and others drafted the Fundamental Orders as the legal constitution of their settlement, and it is upon this early document that Connecticut bases its claims as the first *place in the world* to have a written constitution. Every Connecticut auto license plate remembers Hooker when it proclaims Connecticut "The Constitution State."

TOURIST INFORMATION

The city maintains a visitors' information desk in the Old State House, 800 Main St., Hartford, CT 06103 (tel. 203/522-6766), in Old State House Square, right in the center of town. The desk is open Monday through Saturday from 10am to 5pm, on Sunday from noon to 5pm. There is no short-term parking convenient to the Old State House, so plan to park for the length of your visit in a downtown lot, and then walk to the Old State House to ask questions and pick up maps and brochures.

Another traffic note: Hartford is very much a commuters' town, and traffic is very heavy at rush hours. The best day to visit the city is Saturday, when most everything is open and parking is easily available. On Sunday a lot of places are closed.

WHERE TO STAY

As of this writing, Hartford has none of those wonderful little hotels and inns made from converted Victorian town houses, or from renovated farmhouses on the city's outskirts. The lodging stock here is large, business-oriented downtown hotels and highway motels. Generally speaking, the hotels offer more convenient locations. Many of them are within a few minutes' walk of all the downtown sights. The motels, on the other hand, are not really very far out of the city, and they offer clean and comfortable accommodations at moderate, and even budget, prices. There are some bed-and-breakfast services which will find you a room in a private home, as well. Finally, if you're willing to stay some distance out of the city and just drive in for the day, the surrounding countryside has some lovely old inns in quiet small towns.

When planning your visit to Hartford, you'd do well to make arrangements to stay in a downtown hotel on the weekend. Most of the hotels feature weekend package plans which can save you substantial amounts of money from regular rates. In any case, regular weekend rates are significantly lower than the rates charged on business days. In many cases, this rule holds for the highway motels also.

Hotels in the Center

Here is the rundown of the most convenient downtown hotels, those from which you can walk easily to all of the sights (except of course to Nook Farm, which is some distance from the center of town).

Without a doubt, the most convenient hotel to the Hartford Civic Center is the **Sheraton-Hartford,** 315 Trumbull St., Hartford, CT 06103 (tel. 203/728-5151 or toll free 800/325-3535). It features a pool and health club with sauna and conditioning equipment, a restaurant and lounge, a parking garage, and 55 shops. The bright and modern rooms rent for $108 to $173 single, $108 to $184 double. If you plan to be in Hartford over a weekend, take advantage of one of the weekend specials: a romantic "Champagne Classic" minivacation, which includes one-night accommodation, champagne, and breakfast for two for $119 complete. The Stage Café restaurant specializes in New England and continental favorites that range in price from $15 to $25 at dinner; an extensive breakfast buffet and full lunch are also served.

The **Parkview Hilton,** 1 Hilton Plaza, Hartford, CT 06103 (tel. 203/249-5611 or toll free 800/445-8667), on Ford Street at the corner of Asylum, just a block from the Civic Center, is aptly named. Many of its 410 modern rooms and 20 suites have views of Bushnell Park, of the twin towers of the Civil War memorial arch, and of the ornate Connecticut State Capitol. The benefit of the view is shared by the hotel's various restaurants, including the elegant Terrace on the Park dining

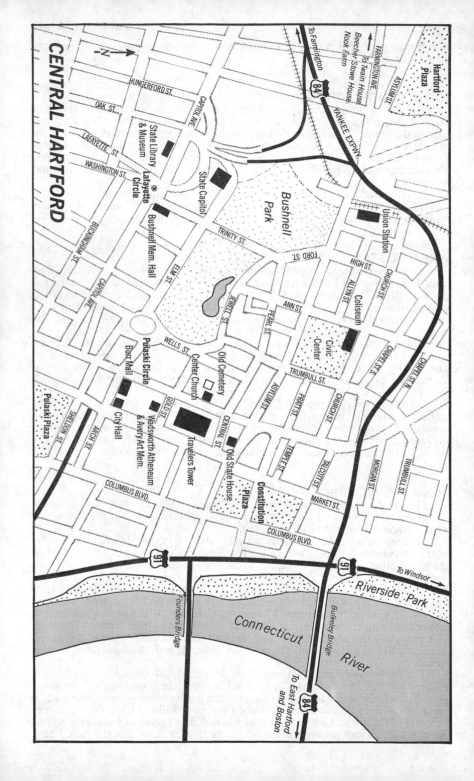

room, and the Glass House coffee shop. There's music for dancing most nights in the Esplanade lounge. The hotel has a full-service health club. With Hilton's family plan, there is no charge for children, regardless of age, when they occupy the same room as their parents. The hotel has several "executive floors" with extra amenities and concierge service. Singles here cost $108 to $158, and doubles are $122 to $188. Rooms at any of these prices have two double beds, making it possible for a family of four to stay for no more than the double rate.

The **Summit Hotel,** 5 Constitution Plaza, Hartford, CT 06103 (tel. 203/278-2000), is an independent 300-room hotel only a few steps from the Old State House and the shops of Main Street. Besides the hotel's comfortable regular guest rooms, the Concierge Floor at the top offers extra amenities such as prompt room service, same-day valet service, bathrobes, and turn-down service; open bar and continental breakfast are included in the Concierge Floor rooms' higher rates. Rooms at the Summit, single or double, cost $138; those on the Concierge Floor are priced at $186.

The **Holiday Inn–Civic Center,** 50 Morgan St., Hartford, CT 06120 (tel. 203/549-2400 or toll free 800/465-4329), is about 2½ blocks from the Civic Center, on the northern side of I-84. Access to Main Street's shopping, to the Old State House, and to the Civic Center is quite good, and the hotel itself boasts 359 comfortable guest rooms, some with views of the river, all with free movies. Other services include babysitting, a game room, an outdoor swimming pool, restaurants, and a kennel for your pet. A shuttle service runs to and from the hotel and Bradley International Airport for a small charge. Singles are priced at $104 to $115; doubles are $115 to $127. These rooms have two double beds, and children can stay for free with their parents. Special weekend rates begin at $63 double.

The **Ramada Inn–Capitol Hill,** 440 Asylum St., Hartford, CT 06103 (tel. 203/246-6591 or toll free 800/272-6232), is very near the Amtrak train station and the Greyhound bus station, just over a block from the Civic Center, facing Bushnell Park near the Civil War memorial arch. The location is very good, with some views of the Connecticut Capitol from the guest rooms and dining facilities. The hotel has the advantage of being small, with 96 rooms, which allows for more personal service, and is also quite moderately priced, considering its excellent location. The restaurant, Honiss' Oyster House, is one of the city's better seafood dining places. To stay here, one person pays $96, and two pay $114.

Motels on the Outskirts

If you're visiting Hartford by car, these motels offer comfortable accommodations at truly moderate or budget prices, and none is more than a few minutes away from downtown Hartford by car.

The **Ramada Hartford,** 161 Bridge St., East Windsor, CT 06088 (tel. 203/623-9411 or toll free 800/272-6232), is at Warehouse Point, near Exit 45 off I-91, on the east bank of the Connecticut River. If you're coming down to Hartford from Boston, you'll see the hotel on your right as you approach Hartford along I-84. Rates are excellent, at $64 single, $64 to $75 double, for one of the 120 very comfortable rooms with one or two double beds, color TV, radio, and air conditioning; some rooms even have their own steambath. The hotel has its own outdoor pool, plus valet, laundry, and babysitting services. A hotel van will pick you up from Bradley Airport.

Another excellent value is Hartford's new **Courtyard by Marriott Hotel,** 1 Day Hill Rd., Windsor, CT 06095 (tel. 203/683-0022 or toll free 800/321-2211), 7 miles south of Hartford at I-91 Exit 38 (Rte. 75, Poquonock Avenue). This new chain of Marriott hotels offers special amenities at moderate prices. For instance, there is an indoor swimming pool, and guest rooms have separate seating areas, full-size desk, king-size beds, and in-room coffee. Room prices are $82 to $104 on weekdays, $60 to $65 on weekends. The hotel has its own restaurant and lounge.

Those in search of budget lodgings will be happy to know that Hartford has numerous inexpensive motels as well.

The **Super 8 Motel,** 57 W. Service Rd., Hartford, CT 06120 (tel. 203/246-8888 or toll free 800/843-1991), at I-91 Exit 33, north of the intersection with I-84, has 104 rooms with air conditioning and color TV within a mile of the center of town, and includes a continental breakfast in these rates: $48 single, $56 double (with two double beds).

Hartford has a **Susse Chalet,** 185 Brainard Rd., Hartford, CT 06114 (tel. 203/525-9306, or toll free 800-258-1980), a 131-room motel at Exit 27 of I-91, with an outdoor swimming pool, and comfortable, television-equipped rooms going for $44 to $46 single, $48 to $51 double.

The 146-room **Motel 6,** 1341 Silas Deane Hwy., Wethersfield, CT 06109 (tel. 203/563-5900), is 10 miles south of Hartford at the Silas Deane exit of I-91. Rooms have individual heating and air conditioning, TV sets, full bath and shower, wall-to-wall carpeting, coin-operated laundry, and direct-dial phones with free local calls. There's a 24-hour restaurant adjacent to the motel. The price for a room is $28 single, $35 double.

Bed-and-Breakfast

For a bed-and-breakfast room priced from $30 to $55 single, $45 to $85 double, contact **Four Seasons International Bed & Breakfast,** 11 Bridlepath Rd., West Simsbury, CT 06092 (tel. 203/651-3045). Rates include full breakfast. Many of these B&Bs will be out in the country or in small towns near Hartford.

WHERE TO DINE

Though it's not a particularly large or cosmopolitan city, Hartford has an interesting selection of restaurants. You should find it easy to satisfy your appetite, your taste buds, and your budget, whatever they may be.

The Top Restaurants

Hartford's best is Chef Chris Pardue's **L'Américain,** 146 Wyllys St., (tel. 522-6500), in a restored brick factory complex at the corner of Charter Oak Avenue in Hartford Square, about a half mile from the Old State House (follow Main Street south and turn left on Charter Oak Avenue; from the Summit Hotel, follow Columbus Boulevard south and it becomes Wyllys Street). Hartford Square is a group of sedate old brick structures across the street from the Episcopal Church of the Good Shepherd. The dining rooms have been remodeled with classical inspiration along clean, modern lines. Queen Anne chairs and heavy tablecloths add to the feeling of luxury. Prepare yourself for an elegant lunch or dinner, for the menu lists priced appetizers of duckling salad, veal pâté, and fresh fruit with liqueurs; or you might choose a clear lobster consommé instead. For a fish course, there was broiled Norwegian salmon filets in a sauce of white Zinfandel with roasted shallots and buttered spinach. Main courses ranged from hickory-smoked turkey through pork schnitzel and Moroccan chicken to a champagne, scallop, and pasta salad. Figure to spend about $25 for lunch (11:30am to 2pm Monday through Friday), about twice that much for dinner (6 to 10pm Monday through Saturday), per person, all in.

At least once, drop in at **Brown, Thomson & Company,** 942 Main St. (tel. 525-1600), just one block's stroll north of the Old State House. The dark stone building (1877), a wonder of American Romanesque architecture with lots of arched windows, columns, and turrets, was designed by Henry Hobson Richardson. The restaurant preserves the feeling of a century ago: matchboard walls, glass that is beveled or etched or stained, stamped-metal ceilings, ceiling fans, and even a great old elk's head. The menu lists everything from French onion soup and buffalo wings to broiled swordfish and prime rib of beef. You'll find pizza and huevos rancheros and fajitas and hot pepperoni. You might get intellectual indigestion if you read the entire menu, but you're certain to find something you fancy. Dessert and drink offerings are equally profuse, from apple cobbler to chocolate-chip-cookie pie, and from frozen daiquiris (with or without alcohol) to Dom Pérignon (at the retail store price!). You can suit your budget as well as your appetite, spending anywhere from $12 to $35 for a meal. There's a special coloring-book menu and a strolling magician most nights for kids. Brown, Thomson opens every day at 11:30am, and serves food most nights until 11pm, till 1am on Friday and Saturday, till 10pm on Sunday.

A View of the Park

For a drink or dining with a view, head for the **Metro Park Café,** 26 Trumbull St. (tel. 246-3355), facing Bushnell Park. Enter the big wooden doors, and the bar is to your right, the dining room to your left. The furniture is of bright bentwood with soft pastel upholstery, comfortable and elegant and modern. The menu lists many favorites of the New American cuisine, on which you can dine for about $30 to $40 per person while enjoying the view of the park (lunch is less). The restaurant opens at 11:30am Monday through Friday, and serves food until 10pm Monday through Thursday, to 11pm on Friday; Saturday hours are 5 to 11pm; closed Sunday. The bar remains open for 3 hours after food service stops. Here you're only a short walk from either the Civic Center or the Old State House.

Civic Center Dining

To satisfy a pang of hunger at any time of the day or night, Hartford's citizens head for the Hartford Civic Center, which has its own collection of restaurants and fast-food shops, some operating 24 hours a day. If you enter from Asylum Street near the corner of Ann Street, you'll be on the Market Level. If you enter from Trumbull Street at the corner of Asylum Street, you'll be on Level One.

Perhaps the most famous of the eateries here is **Shelly's Downtown Deli** (tel. 278-1510), with a 300-item menu and breakfast served all the time. Orders are delivered anywhere downtown. Have chicken soup with matzoh balls ($2) if you wish, or a sandwich of Nova lox ($7.50). I had a good turkey sandwich on rye with bacon, lettuce, and tomato; the orange juice was watery, though.

George's Rotisserie & Bar, on the Market Level (tel. 527-3900), has another of those long and eclectic menus listing everything from chicken curry to seafood kebabs. A full sit-down meal here might come to $15 or $20. George's has a full bar. Lunch and dinner are served daily.

Buon Apetito, at Market Level (tel. 522-4635), is open Monday through Saturday serving seafood, salads, pasta, and those huge sandwiches called grinders in New England, for about $8 to $12.

Upstairs on Level One of the Civic Center are still more places to dine.

Your craving for a dinner of enchiladas, quesadillas, chili, and burritos can be satisfied at **Margaritaville** (tel. 724-3331), a Mexican restaurant and watering hole that opens at 4:30pm every day and serves all sorts of Mexican food and drink until 10pm, till 11pm on Friday and Saturday. Drinks include peach margaritas and banana-rum smoothies. The surroundings are as much fun as the food, with waiters in costume and lots of dark rough wood, stucco, and brightly colored Mexican craft items. You need spend only about $12 or $14 for a meal, but the price can go up if you order a second round of drinks.

Of the full restaurants in the Civic Center, the best is **Gaetano's** (tel. 249-1629), open for lunch (Monday through Saturday from 11:30am to 2:30pm) and dinner (every day from 5 to 10:30pm). The setting here is casual but stylish, the cuisine is continental, inspired particularly by French and northern Italian cooking. Start with bluepoint oysters topped with spinach and hollandaise sauce, or clams casino, and go on to tournedos Rossini or bistecchine (tenderloin tips). Of course there's pasta as well, everything from cavitelli bolognese through capellini angelica and fettuccine to lasagne. A full dinner will cost about $30 per person.

For Chinese Food

What about Chinese food? A long-standing Hartford favorite, indeed a veritable institution, is **Song Hays Restaurant,** 89 Asylum St. (tel. 525-6388), between the Old State House and the Civic Center. Song Hays is what you might call a "neighborhood Chinese place," complete with decor heavy in chinoiserie and a long menu listing heaping plates of Chinese delicacies for only a few dollars each. The luncheon special, for instance, comes in at less than $8; other main-course dishes are only $6 to $8.50. It's open seven days a week for lunch and dinner, and has a full bar.

A Curious Café
The **Russian Lady Café**, 191 Ann St. (tel. 525-3003), just a half block off Asylum (Ann Street is the western edge of the Civic Center), is right in the middle of things. It takes its name from the 1,600-pound solid-bronze statue group atop the building's façade. The statue, executed by the German sculptor Edwin Schulte, was the figurehead of the Rossia Insurance Company for many years, but when the building at Broad and Farmington was torn down to make way for the YWCA, the statue was saved and moved to its present perch. In fact, much of the Russian Lady's decor came from urban renewal: The lamps over the bar are from the ruins of the city's cathedral, which burned down some years ago; the stained-glass windows are from a Russian Orthodox church. The menu specializes in Italian cuisine, with full dinners possible for $18 to $32. The Russian Lady Café is open Sunday through Thursday from 2pm to 1am, and on Friday and Saturday from until 2am. There's live entertainment four nights a week.

WHAT TO SEE
The **Greater Hartford Convention and Visitors Bureau** (tel. 203/728-6789) has organized all the sights in Hartford's downtown into what is called **The Walk,** and a free folder guiding you from point to point along the scenic stroll is available from the office at 1 Civic Center Plaza, or from the visitors information desk in the Old State House. Bushnell Park, the city's central park on The Walk, was laid out by the famous landscape architect Frederick Law Olmsted, the Hartford resident who also landscaped Central Park in New York, the Fenway parks in Boston, and Montréal's Mount Royal Park. Here are the highlights of The Walk.

The Old State House
Pure Bulfinch, the Old State House served as Connecticut's state capitol from 1796 to 1878. You can see the inside Monday through Saturday from 10am to 5pm, on Sunday from noon to 5pm; admission is free. On the Main Street side, have a look at the statue of Hartford's founder, the Rev. Thomas Hooker (1586-1647). Compare this state house with the one in Boston or the Capitol in Washington, both Bulfinch achievements. Outdoor concerts are often held in the precincts of the Old State House, and three galleries inside hold exhibits which change frequently. Warm weather finds farm markets, festivals, and concerts outside on the large lawn. The information center and museum shop are open during regular hours.

The Cheney Building
North on Main Street a block from the Old State House is the mass of Connecticut brownstone built in 1877 by Henry Hobson Richardson for the Cheneys, a Connecticut family of silk manufacturers. It now houses the Brown, Thomson & Company restaurant (see above).

Constitution Plaza
Just east of the Old State House is Constitution Plaza, Hartford's triumph of urban renewal. The plaza has nice copses of trees (one of willows), a fountain designed not to splash or spray passersby in the wind, and the elliptical Phoenix Mutual Life headquarters, perhaps Hartford's most striking building. Hartford is particularly rich in works by Alexander Calder, who had his home and workshop in the state. One of his mobiles is suspended from the ceiling of the commercial banking room in the Connecticut Bank and Trust Company, on the plaza.

The Travelers Tower
Between Main and Prospect streets, right next to the Old State House, rises Hartford's tallest observation point, the Travelers Insurance Company Tower (tel. 277-2431). On weekdays in summer from 10:30am to 3:30pm there are tours to

the top of the building, leaving every half hour on the hour and half hour. In the 15 minutes spent at the top, you'll get the best possible view of the entire city, the suburbs, and the surrounding tobacco country. The Travelers Tower stands on the spot where there was once a tavern. It was in this tavern that Connecticut's royal charter disappeared during a dispute between colonials and royal officials, only to be hidden in the cavity of a nearby oak tree, the famous "Charter Oak" incident. Although the king's men ruled Connecticut illegally for a time (they could not find the charter and so destroy the legal instrument of Connecticut's self-rule), the charter survived, and is now on view at the State Library (see below).

By the way, there are 70 steps at the top of the tower which you must climb to get to the observation area. Also note that tours are run off-season, but you must call and make reservations.

Wadsworth Atheneum

The Atheneum is Hartford's art museum, at 600 Main St. (tel. 278-2670), with a fine collection of over 60,000 items of painting, sculpture, and contemporary and modern art. Don't miss a visit. It's open Tuesday through Sunday from 11am to 5pm. Admission is $3 for adults, half that for children under 13 and seniors. Free on Thursday, and from 11am to 1pm on Sunday. As you enter, ask for a guide leaflet to the collections. Major exhibits change quarterly, so there's always something new to see. The museum's pleasant café serves soups, salads, sandwiches, pasta, and a few heartier dishes at very reasonable prices ranging from $3 to $8.

Burr Mall

Between Wadsworth Atheneum and the attractive city executive office building, Burr Mall is a shady, fragrant spot with a fountain and a fine—if incongruously placed—stabile of Calder's called *Stegosaurus* (1971).

Across Prospect Street from Burr Mall, take a look at the interesting buildings: the **Masonic Temple** and the **Hartford Times Building.** The façade for the latter was once the front of a church in New York, which explains its architecture, odd for a newspaper building!

Center Church and Ancient Burying Ground

Across Main Street from the Travelers Tower is the site of the first church in Hartford, whose pastor was Thomas Hooker (he's thought to be buried under the church). The present church dates from 1807. The gravestones in the cemetery date as far back as 1640.

Bushnell Park

With 500 trees of 150 varieties, Bushnell Park is an oasis in the middle of the busy city. The twin-towered Gothic gateway on Trinity Street is Hartford's memorial to its Civil War dead. Be sure to visit the park's **carousel,** one of the finest restored merry-go-rounds you'll ever see, complete with calliope and automatic drums and cymbals. Rides cost 10¢, and it is by no means only children who take advantage of this low price. The carousel has three types of seating accommodation: "lovers' chariots" for the unadventurous, stationary wooden horses, and horses that move up and down. Remember to grab at the brass ring. Note that the carousel doesn't operate on Sunday, and you must see it with all the lights on and the music trilling to really get the feeling.

The Capitol and Lafayette Square

Richard M. Upjohn is the architect responsible for Hartford State Capitol, a great potpourri of architectural styles and periods—Gothic niches housing soldiers in Civil War uniforms, and more. For all that, the Capitol is fine to look at. Once it was topped by a statue of *The Genius of Connecticut,* a lady. You can see that statue inside the building, and also the battle flags and memorabilia preserved here. Across Capitol Avenue is the **State Library** and **Supreme Court,** a pretty building housing the paper treasures of Connecticut history, including the famous royal charter once hidden in an oak tree. Besides preserving the documents, the library is now the repository of the Samuel Colt collection of more than 1,000 firearms. All together, the collections here make up the **Museum of Connecticut History,** and you can visit it Monday through Friday from 9am to 4:45pm, on Saturday to 12:45pm, closed Sunday; no charge for admission.

Near the Capitol and State Library, in Lafayette Square, is the **Bushnell Memorial Hall,** where many of the city's concerts, plays, and recitals are held. The interior is of the purest 1930s art deco, a style which has seen a resurgence in recent years. The Vienna Boys Choir or the Boston Symphony—you may find either on the playbill here depending on current schedules. For current information, call the Bushnell Memorial at 203/527-3123.

The Civic Center

A complex of several city blocks, the Civic Center follows some of the best modernistic architecture, with fine shopping arcades, lots of open spaces, and mezzanines with hanging plants, small potted trees growing up a story or two, and meeting rooms, restaurants, and clubs. The thing to do, especially on a hot summer day, is to enter the air-conditioned spaces and wander around enjoying the sights, perhaps stopping for a snack or a meal.

The Mark Twain and Harriet Beecher Stowe Houses (Nook Farm)

Hartford has a surprising number of palatial houses, most of them still occupied by wealthy families, and anyone interested in domestic architecture should take a drive through the residential sections northwest of downtown. For a look at two of the city's most impressive houses, drive out Asylum Street and Farmington Avenue about 15 blocks. While you drive, look for the art deco steeple of Trinity Church— the Twain and Stowe houses are four blocks past that point, on the left. You can go by bus—catch any one of the following at the Old State House or along Asylum Street: E1 ("Westgate—Health Center"), E-2 ("Unionville"), E-3 ("Bishops Corner"), or E-4 ("Corbins Corner").

The famous American author from Hannibal, Mo., settled in Hartford in the early 1870s. One of the wealthiest young men in town, Samuel Clemens (1835–1910) had a house designed by Edward Tuckerman Potter. It was finished in 1874 at a cost of $131,000, and is extremely rich in the sort of detail that makes Victorian architecture so much fun to inspect. Twain lived here for 17 years, moving out only after bad investments forced him to take a lecture tour of Europe for some quick money. He loved this place for the best years of his life, and *Tom Sawyer, Huckleberry Finn, Life on the Mississippi, The Prince and the Pauper,* and *A Connecticut Yankee in King Arthur's Court* were all written while he lived here. To see the Mark Twain House, 77 Forest St. (tel. 525-9317), you must take the tour, which is just as well, for the guides have an encyclopedic knowledge of the house and its occupants.

In the same complex of buildings, known as Nook Farm, is a house once lived in by Harriet Beecher Stowe. Although Mrs. Stowe wrote *Uncle Tom's Cabin* while living in Brunswick, Me., she lived and wrote in Nook Farm from 1873 until she died in 1896. Lots of the original furnishings of the author's remain in this Victorian "cottage."

Both houses are open year round, Tuesday through Saturday from 9:30am to 4pm, Sunday from noon to 4pm. They are open on Monday from June 1 to the Columbus Day weekend, and in December; the houses are closed on Monday at other times, and closed on major holidays. A tour of both houses takes slightly over an hour and costs $6.50 for adults, $2.75 for children ages 6 through 16.

Outside Hartford

The region around Hartford has numerous other sights to see. In West Hartford is the birthplace of America's first great lexicographer, Noah Webster. And the colonial town of Old Wethersfield, about 10 miles south of Hartford, has lots of interesting old houses.

Noah Webster (1758–1843) was born in a farmhouse on the outskirts of Hartford. He lived with his strict Calvinist parents and four siblings in this house, helping to work the land, until he was 16. Webster left home to attend Yale on the eve of the American Revolution, and was caught up in the intellectual ferment of the time. He served with the American forces and afterward returned to Hartford to practice law. Webster saw it as his purpose in life to give Americans a new "national language" to go along with their new order of government and society. By 1828, working alone with pen and paper, he had completed his 70,000-word dictionary, which included 12,000 words never previously included in a dictionary. Sales of the dictionary were over 300,000 copies in some years. Along with his *Elementary Spelling Book* and grammar, the dictionary molded and standardized the distinctive spelling, pronunciation, and usage of Americans. His spelling book alone sold more than one million copies annually after 1850, and that was in a nation of only 23 million people! After Webster, Americans no longer had to use schoolbooks and dictionaries written and published in England for Englanders. To Webster we owe such simplified spellings as "honor" instead of the English "honour," and "neighborhood" instead of "neighbourhood."

The **Noah Webster House and Museum,** 227 S. Main St., West Hartford (tel. 521-5362), off I-84 at Exit 41, west of the center of Hartford, consists of Webster's boyhood home, a simple center-chimney colonial dwelling, and a modern museum. The house is furnished authentically in period style, and costumed guides give you a tour and explain what life was like in the America of two centuries ago. There is a typical garden of the period with herbs and dye plants. The house and museum are open from mid-June through September daily except Wednesday from 10am to 4pm, on Saturday and Sunday from 1 to 4pm; from October through mid-June, hours are daily (except Wednesday) from 1 to 4pm. Admission costs $2 for adults, half price for children 6 to 12 years old, $1.50 for seniors.

The town of **Old Wethersfield** has a treasure trove for fanciers of old houses. Take I-91 south for about 10 miles to Exit 26 and follow the signs to the town.

The **Buttolph-Williams House,** on Broad Street (tel. 529-0460 or 247-8996), is a mansion from the 1600s with excellent authentic period furnishings. The kitchen is especially good, and may be the most real-to-life of any extant in New England. Visiting season is mid-May to mid-October, Tuesday through Sunday from noon to 4pm. Adults pay $2, and children pay 75¢.

The **Isaac Stevens House,** 215 Main St. (tel. 529-0612), was a craftsman's home built in 1788, and it still has many of the family's original furnishings. Of particular interest are the collections of toys and ladies' bonnets. It's open all year, Tuesday through Saturday from 10am to 4pm, and also mid-May to mid-October on Sunday from 1 to 4pm. Admission fees are $2 for adults, 75¢ for children. Hours and rates for the Webb House and the Deane House (below) are the same. A ticket to all three houses costs $5 for adults, $2.25 for children.

The **Joseph Webb House,** 211 Main St. (tel. 529-0612), was the site of a strategy conference (1781) between the American commander-in-chief, Gen. George Washington, and his French ally, the Comte de Rochambeau. At the conference, Rochambeau outlined his plan to engage the British at Yorktown. It worked, and that battle ended the Revolutionary War. The house was built in 1752, and now contains period furniture, fabrics, porcelain, and silver.

The **Silas Deane House,** 203 Main St. (tel. 529-0612), was built in 1766 by a member of the First Continental Congress (1774–76) and commissioner (ambassador) to France (1776). It's an elegant place for an elegant gentleman, with interesting architectural details. Though a patriot, Deane was ill-used by some of his American diplomatic colleagues, and he found himself condemned by Congress for profiteering. He lived out his life in exile, but in 1842 Congress made amends to his family and restored his good name and fortune.

If you've now become intrigued by Wethersfield's deep history, drop in at the **Wethersfield Historical Society,** 150 Main St. (tel. 529-7656), located in the Old Academy Museum, a fine Federal-style brick building dating from 1804. The society is in charge of the nearby William A. Keeny Cultural Center at 200 Main St., with permanent exhibits on Wethersfield, and also the Capt. James Francis House, 120

Hartford Ave. (enter from the Historical Society building). This house, dating from 1793, has exhibits which trace a single Wethersfield family through a history of 170 years.

7. Litchfield's Lakes and Hills

Northwest of Hartford is tobacco country. The Connecticut River Valley has very good conditions for growing a premium wrapper leaf for cigars, the famous Connecticut Valley shade-grown tobacco. The long barns next to the fields are for drying; and part of the year the crop will be covered with gauze enclosures to protect it from too much direct sun, hence the "shade-grown" name.

A pleasant morning or afternoon can be spent driving through part of the tobacco country on the way to Litchfield, the town from which Litchfield County takes its name. The county is all forest, rivers, and rolling hills, some of the prettiest country in this exceptionally pretty state, and the town of Litchfield itself is certainly among the most beautiful in New England.

Deeper into the northwest corner of the state you will come upon other charming towns, country inns, and resorts nestled in the Litchfield Hills (Connecticut's "Berkshires") and scattered on the shores of clear lakes. This is vacation country. In the charming old town of Salisbury, you're only 4 miles from the Massachusetts state line, 12 miles from the southern Berkshire town of South Egremont. (For the Berkshires, see Chapter IX.)

ON THE WAY

As you drive west toward the Litchfield Hills, you might want to make several attractive detours. Head out of Hartford on U.S. 44, and soon you will be in Avon, where there is a nice hotel and restaurant. Farther along U.S. 44, just before Winsted, turn for Riverton, the village where Hitchcock chairs are made and Seth Thomas clocks are sold.

Back on U.S. 44, just 8 miles west of Winsted, is the quiet ambience of Norfolk, where you'll find a lovely town green, three state parks, and Yale's Summer School of Music.

Avon

For decades, residents of Hartford have escaped to the country to find the **Avon Old Farms Hotel,** P.O. Box 961, Avon, CT 06001 (tel. 203/677-1651 or toll free 800/228-1651 outside Connecticut), at the intersection of U.S. 44 and Conn. 10. Escaping to the country does not mean giving up the city's comforts, for the spacious rooms at the hotel are furnished with king-size, queen-size, or twin double beds, antique reproduction lamps, mirrors, tables and chairs, color TV, clock-radios, original paintings, and lots of little extras like shower caps, bath oil, and mending kits. You choose from several types of rooms here. Those in the hotel are larger and more modern, and open onto a corridor; they're priced at $118 to $139 single or double. The motel-style rooms are a bit smaller, and they open (as motel rooms do) to the outside; these are priced at $88 single or double. The registration lobby is elegantly done in Georgian style, with comfy sofas and a fine marble fireplace. Guests have the use of the hotel's exercise room and sauna, hairstyling salon, and outdoor swimming pool.

The Avon Old Farms Inn was established in 1757, and a few rooms of the old inn now serve as charming dining rooms. The Forge Room is decorated with blacksmith's paraphernalia, and in chilly weather a fire in the hearth casts an appropriately mellow glow. Two other, smaller rooms near the front door are among the oldest in the inn, and are also charming. A large dining room of more recent construction is decorated with Early Americana, dark-wood beams, old pine boards, and country curtains. The menu is American with continental touches: New England seafood,

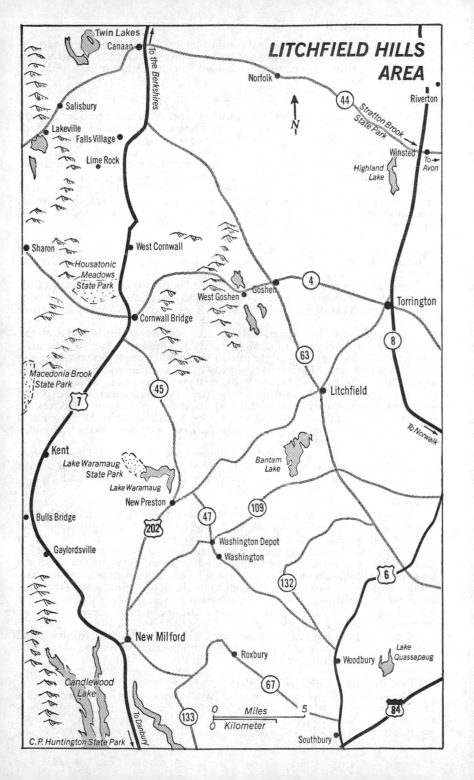

roast beef with popovers, and several continental dishes which change frequently. On Sunday, brunch is an eat-all-you-like buffet. Expect to spend $35 to $40 per person for dinner, with wine, tax, and tip included. Lunch and dinner are served every day but Monday.

Riverton

A few miles west of the vast Barkhamsted Reservoir, in lovely wooded country (much of it state forest land) lies Riverton, a fine Connecticut hill village which looks much like it did in the 1800s. Driving or strolling along the village's main street, you pass the Grange Hall, the new Hitchcock Chair Factory, the Village Sweet Shop, and other shops selling antiques, herbs, and contemporary crafts. The **Catnip Mouse Tearoom** (tel. 379-3745) will serve you lunch from 11am to 3pm, Monday through Saturday, and the **Riverton General Store** (tel. 379-0811) can provide all the raw ingredients for a marvelous picnic, including deli sandwiches, cheese, meat, other groceries, cold beer and hot coffee. The store also sells worms and crawlers if you happen to be interested. It's open seven days a week from 7am to 8pm.

At the **Hitchcock Chair Factory Store** (tel. 379-4826), look over the fine furniture in Lambert Hitchcock's original factory. Visiting hours are Tuesday through Saturday from 10am to 5pm, on Sunday from noon to 5pm, plus Thursday evenings until 9pm; closed Monday.

Another place you won't want to miss is the **Thomaston Clock Discount Outlet** (tel. 379-1077), selling mantel, wall, travel, and grandfather clocks from some of America's best clockmakers. The store is open Tuesday through Sunday from 10am to 5pm.

Cross the Farmington River, and just across the bridge lies the **Old Riverton Inn,** P.O. Box 6, Riverton, CT 06065 (tel. 203/379-8678), on Rte. 20. Originally opened in 1796 by one Jesse Ives, the inn has seen many changes, modifications, and additions over the years, but it retains much of its Early American charm, with heavy wood beams in the Colonial Dining Room, and grindstones from Nova Scotia providing the paving in the Grindstone Terrace. The 12 guest rooms are done in period style, with four-poster and canopy beds, country wallpaper, and some fireplaces. All have cable TV and private bath, and rent for $65 to $100 double; the single rate is $20 to $30 less on weekdays, but the same price on weekends. On the high end, a deluxe suite with a fireplace rents for $168.

Luncheon is served from noon to 2:30pm; dinner from 5 to 8:30pm (till 9pm on Saturday); Sunday from noon to 8pm; closed Monday and Tuesday. At dinnertime expect to pay $17 for veal française and a dollar more for broiled scallops.

Norfolk

In an area full of graceful homes-turned-bed-and-breakfast, the **Manor House,** Maple Ave. (P.O. Box 447), Norfolk, CT 06058 (tel. 203/542-5690), stands with the best. This stucco, timber, and stone inn, on five acres, was built in 1898 by Charles Spofford, the architect of London's underground; that helps explain the English overtones. A massive stone fireplace and authentic Tiffany windows set the tone for the common rooms. The nine guest rooms, most with private bath, have antique beds with down comforters; some rooms boast a fireplace or a private balcony. A full breakfast, with homemade harvested honey, is served in one of three places: in bed, in an elegant dining room, or on the sunlit porch. Prices are in range for the area: $75 to $173 single or double.

From Norfolk, you can continue west on U.S. 44 to Canaan, Salisbury, and Lakeville, or you can take U.S. 44 to Rte. 8 South through Torrington to U.S. 202 West, which will eventually bring you to Litchfield.

A TYPICAL 18TH-CENTURY TOWN

Connecticut's answer to the pretty Massachusetts towns in the Berkshires is Litchfield, a town which a National Park Service writer has called "probably New England's finest surviving example of a typical late 18th-century town." The town was incorporated in 1719, and in the following 100 years grew and prospered as a center for small industry and an important way station on the Hartford–Albany stagecoach route. With this prosperity came the urge, and the wherewithal, to build very fine, graceful houses, which is what the citizens did, making sure that the houses were set well back from the roadway. And while progress in the 19th century robbed Litchfield of much of its wealth—water-powered industry drove Litchfield's small-time craftsmen out of business, and the railroads bypassed the town—the town's decline may have been a blessing in disguise. Today Litchfield retains its late 18th-century beauty, unsullied by the workers' tenements and textile mills that have changed the face of so many other New England towns.

Where to Stay and Eat

Litchfield is an extremely beautiful town. It is also now home to numerous celebrated leaders in the arts, media, and business, who strive to keep it as beautiful and tranquil as it is. Thus you will find few services for visitors, and no lodging places in the town proper. But there is a fine place to stay just outside Litchfield.

Just over 2 miles northeast of the village green along U.S. 202 is the **Tollgate Hill Inn,** P.O. Box 1339, Litchfield, CT 06759 (tel. 203/567-4545), a farmhouse dating from 1745. Originally it stood on the Old East Litchfield Road, where in 1789 it became a tavern to feed, quench, and house travelers on the road between Litchfield and Hartford. But in 1923 it was moved to its present site on Tollgate Hill, where it continues its long tradition of offering fine food and lodging to travelers in the Litchfield Hills. Over the years the inn has been restored and renovated many times, most recently in 1983. The colonial spirit of the house was well preserved, and mated with recent improvements. You'll find a bar made of cherry to harmonize with the original paneling, a formal dining room with a fine fireplace, an arched corner cupboard, and a tavern dining room paneled in wide pine boards. In the ballroom upstairs is a large fieldstone fireplace, lots of windows, copper chandeliers, and a fiddlers' loft from which music issues forth on Saturday nights.

The guest rooms are all different, as you might expect. Ten rooms with colonial furnishings, private bath, and air conditioning rent for $119 double; five rooms with woodburning fireplaces, private bath, and air conditioning are priced at $116 double; and two suites go for $151 double—one of these has a queen-size canopy bed, bar and refrigerator, cable TV with VCR, and stereo tape cassette player, while the other is a small two-room suite with bedroom, sitting room, and color cable TV with VCR. A Continental breakfast, served in your room or on the patio (in good weather), is included in the rates.

If you're feeling in a less formal mood and you're in Litchfield at lunchtime on a sunny day, head over to the **Litchfield Food Company** (tel. 567-3113) on West Street. The white tile floor and built-in wooden shelves give the place an old-fashioned spiffy look. I ordered servings of very creamy pasta salad and chicken pesto, accompanied by blue corn chips and freshly brewed coffee, and my take-out tab came to less than $9. Eat in at one of the few tables or cross the street, pull up a park bench, and enjoy the fine houses all around you. The store is open daily from 9:30am to 5pm.

What to See

At a tiny information booth on the green, you can get a free booklet on the town's history, architecture, and activities, complete with a small map. The sightseeing is simple enough: Drive down South Street just to get the feel of the gracious neighborhood. Stop at the **Tapping Reeve House** (1773), and take a look at the small, unprepossessing edifice beside it, which was the nation's first school of law, established here by Tapping Reeve in 1775 (the school moved into the one-room building in 1784). North Street is as attractive as South Street, and after a drive has given you the lay of the land, park at the green and stroll along either street to see the houses more closely. Tapping Reeve House and Law School is open mid-May to mid-October, Thursday through Monday from noon to 4pm; adults pay $1.

The **Litchfield Historical Society** (tel. 567-4501) will give you a glimpse into the town's interesting past in many of its aspects, political, economic, industrial, decorative, and artistic. The society is on the green at the corner of South Street, and exhibits are open mid-April to mid-November, Tuesday through Saturday from 10am to 4pm.

The **White Memorial Conservation Center** (tel. 567-0015) is out on West Street (U.S. 202) heading toward Bantam, and is the state's largest nature center, with over 35 miles of trails for enjoying the flora and fauna, and several prime perches for birdwatching. Entry to the grounds is free, and they're open all year; the center's museum is open Tuesday through Saturday from 9am to 5pm, and also on Sunday from 11am to 5pm. Displays includes dioramas, mounted specimens, live animals, a touch center, and a 4,000-volume nature library which includes a children's room. Admission to the museum costs $1 for adults and 50¢ for children 6 to 12.

Other Litchfield curiosities: The **Ethan Allen House,** thought to be the one in which the famous patriot and leader of Vermont's "Green Mountain Boys" was born, is at the southern end of South Street, in the road's fork. A **milestone** dating from 1787, which informed the traveler that it was "33 Miles to Hartford, 102 Miles to New York—J. Strong AD 1787," stands on West Street, northern side, just at the end of the town green. And the jail, right on the green at the beginning of North Street, is connected to the bank next door! Whether it's for the convenience of burglars who wish to escape or police who may nab burglars in the bank is not clear.

Litchfield's Winery

Just outside Litchfield is the **Haight Vineyard** (tel. 567-4045), on Chestnut Hill Road off Rte. 118, a mile east of town. This quaint but inviting place prides itself on being Connecticut's first farm winery (established 1975). Besides guided winery tours and wine tastings, you can take the Vineyard Walk, a self-guided tour of the vineyards during which you get to inspect the various types of grapes which make Haight wines.

Some of the favorite wines here are Covertside White, the table wines, a varietal Maréchal Foch, a chardonnay, and a Johannisberg Riesling. There's even a sparkling wine made in the classic *méthode champenoise*. Prices are moderate.

The winery is open all year, Monday through Saturday from 10:30am to 5pm, on Sunday from noon to 5pm.

LAKE WARAMAUG

From Litchfield, drive along U.S. 202 south and west for 12 miles to New Preston. Then head north on Rte. 45, and you'll come to pretty Lake Waramaug. Attractive inns front the lake, as does a state park with picnic and camping facilities.

Lake Waramaug State Park, in New Preston, CT 06777 (tel. 868-0220), has 88 campsites open May 15 through Labor Day. You can reserve in advance, but only by mail. Picnic grounds and swimming are here too.

The Inn on Lake Waramaug, off Rte. 45 on North Shore Road, New Preston, CT 06777 (tel. 203/868-0563, or toll free 800/525-3466 outside Connecticut), is actually a miniresort with all attractions. Indoor swimming pool, tennis court, air-conditioned rooms, restaurant and lounge, gift shop, and water sports (rowing, canoeing, sailing) are among the many offerings. There's even a small launch designed like an old "showboat" for tours of the lake. Even so, the inn retains an antique flavor. Of the 23 guest rooms, only five are in the original inn, while the others are in more modern but attractive guesthouses. All rooms have baths, and most have working fireplaces. Prices range from $182 to $232 per day for two people, breakfast, dinner, taxes, and tips included. The inn offers many special events, like old-fashioned ice harvesting and maple sugaring, which have become traditions over the years.

Not far from where the shore road rejoins Rte. 45, look for signs which point the way to the **Hopkins Inn,** New Preston, CT 06777 (tel. 203/868-7295). This graceful old mansion set on a hill above the lake is most famous for its restaurant, but 10 rooms are for rent as well. If you share a bath, a double room will cost $52; with private bath, prices start at $57. Whether you stay or not, have a meal—but also, have reservations. This is a very popular dining spot, especially on Saturday evenings, when reservations are required. The blackboard menus change daily, but you can be sure of finding interesting, appetizing dishes. I had a difficult choice between clams casino and smoked salmon to start, and an even harder time choosing among backhendl with lingonberries, steamed lobster, wienerschnitzel, and live trout meunière (you can choose your own trout from the tank!). When it came to those Austrian desserts, the choice was impossible. Figure $25 to $30 per person for dinner, with wine. Note these short dining hours: lunch from noon to 2pm and dinner from 5:30 to 9pm (till 10pm on Friday and Saturday), Sunday dinner from 12:30 to 8:30pm. The inn is open April through December every day except Monday; rooms are rented April through November. In warm weather you can dine on the shady patio outside, with a grand view of the lake.

A Visit to a Vineyard

Next door to the Hopkins Inn on Lake Waramaug is the **Hopkins Vineyard,** on Hopkins Road in Warren (tel. 203/868-7954). The quaint red-barn winery is open for tours and tastings from 10am to 5pm seven days a week from the beginning of May through the end of the year. January 2 through April 30, you can visit on Friday, Saturday, and Sunday only, from 10am to 5pm. The winery is closed Thanksgiving and Christmas days.

Whoever heard of a vineyard in Connecticut? You'll be telling all your friends about Connecticut wines once you taste Hopkins' fine, dry Seyval Blanc, perfect for a seafood meal at the inn across the street. Wine prices are moderate and quality is high. By the way, the vineyard is not affiliated with the Hopkins Inn, though the vineyard barn was obviously part of the same estate at one time.

NORTH TO SALISBURY

Back on Conn. 45, head north and you're on your way to **Cornwall Bridge,** which is famous for its picturesque covered bridge. **Housatonic Meadows State Park** (tel. 672-6772) is here with camping and picnic areas, north of town on U.S. 7. You can head north on U.S. 7, then cross westward on Rte. 112 to pick up Rte. 41 north to Salisbury; or take Rte. 4 west from Cornwall Bridge to Sharon, then Rte. 41 north through Lakeville to Salisbury. The distance is about 16 or 18 miles.

Salisbury is an aristocratic, historic town on the edge of the Berkshires. Late in September there's a big flea market here, and at the height of the fall foliage color the Salisbury Antiques Fair is held in the Town Hall. Come any time of year, though. The town is pretty, tranquil, surrounded by gorgeous country, and only 20 miles from the heart of the Berkshires' summer and winter activities.

Where to Stay and Eat

Besides its famed covered bridge, Cornwall Bridge has a choice place to stay. The **Cornwall Inn and Restaurant,** on U.S. 7, Cornwall Bridge, CT 06754 (tel. 203/672-6884), is a mile south of the intersection with Conn. 45. The cozy old inn has a dining room, lounge, and five guest rooms ($106 double on weekends, $95 weekdays). These are supplemented by a half dozen tidy motel-style rooms. Constructed in red-barn style, the rooms have all the conveniences such as television and air conditioning, and cost $61 double on weekdays, $72 on weekends. There's a swimming pool. The location is good, out in the country where it's peaceful and quiet. Note that the dining room is closed on Monday and Tuesday.

You might put up at the **Ragamont Inn,** Salisbury, CT 06068 (tel. 203/435-2372), just off the village green on Rte. 44. You can't miss the inn's two Greek Revival façades with awning-covered dining patio between. The Ragamont rents rooms and suites, most with private bath, for $44 to $58 single, $72 to $82 double, $100 for the suite with a working fireplace. But the emphasis here is on dining as the owner happens also to be a Swiss-trained *chef de cuisine.* On a warm summer afternoon I lunched on vichyssoise, knackwurst Cordon Bleu (who could pass it up?), and pastry, for $18, all in. Fresh fish, the Swiss national dish of raclette, chef's salad, club sandwiches—all these and more were also offered. I caught a glance of the dinner menu (actually, a blackboard) and noted offerings of duck and veal Calvados (that's the apple brandy from France). I'd estimate $38 for a full dinner with wine, per person.

A few miles down the road, you'll do well by dining at the **Wake Robin Inn,** Rte. 41, Lakeville, CT 06039 (tel. 203/435-2515). In the elegant French country dining room, start with a cassolette of snails with fresh mountain herbs or the soup of the day, and move on to medallions of veal simmered with herbs and walnuts or grilled swordfish with lemon butter. With a delectable dessert to top it off, the tab will come to roughly $40 per person, all in. Dinner is served in season Tuesday through Sunday from 5:30 to 9pm, until 8pm on Sunday; Sunday brunch is 11:30am to 2:30pm. Rooms are expensive in this completely renovated former girls' school set on 15 acres, but if you're interested in staying here, they cost $146 to $173 double, more for a suite.

INTO THE BERKSHIRES

Up here in Connecticut's northwest corner, you're very close to one of America's oldest and finest resort areas, the Berkshire Mountains of Massachusetts. The towns of South Egremont, Great Barrington, Lee, and Lenox have great charm, good restaurants, fine old inns and guesthouses, a bewildering array of cultural activities, and more antique shops than you've ever seen before in one area at one time. For details on it all, see Chapter IX, "Central and Western Massachusetts."

NEW HAMPSHIRE

"Live free or die" says the motto on every auto license plate from New Hampshire, echoing the stirring words of Gen. John Stark, victor at the momentous Battle of Bennington (1777) and a New Hampshire native. New Hampshire folk are still very patriotic in an old-fashioned way, and committed to material progress: Modern facilities abound, and the road system is perhaps the best maintained in New England. On a vacation, "living free" in New Hampshire is a snap—mountains, beaches, lakes, amusements, special activities, and good restaurants are all available to the visitor.

On our tour through New Hampshire, we'll look first at the state's seacoast. Yes, New Hampshire has a seacoast! Next we'll visit the charming colonial town of Portsmouth on the border with Maine. Then we'll head north into the state's heart, passing through Manchester, the state's largest city, and Concord, its capital, on our way to Lake Winnipesaukee. From this veritable inland sea, we'll head north again into the White Mountains National Forest and the skiing/hiking center of North Conway, and then even farther north to Bretton Woods. Moving west, we'll cover Franconia Notch, North Woodstock, and Waterville Valley. Finally, we'll visit Lake Sunapee and then Hanover, the hometown of Dartmouth College.

By the way, throughout New Hampshire a rooms-and-meals tax of 8% will be added to your hotel, motel, or inn bill, and you'll also have to pay it every time you have a meal in a restaurant. For your convenience, except where noted, I've added this tax to the prices listed.

New Hampshire's telephone area code is **603.**

GETTING THERE

New Hampshirites are committed to highway travel, so air links and rail lines are played down in favor of bus and car. Amtrak, in fact, has no operations in New

Hampshire proper, although it does run along the New Hampshire–Vermont border for a bit, stopping in Brattleboro, Bellows Falls, and White River Junction on the route between New York and Montréal.

By Limousine and Bus

Airport limousines run regularly from Boston's Logan Airport to many points in New Hampshire. **Hudson Bus Lines' Airporter Limousine Service** goes from Logan to Manchester, Concord, and other southern New Hampshire cities. Call toll free in New England, except New Hampshire 800/367-3885; in Manchester, call 603/883-4807.

C&J Trailways runs hourly daily trips from Logan to New Hampshire's seacoast region and Portsmouth; call these numbers for schedules and reservations: toll free in New York and New England, 800/258-7111; in Portsmouth, 603/431-2424.

Concord Trailways, 7 Langdon St., Concord, NH 03301 (tel. 603/228-3300 or toll free 800/852-3317 in New Hampshire, 800/258-3722 in other New England states), has bus service from Boston through Manchester and Concord to Laconia on Lake Winnipesaukee; from there the bus continues to Plymouth and North Woodstock, and through Franconia. Concord Trailways also has buses from Boston to Conway, North Conway, Glen, Jackson, Pinkham Notch A.M.C. Camp, Wildcat Mountain, and on to Berlin.

Vermont Transit, operating out of Boston's Greyhound terminal near the Park Plaza Hotel, (tel. 617/423-5810), has routes from Portland, Me., to St. Johnsbury, Vt., via North Conway, Bretton Woods, and Bethlehem (near Franconia), N.H., besides running from Logan Airport in Boston to the cities of Manchester and Concord, and thence to Mount Sunapee and Hanover. Vermont Transit also runs buses from Montréal south into Vermont and a few points in New Hampshire, but Montréal visitors will have to transfer at least once to reach most of the vacation locations in the state. Vermont Transit buses depart from the Voyageur Terminal in Montréal (tel. 514/843-4231 or toll free 800/451-3292).

---

1. Hampton Beach

Many visitors to New England forget that Vermont is the only New England state without a seacoast, and that New Hampshire is in fact a maritime state, even though its coastline is only about 20 miles long. The 20 miles are almost all beach, with some rocky headlands and coves, and four state parks with their own uncommercial stretches of beach. **Hampton Beach State Park** is the most southerly, and the public parking and bathing facilities here are run in the clean, well-ordered way of state park management. But just north of the state park is the town of Hampton Beach, two streets wide (north along the waterfront, south along the inland street, as far as cars are concerned). Hampton Beach is a riot of closely packed motels and cottages, ice cream stands and hot dog stands, penny arcades, and watering places. Lights, glitter, and throbbing crowds of the young, tanned, and adventurous make it a nonstop circus, something out of a "beach party" movie, to revel in or abhor as your taste dictates.

FROM HAMPTON BEACH TO PORTSMOUTH

North of Hampton Beach, the state park beaches at **Rye Harbor** and **Wallis Sands** are not as bubbly with activity as Hampton, but to some tastes are all the more pleasant for that. At the state park beaches in New Hampshire, expect to pay a small parking fee, which includes use of all other facilities as well.

The drive along U.S. 1A north to Hampton Beach is very pretty, winding along

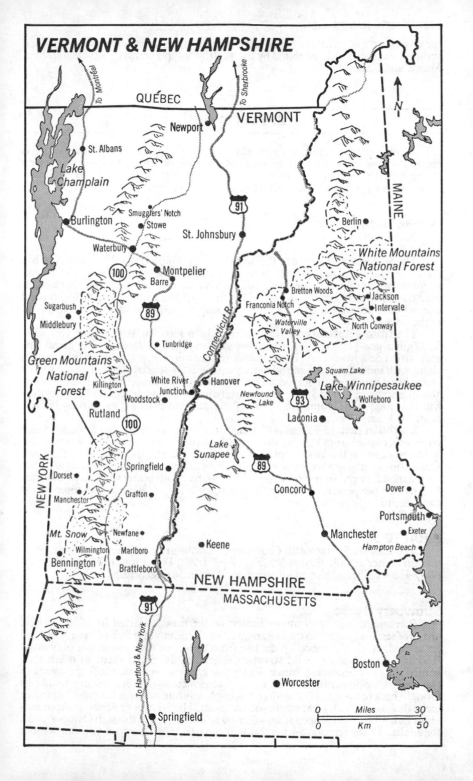

the coast past a succession of ever more sumptuous and meticulously maintained summer mansions, still inhabited by the wealthy and powerful of New Hampshire, Maine, and Boston.

2. Portsmouth

Of the gracious maritime towns along the New England coast, Portsmouth is one of the prettiest and most interesting. A morning or afternoon spent wandering through the town's restored historic side streets, perhaps with lunch, tea, or dinner in one of its restaurants, is both relaxing and entertaining.

WHERE TO STAY AND DINE
Portsmouth has a good place to stay and more than its share of good places to eat.

The **Sise Inn,** 40 Court St., Portsmouth, NH 03801 (tel. 603/433-1200) has 34 rooms and suites all with rich carpeting, private bath, color cable TV, VCR, and telephone. This Queen Anne–style 1881 hotel caters to businesspeople but off-the-road travelers won't feel out of place. Doubles are $113 to $123 depending on bed size, while suites start at $145 to $187. An ample continental breakfast is included in the price.

The **Library Restaurant,** in the Rockingham Hotel at 401 State St. (tel. 431-5202), is a good choice no matter what your culinary preference. The menu lists such varied delights as Long Island duckling, filet mignon, and veal and fish specials, along with more familiar fare and money-saving daily-special plates. The old rooms of the hotel have been preserved without overdoing the decor; books line the walls. You might spend $25 to $35 for a good, full dinner with wine, tax, and tip, less than half that for lunch. Hours are 11:30am to 3pm and 5 to 11pm, Sunday brunch from 11:30am to 4pm.

Szechuan Taste, 54 Daniels St. (tel. 431-2226), is a family-run place offering a refreshing change from Portsmouth's mostly-seafood restaurants. The simple, dimly lit restaurant is the kind of place you go with friends, the kind you might not venture into without a recommendation. There are many Thai and Szechuan dishes on the menu, priced from $6.50 to $8.50, making a full dinner with tea possible for $12 to $16 per person. Szechuan Taste is open from 11:30am to 10:45pm weekdays, until 11:45pm on weekends.

WHAT TO SEE
The **Greater Portsmouth Chamber of Commerce** maintains a visitors information center at 500 Market St. (Exit 7 off I-95), Portsmouth, NH 03801 (tel. 603/436-1118), and also an information kiosk in Market Square.

Strawbery Banke
Portsmouth's jump from wilderness to settlement started in 1630, when a group of settlers sailed into the Piscataqua River's mouth in search of fresh water and good land. As they climbed up the rise from the shore they found not only good land and water but also wild strawberries, which delighted them so much they named the place Strawbery Banke. Today that name serves to identify the center of the city's historic restoration effort, a 10-acre section of 18th-century buildings brought back to life and filled with craftspeople who are not here for show but in fact make their livelihoods right where you see them. The Strawbery Banke outdoor museum (tel. 433-1100) is open from 10am to 5pm daily, May through October, at $8 for adults, $7 for seniors, $4 for children 6 to 16. For this price you can wander

about, looking at the 42 houses and buildings, exhibits, period gardens, workshops, and artisans' galleries on display.

A walk through Strawbery Banke is educational as well as entertaining, for you'll see how chairs, tables, and cabinets were made besides seeing examples of the work itself; weaving and stoneware potting are explained, and early tools and architectural designs are spread out for your examination.

Finding the Strawbery Banke section is easy: Just follow the directional signs, with arrows, posted throughout the town and on approach roads.

Strawbery Banke is the major part of Portsmouth's Old Harbour area, the cornerstone of which is **Prescott Park,** a waterfront park, dock, and amusement area donated to the city by the Prescott sisters in the 1930s and 1940s.

John Paul Jones House

Of the other notable places in this pretty city, none is more notable than the National Historic Landmark house of John Paul Jones (1758), open mid-May through mid-October from 10am to 4pm Monday through Saturday, and noon to 4pm on Sunday in July and August. The stately house, at the corner of Middle and State streets, was actually a rooming house when Cmdr. Jones stayed in it while his frigate, the famous *Ranger,* was being built in a nearby shipyard. It is now the headquarters of the Portsmouth Historical Society, and you can visit the house and museum (tel. 436-8420) on a 1-hour guided tour at $3 for adults, $1 for children 6 to 12.

3. Manchester

Manchester borders the Merrimack River, and the cheap waterpower brought the city wealth in the textile boom of the mid and late 19th century. The very impressive **Amoskeag Mills** still border the river and the canals in the center of town, the brick façades stretching for almost a mile. The mills are used for various purposes today, including the manufacture of textiles and shoes (plenty of factory-outlet stores in town), and continued use preserves these monuments of American architectural and industrial history.

WHAT TO SEE

Although a business and manufacturing town, Manchester has two points of interest besides the giant mills. The **Currier Gallery of Art,** 192 Orange St. (tel. 669-6144), is a fine museum in a handsome building, open free to the public on Tuesday, Wednesday, Friday, and Saturday from 10am to 4pm, on Thursday to 10pm, and on Sunday from 2 to 5pm. The collection is strong in 19th- and 20th-century European and American glass, English and American silver and pewter, and colonial and Early American furniture. It also has a nice collection of paintings and sculpture from other parts of the world. Degas, Jan Gossaert, and a follower of Meliore are represented along with other masters. A beautiful new wing shows off the collections to best advantage. To find the museum, cross the Queen City or Amoskeag Bridge to downtown, and drive along Elm Street (Rte. 3) to Orange Street. Go east on Orange six blocks, and the museum is on your left.

About 5 miles south of Manchester, at Exit 11 of the Everett Turnpike, is the town of Merrimack, where you'll find **Anheuser-Busch Company's Merrimack Brewery** (tel. 595-1202). The company that offers Budweiser and Michelob is the largest brewer of beer in the world, with an annual capacity of about 80 million barrels at 12 breweries across the country.

In the warmer months (May through October), guided tours run continuously every day of the week from 10am to 5:30pm (last tour). In winter, tours run Wednesday through Sunday only, from 9am to 4pm. Assemble in the special alpine-looking tour building.

After the tour there's sampling of the brew, of course, and perhaps a visit to the

Clydesdale Hamlet, home for a dozen of the huge, majestic draft horses. You've probably seen them in eight-horse hitches pulling a brewer's wagon in advertisements or local parades.

WHERE TO STAY AND EAT
The best value is the **Susse Chalet Inn,** 860 S. Porter St., Manchester, NH 03103 (tel. 603/625-2020 or toll free 800/258-1980). The 102 guest rooms, plainish but tidy and comfortable, are bargain-priced at $44 to $46 single, $48 to $51 double. The Susse Chalet is at Exit 1 from I-293/Rte. 101. The motel has a swimming pool, and remote-control cable TV with free movies.

The **Howard Johnson Hotel** is at the Queen City Bridge exit (no. 4) from I-293 (tel. 603/668-2600 or toll free 800/654-2000), Manchester, NH 03102. King- and queen-size beds, satellite TV with HBO, an indoor pool, saunas, a lounge, and a restaurant (open from 6am to 2am) are offered, with rooms ranging from $68 to $79 single, $78 to $86 double; children under 18 stay free in their parents' room.

At the **Holiday Inn West,** 21 Front St., Manchester, NH 03102 (tel. 603/669-2660), there is a restaurant, a lounge, an outdoor pool, and rooms for $64 to $75 double; children, including teenagers, stay free with their parents. Take the Amoskeag Bridge exit (no. 6, Rte. 114) from I-293 for this one.

---

4. Concord

The capital of New Hampshire is a pleasant little city with an appropriate frontier-mountain feeling. First settled in 1725, the town was called Rumford for the first 40 years; the name later found its way into the title of Count Rumford, inventor of a certain sort of shallow fireplace. Since 1816 Concord has been the capital of the state. Granite, printing, electrical equipment, and leather goods, as well as a surprisingly small amount of state bureaucracy, keep the town going.

WHAT TO SEE
Mary Baker Eddy, founder of Christian Science, was born nearby in the village of Bow. Franklin Pierce, 14th president of the United States, was speaker of the New Hampshire General Court (legislature) as well as being among the town's prominent lawyers, and you can visit his house, which is now a National Historic Site called the **Pierce Manse.** The Manse, at the farthest reaches of North Main Street, was saved from demolition by a civic-minded group named the Pierce Brigade, and it is open weekdays from June 12 through September 15 from 11am to 3pm (closed Labor Day). Entrance costs $1.50 for adults, 50¢ for children and students. You might want to make an appointment by calling 224-9620.

The State Capitol, called the **State House,** was built in 1819 of—you guessed it—granite, and is the oldest capitol in which a legislature still occupies its original chambers. Inside are proudly displayed the state's battle flags and portraits of its notable military commanders. A statue of Daniel Webster, one of several native New Hampshire boys who made good on a national scale, stands before the building. The small size of the State House will surprise you; compared with the mammoth buildings in Providence, Hartford, and Boston, it seems barely big enough to hold just the governor's staff. But many of the tax-burdened citizens of other states are lured to New Hampshire every year by the low tax rate, kept low in part by keeping bureaucracy small.

Canterbury Shaker Village
Fifteen miles north of Concord on Rte. 106, on the way to Laconia, you can visit a restored village founded by the Shakers in 1792. Members of the United Society of Believers in Christ's Second Appearing were called Shakers because of the religious ecstasies they sometimes experienced. Their community at Hancock, Mass., in the Berkshires (see Chapter IX, Section 7, "Stockbridge") is the best

known, but there were others, notably at Sabbathday Lake, Me., and here in Canterbury (tel. 783-9511). Two of these villages are still active Shaker communities.

Besides producing the much-admired Shaker furniture and craft items, the Canterbury Shaker community specialized in producing herbs and herbal medicines, which were sold throughout the country. You can still visit the herb garden, as well as the original meetinghouse (1792), an apiary (bee house), the ministry, a Sisters' shop, a laundry, and the schoolhouse (1826).

You can take a guided tour May through October, Monday through Saturday from 10am to 5pm; the last tour is at 4pm. The cost is $6.75 adults, $3.50 for children 6 to 12. On the tour you can see dovetailed and oval box making in the carpenter's shop, and look over reproductions of Shaker designs in quilts, furniture, and crafts in the carriagehouse gift shop.

All year on Thursday, Friday, and Saturday evenings you can also enjoy a traditional candlelight dinner here. There is one seating (family style at long tables) at 7pm sharp. The four-course meal (choose from a poultry, meat, or fish main dish) costs $32 per person. Recipes, ingredients, and cooking methods are all true to Shaker form and philosophy. After dinner has transported you to another era, you'll be guided through the village by candlelight, or if it's off-season and the village is closed, you'll be treated to an evening of folk singing. You'll have an enjoyable evening either way.

---

5. Lake Winnipesaukee

The largest of the lakes in New Hampshire's Lakes Region is grand indeed: 28 miles long, close to 300 miles of shoreline, 72 square miles of water to swim in or boat on, and almost 300 islands. The name has been translated as "smile of the Great Spirit," and while the lake's irregular shoreline might suggest a wry grin rather than a sunny smile, the lake's large size would certainly do the Great Spirit justice. Summer is when the lake is busiest with swimmers, boaters, water-skiers, and the like, but winter snows draw crowds to the **Gunstock** and **Alpine Ridge** ski areas near the lake's shore.

LACONIA AND EAST

Laconia is Lake Winnipesaukee's largest town, and business and commercial center. Many of the companies with large shoe factories in the region have factory-outlet stores here where shoes sell at bargain prices. Downtown next to City Hall, the **Belknap** (pronounced "*bell*-nap") **Mill** (tel. 524-8813), a textile mill built in 1823, has been restored, and you can tour it to see the hydroelectric machinery which ran the mill from 1918 to 1969. The mill now serves as the region's center for culture and the arts. It's open from 9am to 5:30pm Monday through Friday, to 1pm on Saturday, all year.

Where to Stay

Coming to the lake for fun, people stay in the many motels and inns on portions of the lake's shore near Laconia, or in a small, pretty town such as Wolfeboro, due east of Laconia. Skiers stay at the inns located near the slopes or in a lakefront establishment with winterized cabins.

To get away from the hustle and bustle of the highway, drive along Rte. 11 and watch for signs pointing out a scenic shore road off to the left. Rte. 11 has been remade in recent years and is farther away from the lakeshore, while the motels are still along the old road which used to be Rte. 11. Most of the traffic uses the new road, leaving the old one much quieter.

Those looking for quiet, luxurious accommodations with all the conveniences, including color TV and air conditioning, will enjoy the **Belknap Point Motel,** 107 Belknap Point Rd., (R.F.D. 8), Gilford, NH 03246 (tel. 603/293-7511). The Belknap Point has two sections: Down on the shore of the lake, a number of modern efficiency units with kitchens and decks reach out almost over the water; and up the steep slope of the hill between the old road and the new (you can enter from either road) are a number of hotel rooms, all with ceramic tile bath, a little balcony, and gorgeous views of the lake. The owners have put a lot of thought into decorating the rooms nicely, and they work hard to make sure each guest is comfortable. The Belknap Point has its own swimming area and a grassy patio. Prices for the hotel rooms are $84 to $94 a day double, $21 a day less off-season (May, early June, September, and October). You can rent a room here for one or two days at $62 a day if there's an opening for that amount of time. The efficiencies down by the water rent by the week. An additional person in a room is $10; in an efficiency, $52.

The **Estate Motel and Cottages,** Scenic Drive (R.F.D. 4), Gilford, NH 03246 (tel. 603/293-7792), is another of the establishments along the scenic lakefront road. Here there are eight motel rooms and two efficiencies in white buildings. The rooms look out over a grassy lawn down to the lake; the lake boating and swimming dock are convenient. The Estate is secluded and quiet, and it's best to reserve in advance for one of its rooms: $64.25 double in a motel room, $107 double in one of the efficiency cottages, lower rates by the week. Rooms have two double beds, cable TV, shower, and refrigerator; the efficiencies have the same, plus a sink and stove, and kitchen utensils. Three cabins are rented by the week for $348 for one bedroom, $481 for two bedrooms.

What to Do

BEACHES **Ellacoya State Beach,** on Rte. 11 southeast of Glendale, is one of the nicest beaches on the lake. The entrance fee is $2 for adults and children 12 and older, there's plenty of parking, and if you go early in the day you can get one of the picnic tables. A snack bar is in operation, and a lifeguard is on duty all the time the beach is open. The slope of the beach is very, very gradual, making it ideal for small children; for more experienced swimmers, a swimming dock floats in the water farther out.

Weirs Beach, on Rte. 11B near its intersection with U.S. 3, is a town beach with a similar admission charge, free parking at several lots in the town of Weirs Beach (look for the signs to the free lots—everything on the main street is metered). The town is known more for its honky-tonk penny arcades, candlepin bowling alleys, pinball machines, fortune tellers, and fast-food stands than it is for the beauty of its beach. These amusements are open during the day and in the evening in summer, and give the town a character that differs greatly from what it once must have been: The grand old turn-of-the-century mansions seen here and there in the town are some of the finest of their genre, with lots of cupolas, turrets, gables, and all the other paraphernalia that make late-Victorian architecture so intricate. You can stay overnight at Weirs Beach in one of the hotels, motels, or guesthouses, although the low lakefront situation seems to lend a mustiness to most accommodations.

BOAT RIDES A number of large boats make tours of the lake several times daily. Most famous is the M.V. *Mount Washington* (tel. 603/366-5531), which runs cruises from Weirs Beach between May 19 and October 21, with the schedule varying depending on the time of year. The cruise around the lake takes 3¼ hours and costs $12 for adults, half price for children 5 to 12; under 5, free. Breakfast, luncheon buffet, a Sunday champagne brunch, and snacks are available on board. You can also pick up the boat in Wolfeboro every day at 11am. The *Mount Washington* also leaves from Weirs Beach on moonlight cruises on Tuesday through Saturday evenings from July 1 through Labor Day weekend.

WOLFEBORO

Of the other towns on Lake Winnipesaukee, Wolfeboro is certainly the finest. The town escaped the blight that hit such textile-producing towns as Laconia because Wolfeboro never industrialized; and it has escaped the honky-tonk commercialism that has taken over some other lake towns, perhaps because of its "inconvenient" position at the southeastern tip of the lake. So today Wolfeboro is a fine, almost typical, New England town with the requisite historical society, white-steepled churches, gracious old houses, and some very good views of the lake.

There is less hustle and bustle in Wolfeboro than in some other lake towns, less to "see and do," but that makes it all the better for those who really want to relax. The M.V. *Mount Washington* stops here to pick up and discharge passengers for its tours of the lake (see above for details); and a good number of the motels and resorts in town have their own stretches of beach. Wolfeboro is proud to call itself "the oldest summer resort in America," because in 1763 Gov. John Wentworth built what is thought to be the first summer house in the United States within the town's boundaries.

Where to Stay and Dine

Among the most serviceable of the town's hostelries is the venerable **Wolfeboro Inn**, 44 N. Main St., Wolfeboro, NH 03894 (tel. 603/569-3016). The inn was built in 1812, but has been thoroughly modernized, and prides itself on giving the "glitter-weary traveler" a comfortable and tasteful place to lodge and dine. The 43 rooms have some antique pieces, and all have private bath, air conditioning, color cable TV, and telephone, and cost $96 to $114 per night, tax and continental breakfast included. As the inn is often full in high summer, it's best to reserve in advance. In summer, enjoy the sandy lake beach, take cruise in the inn's own launch, or ride one of the bicycles, canoes, or sailboards, all included in the room price. In winter, outdoor activities are cross-country skiing and iceboating.

The dining areas have wooden chairs and tables and several fireplaces, including three in Wolfe's Tavern (open 7 am to 11:30 pm) and a large brick one in the Dining Room (dinner is served from 5:30 to 10 pm). The menu offers a fairly standard selection of the popular beef, seafood, and fowl dishes, but the daily specials (available at both lunch and dinner) are always interesting, and often the best values. Sandwiches at lunch are priced at $4.50 to $6. At dinner, main courses with side dishes cost $15 to $21; the daily specials are usually nearer the lower end of that range.

Staying on the Outskirts

Wolfeboro is surrounded by motels and inns on the outskirts, many of them very nice indeed. Herewith my favorites.

The **Pick Point Lodge**, P.O. Box 220D, Mirror Lake, NH 03853 (tel. 603/569-1338), 4½ miles north of Wolfeboro off Rte. 109, is truly unique. It was formerly a wealthy family's summer estate, and has been converted to accommodate a small number of guests in 10 large cottages (up to four bedrooms) and in two rooms in the main lodge. It would be possible to fill pages with the good points of the Pick Point Lodge, but a quick sketch will give you the idea: Cottages are all very comfy and tastefully done, with fireplaces, porches, full kitchens, and, in the larger ones, two bathrooms; the estate is on a 112-acre tract of forest, with several nature trails plotted for guests' use; guests can enjoy a full half mile of lake frontage, indoor and outdoor tennis courts, a private beach and jetty, indoor and outdoor games, and special cookouts, cocktail parties, and such, which are "on the house" and which you can join or ignore as you wish. The hosts, the Newcomb family, are very gracious and solicitous of their guests' well-being and privacy, and couldn't be nicer. Rates for such quality are not low, but are reasonable for what you get; prices given below include the 8% tax. From late June to Labor Day rentals are by the week only, unless a cancellation or the like leaves a cottage or room open for several days. Cottages range from $700 for a one-bedroom to $1,900 for a four-bedroom for one week from mid-July through Labor Day weekend; prices for May, June, September, and October are in the range of $700 to $950 for a cottage. In the main lodge, rooms cost $90 to $115 double, light breakfast included. This could easily be the finest place on Winnipesaukee.

Just about a mile north of town at 120 North Main Street is the **Lakeview Inn**, P.O. Box 713, Wolfeboro, NH 03894 (tel. 603/569-1335). The simple rooms, with one or two double beds, are primarily in the motor lodge; some of these have kitchenettes. Three of the 14 guest rooms are upstairs in the old inn. Regardless of location all have TV, private bath, and telephone. Summer rates, which include a self-service continental breakfast set up in the lounge, are $80 single, $80 to $91 double. Lunch is served weekdays from noon to 2pm; dinner is served nightly from 5:30pm. The menu includes such selections as roast duckling and a veritable sea of scallops, crabmeat, langoŭstines, and lobster. A full meal will total about $25 per person with tax and tip, but lighter fare is always available for about a third of the price.

What to Do Near Wolfeboro

Several activities in Wolfeboro are worth a special mention.

Dr. Henry F. Libby, a Boston dentist who was born and raised near the shores of Winnipesaukee, devoted the latter part of his life to the study and collection of natural history specimens: fish, animals, and birds. Other interests of his included early Native American lore of the region, and artifacts from the times of early settlers. All these diverse exhibits are brought together in the **Libby Museum,** open from 10am to 4pm daily except Monday during the summer. Donation is $1 for adults, 50¢ for children. The museum is about 3 miles north of the town on Rte. 109.

Around the turn of the century Thomas Gustav Plant decided to build himself a retreat in the New Hampshire wilderness. While he was not alone in this—lots of rich men were building lavish estates in the region—his accomplishment is certainly among the grandest. Lucknow, as the estate was named, cost millions of dollars to build; the name comes from a castle in Scotland, and ultimately from a city in India, although the mansion has distinctly Central European touches to it. Today Lucknow is called **Castle in the Clouds,** on Rte. 171 in Moultonboro (tel. 476-2352), and is open to visitors who pay $7.50 per adult, $5.50 for children from 6 through 12. The grounds are very beautiful, and the view of the mountains and lakes is nothing short of spectacular. Horseback trail rides are available. Castle in the Clouds is open weekends in May and June from 9am to 6pm, daily during July and August to September 10 from 9am to 8pm. To get there, take Rte. 109 north from Wolfeboro for 17 miles, turn right (east) onto Rte. 171, and go 3 miles to the entrance.

MOUNT WASHINGTON VALLEY

The area along Rte. 16 between North Conway and Gorham, including the town of Bartlett on U.S. 302, is organized for tourist reasons as the Mount Washington Valley. The towns of North Conway and Jackson are centers for summer hiking, camping, and biking trips, and for winter skiing at the ski areas of Attitash, Mount Cranmore, Black Mountain, and Wildcat Mountain. The **Mount Washington Valley Visitors Center** (tel. 603/356-3171) has its main information office on Main Street in the center of North Conway, open during business hours and on weekends. The guides will be glad to help you with room reservations if you've had trouble finding a place to stay, and are in general very helpful indeed.

In addition, **North Country Tours,** P.O. Box 747, North Conway, NH 03860 (tel. 603/356-3212 or toll free 800/334-7378), will help you to make reservations at condos, inns, resorts, and motels throughout the White Mountain area, at no charge for the service.

6. North Conway

On the edge of the White Mountain National Forest and at the end of Mount Washington Valley, North Conway is the sports capital of the White Mountains. It's not a particularly large town, although the mile or two of motels and eateries along Rte. 16 south of town do seem to extend the boundaries. But basically one can walk to almost anything except this southern extension by parking downtown, somewhere near the antique railroad station. North Conway has taken well to its role of mountain town, and the people talk hearty and look healthy. And while some of the businesses are old-time mom-and-pop afffairs, a lot of shops obviously have been citified to cater to the hiking and ski trades. But still the town has not been "taken over" by city people. Perhaps the character and charm of North Conway is best exhibited by the town library building on Main Street not far from the railroad station: Although small, it's built of massive granite blocks and has a slate roof which will last forever; it's open to all and sundry on weekday afternoons and Wednesday mornings.

WHERE TO STAY AND EAT

Northway Conway has dozens of places to stay, including a good number of motels along the southern extension of Main Street (Rte. 16), but I'll concentrate mainly on the small inns in the town, and on those in the neighboring towns of Jackson and Glen, most of which have excellent dining rooms. Many of the lodging establishments listed here have midweek and ski packages; be sure to inquire if you are planning an extended or active stay.

North Conway's Inns and Guesthouses

Perhaps the best for price, convenience, and pleasantness is the **Cranmore Inn,** North Conway, NH 03860 (tel. 603/356-5502 or toll free 800/822-5502), just off Main Street on the street leading to the Mount Cranmore ski area, and only a few blocks from the intercity bus stop. The inn is over a century old, with 23 guest rooms in Victorian style; with private bath, the rate is $50 single, $69 double; with running water in the room and a bath down the hall, the price is $37 single, $56 double. Several two-bedroom suites (the two bedrooms share one bath) are available for families and friends traveling together, and can be rented at a price of $106 for three, or $124 for four people. Meal service is family style. There are bonuses: a huge parlor with fireplace, a game room, and a TV room; nice big lawns suitable for games and Frisbee (in summer), and a swimming pool. From the inn you can walk to the slopes of Mount Cranmore in 10 minutes, and the center of town in 5 or less. A 5 minute walk will bring you to the Tennis and Health Club, with full privileges. Note that in winter the rate structure is a bit different: Breakfast and dinner are included in the price of the room, and rates vary depending on whether you come during the week or on the weekend.

On a quiet back street stands the **Sunny Side Inn,** Seavey Street, North Conway, NH 03860 (tel. 603/356-6239), an affordable and cozy bed-and-breakfast place with 10 rooms. Rooms have shared or private bath, and rent for $30 to $53 single and $43 to $64 double, full breakfast included. There's a living room with fireplace and television, and also a reading nook you can use. To find the Sunny Side, turn onto Kearsarge Street at the traffic light, go right again at the top of the hill, and it's on the left.

Another charming guesthouse, 1½ miles north of the center of North Conway, is named **Wildflowers,** North Main Street, North Conway, NH 03860 (tel. 603/356-2224). You'll see the sign on the left as you head north, and behind it the big white house with porch posts made of peeled and painted tree trunks. Homey, simple, convenient, friendly, the six bedrooms at Wildflowers (two with private bath, four with semiprivate) rent for $43 single, $64 to $86 double, continental breakfast included. Add $4 if you want a full breakfast.

The **Cranmore Mountain Lodge,** P.O. Box 1194, North Conway, NH 03860 (tel. 603/356-2044), is off the beaten path, which preserves a spirit of quiet and relaxation. A mile and a half from the center of town you'll come to the lodge, which consists of a nice old inn and a modernized barn loft. Rooms in the inn are the best bargains, as they share several bathrooms; many rooms have sinks; prices are $60 to $80 for two, including breakfast. In the barn loft, rooms have private bath, color TV, air conditioning, and one or two double beds—in short, all the comforts. Prices are commensurate with the degree of luxury, at $74 to $95 for two, again including breakfast. Cranmore Mountain Lodge has a 40-foot swimming pool, tennis and basketball courts, Jacuzzi spa bath, trout pond for fly angling, barn animals, and outdoor barbecues. To find the lodge, turn east at the traffic light in North Conway onto Kearsarge Street; when you can go straight no longer, turn left. This is Kearsarge Road, and the lodge is a mile down.

The **Center Chimney,** P.O. Box 1220, North Conway, NH 03860 (tel. 603/356-6788), is just that: a big center-chimney Federal house built in 1787, now accepting guests. Rates are $38 single, $45 to $55 double, muffins and coffee included. (Extra bed for $10). Look for the house north of town, just off Main Street, near the Saco River.

Hotels and Motels in North Conway

For decades the **Eastern Slope Inn,** Main Street, North Conway, NH 03860 (tel. 603/356-6321 or toll free in New England except New Hampshire 800/258-4709), was North Conway's posh place to stay, a stately white-pillared hotel with a genteel ambience. Swimming pool, clay tennis courts, a restaurant and pub, a summer theater next door, and a village center location are among the inn's advantages. Choose from rooms in the inn or in the motellike Randall House nearby, suites or efficiency suites, many of which are now condos. Rooms cost $92 to $214, single or double, depending on day of the week and season. Children of all ages can stay with their parents for free.

North Conway's snazziest hostelry, always in great demand, is the **Red Jacket Mountain View Motor Inn,** perched on a slope above South Main Street, North Conway, NH 03860 (tel. 603/356-5411 or toll free 800/752-2538). At the height of the season (summer or winter) rooms go quickly because of the inn's central location and luxury accoutrements: a beautiful indoor pool covered by a dramatic wood roof, and an outdoor pool as well; saunas; a headed whirlpool; a game room with table tennis and electronic games; shuffleboard courts; tennis courts; dining room and cocktail lounge. Many rooms have views and balconies, and some rooms offer lofts so that a family can sleep more comfortably. Ceramic tile baths, two double beds to a room, color TV, air conditioning and heat, direct-dial telephones, and other luxury touches add to the draw, but it's the view and the convenience that convince many people to stay here. Rates are $95 to $160 double, and vary seasonally. Package plans are always available. At dinner, main courses are in the $12 to $16 range. Lunch is served in the Birchmont Tavern in the summer.

Staying in Intervale

A mile or two north of North Conway along Rte. 16 are several inns and motels also worth considering. Although you won't be able to walk easily to town from here, these establishments have their own restaurants, and you're only a short drive from most of the hiking and ski points.

Off the main road, on scenic Rte. 16A (a short loop of a few miles), are several more lodging possibilities.

The **New England Inn and Resort,** Intervale, NH 03845 (tel. 603/356-5541), is the largest of the establishments on Rte. 16A, comprising both the inn of that name and the Hampshire House across the road. It's quite a spread, with pools, four-hole golf course, clay tennis courts, and shuffleboard, besides 35 rooms with or without bath in several buildings, costing $66 to $73 *per person;* a normal double room would thus cost about $140 total, per day, 7% tax and 15% service included. A big breakfast and dinner each evening are included in these rates. The one-room cottages for rent here have their own fireplaces and cost between $76 *per person* for up to four, meals included. Rates are 15% higher during foliage and ski season. The dining room, called Anna Martin's, is open to the public for all meals and specializes in Yankee cuisine with home-baked breads and desserts. Besides the pine-paneled dining area, there's a lounge.

Just down the road from the New England Inn is the **Old Field House,** Rte. 16A, Intervale, NH 03845 (tel. 603/356-5478 or toll free 800/444-9245), which is in a field, yes, but which is not old. It's hard to tell at first whether this hostelry is an old building redone from top to bottom or a new building made to look good and last long. Despite its sturdy granite façade and gambrel-roofed wings meant to conjure up the romantic New Hampshire past, it is quite modern. Rooms are all clean and shiny, with beamed ceilings and colonial-style furniture. The bed arrangements are one or two doubles, a queen-size, or a tremendous king-size. There's also an efficiency apartment which overlooks the pool. The room prices are all for two people, including two continental breakfasts: $69 to $106. You get lots of extras at the Old Field House, such as a heated outdoor pool, tennis, laundry facilities, background music, cable TV, a game room, and shuffleboard. The entire place is air-conditioned.

Another place nearby is **The Forest, A Country Inn,** Rte. 16A (P.O. Box 37), Intervale, NH 03845 (tel. 603/356-9772), a large Victorian house converted to take guests. There are 11 rooms in the inn itself and 2 in a nearby cottage, priced from $53 to $101 double, full breakfast included. For these prices you get a private bath, a nice living room (with fireplace) in which to meet new friends, a heated pool in summer, and cross-country skiing in winter on groomed trails, as well as summer hiking trails.

The **Riverside Inn,** Rte. 16A, Intervale, NH 03845 (tel. 603/356-9060) has it all: a quiet brookside location, unpretentious guest rooms, lots of books spilling forth from the bookcases, creative country dining, and a small pleasant porchside bar. Three of the seven rooms have private bath; these rent for $75 to $85, $10 more on the weekends. The other rooms, with semiprivate bath, rent for $60 to $65, $5 more on weekends. A full breakfast is included, and as for dinner, you'd do well to stay put. When I was last there I had a hearty bowl of soup and lightly curried shrimp with candied ginger. My dinner bill was $28 including homemade Amaretto ice cream, tax, and tip.

Staying in Jackson

About 7 miles above North Conway on Rte. 16 is Jackson, right at the geographical center of the Mount Washington Valley, and the central point for cross-country skiing in the region. Besides being right in the middle of the downhill ski areas, Jackson has its own ski touring organization—but more of that below. It also has a collection of delightful inns open winter and summer. The **Jackson Resort Association,** P.O. Box 304, Jackson, NH 03846, will send you information, or you can contact the **Jackson/Glen Information Center** (tel. 603/383-9356). As the phone is answered only in peak season, it's better to write to the resort association for information.

At the center of Jackson is the **Village House,** Jackson, NH 03846 (tel. 603/383-6666), very near the covered bridge leading into the town from Rte. 16. The 10 rooms here have all been redecorated, but the antique flavor of the house has been preserved. Eight rooms have private bath, and there's cable TV in the living room. Rates include use of the swimming pool, clay tennis court, and also a "deluxe" continental breakfast for each person. The basic charges for two are $80 to $92 double with bath.

The **Christmas Farm Inn,** Jackson, NH 03846 (tel. 603/383-4313), is just outside the center of Jackson village proper on the road up the hill to the Black Mountain Ski Area. Here the proprietors hold that "hospitality makes the difference," but one must admit that the resort-style facilities help: The inn has its own pool and putting green (there are two professional golf courses near Jackson), a game room, sauna, lounge, living room, shuffleboard, and a dining room done in Early American. The Christmas Inn has no fewer than five separate places of accommodation, from the original inn (built in 1786) to a maple-sugaring house converted into two modern rooms, with whirlpool, good for family accommodations. There are 35 rooms in all, priced at $185 to $225 for two, tax, service, breakfast, and dinner for each person included. Children under 12 sharing their parents' room are charged $40.

The **Inn at Thorn Hill,** Thorn Hill Rd., Jackson, NH 03846 (tel. 603/383-4242), a short way outside Jackson prides itself on several special features not often found in a huge old Victorian country house, including baked goods from its own ovens. As with several other Jackson inns, rooms here are in several buildings, including the inn itself, a nearby modernized carriagehouse, and three cottages. All rooms have private bath. In winter, breakfast and dinner come with the room at a price of $151 to $191 double.

Whitney's Inn, Rte. 16B (P.O. Box W), Jackson, NH 03846 (tel. 603/383-6886 or toll free 800/252-5622 in New England), has been serving a steady stream of families, skiers, and other loyal clientele since the early 1930s. The 35 rooms come in all shapes and sizes, from small singles to doubles complete with two double beds. The olive-green farmhouse, with rambling additions, is one of the few places in the area that cater to children. There are nightly activities for them, as well as separate earlier dining. After a full breakfast of pancakes or eggs cooked any way you like them, simply ski out the back door and grab one of the four lifts to the top of Black Mountain. When the snow has melted there's swimming and tennis. Rates are high, with breakfast, dinner, tax, and service charge included, but worth it: $150 for a standard double, $45 per additional person over 12. Note that children 12 and under stay and eat free in the summer.

OLD-FASHIONED RESORTS IN JACKSON   Drive out of Jackson village a mile or so, past a series of cascading waterfalls to find the **Eagle Mountain Resort,** Carter Notch Road, Jackson, NH 03846 (tel. 603/383-9111 or toll free 800/527-5022), one of the remaining premier grand old resorts in New England. Originally built in 1879 and completely rebuilt in 1986, the five-story white clapboard hotel commands a magnificent view of the surrounding mountains. Facilities include a heated outdoor pool, tennis courts, health club, a nine-hole golf course, and well-marked walking trails. The lobby is filled with rich leather sofas and the 94 guest rooms and suites with specially made furniture. Rates are reasonable: Doubles range from $65 to $112, suites from $96 to $112; for an extra $30 per person per day, you can have breakfast and dinner daily. (Sunday brunch is particularly nice.) You'll enjoy staying here.

The **Wentworth Resort Hotel,** Jackson, NH 03846 (tel. 603/383-9700), is another turn-of-the-century hotel, complete with rambling frame main building, lounge, elegant dining rooms, various cottages and overnight rooms, an 18-hole PGA golf course, a pool, and clay tennis courts. It's been redone from top to bottom, left to right, and all is shiny and bright. The hotel is definitely of a graceful, older time, though room prices are a modern $85 to $145 double. Condominium units (rentable by the day, week, or month) have been added in clusters.

A MOTEL IN JACKSON   The village of Jackson is known for its country inns, and staying in one of these excellent places is a real treat. But—as you've seen—it is not an inexpensive proposition, especially when you add (as I have here for you) the 8% state room tax and the 15% "service charge," which are often found in the fine print.

For reasonable prices in this high-priced village, look to the **Covered Bridge Motor Lodge,** P.O. Box V, Jackson, NH 03846 (tel. 603/383-6630 or toll free 800/634-2911), an attractive hostelry right near the red covered bridge. The modern units here are designed not to clash with Jackson's forest mood, and prices are reasonable. For a standard comfortable double room with full bath you pay $60 to $81. Three efficiency apartments rent by the week, but another rents for $91 double per night with a two-night minimum.

Mountain Hikers' Huts

The **Appalachian Mountain Club,** the organization that has done so much to preserve and maintain wilderness trails in New England, operates several lodging facilities in the White Mountain National Forest. At the **AMC's Pinkham Notch Camp,** Gorham, NH 03581 (tel. 603/466-2721), 11 miles north of Jackson on Rte. 16, people of all ages, whether AMC members or not, can find inexpensive bunkroom-type accommodations and simple but hearty meals. A bunk and breakfast costs $31.25 per adult; bed and supper is $36.25; bed, breakfast, and supper is $41.25. Children 12 and under receive a discount for the beds and meals, and as a convenience the kitchen will make up trail lunches for $3.50 per person. Note that you must have reservations, and they must be secured by a nonrefundable *per-person per-night deposit.* If you'd like a room alone, you will have to pay $20 extra for each unused bunk in the room, if others are turned away as a result. All these rules seem quite sensible. Note that the 8% tax is already included in these prices.

Besides the Pinkham Notch Camp, the AMC maintains a laudable system of **mountain huts** along its hiking trails in the mountains. Similar accommodations and meals are provided at similar prices, and with similar reservation arrangements. The huts are attended and trail meals prepared by "hutmen" and "hutwomen," a hearty breed of New England youth who pride themselves on being able to pack on their backs all the supplies needed in the huts—to a weight which would make a normal person stagger—and almost *run* up the mountains with the load several times a week. Guided hikes are featured throughout the summer. Write for details.

WHAT TO DO

North Conway is the Mount Washington Valley center for winter sports, but even during the summer there's plenty to do.

Downhill Skiing

The Mount Washington Valley includes five alpine ski areas: Attitash, Black, Cranmore, King Pine, and Wildcat. Altogether there are 94 downhill trails and 21 lifts, and the slopes range from those for the beginner to those that present a challenge even to some experienced skiers. Many of the inns recommended above under "Where to Stay" offer special ski packages which include lift fees for all five areas.

You can get full free particulars on any or all of these areas by writing to the **Mount Washington Valley Chamber of Commerce,** P.O. Box 385, North Conway, NH 03860 (tel. 603/356-3171 or 356-5701).

Besides the five developed ski areas in the valley, it is possible to ski in the cirque at **Tuckerman's Ravine,** where the shadows protect the snow long past the time when the cover on other slopes has begun to melt. The special excitement at Tuckerman, besides the challenge of the *au naturel* slopes, comes from climbing the mountain you're going to ski down, for there are no lifts. This is old-time skiing, with only a run or two a day, and only those with real stamina and strong legs should and will accept the challenge. But going back to the basics is exhilarating, everyone you meet here is your friend, and the fling down the mountain after the climb is a fitting way to end the season. Park in the Wildcat lot, recuperate in the cafeteria or lounge; follow the line of black dots up the mountain to the top.

Cross-Country Skiing

All of the alpine ski areas in the valley have some cross-country trails, some of which are very easy while others are only for experts. The center of the ski touring activity in the valley is Jackson, where the **Jackson Ski Touring Foundation,** P.O. Box 216, Jackson, NH 03846 (tel. 603/383-9355), maintains and grooms over 150km (90 miles) of cross-country trails. The foundation is a nonprofit village organization dedicated to encouraging ski touring in and around Jackson, and it has a small office in the center of the village. Check here for passes, information, maps. There is a nominal fee for the use of the trails. A season membership is available. Clinics, tours, and rentals can all be found both in Jackson and in North Conway at the several ski shops.

Other Winter Sports

Because of the state parks, national forest, and private reserves in the valley, lots of other winter sports are popular here. Winter camping is possible, using a tent or the AMC huts, a few of which are open all winter. Note that many areas in the White Mountains have extremely severe weather—this writer has hiked into a blizzard, in a temperature of 14°F. and winds gusting to 100 m.p.h. on top of Mount Washington, on the last day of *August*. This does not mean you will hit impossible weather, but it does mean you should check with rangers and AMC personnel, and have good equipment and a knowledge of winter camping before you go in.

Snowmobiling is also pretty big in the valley, and places in North Conway will rent you a machine by the hour or the day. **Ice-skating rinks** are maintained by the towns of North Conway, Conway, and Jackson. Various ponds and lakes are not bad for **ice fishing**—the locals will be glad to give visitors tips on the most-visited ice-fishing spots.

Tennis clubs in Glen and North Conway now have indoor courts suitable for winter play, and guest memberships are available. Contact the Mount Cranmore Racquet Club (tel. 603/356-6301).

The Ski Areas in Summer

The ski areas at Attitash and Wildcat Mountain don't fully close down in summer. Indeed, they have developed full warm-weather recreation programs to keep the visitors coming and the bills paid.

At **Attitash** (tel. 603/374-2368), the lifts keep working to take you up to the top of the Alpine Slide, a long track which you schuss down on a little cart—an exhilarating ride, but safe for all ages. You can buy a 4-hour ticket for $15 or single-ride tickets for $5.50 per adult, $4.50 per child.

At **Wildcat Mountain** the cafeteria stays open for those wanting a snack before boarding the gondolas for the 25-minute round-trip ride up the mountainside (in operation late June to early September from 10am to 6pm daily; from September 12 to October 11, it's open on weekends from 10am to 5pm). The area around Wildcat Mountain and its base camp are kept immaculate because they're within the national forest and subject to its regulation.

Summer Activities

Besides hiking and camping in the state parks and national forests, Mount Washington Valley offers many other activities.

Right in Center Conway is the romantic old station of the **Conway Scenic Railroad** (tel. 356-5251), built in 1874 and restored to its present condition in 1974. For $7 (adults) or $4.50 (kids 4 to 12), you can buy a ticket for the scenic ride through the mountain country; choose your seat from among those in the enclosed cars or the open-air "cinder collectors." A steam locomotive and a 40-year-old and a 45-year-old diesel engine are on hand to provide the power, and if you go a little early you can visit the roundhouse to see where the locomotives are turned around. From early May to early June the trains run on weekends only; from mid-June through late October the trains run every day, rain or shine. Departure times are 11am and 1, 2:30, and 4pm. The trip takes about an hour. The "Sunset Special" at 7pm runs Tuesday, Wednesday, Thursday, and Saturday in July and August. On Friday, Saturday, and Sunday of Thanksgiving weekend and on the second and third weekends in December, the train makes special trips at 11am and 1:30pm.

The **Mount Washington Valley Theater Company,** North Conway, NH 03860 (tel. 603/356-5776), currently performs at the playhouse on Main Street in the Eastern Slope Inn complex. The season, from late June through Labor Day, features four lively musicals. Of course, it's most fun to see the entire series, watching the various members of the company take on different roles every other week, but even if you can't afford to stay in North Conway the entire season, you'll enjoy taking in a play here. The box office opens daily at 11am, and curtain time is 8pm sharp. Tickets run $14 to $8. Group rates are available.

A considerable part of northern New Hampshire is included in the **White Mountain National Forest,** which is not to be confused with a national *park*. The forest does have a number of developed sites, however. Camping areas ($6 per night, cold running water, and pit toilets only) are dotted here and there, as are very pretty picnic areas. A maze of trails, both very easy and not so easy, cover a lot of the forest's vast expanse. Signs by the roadside mark the trail's beginning, but don't wander in just for a 30-minute walk if you're not familiar with the area. Instead, buy detailed maps of the trails and a trail guide from the **Appalachian Mountain Club,** 5 Joy St., Boston, MA 02108 (tel. 617/523-0636), or from the club's Pinkham Notch Camp (tel. 603/466-2721) on Rte. 16 north of Jackson. The *AMC White Mountain Guide* ($15.95) will tell you all about the trail: how difficult it is, how long it is, the vertical rise, the average walking time, reference points along the way, and what to see as you walk.

Another option is to rent a canoe for the day or the week from **Saco Bound/ Northern Waters,** 2 miles east of Center Conway on Rte. 301 (tel. 447-2177). The Saco River has lots of smooth and easy areas, and you can go on a Tuesday or Thursday day trip—lunch, guide, and transportation included—for $22 per person. Overnight trips and canoe pickup service are available, as well as daily canoe rental.

Heritage New Hampshire, on Rte. 16 in Glen (tel. 383-9776), has a variety of lifelike scenes and dioramas with talking figures which outline New Hampshire's history, from the docks of an English port town through the Industrial Revolution at the Amoskeag Mills in Manchester. You can walk at your own pace through the maze of displays, and costumed guides will answer any questions you may have about New Hampshire's history. The price is $6.50 adults, $4.50 for children 4 to 12, and it's open daily from 9am to 6pm in July and August, and then to 5pm in June and from early September until late October.

Right next to Heritage New Hampshire is **Story Land** (tel. 383-4293), a children's amusement park with rides, clowns, animals, and lots of other treats. Once you've paid the $12 admission fee, all the rides are free; children under 4 are admitted without charge. Open daily from mid-June through early September, and then weekends only until mid-October.

The **Grand Manor,** 3 miles north of North Conway on Rte. 16 in Glen (tel. 356-9366), is an antique and classic automobile museum with such treasures as a '57 T-bird, '57 Chevrolet Bel Air, '30 V-16 Cadillac roadster, and '34 Packard Victoria convertible. Cars range in vintage from 1910 to 1969. Hours are 9:30am to 5pm daily in the summer and on the weekends in spring and fall. Admission is $5 for adults, $3 for children.

Two Scenic Drives

A private business, the **Mount Washington Summit Road Company,** Gorham, NH 03581 (tel. 603/466-2222 or 466-3988), operates an alpine toll road to the top of the highest peak in the northeast, 6,288-foot Mt. Washington. Start from Rte. 16 in Pinkham Notch. You can drive your own car (no trucks or campers) to the top of the mountain at $12 for car and driver and $5 for each passenger (kids 5 to 12, $3); vans operated by the company will take you to the top and back down again (1½ hours) for $16 per person (kids, $10) if you'd rather not drive. Hours are 7:30am to 6pm for the road, 8:30am to 4:30pm for the guided van tour. The season is normally from mid-May to mid-October, but remember that Mt. Washington's summit has the most severe weather in the Northeast, and it's altogether possible for the road to be temporarily closed because of snow even in June or September. This, by the way, is only one of three ways to reach the Mt. Washington summit, the others being on foot following the Appalachian Mountain Club trails, or by cog railway, described a bit further on in this book.

Route 112 between Conway and Lincoln is known as the **Kancamagus Highway.** Its 33-mile length exhibits some of the finest scenery in the White Mountains, including the view from the 2,860-foot Kancamagus Pass. Almost the entire length of the road is within the boundaries of the national forest, and is therefore protected from any development more civilized than a campground (there are six along the road) or a picnic area. The drive is a must: This is White Mountains beauty in its purest form.

---

7. Bretton Woods and Crawford Notch

North and east on U.S. 302 from Glen will take you through Crawford Notch to the **Crawford Notch State Park.** The park is a fine place for hiking and fishing, and you can see two impressive waterfalls—the Flume and the Silver Cascades—from the highway. Facilities include a 24-site campground, a picnic area, an information booth, and a shop featuring the products of New Hampshire artisans. The ruins of the **Willey House** hold a mystery and a story from the 1820s, when the road was being cut and the Willey family set up house in Crawford Notch to provide for the teams that would pass through the valley. In August 1826 one of the worst storms ever to hit the White Mountains wreaked havoc in the valley, with floods, landslides, wind, and rain which left the Willey House unharmed, but resulted in the death of every member of the household.

WHERE TO STAY

At the **Mount Washington Hotel & Resort,** U.S. 302, Bretton Woods, NH 03575, is a downhill and cross-country ski area, several condominium developments, and three lodging establishments, the new and modern **Lodge at Bretton Woods,** the innlike **Bretton Arms,** and the venerable rambling palace known as the **Mount Washington Hotel** (tel. 603/278-1000 or toll free 800/258-0330). The mammoth hotel was the site of the famous Bretton Woods conference of 1944 which established the world monetary system for the postwar period. Although great old hotels of this sort, with their private golf courses, riding stables, clay tennis courts, indoor and outdoor pools, live nightly entertainment, playhouses, and the like, are almost as rare as dinosaurs, it is heartening to see that this one is still thriving, its gracious service and accommodations open to both the tourist and the conventioneer. The lobby is immense, with a baronial fireplace and lots of color and activity; nearby is a semicircular conservatory with a dome and many small stained-glass windows. The views of the mountains and the grounds are very fine. There are hundreds of rooms, nearly all with private bath, and they rent with two meals included (and tax and service) for about $182 to $342 double per day. If you stay six nights, the seventh is free. There are small fees for use of the golf course, horses from the stable, bicycles, and nursery and babysitting services. If you prefer a smaller place, Bretton Arms, a recently restored house on the property, has 34 rooms renting for $107 to $134 double, with no meals included. Guests are granted access to the facilities at the Mount Washington Hotel.

The Lodge at Bretton Woods out on the highway (U.S. 302) is associated with the hotel, and although the hotel operates only from late May to mid-October, the lodge stays open both winter and summer. Here the prices are for lodging only, but all privileges open to guests at the hotel are extended to guests at the lodge: A double usually with two double beds and with bath is $78 to $118, children are free in the same room with their parents.

At Crawford Notch, one of the most spectacular sites on the East Coast, stands the **Notchland Inn,** Harts Location S.R., Bartlett, NH 03812 (tel. 603/374-6131). Also quite magnificent in its own right, the granite mansion set on 400 acres has 11 rooms with private bath, working fireplaces, and antiques. Rates are set up two ways here: With two meals a day, double rooms cost $136 to $168; with breakfast only, rooms are $98 to $108 double. Take the dinner option—the multicourse repast is served by candlelight. The owners, by the way, keep rare and endangered species in their sanctuary; don't be surprised to see a llama or exotic sheep grazing in the front corral.

WHAT TO DO

Certainly the quaintest way to get to the top of Mount Washington is by the **Mount Washington Cog Railway** (tel. 603/846-5404 or toll free 800/922-8825). It's a 3½-mile track along a steep trestle up the mountainside. The locomotive (powered by steam) drives a cog wheel on its undercarriage which engages with pins between the rails to pull the locomotive and train up the slope. In operation since 1866, the 3-hour round-trip excursion is a lot of fun besides being very scenic indeed. At the portion of the run known as Jacob's Ladder, the grade is a surprising 37%, but the little engine pulls along trustworthily despite the steepness. At the top the average summer temperature is 40°F., and there may be a stiff wind. Stroll to the new visitors center for a snack, drink, or souvenir, and then tour the mountaintop: See the displays highlighting the worst of Mt. Washington's weather. If you pick a clear day to ascend to the 6,288-foot summit, it will seem as though you can see all the way to Europe!

The base station, where you board the train, is 6 miles off U.S. 302 east of Twin Mountain, NH. The season is Memorial Day weekend through Columbus Day (Canadian Thanksgiving), with weekends-only runs until June 10, then daily starting at 8:30am, and continuing on as close to an hourly schedule as possible, with the last train leaving at 4:30pm. Have reservations, or try to take an early train—perhaps the 8:30am—to avoid having to wait in line. From Labor Day through mid-October there are trains daily if weather permits at 11:30am and 2:30pm, and as needed. Fares (round trip) are $32 per adult, kids under 8 free if sitting on a parent's lap, kids 8 and over $16. Remember to take a sweater or jacket, or both, for the cool weather at the top, no matter how warm it is at the bottom.

---

8. Waterville Valley

In 1829 a small settlement in a remote New Hampshire valley was incorporated as a town. A few farms, perhaps a small store, and a tiny library—even here in the remoteness of the White Mountains, the symbol of New England's cultural life —that was all there was to Waterville Valley. Today the tiny settlement is still there, deep within the White Mountains National Forest, but a developer with great taste and tact now owns the valley, and has dictated what shape the new resort community in this beautiful spot is to take. The results so far are very encouraging, almost a marvel: hotels and condominium developments under different ownership, all of striking and interesting design, furnished in good taste and staffed with competent, concerned personnel. Two ski areas are handy, a golf course and lots of tennis courts await, and hiking, bicycling, fishing, and snowshoeing are right at a visitor's doorstep. This is a very fine resort indeed.

All the places in Waterville Valley have the same postal address—Waterville Valley, NH 03215—and the **Lodging Bureau,** provides free reservations service; call toll free 800/468-2553 and 603/236-8371 locally. Or write to Waterville Valley Lodging Bureau, Waterville Valley, NH 03215, for information.

WHERE TO STAY

The setting of Waterville Valley, in the shadow of Mt. Tecumseh, is very beautiful, and the hotels have been designed to fit in well with the town and the natural beauty. Of the six hotels, the majority are of moderate price, one is expensive, and another is very low-priced.

Queen of the valley's hostelries is the **Snowy Owl Inn,** on Village Road (P.O. Box 407; tel. 603/236-8383), a dramatic structure of weathered wood and shining windows which reflect the trees and mountains surrounding it. The interior, like the exterior, is all of natural wood, with a large stone fireplace for accent in the three-story-high lobby. The rooms are modern, luxurious, and decorated with taste that might have come right out of a design magazine. All have two double beds, and some have refrigerator and whirlpool. Many rooms have fine views of the valley and mountains; others look upon Snow's Brook, the stream which runs by the hotel. Even if you don't have a mountain view, you can get one by climbing the spiral staircase at the top of the lobby to the little observation tower. The Snowy Owl has its own Jacuzzi, saunas, and heated indoor and outdoor pool, of course. Rooms cost $68 to $104 single or double in summer, including the 8% "association service charge" (children under 12 free in their parents' room). These are for summer, in winter the rates are about 15% higher.

King of the valley's hostelries is the new **Golden Eagle Lodge** (tel. 603/236-4551 or toll free 800/468-2553). Fashioned in the style of 19th-century grand New England resorts, the Golden Eagle rises proudly to the occasion. It was designed by Graham Gund Architects, one of the most distinguished firms in the United States. The crescent-shaped six-story building with green shutters and turrets is a mass of oversized windows, more than half of which look on to Corcoran Pond, the namesake of the man who has so carefully developed much of this valley. The 139 condominium suites vary in size from 650 to 1,050 square feet, sleeping two to eight people, and are fully furnished with understated accoutrements. In the high summer season rates range from $79 to $98 double; in winter from $101 to $183 double. An extra person pays $25 per day; children 12 and under stay free in their parents' suite. Rates include use of the pool, sports center, and many other facilities in the valley.

The attractive design of the **Valley Inn** (tel. 603/236-8336 or toll free 800/343-0969) adds to the scenery in the valley, and also provides some unexpected bonuses to guests. Many rooms overlook the valley and mountains; others, the forest and settlement. All 45 of the recently renovated guest rooms have air conditioning, king-size bed, wet bar and refrigerator, whirlpool bath, pull-out sofa bed, cable TV, and telephone. The inn's heated indoor/outdoor swimming pool is open all year: part is enclosed by the building, but a huge window comes down just to water level, and you can swim underneath it to the outdoor portion of the pool, winter or summer. The Valley Inn has other athletic goodies: two platform (or paddle) tennis courts, an exercise room, saunas, Jacuzzi, and game room. The inn's dining room has a treetop-level view, and the lounge has live entertainment on weekends and holidays. Rates in summer are $134 to $258 per night double; in foliage season they range from $150 to $292 double; these prices include 13% state and local taxes. Children 12 and under stay free in their parents' room

Long-Term Stays

Several of the condominium developments in the valley have long-term (by the month or the season) rental rates for those who want an apartment rather than a hotel room. Accommodations range from one-bedroom apartments for one or two people to three-bedroom apartments that can take eight to ten people. Each apartment is completely furnished, including kitchen utensils and dinner service, all linens, and cable color TV. The apartments also rent by the day (two-day minimum) for $270 to $540 for a weekend, or $345 to $655 for a five-night ski week. In summer you'll pay $322 to $765 per week. There are various package and weekly plans, both for normal and holiday periods, and low-season specials are available. For more information, contact **Windsor Hill Condominiums,** Jennings Peak Road, Waterville Valley, NH 03215 (tel. 603/236-8321 or toll free 800/343-1286 in New York, New Jersey, and New England except New Hampshire).

WHAT TO DO IN SUMMER

It seems as if they've thought of everything here. First and foremost, the valley is deep within the national forest, so hiking and fishing are easy to find. For tennis, there are 18 clay courts and lessons by a professional staff. The golf course in the valley is nine holes, and not too far away at White Mountains Country Club is an 18-hole course. Guests at the Valley Inn can use its paddle tennis courts for free; the general public can use them, day and night, for a fee. Bikes can be rented from the Golf and Tennis Club. And then, of course, there's shopping in the town square or a ride to the top of Mt. Tecumseh on the "High Country Express," the fastest gondola in the east.

WHAT TO DO IN WINTER

Although snowshoeing, hiking, skating, ana general taking of country-mountain air are all possible and enjoyable in Waterville Valley, most people come to ski the trails and slopes of Mt. Tecumseh and Snow's Mountain. **Mt. Tecumseh** is the larger and more elaborate of the two, with two triple-chair lifts, five double-chair lifts, a T-bar, a J-bar, and a platter-pull lift. The vertical drop is over 2,000 feet, and there are 35 trails and slopes. Rentals and lessons are easily available, as is a quick meal at the base cafeteria. A schuss bus takes guests from Waterville Valley hotels to Tecumseh and back. The other area, **Snow's Mountain,** is right in the valley near the hotels of the village, and has three intermediate and beginners' slopes. It's for first-timers and learners, with one double-chair lift and a vertical drop of less than 600 feet. To keep the crowds down, Mt. Tecumseh and Snow's Mountain operate on a limited-ticket basis (no more than a 15-minute wait for the lift on average). For information about snow at both areas, call 603/236-4144.

Ski packages for two, three, five, or seven nights are offered, and all facilities in the valley participate. Depending on what you want, you can get a package which includes lodging, meals, lifts, lessons, even rental equipment. Prices depend on which hotel you choose, and what options you need to do the sort of skiing you're after. Options are also offered for ski touring (trail fees, lessons, equipment, and lodging) in the packages

9. The Franconia Notch Area

Interstate 93 comes up from Manchester and Concord to pass through the White Mountains National Forest. The towns of North Woodstock and Lincoln form the center of the developed area within the forest, and it's here that most people come to look for a room, a meal, or any of the other services of civilization. At this point the Kancamagus Highway heads east through the most scenic 33-mile drive in the mountains; north of Lincoln and North Woodstock are several natural curiosities, including the famous **Old Man of the Mountains** at the narrow pass called Franconia Notch.

The area centered on North Woodstock and Lincoln is very rich in possibilities for outdoor activities, especially hiking, camping, picnicking, and skiing at Cannon Mountain and Mittersill in Franconia Notch itself, and at Loon Mountain near Lincoln on the Kancamagus Highway.

The local **visitors center** is at the intersection of I-93 and the Kancamagus Highway (tel. 603/745-8720). It is run both by the Lincoln–North Woodstock Chamber of Commerce personnel and also by national forest rangers; hours of operation year round are 8:30am to 6pm daily.

WHERE TO STAY

You can make your base at any of several places in the area. At the southern end of Franconia Notch State Park lies North Woodstock, at the junction of U.S. 3 and

Rte. 112, a small and fairly attractive commercial center with a few inns. Just across the Pemigewasset River where I-93 Exit 32 meets the Kancamagus Highway is the town of Lincoln, basically a commercial strip with some motels and residences.

At the northern end of the state park, near I-93 Exit 38, are the towns of **Franconia** and **Sugar Hill,** with a good number of nice inns. Finally, at I-93 Exit 42, only a few miles from the Vermont state line, is the town of **Littleton,** the largest settlement in these parts. It has two nice old inns for you to consider.

Inns in North Woodstock

The **Woodstock Inn,** Main Street (U.S. 3; P.O. Box 118), North Woodstock, NH 03262 (tel. 603/745-3951), is a century-old Victorian house that's been very nicely redone, and now has six guest rooms which share three baths. Decor is Victorian of course, except for the color TV sets and air conditioners in some rooms. Prices range from $83 to $89 double, full breakfast included. Downstairs in the inn is a full restaurant and lounge (see below). Midweek rates are slightly lower.

The inn also operates a bed-and-breakfast house called the **Riverside,** right by the Pemigewasset River, where each of the eight rooms has its own bath, color TV, and air conditioner, and prices go from $88 to $94 double. You're right in the center of town at the Woodstock, though the Cascade swimming area in the river is within walking distance.

Budget-minded readers will want to consider staying at the **Mt. Adams Inn,** on U.S. 3 south of the center of North Woodstock, NH 03262 (tel. 603/745-2711). A room with full country breakfast can be had for as little as $56 double (share a bath), and the restaurant specializes in home-cooked food. The inn is open all year round. There's also a homey public lounge with a fireplace and color TV.

Motels in Lincoln

Route 3 north of North Woodstock is absolutely packed with motels of every shape, size, and price range, and you're sure to find a room here. But not all of these places are wonderful, and not all of the best places are located in this strip. Here's the pick of the crop, starting with a motel right near Franconia Notch itself.

North of North Woodstock on U.S. 3 is **Woodward's Motor Inn,** Lincoln, NH 03251 (tel. 603/745-8141), which describes itself as "a complete family resort open all the year." It is one of the better motels on this strip of motels and restaurants; its 80 rooms are in buildings set back from the roadway behind a scattering of tall pine trees and a small pond. The pool is heated and is a comfortable 30 by 65 feet; guests get to play tennis on the Woodward's own court; and the Open Hearth Steak House is open to motel guests and the public alike. All rooms are air-conditioned and have color TV and telephone; many have two double beds—the traveling family's boon—as well. Rates for high summer and foliage season are $76 to $90 double in the motel rooms, all of which have private bath. Ski-season rates are slightly lower. The restaurant, by the way, is open for breakfast and dinner, 7:30 to 10:30am and 5 to 9pm, to 8:30pm off-season; the Open Hearth is open only for dinner.

The **Kancamagus Motor Lodge,** Lincoln, NH 03251 (tel. 603/745-3365 or toll free 800/346-4205 outside New Hampshire), is on the Kancamagus Highway a mile west of the Loon Mountain ski area (take Exit 32 from I-93, then drive east on Rte. 112). This modern motel with heated outdoor pool has new rooms in a modern style furnished with private steambath, wall-to-wall carpeting, phone, and color TV. Its attraction is in its location, very close to Loon Mountain and not far at all from the attractions of Franconia Notch. Rates in summer are $62 to $76 for two in a room, fully air-conditioned. In winter, a double room is $43 to $54 Sunday through Thursday nights. The Kancamagus has a dining room and cocktail lounge.

Right in town on Rte. 112, the **Lincoln Motel,** at 5 Church St., Lincoln, NH 03251 (tel. 603/745-2780), is an unprepossessing two-story structure with rooms that constitute one of the best bargains in the area, especially for skiers. Rooms have private bath, air conditioning, and cable TV, and a small kitchenette (fully equipped) is open to guests. Besides the nine rooms in the motel proper, a nearby house has been converted to take transient guests, thereby increasing the chance that a visitor on a budget may find a room here. Rates are $58 to $68 double (the higher price for a room with kitchenette). Good, if basic, rooms, low prices, and Loon Mountain less than 2 miles away. You'll see the Lincoln Motel from the Kancamagus Highway, set back from the road a half block on the left-hand side as you go from North Woodstock east toward Loon Mountain.

Inns in Franconia and Sugar Hill

In the small town of Franconia, a reference point is the confluence of Rtes. 18 and 116. After coming from the south and meeting, the two routes head north to Littleton.

Just over 2 miles south of Franconia along Rte. 116 (Easton Road) is the **Franconia Inn,** Easton Road, Franconia, NH 03580 (tel. 603/823-5542), a nice old white clapboard place built in 1868. It still provides many of the services that once brought wealthy Bostonians here: riding horses, outdoor swimming pool, four clay tennis courts, a family-size hot tub, bicycle tours, and hiking trails. Several golf courses are nearby. Right across the road from the inn is Foxfire Aviation, Inc. (tel. 823-8881), which will take you up for sailplane (glider) rides. Besides all these things to do, there is the tranquillity and beauty of the verdant Easton Valley, with fine views of Cannon Mountain, Mt. Lafayette, and the Franconia and Kinsman mountain ranges.

There are 35 guest rooms at the inn, well maintained and somewhat old-fashioned, but with clean baths. Prices depend on view and room size, and range from $72 to $105 single, $79 to $126 double, with two-room family suites going for $121. An adult can have breakfast and dinner daily for $34; meal plans for children depend on their ages. Add taxes and tips. When you call, ask for a corner room, and also about package plans which may save you some money.

For rainy days and evenings there are movies, a game room with coin-operated games for the kids, a billiards room, an oak-paneled library with fireplace, and a screened porch set with wicker furniture. Downstairs, the Rathskeller Lounge has quiet entertainment many nights. The nice candlelit dining room adds considerably to the feeling that you've settled yourself into a huge old summer estate owned by one of your rich uncles in the heart of Robert Frost country. The "uncles" in this case are innkeepers Richard and Alec Morris. It's comfy here. Ski season, by the way, is one of the inn's best times, with trails radiating from the inn throughout the valley.

The Franconia Inn is open most of the year, but closed for most of April and May.

Lovett's Inn, by Lafayette Brook, Franconia, NH 03580 (tel. 603/823-7761 or toll free 800/346-3802 outside New Hampshire) is a rambling farmhouse (ca. 1784) with 30 modern cottages set amid pine trees or around the backyard pool. The poolside cottages are larger, but all have a sleeping/living area and TV, while some have a fireplace and air conditioning. The seven rooms in the old inn are simple and authentic, nothing fancy. In the summer rates are $125 to $136 for a room with private bath in the house or a cottage in the pines; poolside cottages are $5 more. For one of the few shared-bath rooms in the inn, the rate is $88 to $98 double. When you consider that these rates include breakfast and dinner, it becomes a pretty good deal. There's a TV room with a library of movies for the VCR; in winter cross-country skis are for rent. There is plenty of room and activities for kids here.

The **Horse & Hound Inn,** Wells Road, Franconia, NH 03580 (tel. 603/823-5501), is a real true-to-life country inn according to the old style. It is not plush and fancy, with priceless antiques everywhere, but rather simple, well kept, and attractive. It is well off the main roads, and blissfully, perfectly quiet except for the crackle of a fire in the fireplace on a cool day, or the murmur of conversation in the lounge.

Rooms with private bath cost $54 to $97 double, and come with a double, a queen-size, or two doubles. Rooms sharing baths cost $74. Continental breakfast is included in these prices. The inn's dining room serves good, hearty, honest food such as sirloin steaks and surf and turf; a full dinner might cost $25 to $30 per person, drinks, tax, and tip included. To find the inn, head south out of Franconia on Rte. 18. About 2½ miles south of town, watch for Wells Road, on the right; the inn has a sign here. Head down Wells Road for less than half a mile to reach the inn.

The village of Sugar Hill is a few miles west of Franconia along Rte. 117. Leaving Franconia, turn left off Rte. 18 onto Rte. 117, and less than a mile's drive will bring you to the **Sugar Hill Inn,** Sugar Hill, Franconia, NH 03580 (tel. 603/823-5621), perched up on a hill and surrounded by grassy lawns. The original farmhouse was built in 1789, but I doubt that it had such a commodious and welcoming front porch. In any case, the house became an inn in 1929, still with its original fireplaces (some now fitted with Franklin stoves), old board floors, and wood beams. Now the rooms have very pretty country furnishings, quilts, old paintings, rocking chairs, and hand-stenciled designs on the walls. Each of the 10 rooms has a private bath, and twin beds, a double bed, a queen-size, or a king-size bed. Beside the inn are six small guest cottages with similar decor, private bath, carpeting, and TV set; they're open mid-May through October only. In season, a double room with full breakfast costs $105 to $124, all in. At peak times guests may be required to take dinner here, which would add about $25 to $30 per person to the tab. At other times dinner is served by reservation, and there's usually a choice of meat, fish, and chicken, along with various soups, appetizers, and desserts. Small, quiet, friendly, congenial, authentic—that's the Sugar Hill Inn. Jim and Barbara Quinn are your hosts.

Littleton Inns

White clapboard churches loft their graceful steeples above the solid, four-square brick façades of Main Street's commercial district: This is Littleton, N.H., a fine New England town. Not a quaint village, not an industrial town, but something in between, Littleton may be to New Hampshire what Lake Wobegon is to Minnesota.

The local chamber of commerce and historical society have put together a pamphlet which will take you on a guided tour of the town's landmarks, including the post office and courthouse, Masonic Temple, public library, and Tilton's Opera building.

The **Beal House Inn,** 247 W. Main St., Littleton, NH 03561 (tel. 603/444-2661), is Littleton's prime place to stay, right at the confluence of Rtes. 18 and 302, on West Main Street. Once a farmhouse and barn (1833), the house is now the inn and the barn an antiques shop, both run by the Carver family. The entire place is furnished in antiques and local crafts, and is charming and comfortable. Guest rooms range in price from $44 to $98 double, breakfast and afternoon refreshments included, and the price you pay depends on the size of the room and of its bed; larger rooms with larger beds (queen- or king-size) cost the most. A few rooms share baths, but most have private facilities. The continental breakfast is of freshly made delights such as homemade breads and popovers; if you want a full country breakfast of bacon and eggs, it's available at an extra charge. Behind the inn are lovely lawns and woods, with a deck for sitting and relaxing. Children over 8 are welcome here. By the way, you should know that the inn is actually furnished from the antiques shop, and thus anything you fancy can be purchased; the price tag should be on the object.

Though it's actually in Vermont, the **Rabbit Hill Inn,** Lower Waterford, VT 05848 (tel. 802/748-5168), is connected to Littleton, N.H., by cultural and commercial ties. Established in 1795, the inn was bought by John and Maureen Magee in April 1987, and they now rent its 18 rooms, each with private bath and most with views of the mountains, for $158 to $219 double, full breakfast, dinner, tax, and service charges included. By the way, those mountain views are significant, as the inn is set into the side of a hill with the magnificent panorama of the mountains and the

Connecticut River Valley spread out before it. And the plan to have breakfast and dinner here makes sense, as Lower Waterford is a tiny hamlet with few other dining opportunities.

This inn is antique and elegant in its furnishings, but homey in its welcome. Beautiful antique furniture is in the dining room, pub, book nook, and lounge, as well as in the guest rooms. Across the road from the inn is the village church, built in 1859, and next to that the small library. Besides these public-service buildings, the village of Lower Waterford has fewer than a dozen houses. No doubt, the Rabbit Hill Inn sometimes accounts for fully half of the village's active population! It's idyllic and special here—"like Brigadoon," as John Magee says—and you'll love it.

WHERE TO EAT

Dining possibilities are not particularly rich in this neck of the woods, and you'd do well in most cases to dine at your inn if possible. If your inn or motel doesn't serve main meals, here are the places to look for them.

Perhaps the best full menu hereabouts is at the **Woodstock Inn,** on Main Street in North Woodstock (tel. 745-3951). For a light lunch or a drink before or after dinner there's the Woodstock Station, Lincoln's original railroad station moved to a site adjoining the inn. The favored place to sit for dinner in the inn is on the enclosed porch next to one of the large windows looking out onto Main Street, but there are other attractive Victorian dining rooms as well. Prices are moderate, because the price of your main course includes a choice of appetizer or soup, garden salad, fresh bread, rice or potato, and homemade fresh-fruit sorbet. Main courses range from sole stuffed with crabmeat and tortellini scallops Alfredo (tortellini with mushrooms and gruyère, sautéed with fresh scallops, sauce Alfredo), through roast duckling and chicken curry with coconut and pine nuts, to tournedos au poivre, tournedos Rossini, and steak Diane. You can dine sumptuously here for a mere $20, but your dinner bill will more likely be $26 to $35 per person when drinks, dessert, tax, and tip are included. As the Woodstock Inn provides some of the best dining in the area, it's a good idea to call for reservations.

In Littleton there's a real old diner, like an enlarged railroad dining car, with black-and-white floor tiles, revolving counter stools, and booths filled early and often by local people. It's the **Littleton Diner,** 170 Main St. (tel. 444-6994), a 1928 Worcester-style diner open Monday through Saturday from 6am to 8pm, on Sunday from 7am to 2pm. As in any truly good old diner, breakfast is served all day, and the standard, called "Earl's Favorite," consists of two eggs, home fries, sausage, juice, and toast, plus coffee and tip, for under $5. If you come for lunch or supper, have a slice of homemade pie for dessert. There will probably be a slightly used copy of the Manchester *Union Leader* around for your edification and amusement. A great place!

WHAT TO SEE AND DO

Franconia Notch State Park is surrounded by the **White Mountains National Forest.** The natural wonders of the park are impressive indeed, including the Notch (pass, or gap) itself, the Flume, the Basin, several lakes, and the rock outcrop in the shape of a man's profile which has all but become the state symbol of New Hampshire, the famous Old Man of the Mountains. The state park offers a wealth of outdoor activities: Lafayette Campground, the Appalachian Mountain Club's system of trails and huts, a 9-mile paved bike path, trout fishing, swimming in the mountain lakes, a number of beautiful picnic sites, and two ski areas, one of them with an aerial tramway which operates winter and summer.

The Old Man

The Old Man of the Mountains, also called the Great Stone Face, is one of New Hampshire's most famous features. After thousands of years in the making, it was "discovered" by white settlers at the beginning of the 19th century. The profile is formed by several ledges of granite, and in a cubist sort of way the representation is quite striking. But don't expect a mammoth image: The face is only about 40 feet high, and it's set on a cliff 1,000 feet above the valley floor. Its grandeur comes not from its size, but rather from its fidelity and its impressive perch high in the sky, gazing out over the mountains. In recent years the state has spent a good deal of money preserving the face from the ravages of nature, for even granite formations crumble given enough wind, rain, and ice. From the highway parking lot, a path leads down to the shores of Profile Lake, and descriptive plaques tell you all about the Old Man.

South of the Old Man along U.S. 3 and to the east lies the undulant crest of Mt. Liberty, which to some people resembles George Washington lying in state. Take a look, and feel free to concur or disagree!

The Basin and the Flume

South of the Old Man along U.S. 3, signs will point to a side road and the Basin, a huge glacial pothole in the native granite, 20 feet in diameter. The hole is at the foot of a waterfall, and was presumably made by the action of small rocks and stones whirled around by the force of the water. It's a cool spot, good for contemplation.

Four miles north of North Woodstock, but still south of the Basin, is the Flume, a natural gorge or cleft in the granite. A boardwalk has been erected along the 800-foot length of the Flume, and for $5 ($2.50 for children) you can walk through its cool depths, the granite walls rising to 60 or 70 feet above you, mosses and plants growing precariously in niches here and there. Signs explain how nature formed the Flume, and point out interesting sights along the way. Near the Flume is a covered bridge thought to be one of the oldest in the state, perhaps erected as early as the 1820s. There is a seasonal information office (tel. 745-8391) here, open when the Flume is, from mid-April to mid-October.

Cannon Mountain Aerial Tramway

An impressive view of Franconia Notch and the mountains is yours if you take the Cannon Mountain Aerial Tramway (tel. 603/823-5563) to the top of the line. The tramway operates in the summer from the end of May to mid-October, 9am to 4:30pm, at a cost of $7 for adults, $3 for children 6 to 12, round trip. The tramway station is just off I-93, Exit 2, and U.S. 3 north of the Old Man, and has its own parking lot. In the weathered-shingle building at the base and the summit station are cafeterias, should you be in need of a light meal, and the New England Ski Museum.

Robert Frost's Farm

Only a mile or two from the town of Franconia is the Frost Place, Bickford Hill Road (tel. 823-8038), the farm that the great poet bought in the early part of this century. He lived here with his wife and children during some of the most productive and inspired years of his life, and wrote many of his best and most famous poems to describe life on this farm and the scenery surrounding it. Among these are "The Road Not Taken" and "Stopping by Woods on a Snowy Evening."

Admission to the site costs $3 for adults, half price for children 6 through 15, $2 for seniors. It's open on Saturday and Sunday from 1 to 5pm late May through June and early September through mid-October; in July and August, every day except Tuesday from 1 to 5pm.

The price of admission includes a 20-minute slide show in the barn behind the house. The show explains much about Frost's early life and work, and about the countryside here. The farmhouse has been kept as faithful to the period as possible, and there are numerous interesting exhibits of Frost memorabilia, though much of the furniture is from other places. It is spare and simple, as was the rural lifestyle at the time. Behind the house in the forest is a half-mile-long poetry-nature trail.

Frost's poems are mounted on plaques in sites appropriate to the things they describe. In several places the plaques have been erected at the exact spots where Frost composed the poems. The various trees, shrubs, and flowers along the path are marked, though only some will be in bloom when you visit.

To get to the Frost Place, leave Franconia on Rte. 116 South, and after exactly a mile look for a sign on the right indicating Bickford Hill Road. Then turn left onto Ridge Road, a dirt road, and the Frost Place will be up a way on your right. You come to the parking lot before the house; obey the sign and park in the lot, and walk up the road to the house.

The Lost River

As you travel through New Hampshire, you'll see many bumper stickers proclaiming "I found the Lost River." You can find it too, 6 miles west of North Woodstock on Rte. 112 in Kinsman Notch. Explore the narrow gorge and caverns with the help of walkways, ladders, and bridges. Like most of the attractions in this neck of the woods, it's open mid-May to mid-October. There's a small entrance fee.

Clark's Trading Post

Clark's on Rte. 3 just north of Lincoln has been a traditional stop for families traveling in the White Mountains since 1928. In addition to an old-fashioned photo parlor, water-bumper boats, magic house, narrow-gauge steam locomotive, and gift shop selling moccasins, a family of native black bears performs daily. It's a bit on the campy side, but it's also part of many people's childhood.

Skiing

There are three notable ski resorts in the Franconia Notch area: Cannon Mountain and Mittersill near the Notch itself, and Loon Mountain in Lincoln at the western end of the Kancamagus Highway.

CANNON MOUNTAIN (tel. 603/823-5563) Besides the 70-passenger aerial tramway, Cannon has one triple-chair and two double-chair lifts, one quad-chair, and a pony lift, all with an hourly capacity of close to 7,000 skiers. There are 29 trails, about a quarter of them novice, another quarter expert, and the remaining half intermediate. The vertical drop is 2,145 feet, and besides having snowmaking equipment for the snowless days, the slopes are positioned so that they naturally receive and retain more than the average amount of white stuff. Cannon Mountain is operated by the state, as it is in a state park. Besides the three cafeterias and the base station and lounges nearby, there are a ski school, a nursery, and a ski shop where you can rent equipment.

MITTERSILL (tel. 603/823-5511) This is the junior cousin to Cannon Mountain, with a vertical drop of 1,600 feet, and one double chair and one T-bar for lifts. It's open daily, north of Cannon Mountain, off U.S. 3 on Rte. 18.

LOON MOUNTAIN (tel. 603/745-8146; for snow information, 603/745-8100): A drive 2 miles east of Lincoln along the Kancamagus Highway brings you to Loon Mountain, a modern ski area with a gondola (four-passenger cars), two triple-chair lifts, and five double-chair lifts to take 9,600 skiers an hour up the mountain. The vertical drop is 2,100 feet, and the longest run is 3 miles. Loon has a limited-lift-lines policy (make reservations), and top-to-bottom snowmaking capacity. The Mountain Club on Loon has 240 rooms and a restaurant; other services at the base lodge include a cafeteria, lounge, nursery, ski shop, and rental shop. Lift fees are $32 on weekends, and slightly less on weekdays.

In summer and fall, Loon Mountain's gondolas operate from 9:30am to 5pm daily to take visitors on the 7,100-foot trip (1,850-foot rise) to the summit, at $7.50 per adult, $3 per child, free for kids 6 and under. There are cafeterias at both the base and summit stations.

Several ski areas offer package arrangements through the **Ski 93 Association,** named because the areas involved are all accessible by using Interstate 93. Bretton Woods, Cannon Mountain, Loon Mountain, Tenney Mountain, and Waterville Valley are among the members, and you can get three-day or five-day cut-price lift tickets. Midweek passes good at all five areas are a real bargain. The association will be glad to help with reservations at area hotels, lodges, and inns. Write or call P.O. Box 176, North Woodstock, NH 03262 (tel. 603/745-8101).

---

10. Lake Sunapee

Lake Sunapee is a pleasant regional vacation spot in southwestern New Hampshire, not all that far from the town of Hanover, which is home to Dartmouth College. Besides summer sports such as swimming, boating, and canoeing, the area around Lake Sunapee has its own small ski area in Mount Sunapee State Park. On a trip to Vermont or north to Hanover for a visit to Dartmouth, the shores of Lake Sunapee are a fine place to stop for a night, or even a week.

Of the towns around the lake, Sunapee (sometimes called Sunapee Harbor) on the western shore is the nicest, with a good collection of inns, motels, and resorts. Although in its early days Sunapee held a tannery, gristmill, and several shops for woodworking industries, for many years now it has made its living from summer visitors; and in recent years skiers have brought business to the town in winter as well.

The town of Mount Sunapee, on the southwestern shore, is not really a town at all, regardless of what it may say on your road map. The intersection of Rtes. 103 and 103B, with a motel and the state park and state beach entrance, *is* the "town." Don't plan to get gas there!

INFORMATION

Contact the **Lake Sunapee Lodging Bureau,** P.O. Box 400, Sunapee, NH 03782 (tel. 603/763-2495 or toll free 800/258-3530).

WHERE TO STAY AND EAT

Though the Lake Sunapee region is perfect for vacationers, there is some spirit among the local people to limit touristic growth. Thus many of the inns here are of long standing, and are more like self-contained miniresorts. There are a few motels for those on a vagabond tour.

Dexter's Inn and Tennis Club, Stagecoach Road (P.O. Box F), Sunapee, NH 03782 (tel. 603/763-5571 or toll free 800/232-5571), is hidden away on a back road, but has a fine view of Lake Sunapee and its surrounding mountains. Built in 1801, the yellow clapboard house was renovated in the 1930s and converted to an inn in 1948. It's been owned and run by the Simpson family for well over a decade, and has that family feel about it that makes even first-time visitors comfortable. Some of the 18 rooms have antique pieces, including the beds; other rooms have more modern furnishings. All have private baths. Breakfast and dinner each day come with your room, which may be priced at $149 to $199 double, tax and service included; breakfast will be delivered to your room if you like, and dinner is taken in the dining room.

Amusements include a well-equipped library and piano in the living room, a pretty outdoor swimming pool, and three professional-grade tennis courts (complete with pro and pro shop). Other games include shuffleboard, croquet, and horseshoes. Dexter's is open May through October. Off-season package plans offer good savings on a vacation here.

Right near the entrance to Mount Sunapee State Park is the very popular **Mount Sunapee Motel,** Rte. 103, Mount Sunapee, NH 03772 (tel. 603/763-5592). The motel is modern: tile bathrooms, with tub-shower combinations, TV, and at least two beds in each room. Half of the motel consists of 11 two-room units, each with a kitchenette; the outdoor swimming pool is shared by all. Summer rates are $56 to $63 double in a motel room, $67 to $79 double in a two-room unit. Add 5% if you pay with a credit card.

Out of sight from Sunapee Harbor but only a few hundred feet from it is **Haus Edelweiss,** 13 Maple Street (P.O. Box 609), Sunapee, NH 03782 (tel. 603/763-2100), a nice and homey bed-and-breakfast with five rooms. Guests tend to gather in the living room, where TV, light snacks, and a drink are offered by the hosts. Rates are $38 single, $56 to $62 double, with your choice of a traditional Bavarian or Yankee breakfast.

Sunapee Harbor visitors have been going to the **Woodbine Cottage** (tel. 603/763-2222) for over 60 years, and at my last visit it was as popular as ever: several smallish, but bright and cheery rooms with lots of polished blond wood, and pewter vessels and an old rifle hung here and there for effect. Lots of windows provide plenty of light, especially on a bright day. The daily luncheons are priced between $10 and $14.50, but that's for a full three- or four-course meal. At dinner the prices are in the $14 to $20 range for a favorite such as baked ham in raisin sauce, broiled lamb chops, or lobster Newburg. Remember that these prices include appetizer, vegetable and potato, salad, roll, dessert, and coffee, tea, or milk. The Woodbine is open from May 30 through mid-October. The restaurant is open Tuesday to Saturday for lunch and dinner and Sunday for brunch; closed Monday.

WHAT TO DO

To see Lake Sunapee, there is no better way than to catch the **M.V. *Mount Sunapee II*** (tel. 603/763-4030), which leaves Sunapee Harbor marina at 2:30pm on Saturday and Sunday from mid-May to mid-June for tours of the beautiful, very pure lake. From mid-June to Labor Day there are sailings at 10am and 2:30pm. And until mid-October the ship sails on weekends at 2:30pm. The tour lasts 1½ hours and cost $10 for adults. Kids under 12 pay $5; kids under 5 ride free. The *Mount Sunapee II* holds 150 people, and the tour is narrated by the amiable captain.

In the summer, Sunapee hosts very well-attended **flea markets** out on Rte. 103B at the blinking light (between Sunapee Harbor and Sunapee Lower Village). Both buyers and sellers flock to the intersection's roadsides, and everything from craftwork through antiques to junk is available.

The best **beach** in the area is down near the state park entrance. It's the state park beach, and the entrance fee covers use of changing rooms. Lake Sunapee is a Class A reservoir—the water is about as pure and unpolluted as you'll find anywhere.

Across the large traffic circle from the entrance road to the beach is the entrance to the state park and its chairlift to the summit of **Mt. Sunapee.** In summer the round-trip price in three-person gondolas is $5.50 for adults, $2.50 for children 6 to 12. The trip takes you over 1¼ miles (1,450 feet straight up) to the summit at 2,743 feet. At the top there are walking trails (not difficult) to an overlook and to a glacial tarn named Lake Solitude. At the base of the mountain, near the gondola station, is a cafeteria; spacious lawns, hiking trails, and picnic areas are all open to the public at no charge.

Skiing

The Mount Sunapee area (tel. 603/763-4020 or toll free 800/322-3300 for snow information) has five double-chair lifts, a T-bar, a J-bar, and a rope tow, with a capacity of 6,000 skiers an hour. The vertical drop is 1,500 feet on 23 slopes and trails; in addition, there are 10 miles of free ski-touring trails, novice and intermediate (tel. 603/763-2356 for information). A ski school, a ski shop with rental equipment, a cafeteria, and (weekdays) a nursery are all available.

11. Hanover

The small town of Hanover is the home of one of the country's oldest and most prestigious colleges. **Dartmouth** (named for the earl who was colonial secretary to King George III) was founded in 1769, and its charter gives a hint of why it was located in such a remote place: It was meant primarily "for the education and instruction of Youth of the Indian Tribes," and only secondarily for the education of "English Youth and others." Today Dartmouth is more than a small undergraduate college; its graduate schools of medicine, engineering, and business administration are well respected, and the Hopkins Center for the Arts is the cultural focus of the entire region.

In many ways the college is the town and vice versa. College buildings of exceptional beauty and grace are scattered or clustered throughout Hanover, and most are shaded by trees of a prodigious height and girth. Anyone out for a drive would enjoy a walk through the campus, perhaps on one of the guided college tours (free) that leave from the college information booth during the summer at 9 and 11am and 3pm, and from the Hopkins Center at 2pm (no tours on Sunday); in winter, tours depart from McNutt Hall. To order tickets to performances, or to find out what's showing at the Hopkins Center, call 603/646-2422.

In winter, Dartmouth's **Winter Carnival** is the major fun and social event, with special art shows, drama and concerts, an ice sculpture contest, and other amusements.

WHERE TO STAY AND EAT

The prime hostelry is the **Hanover Inn,** Hanover, NH 03755 (tel. 603/643-4300 or toll free 800/443-7024), right in the center of town. Some rooms have views of the lawns and buildings of the college. It fills up quickly at major college events such as matriculation, graduation, and the big football games played at home. Decor is colonial, to fit in with the rest of Hanover, but the shiny new bathrooms and color TVs show that modern comfort has been given great consideration. Singles and doubles cost $155; larger and slightly newer rooms are in the east wing. Junior suites run from $200 single or double.

The Hanover Inn's formal dining room and new restaurant are supplemented by a lovely outdoor patio, under an awning, in summer. The feeling is very much that of an exclusive country club. At lunch, sandwiches are only about $5, but full luncheon meals (the daily specials) can be had for $8 to $10. The dinner menu offers a good and balanced selection of well-known meat, fish, and fowl dishes: Start with Norwegian gravlax and then have anything from pan-fried brook trout to native spring lamb, and the total bill will be about $35 per person. The waitresses in black uniforms with white trim are silent, efficient, and friendly, waiting attentively at their stations when all the diners have been served. Room service is available for all three meals.

An Inn in Lyme

If Hanover is the busy college town, Lyme, N.H., 10 miles north on Rte. 10, is the peaceful New England village. At the center of Lyme you'll see the high-pillared façade of the **Lyme Inn,** Lyme, NH 03768 (tel. 603/795-2222). Built in 1809, the inn has 14 rooms, most with bath or shower, all with antiques and authentic decor. Prices, depending on which room you choose, are $77 to $83 single, $128 to $150 double, breakfast and dinner included. You should know that the inn has its own tavern, very handy in this otherwise sleepy village.

Across the River in Norwich

Just across the Connecticut River from Hanover, in Vermont, you'll find the **Inn at Norwich,** Norwich, VT 05055 (tel. 802/649-1143), a nice 26-room hostelry known for its charm, dignity, and warm welcome as well as for the excellence of its dining room. The inn has been here since 1797 and its furnishings reflect its heritage, with brass and canopy beds in many rooms, but also television set, telephone, and private bath in all. The cheery lounge is called the Jasper Murdoch Tavern, after the man who opened the inn almost 200 years ago. The current innkeepers, by the way, are the Savidges. Rooms at the inn are priced at $136 double, $30 less in the motel units; these rates include breakfast and dinner in the pretty, formal dining rooms or on the porch. The cuisine is of a high order.

WHAT TO DO

Everyone takes a tour of Dartmouth College, but for a more offbeat view of the campus and surrounding area take a **hot-air balloon ride.** At the Post Mills Airport (P.O. Box 51, Post Mills, VT 05058; tel. 802/333-9254) you can take a sunrise or sunset balloon ride with trained, professional balloonists who will float you up or down the Connecticut River Valley depending on the whim of the wind. After you've helped with the set-up process, you'll be airborne for 1 to 1½ hours, and finish with a champagne reception at the touch-down site. Oh, and don't worry, they'll take you back to the airport to pick up your car if you want. Balloons fly daily, weather and wind permitting. The cost for all this fun is $150 per person, with a minimum of two people. To reach the airport from Hanover, take Rte. 10 north, cross the bridge to Vermont, head south on Rte. 5 and west on Rte. 244.

MAINE

There is something quintessentially American about this rugged and sparsely populated state, the largest in New England. It's as though the vast forests of the north and the jagged coastline of "downeast" Maine are the last American frontier, rich in natural resources but waiting for people equally rugged to tame them.

Although there are still areas of wilderness in Maine, some of the state's potential was exploited long ago, soon after its discovery by Europeans. When the French and English came to these shores, they found miles and miles of virgin growth. The tremendous white pines have been replaced by other varieties, and lumber products again yield a good deal of the state's economy.

Besides its forests, Maine has great stores of granite for building, but they're mostly untapped as yet. Although agriculture is difficult because of the rocky soil and the short growing season, Maine potatoes are known and used throughout the eastern United States. Maine's fishermen yearly pull great quantities of fish, scallops, shrimp, and the famous lobsters from the freezing Atlantic waters. But the largest industry in Maine these days is the vacation trade: campers, hikers, and fishermen in the mountains and lakes, yachting and summer residents in the beautiful old coastal towns. Good food—especially the fresh seafood—and clean air draw the crowds from Boston, Montréal, and New York, and life in the southern coastal towns is lively and interesting from mid-June through Labor Day, after which the visitors become those looking for the quiet of Indian Summer and the autumn foliage season. Most resorts close up by the last week in October.

Of the vacation areas in Maine, certainly the most popular is the southern coast, where pretty towns such as Ogunquit, Kennebunkport, Boothbay Harbor, and Camden provide an atmosphere either restful or lively, cultural or natural, as you like it. Next in popularity comes the famous old resort of Bar Harbor, which is a good ways "downeast." The crowds these days come to commune with the rugged beauty of **Acadia National Park**. Finally, a smaller number of hardy souls head into the hinterland among the mountains, forests, and glacial lakes for a piece of the outdoor life.

Meals and rooms in Maine are taxed at a rate of **7%**, so look for this tax to be added to your bill each night, and at mealtimes. The telephone area code for the entire state is **207**.

GETTING THERE

Amtrak does not operate in Maine, but its trains do connect with buses at Boston's South Station that will take you north into the state. If you're driving, be aware that the Maine Turnpike (I-95) is a toll road. U.S. 1 or its scenic alternate route, U.S. 1A, parallels the Maine Turnpike all the way to Brunswick, and while it's a bit slower, it costs nothing. Besides, it's more scenic, and in my opinion no other highway in the entire country could possibly have as many flea markets, antiques shops, and white-elephant sales as does U.S. 1 in Maine, all the way from Kittery to Ellsworth. Weekends are the best times to catch them, but in July and August any day will do.

Note: If you're heading for Ogunquit, take the exit from I-95 soon after you cross the state line at Kittery—follow the signs for U.S. 1 and the "shore" or "scenic" route through York, and this will save you a toll. And now for some tips on traveling by public transport.

By Bus

Greyhound Lines (tel. 800/237-8211) operates buses from Boston all the way to St. Stephen, New Brunswick, stopping at Portsmouth, N.H., Ogunquit, Kennebunk, Portland, Brunswick, Bath, Wiscasset, Camden, Bangor, and Ellsworth (for Bar Harbor). Two buses daily make the trip all the way to St. Stephen; another goes as far as Ellsworth and then runs down to its final stop at Bar Harbor. There are direct buses along this route from New York with a rest stop in Boston. Greyhound also runs between Montréal and Bangor, and there are connecting buses between Ottawa, Toronto, and Montréal, and between Bangor and Bar Harbor. One can also change at Bangor to go south along the coast. The Montréal-Bangor/Bar Harbor bus goes through Bethel, Me., but for now only on Saturday runs does it stop there. In conjunction with Autobus Fortin Poulin, Greyhound runs between Québec City and Portland, Me.

Vermont Transit (tel. 800/451-3292) works in conjunction with Greyhound and Voyageur to operate on routes between Boston and Portland, and from Portland west to North Conway, Bretton Woods, and Bethlehem, N.H., and to St. Johnsbury, Barre, Montpelier, and Burlington, Vt.; in Burlington, connections are made to or from Montréal.

C&J Airport Limousine Service operates those long airport limousines between Boston's Logan International Airport and points along the Maine coast, including Ogunquit and Kennebunk. In Ogunquit the terminal is at the Dunaway Municipal Building right in the center of town; in Kennebunk it's at the Kennebunk Inn. Places in the limousines are best reserved in advance.

By Air

Bar Harbor Airlines (tel. toll free 800/327-8376), an Eastern Express carrier, one of the older and better commuter lines, flies to many points in Maine—Augusta, Bangor, Bar Harbor, Portland, Presque Isle—and also to Burlington, Vt., Boston, Worcester, Hartford/Springfield, Albany, and New York City (La Guardia).

---

1. Ogunquit

The Indian name means "beautiful place by the sea," and it holds true even today, because Ogunquit's town government has ensured that the town remains tidy and picturesque despite its tourism development. Visitors feel welcome in the town, whether they're strolling along Ogunquit's picturesque "Marginal Way," a path along the rocky coast; relaxing at the Ogunquit Beach; or dining in one of the many excellent restaurants. At Perkins Cove, a tiny peninsula is festooned with the quaint low waterfront shops and shacks from Ogunquit's fishing-village heyday. Right along U.S. 1 is the **Ogunquit Playhouse** (tel. 207/646-5511), presenting Broadway plays and musicals from late June through Labor Day. Ogunquit has been a summer resort for over a century, and it's no wonder that people come back year after year.

INFORMATION

The chamber of commerce maintains an **information office** on U.S. 1 (P.O. Box 2289, Ogunquit, ME 03907), south of the center of town, and as Main Street is U.S. 1, you will come to the office just south of the downtown area. It's open during business hours in the summer season (tel. 207/646-5533) and irregular hours off-season (tel. 207/646-2939).

WHERE TO STAY

Having been a summer resort for so many years, Ogunquit today has a good selection of accommodations in all price ranges, from the extravagant to the inexpensive.

It seems as though every place in town rents rooms, from the gas station to the gift shop. Many are on U.S. 1, however, which is busy with traffic. If you don't find a vacancy among the following selections, search along Shore Road toward Perkins Cove, where it's quieter.

Inns and Guesthouses

As you head down Shore Road from the main crossroads, a few steps will bring you to the **Seafair Inn,** 14 Shore Rd. (P.O. Box 1221), Ogunquit, ME 03907 (tel. 207/646-2181), on the right-hand side. Pass the two millstones at the beginning of the path, walk up through the pretty garden, go through the sunny front porch with wicker furniture, and enter the formal parlor of this one-time Victorian summer house. You've already got a good idea of the inn's charm. Double rooms with shared bath cost $59 to $64; with private bath, $75 to $91. There are also several efficiency apartments. Continental breakfast is included.

Of Ogunquit's cozy Victorian seaside hotels, the **Colonial Inn Resort,** just south of Obed's Lane on Shore Road (P.O. Box 895), Ogunquit, ME 03907 (tel. 207/646-5191), is the notable survivor. These days it's brimming with life, having been renovated by Chet and Sheila Sawtelle. The hotel has 22 suites with kitchenettes ($144 for one to four people), plus some motel units with kitchenettes ($107 double), besides the 45 rooms in the inn. The inn rooms all have private bath, and go for $59 single, $73 to $97 double—the higher price is for the rooms with the best ocean views. From May to late June and after early September until mid-October, rates are about 30% lower. The Colonial has a heated pool, whirlpool spa, a breakfast coffee shop, an elevator, and more important, a spacious veranda in the turn-of-the-century fashion, the perfect place for sitting, viewing, reading, and napping.

Of the several guesthouses on Shore Road near the turnoff to Perkins Cove, my favorite is the **Hayes Guest House,** 133 Shore Rd. (RR1, Box 12), Ogunquit, ME 03907 (tel. 207/646-2277). Elinor Hayes is very kind and friendly, and has decorated her five rooms and two apartments with interesting old pieces such as a rope-frame bed made in Maine (now with a box spring, of course!), old sea chests, and patchwork quilts. Both twin and double beds are available. With private bath, a room is $73 to $75 ($10 per extra person in the room) or $70 with semiprivate bath. Guests have use of a refrigerator and the coffee maker; all rooms have air conditioning and TV. There's a pretty swimming pool. It's a charming place, and Mrs. Hayes a charming lady, and here you're within walking distance of Perkins Cove with its restaurants, shops, and galleries.

Motels

For over a century vacationers have been driving up to the top of Bald Head Cliff, a few miles southeast of Ogunquit, to stay at the **Cliff House,** P.O. Box 2274, Ogunquit, ME 03907 (tel. 207/361-1000). Originally, guests stayed in the large old house perched on the cliff, 90 feet above the surf, but now the house is overshadowed by several large and very modern motel units, all with a view of the sea. Extensive pine-covered grounds, a heated outdoor pool, and tennis courts add to the lure of the Cliff House's remote location and its view. The rooms are luxurious, with tub-shower combination bath in each, picture windows for the sea view, and color TV; all are air-conditioned. From the end of June through Labor Day, they cost $120 to $285 double; off-season, prices are somewhat lower, and special money-saving packages are offered. Cliff House is open April through mid-December. There's free transportation in season into town, to the beach, and to other points of interest in and around Ogunquit.

Ogunquit's modern, "almost downtown" motel is the attractive **Country Squire Motel,** on U.S. 1 at Bourne's Lane, Ogunquit, ME 03907 (tel. 207/646-3162), just four blocks or so from the center of town. The inspiration is colonial, with an arched portico along the front of the motel, bay windows in each room, pots of plants, and colonial-style furniture. The facilities are an uncolonial matter, however, for there's a swimming pool, and each room has a tiled tub-shower, heat and air conditioning, color TV, and wall-to-wall carpeting. The Country Squire is open only from mid-May to mid-October, like most Ogunquit lodging places. In July and August, rates are $94 to $110 double.

Two blocks from downtown on Shore Road in Ogunquit is the **Sea Chambers Motor Lodge,** 37 Shore Rd., Ogunquit, ME 03907 (tel. 207/646-9311). The two-and three-story motel is right down near the water and also has its own heated pool and tennis court. You can walk from your room and get right on Marginal Way, the path along the rocky coast. The whole establishment is quite modern, and all rooms have bath, color TV, air conditioning, balcony, and twin beds or two double beds; most rooms have good sea views. In-season rates for late June through Labor Day, continental breakfast included, are $118 to $127 double, with an extra person paying $14.

WHERE TO DINE

For dinner in a country setting, try **Clay Hill Farm,** on Agamenticus Road (tel. 361-2272), 2 miles from downtown Ogunquit. The farmhouse has been converted into a tavern with several large dining rooms with lots of windows and a very comfortable air. Start with clam chowder or Maine crab cakes and go on to haddock stuffed with lobster; with dessert, wine, tax, and tip, you'll pay $30 to $40 per person. Before and after dinner you can relax in the lounge and enjoy the piano entertainment provided. Clay Hill Farm is open in season (June to October) seven nights a week from 5:30pm to midnight (kitchen closes at 10pm); in winter, you can have dinner here on Thursday, Friday, and Saturday during the same hours, or the Sunday brunch. Call for reservations, winter or summer. To get to the tavern, go south on Main Street (U.S. 1) from the blinker in the center of Ogunquit for .3 mile, to a blinker at a crossroads next to the Admiral's Inn; turn right—this is Agamenticus Road—and go 1.8 miles to the tavern, which will be on your right.

Perkins Cove, at the seaside end of Shore Road, has several good restaurants. In July and August it can be very difficult and expensive to park your car here, and you'd be well advised to take one of the "trolleys" (open buses) that run along Shore Road to the cove.

In Ogunquit, everybody goes to **Barnacle Billy's,** in Perkins Cove, and the reason is clear: good prices, good food, and good service as only you yourself could provide. The routine here is to enter, choose what you want from the blackboard menu, pay the cashier and get a slip, and submit the slip to the counterperson; then wander off into Barnacle Billy's waterfront dining room, done all in pine with tables and chairs to match, and a hardwood fire going in two big stone fireplaces if there's a chill in the air. The view of the marina and the cove is as good as the food: a 1¼ pound lobster for $10.45 (heavier ones for a dollar or two more), steamed clams, corn on the cob, salad, and garlic bread are all available. When the weather's fine, you can even order at a window on the brick terrace and have your meal while sitting in the sunshine, either on the terrace or on a deck a flight up; both terraces are right next to the Finestkind Boat Dock. There's free parking for customers right across the street. Billy's is open May to mid-October daily from 11am to 10pm, more or less, depending on the crowds.

Right downtown in Ogunquit, one of the town's busiest dining spots is the **Old Village Inn**, 30 Main St. (tel. 646-7088). It's popular because of its location, and because of its several low-ceilinged dining rooms with their heavy beams barely six feet from the floor, all decorated with old crockery; if the weather's fine, you'll want to dine in the inn's glassed-in conservatory amid the flowers and plants. At dinner, have the delicious lobster bisque to start, then a dish such as seafood imperial or perhaps roast duckling; the fish-of-the-day is always a good choice; such a meal will cost about $30. At lunch/brunch, main courses cost $8 to $10. Lunch/brunch is served from 10am to 3pm, and dinner from 6 to 10pm; a small bar provides for the thirsty.

Ogunquit is prepared for New Yorkers who come north for the summer, or others in search of good corned beef, bagels, and the like. **Einstein's Deli,** at the corner of Shore Road and U.S. 1, has all these delights and lots more, besides several dining areas and a take-out service (tel. 646-5262). It's open till midnight, as a good deli should be. Note that even the clam chowder is New York style—with tomatoes.

WHAT TO DO

First thing to do is stop in at the town's information office and pick up a map, and then take off to walk **Marginal Way.** Start next to the Sachem Hotel and you'll come out right at Barnacle Billy's in Perkins Cove, a mile or so away. The Atlantic, the rocky coast, the gulls wheeling overhead, and the smiles of the other walkers you'll meet are all part of this Ogunquit institution, and all are a treat whether the sun is shining, or it's misty, or even if there's a gale coming.

Next thing to do is call the **Ogunquit Playhouse** (tel. 207/646-5511) to get seats for a performance, which will no doubt feature a star or two of national reputation. Tickets cost $17 and shows are scheduled for Monday through Saturday at 8:40pm and Wednesday and Thursday at 2:45pm.

As for **beaches,** Ogunquit is well equipped. The town's three beaches—Main Beach, Little Beach, and Fottbridge Beach—are ranged along a peninsula just a few minutes' walk from the center of town. Lifeguards are on duty from 8am to 5pm daily in season.

Some lazy afternoon, be sure to leave time for a stroll around the shops and galleries of **Perkins Cove,** the picturesque old fishing-village section of town.

You can get to know the sea in Ogunquit by going down to Perkins Cove where, next to Barnacle Billy's, the dock of the **Finestkind boats** is located. Each hour during the day (except Sunday) the lobster boats set out to cruise the Maine coast, hauling in the lobster pots and the day's catch. You can go along and have the process of lobstering explained while you view the coastline and the fishing grounds, all at $8 for adults, $5 for children. Make reservations, if you like, by calling 646-5227, or just drop down to the docks for more information. There are cocktail, starlight, and lighthouse tour cruises as well.

Auto buffs can visit the **Wells Auto Museum** on U.S. 1 in Wells, just north of Ogunquit. From mid-June to mid-September, you can view the 1907 Stanley Steamer, a rare 1912 Pathfinder roadster, a 1918 Pierce Arrow, and 75 other classics for $3 per adult, $2 for each child above the age of 6.

An Excursion to York

Just south of Ogunquit is York, or "The Yorks," as the town actually consists of old York, York Harbor, and York Beach

York Harbor, at the mouth of the York River, is a summer resort much like Ogunquit. York Beach is more honky-tonk, with amusements and snack shops.

What you come to see is old **York Village**, first settled by Europeans in 1624. It received a royal charter in 1639, the first English town in the country to have this privilege.

Take a look at the **Old Gaol**, built as a jail in the 1700s, now a museum of colonial and Native American artifacts administered by the Old York Historical Society (tel. 363-4974). Hours are 10am to 4pm Tuesday through Saturday, late June through September.

Jefferds Tavern (1750) and the **Old School House** (1745) are next door to one another, providing an authentic glimpse of two aspects of life over two centuries ago. The **Emerson-Wilcox House** (1740) dates from the same era, and sheltered two presidents over the years; it's now a museum.

Down at the water's edge is the **John Hancock Warehouse and Wharf,** once owned by the great patriot, who signed the Declaration of Independence with a signature so large the king could read it without his glasses. It now holds exhibits on life in York during revolutionary times.

Near Sewall's Bridge on the York River is the **Elizabeth Perkins House,** built in 1730 but preserved with Victorian furnishings.

Finally, you may want to visit the **Old York Cemetery.** Besides having the standard collection of fascinating old New England tombstones, there is a grave said to be that of a witch. Covered with a huge slab of stone to protect the townspeople from a reappearance, it's a real curiosity. One wonders what odd circumstances brought this poor soul such condemnation.

---

2. Kennebunkport

The several communities with similar names—Kennebunk, Kennebunkport, Kennebunk Beach—are clustered together on the Maine coast and constitute one of the state's most popular vacation areas, particularly since they were put on the map by President Bush and his family.

Of the towns, Kennebunkport is perhaps the most interesting. As its name implies, Kennebunkport was the waterfront part of the Kennebunk area. It's been a resort for years, drawing both the well-to-do and the student crowd living on summer earnings. Prices for rooms and meals tend to be a bit high, but for most people the price is not so important so long as they can just find a room open in this delightful Maine town.

WHERE TO STAY

Kennebunkport has every sort of lodging. I've concentrated on inns, the quaint and charming places, with the occasional hotel or motel selected just in case that fits your mood.

Inns

Kennebunkport's inns come in all shapes and sizes, from the rambling old seaside "cottage" to the magnificently restored sea captain's mansion. Here are the best examples.

Lindsay and Carol Copeland's **Maine Stay Inn and Cottages,** Main Street (P.O. Box 500a-F), Kennebunkport, ME 04046 (tel. 207/967-2117), is a charming place, surrounded by gardens and lofty trees, but only a short walk from the center of town. Rates are $118 to $155 double in high summer season. Though the rooms are equipped with all the modern conveniences, the spirit—and the welcome—befits a cozy inn. A breakfast buffet is included, and tea is served to guests at 4pm. The cottages are clean, tidy, bright, and a good value.

At **The Breakwater,** Kennebunkport, ME 04046 (tel. 207/967-3118), the situation is excellent—the open sea is right next door. Prices are $121 to $154 double in season, the cheaper rooms being in the Breakwater building, the more expensive ones in the Riverside building, which is open year round and is more modern and, well, preferable. Off-season rates are 25% to 30% lower, from Columbus Day through mid-June. Continental breakfast is included in these prices. For dinner, The Breakwater has one of the best restaurants around (see below).

The **Captain Jefferds Inn,** Pearl Street (P.O. Box 691), Kennebunkport, ME 04046 (tel. 207/967-2311), is one of those old sea captains' houses so immaculately restored that it made the cover of *House Beautiful.* The house was beautiful, but the owners have improved upon it with unusual antiques, lots of them, and comfortable furnishings. The 12 guest rooms are priced at $118 to $134, including tax and a country breakfast; there's a two-night minimum stay from July through October. Besides being everything a quaint inn should be, the Captain Jefferds is just off Ocean Avenue, walking distance to everything in town.

Kennebunkport has a very special place to stay, and you should consider it. The **Captain Lord House,** P.O. Box 527, Kennebunkport, ME 04046 (tel. 207/967-3141), was built in 1812 by a naval captain whose sailors were blockaded in Kennebunk Harbor by the British. Lord put his men to work on the mansion, and they did an impressive job. Today there are antiques everywhere, private baths all around, and working fireplaces in 19 of the 24 rooms, and you can stay here for $122 to $241 double (the highest-priced doubles are the ones with the fireplaces), full breakfast included. A third person pays $25 in the same room. Driving from Dock Square down Ocean Avenue, keep glancing to your left and soon you'll see the stately yellow mansion topped by its cupola/observatory at the back of a rich greensward a block long: Captain Lord meant this first sight of the mansion to be impressive, and it certainly is.

Guesthouses

You'll recognize the **Welby Inn,** P.O. Box 774, Kennebunkport, ME 04046 (tel. 207/967-4655), on Ocean Avenue across from the Nonantum, by its handsome hand-painted tile signboard out front. One of the owners, Betsy Rogers-Knox, is the faïence artist who did the tiles for the sign, as well as those for all the private bathrooms, and many of the paintings in this graceful old converted summer cottage. Prices for the seven rooms are $83 to $93 double in season, breakfast included.

Of Kennebunkport's guesthouses, certainly the most pristine is the **Chetwynd House,** Kennebunkport, ME 04046 (tel. 207/967-2235), with only four rooms. The house is immaculately clean, which allows you to admire the fine wide-board floors of a rich honey color, and all the very decent furnishings, including many four-poster beds. Extra pleasures at the Chetwynd House include tea and cakes, and a full breakfast with your room; and here you're only two blocks from Dock Square and the center of town. Two rooms have private bath; the other two share a bath. Prices range from $85 to $134 double. Chetwynd House is on Chestnut Street, the second left off Ocean Avenue; the street is not marked, but Chetwynd House is a short distance up on the left, and is marked clearly by a sign.

Among the smaller and more modest inns, the **Green Heron,** on Ocean Drive (P.O. Box 2578), Kennebunkport, ME 04046 (tel. 207/967-3315), has been a dependable Kennebunkport hostelry for years and years. This nice old house owned by Charles and Elizabeth Reid has been converted to hold 10 guest rooms, and a cottage can hold an additional four people. Furnishings are simple but quite comfortable, and there's a cheery breakfast room with lots of big windows overlooking the water. These rates include a good breakfast: $62 to $96 double in high summer season. All the rooms have private baths, with tub and shower. The beaches are within walking distance.

Hotels

The **Nonantum Resort,** P.O. Box 2626R, Kennebunkport, ME 04046 (tel. 207/967-3338) is a very well-kept, classic 19th-century resort hotel, with comfortable and charming public rooms, lawns and a swimming pool, a waterfront location, and even a motel annex. The price, including tax, for a double with bath, is $115 to $170 double; $180 to $190 for an efficiency. This is a real slice of old Kennebunkport. Look for the Nonantum on Ocean Avenue, a half mile from town.

Those who want to be smack in the middle of town, right next to Dock Square, should consider **Austin's Inn-Town Hotel,** P.O. Box 609, Kennebunkport, ME 04046 (tel. 207/967-4241), right next to the Kennebunk River and the dock. The Inn-Town is a new and modern hostelry within an older-style building, and all rooms have private bath; it's possible to fit three, four, or even five people in several, which is good for traveling families to note. A room with a double bed is $107. There's free parking for guests on the dock right next to the hotel.

WHERE TO DINE

Like any good resort town, Kennebunkport has a selection of restaurants in all price categories. Here are the ones I like best.

The Breakwater, on Ocean Avenue (tel. 967-3118), is a local favorite. The dining rooms are elegant without being overly formal, and the sun porch—which is a dining room—affords a beautiful view of the sea. You can order a beef kebab, or baked haddock; the broiled scallops are popular. The delicacies proceed to swordfish and roast prime rib, with the lobster clambake priced according to the day's market. A full dinner costs about $30 to $45 per person. Have reservations, but be sympathetic when you're told that specific tables can't be reserved (the ones with the sea view are the hot ones). The dining room is open every day, for dinner only, from May through October 6 to 9pm. Hours are 5:30 to 10pm in July and August.

The **White Barn Inn,** on Beach Street in Kennebunkport (tel. 967-2321), is a real barn converted to a restaurant. Everything that was found during the cleaning and renovation of the barn was hung on the many rafters and beams for effect, or so it seems. Chef Richard Lemoine's menu includes the popular classics, each with a personal twist: starters of scallops wrapped in bacon with a maple-mustard cream, or cream of asparagus soup with fennel and toasted almonds. Your main course might be baked stuffed lobster, or a thick veal chop with chervil, tarragon, and mushrooms, or poached salmon. Dinner, which will cost you about $5 to $55 per person, all included, is served every day at the White Barn from 5:30 to 9:30pm; closed Monday off-season. Beach Street (or Beach Avenue), by the way, is parallel to Ocean Avenue but across the inlet from it, to the south; if in doubt, ask for the St. Anthony Monastery, and the White Barn's very near, on the other side of the street.

Convenient to Dock Square, and good for a moderately priced supper, is the restaurant called **Arundel Wharf,** off Ocean Avenue a short distance from Dock Square (tel. 967-3444). As you walk across the parking lot to the restaurant, the gulls will be squealing overhead; as you enter you'll see a modernistic back deck, a beamed ceiling, and several windows with water views, for the Arundel is indeed on a wharf by the Kennebunk River. The staff here are young and friendly. For lunch (11:30am to 3pm) there are mostly sandwiches ($3 to $8) with a few platters offered, but for dinner (5 to 9pm) you can have a boiled lobster, steak teriyaki, broiled haddock, or even lobster pie, for $10 to $14. A raw bar is open from 11:30am to 10pm.

The restaurant's name comes from the fact that Kennebunkport was once named Arundel, after England's Earl of Arundel; in fact, it bore that name all through the better part of its maritime prominence, changing it only in 1821. Arundel Wharf is open daily, with dinner served till 9pm.

The **Olde Grist Mill,** on Mill Lane (tel. 967-4781), dates from 1749 and is listed in the National Register of Historic Places. Overlooking an inlet of the Kennebunk River, the restaurant is set back from the street on its own parklike grounds. Seafood is king, of course, but for a change of pace there's also baked stuffed shrimp macadamia and sirloin steak au poivre. Dinner (5:30 to 9pm) will cost $30 to $40 per person, all in. To find the inn, from Dock Square ask for North Street; Mill Lane is a left turn a few blocks down.

Of course, the cheapest way to have a lobster dinner is to wander down to the lobster pound. Although many restaurants have appropriated the name "Lobster Pound," a real pound is simply the place where the live lobsters are kept in saltwater vats until a customer comes and buys them. Most lobster pounds these days have a few simple cooking facilities, and will boil up the lobsters for you if you wish, provide salad and french fries, butter and salt and a paper plate, and charge just a little above the price of a live lobster. There are several such lobster pounds in Kennebunkport, where a cooked lobster will cost between $10 and $14, depending on size and season.

WHAT TO DO

Shops and galleries around Dock Square draw lots of shoppers and window shoppers at all times, and one can spend some time browsing very pleasantly.

Gooch's Beach is right at the southern end of Beach Street, on the western shore of the Kennebunk River; **Kennebunk Beach** is west of Gooch's, along the coast. These fine, gradual beaches are good for swimming, especially on very hot days (the water tends to the chilly), for sunning on any sunny day, and for walking, thinking, or jogging on almost any day.

Be sure to take a drive or a walk along **Maine Street** for a look at Kennebunkport's fine old mansions. For a look at the rocky coast, go south on Ocean Avenue to **Spouting Rock** to hear the crash of the surf.

A Trip to Cape Porpoise

Three miles northeast of Kennebunkport along Rte. 9, on the shore, is the village of Cape Porpoise. This charming little bit of Maine coastal life is a vacation haven for a small, knowledgeable few. Not fancy, not crowded, it has only a few craft shops, a few eateries, a few guesthouses, and a lot of Maine atmosphere. Drive out and head for the pier, with its pretty views of the sea. A brass plaque on a rock atop the sand hill there bears this legend: "August 8, 1782, a British ship of 18 guns attacked a small force of inhabitants gathered on Goat Island and was driven away by severe musket fire, losing 17 men. James Burnham of this town was killed. This tablet erected by the Maine State Council, Daughters of the American Revolution, August 8, 1921."

Well, not an awful lot exciting has happened in Cape Porpoise since that signal victory, and it's just as well, for the quiet is what makes it nice.

Should you decide to stay here, Mr. and Mrs. Lyman P. Huff will rent you a room in their guesthouse, the **Old Garrison House,** Pier Road, Cape Porpoise, ME 04014 (tel. 207/967-3522), for $43 single or $63 twin (shared bath) or $69 twin (private bath). You'll see the big yellow house on the left-hand side of the road at the head of the cove as you head for the pier.

For real Maine lobster, try **Nunan's Lobster Hut** (tel. 967-4362), on Rte. 9 East. Nunan's is an unprepossessing low-roofed shack of a place, open from 5pm for dinner, and serving boiled lobster, steamed clams, salads, homemade pies, beer, and wine such that patrons return night after night. You need spend no more than $12 for dinner, though you may find yourself diving in and spending $16 or $20. Authenticity—that's Nunan's.

---

3. Portland

Cities in Maine have never had a reputation for chic or avant-garde ambience because Maine is a rural state, and it's the farmlands, woodlands, and coastal industries such as lobstering that count. But Portland, the state's largest city and its transportation hub and business center, may be changing all that. The **Civic Center** draws sports events, conventions, and big-name entertainers, and its revitalized waterfront area, known as the **Old Port Exchange,** is now even more attractive than it was in its Victorian heyday when the railroads, the huge sailing fleet, and the trade in lumber and fish made Portland what it is.

You can spend a day profitably in Portland, visiting the city's colonial, Early American, and Victorian landmarks, browsing the **Portland Museum of Art,** or taking a cruise in Portland Harbor or Casco Bay. Portland is also the American end of the Prince of Fundy Cruises, which will take you and your car to Yarmouth, Nova Scotia, on an 11-hour, overnight cruise or on any one of a number of other cruises and tours (details below).

INFORMATION

The **Convention & Visitors Bureau Information Center,** 142 Free St., Portland, ME 04101 (tel. 207/772-4994), next to the Portland Museum of Art can fill you in on Portland life.

WHERE TO STAY

The city has a few lodging places downtown, but many visitors, especially those here on business, stay in motels near Exit 8 of the Maine Turnpike.

Downtown Hotels and Inns

The **Inn at Park Spring,** 135 Spring St., Portland, ME 04101 (tel. 207/774-1059), a few blocks west of the information center, is a restored three-story brick town house with seven guest rooms, most with private bath but some with shared bath. As the house dates from 1935, a colonial or Victorian decor would be inappropriate, so instead the rooms are done in an assortment of nice old pieces and more modern furniture as well. All rooms have queen-size beds, and rent for $93 to $104 double, continental breakfast included.

Down in the Old Port stands the **Portland Regency,** 20 Milk St., Portland, ME 04101 (tel. 207/774-4200), a new hotel in a fine old waterfront building constructed in 1895 as an armory. Here you can walk to everything of interest in the port district, and you're only a few steps from the commercial center of town as well. The guest rooms are decorated in Early American reproductions, not exactly accurate to the hotel's age, but very nice nonetheless. There's a health club. A single room rents for $118, a double for $132.

If you visited Portland years ago, you remember the old Eastland Hotel. In its place stands the totally renovated **Sonesta Portland Hotel,** 157 High St., Portland, ME 04101 (tel. 207/775-5411 or toll free 800/343-7170). Still at the very heart of the city, the Sonesta provides all the up-to-date luxury hotel services at rates of $96 to $134 single, $113 to $150 double. Ask about the hotel's weekend packages when you call for reservations.

Holiday Inn has a downtown hotel in Portland, but out on the turnpike (Exit 8) it's the **Portland-West Holiday Inn,** 81 Riverside St., Portland, ME 04103 (tel. 207/774-5601 or toll free 800/465-4329). The 200 rooms here are all modern, with color TV, and are priced at $104 to $115 double in July and August, a few dollars less per room just on the other side of high season. There's live entertainment in the lounge most evenings in summer.

The **Howard Johnson Motor Lodge** is nearby at 155 Riverside St., Portland, ME 04103 (tel. 207/774-5861 or toll free 800/654-2000), and here the facilities include an indoor heated swimming pool and a sauna, a restaurant and lounge, and rooms with color TV. Special weekend minivacation packages are available, but normally the doubles rent for $97 to $102 in high season. If you're flying, a limo will bring you here from the airport, but you should call in advance.

The bargain place to stay, as ever, is the dependable **Susse Chalet Motor Lodge** (tel. toll free 800/258-1980), and there are two of them here. The 105-room Portland In-Town Susse Chalet is at 340 Park Ave., Portland, ME 04102 (tel. 207/871-0611), adjacent to the Maine Medical Center. Each room has a remote-control cable television, and there's an outdoor swimming pool. Rates are $44 to $46 single, $48 to $50 double, the higher prices being for rooms with king-size beds. To find the motel, take Exit 5A from I-295, go right off the ramp onto Congress Street, then take the second left onto Marston St., which leads you to Park Avenue.

Even cheaper is the Susse Chalet at Exit 8, 1200 Brighton Ave., Portland, ME 04102 (tel. 207/774-6101), near the other motels mentioned above. The motel has a pool and cable TV, but its highway location makes it even cheaper than its sister establishment. The 132 rooms here are priced at only $38 single, $43 double.

WHERE TO DINE

The renaissance of Portland's waterfront district has given rise to numerous restaurants in recent years, and a short walk through the tidy and picturesque restored blocks of Fore, Exchange, Middle, and Moulton streets will reveal interesting and moderately priced places for a snack, a meal, or a relaxing drink.

The **Baker's Table,** 434 Fore St. (tel. 775-0303), is an elegant cafeteria with bar adjoining. Pass through the line at lunchtime for, say, soup and salad, and after you're seated everything else you may need—more wine, coffee, or dessert—can be brought by a waiter. Salad here is almost a meal in itself, but with a big bowl of fish chowder it'll fill you for sure. Such a lunch will cost less than $10 with fresh bread and beverage—that's a daily special. Lunch is from 11:30am to 5:30pm; the heartier and more expensive dinner menu (bouillabaisse, tournedos, or perhaps chicken provençale) is served until 10pm (to 10:30 on Friday and Saturday). Waiters serve at dinner amid linen-clad tables and sparkling stemware. There's soft background music, paintings by local artists, an interesting crowd, a well-stocked bar, and an espresso machine. Dinner might cost $30 per person, all in.

For New American cuisine in an upbeat atmosphere, head for the **Café Always,** 47 Middle St. (tel. 774-9399), a colorful and stylish refuge of the designer set. The menu is as interesting as the clientele and the décor. Lamb loin prepared with sun-dried tomatoes and fresh thyme, Korean-style hot-and-sour chicken, a fancy burrito, and a halibut filet with an orange-and-chive beurre blanc were all on the menu recently. The wine list is heavy with California vintages. Dinner, the only meal served, is on from 5 to 10pm every day but Monday, and will cost about $45 per person, all in.

Go to the aforementioned Portland Regency Hotel, 20 Milk St. in the Old Port (tel. 774-4200), for a sumptuous Sunday brunch buffet, spread out from 10:30am to 2:30pm. The setting is the hotel's restaurant, called the **Armory,** a nice interior court complete with fountains and free-flowing champagne. Drink as many glasses as you like—the champagne is included in the price of the buffet, which is less than $23 once you add the tax.

Portland's choice for Chinese cuisine is **Hu Shang,** 7–13 Brown St. (tel. 774-0800), right downtown near the Civic Center. The cooking is drawn from Hunan, Szechuan, Shanghai, and Mandarin (Peking/Beijing) traditions: Spring rolls, pan-fried dumplings, fried wonton, hot-and-sour or bean-curd soup are among the appetizers. Then lamb with ginger and scallions, chicken with cashews, moo shu beef, fresh scallops with peanuts and scallions—it's difficult not to order half a dozen entrees. But appetizer, main course, and lichee-nut dessert will cost about $18, tea, tax, and tip included. Several people sharing just a few main-course plates can dine very well for much less. This is one of the city's best restaurants, open every day for lunch and dinner from 11:30am to 9:30pm (10:30pm on weekends); no lunch on Sunday.

For Meeting People

The **Seamen's Club,** 375 Fore St., is a good place to meet Portlanders who work in or near the waterfront, particularly at lunchtime, when the sandwiches (about $5) and the low-price table d'hôte ($7) draw a crowd. Sunday brunch is good too. At dinner the menu is filled with the popular classics, tried and proven: baked stuffed shrimp, roast duckling with orange sauce, filet mignon—solid and satisfying. Prices per main course may be anywhere from $6 to $12 (the higher end for lobsters, of course).

The **Old Port Tavern,** right across the street and down a short distance at 11 Moulton St., is another popular watering spot where the people and the drink are as good, or better, than the food.

WHAT TO SEE AND DO

First thing to do is to ask at your hotel for a copy of the Greater Portland Chamber of Commerce's brochure called *The Portland History Trail,* which sets forth details and a walking tour (with map) of all the notable sights in the city. Here are some of the highlights.

Wadsworth-Longfellow House
The Wadsworth-Longfellow House was the boyhood home of poet Henry Wadsworth Longfellow. Built in 1785–86 by the poet's maternal grandfather, Gen. Peleg Wadsworth, the house now holds furnishings that once belonged to the famous Wadsworths and Longfellows, as well as many other period pieces. There's a beautiful garden, and the Maine Historical Society, which received the bequest of the house in 1901, is located right next door. You can tour the house from June 1 through Columbus Day weekend, Tuesday through Saturday from 10am to 4pm, for $3 per adult, $1 per child under 12.

Tate House
The Maine forest was for a long time the prime source of masts for the British navy, and the man who managed the whole trade was one George Tate, who had this house built in 1755. The house is shown by guided tour from June 15 to September 15, Tuesday through Saturday from 11am to 5pm and on Sunday from 1:30 to 5pm. To get to the house, at 1270 Westbrook St. in the Stroudwater section of Portland, go southwest on Congress Street for 2 miles, cross the stream, and turn left onto Westbrook Street, very near the Portland Jetport. The fee to get in is $2.50 for adults, $1 for kids under 12.

Victoria Mansion (Morse-Libby House)
Built between 1858 and 1860, the Victoria Mansion has fascinating Victorian decorations, and many original furnishings, all of which are on view Tuesday through Saturday from 10am to 4pm, on Sunday from 1 to 4pm, from June 1 through Labor Day (in September, hours are 10am to 1pm Tuesday through Saturday and on Sunday from 1 to 4pm). It's at 109 Danforth St. (tel. 772-4841), and costs $3 per adult, $1 per child under 18, to see.

Portland Museum of Art
Portland has a fine museum with a fine collection at 7 Congress Square (tel. 773-2787). Particularly strong are the collections of 19th- and 20th-century American art relating to Portland and to Maine, with paintings by Andrew Wyeth, Winslow Homer, and Edward Hopper. A gift of 17 Winslow Homer paintings is featured in the new building (done by I. M. Pei). Special exhibits change bimonthly. The museum is open Tuesday through Sunday; admission is $3.50 for adults, $2.50 for students and seniors, $1 for kids under 18.

Boats and Cruises
Portland is the prime dock for Casco Bay and indeed northern New England, and you can climb aboard a boat with your car or without, for a few hours or overnight. Here are the major lines.
Casco Bay Lines, Commercial and Franklin streets (tel. 207/774-7871), will take you (but not your car) over to Bailey's Island in summer. While on the 6-hour cruise, you'll be told all about the island's history and its geologic features, plus lots of Portland and Casco Bay lore. On a sunny day, this is a very fine way to "take the air." The price for this cruise is $11.75 for adults, $6 for children. Other cruises are a bit shorter and a bit cheaper: There's a seasonal sunset cruise to the islands (2½ hours), a seasonal music cruise around Casco Bay (3 hours), and the year-round cruise on the U.S. Mail boat which goes to each of the Calendar Islands (3 hours).

Prince of Fundy Cruises to Nova Scotia
May through October on most days, the M.S. *Scotia Prince* leaves Portland in the evening for Yarmouth, Nova Scotia, on an 11-hour overnight cruise. Return sailings from Yarmouth are in mid- or late morning. You can take your car with you, and duty-free shops are aboard. Current high-season (late June to late September) prices

for the cruise are $68 (U.S. dollars) per adult, half price for children 5 to 14 accompanied by an adult; children under 5 go free. The fare for a car is normally $93. A cabin for two costs in the range of $35 to $165. A family of four can easily spend $350 one way. But there are several special fares which might suit your needs and which will save you money. Be sure to call Prince of Fundy Cruises for full particulars, latest fares, and schedules; credit cards now accepted for passage. In Portland, call 207/775-5616; elsewhere in Maine, call toll-free 800/482-0955; in other states, call toll-free 800/341-7540; in Nova Scotia, New Brunswick, and Prince Edward Island, call toll-free 800/565-7900; in the rest of Canada, call 902/742-5164; and in Yarmouth, Nova Scotia, call 902/742-3411.

EXCURSIONS NORTH

Most people head east from Portland, aiming at Camden, Boothbay, Bar Harbor, or the Canadian border. But an excursion up Rtes. 302 and 26, deep into Maine's forested hinterland, will bring you right up against North Woods life.

Sebago Lake

Of Maine's hundreds of beautiful, clear lakes, Sebago Lake is one of the largest and most accessible. The eastern shore of the lake is somewhat developed with small villages, highway establishments, and the like; at the southern tip, the town of Sebago Lake is hardly more than a few dozen houses, two stores, and a gas station. But along the western shore in the area of the settlement called East Sebago there are a number of places which rent rooms and cabins, mingled among the larger private summer cabins and houses.

Although the roads that skirt the lake do have collections of cabins and houses here and there, it's hardly what you'd call thickly settled. You'll come across **Sebago Lake State Park** at the northern tip of the lake, where there's also a fine beach, picnic facilities, and a camping area. Although very busy in summer, the park is yours to enjoy with only a handful of others in early June or after Labor Day.

Sabbathday Lake

Thirty miles north of Portland along Rte. 26 is the settlement of Sabbathday Lake, the last living Shaker community in the country. Founded in the 1700s, the Sabbathday Lake community still has a handful of active members who continue to work and live in the Shaker tradition. A shop selling community products, a museum, and a welcome center are open to visitors, though most of the other buildings are not. For more on Shaker history and beliefs, see in Chapter IX on the Berkshires (Section 7, "Stockbridge") the description of Hancock Shaker Village.

The spare white buildings of the village are plain but extremely well kept. Most notable is the Brick Dwelling House. In the fields near the village are several small, simple cemeteries, each with only one monument, bearing the legend "Shakers" and the dates of interment.

Up the road a few miles is the village of **Poland Spring,** which gained fame in the 1800s when a man was miraculously cured by its waters. The water from the spring has been bottled and shipped throughout the country since that time. Several hotels here cater to those "taking the waters."

Continue north on Rte. 26 and you'll soon come to one of the prettiest towns in Maine, right at the edge of the White Mountains and a vast national forest.

Bethel

Tucked away in the mountains on the western edge of Maine is the village of Bethel. Although the village is on U.S. 2, the highway that heads west to skirt the border of the White Mountains National Forest, there is little else that would bring travelers to the place were it not for two attractions: a well-known preparatory school called **Gould Academy** (founded 1836) and an excellent inn.

WHERE TO STAY The inn referred to above is the **Bethel Inn,** on the Town Common, Bethel, ME 04217 (tel. 207/824-2175). A feeling of tastefulness and elegance is what you get as you drive to the inn's entrance through the greensward in the center of the village. The main inn has a famous dining room, a large lounge with a fireplace to match, and French doors leading out onto a terrace overlooking the mountains and the inn's manicured grounds. Special services include a swimming pool, tennis courts, a music room complete with Steinway, a library, a golf course, a boathouse (for boating and fishing) on a nearby pond, and entertainment and dancing in the evenings. The rooms are done with colonial accents (although the inn itself dates from 1913), and are priced to include breakfast, dinner, service, and tax at $140 to $238 double. The inn has rooms in the main building, and also in a number of old Bethel houses surrounding the Common, so the selection of accommodations is very good.

Also on the green, but moderately priced, is the **Chapman Inn,** P.O. Box 206, Bethel, ME 04217 (tel. 207/824-2657), a bed-and-breakfast place since 1865. The cheery, homey rooms here are priced at $30 for a bed in the dormitory, $46 single, $64 double with shared bath, or $75 double with full bath; full breakfast is included. You get to use the game room, nearby pond, sauna, and hot tub as well.

As you drive into town on Rte. 26 from the south, you can't miss the **Four Seasons Inn,** Upper Main Street, Bethel, ME 04217 (tel. 207/824-2755). This huge, beautiful Victorian house has porches, gables, and turrets to attract any eye. Inside, it's all angles, nooks, fireplaces, antique furnishings, and thoughtful touches such as tea or sherry in the afternoon and chocolates on your pillow. Room rates include a welcoming drink, continental breakfast, afternoon tea, and use of the Bethel Inn's recreational facilities: $62 single, $72 (shared bath) or $88 (private bath) double.

WHAT TO SEE Should you have an hour to spend in Bethel, drop in at the **Dr. Moses Mason House,** 15 Broad St. (tel. 824-2908), on the Common, open in July and August, Tuesday through Sunday from 1 to 4pm, and by appointment (call during business hours) the rest of the year. Moses Mason was a congressman during the Jackson administration, and had this Federal house built in 1813. Today it's furnished in antiques of the period and also holds several murals attributed to Rufus Porter. Admission is $2 for adults, half price for children. There are research facilities, special exhibits, pictures, films, and a gift shop.

Otherwise, there's the great outdoors. North on Rte. 26 is **Grafton Notch State Park,** with a pretty waterfall named Screw Auger. West on U.S. 2 is the White Mountains National Forest. Between Gilead, Me., and Shelburne, N.H., the highway is lined with birch trees, the famous Shelburne birches. Most of us have never seen so many of these unusual, lovely trees in one spot. In autumn, when the birch leaves turn to brilliant yellow with dabs of red, they knock your eyes out.

For more on the national forest in New Hampshire, see Chapter XII.

---

4. Freeport, Brunswick, and Bath

North of Portland, the next major tourist destination is Boothbay Harbor. But you'll pass several interesting towns along the way, each with an attraction peculiar to Maine.

FREEPORT

This small Maine town, nothing special though nice enough, is known all over the country and throughout the world as the headquarters of **L. L. Bean** (tel. 207/865-3111), the company that sells equipment, clothing, and supplies for outdoor activities. L. L. Bean has been in Freeport for decades, but in recent years the store's popularity has burgeoned to epic proportions. A half dozen parking lots, administered by Bean employees, fill up quickly every day with cars bearing license plates from all over America and Canada. The large, attractive store is always mobbed during the day, and busy even at night, for Bean's is open all the time. It *never* closes.

Bean's reputation was built by selling sturdy, good-quality items at reasonable prices. The returns policy is absolute: If you find a Bean item unsatisfactory at any time, return it for a refund. Should you stop at Bean's, remember that the store carries dozens of items for which there is no room in the catalog, and that there's also a "factory store" for end-of-season and distressed merchandise. You should also know that Bean's will mail your packages home for you right from the store at no extra charge. Keep it in mind: If your trunk's too full, take the item you've just bought to the customer service counter, and they'll take care of the rest—for free.

The boom at Bean's has brought prosperity to Freeport, and a dozen other shops—Dansk, Anne Klein, Ralph Lauren, Hathaway, you name it—have opened in order to profit from the press of Bean buyers. In effect it's becoming Maine's town-size shopping mall.

BRUNSWICK

Surrounded by coastal resort towns, Brunswick is the cultural center of this part of Maine, for **Bowdoin College** is in Brunswick along with Maine's only professional music theater. The **Brunswick Music Theater** (tel. 207/725-8769) is on the Bowdoin campus, and presents musical productions from mid-June through Labor Day each summer.

Bowdoin's fame comes not from its theater, although that is certainly famous enough among summer visitors and residents, but rather from the distinguished alumni who have spent their time in Brunswick and then moved on to fame and glory: Longfellow, Hawthorne, and President Franklin Pierce were all Bowdoin graduates. The college is at Pine and College streets, and free tours are available year round. While you're here, visit Bowdoin's **art museum** to see its collection of colonial works.

BATH

A 10-mile drive along U.S. 1 north from Brunswick brings you to Bath, another fine town of colonial and Federal houses built when Bath was a wealthy seaport and shipbuilding center. Take a drive along Washington Street to see what I mean.

While you're on Washington Street, stop at no. 243, the headquarters of Bath's famous **Maine Maritime Museum** (tel. 207/443-1316). One admission ticket ($5 for adults, half price for children 6 to 16, $15 for a family) admits you to the exhibit on the maritime history of Maine, the restored Percy & Small Shipyard and its buildings, the Apprentice Shop boatbuilding school, a lobstering exhibit, and, when in port, a 142-foot fishing schooner. Just about everything you'd associate with the sea is represented in these exhibits: early fishing methods, shipbuilding, small boats, engines and steam yachts, navigation, ship's models and paintings, sailors' memorabilia, and all sorts of coastal lore. There's even a play boat for children complete with crow's nest and a "cargo" of sand.

The museum complex is along the river, with plenty of space for picnickers. Wear outdoor clothing and good shoes. You'll need several hours to see everything; or you can have your ticket validated for the next day also, at no extra charge. The museum is open daily from 9:30am to 5pm.

WISCASSET

Billing itself "the prettiest village in Maine," Wiscasset might live up to its boast if Maine did not have such an abundance of pretty towns. It is pretty, though, and as you pass through the center on U.S. 1 you can confirm this. As you cross the Sheepscot River toward Damariscotta, look right (south) and note the two enormous hulks derelict in the water. The four-masted schooners *Hesperus* and *Luther Little* once carried cargoes along the Atlantic coast. But the many-masted schooners (a few were even built with six masts!) were the last of a proud breed, replaced by the more reliable steamboats. These two sad relics of a romantic age sit forlorn in the mud, awaiting restoration or final destruction.

5. Boothbay Harbor

North and east of Portland, the Maine coastline is a choppy succession of peninsulas, sea inlets, islands, and river outlets. The country here is beautiful, and vacation communities abound. Reaching many of these communities means driving down a peninsular road for quite a number of miles to the tip, and upon departure driving back up to U.S. 1—few bridges or causeways span the inlets or rivers.

Boothbay Harbor is the principal town in a region of vacation settlements which include Boothbay, Boothbay Harbor, East Boothbay, Southport, and Ocean Point. I could write a book on this region alone, and so I've simplified by limiting my recommendations to Boothbay Harbor itself, which is the center of the action.

INFORMATION

As you drive down Rte. 27 from U.S. 1, several miles from town you'll come to a seasonal **information bureau,** on the right. If it's closed, don't worry for there's another one a bit farther along, right at the edge of town, and it's open year round. Or get in touch with the **Boothbay Harbor Region Chamber of Commerce,** P.O. Box 356, Boothbay Harbor, ME 04538 (tel. 207/633-2353).

WHERE TO STAY

As mentioned, Boothbay Harbor and the surrounding region have a plethora of vacation accommodations, hundreds of places in all. I've concentrated on the congenial places, like cozy guesthouses on a hilltop with a splendid view.

Admiral's Quarters Inn, 105 Commercial St., Boothbay Harbor, ME 04538 (tel. 207/633-2474), is Jean and George Duffy's large old white-clapboard sea captain's house built around 1820 commanding marvelous views of the harbor from McKown Hill. Upper and lower sundecks allow you to take in the view from each room. Eight comfortable modernized rooms with bath cost $68 to $96, single or double, morning coffee included.

Captain Sawyer's Place, 87 Commercial St., Boothbay Harbor, ME 04538 (tel. 207/633-2290), is a classic yellow-and-white Boothbay Harbor residence—complete with rooftop "observatory"—now run as a guesthouse by Jerry and Doreen Gibson. Rooms are tidy and bright, with some period furnishings, Martha Washington bedspreads, and very clean bathrooms with showers. A small patio overlooks the pedestrians on Main Street, and the house's long wraparound veranda overlooks everything. The location couldn't be any better, or the welcome warmer. Rates are $70 to $118 for a double room with private bath, continental breakfast included.

Hilltop House, c/o The Mahrs, Boothbay Harbor, ME 04538 (tel. 207/633-2941 or 633-3839), is just that, right at the top of McKown Hill in town, next to Topside (see below). Mrs. Mahr, a real Maine native, will rent you a homey room in her house for $43 double with private bath, $32 with shared bath, $48 to $70 for a family unit. The porch, and its marvelous view, are yours to enjoy any time you like. Homemade muffins and breads and coffee come with the price of the room.

Topside says it all about this charming hilltop house just two blocks from the center of town atop McKown Hill, Boothbay Harbor, ME 04538 (tel. 207/633-5404). Several fine old houses have been meticulously restored down to the marble fireplaces (in the living rooms) and stocked with antiques. All rooms have refrigerators. Several new motel rooms have been added, but in keeping with the architectural style of the house, and these have microwaves as well. And what a view —from many of the rooms or simply from a lawn chair in the midst of Topside's lush green grass, where you can take it all in as the cool breezes waft up from the harbor. Although there are other places on McKown Hill, Topside is smack at the top. Rates are $91 to $102, depending on the size of the room, its degree of comfort, and its exposure (all have private bath). As the number of rooms is limited, be sure to write or call well in advance for reservations. Open mid-May through November.

The **Oak Ledge,** 41 Oak St., Boothbay Harbor, ME 04538 (tel. 207/633-6640), may be the town's prettiest, most pristine bed-and-breakfast house. Located on the road into town, only 2½ blocks from the water, this prim clapboard house offers rooms with blond or honey-colored wood floors, stenciled borders on the walls, and craft items for decoration. Baths are shared; a double costs $70, continental breakfast included. It's great!

For something closer to a motel, check out the **Tugboat Inn,** 100 Commercial St., Boothbay Harbor, ME 04538 (tel. 207/633-4434), a few steps from the center of town, at the lower edge of McKown Hill. The inn has several lodging buildings and a good variety of accommodations, from simple but tidy inn rooms through efficiencies and motel-style rooms to luxury rooms and suites. Prices in high summer season range from $81 to $134 double; all rooms have private bath. You're right on the harbor here, handy to town, with good views, in an attractive and congenial establishment.

Outside Town

The **Ocean Point Inn,** Shore Road (P.O. Box 409), East Boothbay, ME 04544 (tel. 207/633-4200), couldn't have a better location. Way down at Ocean Point by the lighthouse, on the southern tip of a peninsula overlooking the harbor mouth, Ocean Point is all by itself except for a few houses. It's quiet here, and very serene. You stay in the motel, the inn, the lodge, or one of the cottages, and rates depend on which, though all rooms have private bath, electric heat, and color television. Least expensive rooms are in the inn ($74 to $87 double), but the other lodgings are not much more expensive ($74 to $106), though a few suites and cottages are higher in price. The Ocean Point has its own restaurant, as there's no other place to dine without driving into Boothbay Harbor.

The **Lawnmeer Inn and Motel,** Rte. 27, Southport, ME 04569 (tel. 207/633-2544), is a short drive from Boothbay Harbor, across the drawbridge in Southport. In a quiet country setting, the Lawnmeer offers motel-style rooms with private bath, television, and the other modern conveniences for $59 to $106 double. This is the place to go if you need to get away from it all.

The **Five Gables Inn,** Murray Hill Road, East Boothbay, ME 04544 (tel. 207/633-4551), is a superbly restored old Maine coastal inn of 15 rooms, all with a wonderful view of Linekin Bay and also with private bath; five rooms have a working fireplace. Innkeepers Ellen and Paul Morisette obviously love their work. After your buffet breakfast here (included in the rates), enjoy the view from the large veranda, or take the sun on the lawn, or cross the road for a swim. Bustling Boothbay Harbor is 3 miles away; here in East Boothbay, its much calmer and quieter. The Five Gables is open from mid-May through mid-November and charges $86 to $130 double.

Bed-and-Breakfast

I've chosen mostly establishments in town or in special locations outside. The Boothbay region does have a number of bed-and-breakfast houses, most off the beaten track. For information, check (or call) the information booth.

WHERE TO DINE

While Boothbay is no culinary Mecca swarming with gourmet Muhammeds, there are still a few places where you can find things besides fried foods or the infamous surf-and-turf.

For standard American seaside fare, try **Rocktide,** 45 Atlantic Ave. (tel. 633-4455), across the bay from downtown Boothbay Harbor (use the footbridge). Rocktide is a big place with four dining areas. On the Seadeck, in the Chart Room and Buoy Room, you can dress as you like, and no reservations are taken; in the

Dockside and Harborside Rooms diners should observe "jacket" formality, and reservations are taken. The menu is old New England: fried Maine shrimp, ocean scallops, seafood casserole, finnan haddie, New England lobster pie, or a fisherman's platter. But there are unexpected items as well, such as a kebab of shrimp, scallops, lobster, and swordfish and sole Duxelleois and roast duck. Every main course comes with rights to the salad bar, a popover, and rice or potato. Dinner is served from 5:30 to 9pm every evening. You can expect to spend $25 to $35 per person here.

A few steps from the center of Boothbay Harbor, down near the footbridge, is the **Chowder House** (tel. 633-5761), in a building called The Granary. Have a drink in the Loading Dock Lounge, a woody place filled with nautical paraphernalia, then move on to the dining room with its inside waterview room and outside terrace. The clam chowder and lobster stew are made fresh daily and served with freshly baked bread. A bowl of either would make a lunch in itself for only $5 to $9, or you might choose the lobster sandwich or seafood salad, but there's meat and fowl as well. Dinners are somewhat fancier and a bit more expensive, about $20 to $30 per person, all included. Popular choices are the native scallops sautéed in wine and butter with shallots and parsley and surf-and-turf kebabs. Come for breakfast, lunch, or dinner any day of the week from mid-June through early September.

Andrews' Harborside Restaurant, by the footbridge (tel. 633-4074), offers a lobster roll that's not gigantic but is positively stuffed with succulent lobster meat— no filler. With a soft drink, it'll cost you $10. Mako-shark burgers, chowders, and lots of other things fill the menu. Fresh flowers grace the tables covered in nautical blue-and-white cloths, and you have your choice of an indoor dining room with lots of windows or an awning-shaded terrace, both with fine views of the harbor. You can get draft beer or wine by the glass at lunch or dinner any day. For dessert, go downstairs to the Round Top Ice Cream booth beneath the terrace.

At **Gilchrist's East,** on Commercial Street just south of Fishermen's Wharf (tel. 633-5692), the boiled Maine lobster goes for $15 (whole dinner) or $10 (lobster only), which is reasonable; haddock, halibut, and scallops go for a bit less. But the most interesting item on the menu is the Candlelight Dinner, a succession of salads, vegetables, and fish dishes served on miniature china, for $16. The point is to give you various tastes without overfilling you. Otherwise, try the coquilles St-Jacques, the scallops and mushrooms in shells. Liquor is served. You'll like it here. Open for lunch and dinner daily in season.

A place for lobster is the **Lobstermen's Co-op,** on Atlantic Avenue along the east side of the harbor (tel. 633-4900). The Co-op sells lobsters wholesale and retail (from 6am to 8pm), and will cook up a live lobster, clams, and corn on the cob while you wait, at the retail price. Select a few side dishes, a beverage, a hamburger for the one who can't stand seafood, and you're all set to munch lunch at one of the tables (from 11:30am to 8pm). Cheap, fresh, good, authentic. Lobsters are priced from $8.50 to $16.

WHAT TO DO

In Boothbay Harbor, the sea comes first, as it always has. As the rocky, rugged coastline made travel overland virtually impossible until the day of the automobile and the modern highway, Boothbay Harbor was for centuries served from the sea.

Wander down to the shore in town, and you'll see lots of signboards and ticket kiosks for the boats that operate on cruises out of Boothbay Harbor. Ticket prices range from about $10 to $15, and may include a search for seals, water birds, whales, and other marine life, or perhaps a clambake or a chicken bake afloat. When the moon is near full, special moonlight cruises are arranged. Cruises can be anywhere from one to three hours in length. Ask around to find a style, length, and price that's right for you.

A Clambake on Cabbage Island

Go down to the Tugboat Inn on Main Street, look for the Boothbay Steamship Terminal (tel. 207/633-7166), and climb aboard the M.V. *Islander* for a cruise out to Cabbage Island in Linekin Bay and a real Down East Maine–style clambake. Clams and lobsters are steamed amid seaweed the old-fashioned way and served up twice a day from Memorial Day through Labor Day. The *Islander* sails to the clambake Monday through Friday at 12:45pm (returning by 4:15pm) and 5pm (returning before dark); on Sunday, departures are at 11:30am (returning by 2:45pm) and 1:30pm (returning by 4:45pm). Total cost for the clambake is $30 per person, and that includes the delightful round-trip boat cruise, a cup of fish chowder, two lobsters, steamed clams, corn on the cob, new Maine potatoes, and blueberry cake and coffee for dessert. The scenic island has games, paths, and sitting areas for you to enjoy as well. Call 207/633-7200 for clambake reservations at least a half hour before sailing time.

To Monhegan Island

The *Balmy Days* is a sail-assisted motor craft that makes the run 16 miles out to sea to Monhegan Island, Maine's famous windswept resort-at-sea. One trip out, leaving in the morning, and one trip back from the island, leaving in midafternoon, are made daily. You cannot stay overnight on the island without previous hotel reservations, but the *Balmy Days*'s schedule allows you to have between 3 and 4 hours on the island if you go out and back in one day. Monhegan is noted for its interesting paths and walks, and that's mostly what there is to do. A one-way ticket to Monhegan Island is $15; a round trip is $25; children under 10 pay $15 round trip. While it's out at Monhegan, the *Balmy Days* makes one run around the island so you can see the rugged cliffs, and this costs $1 extra. By the way, you can easily hike all there is to hike (pretty much) in one 4-hour stay on Monhegan. For detailed information, call 207/633-2284.

Other Activities

The Brick House, on Oak Street very near the central Town Square, is the present home of the **Boothbay Region Art Gallery** (tel. 633-2703), which arranges three shows of local artists each season. Paintings are on view daily from 11am to 5pm, on Sunday from noon to 5pm. The handsome old house was built in 1807 of bricks brought from England as ballast in ships which came to carry away Maine lumber—in such a forest-rich region, a brick house is a curiosity, as most houses would naturally be made from wood.

---

6. Camden

Picture a small Maine coastal town wedged between the salt waters of Penobscot Bay and a range of rocky hills, and that's Camden. With a population of barely 4,000 souls it's small, picturesque, and manageable. Edna St. Vincent Millay came from these parts, but today Camden's chief claim to fame is that it is the home port for several two-masted schooners which take eager landlubbers for cruises along the Maine coast. The hills behind the town are included in the **Camden Hills State Park,** with campgrounds and picnic spots, and an auto road to the top of Mt. Battie, the highest hill of the range.

TOURIST INFORMATION

The **Rockport-Camden-Lincolnville Chamber of Commerce,** P.O. Box 919, Camden, ME 04843 (tel. 207/236-4404), maintains an information booth on the public landing in Camden where you can get a directory of the area and also a brochure describing the walking and bike tours of Camden and Rockport outlined by the Camden Historical Society. The tours point up all the most historic places, and tell you much about the town as well.

WHERE TO STAY

Camden is not packed with places to stay, and that's part of its charm. Many people stay at the motels scattered along both sides of U.S. 1, north and south of town. Here, I'll mention the best inns and guesthouses right in town, within walking distance of everything.

Inns

For almost a century, the **Whitehall Inn,** P.O. Box 558, Camden, ME 04843 (tel. 207/236-3391), has been Camden's prime place to stay. The graceful old inn, on U.S. 1 just north of the center, is easily recognizable by its pillared porches. Shortly after arriving, you'll learn that Camden's most famous daughter, Edna St. Vincent Millay, gave a reading here when just a girl. The decor is refined in both the public rooms and guest rooms, and the mood in the dining room is semiformal (jackets for dinner). During high summer, your room comes with breakfast and dinner, and costs $128 to $160 double, service and tax included. This is old Camden at its best.

The **Camden Harbour Inn,** atop the hill at the far end of Bay View Street (no. 83), Camden, ME 04843 (tel. 207/236-4200), stays open all year round. A nice big old inn (1874) with white clapboards and, from most guest rooms and from the dining room, beautiful views of Penobscot Bay, the Camden Harbour could be a model for the typical coastal Maine inn. Recent restorations have beautified the inn considerably and added to its authentic Victorian charm. There are 22 guest rooms all with private bath, 20 of them with water views, 8 with fireplaces, 8 with private patios. You can have cocktails or dinner on the nice Victorian veranda, which also enjoys that fabulous view. Prices range from $155 to $198 double for rooms in the high summer season, full breakfast included; prices are lower off season.

The towers and chimneys of **Norumbega,** 61 High St., Camden, ME 04843 (tel. 207/236-4646), will catch your eye as you drive north along U.S. 1 from the center of town. This vast stone fantasy of a Victorian summer cottage has 11 guest rooms, some of them have fine views of Penobscot Bay, and all have private bath. The double rate, full breakfast included, is $189 to $210 per night. Children over 7 are welcome.

Bed-and-Breakfast

The **Blue Harbor House,** 67 Elm St., Camden, ME 04843 (tel. 207/236-3196), is a friendly bed-and-breakfast guesthouse just a few blocks' walk south of the center of town, on U.S. 1. Two of the restored guest rooms share baths and are priced from $75 double; four rooms have private bath and cost $80 to $110 double. Full breakfast is served on the sun porch (for an additional charge). In the separate carriagehouse (built 1806) are two rooms which rent for $96 to $118 nightly. One efficiency apartment rents for $118 nightly or $535 weekly. A fine place!

Goodspeed's Guest House, 60 Mountain St., Camden, ME 04843 (tel. 207/236-8077), is on Rte. 52, a half mile up the hill west of the center. The house has been beautifully redone and furnished with antiques by its owners, who provide a warm welcome and rooms with shared bath for $45 to $49 single and $68 to $79 double. A tiny deck, set with umbrella-shaded tables and chairs, allows you to enjoy the quiet of this location. The suite, $106, sleeps four.

The **Maine Stay,** 22 High St., Camden, ME 04843 (tel. 207/236-9636), is a big white house built in 1813 with very charming rooms, some of which share baths and cost $48 to $68 single, $58 to $77 double, breakfast included. Two pretty living rooms and a deck overlooking the backyard are for guests' use. The Maine Stay is north of the center on U.S. 1, about a 10-minute walk to the commercial district.

Of the new, restored inns in Camden, among the most pristine is the **Hawthorn Inn,** 9 High St., Camden, ME 04843 (tel. 207/236-8842), just a few minutes' walk north of the commercial district on U.S. 1. The big Victorian house with a view of Camden Harbor has been carefully and lovingly restored, and the large, airy rooms furnished with antiques. Rooms come with shared bath at $80, with private bath with a fine harbor view at $85, or stay in a town house apartment at $214 or a town house suite at $112 to $144. Rates include a full breakfast.

The **Owl and the Turtle** (tel. 207/236-9014) is perhaps the strangest name for a guesthouse, but it is explained when one realizes that the building that houses the Owl and the Turtle Bookshop at 8 Bay View St., Camden, ME 04843, also houses a few very nice motel-type rooms, each with a marvelous view of the inner harbor. Prices for the rooms—while they last—are $75 to $80 for two, continental breakfast included, in summer. Believe me when I say the Owl's rooms are nice: Maine-made furniture, color TV, and private bath; but there are so few of them you *must* reserve in advance by phone or mail.

A short distance north from the center on U.S. 1 brings you to the **Edgecombe-Coles House,** 64 High St., Camden, ME 04843 (tel. 207/236-2336), another of those huge turn-of-the-century summer cottages which retains its earlier glory. Period furnishings fill the rooms, and the plumbing (all private baths) has been brought up to date. Cheapest double room here has a double bed with a private bath and a view of the garden, for $97 in summer; most expensive has a king-size bed, fireplace, private bath, and ocean view, for $144. A full breakfast is included.

In recent years the number of bed-and-breakfast houses in Camden has grown dramatically. During the summer high season, many of them will hang out the "No Vacancy" sign. Here's an additional list of places to check. Double-room prices range from $70 to $98, depending mostly on type of bath (shared or private), or breakfast (continental or full), and on view (water views cost more).

The **Swan House,** 49 Mountain St., Camden, ME 04843 (tel. 207/236-8275), is on Rte. 52 four blocks from the town center. The fine Victorian house dates from 1870, has six guest rooms, and specializes in generous full breakfasts.

WHERE TO DINE

Restaurants tend to open and close in Camden. Here are some that have managed to please customers well, and prosper.

The **Waterfront,** Harborside Square off Bay View Street (tel. 236-3747), is true to its name. It caters to the yachting bunch and those who sit longingly gazing at the tall ships, and because of its beautiful location and dockside tables, does a booming business. The restaurant is open from 11:30am to 10pm every day of the week, with the full luncheon menu served from opening to 2:30pm, a light menu from 2:30 to 5pm, and dinner thereafter. While the dinner menu does carry always at least one steak and one chicken selection, seafood ($13 to $20) is what you'll want to eat if you dine here. The seafood brochette (scallops, gulf shrimp, sole filet, peppers, and mushrooms are skewered and broiled) is a favorite.

Cappy's Chowder House, right in the center of Camden at the intersection of Main, Bay View, and Commercial streets (tel. 236-2254), has two dining levels (the upstairs one with a water view and raw bar), has a rich nautical decor, and an eclectic menu. The seafood—clam, fish, and lobster chowders, plates, salads—is excellent and moderately priced at $10 to $14 for lunch, $18 to $24 for dinner; and there are burgers, Cajun specials, stir-fries, and steaks. A bar provides a social center and quick-lunch place; tables and booths are for serious diners. Liquor is served, and you are likely to run into a few local yacht crews. Cappy's is open from 7:30am to midnight daily, so you can get breakfast here as well.

The **Round Top Ice Cream Parlor,** Harbor Square, has delicious ice cream made on its own farm, plus the least expensive light fare in town. Go around to the "Galley" in back for $2.25 hamburgers, $5 lobster rolls, and similar treats. Take your purchases to the picnic tables overlooking the harbor (exclusively for Round Top customers), and you'll have some of the best restaurant seating in Camden at the lowest price.

Less than half a mile south of Camden on U.S. 1 is the **Spinnaker Restaurant** (tel. 596-6804), a trim gray clapboard place much favored by the locals. Chowder, main course, dessert, coffee, wine, tax, and tip will come to $20 to $25 at dinnertime. Come for lunch or dinner any day from 11:30am to 9pm (11:30am to 2pm and 4:30 to 8pm off-season).

WHAT TO SEE AND DO
If you have a car, drive north from town along U.S. 1 and follow the signs to the entrance to **Camden Hills State Park** and the auto road to the top of Mt. Battie. Besides the town itself, the drive up will afford you a view of the rocky hills, the countryside beyond, and of blue, sparkling Penobscot Bay.

Camden's **Windjammer fleet** of schooners provides the adventurous with a very different vacation: dipping in and out of the myriad of small harbors and inlets along the Maine coast. Cruises usually leave on Monday and last a week; they cost about $400 to $450 per person, and space must be reserved in advance. The thing to do is to write to the chamber of commerce (see above) for current lists of who's sailing, and what the cost will be.

Go southeast along Bay View Street a ways and you'll come to **Laite Memorial Park and Beach,** with picnic areas and rest rooms as well as a nice, chilly Maine beach.

For the rest of your time in Camden, latch onto a copy of the walking tour brochure (mentioned above) put out by the Camden Historical Society, and stroll through the town to get the flavor of it.

Vinalhaven Island
From Rockland Ferry Terminal (tel. 207/596-2202), you can take a car-ferry to Vinalhaven Island, in Penobscot Bay, for a taste of island vacation life, cooled by sea breezes. The *Governor Curtis* (State Ferry Service, P.O. Box 645, Rockland, ME 04841) makes the 1¼-hour run to Vinalhaven three times a day, and the return trip two times a day. On Sunday there are two sailings in each direction.

---

7. Castine and Blue Hill

These little villages, set apart on a peninsula in the Penobscot Bay, are gems. Turn right onto Rte. 175 at Orland, east of Bucksport, and continue on Rtes. 166 and 166A to Castine. With only a few places to stay and to dine, these towns draw a steady crowd of summer regulars who come for the beauty, the seclusion, the quiet, the easy summer life.

CASTINE
No small part of Castine's charm is in its history. In the winter of 1613, Sieur Claude de Turgis de la Tour founded a small trading post here among the Tarrantine Indians, but it was not to remain in French hands for long. The struggle for North America's forest, natural, and maritime wealth was already beginning, and the Fort Pentagoët founded by Turgis de la Tour would be conquered by the English in 1628. Treaty returned Pentagoët to France in 1635, and during the tumultuous period until 1676, the place changed hands many times. The British took it and called it Penobscot Fort; the French retook it and built the formidable Fort Saint Peter. At one time the village was the capital of all French Acadia (the lands in what is now Atlantic Canada). Even the Dutch coveted the fort, and ruled here from 1674 to 1676. In the latter year Baron de Saint Castin recaptured the town for France, and opened a trading station. Fortifications were strengthened, and despite raids by the British, the family of Baron de Saint Castin ruled over the town (now called Bagaduce) even after the baron himself returned to France, a wealthy man, in 1703. By 1760, however, the fate of French North America was sealed, and Castin's Fort, or Bagaduce, was to be held by the British after that year.

English settlers brought new life to Bagaduce during the 1760s, and the dissatisfaction that boiled in the English colonies at this period didn't leave the town untouched. Some of the townspeople were loyal to the king, others sympathized—actively and passively—with the American revolutionaries. But in 1779 a British naval force came from Nova Scotia, intent on making the town safe for British Loyalists (and thereby influencing the negotiations that would determine the fledgling United States' northern border). The British built Fort George to defend the town.

The challenge to American sovereignty was taken up by the General Court (legislature) of Massachusetts, which governed the territory at the time, and the ill-fated Penobscot Expedition was outfitted and launched at an ultimate cost of $8 million (in those days!). Bad luck and bad commanding resulted in the destruction of most of the American force, almost bankrupting the Commonwealth of Massachusetts. Fort George was enlarged and strengthened over the years, and the town thrived until the border between the U.S. and Canada was determined. Unhappily for residents of Bagaduce, the boundary was to be the St. Stephen River (the present boundary), and not the Penobscot. Those loyal to the British Crown put their houses on boats and *sailed* them to sites along the coast of what is today New Brunswick, at St. Andrews, mainly. Some of the houses moved thus still stand in St. Andrews.

In 1796 the name of Bagaduce was changed to Castine, and although it was occupied by British forces during the War of 1812, there was never again to be much military action. But in the 350 years of Castine's history its forts—Fort Pentagoët, Fort George, and the American Fort Madison—saw a surprising amount of attack and defense.

You can visit Fort George and the sites of the other forts in Castine, but first, get a place to stay the night.

Where to Stay and Eat

As I mentioned, Castine has only a few places to put up for the night. Have advance reservations to be sure of a bed.

The **Pentagoët Inn**, P.O. Box 4, Castine, ME 04421 (tel. 207/326-8616), a beautiful old gabled-and-turreted pale-yellow house with dark-green trim, is right in the center of the village. Interior decoration harkens back to Castine's fascinating Revolutionary period, although the inn building dates from Victoria's time, 1894. The comforts are modern, though, and a double room, with full breakfast and five-course evening meal, tax and service included, costs between $180 and $206. Drinks are served on the porch daily in the summer. The evening meal offers several choices, usually including Maine lobster. This is a charming place, and I recommend it for those who want a quiet getaway to a beautiful town. The Pentagoet's innkeepers, by the way, are Lindsey and Virginia Miller.

A perfectly delightful reason to go to Castine is to stay at the **Castine Inn,** Main Street (P.O. Box 41), Castine, ME 04421 (tel. 207/326-4365), an elegant old village house stuffed with antiques, fireplaces, and shades of a gracious past. The cheerful innkeepers, Mark and Margaret Hodesh, have 20 rooms and 3 two-room suites on three floors, all with private bath. Dinner is served from 5:30 to 8:30pm every night, before or after which many guests enjoy the big Victorian porch or the lovely gardens. Rates are surprisingly reasonable at $76 to $101 double, and include a full breakfast.

What to Do

Visit the sites for the forts: **Fort Pentagoët,** near the Wilson Museum on Perkins Road; **Fort George,** near the entrance to town; and **Fort Madison.** Fort George is now a State Memorial, kept up by the Bureau of Parks and Recreation.

Historical signboards placed around the village outline Castine's fascinating history. For a closer look, visit the **Wilson Museum,** on Perkins Street, three blocks from Main Street to the southwest. Open daily except Monday, late May through September, from 2 to 5pm (admission free), the museum holds prehistoric artifacts from the Americas, concentrating on the growth of the human ability to fashion tools. Other exhibits explain the rich local history. On Sunday and Wednesday afternoons in July and August, you can also visit the museum's authentic, working blacksmith shop, see Castine's century-old hearses, and take a guided tour (for a nominal fee) of the John Perkins House (1763, 1783).

BLUE HILL

From Castine, it's about 20 miles to Blue Hill, due east across the peninsula. A town of lofty, majestic elm trees, prim white clapboard homes and churches, Blue Hill attracts visitors because it has no outstanding "attractions." Peace, quiet, and an easy pace are its greatest draw.

Blue Hill was settled in 1762 by settlers from Andover, Mass. By 1792 it was turning Maine's forest wealth into ships, and sending these ships around the world. In 1816 granite quarries were opened, and stonecutting complemented shipping. From 1879 to 1881 there was also a copper mine.

Today, if you're not coming to Blue Hill on vacation, you're probably coming to enroll your child in the George Stevens Academy (1803), a preparatory school. Or perhaps you've arrived to attend a concert in Kneisel Hall of the summer chamber music series.

Where to Stay

The **Blue Hill Inn,** Union Street, (P.O. Box 403), Blue Hill, ME 04614 (tel. 207/374-2844) has served as the town's prime hostelry since about 1840, and is an even better place to stay and dine since innkeepers Mary and Don Hartley took over in 1987. The inn's 11 rooms all have private baths, and 6 rooms have working fireplaces and furnishings authentic to the period. Dinner is served by candlelight each evening in summer, and on weekends and holidays off-season. From mid-June through mid-October, rates are $182 to $195 double with breakfast and dinner or $147 to $160 double for room and breakfast, 15% service charge and 7% tax included. Off-season rates are about 25% lower.

Two miles from the center of the village on Rte. 15 (turn at the Exxon station), **Blue Hill Farm,** P.O. Box 437, Blue Hill, ME 04614 (tel. 207/374-5126), is an authentic Maine farm now run as a bed-and-breakfast place by Jim and Marcia Schatz. It's quiet here, with ducks cruising serenely on the pond, and you'll think you're visiting some comfortably established country cousins. Rooms in the converted farmhouse and barn have private or semiprivate bath (two rooms to a bath), and go for $55 to $65 single, $65 to $77 double, breakfast included.

Arcady Down East, South Street, Blue Hill, ME 04614 (tel. 207/374-5576), is one mile from the village, south along Rtes. 172 and 175. As you drive up, you'll see a fantastic shingled castle of a place, looking as though it really belongs in Bar Harbor. If a summer cottage could be called "baronial," it would be this one run by Bertha and Gene Wiseman. Lots of public rooms, views of Cadillac Mountain in the distance, and a great variety of guest rooms, one with a fireplace, all with private bath. A double room can cost anywhere from $85 to $110, full breakfast buffet, tax, and 13% service included.

Where to Dine

Locals rave about the **Firepond Restaurant,** on Main Street right in the center of Blue Hill (tel. 374-2135). The cozy dining room fills up quickly in the evenings, especially on weekends, as diners order roast duckling with almonds and chutney, or veal sweetbreads sautéed with apples and calvados in a rich brown sauce. Dinner (the only meal served from 5 to 9:30pm) might cost $25 to $35 per person here, all in.

At **Jonathan's,** on Main Street (tel. 374-5226), the fare is moderately priced and varied, including everything from New American cuisine to Szechuan stir-fried beef to braised rabbit dijonnaise. Dinner here may set you back only $20 or so.

What to Do

Visit the **Holt House** (1815), home of the Blue Hill Historical Society, open in July and August Tuesday through Friday from 1 to 4pm. The stocky but dignified four-chimney home is little changed from its Federal days. Take a look also at the pretty stained-glass windows in the First Congregational Church.

Those chamber music concerts in Kneisel Hall, performed by students and faculty of the summer music school here, are given twice weekly in July and August, at 8pm.

DEER ISLE

You can continue southward, taking Rte. 15 to Deer Isle and Stonington, its southernmost town. Just after you cross the humpback bridge onto Deer Isle proper, you'll see a little chamber of commerce **information booth,** open in summer. Shortly after passing the booth, you'll enter the village of Deer Isle.

The best hostelry here is the **Pilgrim's Inn,** in the village of Deer Isle, ME 04627 (tel. 207/348-6615). The inn, dating from 1793, is furnished with many antiques, Laura Ashley fabrics, and nice country touches. Eight of the rooms have private bath, and rent for $180 to $192 double; with shared bath, the rate is $156 to $167. These prices include breakfast, dinner, 12% service, and tax. Each evening, hors d'oeuvres are served in the common room, with its 8-foot-wide fireplace, and dinner follows in the dining room, a converted barn. Innkeepers Jean and Dud Hendrick will lend you a bicycle so you can explore on your own, or will give you advice about local excursions, including to Isle au Haut, and to the Haystack School of arts and crafts.

Note that no smoking is allowed in guest rooms or in the dining room and that a two-night stay is encouraged. Should you want to stay for a full week, you can take advantage of special rates. No credit cards are accepted. The inn is open from mid-May through mid-October.

Stonington is a fishing village, summer resort, and former granite-quarrying town. Beyond Stonington is **Isle au Haut,** part of Acadia National Park. A mail boat (tel. 207/367-2468) will take you over to the island in less than an hour, and you can hike along the park trails.

---

8. Bar Harbor

When a Yankee talks about a "Downeaster," he's talking about somebody from Maine, but when somebody from Maine talks about a Downeaster, he means somebody from the region of Bar Harbor or even farther east. Most of the rest of us think of the Maine coastline as running its ragged way north, but a quick look at the map will show that Bar Harbor is at about the same longitude as San Juan, Puerto Rico, and that indeed the Maine coastline heads more directly east than it does north at this point. These are the wilder shores of Maine and the settlements are fewer, the vegetation not so lush, and the climate a bit harsher than in other parts of the state, but at the same time the scenery is more dramatic, the air is charged with life, and a sense of wild nature surrounds one.

The French influence was for a long time paramount in these parts, and many Downeasters today speak French as a second language—the French of Québec, the French brought to these shores by the great Champlain. In fact, it was Samuel de Champlain who gave Mount Desert Island its name, in the form of "L'Île des Monts-Déserts," and even today the local pronunciation is *"dez-zert"* (like what you have after dinner, not like what's in Arabia), following the French style.

When steamships and railroads were opening up America in the 1800s, they also opened up Downeast Maine, and by the end of the century Bar Harbor, a small town on rocky Mount Desert Island, boasted almost as many palatial summer homes as Newport, although the ones here were perhaps not quite so lavish—but pretty close. In any case, only a small number of the original dozens of mansions are still standing, for a great number were wiped out in the Great Fire of 1947.

Today Bar Harbor is a nice town with a wonderful collection of nice little inns; also lots of motels, most (luckily for the town) lining the roads into town from Ellsworth. The big attractions in the area, for which so much housing must be provided, are the town itself, the cruise boats to Yarmouth, Nova Scotia, and of course Acadia National Park. The park takes up something like half of the land of

Mount Desert Island and much of that on the smaller surrounding islands, and is one of the few national parks in the eastern United States. It draws tremendous numbers of visitors every year.

INFORMATION

Bar Harbor's livelihood has been tourism for 100 years now, and so the townspeople know how to treat a guest. The chamber of commerce maintains an **information booth** at the *Bluenose* Ferry Terminal on Rte. 3 (tel. 207/288-3393), and on the village green off Main Street (no phone). In winter, call the business office on Cottage Street at 207/288-5103. You'll get help with information and with any questions you may have.

WHERE TO STAY

While the area draws thousands of visitors each year, there are plenty of rooms to handle the crowds. The problem is to get the room you want rather than one you're forced to take. Reservations are advisable in all recommended places, and as these are some of the choicer spots, I'd suggest that you reserve early.

Inns

Prime among Bar Harbor's elite places to stay is the **Bar Harbor Inn** (tel. 207/288-3351 or toll free 800/248-3351), set amid its own lush grounds on a point overlooking Frenchman's Bay, Bar Harbor, ME 04609. Once a private club, it has been converted, expanded, and renovated to take in visitors year round, and the feeling is that of a posh resort in the 1920s. One dresses well for dinner in the semicircular dining room overlooking the bay; white pillars frame the front porch; attendants pad quietly here and there. The inn's large heated swimming pool is next to a little copse of trees and only a few yards from the waters of the Atlantic, and here, as everywhere else at the inn, the views are magnificent. The rooms are not old-fashioned, however. All have private bath, color TV, and lots of windows looking onto either the bay or the inn's lush grounds; in 1988, 64 new luxury rooms were added, each with private terrace and oversized beds. Prices are $168 to $220 double. The rooms at poolside are cheaper at $130 for two from mid-July to mid-September. The atmosphere is formal but friendly.

In 1900 a retired Boston publisher named Lewis Roberts built himself a "cottage" in Bar Harbor. The sumptuous result of his efforts has gone through several hands since then, lately having been owned by a former dean of Harvard Medical School. Today, however, it is among Bar Harbor's most desirable places to stay. It's called **Thornhedge Inn,** 47 Mount Desert St., Bar Harbor, ME 04609 (tel. 207/288-5398), and the aim of its owners is to "recapture the spirit of Bar Harbor at the turn of the century." This they have done by arranging to purchase many of the house's original furnishings, and so today the large, sunny, gracious master bedroom on the second floor is done in the turn-of-the-century style that suits it; adjoining is the original bathroom, which is a good deal larger than the standard motel *room* today. All rooms have a private bath and cable TV, and many rooms have working fireplaces, in which fire laws allow artificial logs to be burned. You can tell that I like Thornhedge, and when you stay there, you'll know why. The season is May 1 through October 20. In high summer, rooms range from $70 to $134, single or double; off-season rates are lower. There is also one cottage available at a lower rate. Morning coffee, juice, fruit, and muffins are included in these rates. As you're driving or walking along Mount Desert Street, you can't miss Thornhedge, for it's painted a bright, cheery yellow.

The **Stratford House Inn,** 45 Mount Desert St., Bar Harbor, ME 04609 (tel. 207/288-5189), is everything you could imagine in the way of Tudor domestic architecture. Gabled and half-timbered, it looks like Queen Elizabeth I's own summer cottage. Though built by a publishing magnate, Stratford House was the summer home of musical greats Fritz Kreisler and Jan Paderewski. Eight of the ten rooms have private bath (and some have fireplaces), and go for $86 to $134 double; those sharing a bath cost $70 to $80.

The **Manor House Inn,** 106 West St., Bar Harbor, ME 04609 (tel. 207/288-3759), is another huge Victorian "cottage" in which period furnishings fill the guest rooms, each of which has its own bathroom. The Chauffeur's Cottage, two guest cottages, and five gardens also occupy the acre of grounds. The Manor House is right across the street from the prestigious Bar Harbor Club, and Manor House guests can use club facilities for swimming and tennis, plus the reading room, lounge, and grounds. What does it cost to stay in a charming house, now listed in the National Register of Historic Places? Prices are $85 to $135 double, tax included, from June through late September; off-season rates are lower, of course. The inn is open mid-April through mid-November and the price includes a buffet breakfast which you can eat in the lovely garden.

The **Ledgelawn Inn,** 66 Mount Desert St., Bar Harbor, ME 04609 (tel. 207/288-4596), is a palatial mansion fully converted now to a luxurious and elegant inn. Having escaped destruction in the Great Fire of 1947, the "cottage" built for Boston shoe magnate John Brigham now lives on. The public rooms are positively grand in scale, the lawns and trees elaborate, the guest rooms elegant. Many have working fireplace and private bath, sauna-and-whirlpool bath, and prices ranging from $87 to $97 per night double, depending on size, bath, view, or fireplace. The Ledgelawn has a widow's walk on top, open for the view or the warm rays of the sun until 6pm. There's a swimming pool, a hot tub, and access to the clay tennis courts and Olympic-size pool at the Bar Harbor Club for inn guests. By the way, a continental breakfast is included in the price of your room here.

The **Hearthside B&B,** 7 High St., Bar Harbor, ME 04609 (tel. 207/288-4533), run by Susan and Barry Schwartz, is on a quiet street not far from the center of town. The living room of the inn has a fireplace and other touches of past Bar Harbor elegance (re-created here) abound. Afternoon tea and evening wine and cheese are served. Most rooms have private bath, some have fireplace or balcony; all come with an expanded continental breakfast baked at the inn, and cost $68 to $102 double in high summer season. There's a no-smoking policy at the inn. To find the Hearthside, stay on Rte. 3 as it becomes Mount Desert Street and take the third left (High Street), a one-way street just before the Episcopal church.

Mount Desert Street is truly a street of inns. Among them is the **Mira Monte Inn,** 69 Mount Desert St., Bar Harbor, ME 04609 (tel. 207/288-4263 or toll free 800/553-5109 outside Maine), a fine old Victorian house (1864) lovingly restored and maintained by Bar Harbor native Marian Burns. All rooms come with private bath, color TV set, and period furnishings. Each room has something different: a canopy bed, brass bed, fireplace, porch, or bay window. Rates, continental breakfast included, are $102 to $145, single or double.

The **Holbrook House,** 74 Mount Desert St., Bar Harbor, ME 04609 (tel. 207/288-4970), was built in 1880, its 19 rooms providing enough space for even the most enormous Victorian family. Now the family in residence—hardly of Victorian size—is that of Dorothy and Mike Chester, who will welcome you and rent a room for $97 to $112 double in peak summer season, all with private bath. A full breakfast and afternoon refreshments are included.

The **Central House,** 60 Cottage St., Bar Harbor, ME 04609 (tel. 207/288-4242), has what few other local inns have: its own restaurant. The chef is the inn-keeper, and offers rooms with shared bath for $69 double, with private bath for $75 to $90 double, continental breakfast included. Some rooms have working fireplaces. And, yes, the inn is yet another of those lovely, huge old summer cottages, two blocks from the center of town.

Farther from the center of town, 500 yards from the *Bluenose* dock, up on a cliff, is the **Cleftstone Manor,** Rte. 3 (Eden Street), Bar Harbor, ME 04609 (tel. 207/288-4951). What was it like to spend the summer in a 30-room cottage? You can get a taste of it here for $91 with shared bath or $97 to $187 with private bath, double. Breakfast of home-baked breads and pastries is included in the fee, as are high tea and evening refreshments. There's also a new no-smoking policy at the manor. Open April through October, this is one of Bar Harbor's finest.

Bass Cottage in the Field, "in the field" behind the two banks on Main Street, Bar Harbor, ME 04609 (tel. 207/288-3705), is one of the most centrally located and inexpensive, authentic cottages in Bar Harbor, operated and run by sisters in the Maddocks family since it was bought in 1928. Built in 1885, the inn has 10 rooms, most with private bath and some with an ocean view. Breakfast is not included in the rate of $48 to $89 double (there are two singles for $32), but for that price you can walk to one of the many restaurants less than a block away. Relax on the wicker-furnished, glass-enclosed porch. This is a real find!

Guesthouses

Not as fancy or as grand as the Victorian summer cottages, Bar Harbor's guest-houses provide decent accommodations at budget prices. Here is an example.

The **McKay Cottages,** 243 Main St., Bar Harbor, ME 04609 (tel. 207/288-3531), are a mere 1½ blocks from the park and the center of town life. Rooms in the two yellow lodging cottages cost $40 double with shared bath, $45 to $50 double with private bath. No breakfast is served, but it's available nearby.

Motels

The **Golden Anchor Inn,** out on Granite Point off West Street near the Municipal Wharf, P.O. Box 46, Bar Harbor, ME 04609 (tel. 207/288-5033, or toll free 800/242-1231), is a luxurious motel with many seaview rooms, all with a little balcony over the water. The decor is a modern adaptation of Early American, and the luxury extras include a pool, direct-dial phones, color TV (the motel even has its own closed-circuit station), and docking facilities for your boat. The motel is open year round, and the highest prices are charged in July and August, to Labor Day: $75 to $125. The Golden Anchor is easily within walking distance of everything downtown.

On the other side of town is the **Villager Motel,** 207 Main St. (Rte. 3 heading south out of town), Bar Harbor, ME 04609 (tel. 207/288-3211 or 288-3011). The Villager is a very neat two-story motel of moderate size (63 units) and the usual comforts: a heated outdoor pool, modern rooms with private bath and TV, and a convenient location which still leaves you within walking distance of the sights, shops, and restaurants in town. All of these advantages, plus the moderate rates, assure that the Villager is often full, so it's good to make reservations in advance. From July 1 through August 31 the rates are $73 to $87, single or double; from September 1 to October 31 the rooms cost $47 to $59, and in May and June they're $38 to $50.

The **Anchorage Motel,** 51 Mount Desert St., Bar Harbor, ME 04609 (tel. 207/288-3959), is a tidy two-story motel set back from Mount Desert Street, the street with all the inns. Standard motel comforts are yours here for $77 double in high season.

Facing the park right in town is the small **Acadia Motel-Hotel,** 20 Mount Desert St., Bar Harbor, ME 04609 (tel. 207/288-5721). Rooms here are in the budget class, tidy but simple. All rooms have private bath and TV; some have air conditioners and private entrances (the "motel" rooms), while others are entered through the hall ("hotel"). The price range is great: $47 to $53 per room.

Budget Accommodations

Individual women travelers can stay at the **Mount Desert Island YWCA,** 36 Mount Desert St., Bar Harbor, ME 04609 (tel. 207/288-5008). Rooms rent by the night and by the week, and include clean bed linens, use of the laundry room, and kitchen privileges; there are no private baths. Nightly rates are $20 single, $36 double. Weekly rates are $80 single and $140 double. (Weekly rates are available only if paid in full at the beginning of your stay.) Upon arrival you will be charged a membership fee of $10 (for stays of a week or more) and a $25 returnable security deposit. Rooms are hard to come by in the summer so write ahead for reservations. Open year round.

WHERE TO DINE

Bar Harbor is well provided with restaurants to satisfy all appetites, but rather than beginning with the most deluxe, let's start with the one that's the most traditional and also the most fun.

Lobster Pounds

As you drive toward Bar Harbor from Ellsworth, the road is lined with little shacks and stores bearing the magic word LOBSTERS. Outside each is a strange arrangement of backyard barbecues in a row, with large pots or drums on them and stovepipes (in some cases very rickety ones) shooting up. These contraptions are used to prepare a traditional lobster clambake. The drums or kettles are filled with lobsters, clams, corn on the cob, and seaweed, and then salt water is poured in, the fire is started, and the whole business is cooked up and served to the droves of motorists who have been dreaming of such a feast, perhaps for days and for hundreds of miles. Some places have tables where you can sit to consume your feast, at others you take the goodies home with you, but in any case this is the way to get the most seafood for your dollar, and the eating couldn't be better! This is the real Maine experience, and shouldn't be missed.

How does one pick the right place to stop? Every single one seems to have a signboard out front giving the price-per-pound of lobster, and you can go by this to some degree. But the price and poundage depend on how the lobster is stored: The best places will store the live lobsters on ice, and *not* in seawater, as the seawater can add a great deal of weight to the lobster when it's put on the scale. In any case, make sure the lobster is alive, not dead and limp.

Restaurants

The Reading Room at the **Bar Harbor Inn** (tel. 288-3351) is certainly one of Bar Harbor's choice places to dine. The plush semicircular room is filled with brocade chairs and white-clothed tables, all of which share in the view of the bay. Open for dinner from 5:30 to 9:30pm daily. I'd start off here with either the New England clam chowder or the lobster parfait, and go on to a swordfish dijonnaise, or the scallops en papillote (with mushrooms, ginger, snow peas, and soy sauce). By the way, there's a separate, short children's menu, and another for the long list of desserts. Expect to pay $40 to $50 per person for dinner here. Besides the rich atmosphere and good service that comes with the meal, dinner guests have the pleasure of an evening's stroll around the inn's grounds. The Bar Harbor Inn Terrace serves lunch from 11:30am to 5pm. The menu features clam chowder ($3.75), burgers and sandwiches ($6 to $8), and seafood dishes such as grilled shrimp and scallop kebab ($14).

Whether or not seafood is your choice, the best, and perhaps most quietly elegant, meal in town can be found just off Main Street, behind the First National Bank at **George's,** 7 Stephen's Lane (tel. 288-4505). You can dine outdoors in the back garden or inside the softly lit restaurant to the sound of piano music. Start with a seafood crêpe of scallops, lobster, and mussels, or my favorite—baked goat cheese in crispy phyllo. Move on to seared lamb or duck breast sautéed in honey, rum, and mango. Dessert is not for the fainthearted; save room for a rich wedge of chocolate pecan pie or Mississippi mud cake. Dinner will cost about $25 or $30; it's served nightly from 5:30 to midnight. George's is open June through October.

Opera aficionados and lovers of fine food will be delighted by the **Opera House,** 27 Cottage St. (tel. 288-3509). The restaurant is unique in many ways. Although the restaurant is open only for dinner from 5:30 to 11pm, the "listening room" is open throughout the day and everyone is invited to wander through the gallery and listen to a portion of the 90-minute taped program of the day while paying homage to the opera greats whose pictures grace the walls. A placard at the entrance advises Dining for Adults and You Are Welcome Dressed as You Are. The à la carte menu includes rainbow trout ($14) and seafood fettuccine ($15). The seven-course fixed-price menu features roast duck in cognac or Cajun blackened halibut for under $30, all included. If you've dined elsewhere, at least have dessert and a cordial or coffee; the rich crème brûlée ($4) is a wonderful way to end an evening. Reservations are recommended.

Very near the town pier is the **Quarterdeck Restaurant** (tel. 288-5292), at the corner of Main and West streets. Here you can start with sautéed mushrooms and then go on to boiled or broiled Maine lobster or lobster Fra Diavolo (lobster stuffed with Maine scallops, in a spicy tomato and mushroom sauce), and the price will be about $24 to $30 per person. There are a good number of other, cheaper selections as well, such as various spaghetti plates and omelets. The Quarterdeck is modern in decor, and the lights are kept fairly low in the evening so diners can take advantage of the views from the restaurant's many windows. Both lunch and dinner are served; open till 10pm.

The **Brick Oven Restaurant,** 21 Cottage St. (tel. 288-3708), is almost as proud of its decor as it is of its cuisine. Downstairs, the lights are low, lots of stained glass shines, and a turn-of-the-century atmosphere prevails. Upstairs is a Victorian Dining Car room, done up with real fixtures for authenticity. Another room has a cathedral ceiling hung with all sorts of flotsam and jetsam, including an ancient "Whizzer" motorbike. My meal of Maine clam chowder, a plate of fettuccine with scallops and parsley sauce, and a salad came to less than $25, drink, tax, and tip included. Liquor is served.

The **Island Chowder House,** 38 Cottage St. (tel. 288-4905), is a half block off Main Street right downtown. Have a table in the attractive, woody dining room and order the shore dinner of clam chowder, steamed clams, lobster, french fries, and coleslaw, and the bill will be a reasonable $15, tax and tip included. Fish and chips is a third of that price. Lunch and dinner are served. Open from 11am to "late at night" seven days a week, May through October.

Bar Harbor now has a Mexican restaurant, called **Miguel's,** 51 Rodick St. (tel. 288-5117), behind the firehouse and down the street. The quaint, attractive storefront eatery offers delicious quesadillas, burritos, tacos, chilis rellenos, even mole poblano and carne asada. For an appetizer, try the chimitas for $3.50. You can have dinner from 5 to 10pm, for about $12 to $20 per person. Huge frozen margaritas (and other liquor) served. On summer evenings you can dine on the patio.

Another exotic dining possibility awaits you at **The Wok,** 30 Rodick St. (tel. 288-4060). The delicious Thai menu is the same for lunch or dinner, although lunch prices are discounted 10% to 40%. I recently dined on a full meal of golden crisp squid and hot-and-sour fish soup, and finished with the famous Pad Thai noodle dish with shrimp, egg, and bean sprouts, all for less than $18. There are enough choices to please any taste. Lunch is served from 11am to 4pm Monday through Saturday. Dinner is served 4pm to 9:30pm Monday through Thursday, to 10:30pm Friday and Saturday, and to 9pm Sunday. Takeout is available.

For Meeting People

Bubba's, at 30 Cottage St. (tel. 288-5871), is a favorite sandwich-and-drinks place for many of the more interesting people in Bar Harbor on vacation. Soups, salads, and sandwiches ($4 to $10) make up the bill of fare all day, but sipping and socializing are what it's all about. The big bar and the bentwood make it all upbeat and enjoyable.

For a Bit of Nightlife

At **Geddy's,** on Main Street near the corner of West Street (tel. 288-5077), every night in summer is witness to some sort of live performance. Jazz, dixieland, pop, and rock all issue forth from its sidewalk windows. Check the playbill out front and then walk in. There's no cover or minimum, and beer is $1.50 to $3, or a bit more (for Heineken and the like). Happy hour, from 3 to 7pm, sees all drinks reduced to about half price.

WHAT TO DO

As I mentioned above, Bar Harbor has been a resort for many years and town officials, along with the chamber of commerce, throw themselves into organizing activities and making sure there's lots to do.

Special Events

Special events are scheduled throughout the summer, and you should drop down to the information bureau on the town pier for a list of the latest ones. The **Bar Harbor Festival,** with concerts and similar goings-on, is held in July and August, and during the summer months free **band concerts** take place each Monday and Thursday evening on the village green.

Bicycling

Should you want to rent a bike for trips around town or into Acadia National Park, check with **Bar Harbor Bicycle Rentals** at 141 Cottage St. (tel. 288-3886), corner of Eden Street, Rte. 3 (Cottage Street is parallel to West Street but one block south of it, away from the water). Rates are $9 for up to 4 hours, $14 for up to 12 hours, plus deposit.

Cruises

Nothing gives you a feel for Downeast Maine better than some time in a boat on the water. The **Frenchman Bay Boating Company** (tel. 288-3322) organizes all sorts of boat trips: sightseeing, sailing, whale watching, lobstering, and deep-sea fishing. The *Friendship III* motors out to the Gulf of Maine twice daily in search of the leviathans of the deep; the 4-hour whale watch costs $25 per adult, $18 for kids 5 to 11, free for the little ones. If sail power is your preference, hop aboard the schooner *Bay Lady* for one of its four daily 2-hour cruises in Frenchman Bay, the saltwater shushing along its hull, the wind singing in the rigging, and nary a motor's chug or growl. For sightseeing cruises, the diesel-powered *Acadian* and *Frenchman Bay* are the boats to take. Cruise the shores of Bar Harbor and Acadia National Park to a detailed narration of the sights. Cruises last 1, 2, or 2½ hours, and cost from $8 to $12 for adults, $6.50 to $9 for kids 5 through 11 (under 5 free). Perhaps the most thoroughly authentic cruise offered is aboard the 40-passenger *Katherine,* which the captain takes out as a lobster boat to check his traps. Along the way, he'll introduce you to the local seals as well. Fares are $14 for adults, $9 for kids 5 through 11 (under 5 free). As for fishing, morning and afternoon trips aboard the *Dolphin* cost $25 for adults, $18 for kids 8 to 12 (under 8 not allowed); the price includes rod, reel, and bait.

You can also sail aboard Maine's only three-masted schooner, the *Natalie Todd,* or the smaller, but equally impressive two-masted *Janet May.* Both offer 2-hour sails from the Bar Harbor Inn Pier for $16 per adult, $10 for children under 12. The *Natalie Todd* sails three times a day at 10am, 2pm, and 6pm, and the *Janet May* sails twice a day at 11:30am and 3:30pm. Tickets are available at the pier or at the *Natalie Todd* ticket office at 27 Main St. (tel. 288-4585). For information in the off-season call 207/546-2927 or write Capt. Steven F. Pagels, P.O. Box 8, Cherryfield, ME 04622.

A Harbor-View Walk

If you're willing to walk for 30 to 45 minutes, you can enjoy one of Bar Harbor's nicest little hikes. Follow Main Street (Rte. 3) south out of town, past the park on the right, and about a mile down the road (15 to 25 minutes' walk) is a pull-off spot for cars (capacity: four vehicles). If you reach the Ocean Drive Motor Inn, you've gone too far. Walk down the dirt road, closed by a chain, near the little metal sign marking the boundary of U.S. government land, posted on a tree. It's less than a 10-minute walk to Rocky Harbor along the dirt road through the fragrant forests. When you come to a fork, bear left with the road (a path goes off straight). When you reach the viewing point, you'll find a grassy clearing furnished with litter barrels for picnickers (no tables). If you've brought a picnic, you can share it with the gulls and ducks. It's secluded, beautiful, quiet, and in walking distance from town—a fine place.

A Visit to Acadia National Park

The rugged terrain of Mount Desert Island has attracted lovers of natural beauty for over a century, and soon after summer visitors began to arrive here in numbers, preservation efforts were begun. By the end of World War II, Acadia National Park was well along to its present size of over 30,000 acres, or something like half the land on the island (the other half is still in private hands). Focal point of park activities is **Cadillac Mountain,** at 1,530 feet the highest point on America's Atlantic coast. The thing to do at Cadillac Mountain is to hike (or drive) to the top of it for the views. In fact, local people have recognized that those who see the sun break forth on the horizon from Cadillac Mountain are the first people in the United States to greet the new day, so there's a "Sunrise from Mount Cadillac Club." You can join by picking up a blank from the Bar Harbor information bureau, and filling it out with the help of your hotel manager the night *before* you plan to see the sunrise. Then, if you follow through, you get to be a member of this exclusive club.

Besides Cadillac Mountain, the first thing to do in the park is drive the Loop Road, a one-way scenic ocean drive which takes you past many of the most interesting scenic, topographic, and geologic features of the island. Admission to the park is $5 per car; this pass is good for seven days. Stop at **Thunder Hole** when the surf's up to feel the bashing and pushing of the waves, or at **Sand Beach** for a chilly ocean swim. There's national park camping at **Black Woods** (follow the signs). This is the only campground where you can reserve ahead; call your local Ticketron outlet as early as the spring for reservations.

On the island's western peninsula, **Echo Lake** is the park's freshwater swimming area; there's a lookout tower atop **Beech Mountain,** and a park campground is down near the peninsula's southern tip at **Seawall.** And throughout the park are 100 miles of hiking trails (maps sold at park headquarters), and lots of "carriage roads" good for bike trips or horseback riding (horses can be rented in the park).

Not far from the town of Bar Harbor, in the park at Sieur des Monts Spring, is the **Abbe Museum of Stone Age Antiquities,** a wildflower garden, and a nature center. There's no admission charge to the park proper, but there are fees for various activities such as the campgrounds.

The beach at **Seal Harbor** is very fine, and open to the public for free. Park in the lot across the street. Seal Harbor, by the way, is one of Mount Desert Island's poshest summer resorts, with all sorts of famous and wealthy people inhabiting the big houses secluded along the forested streets of the village.

A visit to Acadia National Park wouldn't be complete without tea and popovers ($5) at the **Jordan House** (tel. 276-3116). A tradition for almost 100 years, the restaurant serves lunch on the porch from 11:30am to 2:30pm, afternoon tea on the lawn from 2:30 to 5:30pm, and dinner by the fireside from 5:30 to 9pm. You can get snacks and beverages on the overlook throughout the day from 9am to 6pm. Whether you dine or not, you are invited to stroll around the gardens and spacious grounds; the view of the lake and mountains from the lawn is stunning. Open late May to late October.

Tours

National Park Tours (tel. 207/288-3327) runs two tours daily from Bar Harbor, beginning from Testa's Hotel, 53 Main St. The cost is $10 per adult, $5 per child under 12. The tour takes you through the town of Bar Harbor and stops at many of the mansions left from its heyday, and also past Cadillac Mountain, Sieur des Monts Spring, and Thunder Hole. Traditionally the tours have left at 10am and 2pm, but call in advance to check the times, and to make a reservation.

If you have a car, you can rent a cassette tape recorder with a prerecorded tour narration from **Sightseeing Tapes, Inc.** You pay the $10 rental fee for the tape and player ($7 if you only rent the tape), and start out to follow the description of many interesting points in the national park. The advantage here is that this tour is cheaper overall if you have several people in your car, and you can turn off the tape at any time should you want to spend a while at some point. Tapes and machines are for rent at the National Park Visitor Center (tel. 288-5262) at Hulls Cove, the first park entrance you come to when approaching Bar Harbor from the north on Rte. 3.

A Ferry to Nova Scotia

The Marine Atlantic ship M.V. *Bluenose* sails from Bar Harbor to Yarmouth, Nova Scotia, and back again daily in summer between late June and late September. It's a car-ferry with room for 1,000 passengers and 250 cars, a sundeck, buffet, dining room, cafeteria, bar, casino, and duty-free shop. The *Bluenose* leaves Bar Harbor every morning in summer and returns from Yarmouth in late afternoon, arriving back in Bar Harbor at night. The trip takes about 6 hours each way, and costs $38 per adult, $18 per child 5 to 13 years; cars cost $70; trailers and campers cost $135 up to 30 feet long, with a summertime minimum charge of the normal car's fare. You can rent a day-use cabin for an extra $35. Off-season schedules are such that the ferry leaves Bar Harbor one day and returns the next; fares are about 25% lower. The vehicle fees do not include the driver's ticket, so a car-and-driver crossing in summer would pay over $100, and a family of four with a car would pay over $350 for the journey round trip. Note that *you must make reservations in advance.* Write to the Marine Atlantic Reservations Bureau, P.O. Box 250, North Sydney, NS B2A 3M3, Canada; or call these toll-free numbers: in Maine 800/432-7344; in the continental U.S. 800/341-7981. The number in Bar Harbor is 207/288-3395. In Yarmouth call 902/742-3513.

ON TO CANADA

The coastal highway, U.S. 1, winds east and north from Ellsworth. You might want to wander south along Rte. 186 for views of the scenic **Schoodic Peninsula.** If not, head ever northeastward, toward the Canadian frontier.

When you get to Cobscook Bay, you will have reached the easternmost limits of the United States. Cobscook Bay can boast two state parks, **Cobscook Bay State Park** and **Quoddy Head State Park.** Another park is even more interesting, however.

Roosevelt Campobello International Park

A Canadian island with an Italian-sounding name on which an American president spent his summers? These little mysteries are not at all as difficult to solve as one might suppose. Campobello Island is officially part of Canada, even though the major access road comes from Lubec, Maine. And the "Italian" name is nothing more than the name of a former Nova Scotian governor, William Campbell, with two "o's" added for exotic flavor. When the island was granted to Capt. William Owen by Governor Campbell in 1767, it was still part of the Canadian province of Nova Scotia. (The province of New Brunswick was not formed until 1784, when large numbers of United Empire Loyalists fled New England to live in King George III's still-loyal dominions to the north.)

Franklin Delano Roosevelt's father, James, bought some land on the island in 1883, at a time when lots of important city people were building vast "summer cottages" at Bar Harbor, Passamaquoddy Bay, and other northern coastal locations. Young Franklin—to solve that last little mystery—came here long before he was President of the United States, and spent many a teenaged summer rowing, paddling, and sailing on the waters, and hiking through the woods.

In 1920 FDR ran for the vice-presidency—and lost. Taking on a banking job instead, he looked forward to a relaxing summer at Campobello in 1921. On August 10 of that year the first signs of illness showed, and two weeks later the doctors diagnosed the crippling disease as polio. When he left the island in September, he had no way of knowing that the few more times he would see the summer cottage and his Campobello friends would be brief weekend visits—as President of the United States.

The day-to-day lives of the great and powerful are fascinating to explore in detail, and a visit to the Roosevelt house on Campobello Island gives one a peek at the early years of this incredibly courageous man who went on to become governor of New York and President of the United States after having been crippled by polio. It is no less intriguing to see how a well-to-do family spent its summers at the turn of the century, with long and leisurely days filled by sports, games, and family fun. Servants saw to the chores, and even they must have enjoyed getting away from the city to such a beautiful spot.

The Roosevelt Cottage is now part of Roosevelt Campobello International Park, a joint American-Canadian effort open the Saturday prior to Memorial Day until Columbus Day from 9am to 5pm. Guides at the reception center will point out the path to the Roosevelt Cottage, show you movies about the island, and map out the various walks and drives in the 2,600-acre nature preserve.

Calais–St. Stephen

Residents of Maine and New Brunswick, while the best of friends, cling to memories of their ancestors' fervent support for, respectively, George Washington and George III. With the success of the American Revolution, United Empire Loyalists flocked across the frontier into Canada so as not to be disloyal to the monarch. The "Loyalist" and "Revolutionary" towns preserve this good-natured rivalry.

But things are different in Calais, Me. (pronounced like "callous"), and its sister city, St. Stephen, N.B. Folks in these two towns, cheek-by-jowl on the St. Croix River, make a point of telling visitors how they ignored the affinities of *both* sides during the War of 1812, and St. Stephen even supplied powder-poor Calais with gunpowder for its Fourth of July celebrations! In fact, by the time the war came, families in the twin towns were so closely intermarried that no one wanted to take the time to sort out who should be loyal to whom.

These days residents celebrate this unique plague-on-both-their-houses philosophy with an International Festival in the first week of August. The two bridges over the river between the towns are thronged with merrymakers moving back and forth —through the watchful but benevolent eye of customs, of course—and Canadian and American flags fly everywhere.

Despite its interesting history, there's little to detain you in Calais, and soon you'll be heading onward, into Canada (see *Frommer's Canada*), or back down U.S. 1 to points south and west. When you return home, however, you'll know what the maritime forecasters mean when they predict weather for the coastline "from Eastport (on Cobscook Bay) to Block Island (Rhode Island)." And you'll be able to say that you've been at the easternmost point in the United States.

VERMONT

The Green Mountain State is one of the nation's most rural, with lots of trees and very few people—only about half a million (people, not trees) in the whole state. But the greenery is Vermont's glory, and green has even become the color of the state's auto license plates. To protect the sylvan beauty of the state, and to keep the roads from becoming cluttered with "off-site advertising," the state government has devised a plan whereby participating stores, restaurants, lodging places, and attractions put information on their establishments in a little book called the *Vermont Visitors' Handbook,* yours for free by writing to the Vermont Development Agency, Montpelier, VT 05602. The establishments in the handbook have numbers, and an attractive green sign out on the highway nearby will direct you to the store, restaurant, or motel, and will also bear its number.

Skiing is another of Vermont's glories, and resorts in this state are usually more winter- than summer-oriented. Heavy precipitation gives many ski areas a good, long season, and the mountain scenery and imported "alpine" architecture help get one into the spirit of winter fun. No Vermont lodge would think of opening without its fireplace stocked with logs to give the glow to an après-ski cocktail and conversation.

Although winter is its prime season, Vermont is very much open in summer. Room rates are lower, many ski resorts run their chair and gondola lifts for sightseers, and the state parks do a booming business with campers, hikers, and picnickers. And, winter or summer, most places in Vermont have the distinct advantage of being quite accessible, whether you plan to come by car, bus, train, or air.

The tax on rooms and meals is **6%,** and the telephone area code for the entire state is **802.**

INFORMATION

Vermont rates tourism as its second most important industry, and it's therefore out to tell you what you want to know. In New York City, inquire at the **New England Vacation Center,** 630 Fifth Ave., between 50th and 51st Streets, Rockefeller Center Concourse Shop No. 2 (tel. 212/307-5780). State information booths are maintained on the major access roads to the state; stop at one for a map and for the *Vermont Visitors' Handbook* mentioned above.

---

1. Getting There

For being so rural, resorts and towns in Vermont are surprisingly accessible.

BY CAR

The fastest way to get anywhere by car is to take the Interstates: I-91 from New York City and Connecticut, I-93 to I-89 from Boston, and Canada 10 to 133 to I-89 if you're driving from Montréal. But the heart of Vermont is on and off Vermont's Rte. 100 which winds through the center of the state from north to south, linking most of the resort areas. By the way, Vermont has a law which prohibits skis from sticking out beyond the normal width of the car. Roads are very well maintained in Vermont in winter, but remember that the roads into the mountains are gradients, so it's best to have snowtires. Dry gas, to prevent your fuel lines from freezing, isn't a bad idea either.

BY AIR

Vermont's largest city, Burlington, is served by several major air carriers and their regional commuter subsidiaries such as Business Express (Delta Connection), Metro Airlines (Trans World Express), and Bar Harbor Airlines (Continental Express). In addition, USAir, United Airlines, and Continental Airlines have direct flights to Burlington in large aircraft. Direct flights go to Burlington from Atlanta, Boston, Buffalo, Chicago, Cleveland, New York City, Orlando, Philadelphia, Pittsburgh, and Washington, D.C.

BY RAIL

Two Amtrak trains serve Vermont, both running between New York City and Montréal. The *Montrealer* runs daily between Washington, D.C., via New York City to Montréal, stopping in Brattleboro (for Mt. Snow), Bellows Falls, White River Junction (for Woodstock and Killington), Montpelier, Waterbury (for Stowe), Essex Junction (for Burlington), and St. Albans. Unfortunately, the *Montrealer* is the New York–Montréal night train.

The *Adirondack* runs daily between New York City and Montréal, skirting Vermont as it runs up the Hudson. Stops at Whitehall (for Rutland), Port Henry, and Port Kent (for Burlington) are the most convenient for reaching points in Vermont, although there are lots of other stops. The *Adirondack* is a day train.

BY BUS

Luckily for visitors, Vermont has its own large bus line, **Vermont Transit Lines** (tel. 212/594-2000), which operates from New York (in conjunction with

Greyhound/Trailways), Montréal (in conjunction with Voyageur), and Boston to virtually all points of interest in Vermont. Other services run from Portsmouth, N.H., Portland, Me., and Concord, N.H., to points in Vermont.

2. Brattleboro

The first town you are likely to encounter if you come from New York or Boston is Brattleboro, and in a way this is as it should be, for Brattleboro was the site of Vermont's first colonial settlement. In 1724 a small fortress was built at the spot now marked by a granite commemoration stone, and named Fort Dummer. There had been white settlers in the area before that, but the fort became the focal point of a community as well as its principal defense against the Indians.

Today Brattleboro is one of the state's larger towns, with a population around 13,000, and industries that range from printing and book manufacture to furniture making and the manufacture of optical products. As for famous sons, the great Mormon leader Brigham Young was born (1801) nearby in Windham County, and Rudyard Kipling married a Brattleboro woman in 1892, and they lived near the town for some time.

Brattleboro has some attractive residential sections and a decent collection of lodging places and dining places. The largest collection of motels is on U.S. 5 north of Brattleboro on the way to Putney (Exit 3N from I-95); another collection of places to stay and to dine is on Rte. 9 west of Brattleboro (I-95 Exit 2).

If you have an hour to spend in town before you rush off to the music festival at Marlboro, or the hiking and skiing at surrounding resorts, check out the **Brattleboro Museum & Art Center,** in the town's old Union Station down near the intersection of Rtes. 119, 142, and U.S. 5, only a few steps from the center of town. It's open Tuesday through Friday from noon to 4, on Saturday and Sunday from 1 to 4pm. Donations are accepted.

INFORMATION

The chamber of commerce **Information office** is at 180 Main St., right in the center of town (tel. 802/254-4565), open during business hours.

WHERE TO STAY

Most of Brattleboro's lodging places are highway motels, and most of these are arranged along U.S. 5 (Putney Road) north of Brattleboro.

The best motel buy in town is, as always, the **Susse Chalet Motor Lodge,** Brattleboro, VT 05301 (tel. 802/254-6007, or toll free 800/258-1980). The 59-room motel charges $38 single, $42 double, for a room equipped with a remote-control color TV. The motel even has a small outdoor swimming pool.

WHERE TO DINE

Brattleboro's restaurants are found out in the countryside as well as downtown. **Common Ground** (tel. 257-0855) is downtown Brattleboro's oldest natural-foods restaurant. The location also serves as a popular coffeehouse (live music on weekends) and gallery for local artists. It's at 25 Elliot St. (upstairs), and its second-floor location allows it to utilize a glassed-in patio terrace where diners may sit throughout the year. The menu is interesting and international, with Wednesday night set aside entirely for dishes from Italy, China, Mexico, the Middle East, India, the Caribbean, Japan, and the U.S.A., to name but a few. The prices are certainly reasonable (about $8 for lunch and $16 for dinner), the food delicious, and the staff friendly. Common Ground is open every day except Tuesday till 9pm.

Near Common Ground is Brattleboro's Italian restaurant, the **Via Condotti,** 69 Elliot St. (tel. 257-0094), just a block off Main in the center of town. Stucco walls give the place an old-country air, and copper kitchen utensils hung here and there add to the effect. The menu goes from grinders (the large sandwiches at $4.50) to calamari alla marinara (squid). Pasta dishes, such as baked manicotti, cost less than $7; the price range ascends slowly to a high of $12 for the veal parmigiana. In the restaurant's La Grotta lounge, wine is sold by the glass, half liter, or liter, beer by the mug or the pitcher, and all sorts of cocktails are available. The Via Condotti is open seven days a week, Monday through Saturday for lunch and dinner, on Sunday for dinner from 2pm; the lounge is open from 4pm to 1am daily, with food service until 10pm on weekdays, to 11pm on weekends.

Although Brattleboro is a nice city, it's the surrounding villages and resorts that draw the crowds. One of the most popular of these is Marlboro, home of the famous annual Marlboro Music Festival.

---

3. Marlboro and Wilmington

West of Brattleboro are some of Vermont's—and all New England's— loveliest unspoiled villages, worthy of a few days' stay, or at least a meal or a rest stop. Marlboro and Wilmington are on Rte. 9, west of Brattleboro, in the direction of Bennington.

MARLBORO

The town's name brings to mind immediately the summertime **Marlboro Music School and Festival,** directed by Rudolf Serkin for many years. The festival brings together dozens of the most talented musicians in the country, some famous and some soon to be famous, for two months' practice, consultation, and tutorial. On weekends from mid-July to mid-August the school is opened to concert audiences, most of whom have ordered their tickets weeks or months in advance and have also made early lodging reservations. The auditorium at Marlboro College seats fewer than 700 people, and to keep the spirit of the chamber music, directors and performers resist demands for a larger hall. If you're interested in attending weekend festival concerts, write early to Marlboro Music, Marlboro, VT 05344 (tel. 802/254-2394); this is the address to use from late June through mid-August. From September through mid-June, write to Marlboro Music, 135 S. 18th St., Philadelphia, PA 19103 (tel. 215/569-4690). Or you can phone the box office at tel. 802/254-2394, and ask for schedules, prices and purchase forms. Then, when you've got your tickets, make a reservation either in Marlboro, or nearby Brattleboro or Wilmington, or even in Bennington—that city is only a 45-minute drive away through the forests of southern Vermont.

Where to Stay and Eat

Marlboro is a location more than a bustling town, although when you drive to the dot on the map you will find a church, a small town office building, and several houses. But that's about all, and so for many products and services you must drive to Brattleboro. Several inns and restaurants in the area, however, provide well for travelers year round, as well as for festival visitors.

The only lodging house right in Marlboro proper is the fine old **Whetstone Inn,** Marlboro, VT 05344 (tel. 802/254-2500). The Whetstone has been an inn for close to two centuries: The upstairs was once a "ballroom" where the local gentry could stage their get-togethers; the downstairs was a tavern along the stagecoach route between Boston and Albany. In winter, cross-country ski trails start at the inn's back door. The inn's pond (the reservoir in case of fire) is right out back. As there's no great activity in the town, nothing will disturb you unless you take to your feet or your bicycle to go to the music festival, 2 miles away. Many rooms at the Whetstone Inn have private bathrooms; rates are $32 to $64 single, $58 to $90 double, the higher rates for rooms with a private bath or a kitchenette. During the Marlboro Music Festival a three-night weekend stay is required. Meals are not included, but you can get breakfast each morning (waffles, pancakes, popovers, and home-baked muffins and biscuits), dinners on concert nights during the summer and on weekends and certain weekdays at other times in the year.

Only a short drive from Marlboro College and the music festival is the **Longwood Inn,** P.O. Box 86, Marlboro, VT 05344 (tel. 802/257-1545), on Rte. 9, a fine old Vermont clapboard dwelling over two centuries old. Innkeepers Andrea and Douglas Sauer took over the inn a few years ago, and have maintained a good reputation for warm hospitality and excellent cuisine. The inn's 15 rooms (all but two of them with private bath) are pretty and country-comfortable. It is the dining room, however, that is the center of inn life. The cuisine is up-to-date American regional; the menu changes weekly. During the summer season when the music festival is running, and also during foliage season (till Columbus Day), the inn serves all three meals every day. At other times of the year, breakfast is provided for inn guests, and dinner is served to all Wednesday through Sunday. Rates for the guest rooms are $120 to $175 double in high season, breakfast included. If you want breakfast and dinner (which may at times be required), rates are $164 to $227 double.

The **Skyline Restaurant** (tel. 464-5535) is just across Rte. 9 from a hilltop lookout. The restaurant is open daily in summer from 8am to 8pm; winter hours are 8am to 3pm on Monday and Tuesday, to 8pm. Wednesday through Sunday. Thus you can start the day here with a breakfast of griddle cakes and maple syrup for about $6. Luncheon-special plates cost $8 to $10; entrees à la carte cost about $10 to $15. For dinner, pan-fried trout with almond butter is a good choice, or have baked stuffed sole, or fresh-cut filet mignon with sautéed mushrooms. The emphasis at the Skyline is obviously not on the expensive or exotic, but rather on traditional dishes made with care and with the best local ingredients. Rough-wood furniture and accents make the decor, and fresh flowers cheer up every table in season. During the cold weather, the cheer is provided by a fireplace and as always, by the friendliness of the staff and management.

Hogback Skiing

The Hogback area (tel. 802/464-5494) is small but pleasant, with four T-bars taking skiers to the top of a 500-foot vertical drop. It's a favorite with local people and with families, and has a cafeteria, equipment-rental shop, and plans for ski touring.

WILMINGTON

Almost equidistant between Brattleboro and Bennington is Wilmington, a crossroads town where Rte. 9 meets Rte. 100. Many people pass through Wilmington as they begin their journey northward along Vermont's central scenic artery, Rte. 100. There are many good inns here, partly because it's a crossroads and partly because it is close to the ski slopes of Mt. Snow.

Where to Stay

What's in a name? Well, there's surely some reason why Jim McGovern named his place the **Hermitage Inn,** P.O. Box 457, Wilmington, VT 05363 (tel. 802/464-3511), on Coldbrook Road; follow Rte. 100 north for about 2½ miles, turn left onto Coldbrook Road, and the inn is about 3 miles along. When you see the inn, you'll understand: Jim raises his own game birds, makes his own maple syrup and jam, and has a vast and well-selected wine cellar. If he ever wanted to be a hermit, he'd be set for life. You can become a hermit in this plentiful hideaway, which was once the home of the editor of the *Social Register.* The main house is over a century old, has some of the original furnishings and many others from the same period, and offers 11 of 15 guest rooms with working fireplaces; all have private bath. As you might expect from the bounty described above, the dining here is superb and exceptional, with lots of game fowl, trout, and fresh home-grown vegetables, plus wines from that venerable cellar, which has been abuilding for almost three decades. The inn's other attractions include fine views of Haystack Mountain, lots of ski trails, a tennis court, trout pond, and a shop full of the local crafts and preserves. It's a real country experience, not a citified country inn. Rates are $220 to $244 double, breakfast and dinner included; lunch is sometimes served during the busy summer season, at an extra charge.

The **White House of Wilmington,** Rte. 9, Wilmington, VT 05363 (tel. 802/ 464-2135), could well be this area's most elegant and gracious inn. Housed in an imposing turn-of-the-century (1914) mansion with lofty porticoes and high-ceilinged public rooms with elegant furniture, it has a dozen charming, spacious guest rooms with private bath; five of them have a fireplace. The White House is a complete resort, really, with a 60-foot outdoor swimming pool, an indoor pool, sauna, whirlpool, a lovely rose garden complete with fountain, and lots of hiking and cross-country ski trails. The dining room is very well regarded, and serves breakfast and dinner daily. On Sunday, there's brunch and, in winter, a special skiers' lunch. Rooms are rented with breakfast and dinner included in the price, at $210 to $256 double.

And now for a special place. **Trail's End** is about 5 miles from Mount Snow, 4 miles north of Wilmington, VT 05363, off Rte. 100 (tel. 802/464-2727) on a side road (watch for small signs). Despite its woodland location, Trail's End is no backwoods establishment, for it has a swimming pool, clay tennis court, and trout pond, and a dining room in which remarkably delicious meals are the rule. The rates both summer and winter are usually based on room and breakfast; $70 double for a small room with double bed and shower; a larger room with a queen-size bed costs $90 to $133 double. Service charge of 10% and a tax of 6% are included in these prices. Trail's End is certainly one of Mount Snow's most attractive, architecturally interesting, congenial places to stay.

Where to Dine

You can get good value at the **Roadhouse,** on Rte. 100 at Old Ark Road in Wilmington (tel. 464-5017 or 464-5694). For a full dinner of standard favorites, dessert and home-baked bread included, expect to pay only about $20 to $25. This is not a fancy place, just solid country-casual eating and full bar at a reasonable price. Open daily from 5 to 10pm.

---

4. Bennington

"Vermont's most historic area" is how the citizens of Bennington tout their town. The reason for this civic pride is that the Revolutionary War's Battle of Bennington was fought near here (the actual site is now in neighboring Walloomsac, N.Y.) in 1777. The battle is looked upon as a turning point in the war, since the British troops expected to encounter little resistance at Bennington and instead were forced to retreat after having lost a good number of casualties and prisoners to the Revolutionaries. Soon afterward, at the Battle of Saratoga, the British soldiers thus weakened were forced to surrender, giving the Americans their first great victory of the war.

Although the Battle of Bennington was certainly influential in the winning of the war, it is doubtless remembered so well today because of a 300-foot-high obelisk that was built in 1891 to commemorate it. Both the monument (which has an observation platform) and the well-known Bennington Museum's collection of Americana are open to visitors.

INFORMATION

The **Bennington Area Chamber of Commerce** is at Veteran's Memorial Drive (Rte. 7 North; tel. 802/447-3311 or 442-1162), about a mile from the intersection of Main and North/South streets. Open during business hours, the chamber can give you a good, detailed map of the town and lots of information on both the town and the surrounding region.

WHERE TO STAY

Bennington has dozens of motels on the highways that approach it, but as is my custom I will concentrate most heavily on the establishments right in town. Several are within only a few blocks of the monument, the museum, and Old Bennington.

Inns

The **Four Chimneys Restaurant & Inn,** 21 West Rd. (Rte. 9 West), Old Bennington, VT 05201 (tel. 802/447-3500), is noted mostly for its restaurant (see below), but it does have several spacious, pleasant, comfortable guest rooms priced at $110 to $135 double, tax included. Continental breakfast, served in your room or in the restaurant, is included in the price.

About 15 miles north of Bennington is the village of Arlington, which has a number of its own hostelries, in the town proper or on Rte. 7A between Bennington and Arlington.

The **Hill Farm Inn** is north of Bennington, and 4 miles north of Arlington, just off Rte. 7A (R.R. 2, Box 2015), Arlington, VT 05250 (tel. 802/375-2269 or toll free 800/882-2545). Though the inn has been receiving guests since 1905, it was actually built as two farmhouses in the early 1800s. Of the 11 guest rooms and two suites, seven are in the inn proper, and six in the 1790 guesthouse next door. With shared bath, breakfast, and dinner, the double rate is $96, tax included; with private bath, it's $112.

Motels

Try the **Best Western New Englander Motor Inn,** 220 Northside Dr. (Rte. Business 7A between Bennington and North Bennington), Bennington, VT 05201 (tel. 802/442-6311, or toll free 800/528-1234). The New Englander is a fairly large motel of over 50 rooms arranged around a central court with a swimming pool and the motel's restaurant, which helps block noise from the busy street. As this is Bennington, the rooms have been done with Early American inspiration, although all furnishings are modern. In the clutter and strip development of Northside Drive, the New Englander is a very pleasant oasis, complete unto itself, and rooms are moderately priced at $64 to $88 for a double-bedded room for two, $78 for a similar room equipped with a steambath, $54 to $68 for a room with one double and one twin bed (a slightly smaller room), and $5 for an extra person. Note that the New Englander's rooms have cable color TV, coffee maker, and air conditioning. It's a comfortable, pleasant place.

The **Kirkside Motor Lodge** is just that: right beside the handsome Gothic church, at 250 W. Main St., Bennington, VT 05201 (tel. 802/447-7596). Rates are $55 for a double bed, $62 for a queen-size bed, $69 for a king-size bed, all rooms for two people. Off-season, prices will be about one-third less, but during foliage season they're a few dollars higher. The rooms come with cable color TV and the usual motel comforts, only here they're shiny and new. There's little problem with street noise because of the motel's position and location. If you stay here, you'll be about equidistant from the center of town and the museum and monument.

The **Bennington Motor Inn,** 143 W. Main St., Bennington, VT 05201 (tel. 802/442-5479 or toll free 800/359-9900), has 16 little units right at the base of the hill holding the museum and monument. The little extras here include coffee makers in the rooms, color TV (with cable and in-room movies), individual thermostats, air conditioners, and direct-dial telephones. Some of the larger rooms, designated family units, can sleep up to six people, and these rooms also have little refrigerators for baby's bottle—or for papa's. In one queen bed two people pay $42 to $50; for two beds they pay $46 to $56, and an extra person pays $5. An extra bed is $4; foliage-season rates are higher.

A Guesthouse

Luckily, Bennington is particularly well endowed with fine guesthouses, those establishments which give you more warmth and home comfort than any other type of lodging place. One of the nicest and best located is in the grand old house at 226 W. Main St., Bennington, VT 05201, not far from the Bennington Museum.

WHERE TO EAT

A few restaurants in Bennington (besides those in the motels) provide plain and fancy cuisine for travelers and local folks. I'll start with the fancy places.

Fanciest of Bennington's dining spots is undoubtedly the **Four Chimneys Restaurant,** 21 West Rd. (Rte. 9 West) in Old Bennington (tel. 447-3500), only a half mile west of the Bennington Museum. This imposing and many-chimney'd white mansion shaded by huge old trees set in spacious, well-tended grounds was once the home of a prominent Bennington businessman. Now its formal salons, informal solarium, patio, and terraces are set up for elegant dining. Chef Alex Koks' English-language menu is admirably straightforward: What would be "magret de canard, sauce framboise" in a more pretentious place is "broiled breast of duck with raspberry vinegar sauce" at the Four Chimneys—and just as delicious. Classics such as beef Wellington, rack of lamb, and roast Cornish game hen come in preparations that are interesting and original without being hyperexotic. The food is excellent, the service the same. Luncheon, on a pleasant summer's day, is a special treat, and costs around $15 to $18 per person, tax, tip and drink included. For dinner, prices are $25 to $35 per person, all in. House wines are under $15 the bottle, several good selections cost $20 or less, and most bottles are under $35. Lunch is served daily from 11:30am to 2pm, dinner from 5pm on; Sunday dinner begins at noon.

In Bennington there is a place called the Potters' Yard, a complex of shops and galleries in which local works of art and craft are displayed and sold, and in this same complex at School and Country streets is the **Brasserie at the Potters' Yard** (tel. 447-7922). As the name might suggest, the Brasserie is fashioned on a French tavern restaurant, with beer and wine and delicious dishes such as the pâté maison with French bread or chicken curry. For lunch, have the Yard Special, a platter with Danish pâté, French bread, butter, and a Boston lettuce salad, for $5. A chef's salad or Greek salad and a variety of sandwiches or omelets are about the same. The patio is the choice place to dine in good weather: It's paved in marble, and the little café tables all have marble or granite tops. Note that the Brasserie is open from Wednesday through Monday 11:30am to 8pm. To get to the Brasserie and Potters' Yard, turn off Main Street by the Dunkin' Donuts (which is at 460 Main), and go straight down the street until it ends right at the Yard.

Bennington's purveyor of the daily fresh and delicious is **Alldays & Onions,** 519 Main St. (tel. 447-0043), a combination country store, delicatessen, gourmet food shop, restaurant and bistro, open from 7am to 5:30pm Monday through Saturday, Tuesday through Saturday 6 to 9pm. Drop by and join the assortment of locals and travelers, Bennington College students and professors for freshly baked morning muffins and Colombian coffee, a wonderful create-your-own sandwich, or a cool pasta salad. Evening suppers often feature enticing pasta dishes or fish. Expect to spend about $5 to $8 for lunch, $14 to $18 for supper here. They have a small but good eclectic wine selection.

WHAT TO SEE

The historic sights of the town are mostly grouped along West Main Street, in the section called Old Bennington. You can buy a single ticket which admits you to the town's three most important sights: the Bennington Museum, the Bennington Battle Monument, and the Park-McCullough House, for $8.50 per adult, $6.50 per senior, $6 for a child age 12 to 17, or 50¢ for a child age 6 to 11 (under 6 get in free). The ticket represents a small savings over the price of three individual admission tickets. Pick yours up at the Bennington Area Chamber of Commerce, the Bennington Museum, or the Park-McCullough House.

The Bennington Museum

The Bennington Museum, West Main Street (Rte. 9; tel. 447-1571), has a collection dominated by that for which the town was famous: its Revolutionary and

Early American history. Paintings, glass items (molded, blown, and pressed), American-made furniture and carvings, arms, toys, and costumes are all included, and there are considerable numbers of very attractive treasures. The Bennington pottery, for instance, is more like china with its gold or colored trim; it was made here for wealthy customers for over 100 years. Of the paintings, the most fascinating are the ones in the Grandma Moses collection. Anna Mary Moses (1860–1961) was a farm girl in nearby New York State, and later as a farmer's wife she did all the heavy, hard work that life on a farm demands, yet still found time to paint. After she was 70 years old and could no longer keep up with the heavy farm work, her paintings took on such a charming and primitive character, and such spirit, that one of her paintings now hangs in the Metropolitan in New York, and many others are here in the Bennington Museum. At the age of 100 she was still at work, and she died at 101. You can look back into what life was like for her in the exhibit called "And Life Is What You Make It" in the Grandma Moses Schoolhouse Museum, also in the Bennington Museum.

The Bennington Museum is open daily from 9am to 5pm, March through December; open weekends only January and February. Admission is $5 for adults, $4 for young people, ages 12 to 17 and seniors, free for children under 12, $13 per family.

The Bennington Battle Monument

The impressive obelisk is more than 306 feet tall, which makes it the tallest structure in Vermont. It took four years (1887–91) to build, and when it was finished one could walk to the top by means of an interior staircase. Today the staircase is closed and an elevator hums up and down. Buy your ticket ($1) in the souvenir shop to the west of the monument entrance, and pick up a copy of the free leaflet describing the battle and the monument.

This was not the site of the battle, but of the colonists' arsenal which was the object of the British advance. His supplies depleted by the action at Fort Ticonderoga, "Gentleman Johnny" Burgoyne sent two of his units toward Bennington to capture the Revolutionaries' arms stores. But General Burgoyne misjudged the size of the rebel force, and was unaware that General John Stark, who had fought at Bunker Hill and under Washington at Trenton and Princeton, commanded the Americans. Stark cleverly headed off the British advance at Walloomsac (New York), 6 miles west of the arsenal. Stark is said to have exclaimed, "There are the Redcoats! They will be ours tonight or Molly Stark sleeps a widow."

The pitched battle on August 16, 1777, lasted 2 hours, and when the smoke cleared, the American forces were victorious. On the way back to Bennington, Stark's troops were surprised by British reinforcements, but Colonel Seth Warner and his Green Mountain Boys arrived in time to save the day for the Americans. The losses at Bennington and lack of supplies weakened the British force, and Burgoyne surrendered his entire command in October following the Battle of Saratoga.

The view from the monument is very fine. Though you wouldn't recognize it, you can look west to where the battle actually took place, less than 6 miles away. For a closer view, follow "Bennington Battlefield" signs from the monument through a covered bridge to North Bennington, then west on Rte. 67 to the Bennington Battlefield Historic site near Walloomsac, N.Y. Plaques describe the battle, and shaded picnic tables provide a good place for a rest and a snack.

On the way back, stop in at the Park-McCullough House, just off Rte. 67A in North Bennington.

Park-McCullough Historic House Museum

Of Bennington's outstanding Victorian mansions, one is exceptionally well kept. The Park-McCullough House, at the corner of West and Park streets in North Bennington (tel. 442-5441), is open for guided tours through the house daily, early May through October from 10am to 4pm (last tour leaves at 3pm). Adults pay $3; seniors pay $2.50; students 12 to 17 pay $1.50; children 11 and under accompanied by an adult, free. Besides the house, still stuffed with period furnishings and personal effects, there's a pint-size "manor" for a children's playhouse and a cupola-topped carriagehouse complete with century-old carriages.

While you're here in North Bennington, drive or walk through the campus of **Bennington College,** the unique loosely structured four-year college, which stresses artistic creation and an acquaintance with nature. The situation of the college is particularly beautiful and is particularly well adapted for the creative efforts of the students.

---

5. West Dover and Mount Snow

Because of its southern Vermont location within driving distance of the metropolitan centers of Boston, Hartford, Providence, and New York, Mount Snow is one of Vermont's most popular ski resorts. The ski resort encouraged the inn trade, and the inns began playing host to summer travelers, and now this area is as popular in the warm months as in the cold.

WHERE TO STAY
About 100 inns, lodges, hotels, and motels are clustered near the ski area, on the approach roads, or in the villages near Mount Snow. From this bewildering assortment of choices, several stand out prominently.

Perhaps the most famous inn in the area is the **Inn at Saw Mill Farm,** P.O. Box 367, West Dover, VT 05356 (tel. 802/464-8131). Innkeepers Rodney and Ione Williams, along with their son, Brill, run the sort of inn that appears regularly in designer magazines with lavish spreads of photos showing the guest rooms—Victorian, Federal, turn-of-the-century—in the inn's various buildings. The dining rooms are particularly beautiful, providing the perfect ambience for cozy, romantic dinners of elegant, carefully prepared dishes from a positively sumptuous menu. On the inn's carefully tended grounds are a swimming pool, several fish ponds, and a tennis court. The inn proper, an old farmhouse and barn, houses 11 guest rooms, all with private bath. In addition, there are 10 rooms in other buildings, each with a fireplace and private bath. Rates are $284 to $371 double, breakfast and dinner included. Prices may be a bit higher in foliage season, and between Christmas and New Year's. Note that the inn has an annual closing from mid-March to mid-May, and that *no credit cards are accepted.* Children under 10 cannot be lodged at the inn. To find the Inn at Saw Mill Farm, get to West Dover on Rte. 100, and follow the signs.

Kitzhof, on Rte. 100 in West Dover, VT 05356 (tel. 802/464-8310), is a particularly nice alpine-style lodge set back from the highway, charging quite moderate prices. No two rooms are alike except in their comfort, sparkling cleanliness, and the presence of private bath. Knotty-pine boards and logs and rustic emphasis; a Finnish-style sauna and a whirlpool bath are added luxuries open to all guests. There's a BYOB bar with set-ups. *Per-person* weekend rates in ski season are $70 double, $75 double deluxe, $51 for four in a room. Reductions are in order for lots of things, such as 5½-day economy ski weeks, paying in cash (5%), coming early or late in the ski season. The Kitzhof takes bus tours in summer and can provide lodging for transient guests when there's room.

Where to Eat
A short 5-mile drive north on Route 100 from Mount Snow brings you to the village of West Wardsboro and the **Brush Hill Restaurant** (tel. 896-6100), a late 18th-century post-and-beam barn that's been restored and turned into a romantic dining spot. A 12-foot-long brick fireplace takes the chill off in foliage season; all diners enjoy it, as there are fewer than a dozen tables. Chef Mike Sylva apprenticed at Jaspers in Boston, and while he's in the kitchen creating New American cuisine treats, his wife Lee acts as hostess (but she also makes the desserts). The menu changes daily, but recently dinner started with an unusual antipasto of grilled artichokes, shallots, red pepper, and smoked scamonza, and was followed by a rack of

lamb with mint essence, grilled leeks, and garlic. Dessert may be the dieter's to-order-or-not dilemma, with pastry puffs filled with French vanilla ice cream topped by a chocolate rum sauce. Dinner, the only meal served (Wednesday through Sunday, 6 to 10pm), will cost about $45 to $50 per person, wine, tax, and tip included.

SKIING MOUNT SNOW

The ski area is immense, with three different faces of the mountain covered with trails and lifts—13 lifts in all, including two enclosed, skis-on gondolas. The highest vertical drop is almost 2,000 feet, and you could take the same lift a dozen times and never come down the same trail or slope. It's crowded, yes, because it's close to the cities, and is a good mountain for beginners and intermediate skiers, but it's also got a lot of variety, and certainly a lot of activity. A resort this big has all the facilities: a "Pumpkin Patch" nursery for small children, a bar, a cafeteria, and equipment rentals, a ski school, and 40 miles of cross-country trails.

---

6. Newfane and Grafton

Two of Vermont's most picture-perfect towns, with tall old trees, white churches with high steeples, and gracious old houses designed with classical touches: that's Newfane and Grafton. Come early in spring when they're "sugaring off," and see town children tap the maple trees along village streets. Come in summer and explore for yard and antiques sales. Come in autumn for the blazing color. Or come in winter to hide away in a comfy inn and dine each night from a superb menu.

NEWFANE

The best place to stay or dine in Newfane is the **Four Columns Inn,** P.O. Box 278, Newfane, VT 05345 (tel. 802/365-7713). Except for two weeks after Thanksgiving and three weeks in April, when the inn is closed, you can come for dinner any night Wednesday through Monday from 6 to 9pm. Find a table in the cozy dining room, which recalls a hunting lodge in Europe with its rough-hewn beams, large fireplace, and spindle-backed chairs. Then get ready for such delicacies as a cold salmon mousse, followed by venison or rack of lamb, duck, or steak, finishing up with fancy pastries. The wine list has vintages priced from $14 to $50, and a full dinner for two here might cost $80 to $125.

As for the guest rooms, they are as charming as the inn and the town, and rent for $101 to $132 double, with private bath, air conditioning, and breakfast included.

GRAFTON

Like Newfane, Grafton is a piece of old New England, but there is a nobility about this town—something like Woodstock—that makes it special. Carefully preserved houses and public buildings from a century or two ago are joined unobtrusively by more modern structures on the outskirts. Summer or winter, Grafton is a place bewitching in its beauty. Stop for a cup of coffee, a drink or a meal, or even for overnight. Be careful, though—one overnight easily leads to weeklong stays here.

Grafton's hostelry, the **Old Tavern,** Grafton, VT 05146 (tel. 802/843-2231), is also a town landmark. It's been the center of Grafton's social life since it was built in 1801 as a way station on the stagecoach road. In its long history as a place to stay the night, the Old Tavern has played host to General Grant, Woodrow Wilson, Rudyard Kipling, and even woodsman-philosopher Henry David Thoreau. With its annexes, the inn can lodge about 100 people. Its rooms have private baths and modern conveniences, but the ambience is still old New England. Rates vary with the exact situation, size, and facilities, but range from $58 to $132, and that includes the 6% Vermont tax; *no credit cards accepted*. The Old Tavern is an authentic landmark, but it is not what one would call "quaint." Charming, hospitable, very comfortable —it is all these, though.

You have a choice of dining rooms. The jacket rule is in force each evening. For a drink before dinner, make your way to the Barn, with its own separate bar, several fireplaces, and a TV room. Lunch is served at the Old Tavern from noon to 2pm, and dinner from 6:30 to 9pm, by reservation. At dinner, main courses range from the raisin-stuffed veal steak at $18 to broiled filet mignon at $24, and these prices include soup, relish tray, potato, and vegetable.

What to Do
Grafton is perfect just for relaxing walks and sitting by the fireplace, but there are lots of other things to do as well. Start with a horse-and-carriage ride (in summer) around town. You'll see the driver, her steed, and her buggy at the stand in front of the Old Tavern daily except Sunday between mid-June and the end of October. The ride is not just for fun—you'll get a complete narrative tour of Grafton as you trot along.

Grafton harbors a number of antiques shops, artists' galleries, a village store, and the **Grafton Village Cheese Company** (tel. 843-2221). The Cheese Company makes its own brand, Covered Bridge cheddar, and you can see it being made and buy samples or supplies by following the Townshend Road about a half mile south of the village. Hours are 8:30am to 4pm weekdays all year, 10am to 4:30pm on Saturday from June through October; closed Sunday all year.

By now no doubt you are completely enchanted with the town. To delve into its history, pay a visit to the **Grafton Historical Society Museum** (tel. 843-2584), on Main Street just down from the post office. The exhibits of Grafton memorabilia, old photographs, history, and genealogical files are open from 2:30 to 4:30pm on Saturday from June through mid-October, on Sunday in July and August, and on holiday weekends and holiday Mondays.

7. Manchester and Dorset

MANCHESTER
The town of Manchester was once a summer resort on the order of the Berkshire towns. Settled before the Revolution, the town has a wide main street and handsome houses that retain the charm of the early Federal period.

As the county seat of Bennington County, Manchester was an important place long before Mt. Equinox (3,800 feet), to the west, drew crowds of hikers and skiers. The sprawling Equinox Hotel right in the center of town has undergone an $18-million facelift.

In the modern town of Manchester Center, just a few miles north along U.S. 7, all is bustle and activity, with traffic lights, filling stations, shopping centers, supermarkets, restaurants, motels.

On U.S. 7 is Manchester's modern claim to fame: a beautifully restored house which holds the editorial offices of *Country Journal,* the magazine which has successfully combined city polish with country concerns.

Manchester is busy with locals in the summer, busier with skiers in the winter. Several inns and restaurants serve travelers year round.

Information
The **Manchester and the Mountains Chamber of Commerce** (tel. 802/362-2100) maintains an information office on U.S. 7 in Manchester Center for your convenience.

Where to Stay

The **Equinox Hotel, Resort & Spa,** Manchester, VT 05254 (tel. 802/362-4700), saw its heyday in Victorian times, with four presidents as guests over the years. (It was almost five: Lincoln had reservations for 1865, but was assassinated.) As the inn's fame and clientele grew, wings and additions were added to the original building, making at last a vast, rambling wonder of a place. With its recent facelift, the Equinox is better than ever, and again ready to welcome the best. The 150 rooms here—the management boasts that no two are alike—cost $183 to $231 double. The Equinox has all the facilities of a luxury hotel, and then some: 18-hole golf course, heated swimming pool, five tennis courts, a health fitness center, lounge, restaurant, and Viennese-style bakery. When you get to the old village of Manchester (not the more modern Manchester Center), you can't miss the Equinox, for it dominates the village green.

Close by is the **Inn at Manchester,** P.O. Box 41, Manchester, VT 05254 (tel. 802/362-1793), a restored Vermont Victorian inn with plenty of room for guests in 14 rooms and suites in the inn, and four more in the restored carriagehouse. In the inn proper are six bedrooms with private bath ($111 to $132), five with shared bath ($88 to $99), two two-room family suites ($189), and a suite with king-size bed ($143). In the carriagehouse, the rooms ($134) all have private bath, and there's a separate lounge. The rooms bear the names of delightful mountain and meadow flowers such as primrose, black-eyed Susan, and blue phlox. Antiques are placed carefully in all the rooms, and each bedroom has a different style of coordinated linens and comforters. Old prints, paintings, and posters, picked up by innkeepers Stan and Harriet Rosenberg during their travels, are found on walls throughout the inn. A full breakfast is included in the rates, as are 10% service charge and 6% tax.

What to Do

In winter, this question is easy to answer: You ski. Big Bromley, Snow Valley, Magic Mountain, Stratton Mountain, and numerous ski-touring centers are located within a few miles of Manchester Center. Right in Manchester is the ski-touring center at Hildene, more about which below.

In summer, you can play golf, swim, hike, or ride a bike. Rent a bike from **Battenkill Sports,** in the stone house 1.2 miles east of U.S. 7A along Rte. 11/30, Manchester Center (tel. 362-2734); or from the **Bicycle Shop** in Manchester Hardware, on Rte. 11/30 in Manchester Center (tel. 362-1625). Three-speed, ten-speed, men's, women's, and children's bikes are available.

At the Bromley ski area on Route 11, 6 miles east of Manchester, an **Alpine Slide** (tel. 824-5522) draws downhill racers in summer. You pay the several dollars, take the ski lift to the top, and then choose among the three alpine slide tracks, two-thirds of a mile long, to the bottom. You can control the speed of your little cart as you travel down. The slide is open late May to mid-October from 9am to 5pm, if the weather's good. The slide is fun, and the chair-lift ride that takes you up over the verdant hills is equally enjoyable.

Take in a play at the **Dorset Playhouse** in nearby Dorset (see below for details).

Hildene

Abraham Lincoln had four sons, but only one of them lived to adulthood. When President Lincoln was assassinated in 1865, Robert Todd Lincoln was an officer serving under General Grant in the Union Army. Later a successful lawyer and businessman, Lincoln came to Manchester in 1902, bought 412 acres of land, and began construction of Hildene. The mansion was completed in 1904, and Lincoln spent the summers there until his death in 1926. The estate was inherited by his wife, and then his granddaughter, who left it to the Church of Christ, Scientist, in 1975. It's now owned and maintained by a nonprofit group, the Friends of Hildene (tel. 362-1788).

Robert Todd Lincoln built more than a house here. Hildene's 22 buildings include a dairy barn, horse barn, sugar house, greenhouse, even a small observatory. You can roam the grounds, tour the 22-room Georgian Revival mansion, inspect

Lincoln family heirlooms any day of the week, mid-May through October from 9:30am to 5:30pm. Admission costs $5 for adults, $2 for children. In winter, Hildene is the site of a ski touring center. To find it, go 2 miles south along U.S. 7A from the intersection with Rte. 11/30—the intersection is the main crossroads in Manchester Center.

DORSET

Settled in 1768, Dorset is one of the many villages in New England that is older than the American Republic. It's a gem of a village, having kept its rural spirit and fine buildings intact over the centuries, and any new structures were required to add to the harmony of the village and its setting.

For a number of years Dorset was an artists' and writers' summer resort, but these days it is usually only the successful in those fields who can afford to stay in one of Dorset's few charming old inns; rather, the village now caters to those who have become successful in the city, and who need to get away to the peace of the countryside for a few days or weeks.

In Dorset the sidewalks are marble, and so is a nice church with Gothic touches not far from the town green. There's a marble quarry about a mile south of town, and besides supplying the soft, easily cut stone for a myriad of uses in Dorset, the quarry supplied most of the marble for the New York Public Library building.

For recreation, Dorset has the **Dorset Playhouse** (tel. 802/867-5777), down past the church just past the end of the town green on Cheney Road. Plays are performed June through early September. Also, the **J. K. Adams Company Factory Store,** on Rte. 30 a mile south of town, makes fine wood products—carving boards, butcher blocks, kitchen worktables, even kitchen organizers like a spice block that holds 16 glass jars and revolves on a lazy susan. All the items are available at a reduced price, and the "seconds" are sold at prices up to 40% off the norm.

Where to Stay and Dine

The **Dorset Inn,** right on the town green, Dorset, VT 05251 (tel. 802/867-5500 or 867-9392), claims to be Vermont's oldest continuously operated inn. The inn has several older rooms in the original building, and a larger number of rooms in an artfully disguised modern addition which blends in well with the older part. Room prices include breakfast and dinner, and are $183 double. Tax and 15% service are included in these figures. Dorset Inn guests enjoy privileges at the Field Club, which is virtually next door.

8. Woodstock and Plymouth

Woodstock was chartered in 1761, and within five years it had been designated the shire town (county seat) of Windsor County. The particular significance of these little facts is that they explain why the town is so beautiful today, why so many lovely buildings survive, and why the town escaped the ravages (and riches) brought by 19th-century industry. The industry here was government, the only pollutant from which is hot air, and this rises out of sight at once.

Besides its fine buildings, Woodstock boasts no fewer than four church bells made by Paul Revere. Three are still in service, but one cracked after two centuries of use and is now on display on the south porch of the Congregational church.

Woodstock is particularly well situated, in a beautiful valley of the Ottauquechee River with mountains all around. In winter, skiers can put up in the town while they spend the day on the slopes of Mount Tom or Suicide Six.

INFORMATION

From late June through the foliage season, there is a town information booth in service on the village green. Go here for a free village map and list of town businesses.

WHERE TO STAY
Woodstock has a good variety of accommodations, grouped together here according to type.

Motels
The **Shire Motel** is east of the center of town along Rte. 4, at 46 Pleasant St., Woodstock, VT 05091 (tel. 802/457-2211). It is well kept and has the advantage of being within walking distance of the village green. A room with bath, TV, refrigerator, and air conditioning, and with one queen-size bed, costs $58 for two persons; a larger room with two double beds costs $70. I've found the proprietors at the Shire Motel to be particularly helpful and friendly.

East of town on Rte. 4 is the attractive **Braeside Motel,** P.O. Box 411, Woodstock, VT 05091 (tel. 802/457-1366), set up on the hillside away from road noise. You get the view from here, and also 12 modern wood-paneled rooms with wall-to-wall carpet, cable color TV, and Scottish touches. Prices at the Braeside are $68 to $83 single or double, continental breakfast included.

A Resort Hotel
Woodstock's top of the line is the **Woodstock Inn and Resort,** no. 14 on the green, Woodstock, VT 05091 (tel. 802/457-1100), a very large and plush place which reminds me of a similar style hostelry found in college towns. The guest rooms are all quite new and modern, with color TV, air conditioning, and private baths, but the decorator has tried to keep to the Early American style by using beds, chairs, and papers for a 1700s effect.

Other facilities at the inn include ten tennis courts, two paddle-tennis courts, putting green (the Robert Trent Jones golf course is nearby), and a wading pool. As for food, the Woodstock Inn's "coffee shop" is like many other restaurants, with full-course dinners. The restaurant, then, is super-elegant, and prices there for entrees go from $18 to $24, and you must have a reservation.

As for the rooms, prices are the same year round, and the ones quoted here include tax. Doubles cost $139 to $214; singles are just a few dollars less. No meals are included. You do much better if you avail yourself of a sports package plan—call for details.

WHERE TO DINE
Bentleys of Woodstock is at 3 Elm St. (tel. 457-3232), just a few steps across the village green. In its various dining rooms, Bentleys has captured the spirit of a Victorian tavern but without the heaviness: a pillared bar with potted palms, bentwood chairs, and Victorian sofas. The crowd is eclectic but tends to the young and sophisticated, the prices are moderate, and the food is good and simple or good and fancy. Lunch is burgers and sandwiches, light lunch plates, and salads; for dinner, these same dishes are on order, or you can indulge in a wheel of baked brie, lemon-pepper chicken, Cajun BBQ shrimp, or creative pasta dishes. For lunch, Bentleys is open from 11:30am till about 3pm; for dinner, the hours are 5 to 9:30 or 10pm; there's live entertainment some evenings. Plan to spend around $10 to $14 for lunch, $25 to $35 for dinner per person here.

Very near Bentleys, and right beside the Woodstock Historical Society at 24 Elm St., is **The Prince and the Pauper** (tel. 457-1818), actually down an alley named Dana Lane which runs alongside the society's building. Low-beamed ceilings, candle lanterns casting a golden aura onto the small tables, a worldly clientele, and good conversation are what make the mood here, but the exotic array of dishes and delicacies add to it: Where else would you find calamari in beer batter as an appetizer, or main courses like salmon in pastry? Roast duckling is on the menu too. The menu changes frequently, of course, but the intimate atmosphere and the international flair remain. Expect to pay $35 to $45 per person for dinner, wine, tax and tip included. The Prince and the Pauper is open daily for dinner from 6 to 9:30pm; the lounge opens at 5pm. Reservations are a good idea.

WHAT TO SEE

The Woodstock Historical Society's **Dana House,** on Elm Street (tel. 457-1822), just around the corner from the green, is open for visits Monday through Saturday, early May through late October, from 10am to 5pm, on Sunday 2 to 5pm. Admission costs $3.50 for an adult, $2.50 for a senior citizen, $1 for a child over 12. The collections here are of furniture and paintings, farm implements, and personal effects, and often the displays are as interestingly made as the objects they exhibit.

In your walks around town, you might want to look for the three **covered bridges** across the Ottaquechee, including one built in 1969 and rebuilt five years later—Middle Bridge, just off the green in the middle of town.

On the far side of the Ottaquechee from the town green is a cemetery, and at the east edge of the cemetery is the beginning of a walking trail. The **Billings Park Trails** are maintained by the town, and are yours to enjoy for free.

Quechee Gorge

While in Woodstock, take a spin over to Quechee Gorge, 8 miles to the east. The highway bridge carries U.S. 4 right across the picturesque gorge; below, the Ottaquechee River slips swiftly between boulders and jagged rock walls. The Grand Canyon it's not, but pretty? Definitely.

For the best view, follow the signs to the viewpoint north of the highway. Or enter Quechee State Park, on the east side of the gorge, and take the short hiking trail down to the edge of the gorge. The walk will take 15 minutes, one way. By the way, there's camping and picnicking at Quechee State Park.

SKIING AT WOODSTOCK

Woodstock was the site of the first ski tow in the United States—a rope on a pulley which pulled skiers up the slopes in a farmer's field. Today a well-known ski area is close by, called **Suicide Six.** In addition, the **Woodstock Ski Touring Center,** at the Woodstock Country Club, Rte. 106, Woodstock, VT 05091 (tel. 802/457-2114), has nearly 50 miles of marked trails, plus equipment rental, cross-country ski shop, restaurant and lounge, lessons, ski tours, and midweek ski-free plans with the Woodstock Inn (tel. toll free 800/448-7900). A new indoor sports center is located a mile away.

Suicide Six (despite the terrifying name) is a fine, mid-sized, family ski area with two double-chair lifts, and a free J-bar on the beginners' slope. Located 3 miles north of Woodstock on Rte. 12, it also offers midweek ski-free plans with the Woodstock Inn. Package plans are available through the inn; there is 50% snow-making capability, and lessons and equipment can be had on the spot in a new base lodge which also houses a ski rental shop, restaurant, and lounge (tel. 802/457-1666).

You can stay in Woodstock and ski elsewhere, of course, and the Killington and Pico ski areas present all the challenge and facilities a skier could want. They're just a short drive away.

PLYMOUTH

Calvin Coolidge was born in this tiny Vermont hamlet not far from the intersection of Rtes. 100 and 100A, and you can visit the **Coolidge Homestead** and the **Calvin Coolidge Birthplace** (tel. 828-3226). The former president's early history is interesting, but the story of his "inauguration" is full of fascination. While he was vice-president, Mr. Coolidge came to Plymouth for a vacation in August 1923. Before he could even unwind, news came that President Harding was dead, and that he, Calvin Coolidge, was the 30th president of the United States. But he had to take the oath of office! The local notary public in the tiny town was none other than the new president's own father, Col. John Coolidge, and it was Colonel John who—as the only judicial official handy—administered the oath to his son by the light of a kerosene lamp at 2:47am, August 3, 1923.

You can visit the Homestead, the Birthplace, the **Wilder Barn** (a farmer's museum), the village church, the cemetery where President Coolidge is buried, and **Wilder House,** once the home of Coolidge's mother. Wilder House today holds a small restaurant and lunch counter.

The historic site is open daily Memorial Day through Columbus Day from 9:30am to 5:30pm. Admission for adults costs $2, children under 12 years of age enter for free, and a family ticket costs $6.

But don't miss Plymouth's outstanding attraction, the **Plymouth Cheese Company,** P.O. Box 1, Plymouth, VT 05056 (tel. 802/672-3650). The company's president, Mr. John Coolidge, is a scion of the famous village clan. Come to see the delicious Vermont granular curd cheese being made on weekdays from 11:30am to 1pm, or come to sample and purchase the cheese Monday through Saturday from 8am to 5:30pm, on Sunday from 9am to 5:30pm. Since the first time I tasted it, I've been hooked on Plymouth cheese. It comes cut to order by the ounce or the pound, or in 3- and 5-pound wheels, and it is aged 3, 6, or 12 months to produce mild, medium, or sharp cheddar. Cheeses are also available flavored with sage, caraway, garlic, dill, or pimento. By the way, watching the cheese making costs nothing; the cheese, last time I bought, was about $17 for a 5-pound wheel (I get as much as I can carry).

9. Killington

With many skiers, Killington is the only word they have to hear before they begin thinking snow. The resort is one of Vermont's prime ski areas, and is especially noted for its progressive approach to development of its facilities (for instance, the addition of "gladed" ski trails, which give one the feeling of skiing right in the forest) and its snow-making and grooming capabilities. But in recent years Killington has expanded its breadth of activities so that now you can go there for skiing in winter, organized backpacking and camping trips in the summer, tennis practice and lessons, or for the summer playhouse. The resort is booming, but it is laid out so well on the side of the mountain that there is plenty of room for all the activities and the visitors.

INFORMATION

The whole Killington area, which is part of the town of Sherburne, is organized with the **Killington Lodging Bureau** in charge of making room reservations for you. You can call or write to a lodge or motel directly, or you can call the Lodging Bureau to see what's available at 802/773-1330. The **Killington and Pico Areas Association,** P.O. Box 114, Killington, VT 05751 (tel. 802/775-7070), also maintains an information booth at the junction of U.S. 4 and Rte. 100 in Sherburne, at the Lothlorien Gift Shop; the booth is open during business hours.

WHERE TO STAY AND EAT

Killington is a well-organized resort community, and so virtually all activities here are organized around various package plans which are designed to save visitors money over the normal daily rates. A package would usually include lodging, meals, and the price of the activity: lift tickets, tennis lessons, horseback riding, backpacking trips. In ski season most inns operate on the Modified American Plan (MAP), in which you are required to take breakfast and dinner with your room. Call the Lodging Bureau at 802/773-1330 to ask about the package plans, or to make reservations; or send a card to Killington Ski Area, Killington, VT 05751, asking for information on ski, hiking, or tennis package plans.

Among my favorite places to dine in Killington is **Hemingway's Restaurant,** on Rte. 4 (tel. 422-3886). Established in a restored Vermont farmhouse, the restaurant has won several awards for its dishes. You might start dinner (the only meal served) by ordering hand-rolled fettuccine with smoked trout and scallions, or consommé of rabbit; then go on to shrimp with dark rum and currants, or grilled pheasant with beaujolais. The wine list is full and well balanced, everything from Château Lafitte-Rothschild ($1,565) to Sutter Home white Zinfandel ($12). The restaurant is closed mid-April to mid-May. Expect to pay about $36 per person for a three-course fixed-price dinner which includes hors d'oeuvres and chocolate truffle. There's also a tasting menu which includes wine.

CONDOMINIUM RENTALS

Certainly the most comfortable and luxurious way of all to take a ski or summer vacation at Killington is to rent a fully furnished apartment unit complete with a full kitchen, all linens, a fireplace, perhaps even a dishwasher. A good number of these units, within a half mile of the Killington lifts, are up for rental both winter and summer. Rates vary by what sort of unit you want (a one-bedroom can sleep four, maximum; a two-bedroom does for up to six; a three-bedroom for eight), and also the exact week or weekend you want to rent: a normal Sunday to Friday ski-week rate in the middle of ski season would be $250 per person for a four-person one-bedroom unit. Summer rates run 50% less than the winter rates. For full information and very-necessary reservations, call **The Villages at Killington,** 118 Killington Rd., Killington, VT 05751 (tel. 802/422-3101 or 422-3613, or toll free 800/343-0762).

SKIING AT KILLINGTON AND PICO

Well, here you have it: one of the best-managed ski areas in the United States, with a good snow-making capability, a variety of trails, a well-organized ski school, a very accessible location, lots of parking, three lounges, quick food service or a nice restaurant, several bars, and a long skiing season—what more can I say? The vertical drop is over 3,000 feet, there are six chair lifts, a gondola said to be the longest in the world, and four Poma lifts, all with a total capacity of 10,000 skiers per hour. If that sounds like a mob scene, I must admit that it does get crowded, but also that it's a big mountain, and there does seem to be room for everyone.

The first thing to do when considering a weekend or week at Killington is to send for information on the package plans, for they will undoubtedly save you money. Even if you don't choose a package plan which includes room, meals, and lift tickets, Killington Resort has various packages just for the slopes, including special rates on lifts for two to seven days, or plans with which you get lifts and lessons for two to seven days at reduced rates, or all three—lifts, lessons, and equipment rentals—for one price.

At Pico (pronounced "*pie*-ko") Peak near Killington there are five chair lifts, two T-bars, a vertical drop of 2,000 feet, and plenty of easy parking. It's a good, challenging area in its own right, although today it is too often thought of as Killington's elder sister.

Vermont has two central **ski report phones:** 802/223-2957 and 223-2352. Call either one for weather and conditions reports at any Vermont ski resort.

SUMMER AT KILLINGTON

Everyone coming to the Killington area will want to take the **Killington Gondola,** on Rte. 4/100 north of West Bridgewater. The gondola is the longest such ski lift in North America, traveling 3½ miles up to the 4,241-foot summit. They say that this was the point from which the territory of "Verd-mont" ("green mountain") was christened in 1763. At the top you'll find the Killington Peak Restaurant and a self-guiding nature trail. In winter the gondola carries skiers; in summer it operates from early June to mid-October on Saturday and Sunday from 10am to 4pm. Tickets are $9 round trip for adults, $6 for children 6 to 12, free for those 5 and under.

Killington Playhouse is at the Snowshed Vacation Center, Killington, VT 05751 (tel. 802/422-3333), and has performances of Broadway musicals from the beginning of July through early September, Tuesday through Sunday at 8pm. Tickets are $15 for adults; under 12 and over 65, $12. You can buy tickets at the door, but reservations are requested.

---

10. Middlebury

Like its more famous counterpart of Hanover, N.H., the town of Middlebury is replete with beautiful old Georgian and 19th-century buildings, a small college of a high quality, and a pretty town green. Hanover has Dartmouth, and Middlebury has Middlebury College, but only Middlebury has the Vermont State Craft Center at Frog Hollow and the University of Vermont's Morgan Horse Farm—but more of that later.

INFORMATION

The local chamber of commerce has an **information office** just outside the center of town, on the right-hand side as you come into Middlebury from the south (on U.S. 7) or the east (Rte. 125). The office is open during business hours.

WHERE TO STAY AND EAT

You can't miss the **Middlebury Inn and Motel**, 20 Court House Square, Middlebury, VT 05753 (tel. 802/388-4961 or toll free 800/842-4666), as you enter the heart of town. The great old inn dominates the square even more than the red-brick courthouse just up the hill from it. Guest rooms are in several locations: 45 in the inn itself, 5 in the Hubbard House attached to the inn, 5 in the Victorian-style Porter Mansion, and 10 in a modern motel annex. Rates are $83 to $121 single, $91 to $130 double. All rooms have private bath and telephone, and most have color TV. Price is determined by the size and location (and thus the views) of the room. Children under 18 can share their parents' room for free, and pets are accepted in the motel rooms at a charge of $6 per day. The inn has its own dining room, which serves breakfast, lunch, and dinner.

The **Addison County Chamber of Commerce**, 2 Court St., Middlebury, VT 05753 (tel. 802/388-7951), maintains a list of homeowners who rent rooms to visitors. When crowds of parents swell the town for graduation, or alums return for homecoming, the town's lodging places are always filled. The "Homeowners Listing" is a very useful service. Drop by the chamber's information office at the same address, or call.

Out of Town

The town of East Middlebury is east of Middlebury along Rte. 125, and it's here you'll find the **Waybury Inn**, East Middlebury, VT 05740 (tel. 802/388-4015). Rooms in the cozy, quaint (1810) inn have been refurbished in period style. Rooms, all with private bath and full breakfast, are $106 to $122 double, in summertime. The Waybury's dining room serves dinner and Sunday brunch at moderate prices. At dinnertime, a full-course meal of juice, main course, vegetables, potato, and bread made right in the inn, and dessert will cost between $25 and $30. There's also a fully licensed tavern.

WHAT TO DO

Once you've settled in and taken a stroll around this charming town, wander over to **Middlebury College** for a look at its exceptionally pretty campus and old granite buildings. Those in need of information about the college can get it by dropping in at the admissions office in Emma Willard House on Main Street (Rte. 30). Middlebury was founded by local people in the 19th century and went on to become a high-quality school. Robert Frost's participation in the Breadloaf Writers' Conference (held in Middlebury's mountain campus close to nearby Ripton) spread the college's reputation even further.

Robert Frost wasn't the only person of renown to tramp the streets of

Middlebury. A man named John Deere was an apprentice here from 1821 to 1825, after which he moved to Illinois and invented the world's first steel moldboard plow, making his name a household word in farms across the nation.

Deere's apprenticeship took place at Frog Hollow, which is down the hill from Court House Square, across the river bridge, and down Frog Hollow Lane on the right. The **Vermont State Craft Center at Frog Hollow** (tel. 388-3177) has fascinating craft exhibitions all year, not to mention craft classes and a gallery of Vermont crafts. Gallery hours are 9:30am to 5pm. Monday through Saturday year round, and noon to 5pm on Sundays from July to mid-October.

To see the magnificent steeds at the University of Vermont's **Morgan Horse Farm** (tel. 388-2011), head west on Rte. 125 from Middlebury, turn right onto Rte. 23 (Weybridge Street), and follow signs to the farm for about 2½ miles. Admission to the farm is $2.50 per adult, $1 for teens (kids under 12 get in for free), 9am to 4pm daily, May through October. Once in the farm, you'll get a guided tour of the stables, an audiovisual presentation about the farm and the Morgan horse, and the chance to roam the farm's spacious grounds and perhaps have a picnic at the picnic area.

11. Sugarbush, Warren, and Waitsfield

The area centered on Warren, Vt., along Rte. 100, can boast three well-known ski resorts: Sugarbush Valley, Mad River Glen, and Sugarbush North. Although much of the crowd here comes to stay in its own condominiums, a number of inns, motels, and guesthouses amply provide for the rest.

INFORMATION

The **Sugarbush Chamber of Commerce** will help you out with information regarding lodging, dining, events, and activities if you write to P.O. Box 173, Waitsfield, VT 05673, or if you call 802/496-3409, or toll free 800/828-4748.

WHERE TO STAY

The **Sugarbush Inn** (tel. 802/583-2301) is the area's posh resort inn. Its own pools (indoor and outdoor), batteries of tennis courts, golf course, and nature paths through the woods are all parts of this complex on the Sugarbush Access Road, 2 miles west of Rte. 100. Rooms are tasteful and very comfy, and the inn gives off that quiet *something* that denotes class. Prices for double rooms run $111 to $160, and include free use of tennis courts and 18-hole golf course.

WHERE TO DINE

Right at Sugarbush Village is an eating place that can very easily fill all your alimentary needs: The **Phoenix,** right in Sugarbush Village (tel. 583-2777), has a very fine, second-floor view of the Green Mountains through its large plate-glass windows. The rustic wood and heavy beams of the room contrast with the silver and linen on the tables, and a very impressive antique espresso coffee maker stands glittering to one side. The food is international, from fettuccine with roast duck to slices of veal cooked with oranges and Grand Marnier. Highest-priced items on the menu are the rack of lamb with a currant mustard sauce, and veal. There's also a bar at the Phoenix, fashioned from—of all things!—a Communion rail, and stained-glass windows above finish off the ecclesiastical effect. The Phoenix is closed Wednesday in summer, but any other day you can have dinner from 6 to 10pm, and reservations are suggested. Expect to pay $30 to $45 per person, all included.

SUGARBUSH SKIING

Sugarbush has lots of opportunities for good skiing, and although the resort is not so highly ramified as those at Mount Snow, Killington, or Stowe, well, perhaps that's part of the charm here—an absence of big-time crowds. That doesn't mean you'll have no wait for the lift lines, though. Short lift lines these days are only at places with reserved-seat lift tickets, or at places not worth skiing, and Sugarbush, Sugarbush North, and Mad River Glen are not among them.

Sugarbush Valley

At Sugarbush proper, the slopes and trails come down almost 2,500 feet from top to bottom, and they're laid out so that close to half of them are rated as suitable for expert skiers. Lifts include a gondola almost 2 miles long, four chair lifts, and a Poma. Rentals, instruction, and cross-country ski trails are all part of the establishment. The ski school offers a ski-week "saturation skiing workshop" which claims to instruct students in centeredness and energy awareness as well as techniques on the slopes. Lots of package plans are up for grabs—call the information numbers given at the beginning of this section.

Mad River Glen

Mad River Glen is near Waitsfield, on Rte. 17, an easy drive from the hotel I've named above. It's a smaller area than Sugarbush, but still a good size, with four chair lifts all radiating out from one base station. The vertical drop is 2,000 feet, and the preponderance of trails (four-fifths of them) are for moderately well-trained or expert skiers. Mad River Glen has a rental shop, a ski school, and a nursery. For information contact Mad River Glen, Waitsfield, VT 05673 (tel. 802/496-3551).

Sugarbush North

Sugarbush North's trails and slopes descend 2,600 feet from top to bottom, and about half the runs are classed as good for the median-level skier. But a look at the mountain trail plan will show you that taking the no. 4 chair lift to the top of Mt. Ellen will start you on some very long and pretty tricky runs. Sugarbush North has 36 trails and slopes in all, and usually a good amount of cover for a long season; there's not a lot in the way of snow-making equipment. For lodging information, call 802/583-2381 or toll free 800/451-5030. Equipment and lessons are yours at the base station for the appropriate fees.

SUMMER SOARING

The air currents around Sugarbush make it good for soaring or gliding, and the **Sugarbush Soaring Association,** P.O. Box 123, Warren, VT 05674 (tel. 802/ 496-2290), can fill you in on getting airborne. Call or write for details. Just so you'll know: You can qualify for solo glider flight in less than two weeks of good, full daily lessons and flights.

A SIDE TRIP TO MONTPELIER AND BARRE

The reason to take a detour and visit the state capital of Vermont is to take a look at the capital building, a comely classical structure modeled on the Grecian Temple of Theseus. It's made of granite from nearby Barre, of course, but the dome is of wood covered in copper and then gilded. The State House will surprise you: It's so small, but then you'll notice that the capital city, Montpelier, is pretty small too; and thus it is brought home to you that you are in the midst of the most rural state in the Union, 48th in population (only about a half million Vermonters in all, spread through almost 10,000 square miles). It comes home to you that, as a Vermont schoolchild once wrote, in Vermont "the trees are close together and the people are far apart."

The first thing you must know about Barre is that its name is pronounced like the masculine name "Barry," and not like a drinking place. The next thing to know is that Barre is the granite capital of the world, having the world's largest quarry for the stone, and also a good number of the world's finest craftspeople to work it. Guided tours of the quarries and the workshops are offered daily, and prove a fascinating way to spend a few hours; but even more fascinating is a visit to the **Hope Cemetery,** eight-tenths of a mile north of the U.S. 302/Vt. 14 intersection, on Vt. 14. The cemetery has two gates, and is open until sunset. We speak of making "monuments to survive ourselves," and we usually mean something like a corporation, a law, a charitable institution, or a poem. In Barre the phrase is literal! Stonecutters here create the monument of their dreams for their own resting places. You'll see a balanced granite cube resting precariously on one corner, self-portraits and statues, a ponderous granite armchair (empty, of course!), even a relief of a husband and wife sitting up in bed, hands joined in eternal friendship. Hope Cemetery is more like a sculpture garden, a touching memorial to artisans and artists who came here from many parts of the world.

Details: The Rock of Ages quarry is open from the beginning of May through October, with tours every day from 8:30am to 5pm, free. You can take a quarry train ride from 10am to 3pm Monday through Friday, June through September, for $2 per adult, half price for children.

12. Stowe

The lodges and inns around Stowe adopt alpine or Central European names, and although the terrain here is hardly "alpine," somehow the names make sense. The village is dominated by Vermont's highest mountain, Mt. Mansfield (4,393 feet), certainly no Matterhorn; but there is definitely a European feeling in Stowe, the feeling one has in some tiny Austrian village amid emerald-green rolling hills, winding roads, and steep slopes. Perhaps it is the lushness (in summer) of the lawns, forests, and wildflowers, or perhaps it is the rain and mists—Lamoille County is said to have the greatest amount of precipitation in the state—which make everything so lush. Whatever, there is certainly an especially attractive air about Stowe.

The frequent rain is not a liability, either, for local people learn to plan on it, and the earth scents after the rain are part of the pleasure of Stowe. And besides, it's all this precipitation which makes Stowe one of the best skiing areas in the East, with plenty of deep cover and a long season.

Winter or summer, the narrow rocky mountain defile known as **Smuggler's Notch** is a dramatic place for a hike or a drive, and is just another one of those things that make Stowe special.

INFORMATION

Businesses in the area are organized in the **Stowe Area Association,** P.O. Box 1320, Stowe, VT 05672 (tel. 802/253-7321). The information office, in the center of Stowe very near the intersection of Rtes. 100 and 108 (the Mountain Road), is open daily in ski season from 9am to 6pm, to 5pm the rest of the year. If you don't have a reservation when you arrive in Stowe, drop in here for help.

For information on snow conditions in the area, call 802/253-8521 anytime or toll free 800/247-8693 in the winter.

WHERE TO STAY

Stowe has a good variety of lodging places. Posh or modest, dauntingly expensive or suprisingly cheap, it's here. In summer there is no problem finding exactly the room you want at the price you want to pay. But on busy winter weekends you'd be well advised to reserve in advance. Just give the Stowe Area Association a ring (see above) and reservations will be made for you. In winter the toll-free number is in operation; in summer, call on the regular line.

Most hostelries in Stowe require winter visitors to have breakfast and dinner; in the jargon this is called the Modified American Plan. Smaller places generally have BYOB bars or lounges, which helps greatly in reducing the expense of an after-ski glow. For supplies, trundle down to the Vermont State Liquor Store on Rte. 100 south of town, open from 9:15am to 6pm; till 8pm on Friday; closed Sunday.

What follows is a selection of my favorite places to stay in Stowe, summer or winter. Bus service along Rte. 100 (the Mountain Road) connects the ski slopes to Stowe Village during the busy winter season.

Stowehof Inn, P.O. Box 1108, Stowe, VT 05672 (tel. 802/253-9722 or toll free 800/422-9722), about 3½ miles from Stowe village off the Mountain Road on Edson Hill Road, is a bold, unusual, and exciting place. The inn's inspiration is definitely alpine, and the public rooms give a sense of coziness and charm such as one might get in a small European *Schloss.* But architect Larry Hess's masterful planning of spaces—split levels, strange angles, nooks, crannies, high ceilings, and low ceilings—has resulted in a truly delightful place to spend time. There's a sunken fireplace pit, a cardplayers' nook decorated with giant playing cards (a royal flush, no less), a library seating area, a living room with panoramic view of the valley, several dining rooms, and a downstairs pub. One motif used throughout the inn, from the main entrance to the dining and living rooms, is that of support "columns" of massive tree trunks stripped of bark and dried to a silvery, ringing hardness. All this sounds wild, but it's so well done that Stowehof is truly a delight to be in. Besides the main inn, Stowehof has lovely grounds, a heated swimming pool, tennis courts, shuffleboard, a pitch-and-putt green, a sauna, a library, and a game room. Each of the 41 guest rooms is decorated differently, and each has a private bath and balcony or patio. Some "demi-suites" have extra Murphy beds, or fireplaces or kitchenette. The dining room is among the area's best, with a full, wonderful dinner plus wine costing about $120 for a couple. Rates for a room at Stowehof are $190 to $256 double, breakfast and dinner, tips and tax all included. Weekly rates and special package deals are available as well. This is my first choice in Stowe.

When I wrote of Stowe's having a European air about it, I must have been thinking particularly of the **Trapp Family Lodge** (tel. 802/253-8511), 2 miles along a side road up the mountain slope off Mountain Road, Stowe, VT 05672. The singing Trapp family of *Sound of Music* fame left the mountains of their native Austria before World War II and settled here in Stowe, later using this as home base for their worldwide concert tours. Members of the family still are involved in operating the resort. The Main Lodge, destroyed by fire in 1980, has been rebuilt; there's also a Lower Lodge. All the rooms come with private bath, and many have a balcony as well. Prices, which include breakfast and dinner, range from $160 to $212 double.

To get to the Trapp Family Lodge, start up Rte. 108, Mountain Road, from the center of Stowe, and go 2 miles to a fork by a white church; Rte. 108 bears right, but you bear left and follow this side road up the mountain slope, following the signs to the lodge for another 2 miles until you arrive.

The **Andersen Lodge,** R.R. 1, Box 1450, Stowe, VT 05672 (tel. 802/253-7336), is a small, friendly Tyrolean inn which has an authentic European ambience lent by its Austrian proprietors, Trude and Dietmar Heiss. Mr. Heiss is an Austrian-trained chef as well, and so the meals (which come with your room in ski season) are particularly hearty and "alpine." You can play tennis, the piano, bumper pool, or use the sauna and Jacuzzi, or just sit in front of the fire. Each room is equipped with color TV and air conditioner. Winter rates, with dinner and breakfast, are $91 to $114 double. Summer rates are $40 to $72 double, without meals. The Andersen is on Mountain Road, on the right-hand side as you're coming from Stowe.

The **Scandinavia Inn,** Stowe, VT 05672 (tel. 802/253-8555 or toll free 800/544-4229), keeps close to the spirit of its name. It's a dark-wood building with peaked gables and white trim, decked with Scandinavian flags, right on Mountain Road. In summer there are lounge chairs on the front porch, flower boxes that provide splashes of color, and picnic tables. This inn has a surprising range of services; including a sauna, hot tub, swimming pool, whirlpool bath, fitness room, game room, barbecue grills, and bicycles. In summer, rooms with bath are $52 for two, rooms with bath and color TV are $73 to $81 for two; and these rates include breakfast.

The **Ski Inn,** "on the lower slopes of Mount Mansfield," on Mountain Road (Rte. 108), Stowe, VT 05672 (tel. 802/253-4050), specializes in good food and good conversation. Very near the ski areas (both downhill and cross-country) the Ski Inn is a large white country inn with a big living room/BYOB lounge with a fireplace, a pine-paneled game room in the basement, and simple but bright and pleasing rooms rented with breakfast and dinner during ski season for $74 double without bath, $96 with bath. Mr. and Mrs. Heyer, who operate the Ski Inn, share their conversation, helpful hints, and friendly atmosphere with all their guests, and particularly lucky ones may even get some of Mrs. Heyer's wildberry preserves. In summer, the rooms rent without meals for $32 to $42.

Of the inns right in Stowe Village, I feel **The Yodler,** "first on Mountain Road," Stowe, VT 05672 (tel. 802/253-4836 or toll free 800/227-1108), is a good bet for price, facilities, comfort, service, and food. Besides the lovely old house that serves as the main part of the inn, there are a number of motel units next door, all done up in the white paint and black shutters that is a New England hallmark. Rooms are comfortable and traditional in the main lodge, but all have shower or bath, and telephone; some are more modern in the addition to the lodge, but the motel-style rooms have combination tub/shower, cable TV, and two double beds or a king-size bed, the traveling family's boon. Winter ski-season rates include breakfast and dinner, and can range anywhere from $86 in a tiny "roomette" without private bath in the main lodge, to over $139 for a motel room; a normal lodge room with double or twin beds and either a bath or shower is $127. You can save several dollars per room if you stay five, six, or seven days except during the holiday weeks, of course. Besides breakfast and dinner in the Yodler's well-known dining room, the rates include tea, cocoa, cookies, and canapés every afternoon and also set-ups for the BYOB bar. Although it's not absolutely required, the Yodler recommends that you submit to a 15% service charge rather than bother with tips. In summertime, the Yodler's rates are for room only. Summertime prices are $20 to $110 single, $27 to $110 double, and some of these are housekeeping units. The swimming pool's open in the summer only, and there's a clay tennis court, hot tub, and free shuttle to the ski slopes.

You'll want to take a look at the homey, congenial **Gables Inn,** on the Mountain Road, Stowe, VT 05672 (tel. 802/253-7730), where you can get a room with bath in the inn proper for $64 to $80 double, a larger room with queen-size bed, fireplace, and hot tub for $106. The Gables has a swimming pool, picnic area, hot tub, and a front porch where you can have breakfast (till noon) while gazing at Mount Mansfield.

Motels

I've concentrated on ski lodges and inns, as these places provide the most atmosphere and convenience for the money, but those who prefer a modern, well-run hotel will be happy to know that there are several good choices on the Mountain Road.

An attractive motel is the **Innsbruck Inn** on Mountain Road (P.O. Box 1570), Stowe, VT 05672 (tel. 802/253-8582), a modern place with quite large rooms, each with a full bath plus an extra washbasin outside the bathroom, a color TV, telephone, AM-FM radio, refrigerator, two double beds or one queen-size and one double bed, outside and inside entrances, and with its own restaurant and bar downstairs. As the name implies, the Innsbruck's flavor is Austrian, with an Alpine darkwood-and-white-stucco half-timbered effect, Austrian coats-of-arms and flags. The inn has an outdoor, heated pool, a whirlpool spa, a game room, and a sauna. The rooms are $45 to $80 double in summer, $68 to $102 double in winter, breakfast included. Efficiency suites and a five-bedroom chalet are also available.

Stowe's prime modern accommodations are at the **Golden Eagle Resort Motor Inn,** Mountain Road, Stowe, VT 05672 (tel. 802/253-4811 or toll free 800/626-1010). You can bed down in a comfortable room, suite, efficiency unit, or vacation apartment; such amenities as fireplaces, balconies, refrigerators, and private whirlpool baths are available in some accommodations. The Golden Eagle has many facilities, including a hot tub, indoor and outdoor swimming pools, fitness room, sauna, whirlpool bath, tennis court, and even two stocked trout ponds for fishing buffs. There are three restaurants. Service here is friendly, experienced, and dependable. Rates vary greatly depending upon accommodation and season, but they range from $79 to $132 for luxury motel rooms, $92 to $200 for apartments; weekly and monthly rates can bring the apartment prices down somewhat. You can't go wrong here.

WHERE TO DINE

During ski season, of course, most people will want to eat at their inn, or will be obliged to do so. But for summer, or the odd day out, here are some other dining places to think about.

Look first at the recommendations (above) on Stowehof, the Golden Eagle, and the Yodler, for these are some of the preferred dining places in the valley. Almost every other inn serves meals as well.

An interesting, bright, well-run restaurant right in Stowe is the **Restaurant Swisspot,** right on Main Street just north of the intersection with Mountain Road (tel. 253-4622). The accent is on rusticity of course, with copper buckets hanging from the rough ceiling beams, butcher-block tables, a bar of very rough wood, and the flags of the cantons in the Swiss confederation decked on the walls; for summer supping, tables with umbrellas are set outside with a view of the road. I was not surprised to find on the Swisspot's menu a luncheon hamburger called the burger Verbier, which weighs a half pound and is covered in swiss cheese and curry sauce; you can get one with tomatoes and horseradish sauce for the same price, or you can pick from a dozen other burgers and just as many sandwiches. But there are appetizers, salads, fondues, quiches, daily fish and pasta specials, and main courses such as grilled veal sausages or a char-broiled sirloin, each entree coming with salad and rice or potato. Expect to pay $18 to $20 per person for dinner.

WHAT TO SEE AND DO

Much of the territory around Stowe is part of Vermont's **Mount Mansfield's State Forest and Park,** and for summer visitors that means hiking trails (especially the Long Trail from Massachusetts to Canada), camping areas, and picnicking. Winter visitors will want to note the state ski area, and Spruce Peak ski area.

Skiing Stowe

The trails are down both Mount Mansfield and Spruce Peak, the mountains on either side of the Smuggler's Notch defile, and the variety of trails is such that there's plenty of adventure for everyone, no matter what your ability. In fact, the mountains, the staff in charge of trail maintenance, and especially the Sepp Ruschp Ski School have all worked hard over many years to earn for Stowe the high regard it has among skiers. The vertical drop is over 2,000 feet, and the lifts include five chairs, three T-bars, and a gondola with four-passenger cars. Beginners will want to start off at the Toll House Slopes, near the base of the toll road up Mount Mansfield; the next logical step is to Spruce Peak; and after you've mastered that, go on to the more difficult among the Mount Mansfield trails and slopes. Lessons and rentals are available, and there are restaurants at **Cliff House** (top of the Mansfield gondola) and **Octagon** (top of the toll road), as well as at the base camps.

A big event of the winter season at Stowe is the annual **Winter Carnival,** held during the second week in January, when special races, church suppers, square dances, hockey and skating matches, a snow sculpture contest, and even a Queen's Ball are held—hotel rates are not raised for this event. Check with the Stowe Area Association for a carnival schedule.

Summer at Stowe

Some of Stowe's pleasures are best appreciated during warm weather. The breathtaking ride to the top of Vermont's highest mountain in a gondola (tel. 253-7311) costs $8 round trip for adults, $4 for children. Or you can drive to the top of Mount Mansfield on the toll road, climbing even higher into the mist, past bunches of exotic wildflowers, feeling the air get cooler. The toll road base station is near the ski areas just south of Smuggler's Notch; you pay for your car and then proceed up the road, which is paved only for a quarter of a mile—the rest is stabilized dirt. (But the quarter of a mile at the bottom is so perfect for skateboarding that the management has had to erect a sign prohibiting the fast and fancy rollers from monopolizing this stretch of its land!) Both the gondola and the toll road are open daily from mid-June through mid-October, weather permitting.

It's hardly less exciting just to make the drive through Smuggler's Notch. You approach the mountains and the defile, and start turning the sharp bends in the road as you meet a sign saying "Shift to Low Gear Now"—and it *means* it. The road begins to twist among tremendous boulders fallen from the steep sides of the defile over the eons; the foliage gets very thick, the trees block much of the sun's light, and as you grind along up the switchback slope, a sense of wildness and excitement takes over. Just over the pass is a stopping place (you dare not stop unless you can pull off the road) with benches, toilets, a snack stand, and several impromptu trails which invite one to clamber—at least for a few hundred feet—into the rocks.

Cinema and Theater

Stowe now has a movie house, in the complex called **Stowe Center,** which is exactly a mile north of Stowe village along Mountain Road. Call 253-4678 to see what's playing. When you get there, you can choose a regular theater seat or a comfy corner of the Projection Room—a cocktail lounge—from which to see the film. What a good idea!

The **Green Mountain Guild of White River Junction** brings summer theater to Stowe during July and August, every week Tuesday through Saturday. Performances are at Stowe High School on Barrows Road. Contact the Stowe Area Association for current schedules, reservations, and prices.

Other Activities

It's no exaggeration to say that something's always happening here in June, July, and August. Antique car rallies, horse and dog shows, a craft fair, even a fiddlers' meeting, and a surprisingly authentic Oktoberfest (in October, natch) crowd into the schedule. **Topnotch,** that posh resort on Mountain Road near Mount Mansfield, is the place to rent horses by the hour or for a trail ride: Call 253-8585 and ask for the stables. The going rate is $12 per hour.

Stowe now has an **Alpine Slide,** operated by the Mount Mansfield Company (tel. 253-7311). You start by taking a cool and scenic ride up a chair lift. At the top, you mount a small sled and begin your descent along a concrete runway which weaves and turns like a bobsled run all the way to the bottom of the mountain slope. It's fun! The idea (and the Alpine Slide design) came from West Germany. The slide is open on weekends and holidays from Memorial Day weekend to late June, daily from late June through Labor Day weekend, and then on weekends only through mid-October; on rainy days, the slide closes down. Rides cost $6 per adult, $4 per child, and five-ride ticket books are available. Take your slide-ride between 10am and 5pm, weather permitting. The Alpine Slide is 6 miles north of Stowe village on Rte. 108 at Spruce Peak.

The more familiar summer pastimes are well covered too. **Stowe Country Club** has an 18-hole golf course; tennis courts abound (many hotels and lodges have their own); hiking, bicycling, fishing, and photographing can fill whole weeks.

13. Burlington

The largest city in Vermont is a town of only about 50,000 population, but in this state small is beautiful. Burlington's situation on the shores of Lake Champlain brings it extra attractiveness and aquatic sports opportunities as well. The town is the seat of the University of Vermont, and student activities and cultural events add an extra dimension to Burlington's daily life. Of the city's native sons, the educator and philosopher John Dewey is the most famous, and Ethan Allen, while not born here, chose Burlington as his home in his later years. Today part of his farm is encompassed by Ethan Allen Park.

Besides being a college town, Burlington is industrial: Weapons, data processing equipment, textiles, and consumer products are all made here, and Burlington's medical facilities serve the northern part of the state. Burlington is one of two termini for Lake Champlain ferryboat crossings (the other is Port Kent, N.Y.).

ORIENTATION

Downtown Burlington is a fairly compact area easily negotiated on foot. The heart of town for visitors and locals alike is **Church Street Marketplace,** a four-block stretch of Church Street from Pearl Street to College Street closed to vehicular traffic, beautified with trees, benches, and sidewalk cafés, and busy with strollers, street vendors, shoppers, lovers, performers, and sidewalk bench conversationalists. At the northwestern end of Church Street stands the pretty Unitarian church, built in 1816. Many of the city's recommendable restaurants are near the Marketplace. The **Vermont Transit bus station** (tel. 802/864-6811) is at the southeastern end of Church Street Marketplace across City Hall Park.

In the midst of Church Street Marketplace, near the corner with Bank Street, is an **information gallery** (no phone) with brochures and maps. For more elaborate or detailed information, contact the **Lake Champlain Regional Chamber of Commerce,** 209 Battery St. (P.O. Box 453), Burlington, VT 05402 (tel. 802/863-3489).

WHERE TO STAY

Most of Burlington's acceptable lodgings are a short way from the center of town, but there is one hotel right downtown.

Out at the intersection of U.S. 2 and I-89 is the **Sheraton-Burlington Inn** (tel. 802/862-6576 or toll free 800/325-3535), a prime choice of business travelers to Burlington. The official address is 870 Williston Rd., Burlington, VT 05401, and there are 310 rooms, a restaurant, lounge with live entertainment, a health spa, and indoor and outdoor swimming pool. The heart of the hotel is the Summerhouse, a four-story space with translucent ceiling sheltering fountains, plants, and many hotel services. Room prices in summer (July through October) are $84 to $133 single, $84 to $150 double. Higher prices are for the new Concierge Level rooms, which have marvelous views of Mt. Mansfield, and are connected to the main building by an authentic old Vermont covered bridge. At this location, you're only 1½ miles from the airport, and the hotel has a free shuttle service to take you there.

The **Howard Johnson Motor Lodge,** P.O. Box 993, Burlington, VT 05402 (tel. 802/863-5541 or toll free 800/654-2000), is also here, at the intersection of U.S. 2 and I-89. Prices are on the order of the other chain hotels, but there are several advantages to staying at Hojo's, including indoor-outdoor pool, fitness room, hot tub, saunas, tennis courts, and cable color TV. Lots of rooms are equipped with two double beds, and the family plan allows kids under 18 to stay free with their parents. In the months from May to October, singles are $58 to $70, and doubles are $70 to $80.

Going down the price scale somewhat, **Econo Lodge** (tel. 802/863-1125 or toll free 800/446-6900) has an installation at the intersection of U.S. 2 and I-89, a quarter mile from Exit 14E, at 1076 Williston Rd., Burlington, VT 05403. At the Econo Lodge, in addition to a health spa you get the usual, expected motel comforts —rooms with one or two double beds, color TV, free HBO, full bath, even an outdoor swimming pool—but prices are very reasonable: $50 to $65 for one, $60 to $75 for two, $64 to $81 for three or four (usually a family, but nothing says two couples can't share a room).

Right downtown is the **Radisson Burlington Hotel,** at Burlington Square, Burlington, VT 05401 (tel. 802/658-6500 or toll free 800/333-3333). Many of the 200 rooms have gorgeous views of Lake Champlain, while others open onto the indoor swimming pool. The Radisson bills itself as "Vermont's most luxurious hotel," and although many other hotels may dispute the claim, there's no disputing the Radisson's luxury quality. Tropical plants bring freshness to an enclosed Garden Court next to the pool and whirlpool bath. The price is $102 to $141 for singles, and $118 to $141 for doubles; the more expensive rooms are those with a lake-and-mountain view, and the Plaza rooms with extra amenities. An extra person or bed is $20, but children under 18 stay with their folks for free. Parking is free too.

Of the many motels on U.S. 7 south of town, the **Colonial Motor Inn**, 462 Shelburne St., Burlington, VT 05401 (tel. 802/862-5754), is among the best. A substantial establishment, it boasts 40 modern rooms with air conditioning, color TV, telephones; an outdoor swimming pool is open in good weather. A shopping center with services and restaurants is a short walk away. For one double bed (single or double occupancy) the price is $44 to $55; for two double beds it's $48 to $64. From I-89 take Exit 13 to I-189; take I-189 to U.S. 7 and go north to the Colonial.

WHERE TO DINE

Though not bursting with restaurants, Burlington has good dining possibilities. Several of the best places are located in the area of Church Street Marketplace, right in the center of town.

Best in town is the **Déjà Vu Café**, 185 Pearl St. (tel. 864-7917), near the corner of South Winooski St., just around the corner from the northwestern end of Church Street Marketplace. Dark, cool, and restful inside, its high-peaked roof and ornate trim hint at Gothic style. Cozy booths and simple tables on two levels provide plenty of dining space; in summer, there are tables on the garden terrace as well. The menu is short but varied and well balanced with interesting appetizers (including escargots en croûte), soups, salads, elaborate sandwiches, and light main-course dishes such as fettucine Alfredo, an "American cassoulet," and chicken with corn and achiote. Bretonne crêpes, those large, thin pancakes, are served filled with smoked salmon, sausage and cheese, ham and chicken. In the evening, more substantial plates (veal, steaks, etc.) are added to the menu. The wine list is decent, the beer list long and interesting. Come for lunch, tea (4 to 6pm), dinner, or a late-night snack anytime from 11am to midnight (1am on Friday and Saturday). In winter the restaurant closes an hour earlier.

Alfredo's Restaurant, in the alley across from City Hall on Church Street Marketplace (tel. 864-0854), is three simple but cozy and charming storefront dining rooms with lace curtains, red-and-white-checked tablecloths, and live lobsters in a tank by the door. In good weather, food is served at the umbrella-shaded tables on the small patio. Pasta in all its variations—fettucine, capellini, vermicelli, manicotti, ravioli, linguine, lasagne—is a strong suit here, but there's also delicious veal sorrentino (veal with eggplant and mozzarella in a marsala sauce), chicken in garlic with peppers and mushrooms, and many other Italian delights. Prices are good: A full lunch might be $10 or less, a great dinner $15 to $25 per person, tax, tip and wine included. On Tuesday evenings, pay $6.50 for all the pasta you can eat; on Thursday evening, some veal dishes are priced at only $10. Dinner is served every day, lunch (noon to 2pm) on Monday through Friday.

The **Bourbon Street Grill,** 213 College St., (tel. 865-2800), at South Winooski, is a tidy little storefront bistro with frilly curtains, ceiling fans, and a menu for any time of day. Soups, salads, burgers, and sandwiches share space on the menu with jambalaya, Cajun flank steak, and shrimp étouffée. For a little Louisiana thrill, preface your meal by ingesting an authentic Louisiana Hurricane, a powerful rum-based concoction which calms you down if you're in the midst of a storm, or starts a storm if you aren't. A light lunch can cost as little as $6, a bounteous dinner as much as $25, all in. Lunch is served daily except Sunday from 11:30am to 4pm, dinner every evening from 5:30 to 10pm.

Another choice is **Carbur's,** 117 St. Paul St. facing City Hall Park (tel. 862-4106) at the southeastern end of Church Street Marketplace. Carbur's is done in heavy mod-Victoriana, and tends to the quietly outrageous: a sign in the window says "Famous since 1974." The dining room has a tremendously high ceiling equipped with ceiling fans that spin slowly even on cool days, just for atmosphere. Soup and a large sandwich cost less than $10 at lunch, and huge salad plates go for only slightly more. The menu is a book 25 pages long, filled with sandwiches, soups, salad plates, almost all—with a few exceptions like the monster five-decker sandwich—for around $10 or less. The menu, by the way, is laden with enough drawings and amusing patter to keep you entertained all through your meal. Come for lunch or dinner any day.

WHAT TO DO

Much of Burlington's cultural life centers on the **University of Vermont** campus, and on the campuses of the other three colleges in the area: **St. Michael's, Trinity,** and **Champlain.** The university, of course, has a good museum on Colchester Avenue, called the **Fleming Museum,** open every day of the year and free to all visitors. Exhibits run the gamut: a Kang Hsi vase, Wei terracotta, a Cole painting, 17th-century Persian miniatures, early Roman glass, Coptic carvings, and a bona fide Egyptian mummy.

The University of Vermont also stages an annual summer **Champlain Shakespeare Festival,** held at the Royall Tyler Theatre (tel. 802/656-2094), on the Main Street side of the campus. A **Mozart Festival** is held in summer as well.

Much of the lakefront land in Burlington is encompassed by parks, including **Oak Ledge Park** and **Red Rocks Park** in South Burlington, **Battery Park** near Burlington's center and only five blocks from the ferries, and **Burlington Municipal Beach** on Institute Road north of the ferry dock along the lake shore. **Ethan Allen Park** is north of the center of town; take North Avenue (Rte. 127) starting at Battery Park.

Shelburne Museum

From mid-May to mid-October, visitors to Burlington must make a detour to the town of Shelburne, 7 miles south of the city along U.S. 7, to see the Shelburne Museum, a gala festival of Americana collected into 37 historic buildings arranged on 45 acres, including an authentic one-room schoolhouse, six fully furnished early New England homes, a jail complete with stocks, an Adirondack hunting lodge, a print shop, and a lighthouse which once guided ships on Lake Champlain. The buildings you see date from the 17th, 18th, and early 19th centuries; each was moved here from its original location in Vermont, New Hampshire, New York, or Massachusetts, and all are now filled with the artifacts of earlier American life. The museum is said to have about the best and fullest collection of Americana ever assembled. Among the artifacts are a 1920s carousel, a round dairy barn (1901), and even the huge 220-foot sidewheeler steamboat S.S. *Ticonderoga,* docked here after its last run on the lake. Four art galleries feature paintings and sculpture by European and American artists (Andrew Wyeth, Grandma Moses, Ogden Pleissner, Rembrandt, Monet, Manet, Degas), and other buildings hold displays of folk art both charming and authentic: quilts, decoys, glassware, and furniture, plus the tools used to make these items.

The Shelburne Museum (tel. 802/985-3346) is open from 9am to 5pm daily mid-May to mid-October; admission (good for two consecutive days) costs $12.50 for adults, $4.50 for children 6 to 17, and free for kids under 6. The museum has a cafeteria and snack bars, picnic tables, a bookshop, stores, and free parking.

Lake Champlain Ferries

One of the favorite things to do in Burlington is to take the ferry over to Port Kent, N.Y., whether you're actually interested in getting to Port Kent or not. Ferries, leaving from the King Street Dock in Burlington, operate in spring, summer, and fall, leaving each terminus at about 1-hour intervals from 8 or 9:20am to 5:30 or 6:30pm, a bit more frequently in summer, with 14 trips a day in each direction. You can take your car across if you're going somewhere: price for car and driver, one way, is $11.50; each extra adult pays $3 one way; children 6 through 12 pay $1. The trip, a marvelous way to get to know Lake Champlain, takes about an hour each way. This ferry doesn't run in winter, but ferries between Grand Isle, Vt., and Plattsburgh, N.Y., operate year round. You'll also find a ferry chugging between Charlotte, Vt., and Essex, N.Y., from early April through early January.

INDEX

GENERAL INFORMATION

DESTINATIONS

KEY TO ABBREVIATIONS: (Accommodations): A = Apartments; B = Budget; B&B = Bed-and-Breakfast; Co = Cottages; E = Expensive; Ef = Efficiencies; FC = First Class; I = Inexpensive; M = Moderately priced; MAP = Modified American Plan; Mt = Motel. **(Restaurants):** B = Budget; E = Expensive; I = Inexpensive; M = Moderately priced

NOW, SAVE MONEY ON ALL YOUR TRAVELS!
Join Frommer's™ Dollarwise® Travel Club

Saving money while traveling is never a simple matter, which is why the **Dollarwise Travel Club** was formed 31 years ago. Developed in response to requests from Frommer's Travel Guide readers, the Club provides cost-cutting travel strategies, up-to-date travel information, and a sense of community for value-conscious travelers from all over the world.

In keeping with the money-saving concept, the annual membership fee is low —$20 for U.S. residents or $25 for residents of Canada, Mexico, and other countries—and is immediately exceeded by the value of your benefits, which include:

1. Any TWO books listed on the following pages.
2. Plus any ONE Frommer's City Guide.
3. A subscription to our quarterly newspaper, *The Dollarwise Traveler.*
4. A membership card that entitles you to purchase through the Club all Frommer's publications for 33% to 40% off their retail price.

The eight-page *Dollarwise Traveler* tells you about the latest developments in good-value travel worldwide and includes the following columns: **Hospitality Exchange** (for those offering and seeking hospitality in cities all over the world); **Share-a-Trip** (for those looking for travel companions to share costs); and **Readers Ask . . . Readers Reply** (for those with travel questions that other members can answer).

Aside from the Frommer's Guides and the Gault Millau Guides, you can also choose from our Special Editions. These include such titles as *California with Kids* (a compendium of the best of California's accommodations, restaurants, and sightseeing attractions appropriate for those traveling with toddlers through teens); *Candy Apple: New York with Kids* (a spirited guide to the Big Apple by a savvy New York grandmother that's perfect for both visitors and residents); *Caribbean Hideaways* (the 100 most romantic places to stay in the Islands, all rated on ambience, food, sports opportunities, and price); *Honeymoon Destinations* (a guide to planning and choosing just the right destination from hundreds of possibilities in the U.S., Mexico, and the Caribbean); *Marilyn Wood's Wonderful Weekends* (a selection of the best mini-vacations within a 200-mile radius of New York City, including descriptions of country inns and other accommodations, restaurants, picnic spots, sights, and activities); and *Paris Rendez-Vous* (a delightful guide to the best places to meet in Paris whether for power breakfasts or dancing till dawn).

To join this Club, simply send the appropriate membership fee with your name and address to: Frommer's Dollarwise Travel Club, 15 Columbus Circle, New York, NY 10023. Remember to specify which single city guide and which two other guides you wish to receive in your initial package of member's benefits. Or tear out the next page, check off your choices, and send the page to us with your membership fee.

FROMMER BOOKS
PRENTICE HALL PRESS
15 COLUMBUS CIRCLE
NEW YORK, NY 10023
212/373-8125

Date_____

Friends: Please send me the books checked below.

FROMMER'S™ GUIDES

(Guides to sightseeing and tourist accommodations and facilities from budget to deluxe, with emphasis on the medium-priced.)

☐ Alaska $14.95	☐ Germany $14.95
☐ Australia $14.95	☐ Italy. $14.95
☐ Austria & Hungary $14.95	☐ Japan & Hong Kong $14.95
☐ Belgium, Holland & Luxembourg $14.95	☐ Mid-Atlantic States $14.95
☐ Bermuda & The Bahamas. $14.95	☐ New England. $14.95
☐ Brazil $14.95	☐ New Mexico $13.95
☐ Canada $14.95	☐ New York State $14.95
☐ Caribbean. $14.95	☐ Northwest $16.95
☐ Cruises (incl. Alaska, Carib, Mex, Hawaii,	☐ Portugal, Madeira & the Azores $14.95
Panama, Canada & US) $14.95	☐ Scandinavia $18.95
☐ California & Las Vegas $14.95	☐ South Pacific. $14.95
☐ Egypt. $14.95	☐ Southeast Asia $14.95
☐ England & Scotland $14.95	☐ Southern Atlantic States. $14.95
☐ Florida $14.95	☐ Southwest $14.95
☐ France $14.95	☐ Switzerland & Liechtenstein $14.95

☐ USA $16.95

FROMMER'S $-A-DAY® GUIDES

(In-depth guides to sightseeing and low-cost tourist accommodations and facilities.)

☐ Europe on $40 a Day $15.95	☐ Israel on $40 a Day. $13.95
☐ Australia on $40 a Day $13.95	☐ Mexico on $35 a Day $14.95
☐ Costa Rica; Guatemala & Belize	☐ New York on $60 a Day. $13.95
on $35 a day. $15.95	☐ New Zealand on $45 a Day $14.95
☐ Eastern Europe on $25 a Day $16.95	☐ Scotland & Wales on $40 a Day $13.95
☐ England on $50 a Day. $13.95	☐ South America on $40 a Day $15.95
☐ Greece on $35 a Day $14.95	☐ Spain on $50 a Day $15.95
☐ Hawaii on $60 a Day. $14.95	☐ Turkey on $30 a Day. $13.95
☐ India on $25 a Day $12.95	☐ Washington, D.C. & Historic Va. on
☐ Ireland on $35 a Day. $13.95	$40 a Day $13.95

FROMMER'S TOURING GUIDES

(Color illustrated guides that include walking tours, cultural and historic sites, and other vital travel information.)

☐ Amsterdam. $10.95	☐ New York $10.95
☐ Australia $10.95	☐ Paris $8.95
☐ Brazil $10.95	☐ Rome. $10.95
☐ Egypt. $8.95	☐ Scotland. $9.95
☐ Florence. $8.95	☐ Thailand. $10.95
☐ Hong Kong $10.95	☐ Turkey $10.95
☐ London $10.95	☐ Venice $8.95

(TURN PAGE FOR ADDITONAL BOOKS AND ORDER FORM)

0391

FROMMER'S CITY GUIDES

(Pocket-size guides to sightseeing and tourist accommodations and facilities in all price ranges.)

☐ Amsterdam/Holland	$8.95	☐ Minneapolis/St. Paul	$8.95
☐ Athens	$8.95	☐ Montréal/Québec City	$8.95
☐ Atlanta	$8.95	☐ New Orleans	$8.95
☐ Atlantic City/Cape May	$8.95	☐ New York	$8.95
☐ Barcelona	$7.95	☐ Orlando	$8.95
☐ Belgium	$7.95	☐ Paris	$8.95
☐ Berlin	$8.95	☐ Philadelphia	$8.95
☐ Boston	$8.95	☐ Rio	$8.95
☐ Cancún/Cozumel/Yucatán	$8.95	☐ Rome	$8.95
☐ Chicago	$9.95	☐ Salt Lake City	$8.95
☐ Denver/Boulder/Colorado Springs	$7.95	☐ San Diego	$8.95
☐ Dublin/Ireland	$8.95	☐ San Francisco	$8.95
☐ Hawaii	$8.95	☐ Santa Fe/Taos/Albuquerque	$10.95
☐ Hong Kong	$7.95	☐ Seattle/Portland	$7.95
☐ Las Vegas	$8.95	☐ St. Louis/Kansas City	$9.95
☐ Lisbon/Madrid/Costa del Sol	$8.95	☐ Sydney	$8.95
☐ London	$8.95	☐ Tampa/St. Petersburg	$8.95
☐ Los Angeles	$8.95	☐ Tokyo	$8.95
☐ Mexico City/Acapulco	$8.95	☐ Toronto	$8.95
☐ Miami	$8.95	☐ Vancouver/Victoria	$7.95

☐ Washington, D.C. $8.95

SPECIAL EDITIONS

☐ Beat the High Cost of Travel	$6.95	☐ Motorist's Phrase Book (Fr/Ger/Sp)	$4.95
☐ Bed & Breakfast—N. America	$14.95	☐ Paris Rendez-Vous	$10.95
☐ California with Kids	$16.95	☐ Swap and Go (Home Exchanging)	$10.95
☐ Caribbean Hideaways	$14.95	☐ The Candy Apple (NY with Kids)	$12.95
☐ Honeymoon Destinations (US, Mex &		☐ Travel Diary and Record Book	$5.95
Carib)	$14.95	☐ Where to Stay USA (From $3 to $30 a	
☐ Manhattan's Outdoor Sculpture	$15.95	night)	$13.95

☐ Marilyn Wood's Wonderful Weekends (CT, DE, MA, NH, NJ, NY, PA, RI, VT) $11.95
☐ The New World of Travel (Annual sourcebook by Arthur Frommer for savvy travelers) $16.95

GAULT MILLAU

(The only guides that distinguish the truly superlative from the merely overrated.)

☐ The Best of Chicago	$15.95	☐ The Best of Los Angeles	$16.95
☐ The Best of France	$16.95	☐ The Best of New England	$15.95
☐ The Best of Hawaii	$16.95	☐ The Best of New Orleans	$16.95
☐ The Best of Hong Kong	$16.95	☐ The Best of New York	$16.95
☐ The Best of Italy	$16.95	☐ The Best of Paris	$16.95
☐ The Best of London	$16.95	☐ The Best of San Francisco	$16.95

☐ The Best of Washington, D.C. $16.95

ORDER NOW!

In U.S. include $2 shipping UPS for 1st book; $1 ea. add'l book. Outside U.S. $3 and $1, respectively.
Allow four to six weeks for delivery in U.S., longer outside U.S.
Enclosed is my check or money order for $_____

NAME_____

ADDRESS_____

CITY_____ STATE_____ ZIP_____

0391